KIOWA MILITARY SOCIETIES

The Civilization of the American Indian Series

KIOWA MILITARY SOCIETIES

Ethnohistory and Ritual

WILLIAM C. MEADOWS

University of Oklahoma Press : Norman

Library of Congress Cataloging-in-Publication Data

Meadows, William C., 1966-

Kiowa military societies : ethnohistory and ritual / William C. Meadows.
    p. cm. — (The civilization of the American Indian series ; v. 263)
Includes bibliographical references and index.
ISBN 978-0-8061-4072-8 (hardcover) ISBN 978-0-8061-9009-9 (paperback)

1. Kiowa Indians—Societies, etc.
2. Secret societies—Great Plains—History. 3. Kiowa Indians—Ethnic identity.
4. Kiowa Indians—Rites and ceremonies. 5. Kiowa Indians—Warfare.
6. Great Plains—History. I. Title.
   E99.K5M45 2010
   978.004'97492—dc22

                                         2009013936

Kiowa Military Societies: Ethnohistory and Ritual is Volume 263
in The Civilization of the American Indian Series.

The paper in this book meets the guidelines for permanence and durability
of the Committee on Production Guidelines for Book Longevity of the
Council on Library Resources, Inc. ∞

Copyright © 2010 by the University of Oklahoma Press, Norman,
Publishing Division of the University. Paperback published 2022.
Manufactured in the U.S.A.
All rights reserved. No part of this publication may be reproduced,
stored in a retrieval system, or transmitted, in any form or by any means,
electronic, mechanical, photocopying, recording, or otherwise—except as
permitted under Section 107 or 108 of the United States Copyright Act—
without the prior permission of the University of Oklahoma Press.

To Kiowa veterans,

past,

present,

and future

As veterans they fought for their land and their people, and therefore each dance is like a homecoming for veterans. Therefore they should work together and stay together. Then they can feel good about coming out to celebrate and enjoy the songs and dances that were performed before this part of the country was opened up.
— Gus Palmer Sr.

There are prayers on that bustle. So I tell people to follow that bustle, it is leading Óhọ̀mọ̀.
— Mac Whitehorse

The Kiowa Gourd Clan, they're thinking of their ancestors, and we try to carry on what they left us, what they showed and what they left us.
— Bill Koomsa Jr.

CONTENTS

List of Illustrations   xi

Preface   xiii

Acknowledgments   xv

Pronunciation Guide   xix

Introduction   3

1 Pòlą́hyòp: The Rabbits Society   13
2 Áljóyȋgàu: The Mountain Sheep Society   25
3 Chèjánmàu: The Horse Headdresses Society   33
4 Tòkǫ́gàut: The Black Legs Society   39
5 Jáifègàu: The Unafraid of Death or Skunkberry Society   113
6 Qóichę́gàu: The Sentinel or Scout Dogs Society   215
7 Cáuitémgòp: The Kiowa Bone Strikers   247
8 Óhǫmògàu: The Omaha Society   253
9 Kiowa Women's Societies   307

Conclusion   363

Appendix: Kiowa Military Society Membership Rosters   369

Notes   385

Bibliography   429

Index   445

ILLUSTRATIONS

Figures

1. Horse Headdresses Society meeting positions   35
2. Black Legs Society meeting positions   45
3. Jáifègàu meeting positions   127

Photographs

Unless otherwise indicated, all photographs are by the author.
Kiowa military society whips   6
Rabbits Society dance, 2004   23
Ledgerbook drawing of Kiowa Black Legs Society, 1870s   42
Kiowa Black Legs Society leader Gus Palmer Sr., 1992   64
Gabriel Morgan in traditional Black Legs Society body paint, 1990   69
Kiowa Black Legs Society tipi, staff, and bonnets, about 1994   72
Kiowa Black Legs Society memorial for Joshua Ware, 2007   76
Kiowa Women's Victory Dance, about 1991   85
Kiowa Black Legs Society Turn Around or Reverse Dance, 1999   100
Kiowa Black Legs Society tipi, 2008   106
Kiowa Jáifègàu human hand effigy rattle   134
Kiowa Gourd dancers, about 1915   144
Brush Dance performed at Kiowa Gourd Clan ceremonial, 2004   162
Kiowa Gourd Clan ceremonial with society trophies displayed, 2004   163
Kiowa Gourd Clan ceremonial, 1990   165
Kiowa Tia-Piah Society Brush Dance, 1993   170
Model of Kiowa Dog Society regalia bag   226
Ledgerbook drawing of Kiowa Dog Society, 1870s   228
Ohoma Society dance, about 1915   276
Ohoma Society Pipe Dance, 1993   289
Ohoma Society Initiation Dance, 1993   292
Ohoma Society bustle worn by Mac Whitehorse, 1992   294
Stephen Mopope in Fancy Feather–style dress, about 1950   305
Kiowa War Mothers, 1944   335
Carnegie Victory Club Armistice observation, 1997   351
Kiowa Veterans Auxiliary and Kiowa War Mothers, about 1997   358

PREFACE

In August 1989 I arrived in Norman, Oklahoma, to begin my master's program in anthropology. After participating in a department meeting, I was left with two weeks of free time before my classes began, so I started visiting local museums and historical sites. One day I visited the Kiowa Tribal Museum in Carnegie, Oklahoma. While looking intently at the display cases, I was approached by an elderly woman, who said, "You're not a tourist, are you?" Somewhat startled, I said, "Excuse me?" "You're not a tourist, are you?" she repeated. Actually, I thought to myself, on that day I was. Although I had considered research on the origins of Plains-style dance and the powwow, I had no formal plan at that time. I simply had time on my hands and was "being a tourist" that day.

The woman continued, "You're not a tourist. Most people who come through here, they look at the displays only briefly, most don't even read the displays. They're here about ten minutes, sign our guest book, and they're on their way. But you, you're really looking at our stuff. You're looking at it different. You're interested. Why have you come?"

After I explained the circumstances of my recent arrival at the university, the woman introduced herself and said, "Well, that settles it, you will work with us." Although baffled and thinking she was a little presumptuous, I thought she must see something to make such a forthright statement. As I listened politely, she continued, "We have some doings this weekend that I want you to see." She gave me instructions for getting to her house, told me to be there promptly at 10:00 A.M., and concluded, "And no Indian time!" That woman was Belle Geionety Kayitah, then one of the Kiowa Tribal Museum managers. I picked her up the next Saturday morning, and she graciously began to introduce me to Kiowa elders, dances, and, culture. She was right. I am still working with the Kiowa to this day.

That October I was invited to observe the Kiowa Black Legs Society's fall ceremonial near Anadarko, Oklahoma. During the dance, Belle took me out to dance beside her nephew Reuben Topaum, a society member and a highly decorated World War II veteran. She honored her nephew by placing money at his feet, a common form of honoring among Southern Plains tribes. Reuben handed me his society lance to dance with during the song, after which I returned it, shook hands with him, and received the gift of money. Although I did not immediately realize it, this event dramatically changed the course of my life over the next twenty years. Although I had participated in powwows for many years, this event moved me deeply and prompted me to learn more about it.

With an interest in the origins of Plains Indian dance and music, I eventually focused the research for my graduate degrees on the heart of this topic: Plains Indian military societies, the origin of the contemporary Plains-style powwow. I saw the great enthusiasm and respect the Kiowa had for their veterans and their societies and the importance these organizations held in their rich tribal heritage. While writing my master's thesis on the Kiowa Black Legs Society (Meadows 1991), I discovered that similar knowledge existed for other Kiowa societies, namely, those that had been revived and continued to the present. Elders and members of other Kiowa societies showed great interest in having similar accounts compiled. In 1990 I began collecting information on all Kiowa military societies for my doctoral dissertation on Kiowa, Apache, and Comanche military societies (Meadows 1995, 1999) and with this book in mind. By 1995 I had written rough drafts of the cultural history of each Kiowa military society, which I continued to work on. Many elders asked that this work help them preserve portions of their culture for future generations. Elders indicated that some society traditions and songs had been lost, that others were of more recent origin, and that they were trying their best to carry on their culture. This work is aimed at documenting and helping to preserve these traditions while demonstrating their anthropological importance.

ACKNOWLEDGMENTS

I would like to offer my gratitude to the many Kiowa who contributed to this work, many of whom passed on before its completion. It was their hospitality, generosity, knowledge, insight, patience, and willingness to contribute, to teach, and to preserve that allowed me to complete this undertaking. They included Gus Palmer Sr., Mac Whitehorse, Parker P. McKenzie, Atwater Onco, Bill Koomsa Jr., Harry Domebo, Billy Evans Horse, Fred and Peggy Tsoodle, Oscar and Hattie Tsoodle, Vernon Tsoodle, Rev. David Paddlety, Rev. Bob Pinezaddleby, Reuben Topaum, Gregory Haumpy Sr., Weiser Tongkeamha, Francis Tsonetokoy, George Tsoodle, Victor Paddlety, Rev. George Saumpty, John Emhoola Sr., Ernest Chanate Sr., Dixon Palmer, Ralph Kotay, Blas Preciado, Harding Big Bow, Alice Littleman, Laura Sankadota Tahlo, Joyce Auchiah Daingkau, Belle Geionety Kayitah, Ruby Paukei Williams, Grace Tsonetokoy, Delores Toyebo Harragarra, Della Doyebi, Vanessa Jennings, Carol Flores, Robert Sr. and Martha Nell Poolaw, Martha Koomsa Perez, Christine Two Hatchet Kaulaity, Leonard Cozad Sr., Orville Neconie, Mary Neconie Shane, Dorothy Whitehorse DeLaune, Georgia Botone Dupoint, Gertrude Yeahquo Hines, Lucille Tsalote Aitsan, Sherman Chaddlesone, Tim Tsoodle, Lanny Asepermy, Al Bronaugh, and Anne Yeahquo.

I offer a special thank-you to the Kiowa Black Legs Society, the Kiowa Ohoma Lodge, the Kiowa Gourd Clan, the Kiowa Tia-Piah Society of Oklahoma, the Kiowa Tia-Piah Society of Carnegie, Oklahoma, the Kiowa Warriors Descendants, the Kiowa War Mothers, the Carnegie Victory Club, and the Purple Heart Club. I would also like to thank the Kiowa elders, society leaders, and members who read and commented on drafts of individual chapters. Lanny Asepermy graciously shared his extensive service record data on Kiowa veterans. I also offer my thanks to Hammond Motah and Sherry Tofpi for letting me stay with them during the summer of 1990 and to Hammond for always going out of his way to recognize me to the crowd when he served as a master of ceremonies at powwows. I am most grateful to Carl and Vanessa Jennings for providing me with a home from which to conduct extended fieldwork since 1991.

Many people had a significant effect on my life during the time of my research, and this work would be less without their dedication, encouragement, and input. These were my teachers, friends, and relatives. My late uncle Parker McKenzie taught me much of the Kiowa language, names, and songs and helped translate and standardize the military society terminology and songs for this and other works. I will always benefit from his teachings. Gus Palmer Sr. gave me my Kiowa name. Always patient, he taught me Black Legs and Ohoma traditions and many Kiowa songs. Mac Whitehorse taught me Ohoma Society traditions and showed me the strength and dignity of a quiet man. Bill Koomsa Jr. always made me feel welcome at dances and hand games and took the time to teach me something every time I saw him. My Kiowa mother, Vanessa Jennings, made my moccasins, dubbed me James Mooney Jr., always encouraged me to continue my work no matter how hard things were, and told everyone, "I raised him." She told me that my work had a purpose and taught me the importance of living a traditional life no matter how much the surrounding world changes.

Delores and Kenny Harragarra showed me the true meaning of Christian fellowship. Grace Tsonetokoy gave me a picture of a 1921 Gourd Dance at her father's allotment and told me about the dances held there. Weiser Tongkeamha showed me strength in the face of death and continued to pass on knowledge even as his battle with cancer neared its end. Gregory Haumpy Sr. taught me happiness despite physical limitations. Carol Tapedo Flores taught me about the War Mothers. Blas Preciado always addressed me as "brother." Atwater Onco taught me about what being a traditional Kiowa means, doctored and prayed for me when I was ill, and gave me medicine with which to protect myself. And finally, a Kiowa woman wrote to me to say, "I am counting on your perseverance and tenacity to record events for the unborn generations on the evolution of modern Kiowa history," and told me that my work was important. Whenever times are hard or students ask me why I do the work I do, I pull out this letter and gather strength. With these friends, teachers, and relatives, their devotion to their culture, and their faith in me, I know that I can neither quit nor fail in my endeavor. In light of the numerous legal, social, and economic complexities the Kiowa face on a daily basis, from both Anglo and Indian societies, I have a great deal of respect and admiration for their demeanor and resilience.

In the academic world, I offer sincere thanks to Ray DeMallie, Mike Davis, and Tom Holm, who have always been supportive of my work. Ben Kracht graciously shared his copy of the 1935 Santa Fe Laboratory of Anthropology Kiowa fieldnotes and the Kiowa Agency Files when I first started graduate school in 1989. I continue to benefit from the teachings of John H. Moore and Robert "Boy Chief" Fields (Pawnee) that I received during my graduate studies. Jerrold Levy of the University of Arizona shared data from his Kiowa research. Clyde Ellis has been a pleasure to exchange ideas with. Maurice Boyd of Texas Christian University related his experiences in compiling the Kiowa Voices project. I thank Towana Spivey and Judy Crowder of the Fort Sill Museum Archives, John Lovitt of the Western History Collections at the University of Oklahoma, Candace Greene of the Smithsonian Institution, and the staffs of the National Anthropological Archives, the Chicago Field Museum, the University of Oklahoma Western History Collections, and the Oklahoma History Center Archives (especially Bill Welge) for their assistance during my research. Grants from the American Philosophical Society in 1993 and the Jacobs Foundation of the Whatcom Museum in 1995 financed portions of the fieldwork for this study. N. Scott Momaday, David Lavere, and two anonymous readers provided very useful suggestions on the manuscript for this book. Stacie Gates and Joseph Bowie at Southwest Missouri State University provided the diagrams of Kiowa society meetings. Finally, my thanks to Alessandra Jacobi Tamulevich and Alice Stanton at the University of Oklahoma Press for their assistance in seeing this work completed.

PRONUNCIATION GUIDE

With the exception of quoted historical spellings, all Kiowa names and vocabulary have been standardized in the Parker P. McKenzie Kiowa orthography. Because Kiowa is a tonal language, syllable pitch and length must be marked for accuracy. I prefer the McKenzie orthography because it was developed by a Kiowa who was intimately familiar with the subtleties of the language and because I find it to be the most accurate, thorough, consistent, and easy-to-use orthography for writing Kiowa. The McKenzie orthography was designed using the English alphabet so that it could be written on a typewriter and then have handwritten diacritical markings added. Today, computers and linguistic font programs allow both to be written electronically.

Each Kiowa syllable can be pronounced in five possible ways. The McKenzie system uses five diacriticals in ten possible combinations to mark pitch, length, and nasal quality. Using the letter *a*, the following examples demonstrate these diacriticals. They include two forms of marking pitch: *á* (rising or short pitch, high), and *à* (descending or short pitch, low). A horizontal line over a letter marks length: *ā* (rising long or high pitch long). A horizontal line under a letter, *a̱*, marks a nasal pronunciation, and a circumflex over a letter, *â*, marks a circumflexed or rising and falling pitch. These five forms can be combined to produce five pronunciations of a syllable: *á* (high pitch short), *à* (low pitch short), *ā́* (high pitch long), *ā̀* (low pitch long), and *â* (circumflex). Each of these can also contain a nasal marking, such as *á̱* (high pitch short, nasal), for a total of ten combinations. These markings can be downloaded from the IPA alphabet under the SIL manuscript reg font and made by combining the commands of shift-option with the numbers 2, 3, 4, 6, and = for nasal.

Fourteen of the twenty-two consonants in the English alphabet (*b, d, g, h, k, l, m, n, p, s, t, w, y, z*) correspond to and are thus pronounced in relatively the same way as those in Kiowa. The remaining English consonants (*c, f, j, q, r, v, x*), as they are pronounced in English, have no direct correlation with Kiowa sounds. In addition, the consonants *k, p, s,* and *t* each have two additional variations (soft and plosive) in Kiowa for which English has no counterpart. Thus, six consonants (*c, f, j, q, v, x*) were reassigned to represent other consonants in Kiowa, resulting in the following four clusters of related sounds:

>*f* = a soft *p* sound.
>*p* = a regular *p* sound.
>*v* = a plosive *p* sound.

xix

ch = a soft aspirated *s* sound.
s = a regular *s* sound.
x = a plosive *s* sound, like an aspirated *ts*.

j = a soft *t* sound, as in Jáifègàu.
t = a regular *t* sound.
th = a plosive *t* sound.

c = a soft *k* sound.
k = a regular *k* sound.
q = a plosive *k* sound, like an aspirated *k*.

The six Kiowa vowels are much like their English counterparts except for the Kiowa vowel *a*, which falls midway between the sounds in the words "act" and "arm." Unlike English vowels, which can have more than one pronunciation, there is only one basic sound for each Kiowa vowel. The six Kiowa vowels, with their pronunciations in parentheses, are always: *e* (ay), *a* (ah), *au* (aw), *i* (ee), *o* (oh), and *u* (woo). Kiowa contains four diphthongs (syllables containing multiple vowels): *ai* (ah-ee), *aui* (aw-ee), *oi* (oh-ee), and *ui* (woo-ee), with the vowel *i* (ee) comprising the second element in each. Although Kiowa vowels and diphthongs are affected in varying frequency by nasalization, vowel quality or length, and pitch accent or accentuation, they do not veer from their respective sounds.

In addition, *u* (woo) occurs in Kiowa syllables only after the consonants *g*, *k*, *c*, and *q*. In every occurrence, the *w* sound falls before the vowel *u* when voiced, but because it is a constant, and in order to reduce repetitious spelling, the *w* is retained in pronunciation but omitted in written Kiowa. Thus: *gu* (gwoo), *gui* (gwoo-ee), *ku* (kwoo), *kui* (kwoo-ee), *cu* (cwoo), *cui* (cwoo-ee), *qu* (qwoo), and *qui* (qwoo-ee).

When the consonant *g*, *k*, *c*, or *q* is the first letter in a syllable and is followed by the vowel *a* (ah) or *ai* (ah-ee), the syllable is always pronounced as if a *y* were inserted between the consonant and the vowel. Thus *ga* (gyah), *gai* (gyah-ee), *ca* (cyah), *cai* (cyah-ee), and so on. Because it is a constant, and in order to reduce repetitious spelling, the *y* sound is retained in pronunciation but omitted in written Kiowa. A few words, mostly of foreign origin, occur without the *y* sound and are indicated by an apostrophe, as in C'aiwau (Cai-wau, not Cyah-ee-wau), the Comanche pronunciation of *Kiowa*. For a complete account of the McKenzie orthography, see Meadows and McKenzie 2001.

Whereas English has only the singular and dual forms of the plural, Kiowa distinguishes three forms, the singular, dual, and triplural. These are denoted in the text by the parenthetical abbreviations (s), (d), and (t) and combinations of these such as (d/t) and (s/d), as in "*qópcúgàut* (s)."

KIOWA MILITARY SOCIETIES

INTRODUCTION

Plains Indian warfare and warrior culture have long fascinated ethnologists and lay readers alike. Plains military societies were military and social sodalities, or non-kin-based forms of social organization, that performed a wide variety of services. Known for enforcing codes of conduct during communal bison hunts and the Sun Dance and for providing social control and protection during encampments and camp moves, these organizations also provided the primary fraternal venues for the public display and honoring of the martial ethos and men's prowess through ritual dances and coup recitations. The societies also emphasized moral qualities such as bravery, chivalry, and honesty, as well as the enhancement of social and fraternal relations and group cooperation. They emphasized mutual aid through generosity and benevolence and performed public services such as providing charity to those in need, caring for elders, widows, and orphans, and constructing the Sun Dance lodge. Several Plains Indian women's societies performed auxiliary roles that supported male martial activities. Among other things, they held tribal religious rituals and blessed and redistributed food and goods. Although smaller Kiowa men's medicine and shield societies existed, military societies were the largest and most numerous male organizations. Because the Kiowa lacked purely social dance societies like those of some other Plains tribes, martial recognition and dance-related ceremonies were centered in the military societies. Through annual public dances and initiation rituals, these societies celebrated and publicized their martial and social importance while their members served as role models for younger people. Through their varied activities, military societies motivated people to achieve social prominence and respectability in a culture that emphasized a strong warrior ethos as the means to higher socioeconomic status.

Southern Plains tribes have maintained a strong martial ethos as a distinct enculturative arena for more than two hundred years. Since about 1800, Kiowa, Comanche, and Apache (KCA) martial values, expressed in military society ceremonies, ritual symbols, and some structural and functional attributes, have connected past and present. The evolution and role of these secular sodalities and their symbols comprise four main time periods: pre-reservation (pre-1875), reservation (1875–1901), post-reservation (1901–1945), and post–World War II or contemporary (1945 to the present). These periods encompass larger patterns of social change and development that are applicable to other Native Americans as well. Despite cultural change and syncretism, traditional views and concepts of veterans among the Kiowa, Comanche, and Apache have remained largely intact over time. Because military societies were the largest form of pre-reservation sodality, and because the KCA never relinquished the ideology surrounding the role of the warrior, they were able to regain status in their own terms as "warriors" with large-scale participation in World War II. Because this ethnic identity has been maintained within a larger socioeconomic and politically encapsulating society, the traditional roles of the military societies and the symbols and ethos they foster continue to be significant vehicles for traditional enculturation.

The Societies and Their Characteristics

Ten Kiowa military societies are known to have existed during the nineteenth century. Collectively the societies were known as Yàpfàhêgàu. Often translated as "soldier societies" or "warrior societies," the name actually refers to the temporary authority of these organizations as police and thus means "temporary police or guards" (Meadows 1999:38). Male societies consisted of the Pòlą́hyòp (Rabbits), Áljóyĭgàu (Mountain Sheep), Chèjánmàu (Horse Headdresses), Tǫ̀kǫ́gàut (Black Legs), Ją́ifègàu (Skunkberry or Unafraid of Death), Qóichę́gàu (Sentinel or Scout Dogs, or Dog Society), Cáuitémgòp (Kiowa Bone Strikers), and Óhǫ̀mògàu (Omaha) Societies. Kiowa women's societies included the Xálįchǫ̀hyòp (Calf Old Women) and Sétchǫ̀hyòp (Bear Old Women).

Each society had thirty to sixty members and was based on cross-band membership. The Black Legs and Horse Headdresses Societies included some Naishan Dene, or Plains Apache (Kiowa-Apache), in their membership. A man formally made presents to members of a society upon joining, but there was no concept of purchase in the matter. Although no formal, collective ritual purchase or age-set entry was involved, elements of de facto age grading clearly existed. Each society was graded roughly in terms of status and was composed of a large cohort of men who were approximately but not strictly similar in age. Whereas Robert Lowie (1916b) and Donald Collier (1938) maintained that all adult male societies were of equal rank, James Mooney (1898:230), Alice Marriott (AMP, Box 9), and Bernard Mishkin (1940) stated that beyond the age-graded Rabbits and Mountain Sheep Societies, all were ranked by social status. Jerrold Levy (2001:912) was uncertain "whether these societies had a formal ranking or could increase their prestige by attracting certain members," but a clear correlation existed between progression into the higher-ranked societies and increased age, social status, war rank, and wealth. Correlations between individual societies, society membership, and individual social status are reflected in the four Kiowa social classes (Meadows 1999:40–45). Although Levy (2001:912) believed that society-based "relative social ranking" resulted from the expansion of the men's society system—that is, that wealth required for initiation giveaways and to validate war honors led young men to start new societies that grew in status as their members matured—he offered no examples. I have always suspected that the Mountain Sheep and Horse Headdresses Societies were later developments, and indeed the earliest documentary sources reference the Dog (1790–1806) and Black Legs (1834) Societies. Marriott was told that the Ją́ifègàu was the oldest society but that it was later outranked by the Dog Society.

The Rabbits Society was composed of male children, and the Mountain Sheep Society was viewed as a sort of finishing school for older teens and young males. Membership in the Horse Headdresses Society, which encompassed older men, both commoners and some higher-ranking persons, was viewed as an increase in social status. Status continued to rise with membership in subsequent societies. The Dog Society was the highest-ranking and most prestigious of the men's societies by the mid-1800s. Competition between the Black Legs and the Ją́ifègàu as "second" to the Dog Society was keen, undoubtedly fluctuating with changes in the membership and warfare achievements of each. War honors were required for membership in the Black Legs and Dog Societies and for leadership positions in all the societies. Although Black Legs members were said to be slightly younger and ranked slightly beneath the Ją́ifègàu on average, many were of the second social ranking and went on to become members of the latter society.

Although elder consultants, born in the nineteenth century, stated that all Kiowa men belonged to a society, their estimates of society membership relative to the total male population suggest that perhaps as many as one-third of all Kiowa males were unable to acquire the wealth or military honors necessary for membership (Levy 2001:912). Members could belong to only one society at a time but could leave to join another at any time, and men were sometimes recruited by another society.

The Mountain Sheep, Horse Headdresses, Black Legs, and Ją́ifègàu each had two society leaders (fàujóqį̀) and two whipmen (áljóqį̀). The head leader was known as the tháumjóqį̀ (head society leader), and the other society leader was addressed as fàujóqį̀. The two whipmen served in the capacity of sergeants-at-arms, monitoring members' behavior at all society activities. The whipmen carried badges of office, often a serrated wooden society whip or quirt known as a qópcúgàut (s) or qópcûgà (d) (mountain striker, sometimes called a mountain club) or as a chę̂tą̀óttàgàu or chę̂tą̀òptàgàu (fox pelt handle), named for the small gray and yellow skin of the swift fox (*Vulpes velox velox*), which served as a wrist loop. The whipmen were known as áljóqį̀ (drivers), qį́àlqį̀ or qį́áljòqį̀ (men drivers or men driver keepers), and chę̂tà̀jóqį̀ (s) and chę̂tà̀jóqą̀hyòp (d) (fox pelt keepers). In some societies a whipman might carry a beaded lance (fóséségàu) or a straight sword (hą̨́ujòltǫ̀i or hą̨́ujòltǫ̀ifèjèdą̀u). In some societies men sometimes carried special lances related to their personal power, such as a zébàut (a large fletched lance), a pópǎ́kǫ̀gàut (a spotted feathered lance), or a beaded lance.

Each society maintained four fáuljògàu (drum keepers) who sang and drummed. These four societies also each had two boy members who were called ą̨́udę́tàlyį̀ (s) or ą̨udę́tàlyòp (d/t) (favored boys) and served as errand boys. They were also known as tályį̀yîgàu (boy members), íjèqį̀ (distributors or rationers, from serving food during feasts and meetings), and ą̨́ujòqį̀ (lit. those who keep things handy). The Mountain

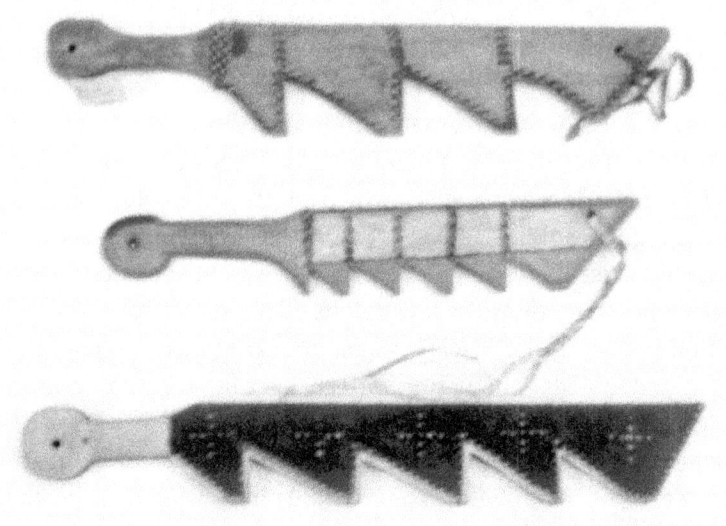

Kiowa military society whips. Smithsonian Institution, Washington, D.C., 1991.

Sheep, Horse Headdresses, Black Legs, and Omaha Societies also each had two female youth positions, or favored girls (ą̀udə́mátàun [s/d]), also known as mátàunyı̀gàu (girl members), who served in honorary positions similar to those of today's princesses. Female members were always from prominent families and frequently were the daughters of other society leaders. When selected from outside the families of society members, they were always from well-to do-families.

The institution of society partners, known as cóm (friend) and châ (the address form for "friend" or "partner"), and the pairing of two men as adoptive brothers permeated society membership. This adoption entailed extensive and reciprocal kinship and economic aid. Members of a society were also considered collectively to be brothers, and a loose network of social services and aid existed among them. The Black Legs and Jáifègàu Societies exhibited strong patterns of father-son replacement. The Dog Society included ten sash owners, who were considered to be among the bravest members of the tribe, their society partners, and several younger, apprentice members known as colts. Each society included several elder members who, because of age, were officially retired (tál) but served as counselors in society and ritual matters. They participated in singing and dancing but were relieved of any warfare or strenuous physical duties. The Kiowa Bone Strikers represent a defunct contrary society that may reflect a widespread but little-known pattern of early Plains Indian military societies. The Omaha Society represents the late-nineteenth-century diffusion of the Omaha Grass or War Dance, which had an organizational basis different from those of the other Kiowa societies.

Two women's societies, the Calf Old Women and the Bear Old Women, served largely as auxiliaries to the men's military societies, performing ritual functions related to the supernatural protection of Kiowa warriors in warfare, aid to the needy, and thanksgiving for recovery from illness. Having war power, the Calf Old Women Society was seen as a counterpart to the men's societies and was viewed as equal in rank to the Jáifègàu. Men commonly presented its members with gifts and requested their prayers before setting out on war parties and feasted them upon a successful return. The women's societies also performed a major role in constructing the Sun Dance lodge. Large initiation fees limited membership to higher-ranking women. Although the Bear Old Women were once closely connected to the Ten Medicine Bundles, a set of tribal religious bundles, and are categorized by some ethnologists as a medicine society, their protective functions in warfare merit comparison with the Calf Old Women Society.

Kiowa military societies traditionally functioned only during the few weeks associated with the Sun Dance, performing numerous functions during the aggregation for, travel toward, choice of, and alignment of the final Sun Dance encampment. For several days before the actual Sun Dance, each society sponsored a series of eight types of society dances, feasts, and parades, which included the initiation of new members. Men validated their war honors and social status by hosting feasts and giving away gifts at this time, which redistributed wealth while demonstrating the generosity and hospitality expected of the higher social classes. Feasts, giveaways, and lavish behavior bestowed on the favored children of wealthy families served similar purposes.

Policing the large aggregated camps, camp movements, and restricted communal hunts and enforcing tribal law and the directives of the Sun Dance priest were all common society functions. The societies participated in selecting the center pole for the Sun Dance, "capturing" it in a sham battle, transporting the pole and arbor materials (an act known as the "Brush Dragging"), building the actual lodge, and performing the ritual Kick Fight upon completion of the lodge. If a man were asked to perform a naming ceremony before the actual Sun Dance, his society might hold War and Scalp Dances as part of the activities. Except for policing duties, society functions were primarily social and economic. Some Kiowa societies conducted raids and warfare ventures that included solely their own members, but this practice seems to have declined by the 1840s. As Sangko, a Kiowa elder, told Marriott in 1936, "Men's societies were organized for dancing, not fighting." Societies also provided some services upon the death of a member and economic aid to fellow members and the needy.

Ethnological Importance

Kiowa military societies are of great ethnological importance for several reasons. First, they were greatly overlooked in early Plains Indian ethnology. The major work on Plains military societies, volume 11 of the *Anthropological Papers of the American Museum of Natural History* (Wissler, ed., 1916), concentrated on tribes whose military societies had not yet received any ethnological investigation and on the Sun Dance.

These writings focused primarily on trait distributions and clusters in order to provide diffusionist explanations and historical reconstructions of the development of these complexes, both within and among the Plains tribes.

Anthropologists largely overlooked Southern Plains military societies for further research. Tribes that had received some earlier investigation by ethnologists were not later revisited, so a golden opportunity for data collection was missed. Lowie (1916a, 1916b) published a total of seventeen pages for the Kiowa and Comanche (both whom he visited only briefly), and the Plains Apache were not investigated at all. The Cheyenne and Arapaho were not researched further because of the earlier, brief works of George Dorsey (1905), Alfred Kroeber (1907), and James Mooney (1907, 1912). The scarcity of data is due to a lack of research and not to a shortage of consultants and existing information. Although other researchers have looked at related topics of Plains and other Indian warfare (Grinnell 1910; Nye 1937; Smith 1938; Mishkin 1940; Newcomb 1950; Voget 1964; Ewers 1975; Biolsi 1984; Ferguson 1984), few scholars have explored Plains Indian military societies. Works that have addressed Plains military societies have focused on the role of societies as police with coercive powers (McLeod 1937; Humphrey 1942; Lowie 1941), classifications of Plains societies (Humphrey 1941), and brief accounts of Southern Plains military society revivals (Bittle 1962; Howard 1976).

Kiowa societies are also of great ethnological importance for other, more recent developments. By the early 1900s, three surviving Kiowa societies had become associated with distinct communities in which the majority of their membership was based. These were the Jáifègàu around Carnegie, Oklahoma, the Black Legs Society near Stecker, and the Omaha Society around Redstone. By 1930 the Black Legs Society was defunct, the Jáifègàu was declining, and only the Omaha Society remained strong. In 1935 a consultant named Mrs. Horse told Marriott that dances were limited to Fourth of July and Armistice Day gatherings.

Although the 1934 Indian Reorganization Act reversed decades of Bureau of Indian Affairs (BIA) policy and guaranteed Indians cultural freedoms, this alone did not prompt a cultural revival. The Great Depression, the Oklahoma Dust Bowl, and widespread poverty inhibited a cultural florescence until large numbers of veterans leaving for and returning from World War II and the Korean War created an almost continuous need among the Kiowa to honor veterans, resulting in the formation of several women's auxiliaries. Veterans returned with improved cultural and political freedom, a renewed and increasing sense of Indian pride, increased economic prosperity, and increased mobility via automobiles, which facilitated and accelerated the frequency of honor dances and powwows and the creation of large numbers of newly composed songs to honor veterans. These activities set the stage for a rekindling of the traditional form for honoring Kiowa warriors—men's military societies focused on ritual song and dance.

The revival of the Kiowa Gourd Clan in 1957 initiated the revival of other Kiowa, pan-Oklahoma, pan-Indian, and eventually non-Indian dance sodalities throughout the United States. It fostered subsequent Gourd Dance and military society revivals among the Kiowa, Comanche, Apache, Cheyenne, and other tribes, including the Kiowa Black Legs Society in 1958, the Apache Manatidie in 1959–1960, the Comanche Little Ponies in 1972, the Comanche Tuhwi Society in 1976, and other Southern Plains veterans' organizations.

These revivals mirrored larger developments and changes in twentieth-century American culture, civil rights, armed forces service, and federal Indian policy. Military society and related dances have become the largest social gatherings among the Kiowa and neighboring tribes and constitute a significant arena for maintaining traditional encampments, giveaways, and naming ceremonies and for introducing new songs and traditions. The Kiowa are also renowned among Oklahoma tribes for composing new songs and providing singers for powwows and society dances of neighboring tribes. Whereas the societies of many other tribes ceased before the 1920s, and few living consultants with knowledge of their traditional practices remain, the revived Kiowa societies and their richer bodies of associated knowledge offer vast research potential, far surpassing that of earlier accounts, which often offer little contextual data and only limited data on dance and regalia.

Need for a Definitive Treatment

Despite the existence of earlier works containing brief portions on Kiowa military societies and dance organizations (Clark 1885; Mooney 1898; Lowie 1916a; Howard 1976; Boyd 1981; Kracht 1989, 1994; Ellis 1990, 2003; Meadows 1991, 1995, 1999; Lassiter 1992, 1995, 1997, 1998), no comprehensive account of these organizations has previously been undertaken. Little research has been conducted on any single tribal sodality except the Black Legs (Meadows 1991), and except for Peter J. Powell's (1981) work on Cheyenne military societies, no recent research has been published on the sodalities of any single population. Most literature continues to be either (1) non-academic and non-fieldwork based, restating earlier data in a very general scope and remaining highly descriptive in terms of regalia and dance traits (Mails 1973, 1998), or (2) academic work on recent revivals and pan-Indianism (Bittle 1962; Howard 1976). More recently, Luke Lassiter (1998) focused on a symbolic analysis of Kiowa song and the various social and symbolic roles that the Gourd Dance and its associated music hold for contemporary Kiowa. Although Lassiter's book offers a rich body of symbolic and experiential data, it takes a postmodern, reflexive approach emphasizing the contemporary (post-1957) form of the dance, with little on sodality structures and earlier developments. Thus, little research of any depth has been conducted for any single Southern Plains military society, and none on an entire tribal military society complex or its cultural, historical, and ritual aspects.

This work provides a detailed account of the ritual structures, ceremonial composition, and historical development of each Kiowa military society. I include the origins, structure, functions, rituals, and society leaders, the respective dances, music, regalia, and paraphernalia, the way these have continued to the present, and their influence on more recent forms of the Gourd Dance, War Dance, and powwow in both Indian and non-Indian communities. The chapters strengthen my earlier arguments (Meadows 1995, 1999) while allowing a more detailed and temporal account of these organizations. Much of this material includes what tribal elders and society members think and feel about their societies. These data are of the greatest interest and perhaps the greatest relevance to contemporary Kiowa, their ceremonies, and their ongoing efforts to maintain them. As one reader surmised, I have written this for the Kiowa people, as my own "honor song" to them. The final chapter summarizes the current role of military and dance societies in maintaining Kiowa culture.

To reconstruct as thorough an ethnohistorical account of Kiowa military societies as possible, I have combined unpublished ethnographic fieldnotes, published sources, native art, extended participant observation, linguistic insights, and oral history interviews with Kiowa and their societies from 1989 to 2008. My approach emphasizes both extensive archival research and ethnographic fieldwork. For the early period, I used early documents, primarily ethnographic fieldnotes, ledgerbook art, and tribal calendars. These sources provide the voices of earlier generations of Kiowa from whom these data were collected. For subsequent periods, I used documents to cross-check and supplement oral history, allowing the Kiowa to express the way they think and feel about these societies and their associated traditions.

The pre-1900 period is constructed primarily from the archived fieldnotes of James Mooney, Hugh Lennox Scott, the participants in the 1935 Santa Fe Laboratory of Anthropology Kiowa Field School, and Alice Marriott (1934–1936), as well as from information in the Doris Duke Oral History Collection, the Fort Sill Museum Archives, the Kiowa Agency records in the Oklahoma State Historical Archives, Kiowa pictographic calendars and ledgerbooks, tribal censuses, and other archival sources. To my knowledge I am the first scholar to combine this wide a range of primary sources with extensive cultural and linguistic fieldwork in Kiowa research.

The reservation (1875–1901) and post-reservation (1901–1945) portions of this work are a combination of earlier ethnographic sources such as Mooney's fieldnotes, oral history collections, Kiowa Agency records and censuses, Kiowa pictographic calendars and ledgerbooks, more recent literature, and fieldwork interviews. The Doris Duke Papers, Kiowa Agency records, and eyewitness accounts from elder Kiowa provided invaluable data for this period, especially concerning society activities and federal government and agency efforts to end Indian dancing (1890–1931).

For the post–World War II period (post–1945), I have relied heavily on firsthand oral history accounts, including interviews with people who were directly responsible for, witnessed, and participated in the initial revivals and developments of the societies. Whenever possible, I interviewed a sample of the leaders and members of each society and examined society publications. These society leaders provided me with interviews and the ability to observe, record, photograph, film, and in some instances participate in portions of current society activities and ceremonies.

Data are lacking in some areas, depending on factors of existing documentation, current tribal memory, and the continuation or cessation of each society. Because some societies (Black Legs, Omaha) have been revived or have continued to the present, more data exists concerning their traditions and histories. These chapters are longer and in some respects more detailed than those of societies that ceased around 1840 (Kiowa Bone Strikers) and 1890 (Mountain Sheep, Horse Headdresses). Although the Dog Society met until 1878–1879, and the two women's societies until about 1905, extensive archival data from the last members of these groups permits a fairly detailed reconstruction of them, clarifying much of the mystery surrounding these societies.

I include numerous song texts in this work. Songs are an integral part of Native American communities. They lie at the heart of Native American sociocultural activities, are a part of everyday life, and are often closely guarded. Although the Kiowa have produced many commercial audiotapes, these generally involve certain types of songs, whereas other types, especially society songs with words, are often more protected. Some scholars (Merriam 1964:187–208; Beatty 1974; Boyd 1981; Lassiter 1997) and elders have discussed the issues of presenting Native American songs in published form, but others have cited the rapid decline of Kiowa speakers—a concern for language survival—and asked that these texts be recorded for future generations that may or may not retain their native language.

To protect the songs, I present only their texts and some of their associated history. Thus the complete musical form is allowed to remain, in its entirety, where it belongs, in the Kiowa community and at the discretion of Kiowa people. For preservation and clarity, I present all song texts in Kiowa, hyphenated by syllable to elicit meaning, followed by a literal grammatical translation and then a free translation in English. For consistency and accuracy, all songs and vocabulary are presented in the Parker P. McKenzie Kiowa orthography system (Meadows and McKenzie 2001). The reader can engage the Kiowa forms for research purposes or simply read the English translations. Because my focus is more cultural than musical, song texts are included to illustrate the Kiowa semantic themes contained in these forms of society and martially oriented music and, in response to the requests of elders, for purposes of cultural preservation.

1

PÒLĄ́HYÒP

The Rabbits Society

The Pòlą́hyòp (Rabbits) or Chą́yòi (an archaic word for rabbits) made up the first society in the Kiowa military society system. Originally including only Kiowa boys, this society served to train boys in tasks they would need as adults. It continued to meet until the adult men's societies became inactive in 1890. Rabbits Society dances were later held in conjunction with the Ją́ifègàu, or Unafraid of Death Society, dances held between 1912 and the late 1930s and, with the revival of this society in 1957 as the Kiowa Gourd Clan, at its annual July ceremonial. Now including all children and displaying few martially oriented themes, the Rabbits Society still aids in teaching Kiowa children aspects of their traditional culture.

The name Pòlą́hyòp denotes "rabbits." However, many Kiowa refer to the group today as Pòlą́hį̀, the singular form, "rabbit," which is also used to refer to the Big Dipper because of the constellation's similarity to a rabbit's ears.[1] The origin of the society is preserved in a Kiowa legend in which a person known as Old Man was exiled from the tribe for breaking a law. Despondent, he lay down to die but later awakened to a multitude of rabbits. The rabbits gathered food and cared for Old Man. Encouraged, he lived with the rabbits and learned their language and way of life. Eventually the rabbits suggested that Old Man teach all the little boys how to become great men (Boyd 1981:77–78).

Moving closer to the camp of his people, Old Man sent a message for all young boys to come and camp by the river. The boys came, and after forming a group with laws, they elected Old Man as the Head Rabbit. Old Man received the name "Grandpa Rabbit" and thereafter trained little boys for manhood. Dancing in imitation of rabbits, the group composed songs. Learning of these events, the tribal council invited the organization and Grandpa Rabbit back into the tribe, giving them a position in the tribal warrior societies (Boyd 1981:77–78).

The Rabbits Society consisted of all boys old enough to walk freely, up to the age when they left to join another men's society (Lowie 1916b:844, 1956:137; Parsons 1929:90). However, parents commonly brought their children to Rabbits Society meetings while they were still in the cradle, before they were weaned. Around the age of twelve, boys were considered members but were becoming ashamed to "still be playing with little boys." Older members were known as jack rabbits (*qómsàugàu*). Some Kiowa elders have stated that they are still officially Rabbits because they never joined another society in adult life. James Mooney (1912:862) and Maurice Boyd (1981:78) wrote that the age of membership was ten to twelve and eight to twelve, respectively.

The adult Kiowa military societies practiced a ritualized forced recruitment or "capture" of boys considered to hold potential as new members. Usually the two whipmen of a society found and escorted the prospective member back to the meeting of their society (Meadows 1999:57–59). According to Rev. J. J. Methvin, a Methodist missionary among the Kiowa:

> The different orders are always watching the Rabbits and as the boys grow old enough for the army [other societies] it is a race to see which order will catch them. In this way the ranks of the "Dog Soldiers" are always kept filled by the captures of the Rabbits.
>
> When a Rabbit is captured by an order he is sent to capture another Rabbit for his file man and close companion in the army [society]. Then the choice is made and the pledge is made and sealed by the smoking of the pipe, which makes them boon companions ready to die for each other. They are no longer "Rabbits" but of a higher order of the Kiowa soldiery.[2]

Methvin (1927:165) wrote that both male and female children belonged to the Rabbits Society, but he most likely confused the Kiowa Rabbits Society with the Naishan Dene, or Plains Apache, Kasowe (Rabbits), which included children of both sexes (McAllister 1935; Meadows 1999). Kiowa girls often sat and danced behind their brothers during dances and feasts, just as adult women did at the men's dances. Although girls participated in portions of the Kiowa Rabbits dances, they were not considered actual members. Goomdaw and Heapobears, two consultants to the Laboratory of Anthropology Kiowa Field School in 1935, both stressed that "there were no girls in the Polaiyi."[3] No formal initiation existed; boys simply went to society assemblies as soon as they were old enough to walk and sat in on the activities. A few favored boys from prominent families were taken directly from the society into the older men's societies to fulfill the positions of male youth society members at around the age of seven or eight.[4]

The Rabbits Society normally had one elderly adult leader who was appointed for life. At one time there were apparently two adult leaders, reflecting the organizational structure of the adult men's societies. HeapoBears stated that there were two leaders, an older adult and a younger one known as the "man driving man" (*qíàlqì*), and that the "captain" was always a Ten Medicine Bundle keeper, or custodian. This tradition apparently changed around the early 1900s, when the men leading Rabbits Society dances were no longer bundle keepers. Although one consultant stated that the leader(s) had no official title, Kiabo, or Edgar Keahbone, who was reported to have been the leader in 1925, gave the term pòlá̰hḭqàjàiqì̀, or rabbit chief (Parsons 1929:111), and Luther Samon (Sahmaunt) and HeapoBears gave the terms pòlá̰hḭfàujòqì̀ (rabbit leader/keeper) and táljóqì̀ (sponsor/leader). This person was also sometimes called the whipman. By 1935 the title fàujóqì̀ seems no longer to have been applied to the leaders of this society, perhaps because of the marked decline of Kiowa military societies with the end of the Sun Dance in 1890. Unlike other adults, Rabbits Society leaders could belong to other men's societies, but their duties for the Rabbits took precedence over those for other societies (Lowie 1916b:844).

Functions of the Society

Although the Rabbits feasted, danced, paraded, and sang like the members of the adult societies, the group's main purpose was to train boys in the skills needed for adult life.[5] Society leaders instructed youths in swimming, running, hiding, riding, archery, and the use of a lance. The leader also gave counsel, supervised play, organized contests and dances, encouraged games and sports that would further the boys' training for adulthood, and maintained order by breaking up fights between the children. Society meetings served to introduce and foster the martial ideology that children would need as adults. To help prepare the boys for membership in an adult warrior society, any qájáiqì̀ (lit. brave man, a man with at least one war honor) could serve as a role model by reciting his war deeds at Rabbits Society meetings (Mishkin 1940:40). Kiowa captive Andre Martinez compared the Rabbits to an Anglo-style school because the leaders set examples for the youths to follow by reciting coups: "When I was young like you, I was a rabbit, when I got older I went and stole horses, took scalps, etc." (Lowie 1916b:844). Mooney recorded from Cûiánáunjè (Guiananti, Wolf [That] Howled):

> Boys in [the] charge of older relatives were frequently allowed to accompany war expeditions in order to accustom them to warlike things. In the Kiowa tribe nearly all the boys from about 10 to 15 years of age were also enrolled among the Polanyop "Rabbits," the lowest warrior society, to receive regular military instruction before their admission to a higher degree. The present Guiananti was born in 1844, accompanied his first war expedition in 1854, killed his first enemy, a Texan, in 1864, and was first married in the winter of 1865–66.[6]

By dancing behind their young male relatives in the Rabbits Society, young girls were taught the role they would play as adult women in honoring Kiowa men as warriors.

Kiowa elders confirm these basic society functions and compare the enculturative functions of the Rabbits Society to those of today's Head Start and Boy Scouts programs.[7] Colonel Wilbur S. Nye (1962:60) also compared the Rabbits to the Boy Scouts, because they often camped in their own tents and had their own activities during the Sun Dance. When asked whether the society was currently important in promoting educational values, society leader Gus Palmer Sr. replied:

Oh yes. It's supposed to be because they were one of them military [societies] to begin with, like I mentioned way back then to them. It's just like any going to school or any training, you just have to start them, train them at home. Yes, you keep teaching them, telling them these things. Step by step in growth and then you practice in dress when you're small and then it stays with you until you get up in age. You feel like you [have] been dressing when you were little and you're going to keep that up. Yes, it's a teaching, that Rabbits. . . . You kind of teach them like you would . . . a kid going to school, home start, head start, that's why, same way.[8]

A new children's care center in Anadarko, Oklahoma, which offers assistance in preparing young Kiowa children for Head Start or kindergarten, was named Kiowa Little Rabbits.[9]

Gilbert McAllister (1935, 1937:139–142, 166) described the Plains Apache Kasowe (Rabbits) Society, which was structurally similar in most respects to the Kiowa Rabbits Society, except that the Apache society included children of both sexes. The Apache Rabbits Society was clearly concerned with the health and longevity of children. For the Apache, the rabbit was one of the most visible symbols of fertility, because cottontails have gestation periods of only twenty-eight days and are capable of producing four or five litters of young per year. The society's name was thus appropriately chosen for its symbolic and protective qualities for children. Parents pledged society meetings for a sick child or to honor a child. Participation was linked to health and victory over sickness (Schweinfurth 2002:102, 149). As Claude Jay explained to ethnographer Charles Brant, "the Rabbit Dance meant health—victory over sickness."[10] The Apache Rabbits Society also focused on child development during the formative years and taught children social discipline in following rules and working together cooperatively. Because the Apache Rabbits leader also cared for the primary Apache religious bundle, the society provided the children with a feeling of unity and importance while promoting tribal integration and continuity through familiarization with the most important religious items and rituals of the tribe (McAllister 1937:166). Because some Kiowa and Apache men's societies participated together during Sun Dances, it is likely that their youth societies also did.[11]

According to the Kiowa consultant Sangko (Seko), the Rabbits Society had no leader when he was a boy in the 1860s, probably because of the large number of deaths in the tribe. So much fighting was taking place among the boys that their fathers gathered and called in Qópcótjè, a Ten Medicine Bundle keeper, to be their permanent leader (Parsons 1929:90).[12] When he became too old, he called upon Boloi or Beidlade, a captive, to succeed him and gave him the society knife, symbolic of the leader's position. Heapobears stated that the successor as keeper of the Ten Medicine Bundle would also be the next Rabbits Society leader. If so, then a pattern like that in the Apache Rabbit Society, with its similar integrative and educational principals, is likely to have existed among the Kiowa. In Martinez's time, Ko'ar and Àiájè (Walking On A Tree, a Mountain Sheep Society whipman) served as leaders (Lowie 1916b:844). Whether the Rabbits Society leader was considered a society leader or a whipman is unclear, but despite variations in terms of address, the position resembled that of a regular society leader, because the other officer positions were temporary appointments made on a meeting-to-meeting basis.[13] When a Rabbits leader died, the remaining leader nominated a successor. When the boys agreed upon a man, they all went to his tipi, and, as in the adult societies, the youths "seized him" and led him to their meeting tipi (Lowie 1916b:844). This further trained them in the behavior expected for later admission into the adult organizations.

The Rabbits' Sun Dance Activities

The Rabbits held meetings from anytime after the event known as the Ride Around Camp, conducted as bands gathered for the Sun Dance, until the beginning of the actual Sun Dance. Feasts could be pledged by anyone, and the families of favored members frequently sponsored them to honor their sons, although not on any regular basis. A father might also vow to sponsor a feast in thanksgiving because his son had recovered from illness. Pledges could be made anytime throughout the year and were fulfilled at the next Sun Dance. A member's father, grandfather, or the society leader announced a feast by riding around the camp and proclaiming which boy had invited the Rabbits for a feast and dance (Lowie 1916b:844). As in adult society meetings, a tipi with its sides rolled up was set up in the middle of the camp circle. The best food was served, and the affair proved quite elaborate, especially if pledged for a favored boy.[14]

According to the consultant Keahbone, after a father informed the society leader of the proposed feast, the leader would respond, "Àhô" (thank you), four times as he moved his hands forward and backward, palms held downward, while facing the pledger (Parsons 1929:111). This practice, known as *thópfásôgù*, is a common Kiowa expression when showing gratitude or asking a great favor. The boy's family placed items in a pile and then had a giveaway in which women came up to receive a gift. Horses or sticks representing the future gift of a horse were also given (Parsons 1929:90). Goomdaw said that sponsored feasts were also given for girls.[15]

Before the Sun Dance, the leader would announce one of the society's favorite activities, a parade. The boys rode horseback, two abreast around the camp circle. They were said to have loved parades but were often unable to maintain control over their mounts, and many young boys experienced humorous riding accidents. Spectators greatly enjoyed these mishaps. Smaller groups sometimes went off on their own, all dressed up, and paraded around without having been formally called together.[16] During the approach to the final Sun Dance encampment, the Rabbits were allowed to shoot toy arrows at any dogs they encountered. This practice is thought to have been a parody of the adult societies, who did likewise. A taboo against dogs during society meetings is found in several Southern Plains military societies.[17]

Like members of the men's societies, the Rabbits danced during the four stops toward the final encampment location. Unlike the feasts and dances of their elder counterparts, those of the Rabbits were limited to the daytime hours. At dances, the leader selected several of the older boys to drum and sing. Lowie (1916b:844) noted that all members sang while dancing, and the leaders also drummed and occasionally took part in the dancing, which must have been entertaining for the youths. The society members danced in a circle, mimicking the motions of a rabbit, with young girls directly behind them. Placing their hands behind their ears with their forefingers extended to represent a rabbit's ears, they danced by jumping up and down in place in time to the music, heads bobbing, while squealing "châ châ" (Mooney 1912:862; Lowie 1916b:845; Methvin 1927:165; Parsons 1929:90). Dances often ended in a tangled mass of wrestling children of both sexes, whom the leaders attempted to separate. Following this, girls sat behind their brothers to eat. The boys are said often to have made creative use of leftover food by throwing it at each other.[18]

At meetings, the society leader sat with a butcher knife, the symbol of his office, lying in front of him. The child members had no regular insignia or badges. As in the adult societies, the leader(s) appointed two older youths to serve as temporary whipmen and servants who forced all to rise and dance. If the children refused, the whipman was obliged to "whack" them with a stick, following the use of society whips in the adult societies. If they still refused or acted reluctant, he was authorized to cut up their blankets with the knife. According to Martinez, three to ten boys danced at a time, after which war deeds were recited by the society leader(s) (Lowie 1916b:844). The leader had no authority to whip or punish any of the children but stopped fights by pulling apart the boys involved. Unlike the ritual offering of a pipe to stop fights between adults (which was reportedly never refused, from fear of supernatural sanction), a pipe was not used in these situations.[19]

Members wore their best clothes for dances, often including a strip of elk hide worn as a headband with an erect feather at the back of the head, buckskin clothing, and face paint (Lowie 1916b:844). Favored boys wore elaborate miniature dance outfits, which included bells, and a special headdress of skunk tail and turkey beard hair with the lower part dyed red and the top black.[20]

In building the Sun Dance lodge, the members of the Rabbits and the Calf Old Women Societies collected and spread sand on the floor of the lodge together. Having started their dancing and fasting the previous night, the Sun dancers took a break on this morning. The Calf Old Women entered the Sun Dance lodge carrying hoes. Occasionally, one of the members took her granddaughter along, for this ritual was believed to ensure the girl a long life. The women made a circle inside the lodge and danced clockwise four times to the left, stopping between each dance. The Rabbits did not dance at this time.[21]

On the following morning, the women sang the first song to prepare the Rabbits for their work inside the lodge. As Gus Palmer Sr. described it: "The main reason is when they have their Sun Dance, the Grandmas they take the little ones, part of their job, they go and they have it near a river where that sand is. . . . They go, they gather that sand and they bring it inside that Sun Dance lodge and they sing to them."[22]

This song had two versions. The Calf Old Women sang the following version as they transported the sand with the children:

1. Má-tàun-yĭ-gàu gàu tàl-yóp pái bát ą̊-hầu
   (Little girls / and little boys / dirt / you all / bring)
   Little girls and little boys, go and pack in dirt [imperative].
2. Jò-dôm bát àui-àum
   (Floor / you all [imperative] / repair-fix or tidy up)
   Fix up the floor.
3. À mâ-kầu-àun gàu qyậu-gà ộ-dèp
   (I / pitiable / and-but / love making / I / love-like)
   I am pitiable, but I still love lovemaking.[23]

Three more songs without lyrics were sung. After feinting four times with their hoes, each of the Calf Old Women Society members cleaned a portion of the ground of all grass and debris. Then the Old Women and the Rabbits went to gather sand, preferably white, for the lodge floor, carrying it in buffalo hides and blankets from a nearby hill or riverbank. Returning, the group lined up west to east at the door of the lodge and marched in clockwise, singing four songs (reported to be the same as the cleaning-up songs) while dancing with the bundles of sand on their backs. Then each woman poured sand onto the portion of the lodge floor she had prepared. After four sets of singing and unloading sand were performed, the Rabbits dumped their smaller loads to finish up. When the sand was approximately one foot deep throughout the lodge, with a two-foot-high cone around the base of the center pole, the Rabbits concluded their duties by smoothing it out. Following this, but before the actual start of the ceremony, the Rabbits "played Sun Dance" at night in the lodge. If one of their parents had so vowed, some of the Rabbits danced with the Sun dancers on the first night of the actual Sun Dance, wearing white body paint like that of the Sun dancers, with a whistle and eagle down feathers hanging down their backs.[24]

The Contemporary Rabbits Society

With the end of the Kiowa Sun Dance in 1890, Rabbits Society meetings and dances declined rapidly, although they continued to be held intermittently at annual celebrations for the Fourth of July and, later, Armistice Day. In the early twentieth century, opportunities for Rabbit Dances existed primarily in association with the revival of the Black Legs Society and the Jáifègàu in 1912 and with the ongoing Omaha Society. Although Edgar Keahbone was reported to be the Rabbits Society leader in 1925, the frequency of dances at this time is unknown (Parsons 1929:111). As the society's functions decreased, so did its role in introducing and preparing children for adult roles and social activities. The society was by no means forgotten, however. The 1915

Carnegie, Oklahoma, baseball team, composed almost entirely of Kiowa, was named the Rabbits.[25]

By the 1950s, many powwows were being held, but as one elder pointed out, "nothing specific for the children." Rabbit Dances returned with the revival of the Kiowa Jáifègàu in 1957 under the new name Kiowa Gourd Clan. Since then a Rabbit Dance has been held at the annual July 2–4 encampment in Carnegie, Oklahoma. Former Gourd Clan vice-president Oscar Tsoodle spoke of the elders' concern for the children and the importance of including them at the time of the Gourd Clan revival:

> They thought of the children. They said, "Say, we need to have something for the children." And that's the way it first begun, in order to do that, at least to recognize them in the first part of the dance. So they have that Rabbit Dance. At least they think of the children and not forget about them, because they were around at that time. They thought about that, "We need to think of our children." . . . It used to be before, way back then, and then came this revival, so we revived it again.[26]

From 1957 to 1976, John Oliver Tanedooah served as Grandpa Rabbit for the group at the annual Gourd Clan dances, advising and singing for the Rabbits. Black Legs Society commander Gus Palmer Sr. served in this position from 1977 to 2006. In 2007 Joe Fish Dupoint began singing for the society. Other Rabbit Dances are held as part of the Carnegie Tia-Piah Society's annual Fourth of July ceremonial at Chieftain Park, south of Carnegie, Oklahoma (see ch. 5).[27]

At the Gourd Clan encampment, the Rabbits figure prominently in cleaning up the dance arena and campgrounds. Whereas the Rabbits once helped to clean and prepare the Sun Dance lodge floor, now they clean up products of the modern age such as food wrappers, soda pop cans, and other debris. Then, in a manner resembling that of parades of past Sun Dances, the Rabbits line up east of the dance arena and parade in as a group, making a clockwise processional inside the arena. Grandpa Rabbit plays a hand drum and sings for them in front of the announcer's stand as they parade and dance. These songs include both nursery rhymes for infants and Rabbits songs for older children. They are generally stories about little animals and their adventures and today include Rabbit Society and Kiowa nursery songs. Some elders state that both types of songs are now sung as Rabbits Society songs and in some cases are difficult to distinguish.

One favorite song is the Prairie Dog Song, which relates how the tribal trickster Saynday (Séndé, or One Who Is Nose Mucous) attempted to kill some prairie dogs to eat. Instructing them to close their eyes and dance in place while he sang to them, he began knocking them over the head with a club. Distrustful of Saynday's intentions, one of the prairie dogs finally opened his eyes to peek. Discovering Saynday's actions, the prairie dog sounded the alarm to save the rest:

> 1 Chá-dàu, chá-dàu, tòn bá jót-jé
> (Prairie dogs / prairie dogs / tail / be wagging)

Prairie dogs, prairie dogs, wag your tails.
2 Repeat.
3 Bá tòn jòt-jè, ôi yá̰ fául-âu-chȅ, ôi yá̰ fául-âu-chȅ
   (Be / tail / wagging, until you're tired and sleepy, until you're tired and sleepy).
   Wag your tails until you're tired and sleepy, until you're tired and sleepy.[28]

A favorite Kiowa nursery song is the Thà̰ukó̰dàugà, or Black Horn Spoon Song. It tells how an elderly woman whose family had once been prominent and wealthy was now nearly destitute. The woman's grandson lost her last valuable and most cherished possession, her black bison horn spoon. After she punished him, he lay pouting in the back of her tipi when, apparently asleep and dreaming, he suddenly received supernatural power:

1 Thà̰u-kó̰-gà váui-xép nàu
   (Horn spoon / black / I lost / and)
   I lost the black bison horn spoon and
2 Tã-lyôi ę́ tá̰-hòl nàu
   (Paternal grandmother/ she / whipped / and)
   My paternal grandmother whipped me and
3 Kòm-dó̰-bà à thà̰u-qá̰u-chȅ
   (Tipi / back of / I / pouting / lay / at the time of which)
   In the back of the tipi I lay pouting.
4 À áu-dé-dà̰u-àum-gà
   (I / favored / state of being / became)
   I became endowed with power.[29]

Another popular song tells of a boy who chased and killed a bison calf, from which he brought the small intestines, a delicacy, to his maternal grandmother:

1 Xá-lȉ gà ál-bá̰u
   (Calf / I / chased)
   I chased a calf.
2 Repeat.
3 Gà hâun-jàu-ál-bá̰u
   (I / exhaust-shall / chased)
   I chased it to exhaustion.
4 Repeat.
5 Thá̰u-yâu gà ję̂ gàu
   (Ear / I / caught / and)
   I caught it by the ear and
6 Há-yá nén kàui-bá-tô-lè-qȉ-gà
   (Somewhere / I / awkwardly back and forth [butterfly]-threw)
   I slung it around back and forth [like a butterfly] and threw it somewhere.

7 Tą̀-jè sé-tháį yán á-càun-màu nàu
   (Maternal grandmother / intestines / I brought / and)
   I brought the small intestines to my maternal grandmother and
8 Gà áu-thą̂-mì-jàu
   (She / licking [lit. sucking] / shall)
   She will lick them.[30]

The following song is another version of the one sung while placing the sand in the Sun Dance lodge, which is frequently sung today:

1 Tà-lyĩ-qí-gàu pái bát ą̀-hàu
   You small boys go and pack/bring in the dirt.
2 Jò̧-dôm bát àui-àum
   Fix it along the lodge floor.
3 Fòi bé yái-gùn yài-qà-jài-gà
   Don't be acting/dancing like you are brave.
4 À mâ-kằu-àun-nàu jò̧-są̂-nà
   Although I am pitiable/humble and have a small house.[31]

Whereas originally only boys were Rabbit Society members, today girls take a greater role in participation and dancing. Elders still note that previously only male children were Rabbits, but all children are generally viewed as members today, at least in terms of participation. Parents often tape-record and film their children in the Rabbit Dances. Gus Palmer Sr. frequently encouraged parents to record and learn the songs and to carry them on. While the youths dance, parents frequently enter the arena to hold giveaways or to pledge beef or money on behalf of their children to the Kiowa Gourd Clan for the next year's dance. I have observed pledges at Rabbit Dances ranging from beef to monetary amounts of $25 to $1,000. Parents and grandparents frequently honor their offspring by placing money, candy, or toys at the feet of their children to give away to others. Several elders report that these giveaways are now much larger than in the past. One or more naming ceremonies for children, followed by a giveaway, are also common today. They are usually limited to families who are able to afford the cost of such events.

Kiowa culture is still learned primarily through observation, listening, and participation, with little formal instruction. In pre-reservation times, physical and athletic training, familiarization with dancing and singing, helping to construct the Sun Dance lodge, imitating Sun dancers, reciting coups, holding society leadership positions, using sticks as society whips, mock-policing one another to encourage participation in dances, participating in society parades, and girls' dancing behind their young male relatives to honor them all mirrored adult military society roles. Although a martial ideology and coup recitations are no longer parts of society gatherings, the Rabbits Society continues several pre-reservation functions and enculturative principals by enabling children to learn through imitation of their elders. Thus the society

Rabbits Society dance performed at the Kiowa Gourd Clan ceremonial, Carnegie, Oklahoma, July 4, 2004.

continues to introduce children to Kiowa dancing, singing, honoring, naming ceremonies, group cooperation, sharing, and giving away.

Oscar Tsoodle described the Rabbits' community service and subsequent public recognition: "Before they Rabbit dance, we make them clean up the area, you know, pick up cups and everything, clean the area up. It's the quickest way we can clean the area up . . . and then after they clean that area up, and bring everything, trash and everything up, when it's all clean, then they start dancing, you know, they start singing for them."[32]

After dancing, the children are given bags of candy, cake, fruit, and soda pop. The morning program concludes with the announcement of who will sponsor the noon meal for the Rabbits. The grandparents of one of the Rabbits usually sponsor this feast in honor of their grandchild.

The role of the Rabbits Society in Kiowa culture has changed, but judging from earlier accounts, it still provides opportunities and functions for Kiowa youths that were present in earlier times. Not all Kiowa children attend the society's dances, because of residential distance or family and individual interests, but a sizable portion does, which suggests the society's continued importance. With the end of the Kiowa Sun Dance, with a larger and more dispersed contemporary population, and with changes in the types of skills needed for adulthood, much traditional training is no longer needed. Although the role of children and the skills they need in Kiowa society today have become adapted to newer circumstances, the importance of the society for enculturating Kiowa children endures. Whereas bringing in sand for the Sun Dance lodge and receiving training in hunting and fighting were important past activities, today cooperation and the preservation of tribal culture are the primary lessons to be learned. The society still promotes cooperation among Kiowa of all ages and serves as a major institution for familiarizing Kiowa youths with both their tribal peers and numerous important ethnic and cultural traditions such as language, society dances and songs, kinship ties, naming ceremonies, and giveaways.

The society also provides Kiowa youths with their own position in the larger Kiowa society, a position that is publicly recognized and honored. The ability of the society to change through time yet retain its enculturative role reflects its adaptability as a unit of social organization, albeit on a brief annual basis. The use of similar society symbols (age, status, songs, dance, feasts) and their associated significance over time demonstrates significant cultural continuity.

Although Kiowa children and some adults may not recognize all the structural and symbolic roles associated with society functions, people often mention the importance of their participation later in life. With smiles on their faces, elders often reminisce about their days as Rabbits, emphasizing the songs, dances, and feasts and the fun they had. Several Kiowa in their thirties spoke of how important it was to have been a Rabbit as a child and to have dressed, danced, and, as one person put it, participated "every Fourth [of July]." On one occasion I was in a group of Kiowa men and women in their thirties and forties who spent nearly thirty minutes reminiscing about being Rabbits. One man even went so far as to say that "being a Rabbit is part of being a real Kiowa."[33] For some Kiowa, society participation retains a recognizable cultural and ethnic importance that transcends the transition from childhood to adulthood and, as an important social symbol, constitutes one aspect of what it means to be Kiowa. For some, this importance is reinforced and expanded with participation in one of several adult societies.

Although the Rabbits Society is currently a stable and functioning society with annual dances, its vitality will depend on future generations of elders, particularly those who will sponsor dances and who can sing the appropriate songs. Many elders lament that younger Kiowa are retaining increasingly fewer of the older cultural forms, especially the language, which is critical for singing, and that children experience too many, often negative distractions derived from Anglo society. It is to be hoped that the younger generations will retain as much traditional knowledge as possible, for one day they will be the elders on whom future generations of Kiowa youths will depend for their traditional knowledge.

2

ÁLJÓYÌGÀU

The Mountain Sheep Society

The Áljóyìgàu, or Mountain Sheep Society, consisted largely of young men with little or no warfare experience. The society served as a sort of finishing school for the skills begun in the Rabbits Society and needed to become an accomplished warrior. Members sought to prove themselves in combat, and by obtaining a coup or battle deed, they increased their chances of being recruited into one of the higher-ranking men's societies. Because members sought to attract wives through their prowess in battle and the attractive dress they wore during society dances, they were often reputed to be reckless in battle and well dressed in society meetings, dances, and parades. The Mountain Sheep Society is one of the least known of all the Kiowa military societies, because of sparse records and the society's cessation in 1890.

The society's name is based on the root words for "mountain sheep," *áljóyì* (s/d) and *áljóyòi* (t), and the suffix *gàu* (people, group, society). The society was also known as Jḛ́bèyòi and Jḛ́bègàu (Bighorn Sheep), from *jḛ́bè̀* (s/d) and *jḛ́bègàu* (t), terms for the Rocky Mountain bighorn sheep.[1] The society has been described under various spellings and ethnonyms, including Sheep (Clark 1885:355); Adaltoyui and Tenbeyu'i, translated as Young (wild) Sheep (Mooney 1898:230); Alto'yuhe (Shepherds) and Te'nbeyu'i (Lowie 1916b:842, 845); Ah-tle-to-yo-ye (Methvin 1927:166); Altoyowe (Sheep) and Taebeyowe (Goats) (Parsons 1929:91); and Goat, by H. L. Scott.[2] Elder Kiowa today typically use the name Àljóyì̀, an abbreviation of Áljóyìgàu, or the English term "Herders," from the similarity of the society's name to the word for whipmen, *áljóqì̀* (drivers or herders) and the association of young men with herding horses. In Kiowa County, Oklahoma, a mountain below Elk Creek on the east side of the North Fork of the Red River is known as Jḛ́bèqòp, Mountain Sheep or Wildsheep Mountain, from the society's having frequently danced at a nearby spring along the river (Mooney 1898:425).[3]

Although the society's origin is unknown, Robert Lowie (1916b:846) recorded an account concerning Sheep Mountain in which an enemy was pursuing a group of Kiowa warriors. Heading toward "a mountain calle'd Altō'yuhe" (Áljóyòiqòp), a

Mountain Sheep Society member declared, "I will not run any farther, I'll make a stand and defend my people, even if I get killed." He sang his song, made a stand, and was killed. The mountain was henceforth named after the society, which adopted the man's death song as a song of its own: "Now I am gone. I am going to leave you" (i.e., "I will not run any more"). This may have been Sheep Mountain in Oklahoma.

Another account records an incident in which a society member named Cî̀èl (Big Meat/Flesh) was shot during a battle between some Kiowa and Anglos at a place written as "Brazo's Ranch" in Texas. Charley White Horse said that his paternal uncle Big Meat was killed at Waterless Mountain (Tǫ́hę́qòp). Mooney (1898:339, 403) wrote that Big Meat was killed in the winter of 1874–1875, when the Kiowa left the reservation in Indian Territory and fled into Texas. Big Meat then joined a raiding party that entered New Mexico. After killing two men and capturing a woman and several horses, the party was surprised and attacked by soldiers. Big Meat "was mortally wounded in the first fire, but propped himself against a rock and succeeded in killing one soldier and wounding another before he died." After another Kiowa was killed, the soldiers were finally repulsed. Big Meat's society brothers who were present tried to cure him, together with the medicine man and fellow member Cûièmhêjè (Entering Wolf), who sang the following song:

1 Jó-gúl fā́-dáu-dè dám-gá-dàu
(Young man / one of them-is / weak-state of)
A young man, one of them is already weak (i.e., dying).

As he lay dying, Big Meat composed and sang the following song, which was later adopted by the society:[4]

1 Ję́-bè-yòi
(Mountain Sheep–[society] members)
Mountain Sheep Society members,
2 Oí-á-qát-jàu à-kó-bà̀-jàu
(Yonder [over there]-they-beckoning-are / I-go-shall)
Yonder, over there, they are beckoning; I shall go now.

These songs reflect the group's sorrow at losing a companion and the warrior's military spirit, his acceptance of an honorable death through combat, and his acceptance of the hereafter.

Because several soldiers were killed in the fight, the Kiowa held a victory dance in spite of Big Meat's death. This was unusual, because the loss of any man typically negated the celebratory Scalp and Victory Dances held when a successful returning party had lost no members. After being shot to the ground while advancing up a hill, Big Meat had managed to get to his gun. With his final shot, he reportedly killed the soldiers' leader, who was wearing a blue cape with a yellow lining. The leader's fall caused the other soldiers to retreat. Big Meat's sister Dǫ́bètâi (Rushed By

Below) danced at the Victory Dance and composed the following song in honor of her brother's great deed:

1. Thá̀-gài jạ́u é jại-dàum-thầu gàu
   My noble brother, bravely on the war party he has acted.
2. Cí-èl-qì̃ qạ́-hyội né hól-gụ̀-jầu cí-còt-dò
   Many men Big Meat has killed fearlessly.
3. Dè yái-gụ̀n-yǐ-jầu há-jêl-chá-hệ̀
   I will dance with joy. Someone will ululate without shame.
4. Án áun-gụ̀-thầu yạ́ áun-gụ̀-thầu
   I shall be sounding (ululating).[5]

Membership

Encompassing mostly postpubescent, unmarried male youths, the Mountain Sheep was the largest Kiowa men's society, ranging from fifty to seventy-five members. Officers included two society leaders, two whipmen, two male youth positions, and two female youth positions. Membership in the society was seen as an increase in maturity and social status over the Rabbits Society and was considered a stepping stone between the Rabbits and the other adult societies. Membership was generally brief, because the other societies actively recruited the most promising members for their own organizations. The role of the Mountain Sheep as a transitional and preparatory stage is also reflected in the fact that they obtained no members from any of the other adult societies except for men in leadership positions.[6]

Elder Kiowa men in 1935 indicated that only ten to twenty men were known to have remained in the society all their lives. Although a favored boy could go directly into one of the higher-status men's societies without passing through lower-status ones sequentially, most Kiowa males who were not of prominent families and were not taken directly from the Rabbits into one of the adult societies were once Mountain Sheep. Only the society leaders generally held war honors and so were *qájáiqì̃* (chief, lit. brave man), because the younger members had not yet proved themselves in battle and the older members were reportedly not great warriors. This correlates with the wearing of feathered bonnets by the four Mountain Sheep leaders during society meetings. After a man had achieved a war honor and thus become a *qájâi*, he normally moved up into another society. Because *qájáiqì̃* were heavily recruited at each Sun Dance, the remaining youths were said to be those who had not yet proved themselves or were unwanted by the other societies.[7]

The remaining society members were described as fiery young men who, sometimes recklessly, tried to maximize their war honors in the shortest period of time, in order to advance into the adult societies. With this came a reputation for great bravado but also unreliability, which might account for the regularity with which members of the other, older societies were selected as hunt and camp police during the Sun Dance.

Because of their youth and unmarried status, most Mountain Sheep members were reputed to be good hunters and lovers who created "a great flutter in the hearts of all the ladies by their good looks and dashing costumes."[8]

Dress and Dance

The Mountain Sheep were known for their elaborate dance attire, which included breechclouts, buckskin or cloth shirts, yellow body paint, yellow painted vests, leggings with red stripes of paint and bells along the outside seams, and necklaces and bandoliers of trade beads. Members wore their hair in two side braids wrapped in otter fur and a small scalp lock, or *câivàun* (lit. fight braid or warfare braid), a braided lock on the back of the crown. The scalp lock supported a porcupine hair roach headdress and a set of *áulhǫ̂ugà* (hair metal), or metal hair plates, attached to a cloth or hide strip that hung down the man's back.[9] Breastplates, silver armbands and earrings, fans, and other items were also worn. Lowie (1916b:845) stated that members "wore feathers on their head," possibly referring to the roach headdress.

Alice Marriott recorded the only known description of a Mountain Sheep Society dance, told to her by Frank Given in 1935. He said, "In dancing, they bent their knees, holding feathers in front of their faces with their right hands and swinging the left behind them. This was an imitation of the dance of the black legs, as was also the dance form itself; moving around the drummer with a dancer outside the circle."[10] Given's description indicates that the Mountain Sheep performed the Turn Around or Reverse Dance (Xàkóigácùngà), as the Black Legs Society did. Elsie Clews Parsons (1929:91) referenced this dance when she mentioned that the Mountain Sheep had the same formation as the Black Legs Society, in that they stood and advanced in a line. The Turn Around or Reverse Dance was referred to as "an old dance" in which one stood in a long line with guns and turned around in portions of the dance.[11] Like the Black Legs, the Mountain Sheep also danced the informally named *émhâcùn* ("to get up and dance in place"), in which performers danced in place while holding their arms outward beside their midsection and bent at the elbows. The Mountain Sheep used a slightly different step from that of the Black Legs; all societies were said to vary slightly in their dance styles.[12] Descriptions of Mountain Sheep meetings suggest similarities with the Black Legs. Both societies had the same number of leadership and youth positions, followed the same arrangement in society meetings, shared at least two types of dances, and used yellow body paint.

Lowie (1916b:845) described the society's dance: "The Shepherds danced differently from the Rabbits, moving slightly or jumping up, and also moving both arms out at the level of the waist." This resembles the Black Legs Society dance that one elder consultant identified as the *émhâcùn*. Lowie also stated that the dancers made no sound while dancing, which probably means that the dancers did not sing. Instead, the Mountain Sheep carried strings of bells in their hands that they shook in time with the drumming and the singing of others.[13]

Insignia

One whipman carried a straight sword with eagle tail feathers attached to the handle, the other a serrated quirt or whip. The quirt often had a "fox pelt handle," a small gray and yellow fox skin, for a wrist loop.[14] Two independent accounts describe the society whip as a flat stick with a "coyote skin loop" on the handle.[15] Lowie (1916b:845) stated that the two Mountain Sheep Society leaders carried society whips with animal skin wrist loops; these may have been common to all societies before newer items such as swords and tomahawks came into fashion with increased Anglo contact. When a whipman arose with his whip, all members were required to get up and dance. At the end of each song, all members sat, except for one or more leaders who recited war deeds. Similar recitations from other members often followed.[16]

A unique feature of the society was its "love sticks," wooden sticks three to four feet in length with feathers or one fluffy eagle feather appended to the tip with buckskin. The entire stick was painted yellow and had a black stripe for every "female conquest." If a member had too many stripes, it was commonly said that he might "be telling lies." According to Parsons (1929:91–93), some members joked by claiming as many as twenty-five. Each society member made a stick to boast of his prowess, and according to Goomdaw, "Belo Cozad won with one hundred, and they were the narrowest kind of stripe!" Members stuck the sticks in the ground in front of them while sitting and carried them while dancing.[17] One society member is reported to have personally owned a spotted feathered lance that did not belong to the society.[18]

Leadership

The best-known leader of the Mountain Sheep Society was Big Bow (Zépcàuiétjè, 1833–1901), a well-known war leader and one of the greatest of the Kiowa *qájáisàupàn* (big chiefs). Big Bow was involved in one of the most unusual instances known concerning society leaders—namely, when the Mountain Sheep were faced with losing him to another society, they made him an officer in order to keep him in the Mountain Sheep. Big Bow was later asked to join the Dog Society but declined.[19] In describing Big Bow's painted tipi, Mooney noted, "Sometimes also fastened above the door was the ceremonial quirt tsen-toni [*chêtòi*, lit. fox weapon, referring to a *chêtàóttàgàu*] of the society to which Big Bow belonged, with serrated wooden handle with nine toothlike notches, and a pendant fox skin, painted green on the under side."[20] This, too, was unusual, because Big Bow was then very young to be a whipman, something inferred from the presence of a society whip on his tipi. But he already had a great war record, and as whipman and later society leader, he would have left his position only for membership in the Dog Society, which never occurred. Big Bow also apparently had a strong following of men who enjoyed helping train the younger men who would soon become warriors.[21]

According to Sangko, the last two Mountain Sheep Society leaders were Big Bow and

Âiá̲jè (Ayante, or Walking A Tree). Two Hatchet (Yíhạ̀utò) held a leadership position, but it is unclear whether he was a whipman or a society leader (Lowie 1916b:845).²² Big Head named Davis (also known as Thôicùtjè, or Spotted Faced [Horse]) and Big Bow as society leaders and Tá̲bái (Tobaccos, also known as Smoky) and Walking A Tree as whipmen. White Horse I (d. 1892) also served as a whipman at one time (Parsons 1929:92–93). Jimmy Quoetone listed Big Bow II and Spotted Faced (Horse) (Toekuete) as the society leaders and Walking A Tree and Tobaccos (Ta.baidw) as the whipmen. Lone Bear listed Big Bow and Thẹ̀nébá̲udài (Bird Appearing) as the two society leaders.²³

Bird Appearing was reputed to have been one of the greatest favored boys ever. He was extremely wealthy, a successful warrior and raider, and the keeper of a spotted feathered lance. He was so fond of his small white dog that he had a miniature bone breastplate and hair plates made for the animal to wear. He had a special cradle attached to one of his mounts for the dog to ride in and even had the dog ceremonially give away horses to visitors from another tribe, after which his relatives gave away horses in honor of the dog. Bird Appearing was killed in 1860 when a Caddo enemy he was chasing shot with his left hand over his shoulder.²⁴ The whole camp was in mourning, and Big Bow, who had been mourning all day, returned late to camp, singing the Mountain Sheep Society song and calling for his society partner (thus Bird Appearing was a society leader and partner of Big Bow). At his burial, the dog was painted yellow and buried alive, with all its decorations, in the same blanket with Bird Appearing's body. The warrior's possessions were then burned, and several horses were shot at his grave.²⁵

Hugh Scott recorded an account entitled "Story of Sheep Mountain" that demonstrates the support a society might give a member in time of need. The Kiowa were camped two miles north of Sheep Mountain, along the ridge on the east side of Elk Creek. A member of the Mountain Sheep Society was attempting to woo the wife of Saddle Blanket, who was not a member of the society. Aware of their activities, Saddle Blanket pretended to go in search of his horse but hid on the nearby hillside. When he saw the two meet in the timber along the creek, he surprised them. Although the man outran the angered husband, Saddle Blanket caught his wife and stabbed her to death with a knife. Determined to kill the young man, Saddle Blanket returned to his camp. The Mountain Sheep Society members took the woman's body to the camp and prepared to bury her. Saddle Blanket announced that if anyone buried her, there would be further trouble. The next morning the society members buried the woman, taking off and throwing in their finger rings and singing a war song over her grave to represent their willingness to fight if needed. Saddle Blanket came out of his lodge with a rifle, mounted his horse, and left camp until late that evening. The Mountain Sheep members moved camp a short distance during the day and were planning to exact revenge on Saddle Blanket. That night four members of the society awoke Saddle Blanket in his lodge and asked him to smoke the pipe they offered to end the matter. After several requests, he consented, and the matter was put to rest. Scott, who was at Fort Sill from 1892 to 1897, recorded this account from a woman named Donety, who stated that the event took place eighty-four years earlier, when she was around ten years old. If that was correct, then the event dates between 1808 and 1813.[26]

Sparse documentation inhibits a complete understanding of the society's role in the larger set of Kiowa warrior societies. With the end of warfare and final confinement to a reservation in 1875, the society's function in preparing young men to be warriors was no longer viable, and the society lost most of its martial functions. With the end of the Kiowa Sun Dance in 1890, the Mountain Sheep ceased to function. Today elders recall little concerning the Mountain Sheep, but the society is still mentioned in conversations, often in terms of its symbols, the fact that its members were young men, its youthful activities, which included herding horses and participating in raiding parties, and its past leaders (through tribal and family oral histories). Most frequently, elders mention the society's position in the Kiowa military society complex as a symbol of young warriors, in addition to the society's role as an educational and social transition in achieving warrior status. It is in this light that the society is perhaps best understood in its pre-reservation context. Some Mountain Sheep Society songs (Áljóyĩgàudǎugà) have been incorporated into the contemporary Kiowa Gourd Dance.[27]

3

CHȄJÁNMÀU

The Horse Headdresses Society

The Chȇjánmàu, or Horse Headdresses Society, did not require war honors for membership, so most members had few or limited such honors. Participating in police duties, this society was ranked higher than the Mountain Sheep but lower than the Black Legs and other men's societies. The Chȇjánmàu danced a form of what is today known as the Gourd Dance. The Horse Headdresses met until 1890 when, with the end of the Sun Dance, they ceased to meet and were never revived. As in the case of the Mountain Sheep, less is known about the Horse Headdresses than most other Kiowa societies.

The society's name derives from a style of headdress worn by the members. On the basis of information from Paul Setkopta (b. 1852), James Mooney wrote in 1902 that the name was "Tsentanmo . . . because all in old times wore *tan* or headdress of feather quills = agotan [ágàujàn, lit. feathered headdress]. [They] did not wear them in Paul's recollection." The name comes from the combination of *chȇ* (horse), *ján* (headdress, lit. brow band area), and *gàu* (people, group, or society).[1] Society member Bert Geikaunmah confirmed the basis of the society name in relation to the wearing of headdresses. The prefix *ján*, from the adverb *jàn-mâm* ("above the level of the forehead") and the noun *jàn-tém* (the frontal or forehead bone), is an old word for headdress that elders say refers to the brow band and not to the feathered portion of a headdress or bonnet. The syllable *ján*, referring to the brow band–forehead area, also appears in several Kiowa personal names (Mooney 1898:424).[2]

The society has been listed by various names and translations in the literature. W. P. Clark (1885:355) listed "Feather Head" but gave no Kiowa pronunciation. Hugh Scott listed Rattle Horse, Scout Horses, and Horse Eaters; Robert Lowie (1916b:846) listed Tse'ta'nma as "Rulers (?) of Horses" but was unable to obtain a complete translation from his consultant, Andele. Rev. J. J. Methvin (1927:166) listed Tsai-e-ton-mo, and Elsie Clews Parsons (1929:91), Tsaeitan'ma, but neither provided a translation. The most accurate translation of the society's name comes from Mooney (1898:230), who gives Tseta'nmo, Horse Headdresses. Although the basis is unknown, the society was also known by the ethnonym Chȇàulkàuigù, or Crazy Horses.[3]

The Horse Headdresses Society is significant because it was often during this stage in a man's society membership that he began to achieve martial success and prominence as a warrior. The society was considered a step up from the Mountain Sheep, with prestige a major determinate for membership. As in the Mountain Sheep, there were no family-owned places in the Horse Headdresses society, so father-son replacements were rare and generally involved only the officers' positions.[4] Members were older and were considered more dignified and not as showily dressed as Mountain Sheep Society members. Kiowa elders in 1935 estimated the membership of the society in the late 1800s at more than forty.[5] Hunting Horse estimated a membership of forty to fifty during the five years he belonged to the society (circa 1877–1882).[6]

Silverhorn (b. 1860) stated that he preferred membership in the Horse Headdresses over the Mountain Sheep because the former were known for their good looks and had more women associated with them. However, Mountain Sheep Society members made nearly equivalent statements, reflecting the intersocietal bragging and rivalry common among Plains Indian military societies, such as those of the Crow (Lowie 1983) and the Iowa (Skinner 1915a:629). Although bias and intersocietal rivalry seem prevalent, girls were reported to be friendlier to members of this society and were faithful in attending its meetings.[7] However, several Kiowa elders in 1935 described the Horse Headdresses as "kind of common" and said that there was "nothing significant about this society."[8]

Meetings

The only detailed account of the society's meetings was obtained in 1935 from Hunting Horse, who reported ten fixed society positions (fig. 1). Beginning at the center of the west side, or back, of the tipi and extending southward sat four *cúnqàjài* (dance leaders) who were graded, probably by war rank or status.[9] Four society singers with hand drums sat on the west-to-northwest side of the tipi and were ranked equally as a group. The position of singers was informal and often varied from year to year. A whipman sat on either side of the door. Hunting Horse described the whipmen as two "ushers or workers" of equal status who were also called fox pelt keepers. Regular members sat along the northwest-to-east and southwest-to-east portions of the tipi. The society also had two young male and female youth society members. If its practices were consistent with those of the other societies, then the boy members would have sat near the door, either inside or outside of the whipmen, while the two society girls sat on the west side of the lodge in front of the leaders.[10]

Before a meeting was held, a member rode through the camp on horseback announcing it. When members began to arrive, the men occupying the ten fixed positions were already in their places. After the members entered, in no particular order, the society held a smoking ritual. The head leader, on the west side of the lodge, lit a pipe and passed it around clockwise to the whipman on the north side of the lodge door. Then the whipman on the south side of the lodge door lit a second pipe and

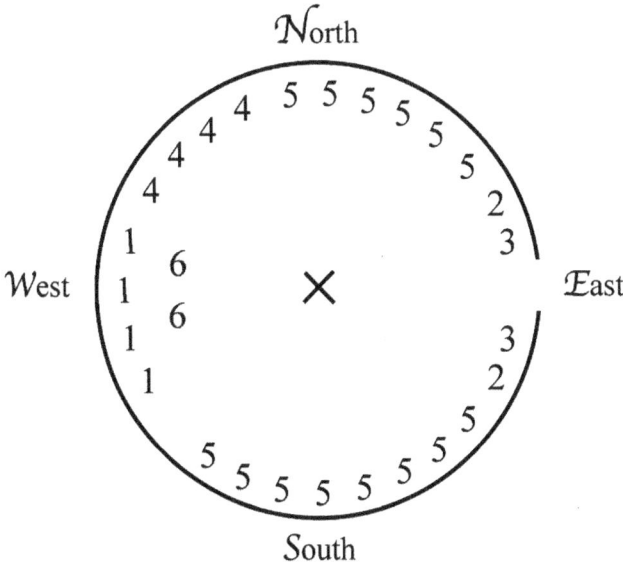

FIGURE 1. Horse Headdresses Society meeting positions.
1, Dance leaders; 2, whipmen, or fox pelt keepers; 3, probable location of society boy members; 4, singer-drummers; 5, regular members; 6, probable location of society girl members. The central X denotes the fire.

passed it around counterclockwise to the second-highest ranked chief, sitting just south of the first. For the next smoke, the pipes had only to be passed from the north whipman to the south whipman at the door and from the second chief to the first on the west side of the lodge.[11]

When the music started, members began to dance as they wished, with no formation to the dance. The dance step was repeated in place. As one elder described it in 1935, "They jump up and down a little, flexing their knees and giving a vigorous downward shake of their rattles." Weapons were carried during the dancing. Between songs the society members sat down, probably to rest and smoke.[12] The higher-ranked leaders then recited war deeds, followed by regular members (Lowie 1916b:846).

Dancing continued until around noon, when the two servants served a dinner prepared by the female relatives of the sponsoring member. As in the case of the smoking ritual at the start of the meeting, food was served in a ritual order. The whipman on the north side of the lodge door served the four singers from the west to the north and then proceeded toward the east to the lodge door. Meanwhile the whipman on the south side of the lodge door served the four dance leaders from west to south and then likewise proceeded toward the east to the lodge door. Meals usually consisted of meat, skunkberries, mesquite beans, and plums for dessert. Before eating, each man offered thanks by holding a piece of meat up toward the sun and then dropping it behind him.[13] After dinner, dancing resumed, occasionally stopping while the men took a smoke break. When the society decided to end the meeting, the members finished with a smoke, probably similar to the one performed at the opening of the meeting.[14]

Society Dress

It is difficult to determine the exact dress code of the Horse Headdresses Society, but members are said to have worn their best clothes, including black vests, breastplates, and eagle feather fans. They were noted for wearing their braids tied together behind them.[15] Members who did not wear shirts and leggings painted their bodies yellow with black spots and the joints of their arms black.[16] Mooney noted that members wore yellow body paint and a black ring on each wrist and ankle.[17] Parsons (1929:91) also wrote that society members painted their bodies yellow, along with stripes of various colors. Although the reason is unknown, the leaders reportedly did not wear the yellow paint that other members did. Roaches reportedly had to be borrowed from other societies on occasion, perhaps reflecting the economic status of the members. According to Bert Geikaunmah, members wore yellow and white paint and, on their heads, eagle plumes, often dyed red or different colors. Such plumes were also placed on the heads of members' horses, which is also said to account for the society's name, Horse Tassel or Horse Headdress. Another consultant described a similar headdress composed of feathers and beads, indicative of the society's name.[18]

Dances

The Horse Headdresses Society danced similarly to the Jáifègàu, focusing on a form of Gourd dancing in which dancers remained semi-stationary while shaking rattles, but shaking their rattles obliquely as well as forward and backward. Members also raised their rattles aloft and shook them at the end of each song. However, there is no mention of a wolf call at the end of the songs (Lowie 1916b:847).[19] According to Big Head (also known as Komalty, Cómàjè, or Friendship Tree; Parsons 1929:91), society members danced in one spot, shaking their rattles forward and backward. Only a few men danced at a time, but all danced if the leaders arose with their badges (Lowie 1916b:846).[20] According to Big Head (Parsons 1929:91), the society leader gave dance directions by blowing on an eagle bone whistle to indicate the desired formation— single file, double file, or arch. This was apparently for parades and outside dances, in contrast to dances held inside a tipi.[21] When the two leaders rode horses during parades, the other members came out in lines, two abreast. Lowie (1916b:846) noted that one leader marched at the front and another at the back of the line, each carrying a serrated quirt. This formation reflects the institution of society brother pairings, with the whipmen in the front and rear positions during group formations to direct the dancing.

Insignia

The Horse Headdresses danced with gourds with feathers attached at the ends.[22] HeapoBears described them as each being different but having two colors painted on them.[23] The society insignia consisted of a beaded lance and a straight sword.[24] The lance was so heavily decorated that it was seldom used in battle. No known code of action was associated with it, and it was usually kept by a young man who was not yet a *qájáiqî*. These aspects are unusual, because individual and society lances in other Kiowa societies generally entailed no-retreat or special-use obligations in battle. The lance was usually buried with its owner, with the rights to it passing to the family. The lack of a code of action associated with beaded lances, in contrast to feathered lances, may explain the distinction between it and a *zébàut* (a large fletched lance) or a *pópákògàut* (a spotted feathered lance). A Horse Headdresses Society's beaded lance was once owned by Tâudèàuljè (The Other Scalp), Big Tree's paternal uncle. Although it was never given to Big Tree, he made one and gave it to Satepeahtaw (Sétfítąu, or Bear Spear), who joined the society in 1883 and was not related to him.[25] Society member Se/osa (Sęąusàn, or Little Bringer/Introducer Of Peyote) was one of two Kiowa who had a *pàubôn* (fur-wrapped crooked staff), the other being Tseptwdle (probably Séttàuljè, or Lean Bear) of the Black Legs. The staffs were reportedly old, inherited weapons that were carried while dancing and then stuck into the ground before their owners were seated.[26]

Leadership

Several of the last society leaders are known. Thęnéàungópjè (Eagle Striking With Talons or Kicking Bird, d. May 4, 1875) and Cûifágàui (Lone Wolf, d. 1879) were the last two pre-reservation leaders of the society. Other officers included Crow Appearing (Mảusáuvédài, often abbreviated as Mapeite or Mảuvéjè), Tòhéjè (No Moccasins or Barefoot), Jòhàusàn (Little Bluff Recess), also known as Dáunfài (Done-pi, or Against The Shoulder Blade Area, or Chuck, d. 1892), and Go.w/ta.gye (Càuáuthágài, or Good Crow, Big Joe). Big Head also listed Càuáuvédài (Kapeita, or Crow Appearing, also known as Mảusáuvédài) as a leader with Little Bluff Recess (Parsons (1929:91). Bert Geikaunmah (b. 1881), who was inducted into the society as a youth, reported Páugùljè (Red Buffalo) and Páutháidè (White Buffalo, probably of the Redstone community) as the society leaders. These three men later joined the Omaha Society. According to Geikaunmah, the society was still meeting at the last complete Kiowa Sun Dance in 1887. Following the uncompleted Sun Dance of 1890, there is no record of the society's formally meeting again.[27] Mooney noted the society's inactivity in 1902 and commented that had it been reactivated, Fágàujògùl (Lone Young Man) and Lone Wolf (the former Mammedaty) would have been the current leaders.[28]

A few Horse Headdresses Society songs (Chèjándàugà) remain in the contemporary Kiowa Gourd Dance. Unlike the following song, they are usually sung with vocables instead of actual words. The lyrics of the following Horse Headdresses song demonstrate many of the warrior themes associated with the society, warfare, and death:

1. Gà fói-ọ̀-àl àn á hẹ-mà
   (Suddenly / unexpectedly [even though everything is peaceful / tranquil],
      you do die (death does come)
   Suddenly, unexpectedly, you do die! (death comes, imperatively).
2. Yí-dè dáu gû, gà thá-gà
   (Two-of us-hit / it is -all right)
   Both of us hit. It is all right.[29]

4

TÒKÓGÀUT

The Black Legs Society

The Tòkógàut, or Black Legs Society, was composed of martially and socially higher-ranking men and required war honors for membership. Many band leaders, warriors, doctors, and priests were members. The Black Legs frequently policed the annual Sun Dance encampment and communal bison hunts. The society met until around 1890. It was revived in 1912 and held dances around Stecker, Oklahoma, until 1927. It was revived again in 1958 and has remained one of the most conservative, veteran-oriented Southern Plains organizations.

Among contemporary Southern Plains military societies, the historical development of the Black Legs is of great ethnological significance because (1) it is one of the oldest documented Southern Plains military societies, dating back to at least 1834; (2) it was the second Southern Plains society revived after World War II; (3) it led to the revival of other, related Southern Plains societies; (4) it retains the most exclusive membership of all Southern Plains military societies; and (5) it constitutes the primary focus of contemporary Kiowa tribal veterans and one of the main forms of Kiowa tribal ethnic identity. The Black Legs are well known for requiring active or honorably discharged military service and Kiowa tribal enrollment for membership. The society is also significant for its continued emphasis on a martial ethos, veteran recognition, and annual dance ceremonials replete with martial rituals and symbolism (Meadows 1991, 1995, 1999).

The society's name, Tòkógàut, is derived from *tò* (legs), *kó* (black), and *gàut* (collective group) and refers to the pre-reservation practice in which members painted their legs black below the knee. Several scholars have correctly translated the society's name, as Mooney did (1898:230) with his "Tonkonko (Black Legs)." Many younger Kiowa refer to the society as Tonkonga (Tòkóga̱), an abbreviated and grammatically incorrect form of the name. This form uses the combining form *gà* ("it is"), as in Tòkógàcùngà (Black Legs Society dance), as a terminal syllable and is not a complete word by itself. Since its revival in 1958, the society has officially used the names Ton-kon-ko, Black Legging Warrior Society, and Kiowa Veterans Association and Auxiliary on its stationery. However, its members also use and are known as Tonkonga, Black

Leggin or Leggins, and Black Legging or Leggings, from the modern use of black leggings or stockings instead of leg paint. Elders recognize the original name, Tǫ́kǫ́gàut, as "Black Legs" and stress its use, as followed here.[1]

Much of the ethnological knowledge about the society was obtained in 1935 from Kiowa elders, several of whom had been members in the mid- to late 1800s. Kintadl (Kį́tàl, Moth, 1849–1938) served as a favored girl in the society in the 1850s. Yellow Wolf (Cûigùtqòjè) joined the society after the Dog Society became defunct around 1882. Frizzlehead joined the Horse Headdresses and then the Black Legs after the Dog Society became defunct. Henry Tsoodle Sr. (Xóól, Packing Stones) and Luther Sahmaunt (Samon) were Black Legs Society members in the 1880s and also provided much information about the society.

Several accounts of the society's origin and name exist. One account states that before the acquisition of horses, Kiowa warriors returned from a war party with their legs blackened from the trail dust. Another account says that members' legs were blackened when they counterattacked after an enemy force attempted to repel the Kiowa by setting the prairie grass afire to burn them out (Bantista 1983:2). Maurice Boyd's account (1981:72) is similar. A small Kiowa party encountered a larger enemy force that tried to burn the Kiowa out by setting the prairie afire. Suffering through the heat and flames, the Kiowa managed to escape and returned to their camp with their legs blackened from the fire and charred grass.[2]

The earliest known documentation of the Black Legs comes from the ledgerbooks of Hugh L. Scott, who mentioned the society in the context of the Walnut Creek Sun Dance, which took place near the west end of the Wichita Mountains the year after the Osage massacre of the Kiowa in 1833—that is, in 1834.[3] According to James Mooney (1898:261), however, the Kiowa held no Sun Dance in 1834 because the Ta̧imé Bundle—the religious bundle used in the Sun Dance—had been captured by the Osage in 1833 and was not returned until the summer of 1835. In 1834 the newly appointed Kiowa tribal chief Jòhâusàn (Little Bluff Recess) appointed the Black Legs as camp guards to keep the entire tribe together during the summer, in case of further Osage or other hostilities. That year a man who had taken his family and left the Kiowa camp to join a Comanche camp to the southwest was whipped and had his horses killed for disobeying the Black Legs.[4] That the society was large enough and sufficiently organized to serve as police by 1834 suggests that it had been in existence for some time. Kiowa elders in 1935 stressed that only the older and more mature societies performed policing duties, which also suggests an earlier origin of the Black Legs. Current Kiowa elders consider the Black Legs to be one of the older Kiowa societies.

Society Dress

Mooney provided the first description of Black Legs Society dress: "Tonkonga = Black Legs, because in [their] dance [they] are stripped and paint most of body yellow, but hands and lower arms, and feet and lower legs [were painted] black from [the] knees down."[5] In 1935 Kintadl stated that during dances the society members painted themselves black from the knees down and from the elbows to the wrists. The upper arms, chest, back, and upper legs were painted yellow. Black circles were painted on the shoulders and outer buttocks. One consultant mentioned the presence of black vertical stripes painted on the thighs. Although black paint predominated, dark blue paint was also used in some instances and shows up in one ledgerbook drawing (McCoy 1987:pl. 31). Members also wore breechclouts, vests, and horsehair roaches. They carried eagle tail fans, and some wore hair plates. They held bells in their hands (Parsons 1929:91). According to Piatonma (Mrs. Horse), members attached two eagle feathers, either erect or hanging (roach feathers?), to the backs of their heads. Bands of bright cloth were tied around the upper arms, under which eagle feathers were placed projecting upward. During warfare, Black Legs members reportedly painted themselves according to personal preference.[6]

At least two Kiowa ledgerbook drawings depict Black Legs members in society dress. The first is from the Julian Scott ledgerbook (Artist B), drawn in 1880. This drawing has the caption "Kiowa Chiefs on a visit to the Agent." The drawing is depicted as "Twelve Kiowa Visit the Agent" in Ronald McCoy's *Kiowa Memories* (1987:pl. 31) and as "Twelve High-Ranking Men" in Janet Berlo's *Plains Indian Drawings* (1996:155, pl. 78). McCoy (1987:5, 64) and Gary Galante (1994a, 1994b) both attribute this drawing to Pah-bo (Tall or Buffalo Head; Fâbô/Fâbôjè, or Large Mustang). Large Mustang was formerly believed to be the author of the Kiowa ledgerbook in the Montclair Art Museum (Maurer 1977:figs 266a–d), which contains a similar depiction of Black Legs Society members. However, recent examination of the drawing attributes it to another artist, on the basis of variation in stylistic details that are used in art studies to identity an artist's "signature" style. It is now attributed to an unknown Kiowa artist in 1880 (Berlo 1996:154), the same year in which the artist Large Mustang died.

The twelve men in this drawing wear black and yellow body paint, porcupine hair roaches, otter caps or turbans, and hair plates and carry eagle-tail fans, which closely matches descriptions of Black Legs Society dress. Another clear indicator that the drawing depicts a military society activity is that the two men in the front of the group each carry a society whip. By the last third of the nineteenth century, the Black Legs are noted as having been the only Kiowa society still to carry two of these clubs as insignia of office.[7]

The leader of the group in the picture wears a red cape with a design on the back that McCoy (1987:63) called a "Saltillo or Rio Grande psuedo-Mexican-type textile." Red military-style clothing in the form of capes and, to a lesser degree, coats was often acquired as gifts from military and government representatives, through trade, and through capture in warfare as early as the late 1700s. Throughout the southern Great Plains, Spanish, Mexican, and later American representatives gave canes, medals, swords, flags, military uniforms, and red capes to Indian leaders as prestige gifts and to recognize and legitimate their leadership. The value and size of such a gift was

"Twelve Kiowa Visit the Agent." Drawing from the Julian Scott ledgerbook, 1870s, depicting members of the Kiowa Black Legs Society. Reproduced from McCoy 1987, courtesy Morning Star Gallery, Santa Fe, N.M.

typically in proportion to the recipient's political and military importance (Kavanagh 1996:181–189, 210–211, 256–257, 377, 479).[8]

Kiowa ledgerbook drawings from the 1870s and later depict numerous red capes and white-selvage-edged red blankets resembling one known to have been owned by Young Mustang. The presence of such items went back much earlier among neighboring tribes and probably among the Kiowa as well. James E. Abert (Galvin 1970:47) mentioned one such cape in his 1845 report, saying that the Kiowa Tohausan had captured the cape and given it to his father. Red capes and coats show up in numerous ledgerbook drawings of Kiowa (see Dunn 1969:pl. 3; McCoy 1987:pls. 4, 31; Harris 1989:33, 69, 79, 99; Viola 1998:58–59; Donnelley 2000:109; Greene 2000:36, 2001:35, pl. 14), and members of other tribes (McCoy 1987: pls. 16, 17, 23; Greene 2001:pl. 16), especially the Ute.[9] Colonel Wilbur Nye (1962:ix) wrote that "Mexicans of Sonora and Chihuahua were probably called 'the red-coated people' because of the scarlet jackets of their lancers and the red serapes worn by the peons."

Although military capes and coats appear frequently in ledgerbook drawings, the body paint and serrated whips shown in "Twelve Kiowa Visit the Agent" distinguish the Black Legs Society. Furthermore, the leader of the group has a design resembling a bull with horns painted in black over his mouth, cheeks, and lower face. Black Horse II (Chêkôgài), an older member and possible leader around 1912, was known to paint in this fashion.[10]

A second drawing identified as representing the Kiowa Black Legs Society comes from the Merritt Barber ledgerbook (Maurer 1977). Barber was an army officer stationed at Fort Sill, Indian Territory, in 1879–1880. In 1954 these drawings were given to the Cincinnati Art Museum by Merritt A. Boyle, a local resident and grandson of Merritt Barber's. The drawing of Black Legs members is attributed to Pah-bo and is also from around 1880 (Maurer 1977:198).[11] Although lacking society whips, the men wear paint and clothing similar to that in the Julian Scott ledgerbook drawing (McCoy 1987: pl. 31). The man in front has a sword and a cape with designs matching the other drawing. The Merritt Barber or Pah-bo ledgerbook (Maurer 1977:198) identifies this man as Feather Head. Feather Headdress (Átàlhâjè) was a Black Legs whipman in the 1870s.[12] Although Kiowa Dog Society drawings exist in the Scott and Barber ledgerbooks, apparently neither McCoy (1987) nor Berlo (1996:147, fig. 70) was familiar enough with Black Legs Society dress and regalia to identify these drawings.[13]

Big Head (also known as Komalty) identified Átàlhâjè (Parsons 1929:92) as "Small Bunch of Feathers" and as a Black Legs Society whipman, but he did not specify when he held this office. The death date of the artist Pah-bo in 1880 and the death dates of other society leaders identified by Big Head date this image to the 1870s. The identification of Feather Headdress as a Black Legs whipman further supports the interpretation of these two drawings as depictions of the Black Legs in the mid- to late 1870s.

Society Dances

According to Kintadl, the Black Legs had at least four dances. The Mountain Sheep and the Black Legs both danced the Turn Around or Reverse Dance (Xàkóigácùngà), in which the society began in a single line with a leader at each end. There were two additional leaders in the dance, one of whom moved in the same direction as the group on the inside of the line and the other of whom moved in the opposite direction on the outside of the group. When the inside and outside leaders met, guns were fired, and the group reversed direction. Several elders stated that the dance formerly began inside the society lodge and proceeded outside, whereas the contemporary form begins outside in the middle of the dance arena.[14]

Charley White Horse and Monroe Tsatoke described the same line formation. The first song was sung in place as the dancers kept time with their left feet.[15] On the second song the group began to dance to the left (turning clockwise). When the inside and outside men met, the head society leader, who was the inside man, gave a shout, followed by the other society leader, who was the outside man. The whipmen, who were generally in charge of the dancing, were at either end of the line. The group then reversed direction (counterclockwise). Although the group periodically reversed direction, the inside and outside men always continued in the original direction in which they began. This continued until one of the leaders saw a dancer sweat and then signaled for the drum to be struck. Everyone stopped, and a war deed had to be recited before the group could be given water. This process was repeated four times, and pistols were occasionally shot into the air. Upon seeing a member sweat, his relatives would give away a blanket, which metaphorically was said to stop the sweating.[16]

Frank Given's and Piatonma's descriptions of the dance differ from White Horse and Tsatoke's in some details. They each said that the man in the center of the circular line proceeded in the opposite direction from the group while the man on the outside of the group danced in the same direction as the group. The drummers remained outside the circular formation of men. Four times during the dancing the leader gave the signal to stop by yelping like a coyote. At each stop a different member recited his war deeds, after which the members shot off guns, producing smoke that hung over the dancers in clouds. A man's sister might dance with him along the edge of the arena at this time and give away in his honor.[17]

The Black Legs alone performed the Shuffle Dance (Tǫ́sódêcùngà, lit. [Legs] Crossing Over Dance), a dance of shuffling one's feet in place interspersed with a series of small steps taken at times when the music changed. This dance could be performed at any meeting and provided a change from the regular dance steps.[18] The other two dances were the émhâcùn ("to rise and dance in place") and a "plain" dance like that performed by the Jáifègàu. Although in-depth descriptions of these last two dances are lacking, they resembled the first two types of dances, which are presently performed by the Black Legs Society.[19] In 1935, Weston La Barre listed a dance form in which a bow and arrows were held in the hand, but he gave no other information or a name. He probably was describing the carrying of weapons during society dances, which most Kiowa societies practiced and which is still done by the contemporary Black Legs.[20] Parsons (1929:91) noted that the Black Legs carried bows and arrows and advanced in a line, perhaps describing the Turn Around or Reverse Dance.

Meetings and Insignia

Jane Richardson recorded the arrangement of some Kiowa military society meetings in 1935. Although her data were associated with the Jáifègàu in the original 1935 Santa Fe Laboratory of Anthropology notes, she later used the same illustration with the addition of typed notes for the Black Legs. The same or a similar seating arrangement was probably used by most Kiowa societies, with the exception of the Jáifègàu, which lacked the two female members.[21]

Society meetings were held in a tipi positioned with its entrance facing east. The society leaders sat inside on the west side, opposite the door. The two female society members sat directly in front of the two society leaders, facing east. The two whipmen sat on either side of the tipi door, facing west, and beside them on either side were the two boy members. Singers and drummers sat on the northwest side of the tipi, and the regular members sat on the southeast-to-west and north-to-northeast portions of the society tipi (fig. 2).[22]

The Black Legs had two types of insignia that were unique to the group: a form of fur-wrapped curved lance known as a pàubôn, which was carried by the head society leader, and two flat, serrated society war clubs, which were carried by the whipmen. The term pàubôn translates literally as "fur crook," from páugá (animal fur) and bôn (bent) (Mooney 1898:415; Harrington 1928:46, 142, 216). Mooney (1896:990) wrote, "The Tonkon'ko captains carried in a similar way a crook-shaped lance, called pabo'n, similar to that of the Bitahi'nena Society of the Arapaho." Parsons (1929:91) noted that

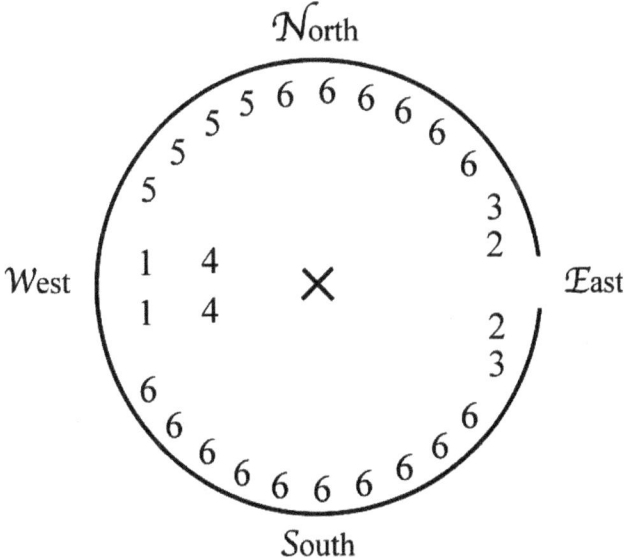

FIGURE 2. Black Legs Society meeting positions.
1, Society leaders (head leader on the south); 2, whipmen; 3, society boy members; 4, society girl members; 5, drummers and singers; 6, regular members. The central X denotes the fire.

one of the two leaders of each society carried the standard for that society. According to Marriott, there were at least two other staffs of this type in the tribe, but the only one associated with a society was that of the Black Legs.[23] At one time as many as ten of these staff-lances existed in the Kiowa tribe. They came in two forms, a straight form and a curved one roughly resembling a shepherd's crook, and they were obtained through dreams or by capture from an enemy. Some of the staffs belonged to individual Dog Society members but were not society staffs. The Black Legs Society is the only Kiowa military society known to have maintained a *pàubôn* as an official society insignia.[24]

A fur crook is a long, curved lance made of willow wood, approximately six to seven feet long and two inches thick, with a leather lacing tied across the bottom of the curved portion to hold its shape. The staff had a sharp metal point on its lower end so that it could be used as a thrusting weapon in battle. These staffs were wrapped spirally with otter fur and were decorated with four sets of eagle feathers attached at intervals along the shaft. Some accounts mention a beaded portion around the midsection of the staff. In combat and during ceremonies the staff served as a rallying point to raise the society's spirit, similar to a flag (Lowie 1916b:847; Bantista 1983:6).[25]

Several Kiowa indicated that there were once multiple fur crooks and keepers in the Black Legs Society. Hugh Scott recorded in the 1890s:

> In the Black Leggings Band there are eight men with lances, four with crooked lances and four with straight ones wrapped with beaver skin, the custom being

in a reverse [a retreat], to stick the lance into the ground, dismount, then turn their horses loose, and remain fighting until they are killed or rescued by a friend, pulling the lance up and take them away on their ponies. Everybody charges back to their assistance to rescue these [men] from the enemy. This is a good way to attain a chief's road.[26]

In 1936 George Poolaw stated that "sometimes the bearer would have a companion. With the spear as a rallying point a whole society might gather and defend the bearer." This suggests the presence of society-based raiding or war parties, society brothers fighting together in battle, and the concentration of a society's members during battle, regardless of the makeup of the entire war party. Frank Given said:

In battle this [the lance] was thrust into the ground and the society made its stand around it. The curved lance keeper wore his society paint and his hair loose upon going into battle. Carrying the curved lance, and a shield that was not associated with the staff, the owner would circle around, probably singing, while advancing toward the enemy. After planting the staff into the ground, he remained until released. One song sung by the society prior to thrusting the staff into the ground emphatically stated, "This pawbon [pàubôn], I'm sticking it in the ground here. That's where I'm going to stay."[27]

If an enemy approached, the owner of a staff would ride around the camp singing and beating on the staff with a drumstick. Upon hearing this, his friends would join him to meet the enemy. The staff held no magic power but was used only as a secular thrusting weapon and to stake oneself down in battle.[28]

This staff was a no-retreat staff, similar in function to the sashes worn by Dog Society members; it required the owner to stake himself down in battle and to hold his ground until either victory or death, unless he was released. However, it represented none of the contrary aspects associated with the Dog Society, such as reverse commands and speech. Retreat after staking oneself down with a fur crook was allowed only if a relative of the owner or a fellow Black Legs Society member released the warrior by pulling the staff up. In the 1930s the proverbial expression "I have staked my pawbon" was still in use, meaning that the speaker had taken a definite stand on some issue. A belief that remaining with a pàubôn ensured protection is illustrated by the following incident in the early 1900s. Someone once hid a barrel of whiskey in Mrs. Tenedooah's house. After local authorities searched and found it, they took the whiskey and arrested several men. The authorities kept returning, prompting Mrs. Tenedooah's friends to ask her to leave. She remained all night, explaining the next day that she stayed because the lance was there and that as long as she did not abandon it, everything would be all right.[29]

If the owner of a fur crook was killed in battle and the staff was captured, it was replaced, presumably by the deceased man's relatives, and then inherited by his most deserving male relative. This also applied upon the natural death of an owner, which suggests that the staff was buried with him. If no male relative existed, the women of the family chose a man upon whom to bestow the staff, and he in turn gave a horse, blankets, shawls, and other goods to the family matriarch. When an owner became too old, he could retire from the position and the obligations of lance ownership by giving the lance to anyone he chose, whether he had sons or not. This act, too, was reciprocated with abundant gifts. According to Henry Tsoodle Sr., the staff belonging to the Black Legs Society was never purchased by a new owner. Instead, the society selected the successor, who was required to be a member. A fur crook owner had to be brave, in order to get close enough to an enemy to use it, and was considered to be as powerful as a Dog Society member. One such staff was used to kill several soldiers in battles. Another was neither captured nor dreamed of by the owner but was simply made and, after being used only once in battle, discarded.[30]

A fur crook that was owned by a society member could not be used or owned by his society partner. According to Frank Given, the Black Legs Society leader carried the lance, and upon staking himself down in battle, he could be freed only by a relative. Whether "relatives" included society brothers is unknown. The lance was uncovered only for use in fighting or dancing. When not in use it was disassembled and kept wrapped in cloth. An owner or his wife could carry the lance when moving camp.[31]

The origin of the fur crook among the Kiowa is difficult to fully reconstruct because several such staffs are known from the nineteenth century, some of which Kiowa reportedly received as gifts from Plains Apaches and some of which were individual and not society-owned staffs. Mooney (1898:272) reported the capture of a medicine lance in a feathered case and a fur crook from Cheyenne who attacked the combined Kiowa-Comanche-Apache camp on Walnut Creek in the Texas Panhandle in the summer of 1837. Kiowa and Cheyenne oral history states that this Cheyenne party was composed entirely of Bowstring Society members, so this fur crook might have been an individual and not a society emblem; the only Cheyenne military society to maintain such society staffs was the Cheyenne Hoof-Rattler Society, which maintained two such curved staffs (Dorsey 1905:18).

In 1935, Frank Given told Alice Marriott that the original fur crook associated with the Black Legs was first captured by the Kiowa-Apaches from another northern tribe, recaptured by that group, and later taken by the Kiowa.[32] The lance Mrs. Tenedooah had in 1936 was from her husband, whose father, Black Legs Society member Bison Bull Recess (Páujòhâudè), had received it from an Apache. When asked about the origins of the fur crook, Henry Tsoodle Sr. stated in 1935, "I don't know where the pawbon originated, or how. When I knew[,] there were a lot of them, but I don't know where they came from. We never captured any pawbons that I know of." This statement suggests that the fur crook may have originated among the Kiowa as a gift. George Poolaw and Frank Given each said in 1936 that Old Lady Smoky had one, or a copy of one, originally received from the Apaches, and another one had been lost. If correct, this origin helps explain the similarities between descriptions of Kiowa lances and the staffs maintained by the past and contemporary Apache Manatidie Society

(McAllister 1935; Bittle 1962; Meadows 1995, 1999), whose name is popularly translated as "Blackfeet Society."[33] One fur crook was reportedly obtained from the Arapaho and given to the Black Legs by the Dog Society at the Oak Creek Sun Dance in 1887.[34] Because some Dog Society members possessed these, and because the society had already ceased by this time, this fur crook may represent simply an additional gift or replacement of this type of staff to the Black Legs.

According to Richardson, the lance originated as a gift and was not a hereditary object. If it was not currently in the possession of a member, then any Black Legs member could make a new one, as Yellow Wolf did and sold to Tonekeahbo, a Black Legs member. Although such lances normally were not sold, Yellow Wolf, having rejoined the Black Legs after the Dog Society became defunct in the 1880s, did this to revive the lance and to receive the payment for passing it on.[35]

Alice Marriott recorded a number of ritual observations associated with owning a fur crook. One never made a fur crook for one's own use. If an owner was killed and the staff captured, another was made, and the family gave it to someone they wanted to honor and considered worthy of having it. If the owner was killed but the staff was not captured, the family still gave it away. If the deceased owner was the head of the family, then the society bestowed the lance on the new owner. Often a male relative of the newly announced owner, usually a brother or uncle, volunteered to make the staff for him. The lance was not inherited and was not considered a private possession; it was considered to be more than a symbol of private power.[36]

These accounts indicate that the Black Legs Society, probably through its head leader, maintained a fur crook. Multiple such lances existed within the Kiowa tribe, and the details of their use and maintenance vary slightly. All except the one captured by the Kiowa from an unspecified northern tribe, the one captured from the Cheyenne in 1837, and possibly the one from the Arapaho that was given to the Black Legs society by the Dog Society in 1887 are accounted for as gifts from the Apache. The giving away of society-related insignia as gifts was common among Plains Indian populations and was likely a factor in the diffusion of the fur crook (Albers 1993; Meadows 1995).

The other society insignia were the two flat, serrated war clubs carried by the two whipmen and used in battle and in enforcing discipline during bison hunts and dances and in camp. Although individuals owned other whips, by the third quarter of the nineteenth century the Black Legs was the only society in which both whipmen still carried these clubs as insignia.[37] At one time, other members of the society carried small metal hatchets. The heads were secured in trade and set on the handles by the members themselves. These reportedly were rare, because "those who had them used them to strike the enemy when counting coup."[38]

Members and Leaders

Between 1850 and 1875 the Black Legs maintained a membership of forty-five to sixty, taking in two to five new members each year, usually as replacements.[39] Before joining the Mountain Sheep Society, Henry Tsoodle Sr. joined the Black Legs for two years to replace one of his older brothers.[40] Tsoodle provided a membership roster for the society at the time of his membership. Judging from the members' ages he provided and their birth dates in agency census records, this was around 1880.[41]

Gilbert McAllister's account of the Plains Apache medicine man Daveko (1970:53–54) indicated that Kiowa societies were still meeting in the early 1880s. In 1881 the Kiowa were camped for their annual Sun Dance and were awaiting the return of a party that had gone in search of a buffalo for the ceremony. After the party's lengthy absence, the Kiowa became concerned, and the Black Legs Society, led by Poor Buffalo, took a pipe to Daveko and asked him to divine or "look for" the missing men. Daveko, whom the Kiowa called "Hand Game Medicine Man" (Jòáudàuqì), was a well-known medicine man with the power to divine, heal, and perform magical feats. Accepting the request, he briefly exited his lodge and then returned to prophesy that the party would return in the morning. With this forecast, the Kiowa societies began to hold their dances. The party returned just as Daveko predicted, and preparations for the Sun Dance continued.[42] Mooney stated that the Black Legs Society ceased to function after the 1885 Sun Dance, but because all the societies were declining at this time, it is likely that the Black Legs still functioned to some degree in 1887, as indicated by the gift of a lance from the Dog Society and the 1890 Sun Dance.[43]

The society maintained two leaders, two whipmen, two male youth positions, and two female youth positions. Because of sparse records, the succession of society leaders and whipmen is difficult to reconstruct and is assuredly incomplete. It is also difficult to determine exact succession, which leaders were head society leaders versus whipmen, and when officers changed. In 1935, HeapoBears stated that it was difficult to name society leaders because they changed so rapidly.[44]

The earliest known Black Legs Society leader was Qáunkíkǫ̀gài (Black Turtle). A man named Black Turtle was recorded as having been an elder brother to Mammedate, Hovakah, Chaddlekongai, and Spotted Bird, all born between 1843 and 1863, but because the society was documented as early as 1834, before the births of these men, earlier, unrecorded society leaders and an earlier Black Turtle must have existed.[45]

Black Turtle was reportedly followed by Gúlhèì (Gool-hay-ee, or Mustang Colt) (Boyd 1981:71; Auchiah n.d.). Although Kiowa oral tradition has preserved much data about this man, conflicting data exist concerning his position as a Black Legs Society member and leader. Nevertheless, because he plays a large role in the current society, he merits discussion. Ethnohistorical and linguistic analysis clarifies much of the mystery surrounding him. Of Hispanic descent, he was captured as a baby in a thicket near a creek by Thépòl (Taybodle, or Packing A Lower Quarter [Thigh] of Meat, also known as Old Colt, 1809–Sept. 15, 1901), who was part of a Kiowa raiding party in Texas. He was reportedly named and trained by Packing A Lower Quarter Of Meat's brother Bohee (Bôhị̀).[46] One version of the story states that the boy frequently turned red in the face when angry and so was named Gúlhèì, which some Kiowa today translate as "Turning Red When Angry." Yet some family traditions, referring to his

Hispanic origin, say that he was very dark complected, contradicting the former assertions. A linguistic examination of the name demonstrates that it is based on the Kiowa name for a domestic mustang colt that is yet unbroken and still semi-wild (gúl-hè [s/d]; gúl-hè-gàu [t]; also known by the modified term gú-hà-lḕ [s/d]; gú-hà-lḕ-gàu [t]). The Kiowa referred to the Quahada Comanche residing near the wild horse herds in the Texas Panhandle as Gúhàlḕgàu, or Wild Mustang People, in a Kiowa pronunciation of the Comanche name (Mooney 1898:405). A small band of Kiowa residing in this area of Texas later became known as Gúhàlḕ or Gúhàlḕgàu, Wild Mustang or Quahada People. In the personal name Gúlhèĭ, the terminal syllable ĭ is a contraction of iyôi, a common suffix in Kiowa names denoting "offspring," "son" or "sons," or "baby of." Hence the name can be read as wild horse + offspring or "colt," and thus as "Young Mustang" or "Mustang Colt" in translation.[47]

Although Boyd (1983:155–158) gave a different account in which HeapoBears was the youth's captor, the data presented here came from family descendants, James Mooney, who personally interviewed Thépòl about Young Mustang, current tribal elders, and the late James Two Hatchet, a grandson of Thépòl. Thépòl's other name, Old Colt—probably a reference to his membership in the Dog Society—and the translation "Young Colt" for Gúlhèĭ further link Thépòl to the role of Gúlhèĭ's captor-father.

On his second war expedition, Young Mustang distinguished himself in a battle against Mexican troops, killing an officer and capturing his clothes, sword, and red cape. During the battle Young Mustang reportedly donned the cape in celebration and was later known for wearing it.[48] Some Kiowa elders have identified the red cape and lance worn by Charley White Horse in a photograph (Boyd 1981:68) as those of Young Mustang.[49] Several Kiowa elders recall White Horse's borrowing these items to wear in parades during the 1920s and 1930s. The Ananthy Odlepaugh Kiowa calendar also depicts White Horse wearing a red cape during the 1929 Fourth of July parade.[50]

Young Mustang is believed to have been born in 1837 or 1839.[51] He was reportedly killed during his fourth war expedition, in a fight with Texans, while still fairly young. Although the exact battle is unrecorded, the date of his death is recorded in the Silverhorn calendar, which was commissioned by James Mooney around 1904.[52] The spring 1872 entry depicts a small horse with a line connected to an owl (a common glyph in some Kiowa calendars, denoting death), beside a larger horse with the caption "Guale-i killed = Wild Horse Son. Killed by Texans." The connection of these images to a tree with leaves indicates that the event happened in the spring or summer of that year. Mooney provides another entry that states, "Guale-i 'Wild Horse Colt' killed by Texans in spring of 1872. Lonewolf Delegation [war party?]. Was Teybodle's adopted son. Shield captured with him. Mexican Captive ... Teybodle had no son and so adopted Guale-i. He was a Mexican captive but was a great favorite."[53]

Family oral history says that Young Mustang's children, George Mopope (Màupóp, Freckled Nose) and Sendehmah (Sḛdémā̀, Sainday Woman), or Sindy Keahbone, were small children at the time of his death.[54] Tribal censuses confirm that both Mopope

(1868–1927) and Sendehmah (b. 1869) were young children when their father died. The Silverhorn calendar also records the birth of George Mopope in the fall of 1868. The entry "First son of Gual-heu-i = Wild Horse Colt" is accompanied by a picture of an adult horse above a smaller one. The birth is indicated by a line running from the name glyph of the colt to a drawing of a cradleboard with a child's face in it, a common stylistic technique denoting births in some of Silverhorn's work.[55] Robert Donnelley (2000:167) and Barbara Hail (2000:31) have both published this page of the Silverhorn calendar. Thus Mooney's fieldnotes, the Silverhorn calendar, and Kiowa census records indicate that Young Mustang died in the summer of 1872 at around the age of thirty-three, confirming family oral history.

After Young Mustang's death, Bôhį̀, a brother of Thépòl, composed two songs in his memory, one of which survives. In many Plains Indian societies, family songs, like personal names and oral history, preserve historical accounts of significant events. The following family song, known as Gúlhèìjèdåugà (Young Mustang's Song or the Song of Young Mustang), was introduced to the Black Legs Society by James Two Hatchet in 1984. Now sung in contemporary society ceremonials, the song recounts how Young Mustang killed a Mexican military officer and captured his possessions, including his red cape.

> 1 Gúl-hè-ĩ dáu-dè só̗-lè-qà-jài-qĩ hól-hèl-gàu
>   (Mustang-colt-offspring / it was / soldier-chief or officer / killed-reportedly-and)
>   Young Mustang Colt it was, I've heard he killed a soldier officer and
> 2 Gú̗-fèl jé án hǻu-hèl gàu
>   (Possessions / all / he / took / and)
>   Took all of his possessions and
> 3 Gúl-kǻu-dáu è dáu-gàu é gő-bàu
>   (Red-cape / it /was-and/ he/ captured)
>   The red cape it was, he captured that.[56]

Oral history, song, and the fieldnotes of James Mooney and Jane Richardson confirm that Young Mustang was a captive of Thépòl and was a *qájáiqĩ*, a man holding war accomplishments. In Richardson's fieldnotes, Young Mustang is identified by elder Kiowa in a list of Kiowa captives taken during raids. The names of the captors are correlated with the names of their captives, all of whom were *qájâi* and members of the Mountain Sheep Society who had never changed society membership during their lifetimes. "Guelheie" is listed as a Mountain Sheep Society member, and his captor is listed as "T'ebodl," a "Koitsenko" Society member. Because Young Mustang was killed at around the age of thirty-three, his membership in the Mountain Sheep is likely. And because most society leaders were inducted after reaching the age of fifty, and whipmen were only somewhat younger than society leaders, his position as an officer is unlikely.[57]

In the Kiowa military society system, a Mountain Sheep Society member who achieved a battle deed was usually recruited by a higher-ranking society shortly afterward. Whether Young Mustang was briefly a Black Legs member before his death in 1872, and whether his song was later introduced to the Black Legs by Bôhį̀, by Thépòl, or only by James Two Hatchet in 1984 is unclear. Perhaps the larger matter is not whether Young Mustang was a Black Legs Society member—because Kiowa societies often adopt and carry forward the songs of other societies and individuals—but that his cape and, more recently, his song and martial spirit became prominent symbols after the society's revival in 1958. In recent years, interest in and knowledge about Young Mustang has rapidly increased. In the mid-1990s a Goule-Hae-Ee Descendants organization was formed and created a distinct emblem containing a feathered bonnet, a red cape, and a shield with crossed arrows and a painted hand on either side. This emblem is sewn on the dance shawls of female members of the organization and is a logo on the organization's monthly newsletters. Although all descendants' organizations celebrate and praise the memory of their respective ancestor, this organization is more aggressive than most in promoting the history of Young Mustang, who has recently emerged as an important apical ancestor.[58]

Sitting Bear, the Dog Society leader who was killed on May 28, 1871, while leaving Fort Sill under guard, is reported to have once been a Black Legs member. His son and namesake, Sitting Bear II, was a Black Legs member at the time of his death in 1870. A Black Legs song composed by Sitting Bear for his son demonstrates the father's affection for his namesake:[59]

> 1 Sét-ą́-gái-dàu-gà gà hâ-fè-jàu-nàu
> (Sitting Bear's-song / it [sing] / sing it [pick it up] / shall / and)
> I am going to sing a song about Sitting Bear.
> 2 Repeat.
> 3 Repeat.
> 4 Qá-jái-qį̀ à dàu
> (Chief / he / is in a state of being)
> He is a chief.
> 1 Sét-ą́-gái-dàu-gà gà hâ-fè-jàu-nàu
> 2 Repeat.
> 3 Repeat.
> 4 Háp-vè-qį̀ è dàu
> (Cute / he / is in a state of being)
> He is cute.[60]

Sitting Bear II was killed while on a war party in Texas in the spring of 1870. Piatonma recounted his death to Marriott in 1935, and its aftermath, as Piatonma described it, stands out as one of the most unusual incidents in Kiowa history. Sometime in 1870, Sitting Bear set out to recover the body of his son. He was grieving so deeply that the other men became concerned that he would commit suicide. One of them asked to borrow his knife, under the pretense that he had lost his own. Understanding their intent, Sitting Bear replied that he had too much respect for the other men to commit suicide. However, they later surrounded him and forced his knife from him, keeping it until the party returned home.⁶¹

When Sitting Bear gathered up the bones of his son, he spoke to them in the "pet voice" he always used to address his son, and he painted them yellow, the color of the Black Legs Society. After tying them up in a blanket, the party started for home, killing a white man they encountered en route. As was typical of revenge parties, they killed only one man, after which Sitting Bear ordered that no other attacks be made. After the men returned to camp, the family set up a tipi with beds. The bones were laid out in the place of honor and covered with new blankets. Sitting Bear frequently slept in the tipi and invited men inside to smoke and feast. He asked visitors what they wanted and gave them gifts of blankets, vests, paint, and other trade goods to demonstrate his great love for his son.⁶²

He also invited the entire Black Legs Society to feasts and dances, presenting each member with a new blanket. Whenever the Black Legs Society held a dance, Sitting Bear II's skeleton was laid out in the dancing lodge, and his favorite horse was tied outside, saddled and available for anyone to use. During dances, one of his female relatives would wail slightly to show that the family still missed Sitting Bear II. Because the Kiowa held great fear of the dead at this time, such activities were considered most unusual. If far from home, Kiowa war parties generally performed hasty burials for casualties, and a future party would return to recover the skeletal remains after decomposition. Although Kiowa families usually recovered, brought home, and reburied the remains of relatives killed on war journeys, no other cases involving the prolonged retention of skeletal remains are known. According to Piatonma, the guests were made to feel that young Sitting Bear was not dead but inside his lodge entertaining his guests. Mooney (1898:327–328) also documented these events, stating that the elder Sitting Bear spoke of his son as sleeping and not dead, kept fresh food and water beside his son's remains, and invited others to feast, telling them, "My son calls you to eat." The guests apparently overcame their fear and accepted the entertainment that was provided. Some young men are said to have taken advantage of the situation by attending just to receive gifts. Sitting Bear cared for his son's remains for nearly a year. After his arrest and death at Fort Sill in 1871, the family buried young Sitting Bear's bones, because there was no one left to care for them and they believed it should have been done long before.⁶³

Although documentation of several other Black Legs Society officers exists, it is less detailed. Pȧutȧuljè (Lean or Poor Buffalo, 1825–1901) was a Black Legs leader dubbed the "singing warrior" for his singing in battle, which was described by Nye (1937:224) as having taken place during the battle of Palo Duro Canyon in 1874. Henry Tsoodle Sr. listed Poor Buffalo and Heidsick, or Càuȧufȋtau (Crow [Feathered] Lance, 1829–July 22, 1902), as having been the society leaders when he became a member in 1880, as did Hugh Scott in about 1892.⁶⁴ Reportedly, while Poor Buffalo was a Black Legs Society whipman, his society partner died. He chose Bȧudài

(Fáibáudài, Sun Appearing, also known as Háunèmídâu, Unafraid Of Danger, i.e., Fearless Charger, b. 1843), a Jáifègàu, to replace his partner.⁶⁵ Mooney indicated that Sun Appearing was chosen by the Black Legs at the 1885 Sun Dance to replace Crow Lance, who was retiring because of his age.⁶⁶ Son of tribal chief Little Bluff Recess, Sun Appearing was listed by Mishkin (1940:54) as the fourth most famous man in the tribe and as chief of the Black Legs Society in about 1870.

Feather Headdress (Átàlhâjè, b. 1835), Kicking Bird's maternal uncle, and Gawky (Cáukį̀, or Ten, also known as Káuqígàcùtjè, or Return From Battle Marks, b. 1836) were Black Legs leaders in 1873. Crow Lance, who later succeeded his father of the same name as one of the two head society leaders, was replaced by Sun Appearing. However, the society reportedly did not meet again following the 1885 Sun Dance. Mooney noted in 1902, "If now kept up, Badai would probably [be] the principal leader."⁶⁷ Stumbling Bear (Sétèmqį́ą̀, or Bear That Runs Over Them, 1830–1903) was a head society leader and society partner with Crow Lance. Sàuǫ́détòn (Squirrel Tail, also listed as Sw'wdetw and Tsaodeto) replaced his own father as a Black Legs society leader and was listed by Richardson (1940:24) as the head of the society.⁶⁸ Other prominent Black Legs members in the mid- to late 1800s included Àunsójèqàptàu (Old Man Long Foot), the Sun Dance leader, the Táimé Bundle keeper, and a band leader; Jángúljè (Red Bonnet Brow); Màyį́tèn (Woman's Heart, 1840–1888), a Fort Marion prisoner; and Mamanti (Cáumámájè, or Goose Flying Overhead, also known as Dáuhájè, Dwhade, or One Who Is Power, 1832–1875), the well-known war leader and owl prophet who died at Fort Marion prison.⁶⁹

The two female youth members of the society were chosen by the society leaders from both inside and outside the members' families. Kintadl (Kį́tàl, or Moth) held one of these positions in the 1850s. In another instance, Wdlpohedlte (Àulpàuhóljè, or Much or Woolly Haired) and Wtote (possibly Mrs. Hauvaht, Áutájè, or Salt) were replaced by W'maite/Oma.ti and Kikw'wdloi or Ka.dloi, the daughters of Kicking Bird (a Horse Headdresses Society leader) and Fâbòjè (Large Mustang [Thépòl's father]), respectively.⁷⁰

The First Revival of the Black Legs Society, 1912–1927

Other than descriptions resulting from Mooney's fieldwork in 1891–1904, Parsons's in 1927, and the 1935 Laboratory of Anthropology Kiowa Field School, early ethnographic descriptions of the Black Legs Society are few and brief. Much of the anthropological emphasis during this time was on salvage ethnography and the reconstruction of aboriginal culture-historical periods, primarily those before much European influence had been felt. Unfortunately, this methodology neglected current events and changes in the cultures being documented.

Like the other Kiowa military societies, the Black Legs appear to have ceased functioning in 1890, the year of the last attempted Kiowa Sun Dance and the beginning of the Ghost Dance, which was held in 1890 and from 1894 to 1917. In discussing the

Ghost Dance, Frizzlehead stated in 1935 that "at that time, none of these war [military] societies were going on at all." Although groups of society members met intermittently after 1890, it does not appear that the Black Legs met again as a society until 1912.[71]

Evidence for the date of the revival of the Black Legs Society comes from a Kiowa pictorial calendar known as the Domebo Calendar. Aside from the better-known Kiowa calendars of Dohausen (Jòhâusàn, Little Bluff Recess/Concavity), Setta'n (Séttàun, Little Bear), Anko (Àunkóvàuigàdédè, Standing In The Middle Of Many Tracks), and Polan Yi Katon (Pòláhikàutǫ, Rabbit Shoulder) (Mooney 1898), many less well-known family and individual Kiowa calendars exist. In contrast to earlier "tribal" calendars, which included most of the larger events known throughout the tribe, Kiowa calendars produced during the reservation (1875–1901) and post-reservation (post-1901) periods contain more local or community-oriented events and thus greater variation. One calendar, drawn by Andy Domebo but listed as the "Alice Soontay Domebo Calendar" in the Doris Duke Oral History Collections, displays drawings from the summer of 1905 to the winter of 1912–13.[72] Seasons are indicated by a tree with leaves for summer and a tree without leaves for winter. Like most other Kiowa calendars, it has two entries per year. The drawings have no dates, but below each entry is a number and a name or description written in English.[73]

One summer entry, number 105, depicts a man with blackened legs standing above a Gourd Dance rattle. Underneath is the description "Ton-Kon-Gah Organize." By using the historically known and documented events on the calendar, one can derive the date 1912 for this entry. Supporting events include those depicted in drawing 94, the beginning of John P. Blackmon's tenure as Kiowa agent (Oct. 10, 1907), drawing 96, the beginning of Ernest Stecker's term as agent (Jan. 1, 1908), and drawing 102, the death of Quanah Parker (Feb. 11, 1911). This places drawing 105, the reorganization of the Black Legs Society, in the summer of 1912.[74]

This date is further supported by the induction of two society girl members in 1912 (Bantista 1983:13) and by the Guy Quoetone interviews in the Doris Duke collection. Robert Lowie (1916b:847), who undertook brief fieldwork on Kiowa military societies in 1915, mentioned a dance and feast held by the Black Legs in the spring of 1914. At this meeting women were allowed to be present, but not members of other societies.

The organization of the society at this time remained largely intact from that of the past. There were two society leaders, two whipmen, and two favored girls in 1912. Rudy Bantista (1983:13) listed Little Joe (Ha-ta-go) and Black Horse (also known as Tàbǫ́hòn, Sage Hat) as the society leaders. Guy Quoetone gave Daniel Boone and Jack Sankadota as the leaders, and later, Big Joe, Aunkoyday, Jim Takone, and Jack Sankadota as leaders and subleaders.[75] The variety of names probably reflects changes in society leader and whipman positions and the popularity of prominent members.

In 1912 the society inducted the future Mrs. Fannie Ahboah, then age 14, and the future Mrs. Lizzie Oyeby (Katt) Silverhorn, then age 12, as its girl members. Participating until she was married, Mrs. Silverhorn was preceded by her mother, Suzie Oyeby (Tine-goo-ah). Mrs. Whitefox (Tahlomah) had been the other former society princess. Following their induction at the encampment, their families held large giveaways in their honor (Bantista 1983:13).[76] There is no mention of the two society boy members at this time. Guy Quoetone confirmed that the society maintained two whipmen but did not identify them. According to Quoetone, the society had ceased to function as an organization before being revived in 1912, but some people occasionally gathered to dance for recreational purposes. Although Quoetone was unsure of the year he was inducted, he participated until about 1918 to 1920, when he left the organization.[77]

Induction methods at this time were similar to those described by Methvin (1927:167) for the Hispanic captive Andele. Quoetone was awakened from sleeping and taken to the society meeting. The participants sang songs, and he was made a member. The principle of society partners continued, and Quoetone was paired with Frank Odlety as a society brother. Society brothers were given a personal song, and whenever it was sung, they led the dancing. Their families then held giveaways for the old and needy.[78]

During this time society dress resembled that of the pre-1890 era. Accounts from the earlier portion of the revival period (1912–1927) describe the wearing of aprons, vests, and body paint. Some members were described as wearing porcupine hair roaches, hair plates, and otter caps.[79] Later the society appears to have ceased dressing as a unit, decreased its use of body paint, and accepted more individual variation in regalia, some of which might have been too difficult or costly for all members to obtain.

The society met at night to smoke, tell stories, sing, and dance. After a meeting started, the tipi door was closed with a piece of stiff rawhide, representing the closed (*dáucâum*) meetings of earlier times. Fines and punishments were imposed on tardy members. Late members were often made to stand outside and perform the comical "Turkey Trot Dance," in which the dancer placed his hands on his hips, elbows out, with the backsides of his hands facing forward. He then had to dance and gobble like a turkey for fifteen to twenty minutes. The latecomer concluded his punishment by performing a society dance.[80]

During one dance at Kiowa Jim Tongkeamha's farm, Guy Quoetone and other tardy members tried to sneak into the camp during dinner. When they were recognized, the leaders ordered the women to remove the dishes, indicating that punishment was to follow. A drum was brought in, and the tardy members were forced to dance until their relatives or someone who felt sorry for them paid their fine. Quoetone commented that he thought he would have to dance forever, because he realized he had no relatives present. Finally, an elderly woman threw a blanket on the ground as his payment, giving away for him. If members tried to run away, their clothes could be cut and torn up by the society. After dinner was resumed and finished, dancing and giveaways followed.[81]

Additional evidence for the continuation of society-based coercive power exists. In

1916 Charley Oheltoint invited a large contingent of the tribe to his home near Redstone, Oklahoma, to repaint the well-known Kiowa Battle Picture Tipi. Among the guests were many of the last prominent combat veterans, who were invited to record their deeds. During this gathering, a portion of the Black Legs Society met and publicly admonished Belo Cozad for beating his wife, continuing the past role of societies in publicly disdaining such behavior.[82]

In the 1990s I interviewed several elders who had attended Black Legs dances between 1916 and 1927. Most of these dances were held around the area of Stecker, Oklahoma. Weiser Tongkeamha, whose father, Kiowa Jim Tonkeamha, frequently sang for the Black Legs during this period, remembered seeing dances between about 1916 and 1919. He reported afternoon and evening dances held annually for four or five days at a time. The Omaha Society was invited to attend these gatherings and held War Dances in the evenings. The Black Legs danced inside a tipi with the sides rolled up. Weiser Tongkeamha believed they danced the Shuffle Dance at this time but distinctly remembered the Turn Around or Reverse Dance, because the men paraded out of the tipi to start this dance. The men ate and rested while seated inside the tipi. Dress at this time included legs blackened from the knee down, bells worn at the ankles or waist or held in the hands while dancing, white waist sheets, moccasins, breechclouts, and other personal items.[83]

Harry Domebo knew of a dance held before 1920 at the allotment of Big Joe (Kau-ti-ke-ah), one mile south of Stecker, Oklahoma. Domebo also witnessed a dance around 1920 at Jack Sankadota's home near Stecker and listed the following dancers: Little Joe (Hautago), Big Joe, Jack Sankadota, Frank Aulty (Odlety), Bert Geikaunmah, Joe Hummingbird, Jim Tacone, James Charley Jackson (Hawzipta), Charlie Domebo, Black Horse (Oscar Tahbone), Aunkoyday (a Mexican captive), Homer Buffalo, Belo Cozad, Daniel Boone, Rufus Tsoodle, and Guy Quoetone. Several other tribal elders confirmed these men as members in the early 1920s. Old Man Tenedooah, Joe Poolaw, Naho (also known as Daingkau), Old Man Bosin, Charley Oheltoint, and Silverhorn were also listed as members.[84]

At this time the society met and danced only once a year, for four days and nights each time, with around twenty male dancers participating. Their dress closely resembled that of earlier periods, with black and yellow paint, breechclouts, roaches and feathers, and waist sheets. Some dancers wore leather or cloth leggings. A whipman used his whip to instruct the dancers when to begin dancing. Society princesses were present, but all women danced outside the arena. Feasting and giveaways were frequent, and the dancers danced only during the daytime.

Alice Littleman camped with her family at a Black Legs dance near Stecker. Mrs. Littleman described the men's dancing, which reflected the linear formation of men's society dances depicted in Kiowa ledgerbook art: "They all danced together . . . in a row. They all dance even." At this time, women were not allowed to dance in the center of the arena but danced along the perimeter. Mrs. Littleman described the women's Scalp Dance at this encampment: "When they dance, they dance together.

They dance like that [indicating side by side with her hands]. Them women, they have those sticks [lances], and they don't scatter out. They dance in a row and then they turn around and go back, and then they turn around and go back [motioning back and forth with her hands]." She also remembered Shuffle Dances performed by men and women at this time.[85]

One of the most important observations at this time concerned changes in the basis of membership. With the traditional means of acquiring male status through warfare and hunting gone, members began to be chosen on the basis of other personal attributes. During the reservation period and into the early 1900s, membership took on a hereditary aspect in which younger nonveterans were inducted to replace older, veteran members. Dances took on a largely symbolic and enculturative form, focusing on honoring past warrior traditions. As Oscar Tsoodle explained, "See, they called it a warrior society, but at the time I danced, none of them were in the war, they were old people . . . it was just a recreational dance." According to Tsoodle, members at this time were taken into the society on the basis of being well off financially, well respected, generous, and of outstanding social status.[86] These characteristics resemble qualities that are usually associated with traditional concepts of ǫ́dè status and reflect the development of a hereditary aspect associated with the differential social status of reservation-era Kiowa families. With the end of warfare, formerly the primary basis for male social status, men's war records became frozen in time, which affected the social status of their families and lineages. This change led to a new basis for replacement as military service and war honors became unavailable; moreover, many Black Legs Society members were traditionally older and in the upper social ranks, so that their families could afford the resources for such giveaways. Referring to military society membership in general at this time and changes in membership requirements from earlier times, Parsons (1929:90) wrote that "members were chosen from the point of view of the help they and their families could give to the society, at its feast or celebration."

Rev. George Saumty, born in 1906, was nineteen when he attended a Black Legs Society dance on the land of Frank Odlety, southwest of Stecker. He stated that this dance was held in 1925 and was the next to the last meeting the society held before it once more ceased to function. The dance took place in a camp of canvas tents with a brush arbor and lasted for three days and nights. No tipis were present. There were approximately twelve to fifteen middle-aged and elderly men dancing, and three or four singers. The dancers dressed in khaki and blue trousers, long-sleeve shirts, and moccasins, although a few men had Anglo-style shoes. The changes in dress may reflect economic hardship, scarcity of traditional materials, and Anglo pressure against traditional practices. As among other tribes during this period, the last piece of traditional dress to be given up was usually moccasins. Members also wore three-inch-wide sashes of red material over their left shoulders, although the reason is unknown. Rev. Saumty saw no society fur crook and no body painting or wearing of black shawls. Several men wore roaches with a single feather.

Saumty also stated that no society princesses were present that day, and the women did not dress out or dance but sat behind the drum and sang. The leaders danced and then called the other dancers to begin. He described the dancing as "slow and dignified," with small steps. On the afternoon of the second day the families of members held giveaways in their honor, to "show their love for the dancers." According to Saumty, the society remained in camp a few days to discuss the future of the group, but he did not know the results of this meeting. He later heard that the last meeting and dance were held at Jack Sankadota's home near Stecker and were similar to the event he attended.[87]

Oscar Tsoodle reported that he was inducted in 1927, at the age of fourteen, at the last Black Legs dance, held at Jack Sankadota's home. He was inducted to replace his older brother, who had recently gone to Bacone College. As he recalled, his father provided a feast and gave away in his honor. Much to his surprise, the gifts included his favorite horse:

> When they initiated me, my parents had to give away. See, that's the reason they take you in. When they initiate you, your parents will have to give away. And my parents had to give away, all of them, four brothers [father and uncles], they give away, and my grandmas and my mother and aunts, you know, all of them give away. During that time they used to give horses away, and sometimes they give buggies away, brand new buggies. And at that time, you know, horses didn't mean nothing to them, they might take five, six, eight, ten head and give them away. Just as I was going to dance they sang a song for me, and my uncle said, "'It's your song." He said, "You gotta get up and dance out there." And they was getting ready, my father and all of them, my brothers was all out there, they had two horses apiece. And just as I looked to my Dad, on to his right, by God there was my Welsh pony that I ride every time. He give it away right there.[88]

Tsoodle's descriptions resemble those of others regarding society dress, members, prominent leaders, and structure. The dancers did not paint themselves at this time. Each member wore his best clothes, and there appears to have been no standard society dress. No one danced with lances. Tsoodle said that the Shuffle Dance was not performed at this time and was danced only when warriors returned from a war journey. He described the Turn Around or Reverse Dance as being much different from today's, beginning in a counterclockwise direction and consisting of seven slow songs with no increase in speed. The tail man fired a gun only at the end. A man then recited a short coup, and his parents gave away for him.[89]

According to all elders interviewed, the last Black Legs Society dances during this period took place on Sam Ahboah's allotment and at Jack Sankadota's home, approximately two miles northwest of Stecker. Three elders stated that the year was 1925, one said 1926, and another 1927. Laura Sankadota Tahlo attended the dance and remembered Jack, Jasper, and Howard Sankadota and Jim Takone as having been prominent society members and possible leaders at this time.[90]

Although various factors contributed to the decline of the Black Legs at this time, one elder stated that the increasingly popular fancy War Dance and the Kiowa Omaha Society might have affected the decline of other Kiowa societies. The increasing number of Kiowa families converting to Christianity also led to a decline of dance-related traditions. The anti-dancing efforts of agents Stecker and Stinchecum from 1915 to 1917 resulted in the blacklisting of numerous families, including those of several Black Legs Society members, and the withholding of annuities and appropriation funds (Kracht 1989:820–875; Meadows 1999:113–126). On the basis of fieldwork in 1927, Parsons (1929:92) wrote that the only surviving societies at that time were the J̨áifègàu and the Omaha Society.

During this revival, from 1912 to 1927, both continuity and change can be seen in the society's structure and functions. The greatest problem in drawing conclusions for this period results from the sparse anthropological records, in comparison with earlier and later accounts. Leadership structure and youth positions remained intact, with the possible exception of the two boy members. Membership was much smaller than in the past. Although a few older members with warrior status remained, new members born after the Indian wars were being inducted, and thus social status came to replace the earlier emphasis on war honors.

In at least the earlier years of this period, the institution of society partners and strict attendance rules for society meetings continued. Many members during this period were prominent tribal members and dancers, as reflected in their being blacklisted by the Kiowa Indian Agency for dancing and giving away. Although many of the activities and functions associated with the Sun Dance, communal hunts, and warfare had ceased, the society continued to provide communal feasts and dances. Families continued to recognize elder warriors and younger men by giving away goods in their honor, thereby maintaining social status and community welfare through redistribution.

The society still provided a place for its members to smoke, feast, sing, dance, recite coups, and reminisce about past individual, family, and tribal warrior achievements. It thus celebrated and enhanced the past experience of warriors through song, dance, and storytelling while performing beneficial socioeconomic services and duties on behalf of the Kiowa community. Although some membership and ceremonial and dress characteristics had changed since 1890, the general structure of the society remained intact.

The Second Revival of the Black Legs Society (1958–)

For the Kiowa and many other tribes, World War II represented the first large-scale return to combat since pre-reservation times. Whereas the Kiowa had only fourteen World War I veterans and a brief series of postwar celebrations and dances, nearly three hundred Kiowa men and women served in the Second World War. Soon afterward, many Kiowa served in Korea, including reenlistments by many World War II veterans. Kiowa elders continued to analogize modern military service in the United States armed forces with the actions of earlier war parties for raiding and revenge.[91] As Atwater Onco explained, this analogy has continued to the present:

> Yes, especially during World War II. It was just like they used to, because the warriors, the soldier boys that went into service, were just class[y] and were treated like they were going on a Kiowa war party years ago. . . . And that's how they upheld not only World War II, but all the wars: Vietnam, Korea, Desert Storm, and other wars and conflicts. Every Kiowa that goes, they—overall, the Kiowa people—uplift the veteran, overall they think highly of the veterans and the person, especially during wartime, that goes to war. It's just in us, in our Kiowa blood, to really think a lot of that person that fights for us, a warrior. . . . Overall, the Kiowa people are like that, they really respect their men that go to service to fight for the country.[92]

The nationwide return of veterans, combined with the resurgence of Native American identity, economic and educational opportunities for veterans, and improved social and political rights, was instrumental in the intensification and revival of many Native American cultural forms. The revival of Southern Plains Indian military societies was but one example of this trend (Meadows 1999). By the mid-1950s, interest in reviving the Black Legs Society had emerged, primarily among the descendants of Young Mustang—the Anquoe family, descended from Sindy Keahbone, and the Palmer family, descended from George Mopope.

In 1954 Kenneth Anquoe and other family members residing in Tulsa, Oklahoma, performed Black Legs songs and dances at the Semi-Centennial celebration in Tulsa. Society songs were learned from tribal elder Bert Geikaunmah, and dance attire included black stockings on the legs, red capes, and associated regalia. As Kiowa tribal director for the American Indian Exposition, Anquoe led a second performance at the exposition that August in Anadarko, Oklahoma. It included Leonard, Jack, and James Anquoe, Lee Tsatoke, Paul Tahlo, Warren Weller, Scott Bradshaw, and others. According to one elder who participated in these dances, many of the Kiowa spectators were unfamiliar with the dance and did not recognize it as their own.[93]

In August 1957 a short performance of Black Legs Society songs and dances was held at the American Indian Exposition by Gus, George, and Dixon Palmer, Hugh, Nathan, and Ernest Doyebi, Puppy Little Joe, Leonard Cozad Sr., Jimmy Anquoe, and Oscar Tahlo. The performance was well received and prompted further interest. Another performance was given at the 1958 exposition as part of a program entitled "The Song of the Redman" (AIEB 1958). On November 23, 1958, World War II veteran Gus Palmer Sr. called a meeting of all Kiowa veterans at the Veterans of Foreign Wars (VFW) hall in Carnegie, Oklahoma. It was this meeting that firmly established the political foundation for the revival of the society, led by the Palmers. With approximately fifty veterans in attendance, the Kiowa Veterans Association (KVA) was formed. With the support of his brothers George and Dixon, Gus Palmer Sr. incorporated the revival of the Kiowa Tòkógàut into the founding of the KVA. Although the society's name actually means "Black Legs," since 1958 the society has commonly been called the "Black Leggins," "Black Leggin Warrior Society," or the "Black Leggings Warrior Society," because the majority of members no longer paint their legs black but wear black leggings or stockings.

According to Gus Palmer Sr., his goal at this time was to organize the men who had served their tribe and country and to explain the importance of maintaining their identity as veterans. Added to this was his desire to develop a more integrated and permanent recognition of tribal veterans than existed and to acknowledge and keep alive the memory of Kiowa who had made the supreme sacrifice for their tribe and country:

> The main thing is that I thought of overseas . . . it was kind of my feeling . . . when I get home, provided I get home . . . there's something I'm gonna do for our tribe, the Kiowa tribe, Cáuigù, that needs to be done. The Tòkógàut, Black Legs . . . they need to revive that because of the men that served this country. . . . World War II was a rough one, it wasn't no easy business. At the same time, when I got home I wanted them to be known as that, Tòkógàut, they protect their tribe and the area they lived in. . . . I didn't want that to die out, because it had been dormant after what the government did to them in 1887 [the last complete Sun Dance], it just died out.
>
>   I'm not going to let that happen, that's the way I felt. I just felt in my heart, I didn't tell anyone I even felt that way. And after I came home I saw how they turned the [November] eleventh into Veterans Day for all wars. And then I saw where these men that gave their lives, how they were recognized—that's what really got to me and I just thought, "No, none of that." I wanted to see that we organize these men that served this country, they know what they did and we need to emphasize that, to do this so they'll know what homecoming is. To be home and celebrate, *háu* [yes], in our Indian way.[94]

In Plains Indian cultures the relationship between brothers was one of the strongest kinship bonds that existed. Besides being an Army Air Corps combat veteran himself, Palmer decided to revive the Black Legs Society in dedication to his brother Lyndreth Palmer, who was killed during World War II, the first Kiowa to be killed in action in the twentieth century, and in honor of all Kiowa veterans. Lyndreth Palmer was posthumously recognized at the 1945 American Indian Exposition. As Muriel Wright (1946:163–164) described it: "The opening parade was held on the afternoon of V-J Day. . . . The outstanding ceremony of the first afternoon's program in front of the grandstand was the presentation of the Bronze Star Medal awarded posthumously to Corporal Lyndreth Palmer (Kiowa), of Anadarko, who was killed in Germany on December 4, 1944. Presentation was made by Brigadier General Raymond E. Lee, Commander, Fort Sill Replacement Training Center, to the young soldier's father, William Palmer."

Palmer said that it was his desire not to see his brother's name and sacrifice forgotten that always gave him the strength to carry on the society, and he has never gotten discouraged through the years. Regarding the revival of the society, he explained:

> You must have a feeling and a reason for starting something, you just can't decide to start something.[95]
>
> When they have this celebration, they [Kiowa killed in action] are gonna be up front — the first ones. We're going to mention their names . . . they fought and they died for it. They didn't surrender. . . . It's just like, it's kind of like the old ways, they don't surrender and they'd rather die in battle. It's a big honor back then, it's still kind of similar. . . . I want their name[s] to be in front, first thing, then we'll do whatever we want to thereafter, celebrate in our own Indian tradition. That's the main thing, and I want my brother's name included also, because he's one of them. I don't want them left out and we would be celebrating and their name there, just like, their life, leaving them out or way back there. I didn't like that. I've said that all the way through, even up to now. So that's the main part. My dedication is especially to him [points to Lyndreth's military service picture on the wall].[96]

The Kiowa Veterans Association was formed and officers were elected before but in conjunction with the revival of the traditions of the Black Legs Society. Since 1958, requirements for membership have included being an enrolled Kiowa tribal member, being an honorably discharged or currently enlisted veteran, and dressing uniformly with the group for society ceremonials. The society prides itself on its exclusiveness and rigid membership requirements, which are stricter than those of many other current Southern Plains societies, most of which allow some degree of intertribal or non-Indian participation.[97]

Reflecting the recent influence of military service and post–World War II Anglo veterans' associations, the leadership structure of the society was initially modeled after that of VFW and American Legion posts. Gus Palmer Sr. was elected commander and maintained that position until his death in 2006. Other officers elected in 1958 included Leonard Cozad Sr. as vice commander, Adam Kaulaity as secretary, David Pinezaddleby as treasurer, Herbert Dupoint as sergeant at arms, Allen Quetone as advisor, Scott Tonemah as public relations officer, and George Palmer and Ernest Redbird as program directors.[98]

The new officers were introduced one week later at a powwow held in the Carnegie VFW building, where the society was reintroduced to the Kiowa people. The first formal Black Legs dance was held in June 1959 at a Kiowa princess contest powwow. Seeing the need to organize and support the veterans, the Kiowa Veterans Association Auxiliary was soon formed, with Celia Auchiah as the first auxiliary president. Red blankets with "Kiowa Veterans Auxiliary" embroidered on the back were soon adopted and continue to be worn by the female members in the processionals at each

Kiowa Black Legs Society leader Gus Palmer Sr. with the society *pàubôn*. Kiowa Black Legs Society ceremonial, Anadarko, Oklahoma, October 10, 1992.

ceremonial. In 1959 and 1960 the society held Veterans Day dances at the Carnegie City Park, where the newly formed Kiowa Veterans Association Auxiliary held processionals (Bantista 1983:7). The Kiowa War Mothers and the Carnegie Victory Club soon joined the KVA Auxiliary in these performances. All three organizations continue to jointly honor veterans and participate in the society's ceremonials today. In 1961, the organizers of Indian City U.S.A. in Anadarko offered the use of their facilities, and from November 1961 through May 1998 the Black Legs Society dances were held at the Indian City U.S.A. campgrounds near Anadarko, Oklahoma.

The request of higher insurance coverage and rental fees from Indian City personnel prompted the Black Legs to relocate their ceremonial to the Lone Bear Dance Ground, southeast of Carnegie. Dances continued there for two years, but attendance declined. The new site lacked concrete bleachers for seating, and people generally preferred the Indian City grounds, which had become the traditional setting for Black Legs dances. In the spring of 2000, the Dixon Palmer's tipi was blown over by strong winds during the ceremonial. Some people took this as a sign of the 1929 tornado, which had leveled the same dance ground and the site of earlier Jáifègàu dances and killed one woman, Mrs. Lone Bear. That summer the owners of Indian City approached the society about returning. Because the May and October Black Legs ceremonials take place slightly before and after the main tourist season in southwest Oklahoma, they draw significant crowds that also visit the Indian City museum and tourist shop. That fall the Black Legs resumed their dances, which presently continue, at the Indian City campground.

The number of active participants during the first years following the revival remained small, consisting only of the "faithful few," as one person put it. From the persistence and strength of a small core of initial members and auxiliaries, the number of participants steadily increased. In 1970 the society began holding two ceremonials each year, one in May, to recognize Memorial Day, and the other in October, to recognize Veterans Day. By the early 1970s the society had steadily grown to form one of the major contemporary Kiowa tribal ceremonies and the primary venue for honoring veterans and recognizing the Kiowa martial ethos.

In 1958, several tribal elders were still living who had been active members when the society ceased to function in 1927. Importantly, these elders remembered the society dances and a number of songs. The elders who taught these to the younger veterans were Bert Geikaunmah, David Pinezaddleby, Daugamah, Henry Tenedooah, White Fox, Oscar Tahlo, Jimmy Anquoe, Homer Buffalo, and Ernest Redbird Sr. Some people say that Charley White Horse taught some of the society songs to Bert Geikaunmah, who frequently visited him. Without their help the revival could not have been carried on with the same rich traditions, and it was to these men that the Tonkonga twenty-fifth anniversary booklet (Bantista 1983:1) was dedicated. When these men were approached for knowledge about the society, they were pleased and encouraged the revival. According to Gus Palmer Sr., "These elders felt that it would be only right if they [the younger veterans] would revive the society and keep it up, keep it going . . . [and that] they had the right to do so, since they were [now] the veterans of the tribe."[99]

Palmer reflected on the origins of the revival and the purpose of the society's ceremonials: "We owe a great debt of gratitude to the Kiowa elders that suggested the revival of this old warrior society and for teaching us the songs, dances, and ceremonial Kiowa warrior traditions of the great men that gave us our roots. The reason for the two ceremonials held in May and October each year are to keep our Kiowa traditions alive and to recognize, honor and express our appreciation for what our servicemen continue to do for our country."[100]

Christian Kiowa and the Martial Ethos

From the 1880s until World War II, two roughly distinct segments of Kiowa socioreligious communities had developed. They may be referred to generally as Christian

Kiowa and Traditional Kiowa. Although many social forms, such as language, kinship, naming, and mythology, continued among both, distinct differences in socioreligious areas developed. Whereas Christian Kiowa followed Christian and more progressive doctrines that prohibited many of the older Kiowa socioreligious practices, Traditional families generally maintained or participated in older cultural forms such as dancing, traditional doctoring, the hand game, sweat lodges, use of the Ten Medicine Bundles, and the Native American Church. Christian Kiowa regularly held prayer meetings for veterans before their departure overseas, whereas other Kiowa commonly held Native American Church meetings and honor dances. Both raised funds to send with servicemen. Once servicemen were overseas, both groups continued to hold their respective forms of prayer meetings for them. By the time World War II began, all the Kiowa men's societies except the Omaha Society had ceased, and older dances had generally declined in the face of the increasingly popular War Dance and other social dances associated with powwows and 49 Dances.

It is often widely assumed that the adoption of Christianity inevitably leads to the loss of all traditional culture. Although Christianity did directly promote and lead to the decline or loss of some cultural forms among some Kiowa—for example, dancing, doctoring, forms of gambling, and certain traditional religious forms—it also introduced new traditions centered on church and community activities. Christianity also modified other traditions such as the style and format for introducing new songs such as church hymns, and it arguably strengthened and continued other traditions by finding common ground in the traditional importance placed upon kinship, family structure, fellowship, and community-based gatherings.[101]

World War II unified Kiowa Christian and Traditionalist segments in the honoring of Kiowa servicemen. Atwater Onco recalled, "World War II, all the customs came back. After World War II, it all started. The church people got stronger in their belief in church. And then naturally with the war going on they all worked together, the non-Christian and the Christian, to honor the servicemen, to pray for the servicemen.... And it just kept a going from then on."[102]

After the war some younger Kiowa began to participate in the revivals of honor dances, powwows, society dances, and other traditional Kiowa activities that were formerly prohibited by Kiowa families who followed strict Christian doctrines. Many "traditionalist" and "Christian" Kiowa were veterans of World War II and Korea, and both were honored.[103] Within a few years, the Black Legs Society included nearly equal numbers of members from Kiowa Traditional and Christian families. Before this time, members of many Christian families were reluctant to participate in dance-related activities because of the wishes of their parents and grandparents, who were strong Christians. With the passing of the elder generation, some people began to attend and participate in more traditional activities during the 1960s and 1970s, particularly in powwows and society dances, in addition to maintaining their Christian practices.

As one society officer in charge of membership records said in the late 1990s, "I would say about half and half, from what I see on the roll. A Christian family and a traditional family both uphold our veterans. . . . Even nowadays . . . we have a lot of people in there that are Christian family, and we have a lot of traditional family now."[104] Recently, a marked increase in the number of inductees from Christian families has been noticed. One member stated that some veterans from Christian families have held back and been reluctant to join and become active because they incorrectly associated the drinking done in American VFW organizations with people's behavior during powwows and society dances. According to this person, many other Christian Kiowa are now discovering that, contrary to earlier Christian church doctrine, participation in Christianity and tribal cultural activities do not have to be mutually exclusive.[105] As one society elder commented, "There is nothing to be ashamed of for any Christian to belong to something that upholds Kiowa traditions and culture. And the younger people are going to see that, and you'll see the younger people that are eligible to join in the future. . . . Christian people or church people are getting more active with our Black Leggins."[106]

Several Kiowa ministers and sons of earlier Kiowa ministers of various Christian denominations have been active society members for decades, and some nonveteran ministers have remained active with the society because of their parents' previous involvement. Indeed, several members from Christian families, including some younger ministers, have recently been inducted into the society. One elder society officer stated, "We've had the backing from Christian leaders all the way, and some of course never did. Some never will now, even in the future, but overall, I've seen a lot of ministers come over there [to the dances]."[107]

Although Christianity qualitatively changed traditional forms of honoring warriors and veterans, it did not terminate these practices. Christian churches are much more flexible today concerning participation in tribal culture, in part because of increased numbers of Kiowa clergy, the high social status of veterans, and the development of greater Indian rights. Some Christian Kiowa and ministers still adhere solely to church activities, but most may attend and participate in dance functions depending upon personal beliefs. Occasionally even an Anglo minister or priest visits a Kiowa dance. Prayer meetings for outgoing and incoming servicemen and for servicemen overseas, as well as collections of money to give to servicemen, have continued throughout Operations Desert Storm and Enduring Freedom and the current campaigns in Afghanistan and Iraq.[108]

On my first visit to Rainy Mountain Kiowa Indian Baptist Church, on Sunday, November 9, 1997, I recognized some members of every current major Kiowa dance society. When I discussed this with one elder church member, she commented, "People are into everything today." Rev. Kerr, then the minister of the church, stated that although the church program had not recognized Veterans Day every year, doing so had been suggested, and it would be included that year. During this service, Peggy Tsoodle rose and spoke of how the Kiowa always recognized their warriors in the past and in recent times. She spoke of the way Kiowa equate the terms *warrior* and *service-*

man and of the way many prayer meetings were held for departing servicemen at the church and in individual homes during World War II. During the war the church also maintained a list of all Kiowa servicemen from the church and the Rainy Mountain Kiowa community on the back wall of the church. Each soldier's name had a star by it. During the December 7, 1997, service, members sang the two Kiowa Christian hymns that were composed during World War II for veterans overseas. During the war everyone would go outside after Sunday services and sing these two songs at the church flagpole. Many Christian Kiowa currently belong to the Kiowa Gourd Clan, the Black Legs Society, the Ohoma Lodge (Omaha Society), and the Kiowa Tia-Piah Society. Christian Kiowa have never forgotten their warrior legacy and the importance of recognizing veterans.[109] Christian or Traditional, the Kiowa continue to support their veterans.

Society Dress

The contemporary dress style of the Black Legs Society is a syncretic blend of old and new martial traditions combining features of the nineteenth-century Black Legs Society and the contemporary United States armed forces. The society decided to adopt a uniform dress code while maintaining society dress as authentically as possible. In keeping with the society's name, the men's legs from the knees down were to be kept black by paint, knee-length stockings, or buckskin leggings. The wearing of a black string shawl around the waist, a porcupine hair roach headdress, and bells would continue (Bantista 1983:6). A *pàubôn* would continue to be the societal insignia, and each man would now carry a straight lance with individual decorations of his military service. Society leader Gus Palmer Sr., for example, had twenty-one eagle feathers on his lance, representing the twenty-one bombing missions he made during World War II.[110]

Although society members did not originally wear capes, upon the Black Legs' revival, Gus, George, and Dixon Palmer gave all society members the right to wear red capes to commemorate the war deed of their great-grandfather Young Mustang.[111] In addition to giving the group a uniform appearance during ceremonials, this was a politically astute move that centered the family and its ancestry at the heart of the modern revival, and the family's influence continues to the present. The family song, composed in honor of Young Mustang by Bôhî̱, is sung today in the middle of the society dance as it gains momentum. During this song, the descendants of Young Mustang and their families dance in the middle of the arena while the other members dance along the sides.[112]

Emphasizing traditional veteran status, members frequently wear their United States armed forces military insignia, service ribbons, and medals on their capes. Other parts of the men's dress remain traditional but are left up to the individual. The society commander alone wears a black waist sash and a set of hair plates on a black base. The leader is also the only member to wear a full-length eagle feather bonnet

Gabriel Morgan in traditional Black Legs Society body paint, with his mother, Vanessa Jennings. Kiowa Black Legs Society ceremonial, Anadarko, Oklahoma, October 1990.

during portions of the fall ceremonial. Today members paint themselves according to individual preference, and only occasionally does a member paint his legs black. The traditional style of society painting was revived around 1980 by Gabe Morgan and has been maintained by his brother Seth and other boy members in the society. They continue to paint their entire bodies in the old fashion and generally carry weapons such as a lance, bow and quiver, and shield, resembling practices of the pre-reservation period. This style of body painting was revived from information provided in 1935 by Kintadl to Jane Richardson, who in turn supplied copies to the Kiowa. Recently, a few adult members occasionally wear the older style of society body paint.[113]

Women wear either Kiowa-style cloth, velvet, or buckskin dresses or everyday Anglo-style clothing and a shawl displaying the name and symbol of their auxiliary organization. Another dress style associated with the society is the "Red Sleeve Dress" (Màunkàugúlhòldà), a cloth or wool dress consisting of a black or navy blue body and red sleeves and sides. The two society princesses wear wool or buckskin dresses and have a sash with their name and the society's name on them.[114]

The Society Lodge

In pre-reservation times societies met in the tipi of one of their members, usually that of an officer. The sides of the lodge were kept down for private meetings and rolled up for public dances. Continuing this tradition, the Black Legs began using a society tipi in 1973 modeled after the famous Jòqígácút (Return From Battle Marks Tipi), or "Battle Picture Tipi," of Jòhâusàn (Little Bluff Recess/Concavity). For the Kiowa this tipi dates to 1840, when the Kiowa, Comanche, and Apache established peace with the Cheyenne and Arapaho. Following this peace, the Kiowa leader Little Bluff and the Cheyenne leader Sleeping Bear formally entered into a bond of friendship, a bond characteristic of military societies and trading partners and known as *cóm* and *châ* (friends). Mooney recorded that the tipi "came originally from the Cheyenne, having been given to Dohausan in the summer of 1845, five years after peace had been made between the two tribes in 1840 by a Cheyenne chief variously known as Two Lances, Big Head and Sleeping Bear. . . . The gift was made in ratification of the agreement and was reciprocated with a return gift of several horses, including a valuable ta-kon [tháukó] 'black ear' racer."[115]

Erected with the door facing east, the lodge may be divided into north and south sides. When Little Bluff Recess received the tipi it had sixteen horizontal yellow stripes painted boldly across the south half of the lodge, from the door to the middle of the back of the lodge. The north side held several battle pictures, including one or two horse figures. Although the Kiowa had many painted tipis, up until this time they depicted battle scenes only on hide robes and calendars.[116]

The yellow stripes are said to have symbolized successful war expeditions led by Sleeping Bear, who instructed the Kiowa leader to add black stripes between the yellow ones to represent successful war expeditions that he had personally led and on which he had brought back scalps and lost no members. Little Bluff subsequently added fifteen boldly painted black stripes between the sixteen yellow stripes. Down the back of the tipi, twenty tomahawks outlined in black with red blades and cloth pendants were depicted in a column from the top of the lodge to its base. These symbols commemorated coups counted by the prominent warrior Ténfìqî (Heart Eater) against the Pawnee with a tomahawk, his weapon of choice. Heart Eater had twenty-seven such coups with this weapon against the Pawnee alone before his death in 1853.

Above the front door, on the north side of the tipi, a column of eight red cloth-covered and feathered lances was added, representing the coups counted with that weapon by Âiá̰gài (Sitting On A Tree), a childhood survivor of the 1833 Cutthroat Massacre. Noted Kiowa warriors filled the rest of the north side with depictions of battle scenes. On the top of the north side was placed a picture of a warrior encircled by enemies. This image originally depicted Feathered Head Pendant, a Comanche ally of the Kiowa, who was surrounded by Mexican troops around 1830 but managed to defend himself from behind hastily constructed breastworks of sand. After killing one of the soldiers, he was able to escape. This portion of the tipi became reserved for a circular picture motif that, although varying from year to year, depicted a single warrior inside a circular breastwork defending himself from an overwhelming number of surrounding enemies. A later picture in this location depicted the noted warrior Big Bow and his wife, Black Bear, who had defended themselves all day in a fight against a party of Mexican troops beyond the Pecos River, he with a bow and arrows and she with two pistols. Although Big Bow received several wounds, the couple escaped the following night. Later this depiction was succeeded by one of Yellow Wolf surrounded by Osage enemies.

Every time the tipi was remade, usually each year, twenty to thirty warriors were invited to participate in its renewal. They discussed events that were considered worthy of depicting on the lodge and selected two or three dozen to display, thereby providing a partial record of recent tribal military history. The scenes were painted by the warrior who had performed the deed himself, by an artist under his direction, or by the current owner of the tipi. Over time these depictions changed with the acquisition of higher-ranking battle feats (Ewers 1978:14–17). Subsequent reproductions and models of this tipi have varied in numbers of stripes, tomahawks, and battle scenes and in the scenes' exact content.

In 1973 Dixon Palmer was commissioned by the Southern Plains Indian Museum to make a replica of the Battle Picture Tipi. Soon thereafter he initiated the idea of using a society tipi for the Black Legs Society, by this time the primary Kiowa society emphasizing military service. Like the contemporary form of society dress, the society tipi blends past and present Kiowa military service by combining portions of the Battle Picture Tipi with symbols of modern Kiowa service in the U.S. armed forces. The Battle Picture Tipi design was chosen for several reasons. First, Little Bluff Recess was the Kiowa tribal chief from 1833 to 1866, and his tipi design is not only known by nearly every Kiowa but remains an important symbol of Kiowa military and political tradition. For the Kiowa, this tipi might perhaps be compared to the United States flag or the Liberty Bell for Anglo Americans—a symbol of freedom, autonomy, and martial ethos. Best known as the leader of the Dog Society, Little Bluff Recess is believed by some to have once been a Black Legs member and the society's leader, thereby add-

Kiowa Black Legs Society tipi, staff, and feathered bonnets. Anadarko, Oklahoma, about 1994.

ing yet another layer of association and tradition. Unfortunately, membership rosters for Kiowa societies do not date back far enough to confirm this. However, because men frequently belonged to several societies throughout their lifetimes, he could well have been a member. In addition, the incorporation of his tipi design directly complements the continuing Kiowa emphasis on honoring tribal martial achievements and the concepts surrounding the revival and focus of the Black Legs Society. In 1974 Mr. and Mrs. Dixon Palmer made the canvas tipi, which Dixon and George Palmer painted.

Facing the door of the current society tipi, the left half consists of yellow and black stripes, or "war trails," like those on the Battle Picture Tipi. The right side of the tipi was originally decorated to commemorate Kiowa participation in modern warfare. This half consists of a red-painted upper portion, said to symbolize the blood given by Kiowa killed in action serving in the United States military, and a white lower portion, separated from the upper portion by a thin blue stripe. On the first society tipi, made in 1974, this portion depicted modern-day battles in which Black Legs Society members had actually participated. Included were four scenes depicting combat. On the north side of the tipi these included, from left to right, two fighter planes shooting an exploding enemy plane, two bombers dropping bombs, a tank, and a paratrooper landing on the ground and wielding a machine gun. This tipi was later replaced with a larger one, which is currently in use. The present society tipi was made and painted in 1986 by George and Dixon Palmer. In 1997, new battle scenes began to be painted on this lodge. On the right side, below the upper blue stripe and extending from the front of the tipi to the middle of the back and then running downward, are military insignia and divisional crests of Kiowa veterans. Near the top of the tipi in the center of the back is a figure of an eaglelike bird centered on a light blue circular background. This figure has the head and wings of a bird attached to a red, yellow, and blue shield that forms the body of the figure. The design has long been used as a society logo on stationery, shirts, and other items.[117]

Facing the door of the lodge and on the upper front portion of the right, or north, side of the lodge is a list of Kiowa veterans of the twentieth century who made the supreme sacrifice for their country and where they fell:

Cpl. Lyndreth L. Palmer—Germany, World War II
Pvt. Matthew Hawzipta—Germany, World War II
Pvt. George Neconie—Pacific, World War II
Pfc. Joe Gouladdle—Pacific, World War II
Sgt. Luke Tainpeah—Korea
Pvt. Silas Boyiddle—(POW) Korea
Cpl. Dennis Karty—Korea
S.Sgt. Donald Bear—Vietnam
1st Sgt. Pascal Cletus Poolaw—Vietnam

Kiowa veterans and Black Legs Society members have served in every major American military conflict of the twentieth and twenty-first centuries, from World War I to the present. Gus Palmer Sr. expressed the importance of recognizing, during Black Legs ceremonials, the supreme sacrifice made by Kiowa who have been killed in action, including his brother: "It's a big honor even though they're dead. They did something far beyond what any man could do. Far more than what I did. He gave his life."[118]

During society dances, the tipi is erected on the east side of the arena with the door facing east. Beside the tipi is a permanent flagpole from which the American flag is flown. A flag for each branch of the United States military and a POW-MIA flag, honoring prisoners of war and personnel missing in action, are placed on the west side of the tipi. Four poles are stuck into the ground behind the tipi, and an eagle-feathered bonnet is placed on top of each, with the society *pàubôn* planted in the middle of them. At some dances the black no-retreat sash is suspended from the top of one of the wooden poles with its end pinned to the ground by the society lance.

Veteran Recognition

The Black Legs emphasize the recognition and honoring of all American veterans. Over the years the society has recognized several outstanding Kiowa, other Indian, and non-Indian veterans at its annual ceremonies, supporting United States military involvements and recognizing the special accomplishments of Kiowa tribal members. These accomplishments and their recognition by the society reflect the ethos, spirit, and willingness behind Kiowa military service and constitute special portions of the society's programs.

In 1964, Kiowa veterans George Neconie (killed in action), Lt. Col. Lawrence Ware, and Hugh Doyebi were recognized for their military service. In 1965 the society announced its full support of the United States' involvement in Vietnam, and on August 27, 1965, it made Lt. Col. Ernest Childers, a Creek Indian and Congressional Medal of Honor recipient in World War II, an honorary member on the day of his retirement from the U.S. armed services at Fort Sill, Oklahoma. In 1966 a special dance was held in honor of returning Kiowa Pfc. Charles Cozad, who had recently been wounded in action in Vietnam.

In 1968, a bust of Kiowa 1st Sgt. Pascal Cletus Poolaw (Jan. 29, 1921–Nov. 7, 1967) posthumously symbolized his induction into the National Hall of Fame for Famous American Indians in Anadarko, Oklahoma, during the Black Legs' Veterans Day dance. Poolaw served more than twenty-five years in the U.S. Army and was the most decorated Indian veteran in U.S. military history, having served in World War II, Korea, and Vietnam. He was wounded in Germany in September 1944 and again in Korea in July 1950. During World War II Poolaw earned a battlefield commission as a second lieutenant but later voluntarily relinquished it to return to active combat duty. His forty-two medals and citations included twenty-two awards for combat service and twelve for acts of valor. Among these awards were the Distinguished Service Cross, five bronze stars, four silver stars, three purple hearts, and one air medal. While serving in Vietnam as a first sergeant with the 1st Battalion, 26th Infantry, 1st Infantry Division, Poolaw was killed in action while attempting to rescue a wounded comrade under fire—an act that was considered one of the bravest possible in pre-reservation Kiowa society (Mishkin 1940:39). After Poolaw swam into open water and carried a wounded comrade to shore on his back, both men were shot and killed. As Poolaw's sister Evalu Russell described it: "This is patriotism from the Indian people, of Kiowas, this family. They weren't afraid to go. He was not afraid to go get that white boy and bring him to shore because little did he know, little did he know, they were both going to be leaving us."[119] In 1968, four of Poolaw's sons—Lindy, Lester, Donnie, and Pascal Jr.—were also serving in the U.S. Army. Poolaw Hall, a remotely piloted vehicle training facility at the Field Artillery Center, was dedicated in his memory at Fort Sill, Oklahoma, on September 14, 1983 (AIEB 1968:17; Bantista 1983:17; Haynie 1984:20).

Other society honors have included recognition of the late Kiowa artist T. C. Cannon (Kiowa-Caddo), a well-known contemporary painter, Vietnam War veteran, and Black Legs Society member; Jack Montgomery, a Creek veteran of World War II and one of four Native American Congressional Medal of Honor recipients; and other distinguished veterans. The society has also recognized prominent Native American leaders such as N. Scott Momaday (Kiowa), who won the 1969 Pulitzer Prize in literature for his book *House Made of Dawn*, and past principal chief of the Cherokee Nation Wilma Mankiller, on October 13, 2002. In 1977 the society decided to begin using more of its own members as guest speakers during society dances, because many of them held significant military records (Bantista 1983:18–28).

On October 6, 1990, the U.S. Army flew an armored OH-58D attack helicopter from Fort Sill to the Black Legs Society encampment at Indian City U.S.A., where the society bestowed the name "Kiowa Warrior" upon the craft. Although the army has maintained a long-standing tradition of naming aircraft after Indian tribes, this was the first one to be given an individual name by an Indian military society. On January 22, 1991, the society participated in a rally supporting Operation Desert Shield and the United States' participation in Operation Desert Storm. On October 13, 1991, four Kiowa Desert Storm veterans were inducted into the society. On October 9, 1994, a bronze bust of Bear That Runs Over Them (popularly known as Stumbling Bear), a signer of the 1867 Medicine Lodge Treaty and a former Black Legs Society officer, was inducted into the National Hall of Fame for Famous American Indians. The induction included an honor guard of six of Stumbling Bear's great-grandsons—all Black Legs Society members—a sign language demonstration of the Lord's Prayer by several third great-granddaughters, and family songs about Stumbling Bear.[120]

On December 28, 2002, the Kiowa Tribe honored three members of the Kiowa Indian Hall of Fame, including Marine veteran Norman L. Sahmaunt, who had fought on Iwo Jima, and inducted four members posthumously at an honor dance at the tribal complex in Carnegie. The last were veterans and Black Legs Society members Rueben Topaum, Frank Kaubin, and Allen Quetone and past Gourd Clan vice president Oscar Tsoodle.[121] Recently, several Kiowa veterans of the campaigns in Afghanistan and Iraq have been inducted into the Black Legs Society.

On November 16, 2005, Cpl. Joshua J. Ware was killed during an ambush in Ubadiya, Iraq, becoming the first Kiowa killed in combat since 1968, during the Vietnam War. A veteran of the second battle of Fallujah, Ware returned to Iraq as a member of Regimental Combat Team 2, 2nd Marine Expeditionary Force. Ware and others had just entered a farmhouse when an explosion went off, wounding another marine. Other marines tried to rescue the man but came under gun and grenade fire from inside the house. Making a flanking movement, Ware kicked in a side door and began firing on eleven Iraqis inside. Ware drew their fire, allowing his wounded comrades to be rescued. Although he killed some of the enemy, he himself was killed, too. In October 2006 a member of Ware's unit brought an Iraqi flag captured during the fight

Kiowa Black Legs Society memorial for Joshua Ware. Ware's father dances with the society staff, facing a captured Iraqi flag. Kiowa Black Legs Society ceremonial, Anadarko, Oklahoma, October 2007.

to the Black Legs ceremonial. It was stuck into the ground beside the curved society lance. During a special event held for the family that day, Ware's service record and an account of the way he died were read. His father danced with the society lance, accompanied by family members and members of the society, all facing the Iraqi flag.[122]

Leadership and Organization

Current society leadership is a syncretic mix of traditional Black Legs Society and modern VFW and American Legion forms of organization, combining older offices such as society leaders and whipmen with contemporary Anglo forms such as chaplains and public relations officers. Gus Palmer Sr. served as commander from 1958 until his death in December 2006. Currently, society leaders include Tugger Palmer, who succeeded his father as commander and previously the late Allen Quetone as vice commander, and Vice Commander Blas Preciado, who was previously a whipman.

Eddie Onco and R. G. Short are the other two officers. Dixon Palmer served as the treasurer for many years. Secretary Lawrence Ware had served as a whipman. Atwater Onco was the society secretary. Parker Emhoola is currently the sergeant at arms. Other officers have included public relations officer Rudy Bantista, who replaced the late Scott Tonemah. Alice Chaddlesone was president of the Kiowa Black Legs Women's Auxiliary from 1978 to 1998. Evalu Russell served as vice president. Annette Emhoola Garza and Tina Emhoola are the current auxiliary president and vice president. Steve Littleman, Eddie Onco, Atwater Onco, Amos Aitson, and McKinley Standing have served as masters of ceremony, and the late Rev. Walter Kokoom, Rev. David Paddlety, and Presley Ware have served as chaplains (Bantista 1983:41).[123]

The two positions of boy society members were revived in the early 1980s, with Gabe Morgan and Christian Palmer serving in them. Commonly referred to as ą̄udę́tàlyį̀ (favored boy), boy members are inducted at around the age of eight and remain in the society up to the age of eighteen. They must then serve in the military before rejoining the group, whereas in the past they were kept in the society. The boy members continue to take care of the coals in the society tipi for cedaring rituals (ritual incensing with burnt cedar sprigs, accompanied with prayer), carry water to the members, and relay messages.

Two society girl members have also been maintained and today are referred to as ą̄udę́mátàun (favored girls). As society princesses they must not yet have been married or had children. They are taken in as young girls and remain until they give up the position or decide to marry. The youth members parade in with the society, after which the boy members dance with the men, and the girl members—as in the 1800s—sit and dance beside the two society leaders.

The youth members' families frequently hold large giveaways in their honor. Giveaways for Black Legs princess Rhea Whetseline included two separate thousand-plate catered meals and four separate instances in which a car was given away in her honor by her grandmother Emma Ware. The giveaway for Gabe Morgan's last dance as a society boy member included a horse with money braided into its tail, women's dresses, blankets, shawls, and other goods. Giveaways reflect the family's love of the person and the honor of having been asked to serve in such an important position.

The Black Legs Society has long been a self-sufficient organization, with all funds and supplies coming directly from the members and their families. Unlike many other dance organizations and societies, the Black Legs hold no benefit dances or powwows and make no use of external funds such as State Arts Council grants. In 2008 the society began to receive partial co-sponsorship from the Kiowa tribal casino. Members and their families contribute beef and other food items, money, and other supplies. The members' wives and female relatives and members of the Kiowa Veterans Auxiliary prepare and serve the food for the entire society encampment, including visitors. Before each annual encampment, several weekly meetings are held to organize, pool resources, practice singing society songs, and socialize, similar to the organizational meetings held at the ride-around camp on the way to the Sun Dance, at which members pledged to sponsor feasts for each day of the Sun Dance. The society has maintained a well-organized, computer-itemized account of its transactions for many years and has recently been considering buying land for a permanent dance ground.

Current Society Ceremonials

As the most visible post–World War II arena of the Kiowa martial and veteran ethos, Black Legs Society ceremonials are replete with martial themes in song, dance, dress, custom, and material culture. The Black Legs Society honors and celebrates all servicemen, but particularly Kiowa veterans, their sacrifices, and the existing freedom enjoyed by all. The women's Scalp and Victory Dances are performed to honor the veterans and their service. Society leader Gus Palmer Sr. emphasized that the society represents the modern manifestations of traditional Kiowa Black Legs Society members of the past, warriors who were protectors of their tribe and encampments. These roles and values have simply been adapted to modern circumstances.[124]

The society's ceremonials reflect the continued emphasis placed upon recognizing and honoring veterans, as well as the ability of military sodalities to serve as enculturative arenas promoting the continuity of sociocultural forms that have been attached to the society's activities. From 1970 to 2008 the Black Legs held two dances a year, one during the second weekend in May, to honor veterans for Memorial Day, and the other on the second weekend in October, for Veterans Day observances.[125] In 2009 the society began to hold only the annual fall ceremonial. Kiowa travel from as far away as California, New York, Washington State, and Washington, D.C., to participate in the ceremonials. The fall ceremonial was originally held on November 11, Veterans Day itself, but the date was moved back because bad weather sometimes developed by that time. Overlap with the Carnegie Victory Club's annual November 11 dances may have also been a factor. Once, someone proposed that the society dance inside on November 11, but members immediately responded that neither they nor their ancestors fought, slept, or ate inside during their military service, and they would continue to dance outside. One man stated that they would continue to "fight like their ancestors did and as they did in modern warfare." On more than one occasion I have seen the society dance in cold, rainy weather. The Sunday, October 12, 1997, dancing was postponed until the following day, Columbus Day, because of heavy rain. Because the annual October dance often falls around Columbus Day, some non-Indians have confused the ceremonial as a celebration of Columbus Day. But as master of ceremonies Steve Littleman clarified on October 13, 1997, "We are by no stretch of the imagination celebrating Columbus Day. We are celebrating our servicemen."[126]

Continuing pre-reservation mourning practices, the society sponsors a feast for the families of recently deceased members before each ceremonial. On Friday evening, all in attendance line up in the campground in front of a small pile of coals brought from a fire. One by one, each is then prayed for and cedared, usually by elders such as Gus

Palmer Sr. and Richie Tartsah, before eating and socializing. This activity continues the earlier practice in which each Kiowa military society was required to visit and mourn with the families of all deceased members before any further society functions could be undertaken. These visits were conducted during the period of society preparatory meetings before the Sun Dance. Prayers and another cedaring ceremony are also performed inside the society tipi on the Saturday and Sunday afternoons of the ceremonials, to purify all of the members before dancing. Today the society feeds the families on the Friday evening to comfort and show respect to the families, to express their shared feelings of loss, and, perhaps symbolically, to ask permission to continue with their activities. The noon meals on Saturday and Sunday bring large numbers of relatives, friends, and visitors together for fellowship in their respective camps and in some ways resemble the daily feasts sponsored by society members during the preparatory stages of the Sun Dance. For the protection of the ceremony, no videotaping is allowed, and in 1987 the society reportedly copyrighted the dress, songs, dances, ceremony, and society name.[127]

Society Songs

During my research I collected fourteen Black Legs Society songs with texts and several more without. Those with lyrics are given in the following section, in their associated portion of the society ceremonial.[128] There are fewer Black Legs than Kiowa Gourd Dance and Ohoma Lodge songs, in part because the Black Legs have fewer personal songs (except those of Young Mustang and Sitting Bear II). In the past, society partners are said frequently to have had their own songs. With the exception of the Chiefs' Song, now called the Induction Song, most Black Legs songs with texts have been composed since the 1958 revival, some as recently as the fiftieth anniversary of the end of World War II in 1995.

Relative to other forms of Kiowa and Indian music, Black Legs Society songs are not well known outside a segment of the Kiowa tribe. Although two commercially recorded cassettes of Black Legs Society songs have been released (by Indian House Records in 1964 and Canyon Records in 1977), they contain only one song with lyrics. Because these songs are sung only during a few private society preparatory meetings and during the annual ceremonial, their performance is limited and thus less well known by some Kiowa and people outside the Kiowa community. The restriction of the drum, or singers, solely to Kiowa at society ceremonials also limits the number of singers who know the songs well. Furthermore, because membership and participation in the society are restricted, no secular version of the society dance is performed outside the Kiowa community, unlike the Gourd Dance and the War Dance, which constitute the majority of powwow programs year-round. Unlike Gourd Dance songs, which are frequently sung without their associated lyrics, Black Legs songs are generally sung with the lyrics.[129] Thus Black Legs songs are not widely used among other tribes or by non-Indian hobbyists, as Gourd and War Dance songs are.

Although the Naishan Apache Manatidie and the Comanche Tuhwi Societies both use many of the same songs sung by the Kiowa Black Legs Society, they use no lyrics in their versions. Thus Black Legs songs take on additional layers of linguistic and cultural meaning through the cultural and martial ethos espoused in their texts. Kiowa Black Legs Society songs exemplify a martial ethos par excellence in that they frequently reference the society's name, reflecting a group orientation as a military and veterans society; the prominent or high social status of young Kiowa men; the warrior status of these men; hope for their safe return home from service; the joy and rights associated with dancing to these songs at society ceremonials; and the fact that these men fought and in some cases died in combat.

Ceremonial Program

Each afternoon program begins around two o'clock with a prayer led by a Kiowa elder, followed by the Kiowa Flag Song (Tháikáuóltádǎugà). In 1919, following Kiowa service in World War I, new words were composed and added to an old Kiowa Scalp Dance song to make the Kiowa Flag Song:

1 Thái-káu-ól-tâ-gàu
 (White / cloth / to raise/ flag or white cloth being raised)
 The flag is being raised.
2 Bét thâ-gà-òl-tǎ-gù
 (You all [plural imperative] / proper or good / to raise/ flag)
 Raise the flag in the proper/respectful manner!
3 Háun-dé-ǫ-dé bà áum-gà
 (Feeling good / for us / what happened)
 What a good thing has happened for us (i.e., in winning the war, acquiring the flag, the veterans' returning, etc.).[130]

Next, the two society processional songs are sung. During these songs a procession of Black Legs Society members carrying the flags of the United States, the Kiowa Tribe, and the four United States military branches is followed by the two society princesses, women wearing Red Sleeve Dresses, the Kiowa Veterans Auxiliary, the Kiowa War Mothers, the Purple Heart Club, the Kiowa Warrior Descendants, and the Carnegie Victory Club. At the request of society leader Gus Palmer Sr., the late Jimmy Anquoe composed the first processional song, which serves as a sort of theme song for the society and reflects the Kiowa community's elation over the return of its servicemen:

1 Jó-gṹ-dáu thǎ-gà yán tén-xò-dǎu-dò
 (Young men / good / you / permitted or allowed-because)
 Because you are privileged to be fine young men.
2 Thǎ-gái dáut âui-chàn-dò

(Good / you all plural [for us embodied] / again-returned-because)
Because they all returned [to us] in good condition.[131]

The second processional song, composed by the late Jimmy Tartsah and presented to the society in his honor posthumously, instructs the veterans to enjoy the day and their dance and to dance in happiness:

1. Jó-gúl-ộ-gòp á dáu-dò,
   (Young men-highly regarded or affluent / they / are-because)
   Because they are highly regarded young men.
   Ám-kǐ-dà báu dáu-dò
   (*You* or *your*-day / you all / is-are)
   Because it is *your* day.
2. Repeat.
3. Repeat.
4. Jó-gúl-ộ-gòp á dáu-dò,
   Bé ộ-tá-gùn
   (You and we all / feel good-dance)
   Dance in joy, happiness (appreciation).
5. Ám-kǐ-dà báu dáu-dò, Bé ộ-tá-gùn
6. Jó-gúl-ộ-gòp á dáu-dò, Ám-kǐ-dà báu dáu-dò
1. Repeat line 4.
2. Repeat line 5.
3. Repeat line 6.[132]

The processional proceeds from the northeast side of the arena southward, making a clockwise circuit. On the second circuit around the arena, the color guards turn to the center of the arena, holding their position and facing west, while the rest of the processional continues clockwise around the arena.

Two Memorial Songs (Câifẽgàudãugà, or War Dead Songs) are sung next. These songs were both composed during World War II and are always sung in unison, with everyone standing. Both songs are part of a large genre of War Mothers' songs and are used specifically as Memorial Songs by both the Kiowa War Mothers and the Black Legs Society. These two songs are sometimes referred to by the English name "Empty Saddle Songs," a name given to them in recent years. They symbolize the return of a war party leading the empty or unsaddled horse of a comrade killed in action. Elders indicate that either Lewis Toyebo or Edgar Newton Gouladdle composed the first song, Gouladdle having lost a brother in World War II.

1. Gáu jḗ-pàui chól bá ạu-gî
   (And / everyone / surely or in that way or manner, like or as / you all / think about it or consider it as)
   Everyone think about/consider it (in that way).
2. Repeat.

82   KIOWA MILITARY SOCIETIES

   3 Gáu jḗ-pàui chól bá fél-dò̱-dè
     (And / everyone / surely or in that way or manner / you all / think about it
       or consider it as)
     Everyone think about it like that.
   4 É câi-hèm-cáui-jò-gù̱-dàu ám-fè̱-dò
     (He / fighting-died-young man / for or on account of you)
     A young Kiowa man died fighting for you.[133]

As this song begins, all Kiowa killed in action in the twentieth century are specially recognized. Their names, as listed on the society tipi, are read over the public address system as "lulus" (ululations) and shouts of remembrance and encouragement resonate throughout the crowd.

The second Memorial Song was composed by Lewis Toyebo in memory of Lyndreth Palmer, who was killed on December 5, 1944. Toyebo first publicly sang this song at a memorial service for Palmer held at Sahmone Church, west of Carnegie, Oklahoma, later that month. Palmer's father, William Palmer, was presented with his son's flag at the service. This song addresses the parents of the recently deceased soldier, telling them to be proud of their son's supreme sacrifice:

   1 Dáu-gà èm thâu-yi̱-thàu
     (Song / you / hear-shall-continually)
     When you shall hear this song,
   2 Ém ò̱-tá̱-yi̱-thàu nàu
     (You / good feeling-shall be / and)
     You shall be feeling good and
   3 Á-í̱ câi-hèm nàu gà sáu-mí
     (Your-son / fighting-died / and / it is / noteworthy, amazing, or prominent)
     Your son died fighting, and it's noteworthy.
   4 Repeat line 1.
   5 Repeat line 2.
   6 Jó-gúl câi-hèm nàu gà sáu-mí
     (Young man / fighting-died / and / it is / noteworthy, amazing, or
       prominent).
     A young man died fighting, and it's noteworthy.[134]

Society chaplain Rev. David Paddlety pointed out, "If you'll notice, one of the things about the ceremony is that they always announce the names of those that didn't make it back. They get the first attention. They get the first honor, and then those of us that survived or come through."[135]

For many Kiowa, these songs and the society dances bring forth strong emotions. In tears, one combat veteran described what the dance meant for him:

Well, the favorite part is, to me, I'm liable to get emotional on you right now [begins to cry]. It's hard. Because of what we go through in life, you know. And one of the requirements is to be in the military, and not everybody is like me, you know a veteran, a combat veteran, and part of our ceremony is not only to celebrate going over and coming back alive, but to honor and remember those that did fight and that were [begins crying again], that died or were wounded, you know, that have to live the rest of their lives disfigured or handicapped. And so it's during those times when we dance that I think of those men. I think of those times, in my mind I, I say "This is for you," you know, and think of their folks, that [continues to cry] the mother and the fathers that had to live the rest of their lives without their sons and or daughters, you know. So that's I guess the highlight for me, because that's what it means to me.[136]

After posting the colors in front of the master-of-ceremonies stand on the west side of the arena, the men exit the arena and enter the society tipi on the east side of the arena to purify themselves before dancing. Using a shovel, the two boy members bring hot coals from a fire in one of the camps into the society tipi, where the men offer prayers of thanksgiving for good health. A cedaring is held in which dried cedar sprigs are placed on hot coals to produce smoke that is fanned over each person. While the participants are fanned and incensed with the smoke, prayers are offered for society members and the members of any families that have recently lost a relative. Society members pray in honor of their recently deceased relatives and ask to receive strength to carry on in life.

Inside the society tipi, the commander addresses the society, emphasizing the importance of retaining its unity. Gus Palmer Sr. emphasized the need to "keep it up," stressing that the unity demonstrated during military service should be continued after service men and women returned to their homes and tribe, by teaching others to work together and stay together as they did in the military. Some members have described these meetings as "pep rallies" aimed at raising group martial spirit.[137]

Current society dances link the past Kiowa warrior ethos to that of the present while maintaining individual and tribal Kiowa ethnicity. Gus Palmer Sr. explained: "As veterans they fought for their land and their people, and therefore each dance is like a homecoming for veterans. Therefore they should work together and stay together. Then they can feel good about coming out to celebrate and enjoy the songs and dances that were performed before this part of the country was opened up."[138]

Society vice commander Blas Preciado commented on the longevity of the society and what it stands for:

> This is a tribal, a Kiowa warrior society. An old warrior society that has been in existence for, my understanding, maybe several hundred years, one hundred and fifty to two hundred years. It's a military society, and it's to honor the ones that have died for this country, to protect the people no matter what color, and that this is ours, the Kiowa tribe. And you know it's been in our culture for these many years and you know that we restrict it to just like a long time ago. It was restricted . . . it was Kiowa, and it was for the people that fought for the protec-

tion of other people, and it is the same way today, the people that went out and are willing to give their lives for the protection of their country, their homeland, the same way.[139]

Atwater Onco, a veteran of World War II and Korea, commented on what the society represented and what being a member meant to him:

> It shows that you were a warrior, modern day warrior. That's what I like about Black Leggins, it shows that I did my part as a Kiowa to do what I could for my country in the past.... We all did this together as a whole. We're a whole group that belongs. We all did it together. And we did it to uphold not only the Kiowas but the United States that we all belong to.... I like being in there, and it's traditional, it comes from way back there.... It's a warrior society... and that's what I like about it, because it upholds the past.... And that shows through the Black Leggins, the Kiowas still, since World War I, through the current wars, they're still doing their share as warriors.[140]

The Women's Scalp and Victory Dances

Following the posting of the colors and the men's exit from the arena, the women's portion of the program begins. As in many other Plains Indian cultures, Kiowa women danced Scalp and Victory Dances upon the safe return of all members of a war party, to honor their returning warriors. In the Plains Indian warfare complex, these dances were closely related to revenge raiding against an enemy. The successful acquisition of vengeance formed a cycle that began with the tribe's suffering a loss or injury from an enemy, followed by mourning (grief, anger, and shame, often including self-mutilation), the seeking of vengeance, and finally a social celebration. A revenge raid often culminated in and was symbolized by the acquisition of scalps and other material items, which were carried in the dances after the warriors returned home. As Marian Smith (1938:455) noted:

> It is important to recognize that these situations, mourning and war, were the only situations in which violence was culturally recognized. Murder was discountenanced, quarreling and bickering were ideally tabu, and nothing could be less violent than the matter-of-fact way in which sacrificial self-mutilation was undertaken. Yet the Plains Indians were decidedly not a calm people and the effect of this cultural concept was to direct all violent emotional expression into warfare and its accompanying ceremonials....
>
> The ideal gamut of excited emotion was that which began with such mourning, ran through self-violence to violence upon an enemy, and terminated in social recognition of success in war.

Smith (1938:461) concluded that the completion of this process was especially important for persons in mourning who were unable to go on such raids and thus relied on

Kiowa Women's Victory Dance performed at the Kiowa Black Legs ceremonial, Anadarko, Oklahoma, about 1991.

"the success of others to allay their emotions of mourning. The scalp was the symbol around which such emotions centered and to receive a scalp was to cease to mourn."

The performance of Scalp and Victory Dances continue today as one of the primary traditional martial roles for Kiowa women. After World War I, a Scalp and Victory Dance was held at Ahpeahtone's, west of Carnegie, Oklahoma. Other Scalp and Victory Dances were held annually during Armistice Day dances on Frizzlehead's allotment on Cache Creek, southeast of Carnegie, and at Whitefox's allotment, west of Carnegie. These last two celebrations became annual events for a number of years. Although the last scalps from the 1800s were "put away' (buried) in the 1950s, the dances retain their symbolic importance. Women's Scalp and Victory Dances are now held at the Black Legs Society ceremonials and at the annual Carnegie Victory Club celebration on Veterans Day.

Keeping with tradition, the women dance before the men on such occasions. Before entering the Black Legs Society lodge, the men stick their lances upright into the ground beside it. The women's portion of the program begins with a clockwise Round Dance step to sets of War Mother songs. These songs all have lyrics and describe the brave deeds of Kiowa veterans, their lengthy journeys, and the happiness felt throughout the community upon their safe return. Next, a set of Scalp Dance Songs (Áuldáucúndàugà) begins, and each woman takes the lance of one of her relatives and begins to perform the Scalp Dance (Aúldáucúngà, lit. Hair Kill Dance, from *ául* [hair], *dáu* [kill], and *cúngà* [dance]). Although the choreography and music differ between the two dances, Kiowa classify the Scalp and Victory Dances under the same name or as two forms of the same dance. Although the two dances are collectively known as Aúldáucúngà, one person informally referred to the Victory Dance as Ǫ́tą́cùngà (Feel Good Dance), a modern and rarely used nickname. Today these dances are referred to by the English name Scalp and Victory Dance.[141]

Elders state that in the past, a series of Shuffle Dances accompanied the Scalp and Victory Dance as part of the celebration held for returning war parties. Today Shuffle Dances during women's Scalp and Victory Dances are rare, although they are a regular part of the men's portion of the ceremonial. Kiowa ledgerbook art depicts line formations in women's dances. As one Kiowa women who has danced the Scalp and Victory Dance observantly pointed out, one ledgerbook depiction (McCoy 1987:pl. 26) labeled a Victory Dance is probably a Shuffle Dance, as indicated by the forward-moving and raised position of the women's feet and by the forward swinging motion of their belt whips and pouches, which conform with the movement of a Shuffle and not a Victory Dance step.[142]

Several elder Kiowa women stated that during Scalp and Victory Dances it is appropriate to dance only with the lance of a male relative or one that is brought by a relative. Women are usually familiar with their relatives' lances and can choose them from among a group of thirty or more at ceremonials. Occasionally, elder women admonish young girls for picking up a lance that does not belong to one of their close relatives. Elder women also insist that once a dancer picks up a lance, she should carry it throughout the Scalp and Victory Dance. More recently a few women have begun to make and bring their own lances to dance with, to honor a male veteran relative.

During the Black Legs processional and the women's dances, women frequently wear the shawls of service organizations (Kiowa War Mothers, Victory Club, or Purple Heart Club) or descendants groups to which they belong. Others don personal shawls displaying the names, ranks, military insignia patches, honors, and medals of their relatives.

Some women dance with weapons captured by a male relative in battle or that hold symbolic representations of their relative's martial experiences. Some of these martial symbols are more obvious than others; many are displayed subtly in forms that may be unrecognizable to the unfamiliar eye. In memory of her brother Pascal C. Poolaw, Evalu Russell danced with a staff featuring several long feathers suspended along the shaft to represent the battles in which he had fought. A cluster of several shorter feathers at the top represented the number of enemies he had personally killed in combat.[143] The late Elva Mae Tapedo, a veteran herself, occasionally danced with an army saber.

Martial symbols are also sometimes incorporated into family dress styles and dance clothing. Some Kiowa women have sewn Army Airborne, 1st Division, and 1st Cavalry patches onto their red and black victory dresses. One woman I saw had sewn

Army 1st Division patches onto the backs of her leggings, in the center of the calf area, where coup marks were traditionally painted during the nineteenth century. In addition to dancing with the officer's saber belonging to her husband, Marine Captain Robert Poolaw Sr., Martha Kauley Poolaw decided to honor his military service by incorporating his service record into a set of dance clothing made by Vanessa Jennings, because, as she explained, "it went back to the warrior theme." The designs of her husband's military medals and ribbons were incorporated into the beaded neckline and dress decorations. Other designs were beaded into her belt pouches, apron, necklace, and legging insteps. A bronze star design was incorporated into her purse. On the backs of Mrs. Poolaw's leggings are twenty-seven coup marks that her husband painted to represent his twenty-seven years in service.[144]

During the Scalp and Victory Dance at each fall ceremonial, women may wear the four society bonnets, which are placed on four poles at the back of the society lodge and face west toward the arena. These bonnets are displayed only at the fall ceremonial and represent the four Palmer brothers, who were instrumental in reviving the society—Gus, George, Dixon, and their late brother Lyndreth, to whom the revival was posthumously dedicated. The bonnets are generally worn by family members. The four bonnets also correlate with the number of society officers in traditional Kiowa military societies. Normally, the only time a Kiowa woman may wear or use a man's lance or bonnet is during these dances.

The women then line up with the men's lances for the Victory Dance. Although similar to the Round Dance, this is the only Kiowa dance performed counterclockwise. It is during this dance that the women's most integral traditional role regarding the military complex—that of honoring and recognizing warriors—is performed. Martha Poolaw explained: "Those dances are to honor the veteran, the warrior at one time and now the veteran, and all those songs are geared to say that.... And there is a certain dance that goes with certain songs, and that's all interpreted to honor that returning warrior."[145]

Society member and master of ceremonies Atwater Onco elaborated:

This is the appropriate time for them to have those dances.... Now that's the way they used to do when the warriors went on a war party, they came back from battle, and they have a Scalp Dance to honor the warriors. And then they have this Victory Dance to honor the warrior. It's all tied together, your Scalp Dance, your Victory Dance. That was done by the women only, not by the men. This is in honor to the veterans, warriors that came back from battle. And that's what that represents every time we have a ceremonial dance, the women do their Scalp Dance and then their Victory Dance that shows that we, the warriors, they are honoring the Kiowa warriors coming back from battle, victoriously with scalps like they used to do. Of course we don't do that now, but it emphasizes that—a return from battle with scalps of the enemy—and now they're over here [the women] Scalp Dancing to show that they appreciate what they [the veterans] did, and also we're having a Victory Dance because we won. That's what that means, the Scalp and Victory Dance.[146]

Evalu Russell, a member of the Kiowa Veterans Association Auxiliary and a long-time participant in Scalp and Victory Dances, described what these dances meant for her:

> When I'm out there dancing, I'm just solely from the heart. I dance because it's a Kiowa version of victory. And the boys have come home, and how much better can a mother, a grandmother, an aunt, and friends feel to see one dancing out there that has been in a terrible battle. And we are so happy that they're back that nothing matters out there where we're dancing. It's just a feeling that really cannot be explained except self-feelings about what you are doing. And when I dance and I take one of those lances, I'm impersonating the idea that he must have gotten in there, and I really dance.[147]

As women pointed out, these dances are strictly for women, and during them "the arena belongs to the women and men are not allowed" to enter. But as the dances take place, the veterans also feel their spirit. Vietnam veteran Blas Preciado said, "It excites me. It's positive. . . . It motivates you. It just stirs me up and gets me charged up. . . . I've never really thought of it honoring me. I mean I always think of the others, I always think of them honoring the other men that had gone out and fought and come back or gone out and died."[148]

Vanessa Jennings expressed her thoughts on the dance: "Physically, it is a demanding dance. And I think that's good, you know, because when you are dancing, it seems like to me you are, whatever pain you experience, I mean that is something you dedicate to those men, you know, for the pain and suffering they went through. This [Scalp dancing] is nothing compared to what you went through, but I'm thinking about you and what you went through."[149]

Kiowa veterans stated that although they did not join the military to be honored or join a society, the honor dances held by the Kiowa women make them feel very good and immensely proud of their military service. As Atwater Onco explained it:

> I didn't join the service to be honored. I went to service twice but that was the least thing I went in there for, was for somebody to honor me. . . . And then you find out that people do honor you because you were in service, and it makes you feel proud that you're a Kiowa and you're upholding the traditions of the Kiowa by doing what the Kiowas used to do, they went to war. And that's what men were for, to go to battle. They went to war and they were highly respected because of their deeds. . . . But that's what I see when I'm out there and they're honoring the veterans. I don't think they are necessarily honoring me as an individual. They're honoring, to me you know, all the veterans. Living or gone, they're covering everybody. That's the feeling I get, you know. They have respect for the veterans and that's the way we're trained, to respect your warriors. That's what they do when they come out, like I said, not for me, they're coming out for everybody,

and because I'm part of the group, naturally it makes me feel good, see. That's the way I feel about those honor dances.[150]

During these dances and throughout the remainder of the afternoon, Kiowa women frequently wear their Red Sleeve Dresses (Màunkàugúlhòldà), red and blue or red and black cloth dresses that are frequently referred to as "Victory Dresses." The front and back body portions of the dress consist of two blue or black panels, and the sleeves and side gussets are red. Among the Kiowa, Red Sleeve Dresses are said to have been worn by women of ǫ̀dè (affluent) status to show their love and support for their male warrior relations during Scalp and Victory Dances, especially in the Black Legs Society. Documented as early as 1857, these dresses were worn by members of several Southern Plains tribes (Ewers 1980:75) and continue to be worn in some of the contemporary veterans auxiliary groups of the Kiowa, Comanche, and Plains Apache. Exclusive claims to the "right" to wear these dresses are found in all three tribes. Today the red and blue version of the dress is claimed and used by the Kiowa War Mothers, the Carnegie Victory Club, and the Purple Heart Club. Some Comanche women wear red and blue forms of the dress at various Comanche dances that include Scalp and Victory Dances. Women in the Comanche Tuhwi Society wear red and black versions of the dress. I have seen both Apache and Comanche women wearing red and blue dresses at current Apache Manatidie Society ceremonials. Although all three tribes have long histories of using these dresses, the Apaches may have revived their use first, in the mid-twentieth century. I have seen photographs of Apache women wearing such dresses in the 1960s in Manatidie, or Blackfeet, ceremonials, and I have interviewed people who participated in these dances.[151]

According to some Black Legs Women's Auxiliary members, the red and black version of the dress belongs solely to their organization. Black Legs members used black and dark blue body paint in the mid-1800s, so their female relatives may have worn both styles. Both colors of dresses are found in ledgerbook art from the late 1800s. One drawing (Petersen 1971:42) depicts a man holding a Gourd Dance rattle and dressed in preparation for the intersociety Sham Battle, beside a woman wearing a Red Sleeve Dress. Both are on horses. Such dresses may have been worn by affluent women throughout the tribe and were not limited to the Black Legs.

Some Kiowa believe that too many Kiowa women are trying to make competing claims about "who has the right" to dance Scalp and Victory Dances and wear the red and black or red and blue Victory Dresses. Some women claim that these dresses and dances belong only at Black Legs ceremonials, whereas others maintain that they belong only at Victory Club Veterans Day celebrations. During my fieldwork I observed from twelve to ninety-five women in the women's dances at Black Legs ceremonials and as few as nine women at one Victory Club celebration. Only a few women wore Victory Dresses at each. However, as one Kiowa woman emphasized, these dresses and dances originally belonged to Kiowa women collectively, and not to any men's or women's military society, organization, club, band, or subsection of the tribal population. The ethnographic record left by Kiowa elders who grew up in the pre-reservation era supports this. These dresses were worn and the dances performed whenever a group returned from a raid or war party, whether in a single band encampment or a larger grouping. Because the entire Kiowa population aggregated only once a year for a few weeks, and military society meetings and dances were held prior to the actual Sun Dance ceremony, Scalp and Victory Dances would have been held throughout the year, by various dispersed bands, and so were not associated with any particular military society.

Some women expressed concern regarding the level of female participation at Blacks Legs dances. One woman stated that the arena "should be packed with women" because their freedoms were obtained only through the efforts of these men, that many women took the men's efforts for granted, and that it "was not too much to come out and Scalp and Victory dance two or three days a year for your freedom." The women's portion of the program lasts less than an hour a day.[152]

Kiowa women noted that as recently as the 1960s and 1970s, Scalp and Victory Dances were regular parts of honor dances held throughout the calendar year to recognize servicemen during the Vietnam War. Women cited several such dances held at the fair building in nearby Apache, Oklahoma, during this time. The family of Vietnam veteran Sherman Chaddlesone had send-off and homecoming events for him at the Apache Fair Building that included Gourd, War, and Scalp and Victory Dances, with participation by the War Mothers. Chaddlesone recalled:

> They had a dance for me when I was leaving, and then also when I came back. . . . It's mainly just a, more of a family-type thing. Of course [it's] tribal, everybody is welcome to participate, and they did, and the situation was ongoing. We were sending a lot of young men over at the time, so every week there would be five or six of these dances going on here in the area. Guys were going over there and coming back. It was a fairly standard procedure and it helped a lot, I know, for the individuals to have that support from at least their families if not from the community as a whole.[153]

Kiowa women reported that none of the "recent" limits or restrictions were placed on these activities, and they described the modern changes as a part of the larger ongoing problem of people and organizations attempting to control activities, tribal traditions, and the "rights" to them.[154]

Among the Kiowa Black Legs, these dresses were reintroduced in 1979 or 1980 through the efforts of Vanessa Jennings, an internationally noted Kiowa beadworker and traditional artist. Today, women who dance at the Black Legs ceremonials specifically claim this style of dress as belonging to that society. It is commonly referred to in English as a "Battle Dress."[155] Although claims to dresses of specific color (red and blue or red and black) are currently maintained, ledgerbook art indicates that both forms were simultaneously present and probably reflected different shades of trade cloth more than social and symbolic distinctions.

A few Red Sleeve Dresses are preserved in museum collections. One, collected in 1860, is in Dunrobin Castle in Sutherland, Scotland. White Horse illustrated this style of dress in ledger art in 1875, as did Koba in 1876, while both were imprisoned at Fort Marion, Florida. Silverhorn illustrated several such dresses in ledger art between the 1890s and his death in 1941. Two other dresses, collected in 1865 and 1909, respectively, were given to the Museum of the American Indian in New York City.[156] Several examples of Kiowa Red Sleeve Dresses have been published in the form of ledgerbook art (Petersen 1971; Harris 1989; Berlo 1996).[157] Black Legs Society member and artist Sherman Chaddlesone frequently incorporates women wearing Red Sleeve Dresses in his ledgerbook-style paintings and drawings.

Vanessa Jennings poignantly described the importance of women's role in continuing to honor the sacrifices of veterans and the relationship of the Red Sleeve Dresses to that role:

> When you go and dance at Black Legs there's a reason for you to be there. I mean it isn't anything to play with. It is a sincere, heartfelt emotion, that's what brings me to Black Legs. You know this country that we live in, the way of life that we have here, to me it's important. It's important because there were so many of our men who were willing to leave. You know they were like those old Kiowas, they were willing to leave their camp, they were willing to leave the safety of their homes. Some of them died, some of them were disfigured, some of them maybe a physical disfigurement, some of them maybe an emotional disfigurement. There was a large price of blood paid for our freedom. So when you go to Black Legs you're honoring those men and their sacrifice, and that's why it's important when you go that you understand why. It isn't something [about which] to go, "Oh, gee whiz, don't I look keen," you know, that has no place at Black Legs. So when you go and you take part, there is a way for you to dress if you really feel strongly about Black Legs, and that's where you dress a certain way. To me that's where you dress in that Màunkàugúl, that battle dress. To me that's the time for the coup marks on the leggings, that's the time for the women to carry out that lance and dance with it because it honors that veteran. That's the one place where no man can come into that arena. You know that's the time for that woman and it's her responsibility to take care of things in a certain way.
>
> My great-grandma had a Màunkàugúl and it was made from a captured flag and it had bullet holes in the flag, and so when they [the veterans] brought it back my great-grandma, it was a battle trophy, and how else could a woman honor that battle deed, you know a man can't—it's not proper for a man to brag on himself—so as a woman that was something that was important to my great-grandma.... It was like World War I ... in this century which is interesting, you know, because it's still a carry over, a holdover of an attitude of the free days. You know they've just updated it and brought it into this century. It still fits with that idea of Kiowas being warriors.[158]

Another important part of women's honoring veterans is their role in "luluing." Common throughout Plains Indian cultures, ululations, known in Kiowa as *sáuàuljògà* (mouth-to voice), are tremolo throat-voiced emissions that sound like "lu-lu-lu-lu." Lulus are traditional women's honor cries to recognize individuals and to show their pride in, love, respect, and support for, and memory of them. Although lulus can be given at nearly any event in which people are being honored, including dances, powwows, giveaways, graduations, marriages, and naming ceremonies, they have long been integral parts of the honoring of returning warriors during Plains Scalp and Victory Dances. They are frequently heard at contemporary Plains Indian veteran-oriented dances. Women may lulu for persons of any age or of either sex. During the dancing, both women's and men's, women can frequently be heard luluing for their veteran relatives, alive and deceased. Several elder women stated that during dances they lulued when they thought of a particular relative who made them feel good. Atwater Onco explained: "Their mind is going back to their former uncle or grandpa, or dad, or brother who was in the service. And it makes them proud that they're dancing the Scalp Dance or the Victory Dance thinking about them. So in turn when they do that, they lulu to show that they're proud, proud of them, they're proud of whoever they're thinking about, see."[159]

In May 1991 I attended the induction of four Kiowa Desert Storm veterans into the Black Legs Society. Evalu Russell described the immense pride she felt when she Scalp danced and lulued for her son Lowell, just back from Operation Desert Storm:

> And I'm out there dancing with my heart and my son came home. When my son came home from Saudi Arabia I put out the best blanket I had, a brand new one on the ground. I said, "Come dance on this. Thank you for what you did over there." We'll never know exactly what he did, but it was pretty tough. I thought about my grandma [who, old and blind, used to sit on her bed praying for the return of her son Pascal Cletus Poolaw]. Am I going to be sitting on the bed waiting for him to come? And just then the good Lord brought him home. Why can't I be out there dancing with the Black Leggins with my heart, from the depth of my heart? And I'm glad we had that opportunity so we can show our patriotism.
>
> It's an honor cry, because it's coming from the heart. We go lulululu . . . , we're proud of you. How else can we tell them that we're proud of them? You know like when he [her son] came and sat on the blanket, oh, the women all around him lulued knowing that he had come back and what he has done for us, in Saudi, and some of the stories he tells us . . . I just know the good lord spared his life. . . . But he came back and I'm really proud of him as a veteran. He did his part.[160]

A large part of Kiowa dancing and other cultural activities includes frequent reflection upon one's elders who used to perform the same traditions and ceremonies and who provided the "road," or way of life, for the younger Kiowa. Women also commonly reflect on their female elders during Scalp and Victory Dances. As Vanessa Jennings commented of her grandmother Jeanette Berry Mopope, "Yes, I think about her. I can hear her lulu. She's with me all of the time, but most especially during the Scalp Dance and the Victory Dance. You know she's the one I watch to keep in step with. You know I may not be able to match her, strength for strength and courage for courage, but I'll sure make an attempt to match her. She really was something. Yeah, she's there with me."[161]

Kiowa frequently talk about the ability of music to make them feel better, both mentally and physically. At the 2003 fall ceremonial, just before the women's Scalp and Victory Dance, I saw an elder friend of mine who clearly was not feeling well. I heard one women say to her, "You don't look like you feel so good." She responded, "I don't. But I'll feel better when the drum starts, when I hear those songs." Soon afterward I saw her dancing enthusiastically and enjoying the Scalp and Victory Dance.[162]

The Men's Dances

Just before the women finish the Scalp and Victory Dance, the men, having completed their cedaring, prayers, and preparations inside the lodge, exit the lodge and stand along the south side of the arena watching the women dance. When the Scalp and Victory Dance ends, the women return the men's lances to their places beside the lodge. The men retrieve their lances, gather in a group formation, and prepare for their processional or parade-in (*kátgà*).

According to Kintadl's account in 1935, the society originally had four types of dances: "Tonkonga alone danced the tonsode, which has 2 different steps in it. They could also dance the emhawgo, and a plain dance like the Daimbega. Like the Adltoyui, they danced the Tsakoigya (turn-around dance)."[163] Today the society performs a parade-in with Dedication Songs (Châtqâutèldåugà, lit. "Door Cut Open Songs"), as well as four types of dances that resemble the preceding categories: the Excite or Stirring Emotions to Action Dance (Yáuldáucùngà); the Arise and Dance (in place) Dance (Émhâcùngà), a regular form of Black Legs Society dancing; the Shuffle Dance (Tǫ́sódêcùngà), which is composed of the Shuffle and Up and Down Dances; and the Turn Around or Reverse Dance (Xàkóigácúngà).

Led by the society leaders and princesses, the society begins its two Opening or Dedication Songs (Châtqâutèldåugà), in which society members sing together as they parade in. This processional resembles the parades made by societies at the Sun Dance. The songs have no words and no pause between them. The first song and half of the second are performed a cappella by the society members, who are then joined by the drumming and singing of the singers. When the drumming starts in the middle of the second song, it begins with a noticeably accelerating pace, and an immediate rise in the spirit and enthusiasm of the dancers, singers, and spectators is heard through whoops, hollers, and lulus. The second song ends with a group yell by the society members, who then plant their lances in front of them and are seated on a long row of wooden benches along the southwestern portion of the arena. Society leader Gus Palmer Sr.

explained that Opening Songs symbolically represent the opening of the ceremony, as if opening a tipi without a door, when a knife is taken out and a door is cut open from within. This song resembles the practice of the *qájáisàupàn* (big warriors, men with four or more coups), who sang four Chátqâutèldàugà, danced, and then recited war deeds at the beginning of the Sun Dance, before placing a stone at the entrance of the Sun Dance lodge to symbolically open the Sun Dance lodge and ceremony.[164]

The next two songs are called Excite or Stirring Emotions to Action Songs (Yáuldáudàugà). They represent the overwhelming joy and enthusiasm felt upon the return of warriors. The name of these two songs and dances is derived from the imperative verb *yául-àum* (excite or stir to action) and the verb *yául-jàu* (to carry on with wild behavior), and it denotes the fervent display of emotions at the veterans' return. Watching the dancers during these two songs, one senses an undeniable increase in excitement and enthusiasm, an energy not yet fully released. The songs not only provide an expression of the immense joy felt upon the physical entrance and symbolic return of the Kiowa veterans; they also provide the dancers and spectators an opportunity to warm up for the remainder of the ceremonial, which continually builds in tempo, symbolism, and emotional expression. As Gus Palmer Sr. described it: "When they return they're happy and they have these songs they sing . . . then they sing this Yáuldáucùn. It means they're so happy they get out there, all of them, and *yául*, it means they're going to dance and holler and all of that, *yául*."[165]

Following these two songs, the dancers are seated, after which they rise and continue with the Arise and Dance (in place) Dance (Émhâcùngà). This name is an informal descriptive reference to the dance's choreography, but is used by some as a proper name today. The men dance in front of their planted lances, with their fists loosely clenched and held near chest level, while keeping time to the music. This resembles the general choreography of many nineteenth-century Plains military society dances in which men danced in a single row. The dance may also symbolize the practice of many past warriors who danced in front of their enemies before battle, thereby showing their willingness to stand their ground and to fight. The dance steps consist of bouncing in place interspersed with small steps and are similar to the steps used in the Gourd Dance.[166] The two Yáuldáucùngà dances and these informal dances most likely make up the "emhawgo" described by elders in 1935. Throughout the afternoon, women frequently dance in place along the outer edge of the arena, entering the arena only to honor an individual or to take part in family songs.

Using a microphone from the public address system stationed beside the drum and singers' on the west side of the dance arena, society leader Gus Palmer Sr. addressed the crowd at this time, welcoming all in attendance and relating aspects of Kiowa military history. Palmer regularly stressed the sacrifice that veterans had made to ensure the freedoms enjoyed today, and the need to honor, uphold, and recognize veterans. He often named all the pre-reservation Kiowa military societies, briefly discussing their functions and relationships to one another, and he often acknowledged the use of "documentation from older men through anthropological notes."[167]

During the next style of songs and dance, the society members pick up their lances and begin to dance with them, holding them point downward, while keeping time to the music with a slow, one-two, forward-moving step common in Plains Indian dances. This style of dancing constitutes the majority of the ceremonial. Elders gave no specified name for this form of dance other than Black Legs Society Dance (Tǫ̀kǫ́gàcùngà). The momentum of the music and dancing continues to increase throughout the afternoon.

The following song, which describes how people view the society in an honorable light as its members dance, is a society favorite that is sung during this portion of the ceremony:

1. Tǫ̀kǫ́gàut jé̜ bé-hâ-gàu
   (Legs-Black-members / all / you-arise [imperative] / and
   Black Legs members, arise—get up and
2. Hét bé gûn-jàu
   (Let / us / dance-shall)
   Let us dance.
3. Nàu báu sáum-bǫ̀-jàu
   (And / they-us / look upon-shall)
   And they shall look upon us.
4. Jó-gúl-ǫ̀-gòp á dáu
   (Young men-outstanding / they / in a state of)
   They are outstanding young men.[168]

At this point, new members may be inducted, historical accounts may be told, new or older revived songs may be introduced, specials and giveaways may be held, and naming ceremonies may be performed. On October 6, 1990, an "Empty Saddle" ceremony was held during this portion of the program, in which a saddled horse was paraded around the arena without a rider, symbolizing warriors who were killed in action and did not return. Memorial songs were sung, speeches were made by deceased veterans' relatives and friends, and horses were given away. Currently the society uses two "Empty Saddle Songs" (Memorial Songs), known informally as Câifḛ̀gàudàugà (War Dead Songs), for their thematic reference to the deaths of soldiers in combat.

These events recognize veterans while giving the dancers a break from dancing and may take place throughout the afternoon. During breaks in the dancing, the masters of ceremonies often relate accounts of society and tribal history. Atwater Onco regularly provided accounts of Kiowa history and kinship connections, combining information gathered from tribal censuses, Mooney's *Calendar History of the Kiowa Indians* (1898), visits with other Kiowa elders, and his own knowledge of Kiowa language, history, and family genealogies.[169] In the Kiowa community, knowledge of genealogies and family connections is highly respected and valued. Persons possessing such knowledge are frequently sought as masters of ceremonies and for performing naming ceremonies, because they can explain kinship connections during specials and giveaways. Emcees also commonly tell jokes, tease participants, and, at the October ceremonial, give regular updates of what many Kiowa say is the most important non-Indian event of the weekend, the annual Oklahoma-Texas football game. However, a serious atmosphere, distinctly different from that of a powwow, is always maintained. As a master of ceremonies stated one year, "This is not a powwow, this is a ceremonial." Consequently, powwow announcements are not allowed during the ceremonial, unlike the custom at other dances and powwows.

When the military records of new members are read, they are taken out to dance with the society to the Induction Song, composed by Gus Palmer Sr. in 1962. During the 1962 Cuban missile crisis, war seemed imminent for the United States. In preparation for that possibility, Palmer composed the following lyrics, which were substituted for those in the song of Sitting Bear's son. This version is known as the Chief's Song (Qájáidåugà) or, informally, as the Induction Song.

1 Jó-gúl-ọ̀-gòp dáu-gà bé hâ-fè-jầu-nàu
(Young men—outstanding or high ranking / song / they / sing / shall / and)
I am going to sing a song to highly respected young men.
2 Repeat.
3 Repeat.
4 Só-lè̱-jó-gú-dáu é dàu
(Soldiers—young men / they / in a state of)
These young men are soldiers.
1 Jó-gúl-ọ̀-gòp dáu-gà bé hâ-fè-jầu-nàu
2 Repeat.
3 Repeat.
4 Qá-jái-jò-gù-dàu è dáu
(Soldiers [chiefs]—young men / they / in a state of)
These young men are chiefs.[170]

This song has since been used as the society induction song when taking in new members. It is said to reflect their willingness toward military service and thus the high social status with which they are viewed as veterans. Also known as the Black Legs Honor Song, this is one of two Black Legs Society songs sung during graveside services for members.

During initiations, members lend the initiates their lances to dance with while relatives give away for the initiates by placing shawls and blankets on their backs. Other forms of honoring, such as giving away cash, blankets, shawls, and other goods at the feet of a dancer, also occur during the regular society songs. Afterward, new members are entitled to attend all society meetings and dances and must adhere to the society dress code for ceremonials.[171]

In a continuation of the emphasis on traditional forms of honoring veterans, members next perform the third type of society dance, the Shuffle Dance (Tọ̄sódêcùngà, lit. Feet Crossing Over). This dance was performed by returning warriors and by women who danced to honor them. According to Kintadl, only the Black Legs Society performed this dance. The Shuffle Dance includes both the Shuffle Dance proper and a dance informally called the Up and Down Dance, which is performed first. The Up and Down Dance consists of slower songs with accentuated drum beats, to which the dancers take higher and slower steps, raising one leg and the opposite arm at a time, as if taking an exaggerated high step, which constitutes an up-and-down motion, while alternatingly raising their opposite arms (bent at the elbow) in unison. Young Mustang's Song is an Up and Down Song that is sung during this portion of the ceremonial. Another Up and Down Song containing brief lyrics reflecting the martial spirit of the society is the following:

1. Tǫ̀kǫ́gáut jé́ ál vâi
   (Legs-Black-members / all / also / fighting)
   Blacks Legs members are all fighting.
2. Repeat.
3. Tǫ̀kǫ́gáut jé́ ál vâi-gòp
   (Legs-Black-members / all / also / fighting)
   Blacks Legs members are all fighting.[172]

The Shuffle Dance proper begins with a slow tempo, to which slow-paced forward steps are taken. As the song shifts to a markedly faster tempo, members begin to shuffle their legs back and forth in place, lifting each foot off the ground in succession. This pattern is repeated with the alternating changes in song tempo. The dance literally "makes the dust fly" on the surface of the grass and earthen dance arena. It is physically demanding because the tempo of several shuffle dance songs increases progressively.

Late in the afternoon the American flag is retired by a group of Kiowa veterans selected to perform the retreat.[173] Many Kiowa songs describe Kiowa military service and the battles into which Kiowa have carried the American flag. If the regular Kiowa Flag Song is not used, then one of two Black Legs Society Flag Songs is used to lower the colors. The great respect for which the Kiowa hold the American flag is conveyed in the following Black Legs Flag Song, which was composed by society member Frank Kaubin:

1. Thái-káu-ól-tâ-gàu thá-gài mài bét hâ-fì-gų̀
   (Flag / good-careful / upward / you all / be raising)
   Raise the flag carefully [with respect].
2. Jé-dàum-tái è câi-jàu-tǫ̀-yằ
   (All over the world / it / been involved in fighting-all over)
   It has been involved in wars all over the world,
3. Jé-dàum-tái ét câi-bà-jằu-dò
   (All over the world / it is / to be respecting-because or for)
   Because it is respected all over the world.

4 Áu-gàu-tâu vą́u + qą́u-chę̀-àl è só-lę̌-dę̀
(Up yonder / moon / is positioned also / it / soldier-standing).
Even on the moon it is standing at attention like a soldier.¹⁷⁴

Leonard Cozad Sr. composed a second Black Legs Society Flag Song:

1 Thą́i-káu-ól-tâ-gàu hét-jáu è góm-dè
(Flag / still / it / waving-standing)
The flag is still standing, waving.
2 Ę́-hàu-dè dàum-tái
(At this point, location / on the face of the earth)
It is still here on this earth (in this hemisphere).
3 Dé è fǫ́-thą́-gà
(Really / it / looks-good)
It really looks good.
4 Qá-cóm-jò-gų̀-dàu kı̌-dà bé thą́-gà
(Life-young men / day / they / well or in good condition)
Let the life of these young men have a good day.¹⁷⁵

The honoring of veterans continues as a prominent part of Kiowa and Black Legs Society activities. It reflects the importance of a past and present warrior ethos and the importance with which military service and the protection of one's people are viewed in Kiowa culture. In recognition of the fiftieth anniversary of the end of World War II, the society held a special recognition of all surviving Kiowa World War II veterans at the May 1995 ceremonial. The veterans were invited into the arena and given an opportunity to speak of their wartime experiences. Some stories were light-hearted and humorous, others so painful that tears flowed from the veterans in the arena and from the audience. Memories of veterans already deceased and expressions of thankfulness prevailed. In honor of all Kiowa World War II veterans, Frank Kaubin composed the following Black Legs Society "World War II — 50th Anniversary Veterans Song," which was introduced that afternoon. It is an emotionally moving song that poignantly and succinctly captures a multitude of experiences associated with the war:

1 Áun-thàu-kı̌-sạ̀i gà dáu
(Fifty-years / it / was)
It was fifty years ago.
2 Á iyòi ém câi-jàu
(Your / offspring (sons) / they / were fighting)
Your sons were fighting.
3 Gà zél-bé-áum-gà-nàu
(It was / fierce, bad, terrible, etc. / became / and)
It became fierce, and
4 Vâi-hı̌ á báu-dà
(Fighting onward / they / appeared)

Fighting onward they appeared.
5 Gér-mán-dàu gàu Jáp-á-nẽe-àl
 (Germans / and / Japanese-also)
 Germans and Japanese,
6 Oí-hyằu bét háun-hèl
 (During that time / they (your sons) / defeated (them)-reportedly)
 During that time they (your sons) reportedly defeated them.[176]

At each ceremonial, this song is sung to honor all remaining World War II veterans, who are brought forward to stand in the middle of the dance arena. One World War II veteran explained why he liked the song: "And that's good because it recognizes the World War II veterans. Because, like I said, there's not too many World War II veterans [left]. They are all gonna be gone. In another ten years I doubt if we'll find another one.... So it gives you a feeling that at least you're still here, you're still here to be around."[177]

The Turn Around or Reverse Dance

The last and perhaps most symbolic and visually martial type of dance performed by the Black Legs Society is the Turn Around or Reverse Dance (Xằkóigácùngà). This dance is performed only on the Sunday evening of the fall ceremonial; at the spring dance, sets of regular dance songs close the program. The dance holds a great deal of symbolic and historical meaning for the society and for Kiowa in general, and it is a good example of the way songs without words can be physically and emotionally moving and can contain multiple layers of spirit and meaning. The dance represents a series of retreats and counterattacks. According to society history, this dance originated with a battle in Texas in the 1830s in which some Black Legs members were outnumbered (Bantista 1983:33). Although the Kiowa name actually translates as "turn around" or "reverse," younger Kiowa often call this the "Encounter the Enemy Dance." During the pre-reservation period, only the Black Legs and Mountain Sheep Societies performed this dance.

The Turn Around or Reverse Dance has two songs.[178] The first is a preparation song that is used to get ready, during which members dance in place in front of their seats and are seen checking, adjusting, and securing their dress, as if prior to entering a battle. At this time the society leaders take off their porcupine hair roach headdresses and don the four eagle-feather war bonnets placed on the west side of the society lodge. The head society leader wears the only bonnet with a long trailer.

There is no pause between the first and second songs, but simply a change in the music, at which time the society begins forming a line on the south and west sides of the arena, facing north and clockwise. There are four positions of choreographical importance during the Turn Around Dance, which were traditionally filled by the four society leaders. The society commander heads the line, and a second leader is chosen

Kiowa Black Legs Society Turn Around or Reverse Dance.
Anadarko, Oklahoma, October 1999.

to take the end position. On the outside of the line is a third leader, while the fourth is situated on the inside of the line of men.

The choreography involves the line of men beginning to dance clockwise from the west side of the arena. The outside man likewise proceeds clockwise around the arena, whereas the inside man proceeds counterclockwise. The directions of these two men do not change during the dance. When the inside and outside men meet, the society members (as a line) raise their lances, shoot off guns, give war whoops, and reverse their direction. This process is repeated every time the two men complete a circuit around the arena and meet, thus causing the line to reverse its direction while the inside and outside men continue in their original directions. As the tempo of the music and dancing steadily increases, so does the firing of guns, the frequency of directional changes by the dancers, the intensity of the women's lulus, and the spectators' concentration. Upon the firing of the guns, the members are traditionally supposed to howl like wolves. Although this tradition is still known, it is not always practiced. The music builds to an extremely rapid pace and the guns are fired more frequently as the dance progresses.[179]

The second song has an emotionally moving, repetitious, and entrancing chorus that continually increases to a faster pace until it reaches a fevered pitch. The dance cannot end until a combat veteran stops the drum by placing his lance across it, after which he must then recite a personal war deed or combat experience (qóitą́ujétjàu).

Earlier in the afternoon the society asks for a volunteer to perform this part of the ceremonial while inside the society tipi. The volunteer is instructed to prepare to tell his combat deed later in the ceremonial. This veteran traditionally stops the drum because he "feels sorry for the men" (the dancers). The drumming and singing stop, as do the society members in the middle of the arena. Catching their breath, they await the recitation from their society brother.

Reuben Topaum, a sniper, squad leader, and member of Darby's Rangers in the North African, Italian, and D-Day campaigns in World War II, performed the public recitation of a war deed in 1991. A recipient of the Purple Heart with Oak Leaf Cluster, the Bronze Star, and other awards, he still carried a German bullet near his heart. Topaum's unit had landed at "Hotspot Annie" on the Anzio beachhead in Italy. As in the landing on D-Day, many men drowned from being let off in water that was too deep. Topaum remembered many corpses being washed out by the tide as he landed. Upon reaching the beach, he saw a good area for cover and headed for it. Reaching a concrete slab, he dug in behind it. A German sniper who had already killed several Americans in Topaum's unit was positioned in a second-story window of a church. Seeing Topaum, he began to fire on him. Topaum kept his head down until the sniper stopped. Later he peered out to see the sniper passing from window to window. Drawing a bead on the window, he waited for the sniper to pass across again. When he appeared, Topaum fired and killed him, the first man he had ever killed.

Later at Anzio, a German sniper had Topaum's unit under fire and had killed two of his fellow soldiers. In the snipers' duel that followed, Topaum was shot in the chest and severely wounded. Thinking he had his third confirmed kill, the German sniper concentrated his efforts elsewhere. Topaum managed to pull himself back up on the line and to sight in on the sniper's fire. He waited and then shot the German out of a tree, killing him. Only then did he seek medical attention.[180]

When the recitation of the combat action is completed, the singers strike the drum hard several times in approval, and everyone shouts words of encouragement in Kiowa (chólhàu, chólhàu, "well done, well done") as the women ululate. In the fall of 1990, Larry Kaulaity told how he and his unit threw grenades to clear out an enemy bunker while pinned down under fire in Vietnam.[181]

The Kiowa Black Legs community cherishes the Turn Around Dance and discusses it with excitement and anticipation throughout the year, but more frequently as the fall ceremonial approaches. Several Kiowa commented that if they could attend Black Legs on only one day of the year, they tried to attend on the Sunday of the fall ceremonial in order to see the Turn Around Dance. Anticipation is visible as the society prepares for the dance. As the dance progresses, the acceleration of the singing and dancing, the directional reversing of the dancers, the shooting of guns and bursts of slowly rising smoke, the calls and whooping of the society members, the women's luluing, and the yelling and calling out by spectators in support of their veterans combine to produce a crescendo and cacophony of sound and action.

This dance is also one of the most visible Kiowa dances in which the expression of spirit permeates the entire encampment as it culminates. The dance is an extremely emotionally moving experience for Kiowa, for visitors from other tribes, and for non-Indians. Both Kiowa and non-Indians have commented on a feeling of complete togetherness during this dance. By attending several years of Black Legs Society dances, I had many opportunities to observe this intensity of focus, to see how people responded to the dance, and to visit with them about their impressions. Although spectators commonly talk among themselves during dances, there is a noticeable increase in attention as this dance begins. People rise to their feet to look on. Several people said they noticed their own heartbeat and blood pressure increase noticeably from the combined tempo of the music, singing, and dancing, a sense of the past, their appreciation of the warriors' sacrifices, and what the society and the Kiowa veterans represent. One elder stated that even his son, who does not understand Kiowa, "goes crazy" when he hears the song and sees the dance.

Society master of ceremonies and World War II and Korean War veteran Atwater Onco said:

> Now, you talk about people being together, that song there, you see that the people are together in spirit there. Everybody's together right there, that song shows you, I don't think Kiowas or not, their spirit is together. . . . It pulls everybody together in spirit, you can tell. I see that every year when that song is sung. The more intense, the faster the singing, everybody's just one there. Everybody's mind is just one there. I bet there's not a person there that's thinking anything else. . . . They're probably thinking it's probably sung way back there by some of our ancestors for the returning veterans. Now they're doing it right here today for the returning veterans. Most of the people I'm sure are thinking that way.
>
> I just feel good. I'm proud to be a Kiowa and I'm trying to carry on Kiowa ways. I don't know who made the song. I don't know how long the song has been here. I heard about the dance a long time ago. Xàkóigà, where the enemy, they find the enemy, they'd run this way, then they'd turn around and re-attack the enemy, and you can't help but think about all those things that they did back there. And we're here trying to show this, what current people did, the current veterans did because of the wars we've been through. And it's still carrying on, that's what I like about it. . . . We do this. I don't know, probably some of my ancestors did that. . . . But to me when I hear that song I can't help but feel good. . . . I'm glad I'm a Kiowa, I'm proud to be a Kiowa. I'm proud to be a veteran. I'm proud I had a little something to do for the service of our country, things like that comes to my thinking.[182]

As the previous quote echoes, one of the most common themes in people's expressions about the dance is its ability to visually transport them back in time. As one younger Kiowa described it: "I could visually image the Black Legs dancing in the past in a long line formation and of what it must have looked like for them to go into battle." A member of another tribe commented how the dance "took him back in time" and how he could "see them rushing into battle almost out of control—into the melee," as the tempo of the music increased. One of the society officers commented similarly that he "could visually see into the past from this dance." Several non-Indians who were viewing the ceremonial for the first time made similar comments independently.[183]

Vietnam veteran and society whipman Blas Preciado described the feelings this dance produced for him:

> The things that go through my mind are how that dance came about and the times, what the old people went through. And how that came about, fighting the enemy, I think about that. It's very emotional for me . . . firing a rifle, it brings back a lot of memories because you know I've been in battle, quite a few times. . . . So I'm thinking about how the dance started. I'm thinking about those rifles, because those rifles they just made me emotional because I've heard a lot of those rifles fired in earnest, and you know that makes me think about those times and then I feel like it's an honor. I always want other people to hear what we went through, no matter whether it was in World War II, Korea, Vietnam, or Desert Shield. I want them to know as much, you know, as another veteran, as much as what actually happened and for them to appreciate those men or women and know the hardships, physical hardships and the mental hardships that we had to endure at those times.[184]

After the recitation of a war deed is completed, the afternoon usually concludes around six o'clock with an evening prayer, followed by a dinner break. Groups of Kiowa and visitors congregate in the various campsites around the dance grounds to eat. Occasionally, because of so many giveaways or specials or the wishes of the society, the dancing continues late into the evening. After dinner a session of Gourd dancing is sponsored by the Kiowa Gourd Clan, followed by a session of social and War dancing sponsored by the Kiowa Ohoma Lodge, which co-hosts the evening program.

Community Functions

The functions and martial ethos of the current Black Legs Society closely resemble those of the past. Since its revival in 1958, the society has undeniably been a warrior-veteran organization. It is organized as a veteran's organization and continues to enhance the past military exploits and current service of its members in song and dance, as well as performing duties on behalf of the Kiowa community as a whole. The society recognizes and celebrates all veterans of the United States while espousing special recognition for past and present Kiowa veterans who have served their country, tribe, and family.

In Kiowa tradition, the society provides rations for each camp in its encampment and a noon meal for everyone in attendance, including all guests. Society chaplains visit members who are ill. When a member dies, the society sends flowers and groceries to the family's home. A contingent of society members attends the funeral of every society "brother" and performs the graveside singing of the Black Legs Society Chief's or Honor Song (previously described) and the official society War Dead or Funeral Song (Câifêgàudãugà), a memorial song that was composed by Bert Geikaunmah in honor of the war dead. I have attended the funerals of several Black Legs members, and such occasions appear to be the only times this song is normally sung.[185] It is an emotionally moving song with lyrics illustrating the continuation of traditional Kiowa values associated with the role of the warrior-veteran:

> 1 Cáui-jò-gǜ-dàu è qá-jái-dàu-gàu
>   (Kiowa / young men / they [are] / warriors / and)
>   Kiowa young men, they are warriors (been to battle) and
> 2 Bé qá̰-hḭ́-tą̀u-jè-bá̰u-dà
>   (You / manlike [he-man] / news / appears — comes about)
>   You hear news [lit. he-man stories] about them.
> 3 Á qá-jái-dàu-gàu chól-hàu á ó-báui-hè-mà
>   (They / warriors / and / that's the way / they / really die)
>   They are warriors and that's the way they die! (i.e., they really die)[186]

The society also holds an annual Christmas fellowship meeting in December for all members and their families. It consists of a dinner, socializing, the singing of Kiowa church hymns, and the viewing of sanctioned videotaped ceremonials. The society also frequently provides a color guard for events across the state such as the Red Earth Festival, the American Indian Exposition parades, religious and sovereignty conferences, and Indian and university educational events. Members of other tribes have commented of their respect for the Kiowa Black Legs Society, which is well known throughout the Native American community.[187]

In 1997 I asked Black Legs Society leader Gus Palmer Sr. what he most wanted future generations of Kiowa to understand about the society. His reflections echo the importance of continuing to recognize the sacrifices of veterans, celebrating their service, valuing freedom, and understanding of the importance of tradition:

> This is just the dance part. The fighting part, you'll never see that. How they fought, just like today . . . you don't see that. Keep this up. You don't borrow from no one. This belongs to our tribe, the Kiowa tribe. And don't give it away. You keep it up just like it is. You don't have to change it or improve it, it's good enough as it is. . . . Bé hâ gàu bé gûn [get up and dance], it's yours. This is a Kiowa tradition. We're keeping it. Bát ǫ̀vàidè, take a liking to it. It's yours.
>
> What it is, is freedom, a celebration of freedom. That's the main thing, protection and freedom. So they won't be worried about being taken over. . . . It's modern today, but it's still the same thing. I said back then they fought and they came home to celebrate. They have something to celebrate about. . . . Look good, dress well, keep it going.[188]

The Fiftieth Anniversary Ceremonial

At the Black Legs' fiftieth anniversary fall ceremonial, held on October 11–12, 2008, the society introduced a new society tipi. The southern half of the tipi (in reference to the door facing east) retained the traditional black and yellow stripes across its entirety. The upper portion of the north side retained the red background. Centered on the upper part of the back of the lodge (west side) was the crest of the Black Legs Warrior Society. The hatchets from the earlier versions of the lodge were retained. The names of the Kiowa men killed in action (KIA) in the twentieth century were moved from the north side of the lodge and placed one by one, in chronological order by date of death and from top to bottom, between the hatchets down the back of the lodge. The names of two Kiowa men recently killed in Iraq, Joshua Ware and Anthony Little Calf Yost, have been added to this list.

The military divisional crests have been kept along the base of the red section on the north side of the lodge, extending to the back of the lodge and then turning downward to the left of the row of hatchets and names of the KIA. The division crests have been changed to include those Kiowa Black Legs members serving since the revival (primarily veterans of World War I through Iraq) and the crest of the Army Women's Corps.

Pictographic images continue to cover the north side of the lodge, portraying the actions of Kiowa warriors involved in and since the society's revival in 1958. The designs were painted to read like a book, from top to bottom and left to right. Beginning with a ledger-style image of Kiowa fighting Kit Carson and the Ute on November 26, 1868, near Adobe Walls, they continue with images of soldiers in World War I (holding rifles with bayonets fixed and wearing gas masks in a trench), World War II (depicting a beach landing in the Pacific and another landing in Europe), Korea (a U.S. soldier taking several Koreans captive in the snow), Vietnam (a scene of troops in paddy fields, helicopters flying overhead, and a U.S. soldier kneeling and firing an M-16 rifle), and Desert Storm and Iraq (a soldier standing over a dead Iraqi with a rocket-propelled grenade launcher). The society plans to add an image related to Afghanistan at a later date.

Sherman Chaddlesone and Jeff Yellowhair painted the pictographic images on the north side of the tipi. Other portions of the tipi, including the black and yellow stripes, were painted by Angela Spottedwolf, Alison Chaddlesone, Russell Bohay, and Russell Bohay Jr. This is the first time I have known Kiowa women to be involved in painting tipis; traditionally, Kiowa women made tipis but only Kiowa men were allowed to paint them. The society tipi remains an ongoing and evolving memorial and tribute to Kiowa military service, periodically changed and updated, just like the original tipi of Tohausen. In front of the military flags and society staff on the west side of the lodge was a memorial-like arrangement relating to the Iraq and Afghanistan wars. It consisted of a pair of military boots in front of an M-16 rifle stuck into the ground, with a helmet covered with camouflage on top of the rifle butt.

Kiowa Black Legs Society tipi introduced at the fiftieth anniversary ceremonial, October 2008.

Several other special events were held during the fiftieth anniversary ceremonial. Sabers were presented to long-time members Dixon Palmer and George Tahbone Sr. The OH-58D *Kiowa Warrior* attack helicopter, named in 1990 and used in Operation Desert Storm, was flown into a meadow beside the camp and throughout the day was periodically flown over the dance ground. In commemoration of their ancestor, the Goule-Hae-Ee Descendants presented a red cape and a lance to the society to display with the society staffs. Families of all eleven Kiowa KIA were called into the arena and one by one, in the order in which the eleven had been killed in action, were called forward to receive a flag in a triangular, glass-topped wooden case, a large framed picture (with the same background and style for each), with a picture of the relative in the lower left corner, and a medal on a ribbon necklace. A representative of each family was then allowed to speak into the microphone about the deceased and his family.

During the Turn Around Dance, Black Legs commander Tugger Palmer went out into the middle of the arena, took out a long hide sash, placed it over his head and shoulder, staked it down with his own lance, and began to dance with the society *pàu-bôn*. This reintroduced the use of a sash that once accompanied the society's curved lance. Palmer danced with great spirit and action as the tempo of the song picked up. The crowd became extremely spirited, and the society members fired off guns and continued to dance faster and faster as the tempo of the song increased.

Finally, Robert Poolaw Sr. walked out to take the curved lance from Palmer, walked to the drum, and held it out over the drum to stop it. He then reported three incidents in which he had participated in Vietnam. First, while he and his squad searched an area with many interconnecting tunnels, Vietnamese kept rising up and firing from holes behind them. The Americans finally took thatch from nearby houses, plugged all the holes, and set them on fire. They met no more resistance from the holes. Second, near the demilitarized zone, Poolaw and a fellow marine crossed a dry riverbed to check the enemy lines. As they followed a trail, a Vietnamese jumped up from a concealed hole and began to run. The two fired on him and killed him. On him they found an AK-47 with a full clip of thirty rounds. Poolaw captured a small bayonet from him and later gave it to his friend, who later returned it to him. Poolaw's granddaughter was named from his capture of this bayonet.

Third, while on a patrol and searching an area, Poolaw's unit had to encamp one night. Poolaw was in charge of the unit. His friend kept hearing something moving in the brush just a few yards from their position. Poolaw told him it was simply rats, which were plentiful in the area, but the friend could not stop worrying about the sound. Finally, Poolaw gave his friend permission to fire several rounds at the position from which the sound came. The next morning the Americans were attacked by Vietnamese, whom they finally fought off in a three-hour fight. When they searched the perimeter after the fight, they found a dead Vietnamese who had been shot several times and who had been crawling through the brush right where they had fired the night before.

Change, Continuity, and Significance

Since 1958, the Black Legs Society has undergone several structural changes relative to earlier periods. Father-son replacement does not occur as commonly as it did in the 1800s, although several sets of fathers and sons are now members. Since the 1920s, the institution of *cóm*, or society brothers, has not generally been maintained. As a result of the large number of World War II veterans and the postwar presence of Anglo veterans' organizations, the structure of two society leaders and two whipmen was blended with forms similar to those of Veterans of Foreign Wars and American Legion posts. However, since I completed my master's thesis (Meadows 1991) and provided to society members, upon their request, the archival materials on Kiowa ethnology from the 1935 Laboratory of Anthropology Kiowa Field School, I have observed a marked, conscious increase in the use of many of the older societal terms for officers and friends (*fàujóqì, áljóqì, cóm*) and in customs that my previous interviews had demonstrated were still known but rarely used. Society leaders Gus Palmer Sr. and Allen Quetone frequently referred to each other as *cóm*. I also noticed a brief revival in the use of two serrated wooden whips (made and donated by the family of Vanessa Jennings) by the whipmen in the early 1990s. As my fieldwork continued, I found that my growing interest in their organizations fanned an already well-lit flame in the Kiowa and Black Legs community concerning the knowledge and customs of their military societies. Society leaders, members, and family members showed great interest in confirming existing knowledge and in gaining additional knowledge from ethnohistorical sources.[189]

The Black Legs Society is of great ethnological importance because of its continued focus on a visible and extremely symbolic martial ethos (Meadows 1991, 1995, 1999; Meadows and Palmer 1992). Despite numerous adaptations, the society continues much of its rich martial ethos and traditions. Although changes in leadership positions have occurred, the functions and symbols associated with the officers continue to reflect Kiowa cultural traditions. The society still provides an opportunity for Kiowa veterans to gather and celebrate their individual and collective military service. It provides social gatherings and feasts for all in attendance and performs duties on behalf of the community as a whole. The Black Legs have retained many pre-reservation martial symbols (the *pàubôn*, lances, whips, offices, oral history, songs, dances) that, despite adaptations, continue to function similarly to antecedent forms. With the decline of other Kiowa societies by 1890, and with a changed emphasis on martial ideologies and recognition of veterans in other societies since 1957, the Black Legs have come to symbolize and define, for many Kiowa, what it means to be a Kiowa warrior-veteran. Several Kiowa spoke of the society's integrative role, which, in its emphasis on honoring veterans, allows participation by the rest of the family as well. As Martha Poolaw commented:

> The way I view it . . . I think they stand for a little bit of the older culture. They're kind of a remnant of just a small part of the whole. If they didn't have that or any

of the other things that they did, then they wouldn't be a tribe within themselves with any culture. They would be like some of the other Indians that have lost everything . . . their songs, their dress, some are using Hollywood stuff now. . . . That particular group [the Black Legs] probably represents a big part of our culture I would say, as a real part of it that you can actually go out and experience. You can give anybody a book and they can read about stuff, but it's not the same as seeing. You know they're actually participating and it's continued and it seems to be pretty much intact, and I think they've done a real good job of explaining and letting people know what they're doing.[190]

Giveaways continue to honor and recognize individuals while redistributing goods throughout the community. The Black Legs Society has maintained its traditional music, dances, and dress with minimal modernization and continues to compose new songs. Much as it once held society meetings during the Sun Dance, the society now holds a number of weekly preparatory meetings for each dance. Traditional mourning practices continue at the funerals of society members and before each dance, with cedaring and meals for families who have recently lost members.

War honors were required for membership in pre-reservation times (Levy n.d.a, 2001:912), and although this requirement lapsed during the reservation and post-reservation periods, active or honorably discharged military service and Kiowa tribal enrollment have been required since 1958. Recently, these requirements have been modified with the induction of men who have served in the armed forces reserves or the National Guard. As a factor behind this change, elder members cite the small number of remaining World War II and Korean War veterans, the decline of long-term warfare and therefore the number of combat veterans since Vietnam, and the need to take measures to ensure the future survival of the organization.[191]

Modern warfare is changing, and much of the initial fighting in wars is now done through technologically complex aerial bombing ahead of ground campaigns. Aware of this, Black Legs Society elders are making conscious efforts to ensure the continuation of the society. Although some members feel that membership should be limited to combat veterans alone, older combat veterans recognize that this restriction would severely limit membership and participation in Indian as well as non-Indian veteran organizations. One society elder explained shortly after Operation Desert Storm:

So we're stressing nowadays that we're taking in membership of people that's in the reserve, or the National Guard, anything that they have been involved with, you know even currently, in protecting the United States government. So if we go by that you have to be in combat, not only the Black Leggins but even the White [Anglo] organizations, they're gonna have nobody left. They'll all be dissolved because there's no war, and we don't want a war. And if there's no more wars, then all the older generation will be gone and who can join? So that's the reason we've changed this and we're keeping it that way now to keep it going for several more years. . . . That's our thinking on that particular part there.[192]

This point is further demonstrated by the fact that although the society maintains a roster of more than two hundred members, only twenty to thirty members dress out for each Black Legs ceremonial, and of them, only a portion consists of combat veterans. The changes in membership criteria should not be viewed in terms of a less-than, more-than dichotomy but simply as expressions of the way Kiowa veterans choose to maintain their martial ceremonies in relation to the larger United States armed forces and international military structures in a changing world. Several veterans stated that they hoped there would be no more wars and that those who served in the military would be able to carry on the society's traditions. Some elder veterans I spoke with stressed that the most important aspect to maintain was that future membership be limited to tribally enrolled Kiowa.

The society has revived the positions of two boy members as helpers. The two female youth positions have been maintained, but the girls' participatory role, like that of all women, has increased since World War II, and women are now allowed to dance along the sides and inside the arena. Although several Kiowa women veterans have been recognized at Black Legs Society ceremonials, none has been permitted to join the society or to dance in the male sector of the arena. Participation by both veteran and nonveteran women remains oriented toward support and honoring of the veterans through Scalp, Victory, and War Mothers Dances, processionals, family honoring, giveaways, provision of meals, and dancing along the sides of the arena in support of the men during their portion of the program. However, the increasing recognition of Kiowa women veterans and the inclusion of the Army Women's Corps crest on the new society lodge raise the possibility of an increased role for women in the future. The maintenance of family camps and preparation of meals are essential for the success of the entire ceremonial, and the Kiowa Veterans Association Auxiliary members and other women who participate in these activities deserve a great deal of appreciation.

Although elements of modernization have been adopted, they remain more in the peripheral structure of the society than at the core. The core elements and ideology on which the society and Plains warrior societies in general were based have remained largely intact or, in some instances, have been consciously revived from earlier forms. The traditional role of the Black Legs Society has been redefined less than that of the post-1957 Kiowa Gourd Clan. Despite grumbling about modernization by some nonsociety members, many Black Legs members and other Kiowa strongly acknowledge a great deal of cultural continuity to the present. Rev. David Paddlety reflected on being a member of the society and on the continuity of a martial ethos:

> But I like it because it's really lively. It gives us a feeling of patriotism. I don't know of any place where there's more activities indicative of patriotism, and it's always related to the early Kiowa warriors, you know, those that protected their homes and villages. That feeling has always transcended right on down to us. So you'll hear a lot of lulus and war whoops when we're out there. Much more

than at the regular social dances, you know. We had just a few, very few officers, but that didn't matter, you know, whether they were officers or not . . . a buck private got the same notice as others. That makes you feel good whenever you're honored like that.[193]

As demonstrated elsewhere (Meadows 1995, 1999; Holm 1996), the recognition of veterans by many Native Americans is more frequent, of longer duration, and often more intense than among non-Indian populations in the United States. For some Anglo Americans, it is unnerving that Native Americans often display greater patriotism than they do. Evalu Russell expressed the importance of patriotism among contemporary Kiowa and the Black Legs Society: "And I want to tell you about how I feel personally about patriotism. Where has it gone? Where is it? If our Indian people can do this, why can't the other people here in America do this. What are they doing here if they are not patriotic? We love the red, white, and blue—and the Black Leggings stand for that."[194]

Postwar adjustments for any veteran are enhanced by the support of other veterans, and for Native Americans, traditional ceremonials and societies help to reintegrate them back into their communities. Over the years, many Black Legs members have spoken fondly of the fellowship and camaraderie shared with other society members. One man described how becoming an active member of the society had been a "positive experience" that helped him immensely in his life's searching and in rebuilding his personal life. This member specifically stated that the society and support from other veterans had helped him with his self-image, feelings of nonacceptance, previous problems with alcoholism and divorce, and posttraumatic stress disorder. Such support had helped him "overcome self-doubt" and the "stigma of being mixed-blood," which was once detrimental to him. This member also said that he felt he was able to join for those Kiowa veterans that never had done so and to dance for those who were physically unable to.[195]

The society also provides an important source of individual, family, and tribal identity. Another member stated that it was aspects of social organization, mainly kinship and family, that attracted him to the organization:

> I don't think it's the dance itself that—I mean the actual, physical part of it being standing and dancing in one position out there—that is a main component. I think it's the whole overall structure. All the different elements of the families coming together, the recognition of the family members and all the other stuff that goes along with it. . . . I don't think about very much while I'm actually dancing, you know. It's all the rest of it put together that keeps drawing me back in it.[196]

When I asked society member Sherman Chaddlesone what the Black Legs represented for the Kiowa people, he spoke of its importance as a source of tribal tradition and identity:

At this point I think it's mainly, it enables us to hold onto some tradition. It's probably the most traditional organization that we have within the tribe. I hear a lot from the younger people, when they talk about Kiowa-ness it always comes back to the Black Legs. Things that happened there . . . all the ceremony that has evolved with it and there's a lot of it that's gradually being brought back. Some of the old family values and things of that nature associated with the organization are gradually being incorporated into the ceremonies. Those things take time to develop and they were suppressed for so long, it has taken time to bring them back. But like I said, for a lot of the younger people that's Kiowa-ness. It's a unique thing. There's nobody, no other tribe in the United States that has anything similar to it.[197]

The Black Legs Society has continued to function as an adaptive form of social organization and as a vehicle of Kiowa enculturation by integrating into the functions of a single sodality a varied number of Kiowa traditions: veteran recognition, community service, naming ceremonies, mourning and purification rituals, song and dance, camping, feasting, social dances, language and kinship retention, and oral history. Although many current Kiowa Black Legs and Gourd Dance songs are new forms of older songs (with changed melodies or new texts added to old melodies) or new, post-revival compositions, they continue ancestral themes. Although many of these cultural forms exist in other types of Kiowa social gatherings, they are fewer or of less variety, which reflects the importance of the Black Legs Society as an integrative sodality. This role is accomplished by a sodality structure that facilitates social integration on a wider basis than that of kin-based groups. Because military and dance-oriented societies continue to be the largest forms of Kiowa sodalities, they are better able to integrate varied social forms and to adapt temporally. The ongoing Kiowa emphasis on recognizing their martial ideology and history and their veterans provides a major arena for cultural continuity. According to one newspaper description, "the society is composed of Kiowa men who have served in any branch of the armed forces, in all wars and conflicts, as well as those who served during peacetime. This ancient society was revived in 1958 to help keep the old Kiowa traditions alive and to recognize and honor all Kiowa service personnel and all American service men and women."[198] Although the society returned to holding only a fall dance after its fiftieth anniversary fall dance in 2008, it remains a strong arena of Kiowa culture based on concepts associated with traditional military societies and tribal traditions and symbols. The Black Legs Society is an adaptive social form that acts as an enculturative tool into which other cultural forms are integrated and thereby continued.

5

JÁIFÈGÀU

The Unafraid of Death or Skunkberry Society

During the second half of the nineteenth century the Jáifègàu was composed of martially and socially higher-ranking men, most of whom possessed war honors. Members in the society included many prominent band leaders, warriors, doctors, and priests. With the Black Legs, the Jáifègàu frequently policed the annual Sun Dance encampment and communal bison hunts. The society continued functioning until the end of the Sun Dance in 1890. It was revived in 1912, continued until shortly before World War II, and was again revived in 1957 as the Kiowa Gourd Clan. Under that name it became well known for its form of dance, now known as the Gourd Dance.

The historical development of this society is extremely significant, among those of other, contemporary Southern Plains military societies, because (1) it is the best-documented Plains military society practicing the form of singing and dancing now known as the Gourd Dance; (2) it was the first post–World War II Southern Plains society to have been revived; (3) it fostered the revival of other Southern Plains societies and the rapid diffusion of the Gourd Dance to other Indian and non-Indian populations; (4) it constitutes one of the primary foci of contemporary Kiowa ethnic identity; and (5) among the Kiowa Gourd Clan it maintains an all-Indian membership and participation. Because the Kiowa first revived the Gourd Dance in 1957, its diffusion to other Indian and eventually non-Indian populations has meant that a Kiowa-style Gourd Dance has had pan-Indian, national, and international effects.

The society has been known by several names. Hugh Scott listed Rattle and Rattle Foot.[1] W. P. Clark (1885:355) gave Horse; James Mooney (1898:230) gave Tanpeko, or Skunkberry People, and Tsen-a'dalka-i, or Crazy Horses; and Robert Lowie (1916b:842) listed Ta-ipeko, or Berries. The translation of Jáifègàu as "Skunkberry People" appears to have originated with Mooney (1898:230), after which it seems to have been accepted without question. However, thanks to the efforts of several Kiowa tribal elders, a linguistic examination of the name suggests another possible interpretation.[2] In the Kiowa language the cone-shaped, fuzzy, clustered red fruit of the skunkberry (*Rhus trilobata*), a variety of sumac, is known as *jái-fè-è-gàu*. The syllable *è* is a combining form representing anything edible, and the syllable *gàu* represents a plural or collective form.³ A noticeable one-syllable difference exists between Jáifègàu, the name of the society, and jáifèȅgàu, the name of the skunkberry plant. It is also significant that whereas the name of Skunkberry Creek is Jáifèȅvàu, the name of the society remains Jáifègàu. In addition, *jái* can be construed as having been derived from the verbal-adjective *jái-dàum* (brave or unafraid), which is found in many Kiowa personal name forms, while *fḗ-gáu*, from the root word for death, *fḗ-gà*, denotes "the dead."⁴

Although scholars and many Kiowa accept the translation Skunkberry People, the exact meaning and etymology of the society name continues to be debated among some Kiowa. Elsie Clews Parsons (1929:91 n.1) stated that none of her consultants could translate the name of the society. Leonard Cozad told Tony Issacs (1975) that "although Tai-pe-go distantly refers to words meaning skunk berry and brave, its translation has become obscure over the years, and today is specifically the name of this society."⁵ When the dance was revived in 1957, some Kiowa were themselves unsure of the correct translation. The Kiowa Gourd Clan wrote in a booklet accompanying its ceremonial (1996:9), "The Kiowa name for the Gourd Clan has been lost and some say that the name is Tdienpai-gah while others say that the name was corrupted by a white historian and called Tai-Pa-Gah and the true name is Tai-Dahn Pa-Goo (Not Afraid to Die)." That a white historian corrupted the name to "Tai-Pa-Gah" is unlikely, because there were so few early scholars and their literature was so small (Clark 1885, Mooney 1898, Lowie 1916b). In addition, seven independent ethnologists, anthropologists, and an army officer all acquired the name Jáifègàu through interviews in the late 1800s and early 1900s with Kiowa elders and society members who themselves used the term. The alleged change of the society's name is not found in the literature of these ethnologists. The names Tdienpai-gah and Tai-Pa-Gah clearly correlate with Jáifègàu. The name Tai-Dahn Pa-Goo correlates with the compositions Jái-dàum-fḕ-gǜ (Brave–Revived From Near Death) and Jái-dàum-fḕ-gàu (Unafraid of Death), both of which are based on the words *jái-dàum* (brave or unafraid) and *fḗ-gáu* (the dead). On the basis of the nature of the society, the nature of related Plains military societies, and linguistic analysis, a translation of Jáifègàu (based on *jái-dàum* and *fḗ-gáu*) as "Unafraid of Death" is likely accurate for the society's name.⁶

Mooney's fieldnotes indicate that he, his interpreters, and possibly even his elder Kiowa consultants were either unclear about the distinction between the two terms and their relationship to the society name or failed to clearly differentiate them. In listing the Kiowa societies he wrote, "Dainpeko [Society]—same word as for dainpe-egau [the fruit], singular - e, plural e-gau."⁷ Parsons (1929:91) noted in 1927 that no one could give an actual translation of the society's name, "Tainpaeko," although the red berry "tanpeigo" was pounded and then cooked with cornmeal as a culinary dish.

All my elder Kiowa consultants stated and recognized that skunkberry was pronounced *jái-fè-ȅ-gàu*, and most of them provided the translation "Skunkberries" for Jái-fè-gàu. But when asked to differentiate the two words, they were unable to further analyze the construction of either. Several elders said that the actual meaning of the name was never explained to them. Some suggested another possible interpretation of the society's name. It is possible that the name, conforming to the pattern of military societies across the Great Plains, was intended to denote "Unafraid of Death," because Skunkberries is a most unusual name relative to the names of other Kiowa and pan-Plains military societies and because the Kiowa pronunciation of Jáifègàu for the name of the society neither clearly nor grammatically denotes skunkberries. A structural and grammatical comparison of Kiowa society and personal names shows that whereas Kiowa personal names are often abbreviated forms of longer expressions and may be used in abbreviated form, society names, which may be similarly formed, are generally used as complete ethnonyms. The name Bear Unafraid Of Death (Sétjàifèjè, also known as Sétáulkáui, or Crazy Bear) supports this interpretation and suggests that Skunkberry Bear is a highly unlikely Kiowa name form. In addition, a few Kiowa elders have independently reported that their elders told them that the name of the society denoted "Unafraid Of Death." A brief examination of Plains military societies possessing similar choreography and ritual also supports this interpretation.[8]

Related Plains Societies

The major problem in tracing the origin of the Gourd Dance lies in the incompleteness of descriptions of Plains military societies written by early ethnographers, who focused more on regalia than on song, dance, and choreography. In addition, many past and present Plains cultures, including those possessing Gourd Dance societies, used or use varied forms of dancing in place and moving forward in a linear formation. Plains ethnography points to a northern origin, especially among the sedentary Mandan and Hidatsa, and a subsequent southward diffusion of many Plains ceremonial forms, including military societies and varied forms of the Sun Dance (Wissler 1916; Wissler, ed., 1916; Lowie 1916a; Liberty 1980:164; Albers 1993). Data supporting a series of chapterlike organizations with similarities in song, dance, and ritual exist for a number of Kiowa, Apache, Comanche, Cheyenne, Pawnee, and other military societies (Meadows 1999:55–57). Recent data from the Kiowa Gourd Clan also acknowledge the likelihood of pre-reservation intertribal participation in the Gourd Dance:

> When the Kiowas moved south from the Black Hills and settled in the area now known as Oklahoma, they continued to hold their annual "Sun Dance" as well as other society or clan dances. This included the Kiowa Gourd dance. As acquaintances were made with neighboring tribes, the enchanting sound and energetic tempo of the Kiowa Gourd Dance attracted these other tribes. These tribes were allowed to participate in the Kiowa Gourd Dance. (Kiowa Gourd Clan 1996:17)

However, this recent statement also serves as a justification for Kiowa claims of exclusive ownership of the dance.

Patricia Albers (1993) examined the way the formation of chains of social connections influenced the production and exchange of specialized goods in Plains Indian trade. She demonstrated widespread effects on Plains trading through the diffusion of religious and military sodality rituals based on formalized friendships, intermarriage, and non-blood (fictive) kinship created through adoption, usually involving sibling or parent-child relationships. Albers suggested (1993:121) "that the convergence of the Plains nomads' kinship systems along generation relationships in military sodalities and under other situations promoted joint collaboration across tribal boundaries." Thus the transfer of Plains economic and socioritual culture was in part facilitated by the presence of larger socioeconomic, kinship, and ritual systems, including chapter military societies. William Fenton (1987) demonstrated several similarities in False Face and Husk Face masking societies among Northeastern Culture Area populations and between Iroquois and Cherokee masking traditions.

A number of military societies that used ancestral forms of ritual and choreography resembling the contemporary Gourd Dance existed among other Plains tribes, including the Comanche, Cheyenne, Arapaho, Iowa, Ponca, Omaha, and Wind River Shoshone (Wissler, ed., 1916; Howard 1976; Meadows 1995, 1999). Because many Plains military societies are known to have diffused, and because some Kiowa attribute the acquisition of the dance to warfare-based diffusion, any serious treatise on the Gourd Dance and its origins cannot dismiss an examination of similar Plains men's societies.

Both the Ponca and the Omaha had similarly named warrior societies with Gourd dancing traditions. The names of several of these societies, along with their cultural content, suggest close linguistically based, if not culturally diffused, cognates. Alanson Skinner (1915b:785–86) described the Ponca E^{x}ga'hre (Not Afraid to Die) Society: "In dancing all stood in a row and danced up and down, remaining 'stationary.' The rattle carriers stood at each end of the line." This society was reported to be one of the oldest dancing societies among the Ponca (Skinner 1915b:783). Its name and its use of a split horned bonnet suggest ties to the Oglala Lakota Strong Heart, No-Flight (Napes'ni, Lone Braves) and Braves (Ca^{n}teti^{n}za, the Dauntless) Societies (Wissler 1912:20–31) and to the Santee Dakota No Flight and Brave Heart (Ca^{n}tet'i^{n}za, Brave Heart) Societies (Lowie 1913:106–109). Sylvester Warrior reported that several of the modern Southern Plains Gourd Dance songs were identical to those of the defunct Ponca T'egaxe (Those Who Court Death) Society songs (Howard 1976:248). Much like older Ponca Gourd Dance–related societies, the modern Ponca Gourd Clan is composed largely of veterans and older men.

The Omaha also had a society that performed a dance similar in choreography to the modern Gourd Dance, in which dancers held rattles and "stood in a row and danced up and down, remaining stationary." James Dorsey (1884:352) reported that the Omaha T'ega'xe watc'i (Dance of Those Expecting to Die) had not been held since 1869. He explained the name as "As one thinks, 'I will die if there are any enemy,' they make the dance." The similarity between the related Ponca and Omaha society names clearly suggests a linguistic if not a cultural cognate for this organization.

This society and its dance pertained to bravery, and members prepared to "meet the enemy and fall in battle." In addition, all members carried rattles made of green hide (probably rawhide). Likewise, the Maca watcigaxe, or Make No Flight Dance, once common to the Omaha, Ponca, and Dakota (probably Skinner's Ponca "Not Afraid to Die Dance" [1915b:785–786]), was a bravery dance in which "the dancers hold gourd rattles and each one carries many arrows on his back as well as in his arms" (Dorsey 1884:352). Alice Fletcher and Francis La Flesche (1911:486) described the society's name this way: "T'e ga'xe (t'e, death; ga'xe, to make, to simulate)—to simulate death was the name of an ancient social society that disappeared before the middle of the last century." The knee-flexing-in-place dance step and the dancers' use of rattles, central to the choreography of the past and present Kiowa Gourd Dance, was also reported among the Dakota Strongheart and No-Flight Societies (Wissler 1912; Lowie 1913).[9]

The name of the Iowa Tc'e'un waci, or Acting Dead Dance, appears to be a linguistic cognate denoting a society similar to those of the Ponca and Omaha (Skinner 1915a:701; Howard 1976:249). Like the Kiowa Jáifègàu, this society was taught to the group's founder by a wolf and included the practice of howling like wolves. Each member was required to furnish himself with a bison rawhide rattle. The society was reported to have contained the largest number of the bravest Iowa warriors.

The names and some of the customs of all these societies refer similarly to a disdain for fear and the acceptance of the possibility—almost the embracing—of death in the face of battle. These traits are found in some degree in nearly every Plains Indian military society, especially among society leaders and a select number of staff or sash bearers. In addition, the choreography of these groups suggests a similar and widespread Plains "Gourd Dance" tradition. Some aspects of these societies resemble those of "no-flight" or "not-afraid-to-die" societies, and they differ distinctly from the characteristics (song, dance, rattles, dress, degree of battle obligations, and number of society sashes) associated with the so-called contrary or Dog Soldier societies. Also, the recorded ethnographic presence of Dog Soldier societies (except among the Cheyenne, who are said to have received all four military societies from the culture hero Sweet Medicine), at least for the Southern Plains tribes (Kiowa, Qóichégàu; Comanche, Los Lobos; Apache, Klintidie), predates the existence of later military societies featuring a choreography focused on the Gourd Dance. If some of the northern and central plains "Gourd Dance" Societies were originally or at least previously "no-flight" or "not-afraid-to-die" societies—and I suspect they were, because Southern Plains Gourd Dance societies were clearly not yet organized, and the society form was still diffusing southward until at least about 1840—then they differed significantly from "Dog Soldier" Societies by the time of ethnological documentation.[10]

Although the name Rattle Dance (Tâucùngà) dates back to the fieldnotes of Hugh L. Scott in the 1890s, I have chosen to use the name Jáifègàu in reference to the earlier society and dance because it is the native term used by the majority of elders I interviewed. Elders frequently speak of the society and its dance as "Jáifègàu" and "Jáifècùngà" (Jáifè dancing") in Kiowa and as the Gourd Dance in English. The name Rattle Dance appears to be a later by-name or nickname for the society and its dance. Milton Toyebo stated, "Way back there they called it straight [Kiowa word]. Later on, they began to call [it] Gourd Rattlers."[11] For consistency, I refer to the society as Jáifègàu and to the post-1957 revival of the dance as the Gourd Dance.

Origins of the Jáifègàu

Several origin stories, some mythological and others more historically documented, account for the beginning of the Kiowa Jáifègàu. The most common account, the Red Wolf version, centers on the gift of the dance and songs to the Kiowa by a wolf. This account closely resembles that of the origin of the Iowa Tc'e'un waci, or Acting Dead Dance (Skinner 1915a 701; Howard 1976:249). In it, a Kiowa warrior (in some versions more than one) who was separated from his war party was traveling across the plains toward where he believed his people were camped. Thirsty and hungry, he traveled on. Some accounts say that he sustained himself on skunkberries. Suddenly hearing a strong, clear, melodious voice singing, he searched to locate the source. From atop a nearby knoll he saw Red Wolf at the bottom of a grassy ravine. Dancing up and down, Red Wolf held a gourd in his right paw, which he shook in a pulsating motion, keeping time with his singing. The warrior watched Red Wolf sing and dance throughout the night (Boyd 1981:112–114).[12]

At dawn, Red Wolf looked at the Kiowa and told him that the dance and songs were a gift for him to take and teach to the Kiowa people:

> I have given you a new dance with many beautiful songs. This is a gift for you to take to your people. These songs and this dance will remain with the Kiowa for as long as they protect and cherish their Kiowa ways. Tell your people to be proud as they enter the dance arena; and remind the children to listen carefully, for this is how the music will live. Go your way now, and teach the Kiowa what I have given you. (Boyd 1981:113)

After resuming his journey, the man reached his people and related his experience with Red Wolf. The people accepted the new dance and its beautiful songs. In memory of Red Wolf and in appreciation of receiving the dance, the Kiowa still end each song with the cry of a wolf and a special upward shake of their gourd rattles.[13] Although this account predominates today, it is peculiar that in light of the extensive earlier ethnographic data on Kiowa societies, including the interviews recorded in the 1960s and 1970s that are now part of the Doris Duke Oral History Collection, the story appeared nowhere until the Kiowa Gourd Clan published it in 1976 (Kiowa Gourd Clan 1976:7).

Some authors (see Ellis 1990:20–23) associate the acquisition of the society songs and dances with the actual development of the society, an association that is supported by some Kiowa who state that "the Gourd Dance started in the early 1800s" (Kiowa Tia-Piah Society 1990). However, other Kiowa maintain that the songs and dances preceded the acquisition and or formation of the sodality. Some Kiowa emphatically maintain that the society has existed from time immemorial and that "the songs have always been with us." One elder said that the Rattle Dance (Tâucùngà, or Gourd Rattle Dance, from *tâu-gàu* [gourd rattle] and *cún-gà* [dance]), preceded the formation of the Jáifègàu, which later became known as the Jáifècùngà (Jáifè Dance). This person was the only elder I spoke with who provided this name and translation. Yet because the vast majority of Plains men's nonreligious dances were associated with military societies, these statements appear contradictory, and interviewees offered no context in their explanations for the alleged separation of dance and society. Reflecting cultural beliefs about concepts of time, many Kiowa show little or no concern for the date of the dance's origin.[14]

A second origin for the Kiowa Gourd Dance was given by a former Kiowa Gourd Clan officer. It focused on a theme of thanksgiving. In this account the Kiowa were starving and suffering during a hard winter in a sandy, desertlike area somewhere southwest of Oklahoma. A Kiowa scout out in search of food climbed a tree on a hilltop to survey the surrounding landscape. He left his bow and arrows on the ground, and an enemy from another tribe found the unarmed Kiowa in the tree. Knowing that he had the Kiowa in a compromising position, the enemy began to dance and sing around the tree. Using the Kiowa's bow as a staff and his arrows and quiver as a rattle, the enemy sang as he danced around the tree four times. Occasionally he stopped and howled like a wolf while shaking the quiver of arrows aloft at the Kiowa. Thinking he would soon be killed, the Kiowa scout collected his composure. But he remembered that he still had his knife, jumped on the enemy, and killed him. Upon returning to his people, the scout related the story and the songs and dance he had seen. When spring came, food once again became plentiful, and the people rejoiced by dancing and singing in thanksgiving. Since that time, the dance has always been held in the summer, in thanksgiving of making it through the hard winter and obtaining plentiful provisions again.[15]

A similar version was given by Ko-sahn (Còsân, or Little Beggar, b. 1882), as recorded by N. Scott Momaday in the Kiowa Gourd Clan ceremonials booklet (Kiowa Gourd Clan 1976:2):

There was a young man who knew that he must go off by himself. It was necessary that he do this, for it was to be done for the people. He went out upon the prairie where it was very dangerous, for there were enemies all around. He came to a high place, a kind of little mountain, which was overgrown with sagebrush and mesquite—and there was one tree. The young man heard something, a voice perhaps, but strange and troublesome, and he was afraid. He climbed the tree and hid among the branches. From there in the tree he watched the approach of his enemy. The enemy was outfitted in the regalia of the wolf clan of his people. He wore the hide of a wolf, and he carried a bow and arrows. The wolflike man crept among the bushes, moving strangely, crouching and peering all around.

By and by he came beneath the tree, and there he stood still. The young man in the tree dropped down upon the enemy and killed him. Then the young man took up the enemy's arrows in his right hand and held them high and shook them. They rattled loudly like dry leaves in a hard wind, and to this music the young man danced around his dead enemy. The people heard the music and came to see what was going on. They were very happy for the young man, and they praised him.

There are many variations of this later version of the origin story. Another recent variation is found in the Kiowa Gourd Clan's own publication (1996:12, 17), which states that the young man was traveling back to his people after completing a vision quest and that the dance was acquired when the Kiowa lived in the Black Hills and Devils Tower area. With their many similarities, it is possible that these accounts and the Red Wolf story are variants of a parent story. Elements of the later two versions are also similar in some respects to more ethnohistorical accounts that involve the acquisition of the Gourd Dance as a result of a battle between Kiowa and Cheyenne war parties.

This fourth, more historically documented origin for the society is found in numerous Kiowa calendars, known as sá-cút (year marks), and in multiple Kiowa and Cheyenne sources. Although the account is unpopular with some Kiowa, there are several indications that the society was obtained following a well-documented battle with the Cheyenne in the summer of 1837. James Mooney (1898:271–72), Hugh Scott (HLS-1, vol. 2:72–74), George Grinnell (1983 [1915]:45–66), E. Adamson Hoebel (1978:78–79), and Peter Powell (1981:38–46, 626–628) all provided accounts of this battle. Mooney and Scott obtained accounts from firsthand participants including Teybodle (Thépòl). A party of forty-eight Cheyenne Bowstring Society members (forty-two according to Powell [1981]) set out on a revenge raid against the Kiowa. They were soon discovered by members of a large composite encampment of Kiowa, Comanche, and Apache who were preparing for a Sun Dance. This encampment was located on the eastern edge of the present-day Texas Panhandle on a tributary of Scott or "Walnut" Creek, a branch of the North Fork of the Red River, and south of the later Fort Elliott, in present-day Wheeler County, Texas. When a Kiowa man approached the Cheyenne, he was shot with an arrow and wounded. After he returned to camp, a sizable party of Kiowa, Comanche, and Apache (KCA) warriors set out in pursuit of the Cheyenne, killing three of them. A running pursuit began. As the Cheyenne proceeded eastward along the north side of the creek into the western edge of present-day Oklahoma, several more of them were killed. Greatly outnumbered, the Bowstrings retreated into a ravine and dug defensive earthworks for the ensuing battle.

The Kiowa are said to have asked their enemies in sign language who they were, to which they replied that they were Cheyenne Bowstrings. According to Powell (1981:40), the Kiowa "signed again, asking about the society, its dances, and what its songs sounded like. The Bowstrings, reckless to the end, now sang their songs for the

Kiowa, so that these enemies would not forget who it was they fought this day." The Bowstrings were noted to have sung and danced in defiance of their enemies, and according to Powell (1981:40), this was "how the Kiowas first learned the Bowstring songs they sang in their Gourd Society dances from that time on." Greatly outnumbered, the Cheyenne were quickly surrounded, overrun, and annihilated. The final location of the fight was along the second stream below Sweetwater Creek, on the western edge of present-day Beckham County, Oklahoma, which became known to the Kiowa as "Creek Where the Cheyenne Were Annihilated" (Sáqàutjàuáàutàundèvãu; Mooney 1898:271–272, 419).

Cheyenne tradition maintains that the Bowstrings were doomed to fail because they had beat and forced Gray (Painted) Thunder, the sacred arrow keeper, to sanction their leaving before the sacred arrows were cleansed and renewed following a recent murder. Some Cheyenne today maintain that it was the Bowstring Society's death songs (which have a Gourd dancing rhythm and choreography) that the Kiowa learned and that became their Gourd Dance songs.[16]

As in some forms of African warfare, singing and dancing before fighting were common among Plains Indian military societies, each of which had its own dance style and extensive repertoire of fraternal songs. But realistically, how could the Kiowa have learned a complete body of Cheyenne Bowstring songs, of which presumably only some and not all of them were heard, and those only once, and assuming that at least some of the songs had lyrics in the Cheyenne language and were perhaps in a tempo different from that used today? If we accept that the dance was captured during this battle, the most feasible interpretation is that the Kiowa learned neither the exact nor complete repertoire of Cheyenne Bowstring Society songs and ceremonies that day. More likely, the Kiowa saw the Bowstring dance and heard the associated style of songs. Although the dance choreography was simple, the style and not the actual repertoire of songs was probably brought home and improvised upon, which is more characteristic of the way cultural elements are actually diffused and innovated upon from one society to another.[17]

Other accounts of this battle are found in the George Hunt and Mary Buffalo calendars (Marriott 1945:293). The entry in the Hunt calendar states, "Arapaho Tai'pego (Gourd Dance Society) killed in a battle with Kiowas" and correlates with other calendar entries for the winter of 1837–1838.[18] Although most of the attacking force was Cheyenne, several Arapaho accompanied them in the 1838 Wolf Creek fight, and the Hunt calendar most likely refers to that fight.

In the summer of 1838, the allied Cheyenne and Arapaho launched a revenge raid on a large encampment of KCA on Wolf Creek, approximately eight miles above its juncture with Beaver Creek, where the North Canadian River forms just east of present-day Fort Supply, in Woodward County, Oklahoma (Mooney 1898:275–276; Powell 1981:51–66; Grinnell 1983 [1915]:45–69). Hugh Scott recorded an account of the fight from an elderly Kiowa woman in the 1890s: "When I was a young woman the Kiowas and Comanches were over near the forks of Wolf Creek (junction of Wolf and Beaver, afterwards Ft. Supply) about 8 miles up Wolf Creek—they were moving looking for the sundance tree—(the Comanches were making sundance with the Kiowas)."[19]

En route to the allied encampment, a party of Cheyenne under Porcupine Bear, the Dog Soldier chief, who had recently been exiled for murder, killed some thirty-one Kiowa women and men who were out gathering plants and hunting bison. In the daylong battle that followed, the Cheyenne and Arapaho were unable to take the confederated KCA village. The center of the battle moved back and forth across the stream, claiming the lives of several prominent leaders on both sides (Powell 1981:51–66; Grinnell 1983 [1915]:45–69). Sporadic raiding and fighting between the two sides continued until 1840, when the Cheyenne sent envoys to arrange a peace between the Cheyenne and Arapaho and the Kiowa, Comanche, and Apache.[20] After this initial agreement, the peace was never formally broken, despite occasional incidents between individuals of the five allied tribes. As the Southern Plains Indian tribes increasingly faced population and hunting pressures from displaced eastern tribes and Anglo encroachment onto the plains, their focus of attention turned in that direction.

Other Kiowa calendar entries correlate with these accounts and suggest that the society began shortly after the 1837 and 1838 battles with the Cheyenne. In a calendar drawn by the Kiowa artist Silverhorn for James Mooney, the entry for the winter of 1838–1839 reads, "Tainpeko Organize this winter, Rattle made of can," with a drawing of a gourd rattle typical of the kind associated with the society.[21] This date matches entries in three of the four Kiowa calendars collected by Alice Marriott (1945:292).

Several oral and written Kiowa accounts of the society's origin also refer to a battle against the Cheyenne, emphasizing the location, a sandy area along a river, and the presence of large quantities of ripe skunkberry bushes (*Rhus trilobata*). A variety of sumac, this bush is also known as polecatbush, squawbush, and fragrant sumac. Some Kiowa acknowledge the bushes as the medicine responsible for the Kiowa's prevailing power in this battle. The plant is common to the Texas-Oklahoma Panhandle area and occurs on a variety of terrains, including sandy graveled soils. It ripens between May and September (normally around early June in the Texas-Oklahoma area), which suggests that the attack took place during the summer, when Plains tribes aggregated and conducted large-scale revenge raids (Boyd 1981:112–122; Barkley 1986:572; Powell 1988:258; Tsonetokoy 1988:32).[22]

In 1971 Yale Spottedbird related the account of the society's origins as told to him by his grandfather:

> The story of the origin of the Gourd Clan as far as the Kiowas are concerns [*sic*] goes back to the year 1840. At that year, the Kiowas had a pitch battle with the Cheyenne tribe up in what we know today as the Panhandle of Oklahoma near a creek called a Wolf Creek. And the fight took place after dinner, lasted all afternoon; and neither side won the battle. As the sun went down, it began to get dark. Both sides withdrew. There were heavy casualties on both side[s].

But just like I said, neither side won. Chief Saintidi, or White Bear, leader of the Kiowas at that battle, had fought other tribes of Indians and particularly along some creek or river, usually where the battle takes place. And two times were [when] Saintati and his warriors fought against hostile tribes, other tribes. They fought in a patch of what we call the skunk berries. They grow very thick in a sandy place along the river banks. And in this one particular instance with the incident with the Cheyenne Tribe, the skunk berries were very heavy, and the fruit was ripe. It's a red berry. It's a red colored berry and they're very tasteful. . . . Chief Saintati told his warriors after the battle was over, he said, "Seems like, we have been fighting our battle in a skunk berry bushes." And along with that there was some—some of these gourd, the wild gourds were growing. And of course they climbed the bushes on the trees, and there were some dried gourd up there. And he told his warriors, "Right here, we're going to organize a clan. We'll call ourselves The Rattle Clan, and we'll take the gourd and use that as our instrument of music. Of course today, we call it the Gourd—they danced this gourd, the Gourd Clan. . . . Now this gourd was growing wild, and it so happened that at that particular time of the year, they were ripe, they were dry. He reached up and cut one, and shook it and made a beautiful sound, a rattling sound. He said, "We'll use this as our gourd—as a Gourd Clan instrument of music." Some kind of percussion deal, and so that's the origin of the gourd. . . . And so that's my version that I got from my grandfather of the origin of this Gourd Clan or Kiowa type of society.[23]

This account may refer to an earlier White Bear, because Dohausan and other elder tribal chiefs were the principal leaders of the time, and the historically known White Bear (circa 1820–1878) would have been very young. Although this account confuses the 1840 KCA–Cheyenne and Arapaho peace with the 1838 Wolf Creek fight, it includes the dominant themes associated with this explanation of the society's origin.

On the basis of information provided by the Kiowa Historical and Research Society, Maurice Boyd (1981:114–115) provided a similar historical version:

The society was originally a Kiowa fraternity of warriors and chiefs, dating from 1838. After one of the greatest battles in their history, the Kiowas offered their gratitude for survival. Their victory at the juncture where Wolf Creek joins the Canadian River against the combined Cheyenne and Arapaho forces called for a dance celebration. Following the dance, the Gourd Dance fraternity was formed. . . . One tradition declares that for four days during the great battle against the Cheyennes and Arapahoes, the Kiowas fought on a battleground of skunkberry (tdie-pei-ai-gah) bushes. Not only were the skunkberries red and in full bloom, but the bushes themselves grew red with the blood of warriors from the three tribes. Because they survived, the Kiowas regarded the skunkberry bushes and berries as a powerful medicine symbol, and they called skunkberries "Feast Food."

Kiowas of varied ages have related versions of this account to me, some comparing the plentiful fruit of the skunkberry bushes to the blood given by Kiowa warriors in the Wolf Creek battle. Some accounts place symbolic importance on the mixing of the skunkberries and Kiowa blood on the field of battle. These accounts generally attribute the formation and name of the society to this battle, to the presence of skunkberry bushes, and, in some versions, to the presence of wild gourds, which were used as rattles, but unlike those used by the Cheyenne. In addition, the singing of Wolf Songs (Cûidåugà), as described in the second version of the society's origins, was a known practice of the Cheyenne Bowstring Society (Hoebel 1978:78), the Kiowa Ją́ifègàu, and the Iowa Acting Dead Dance. Both the Iowa and Kiowa attribute the teaching of the society rituals and songs to a wolf, and many Plains tribes admired and imitated the power and cunning attributed to the wolf in warfare. From the frequent use of wolf hide coverings by their scouts, the Pawnee were known to most Plains tribes, in both spoken and sign language, as "Wolf People."

Thus, similarities among various Kiowa accounts regarding a battle origin (sometimes specifying that the society was acquired through warfare with the Cheyenne), geography, flora, and songs suggest that the society originated in this series of events. Furthermore, several of the accounts and some contemporary Kiowa elders attribute the acquisition of the society to adoption from the Cheyenne in connection with this battle. Others vehemently deny any association of the society or songs with the Cheyenne.[24] The latter view reflects the difficulty of reaching consensus between oral history, which holds important clues but is often difficult to place temporally, written history, and individual family oral histories, tribal calendars, pictographic artwork, and recorded ethnography. Although most of these last sources are difficult for contemporary Kiowa to access and view, and they often deviate from and or exceed current oral history–based traditions, it is important that they were collected from earlier generations of Kiowa elders.[25] Finally, the fact that Cheyenne attended and participated in Kiowa Ją́ifègàu dances in the mid- to late 1800s and from 1912 into the 1920s, and that Kiowa attended Cheyenne dances during this period, further suggests a lengthy ritual connection between the two tribes.

James Auchiah related both the Red Wolf and battle origins in describing the dance's history (Boyd 1981:112):

> Spawned on the field of blood,
> Colored by the Tdiepei-ai-gah, skunkberry red,
> Taught by Red Wolf's vision, his dance,
> The Whip, Rope, and Bugle proclaim us.

Dennis Zotigh (1991:65–66) attributed the gift of song to Red Wolf at sometime before 1700, while the Kiowa were still in Montana, followed by a postmigrational account of the battle against the Cheyenne and Arapaho in the southern plains. Ralph Kotay (Lassiter 1998:158–164) referenced both Red Wolf and the 1830s events, although he positioned his rendition in the Red Wolf account. On the basis of data provided by the Kiowa Historical and Research Society, Boyd (1981:112–122) discussed both Red Wolf and the 1838 Wolf Creek Battle. Of significance is that accounts that reference both origins offer no explanation of their association. Some Kiowa have told me that at this late date, no one can really know for sure.

Although the previous Kiowa accounts and calendars all suggest a historical basis for the origin and name of the society, it is important to recognize that since the post-1957 revival of the Gourd Dance, many Kiowa adhere to the Red Wolf version, which permeates current Gourd Dance ritual. By continuing to cry or howl like wolves at the end of each Kiowa Gourd Dance song, the dancers acknowledge the gifts of song and dance from Red Wolf, thereby reinforcing the connection to this version of the society's origins. With this is a strong association whereby "believers treat the songs, dances, and language that now situate the Gourd Dance experience as God-given and God-centered" (Lassiter 1998:162).[26]

Whether one accepts the translation of Jáifègàu as Skunkberries or as Unafraid of Death, both reference a martial origin. The name Skunkberries references the presence of this shrub at the location of a historic battle, while the name Unafraid of Death references the attributes of a fairly widespread form of Plains men's warrior society and martial ethos.

However, when Kiowa speak of the "community meanings" associated with the contemporary Gourd Dance, the Red Wolf story dominates (Lassiter 1998:162). Because the modern version of the Gourd Dance is seen as being based on song, and the Red Wolf story is about receiving song, this version situates the contemporary Gourd Dance as a tradition founded primarily on song. The longevity and continuation of the songs and dance serve as an affirmation of and evidence for the belief in and correctness of Kiowa life. This continuation reinforces tradition and teaching, the Kiowa way of life, and God's gifts to the Kiowa through song and culture. This basis is further set in the belief in God and that all things are thus God given. Simultaneously, Jáifègàu traditions continue as major foci for many people in the contemporary Gourd Dance in the form of customs, songs, dance, dress, giveaways, and war trophies displayed at annual encampments. Because both the Wolf Creek battle and Red Wolf stories hold various levels of importance for different Kiowa, and because both are integral parts of the development of this dance tradition, both are important to understanding the evolution of the Jáifègàu and the contemporary Kiowa Gourd Dance.[27]

Age, Organization, and Activities

In 1935 and 1936, Marriott's consultants stated that the "Taipego [Jáifègàu] is the oldest order and Koitsenko [Qóichégàu] the next." However, other Kiowa accounts mention the presence of the Dog Society during a fight and subsequent peace with the Comanche around 1790–1806 (John 1985), and Scott reported that the Black Legs Society served as camp police in 1834.[28] Kiowa calendar entries that place the origin of the society at 1837–1838 appear to be the most reliable sources known.

The J̨áifègàu shared practically all the characteristics associated with the other nineteenth-century Kiowa men's societies. It had two society leaders, two whipmen, and two boy members, but no female society members. As one of the two larger men's societies, it had a membership averaging around forty or more at a time. Members were primarily older, more mature men who were accomplished warriors, and they included many of the prominent tribal religious and war leaders. Father-son replacement was common, and because of the group's prominence, leaders for other societies were often recruited from its members. Membership appears to have been somewhat selective, later changing during the reservation era (post-1875). Mooney recorded from Paul Tsaitkopeta (Sétqópjè, or Mountain Bear, b. 1852): "When Paul was [a] warrior [circa 1868–1875] there were not many of these [J̨áifègàu], only about as many as [the] Koitsenko, but now many have been admitted. Not so many as thirty five when Paul knew them, because they were a high order, not common. Thereafter they . . . just picked up all they can."[29]

Society meetings were organized like those of the Black Legs, except for the absence of the two society girl members. The two society leaders sat on the west side of the meeting tipi (fig. 3). To their left, on the northwest side of the lodge, sat the drummers and singers in a group. On the east side, the two male youth members sat on either side of the lodge door, and on either side of them sat one of the two whipmen. Regular members sat on the south and north sides of the tipi. There was no ceremonial smoking as was the case with the Horse Headdresses Society; each man brought his own smoking paraphernalia. During open daytime meetings, the sides of the lodge were rolled up, allowing spectators to sit and watch from the outside. In the evenings the society held closed meetings, limited to members only. If a member was late, he might push a tobacco-filled pipe under the door. If the leaders smoked it, the man was allowed to come in, but he was still teased and cajoled and was occasionally required to dance humorously for the entertainment of his society brothers. If the pipe was rejected, the tardy man was forced to wait outside until the leaders reconsidered.[30]

En route to the Sun Dance, the society performed a special activity symbolizing the pre-horse era. On the day the entire tribe moved to the final location for the Sun Dance, the J̨áifègàu remained behind at the previous campsite. According to Heapo-Bears, the J̨áifègàu and the Qóichégàu stayed behind and walked to the final camp, symbolizing the earlier Kiowa mode of going to war on foot, before the acquisition of horses. These two societies, he said, which always remained on the same side in the sham battle and kick fight, arrived at the final or fourth camp on foot. According to Parson's 1927 research, only the J̨áifègàu remained behind (Parsons 1929:91). Perhaps this reflects the decline in Dog Society membership by the early 1870s. Lone Bear associated the purpose of the Sun Dance with war, which suggests a focus on war revenge or power acquisition, as in the Sun Dance of the Crow (Lowie 1983:297), from whom the Kiowa received their principal Sun Dance Bundle. The J̨áifègàu kept

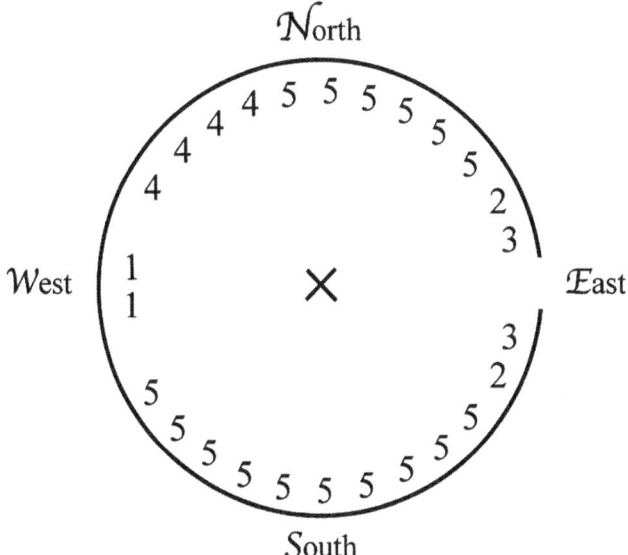

FIGURE 3. Jáifègàu meeting positions.
1, Society leaders (head leader on the south); 2, whipmen; 3, society boy members; 4, drummers and singers; 5, regular members. The central X denotes the fire.

two horses at the old campsite. After waiting until everyone else had reached the final camp, the society sent out two mounted scouts to search for the village, symbolizing the search for enemies during war journeys. When the scouts returned with news of the location of the new encampment, the society set out singing, making four stops to smoke, sing, and dance, as the other societies had done in their approach to the final encampment.[31]

Near evening, the society came in sight of the circular Sun Dance encampment. As the warriors approached, the processional could be heard from afar, with drumming, singing, dancing, and, in later years, the blowing of a bugle by White Bear. Like the other Kiowa men's societies, the Jáifègàu made four stops to smoke as they approached the camp and pointed the end of a pipe toward the Táimé Bundle in the direction of the camp. According to Lone Bear, the two society leaders arrived on horseback while the other members came on foot.[32] At the last stop before the Sun Dance encampment, the two boy members were sent ahead to retrieve the society members' best clothing. All members dressed and painted themselves and then walked to the camp circle. Upon entering, the society paraded a complete circuit around the camp in a clockwise direction, stopping at each cardinal direction to dance. The forth and final stop ended directly in front of the camp entrance, where the society feasted in a tipi situated east of the opening.[33]

According to several accounts, the Jáifègàu were always the first society to dance at the Sun Dance, with the order of the other societies unfixed. Although the reason for this was not stated, it may have been related to the society's symbolic approach to the camp on foot. Because all the societies danced during the series of encampments made before the final Sun Dance encampment and during the four stops made in approaching the final encampment, it is unclear which day these consultants were referring to—perhaps the first day after reaching the final encampment.[34]

Arriving tired and hungry, the society awaited a feast that was always prepared for them. After Lone Bear became a boy member for the society in 1872, the society stopped annually at his family's tipi to feast. Although many people pledged occasional feasts, Lone Bear's mother sponsored an annual feast for the society on this evening because her son was considered to be "so awday" (ą̂udę́, favored). These feasts could be sponsored by a member's sister or by a mother who had privately vowed to do so if a particular relative made it safely through the year, but never by a member's wife. Announcements of feasts were made at the Sun Dance, after which society members convened at the lodge of the sponsoring family. According to Lone Bear, bison hunting during the time when he grew up was variable and often unsuccessful, leaving the society several days with nothing to do except feast while the camp waited for the appointed hunters to bring the necessary bison hide for the center pole.[35]

During feasts the society leaders entered the lodge first, followed by the members, the whipmen, and then the two boy members. Informal smoking and dancing followed until the food was ready. After preparing the food, the women brought it to the tipi door and gave it to the two boy members, who announced to the leaders that the meal was ready. Boiled meat, rice (a reservation-era commodity), and dried fruit were favorites of the society. The boy members served the two society leaders first, and then each served all the members on one side of the lodge. After all had been served, the wives and female relatives standing outside the meeting lodge received a share of the food. Other people might stand beyond the circle of women and receive any remaining food. After eating, the dancing resumed, during which coup recitations were frequently made. It was during such a recitation that Lone Bear received one of the society ropes. When a man rose to dance, his mother, sister, or wife's sister frequently honored him by dancing behind him and giving away a robe or horse in his honor to a fellow member or to a visitor. Although meetings might be held at any member's tipi, and the society had no official society tipi, it often chose to meet in the red-painted tipi of White Bear, who was the fletched lance keeper (zêbàjòqî) of the society.[36]

Choreography and Songs

Early ethnographic descriptions of the society's choreography and songs are sparse. Although the society had an official starting song, it maintained no official quitting song. Elders indicated that the society maintained only two forms of choreography in its dances: the regular form of society dancing, Jái̯fè dancing (Jái̯fècùngà, today called Gourd dancing) and the Buffalo Dance (Pą́ucùngà). At least six types of Jái̯fègàu songs

(Jáifèdå̀ugà) were used in the late 1800s. Beginning with the Starting Song, which dates well before the reservation period, the tempo of the songs increased continuously throughout a dance, with slow, medium, and Fast-Paced songs (Fáuldå̀ugà, lit. Musically Stirring-Exciting Songs) near the end. Changes in the songs were determined more by the pace and speed of the drum and were differences in tempo more than in song structure. A set of four Old Men Songs used to be sung between the Fast-Paced Songs and the Buffalo Dances, during which only elder men could dance. Although these songs are no longer performed, a few singers still know them. No official society quitting song existed until the 1960s.

Today, during the Starting Song (Thàumdǻugà, or First Song), all dancers remain seated, shaking their rattles in time with the music as the singers softly tap the drum. After the song is sung through four times, there is a brief pause. Then the singers hit the drum with an accentuating hard beat and, commemorating Red Wolf, howl "Yo-oooo-ah," after which they begin a faster tempo, singing and drumming vigorously. At this point the dancers rise and stand in front of their seats in a linear formation and begin to shake their rattles in time with the music. The dancers begin to flex their knees, rising and falling on their heels, which produces a graceful up-and-down motion. When the tempo of the music changes, the dancers take a few small forward steps, and when the tempo changes again they resume their dancing, bobbing in place. At the end of each song the dancers lift their rattles upward, shaking them and howling like wolves, "Ya-oooo-ah," in memory of Red Wolf, who taught the dance to the Kiowa. Elders have frequently noted that dancers nowadays do not "howl loudly" and "really put the feeling into it" the way older dancers used to. Several Kiowa described the dance as "a dignified dance," and anyone who has ever watched a Kiowa Gourd Dance can attest that it is performed with much pride, dignity, and respect. As Bill Koomsa Jr. described it:

> The dancing itself, the old-timers danced with respect, they were proud, they were proud that they were Indian, and that they were Kiowa, and that they were part of the Gourd Clan. They danced it that way.... An actual Kiowa, you watch him and he'll dance with dignity, and proud. But when it gets going, some of the old-timers, aw, they used to really dance. They used to come up off the ground, they really danced hard.[37]

According to older Kiowa custom, it is appropriate to sit down after each song until the next song begins. Although this is still practiced at some dances, it is seen less commonly today, because many singers immediately begin the next song without a break, and because many dancers take only a few steps backward and remain standing in the arena for an entire set of songs. Once the dancing begins, women wearing decorated shawls begin to dance behind the men.

On all subsequent songs the dancers slowly advance forward, taking small steps until the music is accentuated, after which they alternate the sets of dancing in place with a series of small steps. Kiowa women are never supposed to begin dancing before the men or to walk in front of the men while they are seated or dancing, unless honoring them. However, this tradition is changing to some degree.

In the past, Ją́ifègàu dances were concluded with the Buffalo Dance. The 1933 Laboratory of Anthropology Comanche fieldnotes and Robert Lowie's Comanche fieldnotes (Kavanagh 2008:478, 486–490; Parsons 1929:85–89), together with several Kiowa and Comanche elders I interviewed, confirm that the Kiowa obtained the Buffalo Dance from the Comanche. Formerly held on the night before Comanche war parties set out, the Buffalo Dance was acquired by the Kiowa leader Wolf Lying Down (Cûiqǎujè) when he returned a Comanche boy the Kiowa had captured to his people. The Comanche performed the dance out of joy, and Wolf Lying Down later brought it back to the Kiowa. Edgar Keahbone (Parsons 1929:88) stated in 1927 that "today it is danced merely as a show. Formerly it was danced before going to war. Men took their shield, quiver, and gun, and put on their war bonnet or buffalo hide with horns attached to it." Those afoot lined up and ran, stopping to dance, while a few of the highest-ranking chiefs rode around the others during the dance on horseback. The first rider to reach the drum recited a war story. Men as well as their horses were painted red to illustrate where they had been wounded in battle.

The martial context of the dance has been deleted, and the dance is now often loosely associated with the herding and migration of bison. Several male and female elders stated that the younger generations do not dance the Buffalo Dance in the manner they themselves had been taught in the early 1900s. Kiowa and Comanche elders stated—in several cases rising during interviews to demonstrate the proper dance form—that the dance is supposed to be performed with a pivoting, side-to-side shuffle in place while the feet are kept together, until the tempo of the music changes, at which time several forward shuffling steps are taken. During a brief pause in the music, the dancers walk farther around the arena, and the process is repeated several times per song. Today dancers continue to carry their gourd rattles but do not shake them during the Buffalo Dance. A variety of steps resembling those of Buffalo, Horse Stealing, and Trot Dances are frequently seen during current Buffalo Dances. Today the Buffalo Dance is performed in a social context as the last portion of the Gourd Dance, but generally only at the larger annual dances. Most of the smaller Gourd Dances held throughout the year that I witnessed between 1989 and 2008 ended with a set of Fast-Paced Songs (Fáuldàugà), and the concluding Buffalo Dances were waning in regularity.

The following song, collected from Charley White Horse in 1935, was considered to be one of the favorite and most important of the society's songs. It addresses the role of the warrior in that period. Commonly referred to as the Chief's Song, it is attributed to the past society leader White Bear:

1 Há-gâi-kò̓ câi-gù é hól-jàu
 (Somewhere-sometime / enemy / they-kill-shall)
 Somewhere / sometime, the enemy shall have killed me.

2 Fòi-bà ấu-lyî-thầu háun yá hái-gá-dấu-thầu
   (Do not / weep-cry-shall / no or not / I / know-state of-shall)
   Do not weep, I shall not know about / of it.
3 Há-gâi-kǒ ầu-sè-cûi-gù é hàn-jầu
   (Somewhere-sometime / spring-wolves / they / ingest [eat] shall)
   Somewhere, sometime, the wolves of spring shall have eaten me.
4 Repeat line 2.³⁸

Today several versions of this song are sung throughout the Kiowa community at Gourd Dances.

Another song, of a more social nature, was sung at the Sun Dance when a man was enjoying himself and did not want to be interrupted:

1 Hé-jâu à yái-tǒ-yà
   (Wait / I am / playing or recreating-going about)
   Wait, I am still going about/around having a good time.
   Há-yâi-kǒ-bèt-jàu–hệ̀
   (Nobody / scolding to me-has-not)
   Nobody has reprimanded or scolded me.
2 Repeat first part of line 1.³⁹

In the past, sets of four to eight songs were interspersed with breaks during which dancers rested, smoked, and recited coups.

Dress and Insignia

Detailed descriptions of the society's original dress are lacking in comparison with those for other Kiowa societies. The best-known form of insignia is still the mescal bean bandolier (*káuhòl*) worn by society members during dances and in warfare. Mescal beans are the hard seeds of the evergreen bush *Sophora secundiflora*, native to south-central Texas, southeastern New Mexico, and adjacent portions of Mexico on the eastern side of the Sierra Madre as far south as the states of Puebla and Oaxaca. The seeds vary in color from yellow, yellowish red, and orange to bright dark red or maroon, and they range in size from 0.8 to 2.0 centimeters in length and 0.5 to 1.5 centimeters in width. Mescal beans have long been confused with mescaline, one of several alkaloids contained in peyote, or *Lophorphora williamsii* (La Barre 1938, 1989:105; Merrill 1977:1; Stewart 1987:4–5). The warriors of several tribes wore mescal bean bandoliers in battle because, like peyote, mescal beans were believed to contain great power for protection in warfare, as well as for divination of lost items. They were widely used in Plains war bundles and in the central Plains Indian "Red Bean Dance." There is considerable evidence for the narcotic use of mescal beans even before the beginnings of peyotism in the late nineteenth century. They were also used as medicine for ear and eye ailments, as a source of stamina for running, and in intoxicating beverages that produced prolonged sleep. Throughout the southern Great Plains, people also used mescal beans as decorative beads on men's and women's clothing, peyote regalia, and other material culture items and for other purposes (Schultes 1937:141–146; Carlson and Jones 1939:537–538; Vestal and Schultes 1939:35; Jones 1972:58; Merrill 1977:94–99, 105–111; La Barre 1989:26, 105–109, 126–127).

The use of mescal beans as protection from contamination by menstrual blood is reported to have been common among Plains tribes (Schultes 1937:35) and appears in the late 1800s among some Oklahoma tribes. At that time, peyote leaders began wearing mescal bean bandoliers as part of their ceremonial attire. Some Kiowa and Iowa peyote leaders wore mescal beans on the lower portions of their leggings and on the heel fringes of their moccasins as protection from menstrual blood (Schultes 1937:140, 141; La Barre 1989:106). The Comanche also used mescal beans for a variety of purposes (Carlson and Jones 1939:537–538). David Jones (1968:3, 1972:58) reported the use of mescal beans as protection against possible contamination from menstrual blood by Comanche *puhakut* (medicine men or doctors), who carried mescal beans or had them sewn into the cuffs of their trousers.

Another item of Jáifègàu dress was the American cavalry waist sash, which warriors captured in battle. The date of first acquisition and the number of these sashes are unknown, but they were worn around the waist and in later days were decorated with beadwork around the tops of the tassels. Modified forms of this item continue to be a standard part of men's Gourd Dance dress today.

Elders in 1935 stated that most Jáifègàu members wore porcupine roaches, whereas the leaders wore owl feather headdresses. The latter are highly taboo today. According to White Fox, the men wore red paint for outside dances. Frizzlehead II (b. 1860, whose father, of the same name, was once the principal society leader) said he never saw society members wear red paint while dancing, but he did see the dance performed with members wearing yellow paint and owl feathers. This dress style and its associated song came to an elderly woman in a vision after the Kiowa had been brought to Fort Sill (post-1875), and the society danced this way only once or twice. Sangko stated, "Once they were told to dress as much as possible like the koiseko, so they wore red paint all over their body, a red vest, and an elk [throat hair] headdress. There were always 4–5 of the owl feather headdresses (just like the koiseko ones) that were owned by the daimbe society."[40] Instead of using red paint, some members are reported to have painted thin white stripes across their bodies by applying paint with their fingernails.

Some members wore regular buckskin shirts, leggings, and moccasins, along with blankets or "sheets" (*tháimáu* [s]; *thái* [d/t]; lit. "white") over their shoulders, which they dropped when rising to dance. Some carried eagle feather fans and gourd rattles. Other members, thought to be less wealthy, reportedly wore only moccasins and breechclouts and covered their entire body in yellow paint. Members who dressed in this fashion are reported to have worn their hair in a single braid with hawk feathers attached to it.[41]

Some depictions of Ją́ifègàu members and dances are found in Kiowa ledgerbook art. Janet Berlo (1996:149, pl. 71) reproduced a depiction of a man identified as Sun Boy dancing in front of a red-painted tipi. He wears red body and face paint, holds a red fletched lance in his left hand, and shakes a rattle in his right hand. Although he is identified as Sun Boy in a caption written in the margin, this drawing probably depicts White Bear, because the red paint, gourd dance rattle, fletched lance (*zébàut*), and red-painted tipi are all traits associated with him. On close examination, the moon and fringe on the back of the red lodge match those of White Bear's Red Tipi, and there is no association of Sun Boy with either the Porcupine or the Red Tipi (Ewers 1978:19–22). Although both Sun Boy and White Bear were Ją́ifègàu members, Sun Boy was of smaller stature than White Bear and is not known to have owned a fletched lance, whereas White Bear was the Ją́ifègàu fletched lance keeper.[42]

Joyce Szabo (1994:8) published a depiction from the Hanna Drawings that is believed to have been drawn by Silverhorn and to have been collected between 1877 and 1885.[43] This drawing shows a military society dance with a line of well-dressed men, each carrying Gourd Dance rattles, being addressed by a society leader on horseback. The depiction contains the caption, "The Indian soldiers, they had dance, and the Captain, he is in the mide [sic] he had talk [with] his soldiers." I have been unable to determine whether this depiction is of the Ją́ifègàu or the Horse Headdresses Society, but because of the dress depicted, the former is likely. Karen Daniels Petersen's book *Plains Indian Art from Fort Marion* (1971:42) includes a picture drawn by Koba of a man and a woman, each on horseback. The woman wears a Red Sleeve Dress, and the man holds a Gourd Dance–type rattle, which probably marks him as a Ją́ifègàu member.

Several other articles of regalia were associated with the Ją́ifègàu in the nineteenth century. According to Big Head (Parsons 1929:91), the society, like the Horse Headdresses Society, used an eagle wing bone whistle to direct single- or double-file and archlike dance formations. HeapoBears stated that one man in the society wore a whistle on a necklace of beads similar to those worn by members of the Dog Society. White Fox, however, said that no whistles were used, because the Dog Society was the only military society to own whistles, reflecting perhaps a contradiction or a change in tradition. Four members with hand drums sat on the northwest side of the meeting tipi. Later, a single large drum replaced these and was relocated to the north side of the meeting tipi. Singers were chosen for their vocal abilities and were generally older members who seldom danced but dressed in the same way as the dancers.[44]

Each member had a rattle (*tâugàu*) that he shook in time with the music while dancing. Harold Driver (1961:201) suggested that rattles made from gourds might have diffused to the western Plains tribes via the adjacent horticulturalists. Rattles made from gourds (wild or domesticated) preceded metal and possibly rawhide forms and were predominant among Plains Indian horticulturalists. Rattles made from dried bison scrotums were also common in many tribal military societies. However, of the forms collected from the Kiowa and other mobile Plains groups, most Gourd

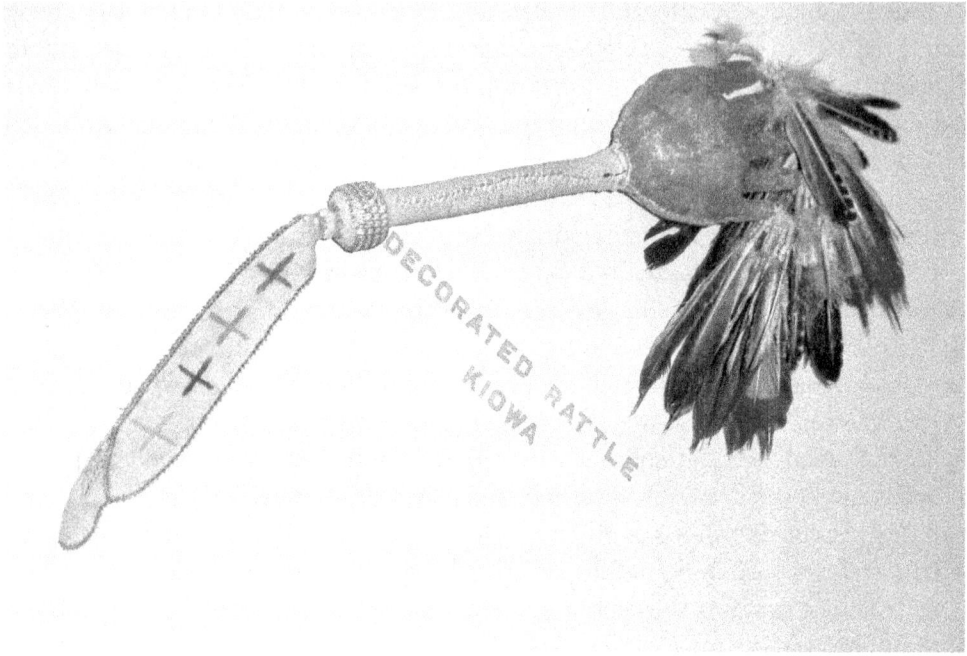

Kiowa Jáifègàu human hand effigy rattle, rawhide.
Chicago Field Museum, permanent display.

Dance rattles were traditionally square, spherical, or globular and made of dried rawhide.

Concerning society rattles, Frank Given reported in 1935: "Taipe in earlier times, they were made of hide, some globular in shape and some in the shape of a human hand, the fingers outstretched." The Field Museum of Natural History in Chicago has a Kiowa rattle of this style on display. It consists of a three-dimensional, red-painted rawhide human hand with flicker wing and tail feathers appended to the tips of the fingers, attached to a yellow-painted, buckskin-covered handle decorated with beadwork. The handle cover, which is sewn together down each side of the handle, extends from the base of the handle proper to form an appendage and is decorated with four beaded crosses and edge beadwork.[45]

With the acquisition of trade goods, the Kiowa replaced rawhide rattles with tin baking-powder cans placed on sticks and decorated with beadwork and feathers on the ends, a trend found among other Plains populations as well. The use of tin cans in Jáifègàu and Horse Headdresses Society dances was common by the mid-1870s, as is depicted in ledgerbook art dating from this period (Petersen 1971:22; Szabo 1994:8) and later. With the help of an older society member, each member made his own dance rattle. According to Big Head, the rattles were shaken from side to side (Parsons 1929:91). At the last part of each song, members of the Jáifègàu and the Horse Headdresses Societies raised their rattles aloft and shook them (Lowie 1916b:847).[46]

The whipmen, who sat on either side of the doorway during meetings, carried a saber and a tomahawk, respectively, as their badges of office.⁴⁷

One of the better-known items associated with the Jáifègàu is White Bear's bugle. Although scholars have mentioned it frequently, little solid documentation has ever been presented on its history. Jean Burroughs's account of the bugle (1974:21–28) gives little in-depth information and is poorly documented. Most references state that the bugle was captured during a battle in Texas. In 1935, HeapoBears said the bugle had been captured by White Bear in a battle with Anglos, but Frank Given said it had been given to White Bear by Anglo soldiers at an army post, which current elders say was Fort Larned, Kansas, built in 1859, and that the society used the bugle to warn the camp of its approach. Mrs. Horse (Piatonma) reported, "No one knows where he got it. . . . He claimed he had captured the bugle from the soldiers. Some people say he traded for it and did not capture it at all." One account indicates that White Bear had the bugle by at least 1864. In March and April of that year, Special Agent H. T. Ketcham spent two weeks among the Kiowa, who were then camped along the Arkansas River about forty miles above Fort Larned. Ketcham spent four days in White Bear's camp. Impressed with White Bear, Ketcham recorded a favorable account of his host, noting that "he has a brass French Horn, which he blew vigorously when the meals were ready."

White Bear reportedly learned to play the instrument and blew contrary calls during battles with the U.S. Cavalry, in order to confuse the soldiers. After its acquisition, the bugle was also used to announce the annual arrival of the society as it approached the final Sun Dance encampment. Using the Ananthy Odlepaugh Calendar, Hugh Corwin (1971a:152, 1971b:109) reported that whereas some elders maintained that the bugle was captured from the army and that White Bear played it, others indicated that the bugler was an African American army bugler who had deserted the army, joined the Kiowa, and, inferably, resided in White Bear's band. HeapoBears stated that Lone Bear still had the bugle in 1935 but could not blow it. HeapoBears thought "perhaps he needed a vision for it."⁴⁸

In the winter of 1869–1870, known as the "Winter When They Were Frightened by the Bugle" (Jôbáutétfédèsài), a party of Kiowa who were returning from scouting for soldiers blew a bugle to announce its return, throwing the encampment into a panic. Mooney gave two versions of this incident (1898:326–327), in one of which the blowing of the bugle was attributed to White Bear. Believing they were being attacked by soldiers, the Kiowa were so badly frightened that they ran for several miles before they realized what had happened. The Ananthy Odlepaugh calendar also contains an entry for the winter of 1869–1870 that states, "This year is known as (Bugle Scare). In this winter a party of warriors were returned [and] had captured an army bugle and while near the camp some one had sent out a few sounds from this instrument which threw the camp into fright."⁴⁹ If this was the bugle belonging to White Bear, then the date suggests that he obtained it in the winter of 1869–1870. Yet Ketcham's 1864 account, which seems reliable, suggests that an instrument was acquired earlier. Reportedly, the Kiowa later used the bugle to warn their own camps of returning Kiowa parties. Numerous accounts indicate that it was also used in warfare and in society ceremonies. In the early 1900s the bugle was blown during Jáifègàu dances by Paul Zotam, and later by Cecil Horse, who stopped after his conversion to Christianity. According to Frank Given, White Bear's arrow, rope, and bugle were in the possession of Tsoodle in 1935.[50]

The society also maintained two society ropes, or sashes, made of red cloth, each accompanied by an arrowlike lance.[51] One of the ropes associated with the society involved White Bear. While a party of Kiowa raiders was returning home, it encountered a group of Mexican or Texan (depending on the account) cowboys, who reportedly wore some type of rawhide armor that was impenetrable to arrows. According to Hugh Scott's account, the Kiowa were just outside of Durango, Mexico, when a group of Mexicans came out to fight them with ropes. After a brief skirmish, the Kiowa retreated. One of the Mexicans lassoed White Bear with a lasso or leather riata and dragged him on the rough ground for some distance, badly skinning up his legs and body. Frizzlehead (1824–1907) charged the Mexican with his lance, causing the Mexican to drop the rope and retreat and thereby saving White Bear. The leather riata was apparently cut with a knife. When the Kiowa returned to camp, the looped end of the riata was still hanging around White Bear's body and thus became a personal war trophy and later a trophy of the society.[52]

Berlo (2000:38–39) published a ledgerbook-style drawing of this incident. The associated caption reads, "White Bear with a war party in Mexico is attacked by a party of Mexicans, who lasso him and are dragging him away; when Red Otter came to the rescue and put a few arrows into the Mexicans, who drop White Bear and run away and the Indians make their escape." The drawing shows four Mexicans on horseback wearing brightly patterned Saltillo serapes. One of them is dragging the lassoed White Bear on the ground. A Kiowa warrior wearing the distinctive sash, red striped face paint, and owl feather headdress of the Dog Society is in close pursuit, shooting arrows at the Mexicans, two of whom have been hit.[53]

White Bear is said to have kept the rope and in one instance to have used it—or possibly a replica, since only the end of the riata was captured after Frizzlehead cut him loose—to lasso and kill an enemy. The Odlepaugh calendar entry for the winter of 1854–1855 states, "Figure relates the deed of Chief White Bear, when while on a big war path looking for scalps he encountered some white men and to show his skill and courage did not use his weapons but used a rope instead by which he overcame his victim." This calendar entry suggests that White Bear obtained the original rope between the time shortly before the 1854 fight with the Sauk and Fox and the Durango raid later that year. According to Thépòl's account in the 1890s (Nye 1962:103–104), White Bear was carrying the shield he had received from Black Horse on this raid, and it had been given to him shortly before Black Horse's death in 1854. Scott (1928:165) reported that this event took place before the Civil War.[54] These accounts suggest that both Frizzlehead and Red Otter were involved in the rescue of White Bear. The rescue might also have involved efforts based on shared society membership, since Frizzlehead was once the head leader of the Jáifègàu.

The second society sash owner is unknown but might have been Jángúljè (Red Bonnet Brow). Along with his rope was a special form of medicine that he kept in a red cloth and wore in the back of his hair.[55] Red Bonnet Brow's arrow was smaller than White Bear's and was reported also to have come from a vision by its owner instructing him to make it. White Bear's father, Red Tipi (Jògúl or Jògúlqáptàu, Old Man Red Tipi) went to Red Bonnet Brow's tipi and tore the fletchings from the arrow, but Jángúljè repaired it and continued to carry it. Still angered, White Bear told the man that his right to carry it would be proved by his actions in the next battle, whereupon Red Bonnet Brow killed a Ute, ending White Bear's protests concerning his arrow.[56]

Jáifègàu sashes were occasionally renewed, but unlike in the Dog Society, no formal ceremony was associated with their repair or replacement. Each man took care of his own rope. There was also no distinction of power associated with the age of a rope; a new rope was considered to be as a good as an old one as soon as it was made.[57] As will be shown, these sashes were associated with no-retreat obligations in warfare.

Society Lances

White Bear's red *zébàut* (fletched lance) is perhaps the best-known lance among the Kiowa. He reportedly was the first man in the Jáifègàu to carry such an unusually long lance. Reconstructing the history of this lance is problematic, because at least four versions of its acquisition are recorded.

The first version was obtained from Frizzlehead II, Henry Tsoodle Sr., and Lone Bear, who was a boy member of the society and who, by his own account, was eleven years old in 1874. White Bear's fletched lance was approximately seven feet long and made of a reportedly scarce form of wood known as "strong handled wood" (*jólcòtą̀*), probably a type of oak. It was painted red (wrapped in red cloth, according to Tsoodle) and had three fourteen-inch fletchings of eagle feathers on the end. For ceremonial purposes (society meetings and dances), White Bear was reported to have used a wooden point, which was replaced with an eight-inch metal point for combat (Mooney 1898:326). In the middle of the handle was a cluster of sage (owl feathers, according to Frizzlehead). According to Frizzlehead, the owner of this fletched lance was prohibited from joining another society, which implies that the lance belonged to the society and was suggested as the reason White Bear, who held the position as fletched arrow keeper (*zêbàjòqî*) and was a renowned warrior, never became a Dog Society member. The lance was associated with war power and was used as a spear in battle, but it did not have a no-retreat requirement associated with it. According to Frank Given, "a man had a vision that he was to make the arrow and give it to White Bear to carry."[58]

The second version of the acquisition of White Bear's lance comes largely from Mooney's fieldnotes. According to his consultants, Red Bonnet Brow, who died in the winter of 1868, was a Black Legs Society member and apparently later a Jáifègàu member who owned a hereditary family fletched lance that originated through his Crow ancestry. White Bear, of the Ją́ifègàu, claimed rights to it through marriage into the family of Red Bonnet Brow and made a similar lance despite Red Bonnet Brow's protests. White Bear later came and broke the fletched lance of Red Bonnet Brow, who later remade one. It was passed on to his grandson Edgar Keahbone, who later took the name Red Bonnet Brow (Mooney 1898:325–326; Parsons 1929:94). Mooney's consultants (1898:325–326) stated that Red Bonnet Brow's family disputed White Bear's claim to the lance through his marriage into the family. Lone Bear said that the fletched lance was given to White Bear by his uncle Black Horse I, a member of the Ją́ifègàu and a brother of White Bear's father, Old Man Red Tipi. Writers appear to have confused Black Horse (Chę̂kǫ́gái) with Black Bear (Sétkǫ̀gài) because of the similarity in name, and multiple sources document that White Bear received his shield (and not his lance) from Black Horse.[59] Lone Bear claimed that the lance was a society possession and not a family one, although it seems to have been maintained over time by various members of that family. Henry Tsoodle said the lance was made by Sabon'ha (Sálbònhâ, or Bent or Warped By Heat). Like the Black Legs, the Ją́ifègàu had many more inherited positions than did the younger societies. At society meetings, White Bear planted the red arrow in the ground in front of him and carried it while dancing. Ownership, which had to be obtained in a vision or in association with custodianship of the special item, entitled the owner to paint himself red all over, because red paint was generally associated with great power, especially in curing.[60]

Parsons (1929:94) recorded a third version of the acquisition of the lance. It describes how White Bear of the Ją́ifègàu and Red Bonnet Brow of the Black Legs Society both owned fletched lances. White Bear broke the lance of Red Bonnet Brow, who later made another one. Lowie (1916b:847) reported a fletched lance owned by Ha'ngul (Jánguljè, or Red Bonnet Brow) that was decorated with reddened eagle feathers and had the entire shaft painted red. Unlike White Bear's lance, this hereditary lance required the owner to stake himself down in battle until released by someone else. Upon the owner's death, the lance was buried with him, and another member made another lance. In the 1920s, Kiabo (Edgar Keahbone) made a fletched lance because his maternal grandfather, Red Bonnet Brow, had previously owned one. The description of this lance appears to be of the type of hereditary lance belonging to Red Bonnet Brow (Mooney 1898:325–326; Parsons 1929:94). Frizzlehead reported that Red Bonnet Brow's fletched lance came from his father, who was also a Ją́ifègàu member.[61] Although White Bear is often mentioned as the fletched lance keeper of the Ją́ifègàu, Red Bonnet Brow's ownership of such a lance is further supported by the fact that he was also known by the personal name Arrow Keeper (Zébàutjǫ̀qì).[62] Red Bonnet Brow was killed in Texas in the winter of 1868–1869 (Mooney 1898:424).

Fourth and last, Corwin (1971a:148), using the Ananthy Odlepaugh calendar, also reported that the lance originated with Red Bonnet Brow's family via the Crow and that White Bear claimed hereditary rights to it through marriage into the family of one of Red Bonnet Brow's ancestors. Despite Red Bonnet Brow's protests, White Bear made a similar lance, which Corwin reported was inherited by White Bear's grandson James Auchiah and was in the Fort Sill Museum.

An ethnohistorical approach combining four independent Kiowa calendars and oral history indicates that White Bear was in possession of the fletched lance for around twenty years, from 1854 to 1874. The Silverhorn calendar includes an entry for the death of Black Bear in the winter of 1853–1854 (not to be confused with a later Black Bear, 1834–circa 1899), with the drawing of a black bear and the fletched lance connected by a line.[63] Both the George Hunt (winter 1853) and Mary Buffalo (winter 1851) calendars (Marriott 1945:295–297) record Black Bear's death, which was remembered because he died while in a sweat lodge. Although some entries are consistently off by two years, the events recorded in Marriott's calendar match up sequentially with those in other Kiowa calendars. Mary Buffalo's 1852 entry notes White Bear's making of the fletched lance during the summer following the death of Black Bear. In addition, the entry from the Silverhorn calendar for the Timber Mountain Sun Dance of 1854 states, "Settante zebat at Ayadalda Pa Kado (Timber [Hill] Mountain Creek Sun Dance). First time Settanti had his zebat, given by Setkongya who died on preceding page. He had given him the rite long before, but this [was the] first time he made it."[64]

Although he had been given the right to make the fletched lance, White Bear had not done so before the summer of 1854, and he is known to have given his lance away upon his release from prison in Huntsville, Texas, in the summer of 1874 (Mooney 1898:338). Kiowa calendars demonstrate that this lance was unrelated to that of Red Bonnet Brow and that White Bear maintained the well-known fletched lance for twenty years, which suggests that White Bear's contention with Red Bonnet Brow may have been personal.[65]

Following the Kiowa attack on the Warren wagon train, White Bear was taken prisoner during a meeting with agency and military officials on May 27, 1871. Tried and found guilty, he was sentenced to hang, but his sentence was changed to life imprisonment. He was later released from Fort Richardson, in Jacksboro, Texas, and returned to the Kiowa on October 8, 1873. Part of his release agreement was that he would cease all raiding and warfare against Anglo settlements (Robinson 1997).

The Red River war began when allied Southern Plains tribes attacked Anglo bison hunters at Adobe Walls in the Texas Panhandle on June 27, 1874. Orders were given for troops to attack hostile Indians in Indian Territory, whereas friendly Indians who enrolled at Fort Sill as neutrals would be protected. The Kiowa were preparing for their Sun Dance while leaders and their bands considered accommodation or opposition to the military forces. Symbolizing his choice of making peace, White Bear appeared at a Jáifègàu meeting and dance that was in progress on the north side of the camp circle. Henry Tsoodle Sr., who witnessed the event and who was White Bear's half brother, said that White Bear and their father, Red Tipi, had been repairing the lance inside a tipi in which no one else was permitted to enter. The men's societies were awaiting the beginning of the sham battle. White Bear, who at this time was reportedly neither a society leader nor a whipman, appeared on horseback and rode around the inside of the society circle with the lance in his hand and announced that he was going to give it away. According to Mooney (1898:338), this was done in celebration of his release from prison. Red Tipi then called for the camp crier, Leg Portion Of A Robe (Káutójè), to announce the event to the entire camp. In contrast to the usual address of a man to his society friends (cóbàu), White Bear specifically addressed his own sons: "My sons, I want you to take this arrow." Odlepaugh (Ôlpàu, or Bison Bird), his second son, who was very young and untried in battle but a favorite of his father's, rose and offered to take it. White Bear did not hear his offer, which others brought to his attention. However, White Bear chose White Cowbird (Áttótháidè, White Blackbird), a distant relative of his and a brother of Sun Boy's.[66]

Odlepaugh and White Cowbird stood up, and White Bear tied a rope around them. Lone Bear said that this was the equivalent to reciting a coup, because everyone knew that it symbolized and referred to the incident in which White Bear was lassoed.[67] The mother of White Cowbird was reported to have been calm, whereas the mother of Bison Bird was reported to have become frantic with grief, reflecting the battle obligation assumed with the acceptance of the sash.[68] Both recipients were also given a lump of medicine tied in a buckskin bag; it consisted of red clay perfumed with sweet grass and beaver testes. The bags were tied on the back of the head to the scalp lock.[69]

White Bear took the two young men to his father's tipi. Following the sham battle, the two returned, stripped and painted red, and were dancing. White Cowbird had the red arrow and was now the official fletched lance keeper (zêbàjòqî), while Bison Bird had a no-retreat sash (ôpàyàipàu, lit. throat-tied-rope, or Jáifèyàipàu, Jáifègàu rope). This sash was made from a one-foot-wide red strip of buckskin or cloth that went over the head and under one arm and trailed on the ground. It obligated the owner to shoot an arrow through it into the ground and remain until released by another. No official title went with the sash. Old Man Red Tipi sang and drummed for the two men as they danced an entire circuit around the dance area, followed by a huge crowd. They then made other circuits with rattles in their hands but with no drumming. They continued to dance most of the night and each following day until the Sun Dance ended. When not dancing, they rested and slept on a nearby sandy knoll, with the fletched lance stuck in the ground. They continued to fast for six days.[70]

As soon as the buffalo skin was positioned in the Sun Dance lodge — at which time people were free to leave the encampment again — Bison Bird went out on a war party. White Cowbird did not obtain much distinction in battle following his reception of the fletched lance in 1874, and all fighting ceased by May 1875. In the fall of 1878, while on a hunting party during which he and Buffalo Calf Tongue crossed the Red River into Texas in search of bison, White Cowbird was killed by Texas Rangers. While Buffalo Calf Tongue retreated, White Cowbird stood his ground and was killed. The fletched lance reportedly was not buried with him, but what became of it is unknown. Bison Bird then made a duplicate of it, "having the right from his father," and was then called zêbàjòqî. Pictures of him holding this lance in the 1920s exist.[71]

According to Lone Bear, the lance and the sash were like brothers, went together, and, when combined, accounted for White Bear's great power as a warrior. Although there were previously several such sashes in the tribe, this one was reported to have had special qualities, because White Bear had received designs to decorate it with. The sash was supposed to have closely resembled those of the Dog Society and could not be relinquished by White Bear because of his position as fletched lance keeper for the society. Whether or not the acquisition of the sash was associated with Old Man Red Tipi, who was a Dog Society member, is unknown.

White Bear's decision to give away his sash and lance is significant. He might have chosen this action as a show of good faith toward the requirements of his probation and to avoid reimprisonment at all costs. Although he enrolled as a neutral at Fort Sill on August 5, 1874, and was forbidden to visit the Wichita Agency at Anadarko, he missed the August 13 roll call and was soon seen at the agency, where a skirmish broke out, leading to the Kiowa's flight to the Texas Panhandle and his subsequent rearrest and imprisonment (Robinson 1997:186). From the Kiowa perspective, he was no longer the official lance keeper of his society. Although his capture and imprisonment undoubtedly hurt his status as a chief, because warriors generally did not let themselves be taken alive, the transfer of these items symbolized that he was relinquishing his position as lance keeper and perhaps that he would never again lead warriors in combat, at least on an official level.

Lone Bear, during a society meeting, received the last society rope from White Bear's son Bison Bird, who had reportedly taken the sash into battle (inferably in 1874–1875). While Bison Bird owned the rope, Bear Shields (Sétkį́jè) borrowed it and kept it for several years, which was permissible by a fellow member. When Bear Shields left the Jáifègàu to join the Omaha Society (sometime after 1884), Bison Bird asked Bear Shields to return the rope, because he was no longer a Jáifègàu member. He then gave it to Lone Bear at a society meeting, and Lone Bear danced with the rope that evening. The next day Bear Shields approached Lone Bear for the rope, and the latter, reportedly being intimidated by the older man, gave it to him outright. After that the rope was put around a drum and used in Omaha Society dances. The rope was considered to have had power in the old days that was lost with the passing of the rope from Lone Bear's possession. Lone Bear was later ridiculed for having given the rope up, and although he had the right to make a replacement, he declined to do so, despite the urging of his fellow society members.[72] Frank Given said that White Bear's younger half-brother, Henry Tsoodle Sr., had his bugle, sash, and fletched lance in 1935, which Tsoodle confirmed.[73]

A spotted feathered lance owned by Not Afraid Of Them (Háunéfę̀gû) and later by his son Beaver Lake (Fótǫ́qį́ or Botone) was kept by the society. As a war lance taken on war parties, it required special treatment and had specific battle obligations associated with it. To lower and point the lance forward obligated the carrier to ride forward with it until he had speared an enemy. Thus the lance was required to be held vertically to prevent obligatory use. The same rules were said to apply to any spotted feathered or fletched lance. Ownership of such a lance required the owner to take it to war nearly every time, in order to avoid accusations of cowardice. Such lances were occasionally loaned to an uncle or brother to use if the owner was not going out on a war party. However, loans of such lances were rare because of the danger and risk entailed in their use. These types of lances were generally buried with their owners. White Fox reported that there were once four such lances in the Jáifègàu, one of which descended through his wife's family.[74]

These characteristics seem to suggest some influence, perhaps indirect, of the Kiowa Dog Society upon the Jáifègàu. The use of sashes, contrary speech, red paint, and owl feathers closely resembles Kiowa Dog Society practices. Specially decorated lances such as the fletched lance, fur crook, and spotted feather lance entailed specific behavior in battle, and the use of sashes, commonly called ropes by the Kiowa, are reminiscent of Dog Society behavior involving the staking of oneself down in battle until released by another. Contrary speech, particularly during a war journey, is reported to have been used by anyone when addressing a Jáifègàu member.[75] Frizzlehead II, however, stated that despite similarities in dress, paint, and associations during the sham battle and kick fight, there was no connection between the two societies.[76] These characteristics may simply have once been common to many Plains military societies.

Leaders

Although White Bear is the best-known leader of the Jáifègàu, the 1935 Kiowa accounts say that he was the fletched lance keeper and neither a society leader nor a whipman. Whether or not these accounts refer to his status during his imprisonment in Texas is unknown. Because the holders of society leadership positions frequently changed, it is now difficult to ascertain the tenures of individual leaders. Several other society leaders are known, including Black Horse I (Chêkǫ́gái), a paternal uncle of White Bear's who was killed in 1854 in the battle with the Sauk and Fox; Black Bear (Sétkǫ̀gái, 1834–circa 1899), who was listed as one of the two head society leaders in 1873 (not the same Black Bear who gave White Bear the right to construct a lance and died in 1853–1854, per the Silverhorn calendar); and Old Man Frizzlehead (1824–1907). The original Big Head (Àultǫ́êl) was a whipman in the society. He died in the winter of 1863–1864 and was replaced by his brother (Mooney 1898:392 says nephew), who took his name, thus becoming Big Head II, also known as Friendship Tree (Cómàjè or Comalty/Komalty), and his position in the society (Mooney 1898:392; Parsons 1929:91–92,139). This appears to be the Comalty who lived from 1851 to 1920.

Richardson recorded Old Man Bird Running (Thę̀néhâlqàptầu) and Old Man Frizzlehead as society partners and society leaders. They were succeeded by Black Goose (Chálkǫ́gài) and Big Head and by Tadli'ekoi and Black Horse as society partners and whipmen, and they in turn were succeeded by Eni'ede and Sun Appeared (Fáibâudài). Comalty, who inherited his brother's name and position as a whipman, listed himself as a whipman in the society from 1913 to 1922 (Parsons 1929:xxii, 91–92). Comalty named Red Wolf (Cûigùljè) as another whipman and Poor Bear (Séttáuljè, Thin Bear, Set'tolta, also known as Ahtapety, 1849–1910) and White Bear III (Séttháidé, d. 1894) as the two society leaders.[77] Mooney wrote: "When last met they tried [to] make Adaltonedal [Big Head] and Set-taudlti [also known as Ahtapety] to be chiefs. Paul [Tsaitkopeta had] not joined since returning from [the] east. These two were not Tainpeko when Paul was one."[78]

Parsons (1929:92) listed Kiowa Bill (Máunhḗdè, or No Hand, 1851–1931), Big Bow III (Qá̱hí̱qò̱yì̱, Male Bison Yearling, or Keinkau, also known as Little Bow, 1853–1934), Big Horse (Chḛ́étjè or Jack Bointy, 1868–1927), and Eagleheart (Cújòténjè, also known as John Eagleheart and Topaum, Thóva̱ui, Middle Of The Face or Cheek, 1875–1939) as society leaders in 1927. In his youth, Rueben Topaum remembered dancing the Gourd Dance at Lone Bear Dance Ground with his grandfather John Eagleheart, who carried the society whip in the form of a riding whip. The whip was passed on to Allie Topaum after Eagleheart's death.[79] In addition, a picture of Kiowa Gourd Dancers (circa 1920s) in the Kiowa Tribal Museum depicts Eagleheart in Gourd Dance attire with the whip.[80] Society boy members included Lone Bear (b. 1863), Red Horn (Gṷéngúl, b. 1875), and Paralyzed (Kṓfèqì̱, b. 1880), a partially paralyzed son of Zêbàèlqì̱ (Big Arrows). In 1935, White Fox gave Mwtsa (by then age forty) and K'la/noi (then age fifty) as having been the two boy members.[81]

Post-1890 Activities

The activities of the Já̱ifègàu from 1890 to 1912 are vaguely known. Clyde Ellis (1990:21; see also 1993:367) wrote, "The practice of the Gourd Dance became culturally vital to the Kiowas in the last decade of the nineteenth century when it began to be used as a substitute for the annual Sun Dance." Luke Lassiter (1992) published similar statements. However, several Kiowa accounts contradict these assertions. Frizzlehead II (b. 1860) stated in 1935 that none of the military societies except the Omaha was meeting during the time of the Ghost Dance. Accounts of the Ghost Dance (1890–1917) suggest that the annual encampment functioned largely as an indirect substitute for the Sun Dance (Kracht 1989, 1992). The Ghost Dance was held around the same time of year as the Sun Dance had been, and although not all Kiowa attended the event or accepted the new doctrine, it became the largest annual aggregative religious ritual. In addition, Kiowa calendars indicate that the Já̱ifègàu and Black Legs were revived in the summer of 1912 and thus were inactive from 1890 to 1912, the majority of the Kiowa Ghost Dance period (1890–1917).[82]

Kiowa calendars and oral history again offer historical clarity. Two calendars contain entries depicting the revival of the Já̱ifègàu in 1912. In the Domebo Calendar, the summer entry for 1912 (no. 105) depicts a man with blackened legs standing above a Gourd Dance rattle. Underneath is the description "Ton-Kon-Gah Organize."[83] No form of rattle has ever been associated with Black Legs Society traditions, so the pres-

Kiowa Gourd dancers, about 1915. Left to right: unidentified; possibly Henry Tsoodle Sr.; unidentified; Newton Gouladdle; Enis Haumpo; Fred Botone; Hunting Horse; Blue Jay, also known as Togamote; unidentified, possibly Charley White Horse or Bob Koomsa. Author's collection.

ence of this instrument additionally indicates the revival of the Ją́ifègàu. The Horse Headdresses Society, the only other Kiowa society that used a similar form of rattle, was never revived after 1890.

A similar entry appears in the Ananthy Odlepaugh calendar. The summer entry for 1912 reads, "The first big dance was held at Stinking Creek," and is accompanied by a picture of a Gourd Dance rattle and a multi-tipi encampment. Parker McKenzie, who was born in 1897, said that he knew of no Gourd Dances held during his youth before the "one which was held on Tsoodle's allotment in 1912, and was attended by several wagon loads of Cheyenne who came to visit." Francis Tsonetokoy, born in 1899, also confirmed the absence of Gourd Dances during this period, prior to "the one at Tsoodle's place in 1912."[84] With the end of the Sun Dance in 1890 and the allotment of the Kiowa-Comanche-Apache reservation in 1901, dances shifted to individual allotments. With the general revival of dancing in the early 1900s, Ją́ifègàu dances, like those of other societies, began to be held in association with the Fourth of July. Dances between 1912 and 1928 were held primarily around Carnegie, Oklahoma, on the allotments of Ned Brace, Eagle Heart, Jack Bointy, Henry Tsoodle Sr., and Lone Bear. Dances were also held at Kiowa Bill Maunkee's, near Hobart. Kiowa elders report the attendance and participation of significant contingents of Cheyenne at the dances held on the allotments of Henry Tsoodle Sr. and Navy Paul "George" Tsoodle (a father and son who had adjoining allotments) and that of Kiowa Bill.[85] The sponsoring of dances by different men resembled the earlier practice by which society members sponsored daily meetings before the Sun Dance began.

During the 1920s, the society held several summer dance encampments on Lone Bear's allotment, southeast of Carnegie, Oklahoma. A photograph of one of these dances on July 4, 1921, depicts sixteen men with rattles seated under a brush arbor on the west side of the arena and twenty-six women, some wearing feathered bonnets and carrying lances, standing on the north side of the arena. Many photographs of dances from the 1920s and 1930s show Kiowa women in similar dress. Five singers are seated around a drum in the middle of the arena, and a large American flag hangs from atop a wooden flagpole. The camp consists of a variety of canvas shades, tents, horse-drawn buggies, a covered wagon, and a few automobiles. Consultants who saw dances during these years reported that Brush Dances, traditionally held by societies as part of building the Sun Dance lodge, continued to be held. In the Brush Dance, the singers were followed by the male dancers, then female dancers, and finally by individuals dragging brush. When horses were used to drag the brush, young men rode with their girlfriends behind them, as in the past.[86] The Ananthy Odlepaugh calendar depicts another Gourd Dance held in the summer of 1926 on Jack Bointy's allotment, during which a contingent of visiting Otoe were given gifts. This entry depicts a Gourd dancer underneath a brush arbor. In the 1920s the Kiowa formally gave the Otoe the right to perform the Gourd Dance, and they remain the only non-Kiowa group to have formally received such permission on a tribal-wide basis. During the 1920s and 1930s the Otoe and Kiowa alternated annual visits to each other's home community, where they camped, visited, and participated in Gourd Dances.[87]

Descriptions and photographs of dances from 1917 and 1921 demonstrate that the dress of the society at this time provided the basis for that worn by the Kiowa Gourd Clan today. Buckskin leggings, silk shirts, mescal bean bandoliers, moccasins, otter fur hair wraps, German silver armbands and earrings, and shawls and blankets wrapped around the waist were worn. The red and blue blankets normally associated with the Native American Church during this period are markedly absent. They appeared en masse in the post-1957 Gourd Dance revival.[88]

The last dance held at the Lone Bear dance grounds took place in July 1928. At approximately eight o'clock on the evening of April 19, 1929, a tornado hit the Carnegie area, killing Lone Bear's wife, To-em-ty (Tòiémdè, or Standing Ready To Strike), injuring five other members of the Lone Bear family, and destroying more than sixty houses. The next day To-em-ty's body was found. With the loss of his wife, Lone Bear declared that there would be no more Gourd dancing at that location; to continue would lead to failure. Following this declaration, Kiowa Gourd dancing practically ceased.[89] Oscar Tsoodle, who witnessed the destruction, described how the loss of Lone Bear's wife resulted in the cessation of Gourd dancing at the Lone Bear allotment: "We had a tornado through here. His wife got killed in the storm right here where they danced, Lone Bear's wife. And right then and there he told the elders, my dad and all of them, he said, 'From this day forward there will be no more Gourd dancing there,' because he lost his mate there. And that's the way it just died down."[90]

Although most tribal elders report having seen Jáifègàu dances until 1928, some report smaller, occasional dances until 1938. Alice Marriott attended and documented a large dance at George Tsoodle's home near Carnegie from July 14 to 18, 1937. A large contingent of Otoe who had visited in 1926 on Jack Bointy's allotment, as well as groups of Pawnee, Ponca, and Osage, attended.[91] Although the program focused primarily on fancy War dancing, hand games, and other social dances, a small "Gourd Society" dance was held by some of the remaining elders. As Marriott described it:

> Such members of the old soldier societies as are still living took part in the dancing and served as camp police. The few members of the Gourd Society, for instance, danced on the first day, as was their privilege during the Sun Dance. The camp caller [crier] was a member of the Horse Society, the principal host was a member of the Herders. He was assisted in his hospitality not only by his sons, but by other members of his society.[92]

Participation by members of several societies as well as intrasocietal support for the sponsors was demonstrated. Although Brush Dances were held each afternoon, it was clear that a more mixed program of social dances dominated the activities. The fewer, elder people participated in the older, traditional Gourd Dance, whereas younger people took part in the more modern social dances: "The afternoon dances were primarily for the older people, few of the younger ones taking part. . . . The dances in the evening were largely for the younger people, but a few of the elder men and women took part. Most of the dancers were men."[93] Marriott's fieldnotes also indicate that by 1935 the Kiowa were using the term *gourd* for the rattles of both the Horse Headdresses Society and the Ją́ifègàu, and "Gourd Dance," "Gourd Dancers," and "Gourd Society" for the Ją́ifègàu and their dance.

By 1935 the Ją́ifègàu and the Omaha Society were the only Kiowa societies still meeting. White Fox (1870–1959), although he listed thirty-one Ją́ifègàu members, reported only twenty active members in 1935. All were then elderly men, the oldest of them eighty-four. White Fox was one of the last two whipmen, and Henry Tsoodle Sr., who died in 1941, was one of the last two society leaders. Big Bow III (Qą́hį́qòyì, or Male Bison Yearling, also known as Kein-kau, or Little Bow, 1861–1934) and Bald Face Buffalo (Páuthòcáui, also known as Bo-hay, 1859–1935) were the remaining society leader and whipman, respectively.[94] As Henry Tsoodle Sr. stated in 1936, "None of the old societies are going on now. There are some men who call themselves tampeigo [Ją́ifègàu], but they are not the real members. They are just boys."[95]

A "Gourd Dance of the Tia-pe-ga Society" was performed as part of the National Folk Festival programs in Washington, D.C., in the late 1930s (Bureau of Indian Affairs, Anadarko Agency, letter to M. Pickering, 1938). Elders recall a small society dance held southwest of Carnegie in 1938 that was performed by mostly elderly men. Fred Tsoodle reported that the last dance held at his grandfather's allotment was in 1941, the year Henry Tsoodle Sr. died. As in neighboring tribes, participation in the older, traditional tribal dances such as military society dances was limited primarily to middle-aged or elder men, while the younger generations were attracted to and participated in newer and more social forms of War, Round, and 49 dancing. Following this, Kiowa Gourd dancing is reported to have ceased until 1946.

The Revival of Kiowa Gourd Dancing: The Kiowa Gourd Clan

In 1946 a large celebration was held in the Carnegie City Park for the returning Kiowa World War II veterans. Although the men participated in social and War dancing (Fancy Feather) and the women held Scalp and Victory Dances, participants report that no other forms of dances were held. On Armistice Day 1946, a Gourd Dance is reported to have been held on White Fox's allotment, west of Carnegie, to honor returning World War II veterans and celebrate the end of the war. At least two events sparked the eventual revival of Kiowa Jáifègàu traditions and the Gourd Dance, one in 1942 and the other in 1955. During an Armistice Day encampment held by the Carnegie Victory Club in the Carnegie City Park in November 1942, Bill Koomsa Sr. was lying under an arbor on a pallet singing old Gourd Dance songs for his own pleasure. Mrs. Henry Tsoodle Sr. (1874–1951) became so emotionally moved that she began crying and came over and gave him a gift of money, telling him that "it made her feel so good to hear them singing, to hear the old songs."[96]

The return of World War II and Korean War veterans necessitated honor dances, which reinvigorated and increased the frequency of honor dances and powwows. Fred Tsoodle remembered a dance that was held for him upon his return home from the war: "[in] 1945 I came back and what got me was when I got back they were dancing. They had a dance for me, a special down there at Carnegie, but they didn't do any Gourd Dance and I couldn't understand what was going on, I mean it was all just War Dance, no Gourd dancing."[97] With the widespread postwar resurgence of Indian culture, ethnic pride, and political and social rights, the time was ripe for a cultural revival among the Kiowa. One Kiowa woman recalled two or three small dances that were held between 1954 and 1957 on the allotment of Kosan, just south of White Fox's, west of Carnegie. The dancers were mostly elder men.

By 1955, talk of reviving the dance had emerged, but no formal effort to do so had been made. As Fred Tsoodle explained, "So anyhow they had a dance for me and everything like that and after that they was trying to start something. They was trying to start the Gourd Dance. Seemed like they could not get it going. So Peggy and I, we sat down and we talked about it and I said, 'Let's present it at the fair!'"[98]

In August 1955, Fred Tsoodle was serving as the Kiowa tribal director for the American Indian Exposition. Every year each tribe was asked to prepare a short performance to represent its culture in the Tuesday evening program known as Tribal Night, a competition that was judged for an annual award. Tsoodle, who had grown up seeing Gourd Dances on his grandfather Henry Tsoodle Sr.'s allotment, began making plans to present the dance. He planned to present the dance as traditionally as possible, as he had seen it as the 1930s. He called together prominent Kiowa men who were knowledgeable about the dance, knew how to dress traditionally, and still wore their hair in braids. Great efforts were also made to acquire traditional, older-style buckskin clothing for the performance. Some clothes were borrowed from families, often after having been packed away in old trunks and not used for many years. Others were bought from local pawnshops to which people had sold items. As Peggy Tsoodle recalled, "One or two were reluctant because they said, you know, it really wasn't a show, you know, meant to be shown. Fred explained to them that the people need to see it, so they agreed to it."[99]

In full dress, Clyde Ahtape, Harry Hall Zotigh, Fred Botone, J. O. Tanedooah, and Able Big Bow performed the Gourd Dance at the 1955 American Indian Exposition while Bill Koomsa Sr. and William (Cornbread) Tanedooah sang and drummed. The presentation was reportedly so emotionally moving that it produced "tears and soft crying" among the elder spectators. Fred Tsoodle recalled, "It got silent, sort of quiet. It was just a short time, they limited us to only two songs. A hush came over the grandstand and you could hear the women crying. They were crying. They knew it, but they hadn't seen it, the Gourd Dance, because it hadn't been performed in so long. . . . It hit those people and that's where the beginning was."[100] Although sporadic small dances had been held in the 1930s and early 1940s, many spectators were unfamiliar with the dance.

This event rekindled a flame that led to the revival of the Gourd Dance among the Kiowa within two years (Kiowa Gourd Clan 1976:22). Daugomah, James Honey-Ho Haumpy, White Fox, James Littlechief, Harry Hokeah, Leonard Cozad, Rogers Tofpi, Quay Tonemah, and others soon joined in (Poolaw 1981). Efforts to revive the dance were publicly acknowledged during a meeting in 1955. By 1956 plans to revive the society were under way by a group of Kiowa, many of whom were descendants of White Bear and who still knew some of the society songs. Singing practices began to be held at Sam Satepauhoodle's home near Carnegie.[101] These activities led to the formal revival of the Jáifègàu under the name Kiowa Gourd Clan on January 30, 1957. Another presentation of the Kiowa Gourd Dance was reportedly held at the 1957 exposition. In 1958 the Kiowa Gourd and Black Legs Dances were two of eighteen tribal dances presented in the American Indian Exposition pageant, entitled "The Song of the Redman" (AIEB 1958). However, it would be the symbolic importance of the songs and not the dance itself that formed the foundation for the society's revival.

Music

Current Kiowa Gourd Dance music is a mixture of Jáifègàu, Mountain Sheep, Horse Headdresses, and Dog Society songs, at least one Black Legs Society Song, and Brush Dance, Sweat Lodge, Sun Dance, Ghost Dance, Buffalo Dance, and numerous individual family songs.[102] At the time of the revival, a relatively limited body of society songs remained, most of which had no lyrics. Since 1957 many old songs have had lyrics put to them, and many new songs, both with and without lyrics, have been composed. Those featuring lyrics reference a wide variety of topics, including the Jáifègàu, the Sun Dance, past society leaders (notably White Bear), the world wars, the importance of songs, elements of Kiowa family histories, and Kiowa elders. For songs with lyrics, there are often several versions that vary slightly in content but are generally similar in overall meaning. These variations stem largely from differences in the ways the songs were taught. I found several such cases when I compared song texts collected in 1935 with the versions sung by Kiowa singers today.

Songs with lyrics may be sung with or without the lyrics, depending on who is leading the song and on the context of the dance and level of spirit involved at a particular time. More often than not, Gourd Dance songs are sung without their lyrics, because of factors of possessiveness, family ownership, and concern for correct pronunciation and meaning. Often, lyrics are not sung unless there is a special reason for doing so, such as a request for a family song. In such instances, an elder singer at the drum often explains the reason for singing the song, its history, and the meaning of the lyrics before the song is sung, to prevent a potential conflict (Lassiter 1998:170–171). At annual celebrations like the Kiowa Gourd Clan ceremonials, this restriction is much more relaxed, and songs are generally sung with their lyrics, often even without being requested.[103] Because so many different tribes now perform the Gourd Dance, the inclusion of Kiowa lyrics may initially present a problem for an intertribal group of singers.

One Gourd Dance song with lyrics addresses the positive feelings associated with the dance. This song was originally from another society and was brought into the Kiowa Gourd Clan in the late 1950s by William Tanedooah, who put new words to it. Today this song is known as the Tanedooah Family Song:

> Jáifègàu ém ǫ́-tâ-gûn-màu
> (Jáifègàu / they / feel good-dancing-be)
> The Jáifègàu are dancing and feeling good.[104]

Another version of this song is one of the most commonly heard Gourd Dance songs with lyrics:

> Jáifègàu há-bé ǫ́-tâ-gûn-jàu
> (Jáifègàu / at some future time / feel good-dancing-shall be)
> The Jáifègàu, they shall be dancing because they feel good.[105]

Several Mountain Sheep and Horse Headdresses Society songs, which are similar in composition, have been adopted or changed since the 1957 revival and serve to keep alive the memory of these societies. As singer Bill Koomsa Jr. described it: "Them clans [military societies], you know they're all about forgotten and some songs that sound very similar, they change them and put them into the Gourd Dance now." Some old Brush Dance songs, which are described as "real peppy," have also been mixed in with other Gourd Dance songs.[106] One elder singer described the innovation involved in creating new songs:

> There were words added to some songs. Some of the older songs got words put into them and then some of them are just new songs. At one time my dad told me that there were just so many songs and after you sang them, if you sang them

over, you know, there was nothing you could do about it, that's all there were. But anymore, there's been a lot of new songs that have been made and sung. Some of them are good songs. It's just like any other dance, they are making some of the songs.[107]

The role of music in the revival of the Kiowa Gourd Dance is of great significance in understanding the importance of the dance to the Kiowa. Between 1890 and 1957 the music underwent several active and inactive periods (Goldstein 1972:62–67; Lassiter 1995). Although the Jáifègàu and the Gourd Dance were largely dormant between 1890 and 1912, the songs were still known by people upon whom the later revival of the dance would depend. Following a period of renewed activity from 1912 to 1928, Gourd Dances and their songs again became increasingly inactive. In time, fewer persons retained the songs. The scarcity of dances between 1928 and 1957 and the decline of active elder participants threatened to end the dance. As in the Black Legs' revival in 1958, a limited number of people who had participated in the dances from 1912 to the late 1930s were sought out for their remaining knowledge of Gourd Dance songs, ending this second period of semi-dormancy. It was during this period that pivotal musical changes occurred as the songs began to develop a significance separate from the associated dance of the society's earlier tradition. Thus, whereas the dance largely ceased, the songs retained their coherence (Lassiter 1992:35–36).

Significant in the revival of the dance was that the elders who still knew the songs had received them directly from the last generation to experience pre-reservation culture. They in turn passed them on to the World War II generation, whose members had no direct relationship to this nineteenth-century lifestyle, except through the history of the songs. The "performative responsibility" of those possessing knowledge to perform the dance (see Lassiter 1992, 1995) shifted from the nineteenth-century men's military society to the participants in dances in the 1920s and 1930s. Although the songs and their meanings changed, they nevertheless continued. This relationship was central in reviving the Kiowa Gourd Dance. Gourd Dance and other incorporated songs that formed the core of the revival were the very songs the younger people's grandparents had sung and danced to. Because dancers depend on singers in order to dance, it was the songs more than the form of choreography that formed the foundation of the Kiowa Gourd Dance revival. A similar basis of events associated with inactivity, song retention, and reactivation underlay the subsequent revival of the Black Legs Society in 1958 and the revival of the children's Rabbits Society through the Kiowa Gourd Clan (Meadows 1991, 1995).

As defined by Bruno Nettl (1985:26; and see Lassiter 1998), "the combination of style elements from diverse parts of a native repertory into a musical style with broadened cultural significance in the face of Western contact" is known as "consolidation." Nettle wrote that consolidation "has occurred often as a function of the creation of nation-states from what once were groups of politically separate entities, tribes, chiefdoms, kingdoms, or of the change of a people from independence to colonized minority. The establishment of a reasonably compact and, in terms of musical energy, not very demanding North American Indian style to replace what was once a large variety of tribal repertoires is an example" (1983:352).[108] In light of the events leading to the post–World War II cultural and political revivals, the Kiowa Gourd Dance, by consolidating varied types of songs, became one rallying point for Kiowa song revival in general. Songs maintained in the Gourd Dance became the most public forum for the expression of several now defunct military societies and religious forms. The children's Rabbits Society has similarly consolidated several types of children's songs into its current repertoire.

Facilitating the separation of music from dance and the dissemination of cultural forms has been the growing use of tape-recorders and broadcasts of Indian music over local radio stations. One early example was Don Whistler's "Indians for Indians Hour," a radio broadcast that first aired in April 1941 on WNAD at the University of Oklahoma.[109] New technologies provided a means to spread music throughout the Kiowa and intertribal community and to encourage others to learn and preserve musical traditions. Although many younger people were not singing the old songs, many people enjoyed listening to them, and by 1946 some seventy-five thousand Native Americans throughout Oklahoma were regularly listening to the "Indians for Indian Hour" (Hatton 1989:59).

Today the Kiowa tribe produces an hour-long live musical program entitled "Indians for Indians" every Saturday morning on KRPT AM 850 in Anadarko, Oklahoma, on which Kiowa Gourd Dance music is frequently performed.[110] Members of many tribes listen to this program regularly for its live music, news, and dance announcements. With the revival of the Gourd Dance through the Kiowa Gourd Clan, the relationship between the music and the dance was reestablished. Radio programs and audiotape recorders enabled music to develop a new and distinct significance that was entirely separate from its former intimate association with dance, in which it was limited largely to live performances. Kiowa who obtained reel-to-reel and later cassette recorders began making recordings of themselves and others for personal use. Some people have amassed large audiotape collections of Kiowa songs. These practices continue and have helped in both the preservation and diffusion of various forms of music. Since the early 1960s, Indian House Records and Canyon Records have produced commercial records, cassette tapes, and more recently, compact discs of Kiowa music. As with other Kiowa military societies, if a handful of elders had not retained the songs, there most likely would be no Gourd Dance today, at least not in terms of the historical and symbolic continuity with the past that these songs and the dance hold for many people (Lassiter 1992:37).

Leadership

On January 30, 1957, a meeting was held at the home of Taft Hainta, and an association was formally organized, voted on, and adopted under the name Kiowa Gourd

Clan. As Fred Tsoodle explained, "Well, we picked it, you know, when we was at this meeting. And we said, 'What should we call it?' you know. So we said we had different names, and we could've called it in the Kiowa, Jáifègàu, we could've called it that. But somebody said, 'How would you spell it?' you know. So we said, let's have it Kiowa Gourd Clan, so we voted and that's the name we took."[111] From this point the Jáifègàu and its dance were redefined and became officially known as the Gourd Dance. Several tribal elders, including former society members White Fox, Henry Tsoodle Jr., the three brothers Daugomah, and William and Henry Tanedooah, selected the new officers for the organization. Sam Satepauhoodle, Rogers Tofpi, Quay Tonemah, James Honey-Ho Haumpy, George Tsoodle, and other elders were also involved in the revival. Daugomah's son-in-law Taft Hainta was selected as president of the organization. The other original Gourd Clan officers were Bill Koomsa Sr., vice president; Moses Botone, treasurer; James Auchiah, secretary; Henry Tsoodle Jr., historian; Joseph Kaulaity, advisor, and Henry Tanedooah, spokesman (Kiowa Gourd Clan 1976:22; Poolaw 1981:2).

Originally the society had no female members. In 1957, Tomascine Tsoodle was the Kiowa princess for the American Indian Exposition. The following year the Gourd Clan elected her to serve as Gourd Clan princess, and James Henry Tsoodle and Moses Botone danced with her at the Gourd Clan annual ceremonial. In her honor, her father, Oscar Tsoodle, in 1957 began pledging a beef to the Gourd Clan every year; later he increased the pledge to two beeves a year. The princess position was established for life or until Tsoodle retired and passed it on to someone else.[112]

Some Kiowa state that their elders initially advised them not to elect officers but simply to keep the dance open to all Kiowa, believing that leadership positions would lead to conflict and be a potential source of fission in the society. Many Kiowa elders maintain that the installation of officers for life terms and the competition and jealousy over a small number of leadership positions immediately created factions in the newly revived society and ultimately caused the breakup of the Gourd Clan. When I asked the reason behind the split, one former Gourd Clan officer said, "Everybody wanted to be chief . . . that's what happened. . . . I don't care what kind of organization you've got, there's gonna be somebody who's not gonna agree and everything like that, and just like a little old kid he's gonna run off and that's it. And that's what happened, see. I hated to see that because they're all my kinfolks." Other elders also referenced this problem, saying, "Everyone wants to be the chief, no one wants to be just an Indian anymore." That is, too many wanted to be leaders and not just supportive members. Pervasive factionalism resulting from dissatisfaction with existing leadership structures and competition to acquire subsequent leadership continues in many Plains Indian communities.

In 1958, Bill Koomsa Sr. resigned his position as vice president and was replaced by Oscar Tsoodle, who remained in that office until he retired in 1985, when he named his nephew Fred Tsoodle as his replacement. Oscar Tsoodle continued as an advisor to the Kiowa Gourd Clan until his death in 2000. Taft Hainta remained president until his death in September 1990. After Hainta's passing, an election was requested by Vice President Fred Tsoodle and Secretary Glenn Hamilton. It was held on Thanksgiving weekend in 1990; Glen Hamilton defeated Fred Tsoodle and was installed as the new Gourd Clan leader in July 1991. Citing health problems, Fred Tsoodle requested that Curtis Horse replace him as vice president. James Auchiah resigned his position as treasurer after one year and was replaced by Joe Kaulaity, who has since been succeeded by his brother Henry's grandson Walter Kaulaity.[113]

Upon Hamilton's installation as president in 1991, he named Gary Kodaseet as the new secretary (Kiowa Gourd Clan 1996:7). From 1991 to 2004, Gourd Clan officers included Glenn Hamilton, president; Curtis Horse, vice president; Gary Kodaseet, secretary; and Walter Kaulaity, treasurer. In 2004, Tim Tsoodle was installed as vice president in place of Curtis Horse, who resigned for health reasons, and Jesse Kaulaity was installed as the Gourd Clan whipman to succeed his father, Adam, who had passed away in 2003. There are indications that earlier attempts to revive the dance between the 1946 Armistice Day dance and the 1957 revival were prevented because of a personal rivalry between Taft Hainta and Bill Koomsa Sr., both of whom were descendants of White Bear, which undoubtedly strengthened their potential as society leaders.[114]

Although no standardized form of recruiting existed at this time, participation increased as more and more Kiowa, many of whom were descendants of earlier society members, began to join the Gourd Clan. The first celebration of the revived society was held at the Carnegie City Park during the 1957 Fourth of July weekend. Whereas the sodality had functioned as a warrior society before 1890, its purpose and function were clearly redefined at this time, with a new focus on the promotion of Kiowa ethnicity and cultural heritage through a conscious effort to maintain and strengthen both Kiowa culture and Jáifègàu traditions through the Kiowa Gourd Clan. The Kiowa Gourd Clan ceremonials booklet (1976:22) states, "The purpose and function of this organization was to perpetuate our Indian Heritage and to revive the Kiowa dance as near as possible from the past original ceremonies." Symbolic of the pre-reservation era and the group's role as a prominent military society, several well-known society war trophies were incorporated into the Gourd Clan ceremonial, including feathered lances, a bugle, and a lariat (Kiowa Gourd Clan 1976:22). Member's families soon pledged beeves to support the next year's celebration and money for the Kiowa Native American Church.

Societal Themes

The Kiowa Gourd Clan and the Gourd Dance emphasize several themes, including preservation and upholding of Kiowa cultural heritage and Jáifègàu and martial traditions, respect and appropriate dress for the dance, and the memory of elders. The attention given to preserving Kiowa cultural heritage, the Gourd Dance, and the memory of ancestors is prominently visible in the Gourd Dance. Numerous Kiowa have described to me the great emphasis placed on remembering elders and commemorating past Kiowa heritage through the Gourd Dance songs, dancing, camping together in the old fashion, "taking care of visitors" (feeding and showing hospitality to guests), and general fellowship. One member stated that the songs, dances, rituals, and prayers were the most important part of the organization, stressing that there were many prayers offered at various times throughout the years. These older traditions remain a significant part of Gourd Clan and Gourd Dance traditions.

Elevated social status has also continued to be an important feature of the Gourd Clan. Some Kiowa maintain that Gourd Clan members see themselves as socially more important than others and that the organization also serves as a de facto social and political network. When I asked one society member what he thought the Gourd Clan represented for Kiowa people, he replied, "To me it's more of a class-social thing. If you belong, if you dance, if you participate, then that raises your status a little in the tribe and the class structure. To me it's more of a social [thing]."[115]

The 1957 revival of the dance unquestionably redefined it as a broader expression of Kiowa ethnic identity, with a decreased focus on the martial or military society aspect (Lassiter 1998:243). Yet distinct elements of Jáifègàu traditions and frequent acknowledgment of veterans remain. One Gourd Clan member explained: "I was also inducted into the Gourd Clan, but I've had a lot of personal issues with that, you know, the structure of it and all that, and I haven't been as active as I could and should be. . . . The Gourd Clan is not a veterans' organization like the Black Leggings is. The Black Leggings is a true warrior's dance. Now as it's observed today, the Gourd Clan was at one time but that has changed, and that's one of the issues that I have with it."[116]

Despite the post-1957 redefinition, and contrary to Lassiter's findings (1995:254, 289), both elder and younger consultants indicate that elements of both past Jáifègàu and present Kiowa cultural traditions are of conscious importance to members and are currently stressed. Some elders make strong Jáifègàu and martial associations with the dance, what it stands for, and the way people should act while in the arena. Harry Tofpi explained that when he returned from the Korean War, he was welcomed home, "just like in the old days—songs, dances, prayers. They had a big Gourd Dance for me. I talked about what I had done in combat, just like those guys did a long time ago" (Ellis 2003:23). World War II veteran Scott Tonemah said that the revived Gourd Dance "reminded Kiowas of the importance of warriors and their obligation to protect and defend their people" (Ellis 2003:23). Christopher Glazner (2002:62) reported that during the honoring of a female Kiowa Marine at the July Fourth, 2002, Gourd Clan celebrations, "the M.C. took the microphone and announced above the song, 'This is what it means to be Kiowa. We are proud of our Kiowa soldiers who risk their lives for us every day. We are proud of these Kiowa ways God has given us. We are KIOWA and we are still here! Aho!'" The addition of Vernon Tsoodle's Marine Corps saber to the society's trophies also acknowledged the role of modern military service. Although general Kiowa cultural traditions are perhaps more visible in the Gourd Dance than many past Jáifègàu traditions, the latter are by no means obsolete.[117]

Several elders I interviewed stressed the martial origins stemming from the nineteenth-century society as well as the importance of maintaining Kiowa culture. It is important to recognize that just as songs, ownership, and other elements of the dance are contested and interpreted differently, so are individual and group emphases concerning the origin of the society, as well as the associated degree of former society characteristics. Some Kiowa continue to attribute strong military links to the present Gourd Dance societies, whereas others do not. Several current Gourd Dance songs directly reference the association of the dance with its ancestral military society through the inclusion of the name Jáifègàu in their lyrics. Although veteran status is no longer the basis for membership, the society's history, the continued stewardship of society trophies, the use of the name Jáifègàu in speech and songs, and other customs point toward the need to recognize this diversity of current foci. The Kiowa Black Legs Society, widely regarded as a military society, and the Ohoma Lodge, a War Dance society, are firmly associated with the maintenance of many of the same Kiowa traditions.

When asked the purpose of the Kiowa Gourd Clan, Bill Koomsa Jr., who is often the head singer at Gourd Clan ceremonials, said:

> The Kiowa Gourd Clan, they're thinking of their ancestors, and we try to carry on what they left us, what they showed and what they left us. . . . People always say, "We're trying the best we can." There's nobody to look up to anymore, they're all gone, so we're going to do the best we can, how we're doing it, that's the best we can do. We don't have anybody to tell us anymore, they're all gone, which is true, you know, there's even a song that says that. We got a certain song that says, "Where have all the Kiowas gone? Where are they? The only thing they left us was these songs."

The song he referred to has the following lyrics:

1. Cáui-qá-còm-bàu há-yá á hái-ài
   (Kiowas / where or to some place / they / went on or proceeded us)
   Where have all of the Kiowa gone?
2. Dáu-gà jé-kúi dâu tái-dò
   (Songs / all / they-to us / left [i.e., staying or remain with])
   All they have left us are these songs.[118]

Although many original Kiowa Gourd Clan members were veterans of World War II and Korea, and the society continues to count many veterans among its members, military service is not required for membership, as it is in the Black Legs Society. Similarly to induction changes in the late 1800s, membership is now based largely on Kiowa concepts of individual and family social status and the positive attributes that an individual can bring to the society. As one elder put it, "Even the Gourd Clan now, they kind of recruit them, not only veterans, but anyone they think can help the club, in other words. That's the way they recruit anymore . . . they always recruit four or five guys a year. . . . Anymore it's just more or less if they are from a pretty outstanding family or he's done something worth honoring, I guess you'd say."[119]

Despite its aspects that reflect martial and past Jáifègàu traditions, the Gourd Clan is clearly no longer structured as a military society. Although non-Indian participation in singing, dancing, and membership is prohibited, the Gourd Clan has occasionally inducted members of other tribes, some of whom are married to Kiowa. Yet the Kiowa Gourd Clan is undeniably a Kiowa-based organization that frequently and publicly espouses the maintenance of Kiowa ethnicity and traditions. Elders regularly indicate the need to show respect for the dance by maintaining an all-Kiowa drum during ceremonials, dressing appropriately, and prohibiting non-Indian participation. Non-Indians who have attempted to sing or dance have promptly been asked to leave the arena.

Dress

At first notice, contemporary Gourd Dance clothing bears little resemblance to that of the past. It reflects a syncretic blend of Kiowa, Jáifègàu, Native American Church, and pan-Indian dress styles that vary with the resources available to individual dancers. A conservative and respectful dress code is a major tenet of the Kiowa Gourd Clan, serving as a source of pride and dignity as well as one means of differentiating itself from other Gourd Dance societies. Elders often emphatically and publicly state that respect for the dance must be shown by "wearing respectable clothing," such as moccasins, traditional Kiowa apparel, and a roach, an otter cap, or no headgear at all. Long pants and long-sleeve shirts with moccasins or dress shoes are also considered appropriate for those without traditional Kiowa clothing. The Kiowa Gourd Clan considers jeans, cutoffs, cowboy boots, tennis shoes, ball caps, and cowboy hats inappropriate, whereas they are commonly seen at some other Kiowa Gourd Dances and those of neighboring tribes. Although the Kiowa Gourd Clan strongly emphasizes a dress code, the dress of some younger members varies, and a few have been verbally reprimanded by elders.[120]

Oscar Tsoodle spoke of the importance associated with looking presentable in public and respecting the society:

> The elders told us. When you're going to get out there and dance, look presentable, look your best. Put your regalia on. If you have buckskin leggins and buckskin shoes, put them on. Look presentable. And don't wear a hat. . . . And always shave, and get a good haircut, or braids. Look presentable, that's what it is, because you're out there dancing and people are going to see you. . . . Don't get out there dirty. Uphold the dance, enjoy it, and at least respect the organization.[121]

Bill Koomsa Jr., one of the most highly respected Kiowa singers, similarly stressed the emphasis on appropriate dress for the Gourd Dance:

When you're the center of attraction, when you're in the center, you better be dressed up. That's one of the codes I try to stress whenever I'm head singer. I don't allow anybody with sleeveless shirts on. I frown upon that. There is some other tribes, you know, that do that ... but we're representing our group and we try to dress up, you know, proper. When we go to the drum, we try to dress up a little. That's one of the things that our people always taught us, when you're—they say, Dǫ́gà à hòtgôm—when you're in the center, when you're within the dancing arena, you should be properly dressed, you know. And that's something I try to follow.... Just be presentable, that's what we stress.[122]

James Howard (1976:249–50) described the typical contents of Oklahoma Gourd Dance clothing. Few Native Americans, however, dress in complete sets of traditional clothing for Gourd dancing today. Although appropriate dress is essential, and a set of traditional dance clothes is highly valued, the Kiowa place more emphasis on participation, community, meaning, and the "spirit" of the songs and dance than on how fancy a person's set of clothing is—a distinction that many Anglos and Anglo hobbyists fail to recognize or understand. Many Kiowa state that the practicality of the modern style of Gourd Dance clothes is a Native economic adaptation that enabled many people with limited incomes to participate. It must be remembered that a dancer's outfit is largely dependent on his available funds and the number of craftspeople in his family. One man remarked, "Not everyone can afford to be dólbé [showily or well dressed]." Throughout Oklahoma, most dancers wear standard contemporary Gourd Dance apparel over their everyday clothing. This apparel usually includes a rattle of the salt shaker variety, a tail or loose feather fan, a two-string bandolier of mescal beans and silver metal beads, a red and blue wool trade cloth blanket worn over the shoulders, a fringed and beaded waist sash commemorating earlier cavalry waist sashes, and personal jewelry. Although some dancers still wear moccasins, boots and dress shoes are common. Only rarely, usually at some of the annual celebrations, do a few dancers wear entire sets of Indian clothes for the Gourd Dance.

Several items of post-1957 Gourd Dance dress were borrowed from the Native American Church. In photographs of Kiowa Gourd Dances from before 1930, one sees a notable absence of the red and blue blankets that became a standard part of Gourd Dance dress after the 1957 revival. Red and blue blankets (kǫ́hą́ubáup [s], kǫ́hą́ubá [d/t], lit. "dark") date to the 1850s on the southern plains as a high-status luxury trade item, acquired and made by prominent families. Such blankets can be seen in Kiowa ledgerbook drawings from the 1870s and 1880s. Later, with the introduction and growth of peyotism (roughly post-1885 for the Kiowa; see La Barre 1938; Stewart 1987) and the Native American Church (post-1918), the blankets became a regular part of church dress. Similarly, the use of gourd versus metal rattles in the contemporary Gourd Dance is disputed by some, who feel that gourd rattles should be used only in the Native American Church, and metal salt shaker rattles in the Gourd Dance.

Upon the revival of the Gourd Dance, many Gourd Clan members who were also

Native American Church members brought red and blue blankets into the Gourd Dance, where they became a standard item of dress that has continued. Although now worn by nearly all dancers, some elders have expressed disapproval of the wearing of red and blue blankets in the Gourd Dance. One man stated, "It has no place in the Gourd Dance, it belongs to the [Native American] church." Older generations of Kiowa frequently wore sheets that they used for various purposes by tying them up to carry firewood, groceries, and personal belongings. Consequently, many old photographs of Kiowa and Kiowa Jáifègàu dancers depict men wearing white sheets (thą́imáu [s]; thą́i [d/t]) around their waists.

As Oscar Tsoodle, a long time Gourd Clan officer and a Native American Church leader, explained it:

> That red and blue blanket is in the Native American Church [NAC]. It's not supposed to be worn in the Gourd Dance. The Gourd Dancers are supposed to wear a white sheet.... The elders call it pure. It's pure, it's white, you know. But the NAC people, when they go into worship, they wear them red and blue blankets. And you always want to wear the red to the right.... And you must remember you wear the red to the right, representing the blood of life. They always say that, this is life right here to your right, at daylight. 'Cause the sun's coming up, it's red, and the blue means that the sun is going down, that's the reason why. The red is always over to the right because you meet the day, you know, just like that, and at the same time you're looking for good life, you're going, it represents the blood.[123]

Tsoodle also explained that in using red and blue blankets in the Gourd Dance, one is always fighting the blanket and adjusting it as it slides around, whereas with a waist sheet one's hands are free for holding the dance rattle and fan. The wool blankets also get hot when draped over one's neck in dancing. Recently, more men have been wearing a smaller red and blue "waist" blanket, worn like a sash around the waist, in place of the larger shoulder type.

Other Kiowa similarly stated that Native American Church "priests" or "roadmen" wear this type of blanket. Still others have argued that because the Gourd Dance and the use of various types of sheets and blankets precede the peyote and later Native American Church religion, they are appropriate to use in the Gourd Dance. Some Kiowa consider the red portion of the blanket symbolic of blood spilled by past Kiowa warriors. Nevertheless, the red and blue blankets, mescal bean bandoleers, and Native American Church–related jewelry such as German silver waterbird pins and "loose" or "peyote feather fans" have been redefined and placed within a whole host of new social and ritual contexts that are now trademarks of Kiowa and intertribal Gourd Dance apparel.[124]

The Current Gourd Clan Ceremonial

In order to convey the importance of the Kiowa Gourd Dance and some of what it means to the Kiowa people, I next describe the Gourd Dance ceremonial as it takes place today.

After the first thunder of each spring, the Gourd Clan officers meet to choose a date for their annual pilgrimage, usually the last Sunday in March. The Kiowa Ten Medicine Bundle keepers are contacted, and visits to their homes are arranged. Some keepers currently care for more than one bundle, and some bundles are brought to the residence of another keeper for this day. A contingent of Gourd Clan officers, members, and others travel to visit, offer prayers, give thanks, and leave offerings at the site of the Kiowa Táimé Bundle, the primary bundle in the Kiowa Sun Dance, and each of the Kiowa tribal medicine bundles. This constitutes "a pilgrimage to the sacred places of the religion of their ancestors to 'renew' their right to perform this dance for the coming year, and for the successful gathering of the people" (Kiowa Gourd Clan 1996:7).[125]

> The pilgrimage is made by the leaders and recently, in trying to keep the Kiowa heritage from being lost, other members have been allowed to participate in this spiritual journey. Prayers are offered at different locations and sites known only to Kiowas. The prayers are made to the Great Spirit thanking him for guiding the Kiowas and other peoples through the year and asking him for another safe and plentiful year for the Kiowas and also for the Kiowa Gourd Clan. (Kiowa Gourd Clan 1996:15)

One Kiowa woman described the 1999 pilgrimage to me. Out of respect for the bundles and their keepers, I have omitted their names and exact locations. Starting early in the morning, the delegation made four stops, including one in Anadarko, two near Carnegie, and a final one near Hobart. Although the Gourd Clan officers and a few others completed the entire set of visits in the pilgrimage, many people attended only one bundle visitation, so the size of the contingent fluctuated from one stop to the next. One woman estimated that the contingent averaged fifteen to thirty people. Each bundle or group of bundles was placed out in view, and the owner's house was made ready for the visiting contingent. At each home the men entered the room containing the bundle or bundles first. When the men had finished, the Gourd Clan headmen remained, and the women entered as a group. Each person was allowed to go up to the bundle, where they could pray or ask for help or a blessing and then leave virtually any form of offering they chose.[126] At the first stop, several women entered wearing strips of calico cloth across their backs and shoulders that were left as offerings. Offerings of tobacco and money were made at each stop and were the most common forms of offerings. After the last stop and visitation, a meal was served to all in attendance. Many groups and societies hold cedarings after the first thunder in the spring, but the Kiowa Gourd Clan is the only group that makes a pilgrimage to the Kiowa medicine bundles.[127]

The annual Kiowa Gourd Clan ceremonial is held July 2–4 at the Carnegie City Park in Carnegie, Oklahoma. In preparation for each annual celebration, three monthly benefit dances are held, in March, April, and May, to raise funds. In 1993, one Gourd Clan officer reported that around $8,000 a year was needed to sponsor the annual encampment and provide rations for all the campers. A cedaring ceremony, usually held in February at the Kiowa Tribal Elders Center, is conducted for all Gourd Clan members, their families, or anyone who has lost a loved one during the past year. At each benefit dance a meal is held, for which the society furnishes the meat, and members' families and others bring covered dishes, desserts, and drinks.[128]

About two weeks before the annual July ceremonial, usually on a Saturday, members assemble at the Carnegie City Park with trucks and tools to clean and repair the grounds and to build an arbor around the dance arena. The members' wives provide a lunch. Although the ceremonial lasts for three days, many members set up camp several days in advance and may remain to visit for one or two days after the dancing ends. The encampment is not associated with the celebration of American independence, but because of the practicality the Fourth of July holiday presents for people who work, it is used as an occasion to gather. As Oscar Tsoodle stated on July 4, 1991, "This is not a Fourth of July celebration. The occurrence is due to free time from jobs. We are in no way promoting or celebrating the American Fourth of July."[129] Martha Poolaw described the symbolic role of the annual encampment and ceremonial: "It is the Kiowa Homecoming, July Fourth. . . . It is more or less the homecoming dance for the Kiowa people, without calling it a homecoming."[130]

The annual celebration is replete with symbols of the old Sun Dance and Ja̧ifègàu military society ceremonies, and analogies between past and present activities are easily made. The dance is held at approximately the same time of year that the Sun Dance once was. It continues the use of a large, circular arbor that is indirectly similar to the Sun Dance arbor built by military societies in the past. Brush, Gourd, Rabbit, War, and social dances all relate to activities that were originally focused on the period of socialization that culminated with the annual Sun Dance. Since the revival of the Gourd Dance in 1957, many families have maintained individual camping locations at the annual encampment. Although this practice resembles that of assigned camping units during the Sun Dance era, I have found no correlation between these arrangements and any earlier band formations, and little evidence of relationships to later reservation communities. Personal custom and kinship and marriage ties with the camps of elders appear to determine camp selection more than any other factors. Although communal hunts are no longer held, society members distribute rations every morning during the encampment. As in the case of individually sponsored feasts in the past, pledges of money and beef provide resources for these meals.

Atwater Onco commented on the analogy between the contemporary Gourd Clan encampment and the old Sun Dance, the Gourd Clan's emphasis on maintaining Kiowa ethnicity, and the continued association with the original society name:

It's not a Sun Dance . . . but this summer gathering over there, it goes to show that were still trying to get the Kiowas together once a year, to be Kiowas, to live like Kiowas, to fellowship and go around and visit, and just have a great time like Kiowas. That's why we have the Kiowa Gourd Clan. It's strictly Kiowa. A lot of Kiowa talking. Its strictly Kiowa, singers, everything, dancers, you've got to be Kiowa to dance there. . . . At least once a year we keep it Kiowa and show other people that it is a Kiowa dance. That's the reason of it, the Jáifè.[131]

The Gourd Clan encampment is situated on a low floodplain along the Washita River that is shaded with large cottonwood trees. During the encampment, many Kiowa set up tipis and wall tents around the circular dance area in the center. On the evening of July 1, all head staff are called to a meeting during which rules and protocol are stressed, especially concerning the maintenance of a proper dress code. Each morning, activities begin around six o'clock, with a devotional and a flag-raising ceremony. In some years, a camp crier (óèljòqî, "big-voiced talker") such as Evans Ray Satepauhoodle either walks or rides a horse around the encampment announcing the news verbally. Recently, the use of a public address system has become more common. Around nine o'clock in the morning, rations are distributed to the entire encampment. The food is acquired through donations and pledges of money or food from the previous year's dance and is distributed daily to each camp to use in feeding members and visitors. At ten o'clock, the leader of the Rabbits Society, informally known as Grandpa Rabbit, calls (with the help of either a camp crier or a public address system) for the children to gather in the arena for the Rabbit Dances. The Rabbits gather near the master of ceremonies' stand in the arena, where they are given trash bags to use as they rapidly clean the dance grounds of all debris. After this public service the children are led in a parade around the inside of the arena, and then songs are played for them to dance to. Finally they are rewarded with treats and invited to eat lunch at a sponsor's family camp (see chapter 1).

Around eleven o'clock, a series of Brush Dragging Songs (Ãkùidåugà) is sung while men and women perform the Brush Dragging Dance (Ãkùicùngà) for approximately thirty minutes. Singers say that approximately ten Brush Dance Songs have survived. During these songs, a small group of women gathers on the east side of the dance arena, just outside the entrance. These women go to the numerous large cottonwood trees in the camp and break off small branches, some of which are made into crowns that are worn on the head. During the Brush Dance, women hold other branches upward, shaking them in time to the music as they dance. A processional led by several Gourd dancers is followed by the singers, singing and carrying a drum, and then by the women who accompany the singing. The processional slowly proceeds through the entrance and into the middle of the arena. At the end of the Brush Dance, the women walk over to the edge of the arena and place the crowns and branches on top of the circular shade arbor, reminiscent of the old Brush Dragging, in which entire societies met to cut and bring in the brush necessary for building the Sun Dance arbor.

Brush Dance performed at the Kiowa Gourd Clan ceremonial, Carnegie, Oklahoma, July 2004.

Despite the large encampment—several hundred people—today's Brush Dances are very small. Over five years of observations in the early 1990s, I recorded an average of ten male Gourd Dancers and eight female dancers who participated in the annual Brush Dance. In 2004, thirty women participated. The dance holds more importance on a symbolic level than on a social and participatory level.

The Kiowa Gourd Clan displays several war trophies, all but one of which were obtained by the Jáifègàu in the nineteenth century. Several of them relate to White Bear. Before the first day of the annual ceremonial, these trophies are taken into a tipi where they are "smoked" or cedared, prayers are offered, and other rituals are conducted. On July Fourth, the custodians of several war trophies gather at the camp of one of the Gourd Clan officers around noon. Prayers are offered and the trophies are cedared. Just before 1:00 P.M., several Kiowa men enter the center of the arena and plant four forked poles painted solid red in the ground from south to north. A red cloth sash is placed on the first (southernmost) forked pole, representing the no-retreat sashes

Kiowa Gourd Clan ceremonial with society trophies displayed, Carnegie, Oklahoma, July 4, 2004.

of the past. Some members indicate that this is White Bear's sash, whereas others say that White Bear's original rope is encased within the sash. Between the first and second forked poles is a red and white beaded lance commemorating White Bear's fletched lance, now kept by the Spottedhorse family. On the second forked pole is a bugle commemorating that of White Bear. On the third forked pole is a saber belonging to Vernon Tsoodle, a career Marine who served in Korea. Around 1990 Tsoodle was presented with the saber as a retirement gift from his sons. He asked the Gourd Clan officers if the saber could be displayed with the older trophies to represent contemporary Kiowa military service in the twentieth century, and the officers gave him the right to do so.[132] Between the third and fourth forked poles is a fur-wrapped *pàubôn* with attached eagle feathers. Although originally it had no historical association with the society, it is now kept in the Yellow Wolf family.[133] On the fourth forked pole is an eagle-feather bonnet from the Hainta family, which is descended from White Bear. Once these items are set up in the arena, members are instructed not to go between the posts and their trophies.

    The afternoon program begins with a parade-in of the dancers led by the Gourd Clan leaders and princess. Following a prayer, the Kiowa Flag Song is sung, followed by the Starting Song. As the singers begin the Starting Song they tap lightly on the rim of the drum. Seated on the benches around the arena, the dancers begin to shake their rattles lightly in time to the music, producing a distinctive metallic sound from aluminum salt-shaker rattles filled with pebbles, beads, or BBs. Although the Starting Song has no lyrics, it has a rhythm distinct from those of other songs and is recognized by all. The song serves to announce the beginning of the dance and focuses attention toward the center of the arena. After the song is sung through four times, the singers strike the drum, and after a pause of one to two seconds, they begin to ruffle the drum with their drumbeaters and all call out a resounding "Yooooooo-ah" in memory of Red Wolf. The singers then immediately increase the tempo of their drumming, now on the drumhead, and continue singing the song louder and faster. The dancers rise and begin to dance in place in front of the benches, shaking their rattles louder and faster in time to the music. At some dances the song may be sung two to four more times before the dancers arise and begin dancing. At annual dances like those of the Kiowa Gourd Clan, a whipman is often present. When the leaders of the Gourd Clan arise (especially the society whipman, who carries a whip), all the members stand up and begin to dance.

Kiowa Gourd Clan singers whom I interviewed stated that following the Starting Song and two to four "slow dance songs," the order and number of songs is not formally set but varies according to the head singer for that session. Often the lead is passed around the drum in "round-robin" style, allowing each singer to start a song in succession. A break is usually taken after one round. If the emcee calls for a break before each singer has been given an opportunity to start a song, the singers usually start up again in order with the next singer around the drum.[134] However, the Chief's Song, commemorating White Bear, is usually sung within the first four songs after the Starting Song; these are a body of three to four "slow songs" used to build a slowly increasing tempo for the dance.

The remainder of the afternoon consists of Gourd dancing, usually in sets of four to eight songs, interspersed with rest breaks and specials during which initiations, naming ceremonies, speeches, giveaways, pledges, and honorings are held. Giveaways are often signaled by the singing of family songs, which are previously requested, during which a processional is danced around the drum. In some instances a "one and one" is called for, in which one family or War Dance song is played and a processional is danced around the drum, followed by one Gourd Dance song, to which the men Gourd dance while the women and other relatives dance behind the person being honored. Honoring continues throughout the afternoon, growing in frequency and intensity in response to the feeling derived from the songs and the "spirit" of the dance. Members occasionally take down one of the society war trophies and dance with it. Descendants of White Bear frequently dance with his beaded lance when his personal song is sung. Other members often dance with the Marine saber.

Giveaways are held to honor an individual, to express gratitude for one's having served in a position, overcome an illness, reenter the dance community after a death in the family, or for other special purposes. Gifts of Pendleton blankets, shawls, money, and, on rare occasions, horses are given away in honor of the person being recognized. Although the Kiowa Gourd Clan is noted for its numerous, large, and

Kiowa Gourd Clan ceremonial, Carnegie, Oklahoma, July 4, 1990.
Note society war trophies in center of arena.

lengthy giveaways, many elders complain that giveaways have become extravagant and that people are simply showing off their wealth. Elizabeth Grobsmith (1981b) suggested that Plains Indian giveaways had shifted toward marking and symbolizing social status more than promoting economic redistribution. During my fieldwork, several giveaways held at Gourd Dances lasted for an hour or more. Elders frequently recall that in the past, giveaways did not stop the program, the dancers did not get cold and stiff waiting for the next set of songs, and, as one person put it, "there wasn't so much down time." Yet others point out that things must be taken care of in the "right way" and that the traditional importance of generosity, public honoring marked by the redistribution of wealth, and attention to protocol must continue. Waiting for each person called up to receive a gift as he or she walks to the forefront consumes most of the time. Another form of giving away involves relatives placing money or goods at the feet of an individual during the dance—either someone who is already dancing in the arena or someone who is brought into the arena for this purpose. The person chosen by the relatives to receive the gift is then placed beside the dancer for the extent of that song, after which he or she picks up the gift and shakes hands with the honored individual.

Initiations of new members are also held during the afternoon dances. As one elder Gourd Clan officer explained, when inducting someone, the society should ask the parents of the potential recruit for their consent, because they will be the ones to support him and give away for him. If the society does not do this, but initiates the man on the spot, his parents and family members may not be present or prepared for his giveaway, which would embarrass the entire family.[135] The recruiting song (Yîqàuàumdàugà, lit. Member Making Song) is sung when initiates are brought to the center of the arena, where they are joined by the society members, relatives, and friends, many of whom give away in their honor. This song is the Tanedooah Family Song with new words put to it that directly reference the initiation process and the old military society:

> Jái-fè-gàu áu-yà-kạu-màu nàu á-kó-bà-chá
> The Jáifègàu are calling me and I must go.[136]

An elder then speaks for the inductee, mentioning his community, lineage, educational level, military service, significant achievements, and, in some cases, Indian name. The initiation concludes with family members holding a giveaway or pledging beef, money, or both for the society's next annual ceremonial.

Throughout the afternoon, a bugler periodically sounds calls during the dancing. The use of a bugle during the Gourd Dance is generally limited to annual celebrations. Over the years I have seen a Kiowa man in Gourd Dance dress and a soldier in period dress uniform perform this role. Currently, a non-Indian son-in-law of Vernon Tsoodle's dresses in period uniform and performs the bugle calls at the annual Gourd Clan ceremonials. Although the right to use a bugle in the Gourd Dance is claimed by White Bear's descendants, other Kiowa and some Navajo are now using a bugle in their Gourd Dances.

Kiowa author and Gourd Clan member Scott Momaday (1976b:35–37) described the encampment, regalia, dancing, and giveaways of the celebration in his poem "The Gourd Dancer." One part in particular captures the essence of the Gourd Dance:

> Dancing,
> He dreams, he dreams—
> The long wind glances, moves
> Forever as a music to the mind;
> The gourds are flashes of the sun.
> He takes the inward, mincing steps
> That conjure old processions and returns.
>
> Dancing,
> His moccasins,
> His sash and bandolier
> Contain him in insignia;
> His fan is powerful, concise
> According to his agile hand,
> And holds upon the deep, ancestral air.

Whereas some dances are performed closer to the edge of the arena, during others the dancers begin to move around and spread out. At some dances the dancers start a Tạudàugà (Rattle Song) while the singers take a smoke and water break. The seated dancers begin to shake their rattles, and after they sing the song three to four times, the singers pick it up and the dancers rise and being to dance.[137] Throughout the dance, elderly Kiowa singers maintain a rather strict protocol concerning the order, speed, and tempo in singing specific songs. The tempo gradually increases throughout the dance. Toward the end of the program, a number of Fast-Paced Songs (Fáuldàugà), sometimes called Rhythm Songs, are sung as the momentum of the dance increases.[138]

Around 5:30 P.M. the dancing concludes. At some dances the Fịdàugà (Eating Song) is sung prior to stopping for the evening meal, but this song is becoming rare. A Kiowa elder or minister usually gives a prayer, after which all return to their camps for supper. Continuing the tradition of Kiowa hospitality, families often invite visitors to eat with them, an old custom that should never be refused. Often, twenty to sixty people may eat at a single camp during a meal.

Oscar Tsoodle explained the tradition of redistributing rations and of having open camps at the Kiowa Gourd Clan ceremonial:

> That's the reason why our camps are open to anybody. Just like ours, she [his wife] cooks and put up a big long table there. Anybody can come there and eat, breakfast, dinner, supper, just enjoy. . . . That's our Indian way, we just welcome anyone. I have a lot of visitors and non-Indians come to visit. . . . That's the reason that whenever you come down to Fourth of July you just go to anybody's camp and you're welcome. You're welcome. That's the reason we give out rations and then we tell them, "Feed your visitors, feed your friends." . . . Fellowship and eating together, that's what it is, and we do that.[139]

After supper, dancing resumes at around seven o'clock. Beginning with the Kiowa Flag Song, a single-file processional parades in from the east side of the arena. This processional is led by the Gourd Dancers, followed by the male Fancy, Straight, and Traditional Dancers and then women and younger girls who will later participate in the program. After a final session of Gourd dancing, culminating with several Fast-Paced or Rhythm Songs, the program changes to intertribal men's and women's War and social dancing.

On the evening of July Fourth, the last session of Gourd dancing culminates with a series of Fast-Paced Songs. The last of these songs is usually known as "Charlie Brown." Originally a Jáifègàu Fast-Paced Song, it was known as the Komalty Family Song, but General Charles Brown took a special liking to a performance of it during a dance at Fort Sill in the 1960s. It was sung again for his pleasure and nicknamed "Charlie Brown."[140] Although the old society had no official Quitting Song, the Kiowa Tia-Piah Society of Oklahoma began using this song as a Quitting Song in the 1960s, and this use has continued and spread to nearly all Kiowa Gourd Dance groups. Though it is often popularly called "Charlie Brown," elders stress that it should be referred to as the Komalty Family Song.

Other than an occasional War Dance song during a one-and-one (one War Dance song followed by one Gourd Dance song for a giveaway), the afternoon and early evening program is all Gourd Dance, concluding with a series of four Buffalo Dance songs. The Buffalo Dance's slower pace serves to suspend the tremendous momentum and crescendo achieved during the Fast-Paced Songs. Although the Kiowa Gourd Clan stresses that no Gourd dancing should occur after dark, activities in some years stray from this edict. Many Kiowa say that it is not "good luck" for society dances to go beyond daylight hours, so the pre-reservation practice of all-night society meetings and dances no longer continues.[141] A session of social and War dancing for male and female dancers of all ages concludes the evening program each day. Around midnight the program ends, and people return to their camps or homes. Some younger people prepare for a "49," a social event held at various locations in the surrounding countryside, where younger Indians sing 49 songs, dance, drink, and socialize throughout the night.[142]

Popularity, Fission, Secularization, and Diffusion

The response to the Gourd Clan revival was immediate and overwhelming. As in the Black Legs revival and the growth of the post–World War II powwow, most initial participants were traditionalists, but they were soon joined by members of many Kiowa Christian families. One woman remarked, "Well, after the momentum [began], boy, people came to powwows who would never set foot on them." At the time of the 1957 Gourd Clan revival, elders warned that lifetime leadership positions would lead to factionalism and were a potential source of society fission. They were right. Following the revival of the Kiowa Gourd Clan, three other independent Kiowa Gourd Dance groups emerged through factionalism and differing interests: the Kiowa Tia-Piah Society of Oklahoma, the Kiowa Tia-Piah Society (formerly the Kiowa Tia-Piah Society of Carnegie), and the Kiowa Warrior Descendants. One Gourd Clan officer stated that two issues lay at the heart of the divisions. Foremost was the fact that a limited number of officer positions existed, and many people, when they found that they could not become officers, broke off to form their own organizations. Some left the Gourd Clan because of its strict adherence to tradition and because they wanted a more "casual" and "lenient" protocol.[143]

Another major point of contention involved whether membership would be limited to Kiowa or whether members of other tribes and non-Indians would be allowed to participate. By this time many Kiowa were married to members of many other tribes and to non-Indians. These issues led to the fission and diffusion of the society that continues to the present. Newton Poolaw (1981) stated that Bill Koomsa Sr. was ousted while in New Mexico on a dancing trip because of jealousy and because of his insistence that the organization maintain an all-Kiowa membership, dance only during the daytime, and not dance on the Anglo Fourth of July, which had been chosen because of vacation time. Although the Kiowa Gourd Clan is considered by Kiowa to be the "granddaddy of them all," the three other major Kiowa Gourd Dance societies are essential in understanding the post-1957 diffusion of the Gourd Dance.

The first group to branch off from the Kiowa Gourd Clan initially adopted the name Kiowa Tia-Piah Society of Carnegie. Led by Nelson Big Bow, Tom Little Chief, James Auchiah, Bill and Vincent Bointy, Yale Spottedbird, Bruce and Gregory Haumpy, Jasper Sankadota, and others, this organization began to hold an annual dance near Lawton, Oklahoma, at Tia-Piah Park, a dance ground located on a Comanche allotment owned by Nelson Big Bow's wife, who was Comanche. The society held its first dance in 1962. Whereas the Gourd Clan sought more exclusive membership, the Tia-Piah Society sought to integrate its membership, recognizing that many Kiowa were married to other Indians and non-Indians. In the early 1960s, under the leadership of Nelson Bigbow, after another fissioning, the group became known as the Kiowa Tia-Piah Society of Oklahoma. Today this organization draws a considerable number of Kiowa families, but a smaller number than the Kiowa Gourd Clan or the extant Kiowa Tia-Piah Society of Carnegie. Because the dance is geographically located in the Comanche community, it draws considerable Comanche participation.

Splintering off from the preceding group was a second independent group that included many original Gourd Clan members. It was incorporated as the Kiowa Tia-Piah Society of Carnegie and was led by, among others, James Auchiah, Bill Bointy, Yale Spottedbird, Lynn Pauahty, and the Kauahquo family. Relocating to an allotment thirteen miles south of Carnegie, the group began holding annual July 2–4 dances in 1966.[144] The location came to be known as Chieftain Park. In 1992 the group returned to the site, having held the previous five annual ceremonials at the Wichita tribal dance ground because of disputes over use of the Chieftain Park grounds. That same year the Kiowa Tia-Piah Society of Carnegie officially changed its name to "Kiowa Tai-Piah Society."

The distinctive feature of the society's dress is an attractive red vest with the group's name embroidered on the back in blue letters. These vests are typically worn at the group's monthly benefit dances, which are often held at the Wichita tribal facilities north of Anadarko. Although some Kiowa Tia-Piah Society members wear traditional Gourd Dance clothing, most wear more formal daily dress clothes such as slacks, long-sleeve shirts, and dress shoes or informal clothing such as blue jeans, T-shirts, tennis shoes, and baseball caps. The dress code is generally more relaxed than that of the Kiowa Gourd Clan.

The Tia-Piah Society maintains a group of four headmen and a princess. During its ceremonials, Rabbit Dances and games such as horseshoe throwing contests are held in the mornings, and Gourd dancing is held in the afternoons. On the evening of the first day of dancing, a cedaring ceremony is held. The entire camp is invited in small groups into a large tipi in which several of the Tia-Piah members bless each person with cedar smoke, prayer, and gifts of sage picked that day from the surrounding

Kiowa Tia-Piah Society Brush Dance, Chieftain Park, near Carnegie, Oklahoma, July 3, 1993.

area. In the evening after supper, Brush Dances are held, with two processionals led by small boys dragging cottonwood limbs, followed by the Gourd dancers, women, and then the drummers and singers. Starting on the east side of the arena, each group makes a circular procession until meeting up on the west side, where all turn inward to face the drum, dancing in place. Gourd dancing resumes, followed by War and social dancing. Two adjacent dance arenas are used, the afternoon dances being held in a well-shaded arena beneath the canopy of a large grove of cottonwood trees bordered by a creek, and the evening dances in the more open arena to the east. During the annual dance, a set of six society trophies is positioned north-to-south on the west side of the arena. From south to north these items consist of an eagle-feather bonnet, four beaded and fur-wrapped lances of various types, and another bonnet with a bugle hung beside it. Bugle charges are blown frequently throughout the dancing by an Anglo member from the Texas Tia-Piah Society, an Anglo hobbyist Gourd Dance group. References to White Bear and to old Ją́ifègàu traditions are made frequently during speeches, at which time some members often demonstrate their descent from White Bear. Individual veterans are recognized with speeches and dancing during the program.

The atmosphere of the Tia-Piah Society dances is tremendously warm and friendly, especially to visitors. With typical Kiowa hospitality, visitors are fed in the many camps surrounding the arena, and the society provides rations to each camp. Membership is one of the primary differences between the three societies. Whereas the Kiowa Gourd Clan does not permit non-Indian participation, the Kiowa Tia-Piah Society has opened its membership on the intertribal and non-Indian levels. The Kiowa Tia-Piah Society of Oklahoma has incorporated a large degree of participation by Comanches and some participation by non-Indians.

The third independent Kiowa Gourd Dance group is the Kiowa Warrior Descendants. According to members of the Lone Bear family, the Kiowa Warrior Descendants' dance began with an honor dance held in 1972 in recognition of new Kiowa Tribal Princess Huberta Jean Tsotigh. This dance included Gourd and Brush dancing. With the election of Lynetta Gay Kaulaity as Kiowa Tribal Princess in 1975 and with further honor dances, the organization grew. Since 1977 it has held the Kiowa Warrior Descendants Annual Labor Day Powwow at the old Lone Bear dance ground southeast of Carnegie. At its functions, some dancers dress conservatively in buckskin leggings, moccasins, silk or ribbon shirts, waist shawls, silver work, and Gourd Dance accessories. Others may be seen in dress clothes or occasionally jeans. With the exception of Brush Dragging Dances, which I did not witness during my visits, the format regarding Gourd, War, and social dancing generally follows that of other Kiowa organizations. At the dances I witnessed, the Warrior Descendants drew a sizable but smaller following than the Kiowa Gourd Clan and the Kiowa Tia-Piah Society.[145]

The Kiowa Warrior Descendants promote the same basic Kiowa traditions espoused by other organizations in a very respectable fashion. Nevertheless, gossip and rumors from other organizations abound. In the early 1990s, strong winds knocked over the arbors at the dance ground, forcing the group to hold its dances at Red Buffalo Hall at the Kiowa tribal complex in Carnegie. Rumors of a decline in attendance and of leadership struggles and shifts continue. These rumors differ little from those both alleged and actually experienced by the other Kiowa organizations over time. Several elders have stated that the cause of the bad luck suffered by the organization was its persistence in dancing at the Lone Bear grounds after Lone Bear declared that no more dancing would take place there.[146] Geographically, the dance ground is on a fairly high, plateau-like ridge and is prone to strong winds.

Fission and Fusion, Past and Present

Luke Lassiter (1995:196, 207n.6) maintained that these processes of fission did not represent factionalism as much as they reflected evolution, which he compared to the earlier tradition of fluid membership in band structures, which ebbed and flowed with the popularity and success of each respective band leader (*jòfàujóqî*). In some respects, I agree that the growth and fissioning of Kiowa Gourd Dance organizations parallels the flexible membership and frequent changes in band residence that characterized pre-reservation Kiowa society. When individuals and families opposed the leadership of the headman of their own residence band, they were free to leave and take up residence in another community. This process continues today as members and even some society officers or headmen change their membership and attendance back and forth between organizations, particularly between the Kiowa Gourd Clan and the Kiowa Tia-Piah Society.

However, although fission and fusion were common among pre-reservation bands, they are less well known for Plains Indian sodalities. Vertically structured, lineage-based residence bands are known to have shifted and reorganized more frequently than horizontally structured sodalities such as cohort-based military societies. Membership change in residence bands was typically lineage oriented, whereas in sodalities it resulted from individual choice or recruitment into another sodality. Thus, significant structural differences between the two kinds of groups existed. In addition, Lassiter's consultant, referring to fissioning, stated that "they didn't split off; they were just under the leadership of those Kiowa who couldn't get in one box. They couldn't come together" (1995:207n.6). This statement is contrary to the organizational basis of pre-reservation Kiowa military societies, which had pan-Kiowa membership, and is also suggestive of pervasive factionalism, which might have contributed to frequent shifts in band membership.

The fissions that have taken place among Kiowa Gourd Dance groups are significant in that they demonstrate that although sodalities provide essential integrative features of social organization that supersede and cross-cut kin-based structures, they are not immune to kin, family, and communal political factionalism. In order to avoid conflict, some singers and dancers choose not to belong to any society or descendants' group but to try to help any and all organizations whenever asked. The three independent organizations are reported rarely to have collaborated with one another. Today their antagonisms have generally lessened, and some members of all organizations support each other at benefit dances held throughout the calendar year, on which they depend to raise sufficient funds to sponsor their annual celebrations. However, nearly all Kiowa say it is unlikely that all the organizations will combine forces again.

Relatively recently, two other Kiowa Gourd Dance organizations have emerged. These are the Chief Sa-tan-ta (White Bear) Descendants, formed around the Washburn family in Apache, Oklahoma, and the Satethieday Khatgomebaugh (Sétthái̯dé̜qàcôm-bàu, or White Bear's People/Descendants), centered near Carnegie. Both are structured as descendants' groups focused on the life and achievements of White Bear and on Gourd dancing. The former group incorporated to clear White Bear's record of criminal charges, particularly his 1871 conviction and subsequent sentence for alleged responsibility for the Warren wagon train massacre, in which descendants maintain that he did not participate, and to locate and repatriate his lance, shield, rope, and bugle. Formed in 1987, this organization held its first annual powwow in July 1990 and continues to hold its dances in Apache, Oklahoma. The latter group is a community service organization inspired by "the spirit" of White Bear's service (Lassiter 1998:167). It held its first annual celebration in the early 1990s. Lassiter (1995:144) characterized the two groups as a "descendant/Gourd Dance organization" and a "descendant/service organization," respectively. Both groups maintain and celebrate their descent from White Bear, Gourd dancing, bugle calls blown in his memory during the dances, stories of his life, and numerous versions of songs, some of which were his personal songs with lyrics that refer to him and are now considered to belong to his descendants (see Lassiter 1998:164–169).

Functional Changes

Over time, the general and specific functions and uses of the Ją́ifègàu and its dance and music have broadened. Before 1890 the dance was performed during military society meetings prior to the Sun Dance by a select sodality of male warriors. Later, during the reservation and post-reservation periods, nonveteran members of high-status families, often descendants of earlier members, were inducted (Meadows 1995:396–397). The functions and uses of the society changed dramatically, because many of its roles in policing the communal bison hunt and fostering a martial spirit for warfare were no longer available. By 1912 the dance had been revived, but it was performed by a group of middle-aged to elder men, some of whom were veterans who had had their martial status frozen with the end of warfare in 1875, as well as by younger men who were not veterans. Yet all these men had been raised with a continued emphasis on the earlier martial and Ją́ifègàu traditions.

In 1935 White Fox described the purpose of the Ją́ifègàu as "part social [and] part honorary."[147] His comment suggests that the organization still held value in commemorating Kiowa and Ją́ifègàu heritage and that it fulfilled significant social, political, economic, military, and cultural roles. Participation also provided a means for descendants to commemorate ancestral society members.

By the time of its revival-revitalization in 1957, the Gourd Dance had changed significantly, by essentially opening membership to all Kiowa men and by combining or consolidating new functions and uses to shape the contemporary form of the dance. Foremost among the society's goals was the perpetuation of Kiowa heritage, along with an emphasis on Ją́ifègàu martial traditions and heritage:

> The purpose and function of this organization was to perpetuate our Indian Heritage and to revive the Kiowa dance as near as possible from the past original ceremonies.... It was also decided to display early day trophies taken from enemies during frontier encounters. The Army bugle taken at one of the Frontier Posts, a lariat rope captured from the Texas Rangers; also feather staffs and lances owned by the past members. These trophies are regarded as mark and symbol of courage and bravery of the Kiowa tribe. (Kiowa Gourd Clan 1976:22)

Lassiter (1992:30) wrote that "the Gourd Clan became a rallying point for continuing the unique heritage that had unfolded among the Kiowa." As a performance, the Gourd Dance was now a conscious symbol of "what it meant to be Kiowa," at least as seen by Gourd Clan followers. Several Kiowa have made statements to this effect. One Gourd Clan elder reinforced this ideology at the 1993 annual dance, stating over the public address system that "the Kiowa Gourd Clan will be used to revive and strengthen several Kiowa traditions" for which there was concern about obsolescence.[148] The same can be said for Black Legs and Ohoma Lodge traditions, each of which maintains its distinct set of society and Kiowa traditions while integrating segments of the Kiowa population.

In addition to the conscious emphasis on promoting Kiowa culture and identity through the Gourd Dance, a variety of revived and new interrelated functions and uses of the Gourd Dance have developed. Although both continuity and change clearly exist in contemporary Kiowa Gourd Dance societies, attempting to characterize the society in either-or terms is difficult because of its long history and varied changes. Lassiter listed the Kiowa Gourd Clan as a "revived Plains military society" but later stated, "No longer a warrior's society, the Gourd Clan focuses exclusively on the dance of the Taimpego, which would be called the 'Gourd dance'" (1995:144, 190). Yet the performance of the dance to honor World War II veterans on Armistice Day in 1946 and the maintenance of early society war trophies continue previous military society practices. According to Ellis (2003:23), "Scott Tonemah recalled that the revived Gourd Dance reminded Kiowa people of the importance of warriors and their obligation to protect and defend their people." Although Gourd Clan membership does not require veteran status, many members are veterans, some of them highly decorated. But the dance has also brought about changes in Kiowa social integration, including the use of the Fourth of July weekend as an annual encampment, the ability of all Kiowa men and some older boys to participate, the increasing role of women in singing and dancing in powwows since the 1950s and later in Gourd Dances, and increased participation by children in Rabbit Dances and by all ages in Gourd and War Dances. Modern Gourd Dances can thus be viewed as adaptations that hold multiple significant levels of ethnic expression and integration for contemporary Kiowa.

One elder Gourd Clan and Kiowa Tia-Piah Society member explained what he saw as the major difference between the Kiowa Gourd Dance organizations: "The *way* it is done at Carnegie is the distinguishing feature between the Kiowa Gourd Clan and other Gourd Dance organizations."[149] Other Kiowa elders stated that they could feel the difference between the dances held by the Kiowa Gourd Clan and other organizations. Additional criteria that differentiate the Kiowa Gourd Clan include no non-Indian participation, a stricter and more conservative dress code, maintenance of an all-male leadership, and male control at dances and business meetings. Interpretations of dress code and the level of respect associated with the dance were the most frequently cited differences. It is important to recognize the contribution of Kiowa women, without whom any large-scale activity would never succeed. Although women play a large and important role in terms of organizing and running the family camps, meals, and giveaways, their contribution remains overshadowed by the traditional and more public roles and statuses of men. One elder commented, "Women have no say so over there. Men make the rules."[150] Some Gourd Dance organizations have women officers, prompting some male Gourd Clan members to attribute all the organizational and monetary problems of the other organizations to the inclusion of women. These assertions must be taken in perspective, and although the women may dance behind the men around the arena, their roles are essential and well known in the Kiowa community.

Viewing the dance as a ceremonial and not as a social dance, regardless of the social qualities found in any gathering, is essential because of its origin in a warrior society and chieftain organization. As Atwater Onco explained, when the dance is considered a social dance, it loses its meaning—an essential part of the Kiowa Gourd Dance tradition: "The only time we have that feeling, Jáifègàu, is when we meet over here at Carnegie. Outside of that, every weekend, I don't care where you go, you're gonna see Jáifè dancing. It's lost the meaning. But right there at Carnegie we're still carrying on the ways that were taught in the sixties when they got reorganized to keep it this way."[151]

Secularization and Diffusion

From the fission and re-formation of other Kiowa Gourd Dance groups and the popular growth of the dance into other Indian and later non-Indian communities, two distinct forms of the Gourd Dance emerged. The first is a more ceremonial form that is typical of the more conservative annual organizational dances. This form is generally limited in the type, context, and frequency of performance, has a more rigid protocol, and contains a greater percentage of songs sung with Kiowa lyrics. The second is a more social form that has a less rigid dress code and protocol and may be found nearly every weekend as a main component of Kiowa and intertribal powwows and benefit dances. Following the first non–Fourth of July Gourd Dance, held by the Kiowa Warrior Descendants in 1972, other groups began to hold non-annual and more powwow-oriented Gourd Dances. This dichotomy constitutes a major development in the evolution of the Kiowa Gourd Dance. The two forms soon spread throughout southwestern Oklahoma Indian communities. While the first form continued in more tribal- and military-society-oriented contexts, the latter form functioned as a more popular expression of the dance and began drawing increased participation at powwows and, in time, by non-Indian hobbyists.

Economically, the Gourd Dance has become a major part of nearly every Kiowa and neighboring Southern Plains Indian social dance or powwow, and it serves as a major arena for numerous forms of fund-raising. Just as the Kiowa's understanding of the dance's significance has continued to change, so have the ways in which the dance is now used. The social form of the dance has played a significant role in drawing sufficient numbers of people to benefit powwows to raise funds for charitable causes or the next annual dance. This use of the Gourd Dance as a "drawing card," as one elder described it to me, generally occurs at dances in which the Gourd Dance is not the primary purpose for gathering. This is a seminal difference between the two types of dances, which affect each other. Today the Gourd Dance is often the principal activity for many events or for many afternoon and early evening portions of mixed program (Gourd and War Dance) powwows that later shift to a social and War Dance program.

The neighboring Apache, Comanche, and Cheyenne regularly use the Gourd Dance as an afternoon or evening program and as a drawing card to attract people to nearly all their dances, including benefit dances, mixed-program powwows, and ceremonial performances by societies such as the Apache Black Feet Societies. Intertribal participation by head staff, dancers, and spectators is typical of most Southern Plains dances today.

Whether held as all–Gourd Dance programs or mixed-program powwows, benefit dances include efforts to raise spirit and support for local (Carnegie and Anadarko) high school basketball teams before and after sectional, regional, and state level tournaments and to raise funds for athletes to attend special events. A March 16, 2002, benefit was held for Hyde Toppah, a Weatherford, Oklahoma, high school junior who was selected to play in the Maui Football Pigskin Classic in Wailuku, Hawaii. Dances have been held to raise funds for the Kiowa Tribe's Education Department and annual Kiowa Recognition Banquet. Benefit dances are often held to help a family with housing, medical, or financial problems. On June 1, 2000, Ruth Wetselline's home was severely damaged in a fire. Benefit Gourd Dances including several Kiowa head staff were held at the Apache tribal gymnasium on June 5 and at the Wichita tribal dance ground on June 15, to raise money to help the family repair its home. A June 3, 2001, benefit Gourd Dance was held to raise funds for Vernon and Juanita Ahtone to repair damage to their home from a recent storm. On March 8, 2002, the family home of Lupe Gooday Jr. burned. On March 14, an all–Gourd Dance benefit was held at Red Buffalo Hall at the Kiowa tribal complex to raise money for the family. A June 21, 2002, benefit was held to raise funds for John and Geneva Emhoola to help them defray costs from an automobile accident incurred on June 9. Other benefit Gourd Dances have been held to raise funds for organizations such as the Carnegie High School junior class, the American Cancer Society, and the Hobart Native American Heritage Centennial Celebration. Benefit Gourd Dances are even beginning to attract Christian organizations. The South District of the Oklahoma Indian Missionary Conference hosted a benefit Gourd Dance to raise funds for the purchase of a multipurpose metal building to be located at Hog Creek. The Southwest Region United Methodist Youth, composed of members from several Kiowa and Comanche Indian Methodist churches, held a benefit dance to raise funds for its Summer Youth Camp. Similar all–Gourd Dance programs may be used to honor individuals, such as a November 7, 2002, dance held for the Carnegie High School girls' cross-country team, which won the state championship that year.[152]

Benefit dances, especially those employing all–Gourd Dance programs, are among the most readily available forms of communal support and insurance in times of need. Today a family or organization can hold a benefit Gourd or War Dance for practically any good cause. In contrast, at annual Gourd Dance celebrations, the Gourd Dance is the primary dance form and the purpose for gathering and thus comprises the majority of the entire program. Although pledges are commonly made and recorded, few or no benefit activities are held, relative to those held at a benefit dance. In both forms the Gourd Dance increasingly draws Kiowa, other Indians, and an increasing number of non-Indians together for a variety of socioeconomic reasons.

This differential use of the dance is a major point of contention between Kiowa who view the dance as derived from a men's society and to be performed only on special occasions, with strict protocol, and Kiowa who adhere to the more frequent and increasingly popular use of the dance. This difference of opinion has also led to feelings among some Kiowa that the current manner and frequency of the dance has led to the loss of its essence and "spirit" and to a loss of respect for it. Claims by elders that individuals and organizations are not performing or upholding the dance as it used to be are common.[153] Others have accepted the changes and are largely unconcerned with the increasing frequency of Gourd dancing. The growing interest in the dance by many non-Kiowa (both Indians and non-Indians) has resulted in other issues.

The formation of the Kiowa Gourd Clan in 1957 undeniably heralded a general cultural revival of military societies and dancing throughout the Southern Plains tribes. The Gourd Dance grew in popularity among other Native Americans in Oklahoma and among non-Indians (Howard 1950, 1955, 1976, 1983; Kracht 1989; Stahl 1989; Ellis 1990, 1993; Meadows 1991, 1995, 1999; Lassiter 1992, 1995, 1998). Howard (1976:249) attributed the Gourd Dance's rapidly gained popularity to the growth of the "Pan-Indian powwow complex." At this time the Gourd Dance was centered in Oklahoma and included a connection to Plains culture, with its appealing music and its simple and affordable dance attire, and to a heightened level of Indian identity and awareness. The rapid growth of the dance was strongly influenced by the strengthening of Native American civil rights and the revival of Native American awareness following World War II and the Korean War (Meadows 1995). Ellis (1990:25–27, 1993:370) attributed the rapid growth and strength of the dance to the increasing Indian activism of the 1960s and 1970s. The Gourd Dance also served as an Indian representation of Indianness, not a white one (Ellis 1993:370). The Gourd Dance today is being appropriated and woven into myriad tribal cultures, traditions, and programs. A December 4, 2004, program sponsored by the Shawnee at Shawnee, Oklahoma, included an afternoon Gourd Dance followed by an evening Stomp Dance.

Billy Evans Horse explained how his grandfather predicted the spread of the dance to him as a youth:

> He said, this dance, once it's introduced, it's going to go all over the world. He said, you're gonna see black men, you're gonna see white men, you're gonna see Mexicans, all races of people will dance this dance. He said, you're gonna see that. Whenever you go . . . this dance is going to go all over, he said. I never knew why, but today it's true. . . . It must be good because other people are joining in and they want to be a part of that something, whatever it is that they identify [with] and when you realize the songs, see, they're not just today or yesterday, they were a hundred years ago and even farther than that . . . and they have a deep meaning with them once you understand them.[154]

The key issues concerning the use of the dance by non-Kiowa are centered on (1) a concern for performing the dance in a dignified and respectful manner (dressing properly, not dancing too wildly, not popularizing the dance); (2) the fact that the Kiowa songs belong either to the society or, in many instances, to particular families; (3) the fact that outsiders cannot fully relate to the songs on either a linguistic or a family level; (4) a concern that outsiders do not fully understand the history and meaning of the dance; (5) a belief that no Kiowa has the right to give the dance away to outsiders; (6) the perception that the songs are now being sung too fast (by non-Kiowa and sometimes by Kiowa); and (7) the fact that many people know only the popular form of the dance performed at powwows and not the traditional form performed at annual ceremonials. One Gourd Clan elder stressed to me:

> You can imagine how you'd feel if there's something that you want done right and they don't do it. That's what's happening nowadays. . . . I want them to dance it like it's supposed to be, you know, and do the things that's supposed to be right. We're very strict about what we do out there, 'cause I want them to keep it that a way. I don't want it just any old way. That really makes me mad because they don't respect it. It's not their dance, you know. If they're gonna use it then use it in the right way.[155]

Similarly, the wife of an elder Gourd Clan member remarked, "We have a lot of pride in that. That it's a Kiowa dance and that we try to keep it that way and do it the way it was intended to be."[156]

Although some Kiowa feel that it is permissible for members of other tribes to Gourd dance as long as they do so properly, others feel that only the Kiowa and the Otoe have a legitimate right to perform the dance. Kiowa who welcome and encourage non-Indian participation are mainly members of the Kiowa Tia-Piah Society and some Kiowa living outside the Kiowa community. Reflecting their disapproval of what is known today as cultural appropriation, Gourd Clan members whom I spoke with said they would prefer that non-Indians not perform the dance.

Scholars have attributed the popularity of the Gourd Dance to factors of simple choreography, limited and affordable attire, and pan-Indian social aspects. Kiowa participants offer additional reasons, including the rhythm of the dance, the bonding involved in creating new friendships, the spiritual significance, which one elder singer said "makes you feel like something," and, most important, the strength of the songs. One elder Kiowa woman stated that had the dance continued to require the wearing of a full set of traditional Kiowa clothes, it would not have spread as much. Most dancers use only a blanket, sashes, bandoliers, and a rattle and fan—items that practically anyone can obtain—making participation easy. One elder male maintained that non-Indian Gourd dancers had no real understanding of the dance: "They take it at face value. It's just a dance to them."

Gleaning information from the brief literature on and commercial tapes of Gourd

Dance music, many non-Indians have no real understanding of the full history, songs, and dance. My observations of non-Indian and hobbyist dance organizations corroborate this trend. Most non-Indian Gourd Dance participants learn about the dance and its traditions through limited literature and commercial tapes, and not from Kiowa who are knowledgeable about the history, purpose, and appropriate use of each song. Another elder male expressed concern that the Gourd Dance "has been given away" and "is out of control, being performed . . . [by those] who do not understand what the dance represents and is about." Some Kiowa recognize that many non-Indians who become interested in the dance are people who are searching, often spiritually, for things to meet their needs. One elder explained that in searching, non-Indians have to know what they want, and for non-Indians to truly understand the Gourd Dance, they would have to come to their own understanding of it by "bonding with it."[157] To truly achieve this level of understanding requires a significant amount of time in the Kiowa community and an intimate knowledge of the dance and songs. This is impossible for most non-Indians because of work and family commitments. Moreover, voluntary assimilation by people already raised in another culture, no matter how extensively undertaken, is always an incomplete rite of passage to some degree, qualitatively different from enculturation in one's own culture, and is a bridge that on some levels can never be fully crossed.

Some Kiowa attributed the popularity of the dance to other factors. The individual and collective experiences that are derived from hearing the Gourd Dance songs, an understanding of their collective and multilayered meanings for the Kiowa, and participation and sharing in this experience on an ethnic and communal level are what many Kiowa stress as essential to understanding the dance. Through song and dance and the depth of good feeling that these forms bring, the Gourd Dance represents a major social form for the continuation and expression of Kiowa tradition and culture, and for many, that is reason enough for celebration.

The Kiowa have played a seminal role in the dance's diffusion across the country to other Indian and non-Indian groups. By actively introducing the dance to other Native American communities, the Kiowa are considered to have been the catalyst for the dance's rapid growth (Howard 1976:253–254). Much of non-Indians' interest in the dance has been spurred by Kiowa who have relocated to urban areas where they started their own Gourd Dance organizations, many of which later took in non-Indians as full or auxiliary members. Throughout the United States, the majority of non-Indian hobbyist interest in Indian dancing in general, including the Gourd Dance, has been through membership in Boy Scout, Order of the Arrow, and Explorer Post organizations. Although all the Kiowa Gourd Dance societies have furthered the diffusion of the dance to Indian and non-Indian groups, the Tia-Piah Society of Oklahoma and the Kiowa Tia-Piah Society are responsible for much of its diffusion to non-Indians. As the Kiowa Gourd Dance grew in popularity after 1957, members of several other Indian and non-Indian communities sought out Kiowa, especially members of the Kiowa Tia-Piah Society, for aid in forming their own Gourd Dance groups. Some Kiowa traveled to more distant dances to serve as head staff, especially in Oklahoma and the Dallas–Fort Worth area.

Because Kiowa Tia-Piah Society dances are essentially open to anyone who respects the dance, they attract Indians and non-Indians from across the United States. Although membership is determined by the society itself, participation is more open. Significant numbers of Anglos drive to participate in the annual Kiowa Tia-Piah Society Fourth of July celebration at Chieftain Park. The high level of non-Kiowa and non-Indian interaction can perhaps best be illustrated by a comment the master of ceremonies made repeatedly during the 1992 Kiowa Tia-Piah Society ceremonial: "Let's everybody come out and dance. This dance is intertribal, interracial, interdenominational."[158] Factors of intermarriage, political correctness, non-Indian-based financial support, and genuine fellowship all affect this level of accommodation.

The Kiowa Tia-Piah Society has strong ties with Anglo hobbyist groups, particularly those in Texas. Several Kiowa living in Texas have also sponsored Gourd Dances in their respective urban locales and have invited non-Indians to dance at their July ceremonial. In the early 1970s, members of the Kiowa Tia-Piah Society helped form the Texas Tia-Piah in Crowley, Texas, the first Tia-Piah-related organization outside the Kiowa community in southwestern Oklahoma. By the late 1970s the Gulf Coast Tia-Piah had formed in Texas. In the early 1980s, Kiowa living in Georgia helped form the Georgia Tia-Piah, which is now reportedly defunct. Kiowa in Denver formed the Tia-Piah Society of Colorado. The formation of similar groups has led to the use of the name "Tia-Piah" by numerous Anglo hobbyist groups as widespread as California, New York, and Memphis, Tennessee. Several Texas groups have adopted the use of the Kiowa name—for example, the Texas Tia-Piah, the Dallas–Fort Worth Tia-Piah, and the Houston Tia-Piah. There are also the Gold Coast Tia-Piah in California and recent rumors of a Tia-Piah Society in Hawaii. At least six Gourd Dance societies using the name Cherokee but not federally recognized as Indians claim the right, acquired from other Tia-Piah organizations, to use the name Tia-Piah for their Gourd Dances. Intertribal and non-Indian groups have appropriated the dance to the point that it has become a pan-Indian part of most Anglo and many Indian powwows in the United States. Although several groups now using the Kiowa Tia-Piah name were originally started by Kiowa who had relocated to large urban centers for jobs, most have members predominantly from other tribes or non-Indians. They often invite Kiowa to serve as head staff at their annual dances. At one powwow sponsored by the Housing Authority of the Cherokee Nation in Talequah, Oklahoma, which included a Gourd Dance segment, four of the seven head staff members were Kiowa.[159]

The growth of the dance is also evidenced by its endorsement by various non-Indian groups. Although Caucasians predominate, a few Hispanics, African Americans, and Asians participate in Gourd Dances. This is but one arena in which non-Indian Americans appear to be searching for a historical and ethnic connection, perhaps owing to the relatively recent displacement of many from their own European backgrounds.

Many Anglo Americans and Europeans are involved in historical period reenactment movements, including those of American wars, mountain men, medieval fairs, and Indian dancing. It is significant that although some Native Americans participate in historical reenactments, primarily of military engagements with U.S. cavalry reenactors, they participate as Indians and not as Anglos. Also, relatively few Native Americans are involved or interested to the extent that non-Indians are in using historically correct period clothing, camping equipment, and, in some cases, even speech and mannerisms. Native Americans typically display little interest in imitating non-Indian cultures through historically based reenactments.

Non-Indian Gourd Dance participants are generally familiar with the choreography of the dance and the production of associated contemporary or historical period clothing. However, many non-Indian dancers with whom I visited said that they had never met any Kiowa or ever been to a Kiowa Gourd Dance in Oklahoma. Most who have attended Kiowa dances return home after each dance, spending no real time in the community. My personal experiences, the opinions of several tribal elders, and the observations of other scholars (Stahl 1989; Lassiter 1992:61; Ellis 1993:371) suggest that few hobbyists have in-depth knowledge or understanding of the historical origins and development associated with the dance, familiarity with the Kiowa language, accurate translations of the Kiowa songs, or, more important, an understanding of what the dance entails for the Kiowa.[160] Hobbyists tend to emphasize the visual, material culture, and status aspects of historically "correct" materials and late-nineteenth-century construction techniques of period clothing (a style worn by only a few Kiowa today), rather than the more current social and cultural functions. It is the social, cultural, and symbolic attributes, especially those conveyed through song and a shared sense of historical and ethnic community, that hold more significance for the Kiowa themselves. That song is emphasized over dance and attire reflects its foundational importance for the entire Gourd Dance experience. As one Kiowa Gourd Clan member in his forties expressed it: "From what I understand, I hear they've got better regalia than we've got! They've got better drums than we have, you know. And that's because of *áulhàugà* [money]. I mean they've got prettier beads and stuff like that and they're able to do that ... but to me that's superficial, that's not the real thing, you know, among Indian people."[161]

A few non-Indians become much more knowledgeable about the dance and may be accepted into Kiowa circles, some as dancers and singers, others as anthropologists. Although many hobbyists devote great amounts of time to material culture, song, and dance, few significantly alter their manners, values, thinking, and the social, economic, religious, linguistic, kinship, and other related aspects of their lives to such a pervasive level that it reconstitutes their entire identity, as acknowledged by the individual and others. A few have altered their lifestyles to the degree that they enter into what I would characterize as an elevated form of Indian hobbyist subculture.

Robert Stahl (1989) provided an account of one such Anglo hobbyist from Texas, to whom he gave the pseudonym Joe True, who was adopted by a Kiowa family and who sought an alternative lifestyle to the point of attempting to restructure himself into a Kiowa. In a case of convergent needs that served both True and the Kiowa, the young man attempted to assist his adopted family in helping to spread the Gourd Dance to a non-Indian chapter in Texas. Meeting strong, stereotype-based misunderstanding from other Anglos, who were largely unfamiliar with acceptable Kiowa protocol and cultural knowledge, he was politically ousted from the chapter. This led to growing resentment by some members of his adopted Kiowa family, which resulted in strained relations with them as well. True's phenotypical identity as a non-Indian also served as an easy line of demarcation for both Indians and non-Indians when they decided to distance themselves from him.[162] Subsequently, True experienced tremendous stress, anxiety, and disaffiliation with the Kiowa and their culture, as well as with a segment of non-Indians. In the end, his conversion was incomplete, impermanent, and not fully accepted by either his native Anglo community (which responded to his efforts on the basis of common non-Indian stereotypes of Indians) or the Kiowa community (some of whom resented him or were jealous of his standing in his adopted family). This case study is a valuable lesson in how some hobbyists can go too far in attempting to adopt Indian culture, as well as in the intricacies of Native and non-Native perceptions of race, ethnicity, and ethnic identity and the problems that can result when support from the Indian community can readily be given or taken away. Some of the features of the Joe True story closely mirror my observations of non-Indians in Southern Plains tribal cultures and some of my own experiences among Southern Plains groups.[163]

For the Kiowa, the Gourd Dance is not a hobby to dress up for and occasionally perform. It is a part of everyday life, of recognizing and maintaining their tribal heritage and kinship, and of sharing, embracing, and celebrating their tribal history, ethnicity, and physical and cultural survival. Although the dance spread to non-Indians, its distinctive practice and, particularly, its ethnic and cultural basis as performed by the Kiowa did not. Hobbyist Gourd Dances in the Midwest that I have attended and participated in do not have the same atmosphere, look, or sense of sodality, community, or ethnicity as those of the Kiowa or neighboring Southern Plains tribes. Clearly, non-Indians of diverse ethnicities and dispersed geographical locations who periodically gather to Gourd dance cannot lay claim to sharing these criteria, because they lack the ethnic, kinship, historical, geographical, linguistic, and cultural background on which the dance is based.

In Kiowa Gourd Dances, the words to many songs are sung only during the annual ceremonials. Hobbyists groups are increasingly singing more and more Kiowa songs with words in them, the pronunciation of which often leaves much to be desired. Even with correct translations, hobbyists cannot relate to the Kiowa songs and history on the same level that the Kiowa do. Although some non-Indians are talented singers, they generally do not compose their own songs and thus are dependent upon borrowing the necessary repertoire of Indian-composed songs. Furthermore, because songs were the basis for the revival of the Gourd Dance and are the most crucial element of the dance and its history, their use by outsiders and non-Indians angers some Kiowa, who see the dance as derived from a military and religious background associated with the Sun Dance and not as a secular dance for the taking at will. Conversely, there are also Kiowa who welcome non-Indians who demonstrate a sincere interest and are gladly willing to teach them. In the middle is perhaps the largest segment, those who would rather see outsiders remain spectators but who are too polite to deter those attempting to learn.

For the Kiowa, the dance is an ongoing form of direct family and tribal history, culture, and ethnic identity—not an abstract avocation to be imitated. Although some outsiders come to understand the "spirit" of the Gourd Dance through participation, many fail to identify with the intricate concepts and values that permeate the dance, and thus with the multilayered, interwoven content and significance that the dance holds for the Kiowa. The complexity of the tonal Kiowa language makes it difficult for non-Kiowa to learn and thus to fully understand these topics. The full significance of the dance, the language, and especially the Kiowa definition of "spirit" and what the dance means for them is often difficult for outsiders caught up in the popular and material culture dimensions of the dance to perceive and understand. As the Kiowa Gourd Clan (1996:17) stated:

> In this age of mobility, the gourd dance has spread across the nation throughout "Indian" country. Since then many tribes have formed gourd dance clubs and the popularity of the dance can be observed at most Native American gatherings. Although each tribe has their own singers who sing the gourd dance songs, the true meaning of the gourd dance can not be felt or the melodies can not be enjoyed in their truest beauty and form until a visit is made to the Kiowa Gourd Dance celebration where the Kiowa singers are heard singing in their Kiowa language.

The heavy inclusion of non-Indian participants and especially the use of the Kiowa "Tia-Piah" name by Anglos have produced some hard feelings between various Kiowas Gourd Dance groups. Although Native American tolerance and accommodation of hobbyists varies widely, extremely courteous accommodation prevails, in accordance with the traditional hospitality shown to strangers. Many Anglo-based Gourd Dance groups assert that they were "given the right" to perform the dance by a visiting Kiowa or Indian authority who "had the right to do so." In many cases this "gift" did occur. However, many Kiowa do not find this basis of authority for giving, receiving, or performing credible. Frequently, a person who has limited contact with and participation in the home community is sought out in an urban locale to provide leadership for non-Indians interested in the Gourd Dance. Often these people are sought out more because they are Indian, which in the Anglo viewpoint serves to validate their interests, than because they are truly knowledgeable, are active Gourd Dancers, and, more important, have the support and authority of the tribal community to do so. More often that not, the home community does not recognize such persons' authority as leaders or their right to give outsiders permission to perform the dance.

Context, tradition, and the way the dance is conducted are major criteria by which Kiowa view the way the Gourd Dance is performed. One Gourd Clan member expressed his concern over and disapproval of non-Indians performing the Gourd Dance:

> If I knew there was a non-Indian Gourd Dance society I wouldn't even go to it. I wouldn't mess with it anyway. I'm against it. I don't think that they should have it, and whoever, whatever Kiowa went down there and gave it to them, who gave him the right to do that, you know? Among Kiowa people that's very important. Who has the right to do this, you know? I mean the issue of the right to do something is big, you know, very big. And you have a lot of people who are, that have mixed emotions about it, and I'm one of them.[164]

However, non-Indians' willingness to follow is attractive to people who are willing to lead them. And for Indians who live in off-reservation, non-Indian environments, such leadership serves to establish as well as to reinforce their Indian identity. As one elder Kiowa Gourd Clan singer described it:

> When it comes to that, we kind of feel offended. Our people, we are direct descendants to this dance, right in it. Yet we don't really go out and try to be the leaders. We know our part and we stay within. But to go out, see someone who don't really take part around here, to be a leader or whatever, kind of burns us a little bit. But we keep it within ourselves. We know it's not right, but we'll go along with it. But it gets kind of offensive sometimes, some things that are "uncalled for" that happen.[165]

Most non-Indians are oblivious to this distinction and form an allegiance simply because the person is an Indian and represents the most direct link to what they desire — a level of acceptance and inclusion that permits them to dance. Although long-term and sincere bonds exist between Indian and non-Indian people, non-Indians look to Natives for information and, even more, for approval and permission. In some instances Native people sincerely welcome non-Indian participation, and in many cases they tolerate hobbyists because they are an important source of resources through the dance clothing, food, money, and other items they provide as gifts, through giveaways, or simply out of hospitality. As one non-Indian Gourd Dancer said, "I was dancing at a benefit dance of one of the organizations. During a break about halfway through the program, one of the officers picked up the microphone, looked directly across the arena at me, and said that non-Indians were not welcome to dance. . . . Of course they didn't return any of the money I had donated up to that point."[166]

Some elder Kiowa feel that the diffusion of the Gourd Dance, including the use of the name Tia-Piah by others Indians and non-Indians, has resulted in a relatively widespread corruption of its rites and a blatant disregard for their heritage. Many feel that the name is a Kiowa name and should remain so. One elder emphatically stated: "It's okay if those other groups gonna dance. I know a lot of other Indians and non-

Indians, they like to dance. But Tai-Piah, that's our name, our society. It's a *Kiowa* name. It shouldn't be used by any other groups, Indian or non-Indian. They got no right to it and no one's got the right to give it away, either."[167]

Elders whom I visited spoke at length about other tribal and non-Indian Gourd Dances they had attended and were quick to point out differences and inaccuracies. Though not approving of them, most laugh and make light of the situation, saying that although many people do not have the right to perform the dance and that they are sometimes offended, there is little they can do about it. One elder remarked, "If they want to dress up and hop around, they can do that, no matter how ridiculous they look. So be it. That's their business." Two Kiowa men described how someone came up to them at an out-of-state Gourd Dance and asked them to initiate him because they were Indian. They declined. Although permissions continue to be given, many Kiowa in the home community are outraged, feel that no one has the right to give away either the dance or the Kiowa Tia-Piah name, and believe that the dance belongs to or is "owned" in only a tribal or collective Kiowa sense.

One Gourd Clan member expressed his concern over the way other Indians and non-Indians performed the Gourd Dance and the fact that many knew only the popularized form of the dance:

> In regards to other tribes doing the dance, I think most tribes, most people who are doing it, try to respect it. . . . For me, if they come to Carnegie, see how it's done, and then go to their respective place and do it correctly, then I'm okay with it. But then I have this problem with who has the right, who authorizes the right of people to go and give this dance to somebody else? You know, that's the problem that I have, who is the person who has the authorization to go to down to Texas, or to, you know, the Gulf Coast Tia-Piah Society, you know, and to start these Gourd Dance Societies? I feel that way because this Jáifègàu Society is really sacred to me. Very, very important, and we don't want any lack of respect whatsoever to get involved into the Gourd Dance, you know. So I mean I have mixed feelings on it, you know, and you never really know if they do it like us, you know, like I see people that Gourd Dance in other places in shorts, you know, short-sleeved shirts [laughing]. You know, they got cowboy hats and stuff like that, you know. Huh-uh. I don't like that, no, no, that's no good. They do it like us, heh, I'm okay with it, and that to me, that's showing respect, that's showing respect for our Jáifègàu, our warrior society, then you know I'm okay. But, if you go out there and you Gourd dance in tennis shoes, and then you know, not looking your best, to me that's a lack of respect and I don't like that. . . . I have mixed feelings on that. I'm against societies doing our dance because I feel like they don't take the time to understand what we do and realize the historical aspect, I don't know, maybe like a cognitive approach to what Kiowa people are all about. I feel like if a person wants to Gourd dance they need to come to Carnegie and see what it's all about, and I've talked to

several people who have Gourd danced before, and when they went to Carnegie and seen how it was really done, how it was supposed to be done, they're going like, "Man, we never realized how important, how Gourd dancing is," you know, to Indian people, or to Kiowa people, and they went away with it with a new respect, with a newfound motivation, you know . . . and these were Indian people.

Every time I go to a powwow and I see these Gourd Dancers and they're not, they don't give Gourd dancing the proper respect, you know. One of the reasons why is because they're not educated about it, they don't know the history about it, they don't know why we Gourd dance, you know. If they come to Carnegie and if someone can sit down and explain it to them, I can guarantee you they would have a different perspective on Gourd dancing. Because today, you know, [many people think that] Gourd dancing is just something that you do, it's just the precursor to supper. It's the precursor to the Grand Entry, and then . . . some people think that's when the real powwow starts. That's when the real dancing starts, you know after the Grand Entry when they have contests. Not to Kiowa people. Gourd dancing is, uh, Gourd dancing is *the* dance, you know? Because, what's interesting about it is Gourd dancing is a ceremonial dance of an ancient and old warrior society.[168]

Anthropologists might view these scenarios as parts of the normal processes of diffusion and innovation associated with cultural borrowing between groups. Kiowa, however, look at these changes largely in terms of the degree to which they follow existing concepts of tradition and protocol. Yet the way others perform the dance outside of the Kiowa community has little or no affect on the way the dance is performed in the home community, and it is this performance that is most significant to the Kiowa and to the maintenance and continuation of their traditions.

Following the formation of the Kiowa Gourd Clan in 1957, numerous other tribal Gourd Clans formed. Today one can find the Otoe Gourd Clan, the Cherokee Gourd Clan, the Osage Gourd Clan, and the Cheyenne and Arapaho Gourd Clan in Oklahoma. The revival of the Kiowa Gourd Dance not only served as a catalyst for its revival among other tribes such as the Comanche, Cheyenne, and Ponca, but it also stimulated revivals of other military and formal War Dance societies among neighboring tribes during a time of tremendous growth and revival of Indian awareness, dancing, and culture between 1958 and 1975 (Meadows 1999). Although the dance was practiced by a number of pre-reservation Plains tribes, the contemporary Gourd Dance revival is based on the revived Kiowa form, as is demonstrated by a considerable historical record of its existence and the heavy use of Kiowa dance style, dress, and music. The singing of Kiowa Gourd Dance songs with Kiowa lyrics is now common among Plains, Woodlands, and Great Lakes tribes and Anglo groups.

The Kiowa helped to disseminate the dance by performing it throughout the United States. The dance has been adopted by the Alabama-Koasati near Livingston, Texas, a Southeastern group that originally never performed the dance. Its members continue to be assisted by Kiowa, who often serve as head staff, singers, and dancers at the annual June tribal powwow, at which the Gourd Dance constitutes the principal dance. The Otoe have maintained a friendship with the Kiowa since the late 1800s and have attended Kiowa Gourd Dances since the 1920s and 1930s. Several Otoe have been inducted into the Kiowa Gourd Clan, from which they also formed a Gourd Clan modeled after the Kiowa group. The Kiowa Gourd Clan (1996:10) states that only "the Otoe Tribe was given the right to dance the Gourd Dance in the 1920s. Although members of other tribes have been initiated and retain membership in the Kiowa Gourd Clan, it is said that only the Otoes were given full permission to dance." Members of the two tribes continue to attend each other's annual dances. The performance of the dance by the Otoe in north-central Oklahoma has helped increase its exposure and diffusion to other tribes.

In April 1970, two Omaha men who had recently been inducted into the Kiowa Tia-Piah Society in Oklahoma brought the Gourd Dance to the Omaha reservation in Nebraska (Liberty 1973). In addition, several intertribal Gourd Dance organizations have been started and influenced by Kiowa in urban communities such as Oklahoma City, Tulsa, Dallas–Fort Worth, Denver, and San Francisco. These cities have large numbers of Native Americans as a result of the relocation program of the 1950s and subsequent urban migrations for employment opportunities. These groups have further attracted and influenced non-Indian hobbyist organizations, some of which have adopted the Kiowa name Tia-Piah.

Ellis (1990) and I (Meadows 1999:134–161, 389–403) have each summarized the role of the Kiowa Gourd Dance in light of national governmental policies and Native trends. Our work affirms that the political and ethnic activism of the Indian awareness movement of the 1960s and 1970s aided in spreading the dance across Indian communities who were reclaiming their heritage during this time.[169] Although military societies were revived among several tribes after 1957, the revival and subsequent enormous popularity of the Kiowa Gourd Dance produced an unparalleled pan-Indian diffusion, paralleling the role the Kiowa, Comanche, and Apache played in the spread of peyotism in the late 1800s. The Gourd Dance initially spread after 1957 to include the majority of Plains and Prairie tribes (Howard 1976), but it has continued to grow in popularity and can now be found from coast to coast in the United States. The dance has also become popular among many other tribes in Arizona, California, New Mexico, and Texas, among some Lakota in South Dakota (Howard 1976), and, more recently, among the Navajo. Although the use of the Kiowa name by other tribes and non-Indians bothers some Kiowa, others embrace and even encourage interested outsiders. The effects of the post-1957 diffusion of the Kiowa Gourd Dance remains strong in many contemporary Southern Plains Indian–style powwows. Throughout much of Indian and hobbyist country today, a Gourd Dance can be found in nearly every program, and Kiowa frequently serve as head staff for both Indian and non-Indian powwows and Gourd Dances.

Anthropological Classification

Howard (1976) classified the Gourd Dance as a "revitalization movement" and further related it (Howard 1976:257) to Nancy Lurie's (1971:418) "articulatory movement" on the basis of the absence of "identifiable leadership and spokesmen." Although a revival aspect is present, the dance is probably not best understood as a total revitalization or articulatory movement (Wallace 1956:265–268), for two reasons. As Lassiter (1992:66) explained, these are, first, that no distinct belief system linked to the dance's historical development is present in the Kiowa community, and second, unlike in the Ghost Dance, which encompassed a well-defined conviction that facilitated the rapid spread of the dance—thereby making it a revitalization movement—no such distinct conviction or canon associated with the Kiowa Gourd Dance has spread to other communities. Although acknowledging that the dance did periodically stop between 1890 and 1957, until it became the subject of renewed interest, Lassiter (1992, 1993, 1995) further argued against categorizing the Kiowa Gourd Dance as a revitalization movement because the "dance never left the Kiowa because the songs never left them. . . . The songs were never truly at rest, i.e. they were never 'revived because they never ceased'" (1993:377). Despite the lack of attention given to songs in earlier ethnographies and the fact that songs are the most central aspect of the Gourd Dance and its resurgence, their overall inactivity in a sodality-based format, the formation of many new songs based on the older, traditional style, the incorporation of songs from several other societies into the current Gourd Dance repertoire, and the Kiowa's conscious attempt to revive the dance suggests that elements of revitalization are present. From another viewpoint, with intermittent Gourd Dances being held from the 1920s through World War II, the 1957 formation can be seen more as a reconfiguration or reorganization than a complete cessation and revival. Perhaps more important than distinctions over the meaning of the words *revitalization* and *revival* is that most Kiowa, including the Kiowa Gourd Clan (1976:22, 1996:6, 9), Comanche, and Cheyenne with whom I have visited speak of the Gourd Dance and many other cultural activities in terms of "revival" or "being revived," indicative of their conceptions of the post–World War II events associated with the dance.

On the basis of dance style, Howard (1976) briefly discussed several Plains and Prairie groups that had military societies that used similar choreography, including the Cheyenne, Arapaho, Comanche, Ponca, Omaha, and Iowa, some of whom make their own claims to the modern Gourd Dance. Southern Cheyenne and Bowstring Society members I have spoken with maintain that the dance was "stolen" from them by the Kiowa during a battle in the 1830s.[170] From an emic point of view, Plains tribes usually considered such warfare-based acquisitions as honorable. As Lassiter noted (1992:66), whether or not these claims are true is not really the question. What is most relevant today, especially among younger Kiowa, is that the Kiowa unquestionably revived their distinct version of the Gourd Dance, which produced the popular expansion to other Oklahoma groups, some of whom once had historically similar dances and societies. Some younger Kiowa and other Native Americans (Lassiter 1998:243n1) attribute the origins of the dance to the Kiowa and are concerned only with the modern manifestation of the dance. Yet popular opinion about and historical evidence for any event or activity often differ significantly. Assuredly, we would not dismiss firsthand accounts by Civil War veterans concerning their military experiences in favor of the popular viewpoints of the current generation. What is significant is that there are two different perspectives concerning the Plains Gourd Dance and its origins, one rooted in Plains historical and ethnographic sources and pictographic calendars dating from the 1830s to the late 1930s and the other a contemporary perception of the post-1957, Kiowa-dominated revival. Some Kiowa and other Native people associate with the former, others with the latter. It is imperative to distinguish between the current popular view and the historical-ethnographic view, because both are important in understanding the historical origins, development, and present effects of the dance.

When the Kiowa revived their Gourd Dance, they provided the Comanche, Cheyenne, and Arapaho with a renewed historical connection to the dance, but in a modern (revived) Kiowa form. My fieldwork and participation in Kiowa, Comanche, Apache, and Cheyenne Gourd Dances, in addition to Lassiter's work (1992:66, 1998), indicate that the dance was conceptually changed to be Comanche-specific or Cheyenne-specific.[171] With its similar dance and music styles, the Gourd Dance underwent what William Powers (1980:217) called "homostylic diffusion." Within the geographical proximity of Oklahoma, the selective traditions associated with the revival originated with the Kiowa version, providing them with a specific relationship to the songs in a modern context. Thus, whereas several pre-reservation groups had similar societies, the post-1957 form is Kiowa based. Numerous Kiowa Gourd Dance songs, especially those with texts, provide the Kiowa with claims to the songs, which in turn strengthen their claims to the tradition, because Gourd Dance songs with texts have been lost and not replaced in most neighboring tribes. Although critics say that anyone can put words into a song, one might ask why others have not done so.

The revival of the dance first as a Kiowa representation of Kiowa culture and then, as it diffused, as "an Indian representation of Indianness, not a white one" (Ellis 1990), made it even more popular. During the 1960s and 1970s the Gourd Dance grew in popularity, eventually becoming a major part of the Southwestern Oklahoma Indian powwow after 1972. Over the last thirty-five years, numerous organizations have formed that concentrate exclusively on the Gourd Dance as their main activity. Nearly all sought out reputable Kiowa singers who composed individual and "club" songs for the respective groups, providing them with a sense of distinction among the Gourd Dance organizations of southwestern Oklahoma.

Some organizations that were previously and exclusively War Dance groups adopted the Gourd Dance in part because it enabled larger numbers of people to participate and because of the lower cost of Gourd Dance clothing relative to War Dance clothing. Each organization normally holds an annual dance and several benefit dances through the year, so one or more Gourd Dances of eight to ten hours in length usually take place every weekend of the year in southwestern Oklahoma. Interviews and a review of old powwow fliers show that by the early 1980s, Gourd dancing had replaced War dancing at many organizational benefit dances held by powwow clubs, veterans groups, and descendant organizations, except at those hosting War Dance contests. Gregory Haumpy Sr. recalled how the Gourd Dance began to supplant the War Dance in popularity and frequency in the mid-1980s: "The War Dance was popular. But when the Gourd Dance came in, everybody was out Gourd dancing, whooping and hollering. And when they change programs, well, after the last four songs, Gourd Dance songs, they change the program over to War Dance, people would start getting up and heading home. Yeah, they'd leave. The crowd gets thinner."[172] One elder even said, "The Gourd Dance has ruined the powwow." Although this person came from a War Dance–oriented family, the point is taken. At dances containing both Gourd and War dancing, Gourd dancing generally makes up the afternoon program as well as a short session after the supper break, before the program changes over to other types of social and War dances. Organizations with all–War Dance programs are more societal organizations with formal dance protocols, such as the Kiowa Ohoma Lodge and the Comanche War Dance Society. Yet occasionally, even some War Dance groups include a Gourd Dance portion of the program. As in the cases of the hand game, the Native American Church, and other cultural forms, distinct Gourd Dance and War Dance "crowds" (people who frequent a certain form of cultural activity), as well as singers who sing primarily in one genre over others, perform nearly every weekend.

With the increasing popularity of the Gourd Dance and its spread in the pan-Indian movement, the dance came to symbolize in some ways what it meant to be Indian rather than what it meant to be Kiowa, as the conceptualization of the dance beyond Kiowa country became increasingly diversified. The spread of several regional War Dance styles that have evolved into contemporary powwow forms mirrors this development. Powers (1980:217) called this process "transcultural diffusion," which occurs when "songs and dances retain their original structure, but either most of their functions are lost or new functions added." Lassiter (1992:67) referred to the Gourd Dance revival as a "popular revival," because it was a revival within the context of the Kiowa community that is also popular outside this center.

Examination of how the Kiowa version of the Gourd Dance is used outside the Kiowa community greatly determines how the dance revival should be categorized. Its classification as a "revitalization movement" does not fully reflect the character of the dance's diffusion, for it is instead characterized by an activation of selective traditions, in this case Kiowa traits, that have taken on new meanings and connotations — primarily Indian identity in terms of pan-Indianism — once outside the Kiowa community and Oklahoma. Because the Gourd Dance has a specific (still known) history and a specific meaning for the Kiowa, they perform the dance much as the original 1957 revivers did — revivers who were reinforcing their own identity, albeit during a period of rapid pan-Indian development — and not as a result of pan-Indianism (Lassiter 1992:67). Thus, concepts of revitalization are not totally useful in discussing the Kiowa revival of the Gourd Dance, because the dance did not diffuse to other Indian communities in forms culturally and qualitatively the same. However, elements of the concept are applicable, because the Kiowa revived the dance to perpetuate their own heritage, and they perceived the new formation as a revival themselves (Kiowa Gourd Clan 1976, 1996). As the predominantly Kiowa-influenced version of the Gourd Dance continues to grow in popularity among other tribes and non-Indians from coast to coast, it will be interesting to see the relationship and attitudes that will develop, at home and abroad, from such an undeniably influential dance form.

The Role of the Gourd Dance and Music in Kiowa Ethnic Continuity

Anyone who has witnessed, let alone participated in, a Kiowa Gourd Dance can attest to the intensity and spirit of its emotion, concentration, music, and dance. From a Kiowa perspective, participation and personal experience is essential to gaining a feeling for and understanding of the music and dance. There is simply no other substitute. Albert Bronaugh enthusiastically described what he thinks about while dancing at the annual Gourd Clan ceremonial:

> Oh, man. I'm out there from the starting song on the first day. The starting song is one of my favorite, favorite, Gourd Dance songs. It's just an unbelievable song. I don't know how old that song is, or who did it . . . but the music is so powerful . . . it just goes through you, it just gets in you, you know? And when you're out there dancing and it's hot, you're sweating, your adrenaline is going, physically, you know, you're just really, really into it. You're out there shaking your gourd in time with the drum, you know, the drum is beating like your heart, and you hear that bugler come in, and oh, man, it's just spirituality, spiritual-wise you're just, I mean, you're in a trance. I mean, it's like you're in a trance. And I understand, you know, when they're talking about the Ghost Dancers, you know, long ago, you know, doing the Ghost Dance movement, and how they danced and danced and they were in a trance and they were in like another dimension. That's the way it is down there at Jáifègàu, you know? To many of us dancers down there, we feel that way. It is so important to us, you know, because it's like the Old Ones are out there with us, you know? I mean, you got Séttháidé's, you know, the war trophies, we got different things out there from our past warriors there, [that] we're dancing with. And there is just something out there in the arena that is just strong, it's really powerful and it's just, ah man, it is such a great feeling you know . . . it's just a permeation. It just goes through me, it's just in me, you know? So the reason I feel that way is because I now understand who I am. I understand who my family is, and everything, uh, what they were about. And so to me everything about their life, I'm talking about my ancestors now, and even of today. Everything about their life—whether it's their way of life, the tipis that

they lived in, the buffalo meat that they ate, the buffalo that they killed, their weapons, their language, their dance regalia, you know? Their eagle feathers, all of it's so sacred, so, so sacred. And you have that respect, you have that respect for them. Respect for the regalia and their way of life, the way of life, everything about them is just unbelievable.[173]

From my perspective, as well as that expressed by several Kiowa, knowledge of the song texts is also necessary to fully understand and appreciate Kiowa songs. Alan Merriam (1964:207, 280) showed that song texts, as language behavior, are a reflection of culture and often function as a vehicle of history. Many types of Kiowa songs serve as a means of maintaining oral history (Meadows 1991, 1995). Although Westernization has caused drastic changes in many aspects of Kiowa life, Lassiter (1992, 1995) maintained that Kiowa's reactions to enormous cultural transformations have actually been in favor of cultural retention, by producing a unique ethnic continuity for the Kiowa Gourd Dance. Many cultures have preserved and maintained their musical repertoires despite the effects of Westernization (Nettl 1985). The Kiowa have maintained the Gourd Dance and its music in new ways that, while clearly undergoing changes and the loss of some aspects, have been adapted to preserve the vitality and intactness of the performative aspects of the dance and Kiowa ethnic identity. Performances of traditional dances, songs, and speeches are the products of unique histories of Native American communities and maintain and preserve a specific ethnic continuity in American society. Whereas some of these performances, such as the powwow, are more pan-Indian, other, more ceremonial performances continue to address and maintain more specific ethnic distinctions.

The Kiowa Gourd Dance continues to connect Kiowa ethnic identity with cultural and artistic performance. The maintenance of a tribally specific and distinct form of the dance provides the Kiowa with a unique cultural boundary that allows them the opportunity to reinforce uniquely Kiowa concepts and values. With its own specific history, the dance contributes to the continuation of Kiowa culture. In essence, the Gourd Dance represents the way an older tradition, redefined through revival or revitalization, serves as a unique source of ethnic identity for Kiowa as both Kiowa and Americans. Inducted into the Gourd Clan in 1999, Albert Bronaugh spoke of the multifaceted relationship between membership in the society and Kiowa family history, the maintenance of tradition, and ethnicity:

It's how you conduct yourself, how you present yourself, and how you represent your family.... It's if you practice what you preach. If you talk about language, you know, if you speak your language. If you adhere to your tribe's and your family's customs and you do what you're supposed to do.... Like this past year I couldn't dance at Ją́ifègàu, you know [because of a recent family death]. I mean, right there's an example of doing what you're supposed to do. I didn't like it, and I still don't like it, because of how I feel about Gourd dancing. I mean, Gourd dancing is a state of mind. Gourd dancing is a state of being. I mean, it's not just [being] out there, just shaking a gourd and listening to music and getting all hot and sweaty and then go back to camp and eat. To me, Gourd dancing, like I said, is so important to me. It's just in me, and I have no desire to be a fancy dancer. I have no desire to be a straight dancer, I have no desire to be anything else . . . because that's what my ancestors were. And whatever's good enough for my ancestors is good enough for me, because that is who they were, that's who I am. I don't have to be anybody else.[174]

Kiowa feel deeply for their music, and Gourd Dance music plays a major role in the relationship of music to the maintenance of ethnic continuity. Song takes on a unique meaning in the southwestern Oklahoma world of ceremonial and social dance. As in many other human communities, music is extremely meaningful for participants and serves as the drawing card to events (Nettl 1985; Lassiter 1992:8, 1998:117; Meadows 1995:290, 428–434). Many Kiowa have stated that they go to powwows and society dances to listen to the music, and indeed, spectators always outnumber the singers and dancers combined. Many dancers have also stated that the singing is their favorite part of dances. For some the music has a medicinal quality that, beyond serving simply to take one's mind off everyday problems and worries for a while, provides an observable social and psychological stimulus that actually makes people feel physically better.

"Spirit" in Gourd Dance Music

Central to the role of Gourd Dance music in maintaining ethnic continuity is the "spirit" of the music, which many elders state is the most important and most difficult aspect to understand. Lassiter (1992, 1998) discussed the concept of spirit extensively but provided no Kiowa term for it, only an English definition of spirit as "Power Felt." From the Kiowa perspective, the soul is contained in the mind. As one Kiowa elder explained it: "The Being is in the mind and not the heart. That's the difference between Kiowas and Anglos." Another elder said, "Fégà, mind. Fégàǫ̀tàthàu, when your mind feels good. People say it's heart, white people, but it's all the same. Fégà, that's the same thing, heart. See, the mind has a lot to do with your body. When your mind is, well, you know, fégàǫ̀tàthàu, yeah, mind feels good. When your mind feels good, naturally it's gonna tell your heart to feel good." The Kiowa term for mind, *fégà*, is also commonly used to denote the Christian concept of soul when translated into English.

The feeling one gets from pleasing music, which often leads to one's tapping a foot, is known as *fáultàgà*. This term is based on *fául-tà*, a verb meaning "to become musically astir," and *tà-dáu*, a verbal adjective meaning "to be in a happy state" or to feel good. In Kiowa, many intellectual processes, such as *féljàuqĭ* (thought) and *sàǫ̀qĭ* (mentally or physical apt), and physical ailments are personified in the masculine gender (McKenzie n.d.e). Spirit of the kind associated with emotion, song, and religion is known as *fégàqĭ* (Meadows 1999:151). This term is taken from the root word *fégà*, a noun that Parker McKenzie (1991) defined as "the mind, the will," plus the male personifying suffix -qî. People become fégàǫ̀tą̀mà when they become overjoyed in spirit, as from songs or singing, prayers or praying, or talks and talking. McKenzie translated fégàǫ̀tą̀mà as becoming "spiritually pleased."[175] This is the quality of spirit associated with emotionally moving performances of the Kiowa Gourd Dance.

Similar to many other Kiowa cultural activities, the essence of a Gourd Dance is to feel good while simultaneously practicing, enjoying, respecting, and upholding the traditional activity. Feeling spirit during a Gourd Dance is what makes the event most successful. Just as people experience and feel song individually yet in a culturally patterned manner, so spirit is, to a degree, similarly experienced. Each Gourd Dance forms an arena for the exchange of this shared feeling on a community-wide basis. It is the important and dynamic level of exchange between individuals and the group that makes every dance unique. Although feeling and "spirit" are difficult to fully describe, they are present and observable and can be felt. Because spirit most frequently emerges through song, it centers the Gourd Dance experience. When the songs begin to be felt, spirit manifests itself, and because song makes spirit tangible in the Gourd Dance, song serves as the central feature on which the entire Gourd Dance is based. As Lassiter described (1992:8–9) from his research and participation in the Kiowa Gourd Dance and singing:

> For the Kiowas, Gourd Dance songs have a special power of their own, a power beyond the comprehension of many untrained outsiders. "I may sing these songs for ten hours, and if the Spirit hits me for five seconds, it's all worth it," one singer told me. Each Gourd Dance must ideally invoke the "Spirit of the Dance," and this begins with the songs. . . . No matter how one might define it, this Spirit is apparent when one attends a Gourd Dance and hears the music about which the Kiowas feel so strongly. . . . The Gourd Dance songs invoke a Spirit that is a multi-faceted relationship entailing a dialogue between God, the natural and cultural environment, and human beings. An important part of this dialogue is the retention of Kiowa language—the songs now an important container of tradition. In addition, the Spirit ultimately involves a link to both the historical and mythological past through song. These combinations are the circumstances that allow for the expression of an unique ethnic continuity of a Kiowa-specific life. Seen in this light, the songs are the soul of the Gourd Dance. They embody and preserve precious and vital knowledge that defines the Kiowa people. Gourd dance songs are not merely a reflection of Kiowa traditions; they are an embodiment of their religion, their connection to God. As a potent symbol, both of the Kiowa struggle with the U.S. government and the Kiowas' persistence, the songs are about Kiowa people, by them, and for them.

The songs themselves have the power to invoke the spirit of the dance. The Kiowa have sustained their identity through these songs while undergoing immense cultural transformations. As the functions and uses of the music changed over time, the music took on new roles for Kiowa people, and this broadened cultural significance of the music has become a new rallying point for ethnic continuity in both the Kiowa community and the intertribal community.

Spirit as a Dialectical Process

At this point I offer a discussion of "spirit" as a synthesis of what I have learned from interviews, discussions, observations of Gourd Dances, and my participation as a dancer in Kiowa and other Gourd Dances between 1989 and 2008. Discussions of the Kiowa Gourd Dance and its associated music have been primarily from the viewpoint of the singers at the drum, and little has been offered from the perspective of the dancers.[176] There is no precise scientific formula for observing or discussing spirit, and this would miss the point in any case, so I offer a descriptive analogy for purposes of discussing and comparing the phenomenon of spirit. No exact or precise canon exists for the way spirit is produced or when it will come. Spirit is not a quantifiable, measurable physical entity that can be scientifically examined. It is an emotionally laden metaphysical entity that can be physically felt and experienced or observed as people embrace it, react to it, and in turn produce it and affect others.

As several Kiowa described it, in some dances spirit comes several times, whereas in other dances it never comes. Although spirit usually does not occur on the first song, it can. Spirit can occur any time throughout a session or day of Gourd dancing, up to and including the very last song. It can also occur more than once in a single session. In some instances spirit occurs on a special song such as a favorite organizational or society song, and it may occur during the singing of the same song more than once during a session or dance. In other instances it may arise from a song that holds special significance for one or more of the singers, dancers, individuals, or families present.

Spirit is a multifaceted phenomenon involving song, singers, dance, dancers, organizations, and the reaction and participation of the spectators. It often includes getting up to dance, giving away, and "throwing down" money by anyone present. The ways in which these elements combine to produce spirit are immeasurable and almost innumerable, because no two Gourd Dances are ever exactly the same. Often, spirit emanates from the drum, starting with the song and the singers and then spreading to the dancers and the crowd. In other instances, spirit may start with the intensity of reaction of one or more dancers to a particular song. Spirit may then spread to the drum, and the singers intensify their singing and drumming and return it to the dancers. It may then return to the drum again, and so on, as the dancers and singers build off of one another.

Regardless of the exact order of action and reaction, several phenomena are observable when spirit develops during a dance. The dancers begin to dance harder and faster, often shaking their gourd rattles more intensely and calling out as they dance. The male singers begin to drum harder and sing louder, often leaning inward more toward the drum. One girl said that when the drummers begin to lean inward, it reminds her of the way men look when beginning to ride a horse fast. The female singers also begin to sing harder and louder, often standing up from their chairs behind the drum and dancing in place behind the singers. Some begin to keep time to the song with a drumming-like motion made with their fists closed and held in front of their bodies. Spectators are also affected, often entering to dance along the edge of the arena or, more frequently, to "throw down" money (place money on the floor in front of dancers in the arena or in front of a singer being honored at the drum or in the arena). Although men will enter the arena to throw down money to honor a dancer, often more women do so, putting on their shawls, throwing money down to honor a dancer, and then dancing behind him.

In other words, energy (emotional, spiritual, visible, auditory) is produced and is perceived and felt by others, who acknowledge and react to it and, through their reactions, produce further energy. Thus, what I call a dialectic transmission of energy or spirit occurs as the intensity of the actions and reactions increases, and they periodically and repeatedly react to or play off of one another. The process repeats itself through one of innumerable combinations of the aforementioned elements. This process may involve dialectical exchange from one element to another or back and forth between two elements (such as the singers and dancers), producing an increasingly intense, dynamic crescendo of dancing, singing, and drumming and, inevitably, of increased spirit, giving away, and honoring.

Although many people describe spirit as always emanating from the drum and the singers, and often it does, it may also start and spread from other sources, including dancers in the arena, people giving away, or spectators who are suddenly moved by a particular song to rise and dance. Gregory Haumpy Sr. described how spirit comes to him while singing, and how spirit may start with either the singers or the dancers:

> Yeah, it happens there, Gourd Dance . . . it comes about anytime. . . . I just sing the best I know how, and the songs that come out, I put my heart into singing, and then I like the people that sing and dance and holler, raise cain. Yeah, make the people feel good. . . . There's a lot of times I get that feeling. . . . It's funny . . . I like to sing, and [when] something comes on like that, well, continue. Well, it feels like this air, cold air, cool air, just comes right down here to the bottom [points to the back of his head] and it goes all through my body. . . . When you hear a certain song and just one dancer there, that gets [him], he likes that song, and he hollers, and boy, he starts it. And that spirit will come in. And then that starts and they'll dance their heads off. It comes to the dancers too.[177]

Haumpy described another instance of spirit coming during a benefit dance and the subsequent transfer of energy:

> They was having a benefit dance for a certain person that was ill and they needed help. And we was singing, we wasn't singing too hard. I started a song and every-

body started to help with that song and then all of a sudden, just like that hand game, that cool air come up and hit me. I guess it hit everybody right here and then I beat that drum hard and then I started singing loud, with all I've got. Boy, I tell you what, those people came out with that money. They gave it, they put out that money on that blanket, man, there was a bunch of it. And that one time I seen it happen that way. That dance, that song made them people feel like giving, and I mean they gave. . . . Them kind of deals you don't forget, you think about that all of the time. That's what makes me want to sing some more.[178]

Billy Evans Horse essentially described the same process of the dialectic transfer of spirit from the singers to the dancers in the Gourd Dance: "You have to be careful with the singing portion of it, so you can make sure that if you've got the feeling, the dancers get the feeling. And transmit it back and forth. Then your audience will get the vibes, so to speak" (Lassiter 1997:83). Glazner (2002:61) similarly described this process during the honoring of a female Kiowa Marine at the Kiowa Gourd Clan ceremonial on July 4, 2002: "The singers . . . put every bit of their voices and hearts into the song for this young lady. It continued to build in intensity with every push of the song. The dancers could feel it as the pulse of the song quickened, and they responded by dancing even more vigorously as they yelled war cries into the night air." Non-Indian spectators have also described the transfer of energy they perceive from the Gourd Dance, which speaks to the cross-cultural power that music can sometimes possess.

When spirit is achieved, people usually comment on its presence after that song. Often, when the spirit hits, several songs are sung, one after the next, as the momentum continues. Although people can and do throw down to honor individuals throughout a session of Gourd dancing, the frequency and intensity of the act increase dramatically when spirit manifests itself and are directly related to the level of spirit present. People often speak of getting the "feeling" to give. Once the spirit hits during a song, dancers and spectators often use the word *contagious* to describe the overwhelming pull to honor persons by throwing down money for them. Many times when I have been Gourd dancing, I have felt this urge and have thrown down money for someone being honored, whether I knew the person or not.

During the Gourd Dance at the 1997 Carnegie Victory Club Armistice Day celebration, emcee Martha Koomsa Perez addressed the crowd, describing the emergence of spirit from the drum, the importance of the singers for its transfer, and its effects on people:

Mr. Leonard Cozad and my late father, Bill Koomsa [Sr.], they each told me that the drum has a spirit inside it. And it's going to take these singers [points at the drum] to bring out this spirit, and when that spirit catches you, you're gonna do something. You're going to want to dance, you may want to sing, you may want to say something. We all wait for that, we watch that. And it depends on those singers to touch us in some way, by singing the songs that we love so much, knowing and believing that that spirit is within that drum.[179]

Similar expressions of spirit and the dialectic process that follows are found in many other Kiowa cultural activities, including Kiowa Black Legs and Ohoma Lodge ceremonials, the activities of Christian churches, and hand games. Although qualitatively different in each tradition, these expressions are nevertheless similar and easily observable.

Songs and Language Retention

Related to the Gourd Dance's role in maintaining Kiowa ethnic identity is the relationship between song texts and language. Among an enrolled population of more than twelve thousand, there are presently fewer than one hundred fluent Kiowa speakers. Indications are clear that the younger generations are not becoming fluent speakers. These developments produce a change in the way songs are understood and sung and in the way Kiowa identity is identified.[180] As Lassiter has shown (1992:52), the way "some Kiowas understand the Kiowa language is shaped by their participation in the Gourd Dance and not by directly speaking the language, they know the language through the songs they sing." This is true of many younger singers who are gifted and knowledgeable but not fluent speakers of the language. Most currently prominent singers who are fluent speakers are now over the age of seventy.[181] I have heard members of Kiowa Christian churches comment about how important it is that younger Kiowa who do not speak Kiowa learn Kiowa church hymns, all of which contain texts, so that they can know their language to some extent through songs. Whereas the spiritual significance of the Gourd Dance is variable, the meanings of song texts are more precise and easily observed. And while linguistic fluency is not needed to sing and understand brief song texts, it greatly enhances the degree of cultural understanding a person has in relation to songs and singing. Although many younger singers cannot speak conversational Kiowa, many of them understand the basic meanings and translations associated with songs. One young man from a neighboring tribe who frequently serves as a head singer and sings Kiowa songs with words stated that he did not speak any Kiowa or know the translations of the songs but knew them largely through memorization.

Although songs with texts have become an important repository in the preservation of language and clearly serve to recount Kiowa history and reinforce Kiowa cultural continuity, they do this perhaps more symbolically than on a truly linguistic level. Though extremely important in terms of exhibiting ethnic identity, songs with occasional texts do not function as a full language. The repercussions of this situation are already visible. Occasionally, fluent elders capable of offering invocations or prayers in Kiowa are not present at public functions. At some dances an insufficient number of singers is present who are capable of performing certain songs, and in one instance a dance had to be canceled because of an insufficient numbers of singers.[182]

Several of my elder consultants stressed that understanding the meaning and association or context of song texts was integrally important in beginning to understand the complexity of the Gourd Dance.[183] As Lassiter (1995:226–227) wrote: "Knowledge is what makes sound meaningful; to know a song is to know its meaning. To know a song's meaning, in turn, is to know its power—that which inspires, uplifts, and edifies." In many ways, songs remain a major symbol of contemporary Indian culture among the Kiowa and other tribes because they evoke such deeply layered meanings and sentiments and serve as a source of cultural and individual inspiration. At annual Kiowa dances, songs with texts linguistically reinforce the distinctly Kiowa quality or orientation of the event and the symbolism of the performance while conveying the associated meaning in a form more meaningful to elder Kiowa who understand the language. One Kiowa woman in her sixties commented, "The words do have a lot of meaning. I seem to get a lot more out of the ones that have the words."[184] In Oklahoma, only Kiowa Gourd Dance songs contain texts. Only recently have some Omaha and Navajo placed texts in some of their Gourd Dance songs (Lassiter 1995:290). The Kiowa song texts reference a broad spectrum of Kiowa cultural experience, including the Ją́ifègàu, past society leaders, the Sun Dance, individual families, World War II, tribal elders, the Kiowa Ten Medicine Bundles, ethnicity, cultural preservation and loss, good feelings obtained from song and dance, and more.

The origins and meanings associated with songs are essentially individual but culturally patterned experiences such as battle deeds and personal experiences or thoughts that are then introduced and shared through the context of song and community events. Thus every song can hold multiple symbolic meanings and statements at any given time and for any individual. Much as in individualistic religions, people feel and experience songs on different yet culturally patterned levels. Knowledge of family or society connections and of the history contained in songs deepens the symbolism and power of songs by providing a means to ground or reference what is understood. However, even without a means to ground a song's meaning, the Kiowa still share a collective and general knowledge of songs and their power and ability to evoke feeling and meaning. These varied levels of feeling and experience are visible in the way meaning is constantly discussed within the community. The feeling that emerges from Gourd Dance songs is unique to the Kiowa community while it simultaneously marks the distinction between the Kiowa and other communities through song.

Consultants speak of both understanding the meaning of a song and of feeling it on a deeper level, much of which is based on the grounding of personal experience through belief. Understanding what it means to feel song is central to appreciating the unique quality of the Gourd Dance experience. "The deepest significance of song, then, lies in how people *experience* it" (Lassiter 1995:282). Although all songs contain and convey meaning, and all songs have history, those with texts or lyrics communicate more than is referenced by the song's vocals alone—a range of distinct qualities surrounding Kiowa identity. Feelings that are expressed through song differ than those expressed through language alone, perhaps creating a reason for singing them—to express the unique feelings and communications that song conveys. With the addition of texts to the songs comes an additional layer of language, meaning, and history.

Song texts can resemble prayers in that prayers are usually given in Native languages and have come to possess sacred qualities by reinforcing the unique relationship between the Kiowa and God, the environment, and their history. As a part of language, songs embody much of a culture's ethos. Language retention represents the continuation of a distinctive Kiowa heritage and ethnicity. As the language declines, the song texts have began to absorb some of the role of maintaining a Kiowa ethnicity for nonspeakers.

The debate over whether the retention of language is necessary in order to retain culture affects most tribes, including the Kiowa. The Gourd Dance adds to the retention of Kiowa language and culture through the use of song texts as extremely meaningful ritual symbols. Ownership of music is prominent among the Kiowa. Whereas some songs are considered "open," "let go," or "public" and can be sung by everyone, others are "owned," often by individuals, families, or societies. The definition of ownership and extent of use is varied and frequently contested. Some songs are sung in two versions, with and without lyrics, and those with lyrics, especially those including personal names, are more precisely defined, often as owned by or belonging to a specific family. Family and organizational songs are closely guarded, and a strong degree of possessiveness is associated with their use. In song texts that explicitly express elements of Kiowa or family history, the "spirit" of the dance is arguably more specific. By clearly referencing and reinforcing the Kiowa's collective story of cultural survival, songs and their texts unify Kiowa as a distinct group. The survival of the songs alone is often used to justify the Kiowa's historical struggle (Lassiter 1992:50). Because song texts are sometimes reserved for and sung only at "special times," they "help to invoke a unique relationship, they authorize a special distinction, giving them a 'sacred' quality" (Lassiter 1992:53).

The Spiritual-Religious Significance of the Kiowa Gourd Dance

Although no truly integrative Kiowa tribal ceremonies currently take place, the July Gourd Clan ceremonial is the largest annual encampment and integrates a sizable sector of the tribe. Yet the dance continues to hold diverse meanings for different Kiowa. According to the Kiowa Gourd Clan (1976:22), "the present day Kiowa Gourd Clan celebration comes at the time of the Sun Dance and has replaced the Sun Dance." Some people describe what they feel upon hearing Gourd Dance songs by reference to emotional experiences filled with knowledge, personal memories, and the ability of songs to touch and inspire in various degrees. Some compare their feelings to those felt during religious experiences such as peyote meetings, sweat lodges, and Christian church services.

Many Kiowa stress that the dance and music have a sacred or spiritual character, often with reference to the Sun Dance of the past and to the religious association of songs. However, some Kiowa feel that because the Gourd Dance exists under conditions completely different from those of the past and is no longer associated with the Sun Dance, it has lost some of its earlier religious power. Some Kiowa Gourd Clan members were against the Kiowa's accepting the 1997 gift of a Big Lodge (Sun Dance) ceremony from the Crow, from whom they had originally obtained the Sun Dance. Yet Kiowa elders and Jáifègàu members as late as 1935 clearly described the society's dance as a secular, martial-oriented affair and said that the society was associated with the Sun Dance only in the preparation of the camp and Sun Dance lodge. Once these were ready, the society's duties were finished.

Atwater Onco described some of the social and communal aspects of the annual Gourd Clan encampment:

> The songs mean so much. A lot of them have a Kiowa interpretation. The Kiowas know and can't help but feel about our deceased relatives that are gone. The elders. A lot of songs have words in them about our elder people that are all gone. A lot of things, I belong to Jáifè and I'm gonna enjoy myself. It's just the Kiowa words in them. That's why I say it's pretty much like the, it's not the Sun Dance, but what I'm saying, it pretty much functions like it, the social gatherings and all that—tie in with the Sun Dance that was stopped years ago.[185]

Some Kiowa believe that all elements of life are God given and that because songs are religious in quality, one can worship God through song as well as by other means (Lassiter 1998). On a deeper level, the Gourd Dance has always evoked a Godlike presence through song, although in a new form with new purposes. Kiowa songs include a lengthy relationship between God, the Kiowa people, and their culture and translate this unique relationship into "spirit," which allows that power to be tangibly felt. Indeed, the story of the dance's continuity and its songs entail a God-centered perspective that acknowledges all life and cultural components as God given. Because some people view the Gourd Dance primarily as a spiritual or religious expression, analogous to the Sun Dance, they are irritated by the popular expression of the Gourd Dance. As the dance spread beyond the Kiowa community, songs became a symbolic means for Kiowa people to affirm their Kiowa-specific relationship to the dance.

Some younger Kiowas say that religious connotations are part of the importance of the dance. The elders I have interviewed say it is spiritual and has spirituality, but it is not religious, although they agree that the Gourd Dance has been elevated in socioreligious importance as a Kiowa tribal ceremony. There is no doubt that the dance is highly respected, even revered and venerated among the Kiowa. The Kiowa Gourd Clan (1976:23) states, "There are several other gourd clans that have branched off from the original clan and the dance itself has spread to the other tribes over the

United States. BUT ONLY THE KIOWAS venerate, in other words, look upon with feelings of deep respect, THIS, OUR DANCE, OUR SONGS, AND OUR HERITAGE."

Twenty years later the Kiowa Gourd Clan voiced this association in similar fashion:

There are other gourd dance organizations that have branched off from the original clan and the dance itself has spread to other tribes over the continent, but only the Kiowas look upon with feelings of deep reverence for THIS IS OUR DANCE, OUR SONGS, OUR HERITAGE, AND A SACRED PART OF OUR KIOWA CULTURE.
REMEMBER THE GOURD DANCE IS CONSIDERED SACRED AND THE DANCE ARENA IS CONSIDERED SACRED. . . . The Kiowa Gourd Clan is a spiritual and religious organization. (Kiowa Gourd Clan 1996:7, 10, 15)

However, it is important to recognize that the importance and meaning of the dance vary greatly among individual Kiowa. Personal opinions from consultants ranged from "purely social" to "highly respected and dignified" and "spiritual—but not religious" in the sense of other tribal religious forms such as the Sun Dance, the Native American Church, and the Ten Medicine Bundles. Most elders over the age of seventy spoke of the dance in terms of being "dignified," "serious," "spiritual," "highly respected," "traditional," and "cherished" but in no way "worshiped" in a formally religious sense.

That secular and sacred are nearly always interwoven in Indian activities calls for non-Indians to view the situation differently from the Anglo polar distinctions of sacred and secular. Some Kiowa describe the Gourd Clan ceremonial as a homecoming that in effect has replaced many aspects of the Sun Dance. Gourd Clan vice president Tim Tsoodle explained: "I think it does. I think it took its place. A lot of the spiritual feelings you get on the main day, I think that's probably what they're looking for. 'Cause like I said, on that day alone I think that arena becomes holy because you bring the trophies out there. I think it's a whole different setup then."[186]

Gregory Haumpy Sr. stated, "I take it as a social dance, that Gourd Dance. But there's always a prayer brought in. God always comes in on that."[187] Billy Evans Horse offered clarification when he said, "When we say that the Gourd Dance is sacred, it means we respect it, we cherish it."[188] Oscar Tsoodle elaborated on the dance's connection to celebrating life: "See this dance is just something like rejoicing, you know. Enjoy yourself, you know . . . thank the Lord for their lives, that's what it is. . . . This dance is not supposed to be sacred. Sacred, no. It's just a rejoicing dance. . . . Enjoy it and just thank the Lord that it's summertime, another year and you're still here."[189]

Clearly, the dance and its history and traditions hold many different, though often overlapping or correlating, layers of meaning for its practitioners. When asked to elaborate on how they viewed the dance, several other Kiowa provided similar descriptions, including the interpretation of sacredness as respect rather than the strictly Christian usage. Understanding the Kiowa use of the word *sacred* to mean an especially elevated level of respect is essential to understanding Kiowa views and classifications of the Gourd Dance. Perhaps the dance is best understood as a significant part of a highly cherished way of life in which the Kiowa have never lost their faith. Although Kiowa often use English terms such as *sacred* and *religious* in describing the Gourd Dance, these terms hold very different meanings for them than those they hold for clergy and religious scholars.

Beyond being a spiritual and ethnicity-based expression, the dance holds other meanings for some persons who emphasize martial themes stemming from the dance's earlier military society origin. In describing how he felt about the dance, Atwater Onco mentioned some of the varied socioreligious meanings that the dance holds for contemporary Kiowas:

> It's an organization that's highly respected. It's a traditional Kiowa chieftain dance, and I look at it that way. When a person dances that, you're saying that I'm not afraid to die. And a lot of people are dancing, that don't know what it is all about, especially non-Indians.
>
> I can't help but think that this is a sacred dance and it should be carried on that way. It shouldn't be taken lightly.
>
> It's a dignified sacred dance. It's not a social dance. When I get involved in Jáifè dancing, when I really get involved, there's spirit involved in there. When you're really at a Kiowa dance, you feel like you're the only one out there dancing. You don't know if there is anyone dancing out there. That's what I get out of it when I dance the Jáifè dance. I don't care if there's a hundred there, I feel like I'm the only one there. There is spirit involved, spirituality involved. You can't help but think of your ancestors that carried this on, no telling how many years back there, and it's still here today. I look at that and it's not a social dance. It's a ceremony.[190]

Lassiter (1995:313) offered additional insights into the dance's varied descriptions and meanings:

> The tendency of outsiders to ignore this experiential complexity often leads them to talk about such deep experience in traditional Judeo-Christian terms, where so-called "religious" feelings should emerge only within a delimited realm of dogma or belief. Experiencing song does indeed turn the mind toward the "sacred" on many levels. Yet powwow people do not situate this experience within a distinct religious system. Although this feeling can be as deep as religious experience (thus prompting many to compare it with religion), it exists unto itself without the trappings of a set of dogma. Instead, it occurs with the "good dance," a realm which also turns the mind towards pure "fun." And this "fun" is the kind also experienced in recreation and diversion; in play, teasing and laughing, in eating and visiting, and in singing, dancing, and honoring.

Maintaining tradition while producing a good feeling for all permeates the Kiowa approach to the dance. One Kiowa woman's description of the Gourd Clan's annual encampment focused on its more ceremonial and socially integrative aspects:

I don't think they consider it to be sacred, but I think they kind of think of it as more like a ceremonial to honor the beginning of it. At the same time, it's kind of a gathering time, I think as a time to socialize now in modern day.... Kiowa people are kind of a people that like to be together, that like to do things together, that like to share things. And I think that they like being among each other and they like to have this interaction, and for them that's time for their families to come back now from somewhere. But underlying all of that, there is a ceremonial basis for it . . . there is a certain way they handle things, a certain system to the way they dance. . . . There is a system to the way that they are structured out there.[191]

But what has led to the dramatic elevation in importance of a military society dance and set of traditions that was once subordinate to the Sun Dance? With the end of the Sun Dance in July 1890 and the emergence of the Ghost Dance from the fall of 1890 to 1917, the latter absorbed some, but by no means many, of the functions of the former. The Ghost Dance provided an annual, communal, tribal-level religious aggregation for those who wished to attend. Some devout Ghost Dance participants met weekly to sing throughout the year. Although a sizable segment of the Kiowa tribe participated in or attended Ghost Dance rituals, others attended largely to socialize and visit, and a growing Christian segment formed another community focus. The opening, repairing, and cleansing of the Kiowa Ten Medicine Bundles in a sweat lodge ceremony at each Sun Dance was continued at Ghost Dance encampments.[192] With the end of the Ghost Dance in 1917, the opportunities for large-scale, tribal-level religious aggregations that included bundle renewal were gone.

The respect and reverence in which Kiowa currently hold the Gourd Dance suggest that the elevation of the dance is in part a result of the loss of larger, tribal-level integrative religious ceremonies such as the Sun and Ghost Dances, even though not everyone participated in either. Among the Southern Cheyenne, who perform the Gourd Dance in both societal (Bowstring Society) and nonsocietal (powwow) contexts, the Gourd Dance has not been elevated to the same level that it has among the Kiowa and Comanche. The four Cheyenne societies continue to play their integral roles in sponsoring, funding, and preparing for the annual Sacred Arrow and Sun Dance ceremonials. Each spring the four Cheyenne societies meet, and every man who speaks donates money that is in turn given to the pledger for that year's dance, to help defray costs. Afterward the societies bid against one another, and the highest bidder is allowed to set the date of the ceremony. The funds raised this way are likewise used to defray the cost of the ceremonials. Among the Southern Cheyenne, one or more societies may also hold a benefit dance to raise funds for the summer ceremonials, especially if one of their members is the pledger. The Bowstring Society, from which the Gourd Dance originates among the Cheyenne, remains integrally connected to ensuring that the preparations necessary for the Sun Dance are completed. Before the beginning of the Sun Dance, one day each is designated for two of the four societies. At the 2002

Cheyenne Sun Dance, held at Seiling, Oklahoma, July 1 was the Dog Soldier and Kit Fox Society Day, and July 2 was the Elkhorn Scrapers and Bowstring Society Day. July 3 was the Chief's Day. The actual Sun Dance began on July 4. July 5 was the day for the erection of the Sun Dance arbor, and the Sun Dance was held on July 6 and 7. Cheyenne military society functions continue to be formal, tribal events focused on serving a larger cause such as the Sun Dance and Sacred Arrow ceremonials.[193]

Unlike the contemporary Kiowa, Comanche, and Apache military societies, Cheyenne societies do not perform large-scale public dances with elaborate society dress. The Cheyenne distinguish between society functions linked to the Sun Dance and Sacred Arrow ceremonies and more secular Gourd Dances held at powwows.[194] For the Kiowa, the end of the Sun Dance led to the elevation of other, more secular events—namely, revived military societies (Kiowa Gourd Clan, Kiowa Black Legs) and transformed manifestations of these earlier societies, such as the War Dance from the Ohoma Lodge and the Gourd Dance as found in contemporary powwows—to meet the various roles of tribal-level social, cultural, spiritual, and political integration fulfilled by the earlier, single, tribally integrative, pan-Kiowa ceremony, the Sun Dance.

As the Gourd Dance continues to spread throughout the United States, some non-Kiowa and non-Indian adherents have begun to identify with the dance to the point of religious or spiritual fervor (Howard 1976:255; Ellis 1990:25–28; Lassiter 1992). However, this is usually limited to popular ideas of the dance as associated with being "Indian" rather than pertaining to a distinct tribal ethnicity. One Kiowa woman who is active in the Kiowa Gourd Clan explained how she was verbally accosted by a Navajo for "taking pictures of 'their' sacred dance" at a Navajo Gourd Dance in Arizona. She promptly informed him that she was a Kiowa and reminded him where the dance had come from.[195]

The accounts of Kiowa elders in the 1935 Laboratory of Anthropology fieldnotes indicate that during their lifetimes, most military society functions were limited to the preparatory phase of the Sun Dance. Kiowa today increasingly espouse the elevated importance of the Gourd Dance and its semireligious character. As such, it serves as another example of the way military society dances have been redefined. The contemporary Kiowa Gourd Dance and songs reflect the importance placed on belief and faith in Kiowa life (Lassiter 1992:41). Yet by no means do all Kiowa associate this significance with the dance. The various traditions, functions, and uses of the dance produce varied meanings for individual participants, nonparticipants, and families, which continue to differ among the Kiowa. Some Kiowas resent outsiders overemphasizing alleged "sacred" aspects of their dances. They feel that some outsiders place too much emphasis on concepts of Indian spirituality and fail to recognize the social aspects and emphasis on "enjoying the dance" and "having a good time" associated with the dance arena.[196]

The Kiowa's role in reviving and helping to disseminate the dance has resulted in its taking on an ambiguous religious and spiritual character. In terms of personal meaning, the dance may appear homogeneous, but it is actually heterogeneous (Lassiter 1992:42). For the Kiowa, meanings and interpretations are diverse, situational, multifaceted, and sometimes contested, because experience holds different meanings for different individuals and multiple layers of complexity simultaneously at any given dance (Lassiter 1995:217).

Although other Native American groups and even non-Indians have undoubtedly been affected by the social, historical, and spiritually reawakening qualities of the dance, as commonly occurs with popular revitalization movements (Wallace 1956:267, 279; Howard 1976:255), they have been affected on a less specific level. The Kiowa-based origin of the revival, an intimate knowledge of the music and texts, and the gift of the dance from the elders provides the Kiowa with defined, concrete boundaries that non-Kiowa and non-Indians can neither claim nor experience on the same level.

Back to the Basics: The Gourd Dance Songs

Many of the complex, multifaceted relationships associated with the Gourd Dance are integrally linked and symbolized through song. From the Kiowa viewpoint, the songs have an association and continuity that is distinctly Kiowa and cannot be claimed by others. Although other tribes make claims to the Gourd Dance, Kiowa more than others openly contend with pride that the Gourd Dance is distinctly theirs.[197] Although some form of the Gourd Dance was common to many Plains groups (Howard 1976) and is adequately documented for the late 1800s, most Kiowa refuse to recognize its existence. Although many groups did perform a similar dance, sometimes with the Kiowa, the post-1957 revival of the dance is Kiowa. Already a higher-ranking pre-reservation society, the Gourd Clan in its revived form became an important focus of social status and ethnic identity. Consequently, Kiowa in the home community are typically protective of the dance and vocal in their claim to it. In addition to reviving their style of Gourd Dance, the songs and the fact that only the Kiowa retain song texts clearly provide them with a stronger claim to the origins of the modern manifestation. Thus the songs provide the basis for Kiowa claims to the right to the Gourd Dance and, in turn, to their right to define the appropriate means of expressing the dance, which is frequently obscured by its popularity. As the annual Kiowa Tia-Piah Society program (1990) illustrates, "Cheyenne say this is their dance, but all of the old Gourd Dance songs are Kiowa. Of course, a lot of songs were recently composed and some by different tribes besides the Kiowas, but even today most of the Gourd Dance songs are Kiowa. The older Kiowas say that this is a Kiowa dance."

Former Gourd Clan officer Oscar Tsoodle maintained, "It originally came from here.... Their way of dancing, respect, and everything. That's what they did. That's the tradition. You know, whenever they take you in as a member, they dance with you, you know, uphold it, just like a lodge or any organization."[198] Lassiter (1992:44, 1998) maintained that from the Kiowa point of view, the songs were the determining factor in distinguishing cultural boundaries. Indeed, the Kiowa style of song, dance, and dress that was presented in 1957 heralded the subsequent pan-Indian and non-

Indian adoption of the Gourd Dance throughout a significant portion of the United States.

The widespread pre-reservation existence of Plains military society chapter organizations (Meadows 1999:55–57, 363) explains much of the widespread similarity of Plains song and dance forms, including the Gourd Dance. Citing similarities of ceremonies, songs, and dances among several Plains tribes, Billy Evans Horse stated that although tribes traditionally learned, shared, and copied songs and dances from one another, the songs did not come out exactly the same. As Horse explained, older songs are always being lost as newer ones are made, as is evident when he sings an old song and younger Kiowa think it is a new song.[199] This issue is readily pointed out when Comanche or Cheyenne sing songs with Kiowa lyrics or make claims to the dance, which only reinforce Kiowa perceptions of the dance as belonging to them.

It is the use of the same songs that transcends organizational differences, issues of revival and ownership, divisions between men and women, and conservative and popular views of the religious and social aspects of the dance and that unifies Kiowa involved in the Gourd Dance (Lassiter 1995:218). It is the songs and social networks that unify, draw, and maintain participation in the Indian community. The songs and the Gourd Dance bring many Kiowa together as a community with a shared ethnic and historical background. Non-Indians who do not Gourd dance often find Gourd Dances lacking the excitement they expected of Indians and the way they dress and dance. Some non-Indians attending Gourd Dances have made comments including, "Boring," "That's all they do?" "It's not what I expected," and, my favorite, "It's definitely not a spectator sport." What outsiders experience is an unfamiliarity with and inability to comprehend the full significance of the songs, the extended kinship and social networks, and the cultural history they are seeing and hearing. For community participants, these networks and songs center their Gourd Dance experience. Outsiders, by placing too much emphasis on what they can see, fail to hear, feel, and understand.

The role of Gourd Dance songs in maintaining Kiowa identity is significant. Lassiter (1992:44) noted, "More critical to understanding the importance of the Gourd Dance is comprehending how Kiowa people maintain a connection to their larger group of traditions through this musical repertoire." Gourd Dance songs connect Kiowa to their historical and mythological origins, whether it be Red Wolf or the Ją́ifègàu. That the musical origins still hold significance is demonstrated by the "wolf cry" at the end of each song, which recognizes the gift of the dance and songs from Red Wolf and thereby connects the dancers to the dance's origins. By spiritually linking Kiowa to their past, songs maintain a shared performance that heightens group identity. As Lassiter (1992:45–46) described it, "through the musical enactment of traditional Kiowa mythology, Kiowa Gourd Dance songs establish a link between the performers, the natural environment (the wolves), the mythological past (the Red Wolf Legend), and God" (Kiowa religion). Intimately intertwined, these elements create "yet another factor of what it means to be Kiowa."

Because the song texts specifically address Kiowa people and their cultural heritage, they affirm, reiterate, and transmit Kiowa ethnicity, the perpetualness of their environment, and the transitory life of Kiowas as mortals, and they provide assurance and hope for the future. Through singing, songs become personified, as is experienced in the feeling of "spirit," which can be evoked with the appropriate singing and which is more personable and enjoyable in a group performance. Ideally, a good dance is considered to be one in which people are having fun and in which a good feeling emerges and resonates throughout the entire event. Numerous Kiowa song texts contain references to individual and group levels of feeling good and to statements that everything is good or well, such as the feeling upon the return of veterans. Thus songs are clearly linked to and reference concepts associated with good feelings. Yet to produce this feeling and for it to develop into spirit, song must first be felt and then heard, because song is the central basis for the constantly reciprocal, multilayered exchange of meaningful relationships between the singers, dancers, and spectators that ideally and progressively develops into spirit as a dance proceeds.

Songs also link Kiowa people to their past, to their ancestors, and to their memory and history, something that serves as a foundation for and a major function of the contemporary Gourd Dance. Nearly everyone with whom I discussed Gourd Dance songs spoke of reflecting about his or her elders who had performed the dance before, of spirituality, and of having a good feeling from the spirit derived from the dance. When asked what he felt while singing Gourd Dance songs, Bill Koomsa Jr. said:

> There's certain songs that makes me feel of certain people that sang them at one time. You know, and that gives you a good feeling to really sing it hard. You know these people sang them or you heard them sing them at one time or whatever. That's the way I look at it. . . . Certain times you feel good. Well, in this arena when you see some of our older people take part, it makes you feel good. You picture their fathers and mothers that were actual members that took part all the time. You think of them and it makes you feel good sometimes when you sing some of these songs and there's a lot of spirituality in it. You get going and it makes you feel good. On certain songs you think of some of these older people.[200]

Billy Evans Horse spoke of the temporal and spiritual depth of song and dance and of the cross-cultural connection between song and spirituality:

> To me it's a spiritual, I have a spiritual feeling. . . . The song and the spiritual aspect of it is based on their prayers and what they believe in, in their existence. And then even if you read the Bible enough, you're going to find out that it says the same thing in there too. So no matter what race of people it is, wherever it's at, you've got them all over the world. You know you got the Hindus, they got their chants and they got their dances. And you got the guys in Africa and they

got their style and they got their spirituality with it. I kind of like that biblical saying, "Make a joyful noise unto the Lord." I look at it from that perspective.

It must be good because other people are joining in and they want to be a part of something, whatever it is that they identify [with]. And when you realize the songs they're not just today or yesterday, but they were hundreds of years ago and were even further than that.... So it's got a deep meaning once you understand that.[201]

Memory of the past and of Kiowa ancestors is an integral part of the overarching ideology and spirit associated with the Gourd Dance. This can be invoked and communicated through music. Many Kiowa state that the songs remind them of their deceased relatives and friends, especially elders. The Gourd Dance and its songs are a constant reminder of the past, the elders, and the cultural legacy they left for contemporary Kiowa. Taken in a larger view, Kiowa Gourd Dance music functions as a reminder of Kiowa perseverance and cultural survival, as a reminder never to give up on who they are as a people or their belief in their way of life. Together, Gourd Dance music and shared heritage produce a "spirit" that is distinctly Kiowa and that forms a cultural boundary between Kiowa and non-Kiowa. Song texts affirm and transmit Kiowa identity by specifically addressing Kiowa people and their unique ethnic heritage (Lassiter 1992:48), but such connotations are not limited to songs containing words. The majority of songs sung today are wordless "vocable" songs.[202] The Kiowa refer to this difference simply as "songs with words" and "songs without words," or "straight" songs. Songs without lyrics or texts also have meanings, histories, symbolism, and individual significances that are conveyed in singing and speech. One elder stressed, "To completely understand a song, you've got to know its history in addition to the meaning of the words."[203] Both types of songs can invoke spirit. Because songs can be sung with or without lyrics, those with texts provide a deeper, more intense feeling for people fluent in Kiowa, and it is when they are sung that an understanding of the history and meaning of songs is often stressed and more apparent.

As Lassiter noted (1992:48–49), "these song texts do not merely reflect about the past; they invoke several layers of belief. They open a dialogue with history and heritage, and in so doing, link past, present, and future." The references to these topics in songs and in the previous quotations reflect the prevalence of this interlinked ideology, which in turn reflects the long persistence, and not the resistance, of the Kiowa people. In taking on new functions and uses over time, the songs have played a major role in the transformation of the cultural, religious, and symbolic character of the Gourd Dance and its music. The reinforcement of a uniquely Kiowa heritage is what many Kiowa stress as integral to "what it means to be Kiowa" in contemporary America.

Diachronically, the Gourd Dance reflects Sherry Ortner's (1973) "summarizing" and "elaborating" symbols. Symbolically the dance summarizes and elaborates the evolution and persistence of the Kiowa. "The Gourd Dance is clearly a powerful symbol of the Kiowa struggle to be Kiowa in American society" (Lassiter 1992:56). Although the songs convey Kiowa history, they are not just symbolic relics of the past but an active, growing, and adapting cultural form that links past and present. As a performance participating in "spirit," the Gourd Dance gives meaning to contemporary Kiowa life and serves as one means of rejuvenating Kiowa spirit, similar to the Sun Dance (Lassiter 1992:56–57, 1998:91).

In order to achieve this, a combination of circumstances and procedures that Lassiter (1992:57) referred to as "dialogue" must be reached in order for spirit to form completely:

> Through the Gourd Dance, Spirit invokes a dialogue between song, dance, and the Kiowa people. From the musical center, the songs increase this multi-layered dialogue to encompass the mythological past, the natural and cultural environment, and God. Furthermore, in the core of the music itself, we find that the song texts, as a set apart and sacred entity, augment the dialogue further to include, through language, the incarnation of a selected group of traditions that express a vital history important to the Kiowas. That is, being a symbol of Kiowa cultural survival and continuity, song texts explicitly and precisely affirm and transmit Kiowa traditions and heritage. Yet while song texts make a unique ethnic heritage specific, as a contemporary container of language, the Gourd Dance transforms to become a forum for negotiation in an ever-changing dialogue about the retention of Kiowa language and culture within the Kiowa community. Thus, the Spirit of the Dance is a complex dialogue between all aspects of the Gourd Dance: past (historical and mythological), and future, human and environment (natural and cultural), human and God, dance and song, song and text.

The three Kiowa Fourth of July Gourd Dances remain the locations where this dialogue and spirit occur in their most complete forms. Of the three Gourd Dance organizations, the Kiowa Gourd Clan is considered the most conservative. That some animosity and rivalry remain between the groups is clear. When I asked one Gourd Clan member what he thought about the other Kiowa Gourd Dance societies, he replied, "I don't even hardly think about them" and laughed. Members of other Kiowa Gourd Dance societies have similarly dismissed the Gourd Clan or have described it as being too rigid, controlling, and self-centered. But as one Gourd Clan officer noted, "The door's always open, we've always said that. Gourd Clan has always told them that the door is always open." Although some members of the three organizations have periodically danced at one another's annuals, each has continued to maintain its independence, and a reunification does not seem imminent.

Dances outside of the Kiowa community are complicated by the problems created by a lack of understanding of the full significance of the dance and knowledge of the Kiowa language. The absence of this historical and linguistic knowledge inhibits a complete dialogue with the songs and dance. However, even when performed elsewhere, the contemporary Gourd Dance emanates a uniquely Kiowa-specific quality or spirit.[204] Cross-culturally, each generation varies to some degree in its interpretation and practice of cultural forms. If the decline of the Kiowa language continues, additional redefinition of the dance and songs in relation to other parts of Kiowa culture is likely. Nevertheless, the dance and songs will most likely remain an important part of Kiowa culture.

The processes involved in the redefinition of the Kiowa Gourd Dance resemble those described by Jimmy Duncan (1997) for the way the Omaha or War Dance was redefined and reinterpreted across the Great Plains in the early 1900s. The dance gradually changed from being an integral part of the military society system to being a more secular and ethnic body of ritual. Integral to this change was the retention of the memory of "old ways" and tribal values cherished by then middle-aged Indians and their elders in their past. This process was essentially a continuation of what was happening in most Plains Indian dance sodalities, which were becoming ethnic and honorific groups rather than active warrior societies in the late 1800s. This adaptation provided a means to maintain important cultural forms in the contexts of rapidly changing sociocultural influences. The purposes behind the dance were redefined to serve as a much broader source of ethnic revival and continuity, rather than as a strictly military institution. Increased secular features, less rigid (nonveteran) membership requirements and rituals, simple dance choreography, and convenient and limited regalia contributed to the dance's rapid acceptance among many peoples during the great cultural readjustment of the 1950s and later. The rapid spread of the Grass Dance in the late 1800s was accompanied by similar widespread introductions or revivals of the Ghost Dance, peyotism, and hand games. Similarly, the 1957 revival of the Kiowa Gourd Dance aided in the reestablishment of Indian ethnic identity, awareness, and self-determination.

The ability of the Gourd Dance, much like the Grass Dance, to be flexible partially explains the dance's growth (Howard 1951:85). Although the Gourd Dance retained a conservative form in annual ceremonials, its flexibility allowed the secular form of the dance to merge simultaneously into the existing powwow structure. In either form, it is the high esteem in which the dance is held and the persistence of the Kiowa people to adapt and move forward that reflect the spirit of the Kiowa Gourd Dance and what it stands for.

The Gourd Dance integrates Kiowa through a shared sense of community and provides a form of ceremonial integration as well as a cultural diversion from the problems of everyday life. Although not held every day, for many it is truly a part of everyday life—from annual society dances to weekly benefit dances, from ceremonial expressions to popular forms, from time spent composing and practicing songs or preparing for a giveaway or benefit to time spent reflecting on one's ancestors or anticipating the weekend. Many Kiowa describe a need to return home every summer "to go to Gourd Clan," a need "to hear the songs" and feel the intense emotions and reinvigoration that the songs produce for individuals.

Like other forms of music, Gourd Dance songs have the power to make people feel better. In some instances this transformation is on an emotional or psychological level, as in raising one's spirits. On a deeper level it sometimes involves actual physical responses such as increased blood circulation, better mobility, and an overall general improvement in the way a person feels. Mental and physical conditions are ultimately interconnected, and state of mind often plays a significant role in a person's outlook, physical state of being, and ability to heal. This view often coincides with the way people speak about power in terms of its healing ability in association with music and dance. On other levels, song and dance represent ethnic and cultural survival and the power entailed in that continuity. In 1997, at a dance in Apache, Oklahoma, I saw a truck with a bumper sticker that read, "Gourd Dance Power."

Many Kiowa describe the "medicine" and "healing qualities" that the songs contain. Several persons who were troubled or feeling poorly prior to a dance indicated that they felt better, mentally and physically, after the songs began.[205] At a Kiowa language class in 2004, one elder woman asked another how her health was. She responded, "Well, if I'm at Carnegie on the Fourth, and at Ohoma, and Black Legs, then I'm okay." The importance the dance holds for elders was apparent at a dance I attended in 2004 at Red Buffalo Hall. When a certain song began, an elder woman seated near me struggled to get to her feet. After being helped up by others, she danced in place with the aid of her walker until the song ended, then sat back down.

The modern Kiowa Gourd Dance is based on traditions and songs that have been safeguarded and handed down for generations. Although the performance of the dance waned, the tradition associated with the songs, the critical basis for the entire phenomenon, was sufficiently maintained to permit a revival and subsequent composition of new songs. Because the continuity between the ancestral and modern form of the Kiowa Gourd Dance is clear, it possesses a perceptible sense of historical importance and cultural continuity that other forms of the dance lack and that distinguishes the Kiowa version from other tribal forms. Ever conscious of its historical importance, Kiowa have bestowed upon the dance a level of honor and veneration unlike that given to most other contemporary forms. Although multiple groups exist, all provide a meaningful and important expression of the Gourd Dance, Kiowa ethnicity, and identity.

Eventually the Kiowa became victims of their own generosity as the popularity of the dance led to its widespread adoption by many non-Kiowa. In many circumstances it was stripped of its Kiowa-specific identity, customs, protocol, values, and cosmology, which resulted in a transformation of the Kiowa Gourd Dance into a largely social and informal pan-Indian dance outside the Kiowa community. Yet as a marker of cultural resiliency in a form that is uniquely suited to the modern world, the revival and growth of the Kiowa Gourd Dance should be viewed as a watershed event in the revitalization of Native American song, dance, culture, and ethnic identity in the twentieth century.

Despite the diffusion and popularity of the dance, the more conservative forms of it and perceptions of what it stands for remain in the Kiowa community. Albert Bronaugh, a younger Gourd Clan member, described the importance of the Gourd Clan ceremonial to his family's history with the society and to following the tradition of sitting out society activities following a death in one's family:

> Kiowa Gourd Clan, I'll tell you what, that is probably one of the things I'm most proud of. That my family, the Horse family, the Chêjòqĭ family, associated with the Jáifègàu for a long, long, long time. And that's one of the things about Kiowa families, the line of a Kiowa family, your descent, all that is so important to us, even when we're dancing up there, it's all family, we're all family, you know. And this past weekend, it was literally killing me to not be able to dance out there, because I focus everything for this, for the Jáifègàu, I focus everything—my financial resources, my mental resources, my spiritual resources, everything about me that, everything that permeates my soul. The Kiowaness of me, it just is all focused for Jáifègàu. But then we had a family tragedy Fathers Day weekend, you know, two weeks before Jáifègàu, and I had to sit out. With the passing of my niece, you know, it was her birthday, nineteen years old and she died in a car wreck. So sad, so tragic. But I'll be back next year, I'll be back. I can regroup, reorganize, and just get everything back together again, and focus again. And I'm determined next year that I will dance again and be out there with the bugler, be out there with the war trophies, and be out there with the Old Ones, with all of them old songs that they sing, you know, it's just, oh, it's unbelievable.[206]

Gourd Clan Vice President Tim Tsoodle described his views of the importance of the society for the Kiowa:

> I think it's our heritage. It's our inheritance. It's our identity. It's who we are. It's just a statement of who we are. I mean I know other tribes do it, and claim it, and have their own stories, but it's Kiowa. There's nothing they [can say], they can talk till they're blue in the face, it's Kiowa, it's who we are, and it's what makes us who we are. . . . Black Leggins, yeah. I feel like that with Ohoma too. Those are all just parts of a whole that we have to continue and keep up, almost like a covenant we have to keep with God to keep who we are. And that's the way I look at it. Because it's got a lot to do with our religion.[207]

Although the Kiowa Gourd Dance is only one arena in a larger lifestyle involving what it means to be Kiowa, it is an important one because the dance addresses the ideology integral to the maintenance of Kiowa ethnic identity. Those who understand the Kiowa language, the Gourd Dance songs, the lengthy history of the dance, and the social and cultural makeup of the Kiowa community best understand this complex ideology. Songs serve as a reference point that enables the specificity of Kiowa identity, despite diffusion and participation by others. The description and interpretation of spirit can only begin to approach what those who hear, understand, and feel Kiowa songs experience on a deeper level. The Gourd Dance is a complex experience that is uniquely Kiowa. Direct participation in Kiowa community celebrations, including the Gourd Dance, and in the spirit of the dance, with an emphasis on maintaining tradition, an appreciative commemoration of what earlier generations of Kiowa provided, and a remembrance of one's elders, is a major part of the way Kiowa define what it means to be Kiowa. As Anne Yeahquo, who has danced at the Kiowa Gourd Clan Fourth of July celebrations, described it: "During that last [Gourd Dance] song, when all the men are dancing hard, everyone is dancing so hard, and the women's shawls are swinging, and all that money is being put on the ground [given away], I can imagine the past and what it was like for the old people way back there in the buffalo days. That's what it means to be Kiowa."[208]

6

QÓICHḬGÀU

The Sentinel or Scout Dogs Society

The Qóichḛgàu is one of the best known but least understood of all the Kiowa military societies. Associated with warfare, it included several of the leading war chiefs and band leaders, and its members were selected for conspicuous bravery and merit. Considered the bravest of the Kiowa military societies, the Qóichḛgàu was seen as equivalent to the highest-level men's or "Dog" societies in other Plains Indian tribes.[1] The generic label "Dog Soldiers" has often been applied to all Plains Indian military societies, especially those with features of contrary behavior. However, the accuracy of this usage is highly varied, because the names of some of the societies relate to dogs whereas others do not. As I demonstrate later, the application of this genre name to the Kiowa Qóichḛgàu is valid.

Plains Indian "Dog Soldier" societies generally involved forms of contrary speech and action, origins relating to instructions from a supernatural dog, elevated bravado and warfare obligations, the wearing of sashes, and the obligatory staking of oneself down in battle (choosing a place to make a stand and pinning one's sash to the ground while in combat). Although some of these features apply to other Plains Indian military societies, the nature of their use in contrary societies is unique to that type of society. The Qóichḛgàu held its last initiations in 1868 and continued to function until 1878, when it became inactive.

Name and Origins

Because of the tonal complexities of the Kiowa language, the name of this society is difficult to translate with total certainty without in-depth linguistic analysis. Often listed as Koitsenko, the Qóichḛgàu have been described by various names. James Mooney (1898:230) gave the name as Ka-itsenko, "Real or Principal Dogs (?)." Later in the same publication (1898:409) he stated that the name seemed to mean "Kiowa Horses from Ga-i or Ka-i and tsen" (which would be Cáuichḛgàu instead of Qóichḛgàu) and that the society was analogous to the Horse and Big Horse Societies of the Kiowa and Plains Apache, respectively, as given by W. P. Clark (1885:355). Hugh Scott gave

"Elk Horse" in three different lists from the 1890s and stated that the society "had the hardest road due to the obligation to stake oneself down in battle." In one of his interviews, his consultant (probably Isseo) referred to the society as Elk Horse Soldiers, which would be Qóichégàu, an abbreviation of Qócáuichégàu.[2] In 1927 Spotted Bird told Elsie Clews Parsons that "they alone were entitled to wear the elk hides from which the Society took its name (kok'owi [qócáui], elk)," but Parsons supplied no full translation of the name (1929:93). Robert Lowie (1916b:847–848) was unable to acquire an exact meaning for the name but cited one consultant's translation as "Horses with additional honorific epithet, possibly connected with the office of scout." In 1935 Jane Richardson recorded, "After much hesitation, inft [Frizzlehead II] said that the word koiseko meant: k'oi = fox, from k'ode (foxes); and se, meaning 'horse', therefore fox-horses."[3] Despite its various interpretations, Qóichégàu is still the name used for the society. Some elders have suggested that the Kiowa's name for themselves, Cáuigú, is derived from the word qócáuigú (the triplural form for "elk"). In addition, two of the Kiowa divisional bands were known as Cáuigú (Kiowa Proper) and Qógûi (Elk), names that are clearly derived from this compound, and an individual bore the personal name Elk Horse (Qócáuichẹ̀).[4]

Linguistic analysis of the society's name and associated attributes elicits integral information behind the meaning of the name form. Paramount is whether the society's name refers to elk, horses, dogs, scouting, bravery, the Kiowa, or some combination of these. In fact all these elements are related to aspects of the society's origins (dog), behavior (martial bravery, scouting), and material culture (elk hide sashes). Some information suggests that the name is based on concepts of bravery. According to Mooney, "Koitsenko—koi refers to surpassing bravery, or full of deeds of a chief, imkoi-tan-det [ém qóitáujét] = 'he tells chief stories', said of a warrior who recounts [war] deeds in dance."[5]

Kiowa elder and tribal linguist Parker McKenzie provided insights into the name of the society that suggest that a more accurate translation might be "Scout Dogs" or "Sentinel Dogs." The first syllable of the name (qói) can refer to three items: a root form from the word qó-dè, for scout; the use of qói to signify a scout or a sentinel or sentinels; and the use of qói as in qói-táu-jét-jàu, "to recite battle or war deeds." In addition, qó̂-dè refers to the swift fox, prevalent in Plains military society names. The pelt of the swift fox was commonly used as a wrist loop and appendage on Plains military society whips. The behavioral aspects of the society and its role in taking the most dangerous positions in battle suggest that qói (serving as a brave scout or sentinel) is the intended reference, which is also associated with the prevalent scouting behavior of wolves and foxes.[6]

Regarding the second and third syllables of the name Qóichégàu, the earliest known Kiowa word for "dog" is sâ-lé (s/d), or sâ-lé-gàu (t), the term for travois dogs. After the introduction of horses, which replaced dogs as pack animals, dogs became known as ché-gùn (s/d) and ché-gṵ̀-dàu (t), from which is derived the term chệ-gàu (lit. "beasts of burden," in reference to their use in carrying materials on their backs). The term chê̜-gàu was then applied to the horse while a new term, ché-gùn ("discarded beast of burden"), was applied to the dog. Dogs also became known as chê̜-hį̀, with the second syllable denoting "real" or "original" to distinguish them from horses. At some point the nasal and circumflexed tone in the first syllable in chê̜-gàu changed, and ché-gùn became the accepted vernacular term for dogs.[7]

Clearly, nominal and cultural elements relating to elk, dogs, horses, foxes, warfare bravery, and scouting are all associated with the original name and cultural practices of the society. These similarities are further complicated by the tonality of the Kiowa language. Whereas later data suggest that the name Qóchę́gàu was altered to Qóichę́gàu, both of which imply "Scout or Sentinel Dogs," the earliest data indicate that Qóichę́gàu is abbreviated from Qócáuichę́gàu, denoting Elk or Kiowa Horses.[8] Details of the society's origins, however, suggest that the name pertains to dogs.

Jerrold Levy (2001:912), using Alice Marriott's data, placed the origins of the Qóichę́gàu after that of the Jáifègàu and attributed the formation of the former to a setting apart of the great and wealthy warriors. Existing documentation, however, indicates that the society dates back at least to the late 1790s. According to Frizzlehead II (È̜máuthâą̂, or Arising Crying) and Quoetone (Kuito, Guito), a shaggy, poodlelike dog once spoke to a man, instructing him in the way to dance and dress. With these instructions came a taboo prohibiting a society member from touching a dog. This taboo had to be observed until a man had retired as a sash owner and given his sash away, whereupon he was once again permitted to touch dogs. According to Sangko, society members were afraid of dogs and always drove them as far away as possible, because the spirit in the society ropes and feathers would not permit their presence.[9] Mooney (1898:230) wrote, "According to the myth, their founder saw in a vision a body of warriors dressed and painted after the manner of the order accompanied by a dog; which sang the song of the Ka'-itsenko and commanded him, 'You are a dog: make a noise like a dog and sing a dog song.'"

Judging from the prominent role of dogs in the society's origin story, attributed society behavior, and the widespread relationship of dogs to other Plains Indian Dog or Dog Soldier societies, a translation of "Sentinel Dogs" or "Scout Dogs" appears to be the most accurate one for this society's name. For simplicity, I use the translation "Dog Society" to refer to the Qóichę́gàu.

Early History

An early account of the society was told by Silverhorn in 1935 and involves a well-known story of a battle between the Kiowa and the Comanche. Although alleged to have occurred in 1790, it may, according to Elizabeth John (1985), date to just before 1806, when a formal peace was established between the two tribes.[10] As a young chief, Lone Young Man (Fǽgàujògùl) led a war party of Kiowa and a few Plains Apache against the Comanche. Upon meeting the Comanche, the entire Kiowa and Apache contingent was killed, except for the Kiowa leader, whom the Comanche could not kill. Finally the Comanche leader called his warriors back, leaving the sole survivor to carry the news back to his camp.

Lone Young Man slept among his dead comrades that night and arose the next morning to discover that his society insignia, a black rope, had been shot to strings. Mourning his comrades' fate, he rode to the Comanche camp determined to die fighting. Upon his arrival, the Comanche leader would not let his warriors kill him and rode out alone to meet the Kiowa. Lone Young Man approached slowly, rode a few steps, dismounted, sang his war song and danced, and then remounted. He repeated this process several times before reaching the camp, where the two leaders then conversed in sign language. Lone Young Man asked to fight to the death, but the Comanche leader responded that his men would not fight him and invited him to his lodge. Lone Young Man accepted the invitation but continued to dance, sing, and whoop on his way to the Comanche leader's lodge.

The Comanche leader gave him a bed, where he remained until his wounds had healed. Later the Comanche leader adopted him as a brother and told him, "When you kill four fat buffalo I will let you return to your home." One day he asked Lone Young Man to go on a war party with him, the fourth such venture, in which he distinguished himself against the Arapaho. The Arapaho had retreated into some timber that the Comanche were hesitant to enter. Dismounting, Lone Young Man sang and led a charge into the timber, brandishing a tomahawk effectively. The Arapaho were all killed, save for one man who hid under the dead and returned with the news to his tribe.

The Comanche honored Lone Young Man, and their leader told him, "When I said four buffalo, I meant four war parties. This was the fattest of all." He then released him and gave him a mount, a packhorse, food, weapons, and clothing. The Comanche leader instructed his warriors not to molest the Kiowa, and after four long years he started for home. He came to an Arapaho village that he thought might be his own, and several warriors rode out shooting at him. Although he was alone, he told them he would fight them if they wished. The Arapaho who had survived the Comanche attack recognized the Kiowa and told his people of Lone Young Man's attack. This frightened the Arapaho so badly that they would not fight him, and they left him alone.

Upon returning to the Kiowa he met a man who informed him that he was believed to be dead, and his black society rope was being given to another man at that year's Sun Dance. Furthermore, his soon-to-be successor had married his younger wife, although his older wife had remained faithful. Continuing toward the camp, he met his mother, who embraced him and cried. He informed his mother that he was not upset about his younger wife, since he had been believed dead. His relatives held a large reception for him at which his presence was announced to the camp, and he was asked to come to his society's meeting. Upon entering the meeting he saw his successor sitting in the place of honor. The successor immediately left the meeting, picked up his new wife, and left camp. Singing his war song, Lone Young Man instructed some people to bring the couple back, but they could not be found. Thus Lone Young Man remained chief of the society.¹¹ The presence of the Dog Society as a well-established group by the turn of the nineteenth century is of historical importance because it provides the earliest known reference to a Kiowa military society.

Membership and Status

The Dog Society was considered to be the warrior elite of the Kiowa tribe. Lowie (1916b:842) wrote that the society was "superior to the others [Kiowa military societies] in social prestige, being composed exclusively of eminent warriors." Members were generally near middle age, although outstanding younger warriors were occasionally inducted. Lowie (1916b:848) stated that members were twenty-five years of age and up. Regular membership accorded a higher rank than any position in the other men's societies. Membership in the society was the highest societal level a Kiowa man could achieve. A man would therefore never leave to join another, lower society but would remain a member until he was either killed or retired.

Society members also held other forms of prominent social status; many were Ten Medicine Bundle keepers or band leaders, and some were both. In 1935, Frizzlehead II stated that although he believed the society was closer to the Ten Medicine Bundles than any other society, there was no special connection between the two. That members were often Ten Medicine keepers was because Dog Society members were eminent members of the tribe; it had nothing to do with the association of the number ten.¹² Jimmy Quoetone noted that whereas many Plains groups had (contrary or military) societies equivalent to the Kiowa Dog Society, none had a system of Ten Medicine Bundles and keepers.¹³ In society meetings, no Ten Medicine Bundles were present, no bear taboo—associated with Ten Medicine keepers—was observed, and no sweat lodge ceremonies were held, as was common for the bundles.¹⁴

Like the other Kiowa military societies, the Dog Society had two leaders and two whipmen. However, it had no youth members. Membership was divided into three groups that varied in age and martial status: regular members, colts (*chêyòi* or *chêyòp*), and retired (*tál*) members. Regular members were men of adult age who were of at least *qájái* (lit. "brave man," but often translated as "chief") status, men who had distinguished themselves at least once in battle. All sash owners appear to have been *qájáisàupàn* (lit. "big brave men"), or warriors who had at least four war accomplishments. In light of these warfare requirements, and because much of Kiowa wealth and economic status was warfare based, the society served to distinguish the great and wealthy warriors from the rest. Possessing war honors, these men were organized into pairs of society partners, with one wearing a sash while the other carried the end in society dances and parades. Archival sources indicate that no status difference existed between the members of the pair, but that the sash wearer had been a society member longer than the other.¹⁵

A position in the society that has been forgotten by contemporary Kiowa was that of the colts. In listing these members Mooney stated, "These are all of the variety called

'Tsenyui' or colts, younger men in training by older warriors but in the same dances, paint, etc." These apprentice members were referred to as colts (chêyòi) or replacers (cõthát) and occasionally as wild colts (thàuchéyòi).[16] They were young men, aged fifteen to thirty, who were from socially prominent or "good" families, showed military promise, and had not yet joined another society. They were usually much younger than the men selected as attendants or society partners for older sash owners and were brought in approximately every twenty years as a reserve to replace the regular members as they died. Yellow Wolf maintained that the society had always had the position of colts, and it was not a late development to bolster the membership of a declining organization.[17]

Promising men with war honors in other societies were occasionally taken in upon consent of the leader of the other society. Upon induction into the Dog Society, colts did not receive a sash but could borrow one for use in dances or warfare. Sashes were not received until the next time they were made, which was sometimes as long as twenty to twenty-five years. Frizzlehead II and Yellow Wolf were waiting to receive sashes, but the society ceased before they were made again, so they never received theirs. Colts who had belonged to the society for several years were sometimes called old colts (probably qómchêyòi). Colts were not paired off as regular members with each other but were a collective group of equal status. All were considered to be society partners or friends (cóm) to one another and addressed each other as châ, the address form for "friend" or "partner." The families of colts interacted congenially but did not use the full set of kinship terms employed in regular society partnerships.[18]

The third classification of membership was elder men who had retired from active service by giving their sashes and thus their positions to younger members. They were henceforth known as one who had retired (tál). Free from active warfare, retired members retained honorary membership for life, attended meetings and feasts, and maintained a prominent role in the performance of initiations. Old Man Red Tipi, for example, had been a retired member for fifteen years in 1866.[19]

Membership estimates for the society vary considerably but can be reconstructed in the context of society social organization and Kiowa warfare patterns. Mooney (1898:230) wrote that there were ten members, then later (1898:285) stated, "The membership was always kept up to the requisite number of ten.... Usually each one had a younger partner (tsa)." This statement, as well as the presence of society partners, indicates that the number ten refers only to the sash owners; it is the number usually given by Kiowa elders today. In his fieldnotes, however, Mooney wrote that there was "no fixed number formerly for [the] Koitsenko had at least thirty-seven when Setangya [was] alive by count, and he was their chief."[20] Although Lowie (1916b:842) had only three Kiowa informants, the Kiowa captive Andrew Martinez, or Andale, reported fifteen to twenty members, and the other two Kiowa consultants reported thirty members. Spotted Bird (Parsons 1929:93), born in 1856, said that there were fifty members, which is possible but probably a slightly high estimate. In the 1935 Laboratory of Anthropology fieldnotes, the membership roster given for the 1867 society initiation lists a total of thirty-two members, including two society leaders, two whipmen, two red blanket wearers, sixteen regular members, two retired members, and eight initiates, or colts.

Variations in membership estimates are best explained as follows. First, Dog Society initiations did not take place annually as in the other men's societies. Therefore, membership gradually declined between the infrequent initiations from deaths, warfare, and the dangerous battle obligations entailed by membership. The last surviving members of the society, Frizzlehead II and Yellow Wolf, clearly indicated that the common figure of ten members referred only to the sash-owning members and did not include their society partners, the colts, and retired members. Likewise, as Sangko stated in 1935, "at one time the koitsenko had a very large membership." Therefore, a base figure of membership would consist of ten sash owners and ten assistants (some of whom might be retiring), a group of colts, and a remainder of retired members who were still active in society ceremonies and social activities. Thus membership could easily have been fewer than thirty members before an initiation and many more members immediately afterward.[21]

Contrary Speech

One of the best-known characteristics of the Dog Society was the use of contrary or backward speech. In speaking, a member said the opposite of what he meant. This style of speech was especially common during battles, initiations, and dances. The society leader used contrary speech in battle. If one man released another who had been staked down in battle, he was told "not to retreat," after which he was free to do so. Contrary speech was required not only for members but for anyone else addressing a member. For example, Spotted Bird stated that if a member of the society sighted an approaching enemy, he would say, "I see no enemy," and if a member gave the call for sighting a buffalo herd, the people would say, "That is a Koitsenko man, let us find out what it really is." By 1927, some Kiowa would say to a liar, "You are worse than a Koitsenko," referring to the society's contrary speech (Parsons 1929:93).[22]

Feasts

During preparations for the Sun Dance the society danced during the four stops to the final encampment. The society appears not to have met as often as the other men's societies. Although one person indicated that nightly dances and meetings were held, others stated that the society lacked the regular nightly meetings, holding the majority of its social functions in the form of feasts during the daytime. Daytime feasts were sponsored by regular society members or by colts, with four to six feasts held per Sun Dance. Feasts began with singing, followed by the serving of a meal, and then dancing inside a tipi. Nighttime meetings were held infrequently, primarily for initiations. At this time, social feasts were not conducted, because all activities focused on the lengthy and arduous induction ceremonies associated with the renewal of sashes. A sponsored feast took place five Sun Dances before the last Sun Dance. At that Sun Dance, society members acted as fire builders in the lone tipi and in the Sun Dance lodge itself. Frank Given recalled that the camp crier was a Dog Society member but did not know whether the society was obliged to furnish a man for this office.[23]

Society Offices and Sashes

Jane Richardson recorded a partial account of the organization of a Dog Society meeting. The two society leaders sat at the west end of the tipi while the whipmen, who directed the dancing, sat on either side of the tipi door. The drummers sat on the south side of the lodge instead of on the northwest side as in the other societies. The other members and colts appear to have been seated around the remaining portions of the lodge.[24]

The two Dog Society leaders owned a single black sash. This was the highest level to which a *qájáisàupàn*, or great warrior, could aspire. There were ten such great warriors in the society, which probably accounts for contemporary Kiowa's use of the term "ten bravest" in reference to the society. It is possible that the rank of great warrior was required before a man could be a sash owner, again correlating with the number ten. Unlike in the other Kiowa societies, the two Dog Society whipmen did not carry flat serrated quirts or whips. As a symbol of office, one whipman, Many Camp Fires (Áisèàuidè), an uncle of the later Iseeo, carried a spotted feathered lance (*pópákǫ̀gàut*), and the other, Killed A Man (Qá̱hí̱hóljè, who died in 1869), carried a sword (*hǎujòltǫ̀i*). Upon the death of Many Camp Fires the lance was buried with him, and presumably a new one was made. At the 1867 initiation the two whipmen were reported to have had no sash and to have had to borrow one to dance with at a feast. This more likely resulted from the sash's not having yet been conferred on them than from such a high position's not having had a sash.

Long romanticized in literature, paintings, and movies, the most conspicuous items of society dress worn by Plains Indian Contrary or "Dog Soldier" Society members were their sashes, used for staking themselves down in battle. A Kiowa Dog Society sash consisted of a strip of soft elk hide (perhaps related to references to these men as Elk Horse Soldiers) or buffalo hide or a strip of blanket. Each measured approximately eight inches wide and nine to twelve feet long. Near one end the sash was split for perhaps two feet. The wearer's head and left shoulder were passed through the slit, leaving the sash trailing under his right arm and off his right hip. At the other end of the sash were small holes made by staking oneself down in battle. During dances, a sash wearer's society partner placed his fingers through the holes in the trailing end to carry the sash and prevent it from dragging on the ground (Lowie 1916b:848; Parsons 1929:94). When men went to war, they rolled the sashes up and carried them under their arms. Hugh Scott obtained a description of their use from Kiowa in the 1890s:

When he [the sash wearer] wants to make an example to keep the young men from retreating in a fight, he unrolls the streamer and shoots an arrow into the hole pinning it to the ground and he is like a horse tied to a peg. He can only go around his arrow until he is either killed or some have [a] friend at the risk of his life pulls up the arrow and liberates him. These are both very brave deeds.[25]

Three categories of Dog Society sashes existed in the nineteenth century: black rope (*yáifáukógá*, black elk-skin sashes), red rope (*yáifáugùl*, red cloth sashes), and red Dog Society rope (Qóichêyàifàugùl, red elk-skin sashes), also known as a "choking rope" (*ôpàyàifàu*, red elk-skin sashes). The exact number of society sashes varies by source. Scott reported ten sashes. Mooney (1898:285) also reported a total of ten, including one black elk-skin sash (*yáifáukógá*) for the two society leaders, three *yáifáugùl*, or red cloth sashes, and six red elk-skin sashes (*ôpàyàifàu*). Parsons (1929:94) described an unspecified number of sashes, of which two black sashes belonged to the two leaders and their "chums," which implies that the two society leaders were not society partners to each other. The 1935 Laboratory of Anthropology fieldnotes report thirteen society sashes, each of which was held in common by two men. They had no designs or beadwork but were simply of a solid color. These thirteen sashes fell into the same three categories previously listed: one black rope that was painted black on one side and red on the other, one red blanket rope, believed to have been held by the two whipmen, and ten red elk-skin ropes. Additionally, Sangko reported to Marriott that there were two black sashes, whereas Atah indicated only one, thus totaling thirteen and twelve sashes, respectively.[26]

The well-known historic picture of Sitting Bear depicts him wearing a thin sash across his torso and left shoulder. Although many Kiowa believe this was his Dog Society sash, the sash in the picture is much thinner than that described by elder Kiowa of the period. Furthermore, because he was then the head of the society, his sash should have been black, but it appears to be white in the photograph. Although some sources indicate that every society member owned a sash, ledgerbook depictions in the Chicago Field Museum and in Ronald McCoy's *Kiowa Memories* (1987:pl. 46) clearly show that two society members shared each sash. During society dances and parades, each sash owner wore his sash while his partner danced slightly to one side, holding the trailing end of the sash off the ground. Colt and retired members did not have sashes.[27]

Although sources vary, the earliest accounts, obtained by Scott and Mooney, and the almost universal descriptions of ten sashes in Kiowa oral history suggest that a total of ten society sashes existed during the third quarter of the nineteenth century. In light of the Kiowa use of the institution of society partners and the prevalence of society badges of office, it is likely that one black sash was shared by the two society leaders and that the two whipmen shared another sash, probably a red cloth sash. An initial account in 1935 stated that there were two of these sashes, and a later statement clarified the sharing of each sash by two men: "Two men owning the sash of a red blanket. They could sit anywhere." Furthermore, in Frizzlehead II and Yellow Wolf's account of their initiation in 1867, both stated that neither whipman had a sash in the meeting, yet they could not explain why a pair should be lacking one. I suggest that this was the normal pattern for the two Dog Society whipmen.[28]

One sash in the collections of the Smithsonian Institution (no. 152897) fits the description of the third type of sash, Qóichêyàifàugùl. This sash is approximately six feet long, made of thick (possibly elk) hide sewn together in sections, and painted with red pigment on both sides. It has a cluster of stripped turkey wing feathers below the opening for the wearer's head. Several small holes on the opposite end of the sash appear to have been used to stake the owner down in battle.

Pairs of sash owners and their wives used special terms of address. The man wearing a sash was known as "choked (around the throat) man" (ṓpàqî), and the man carrying the end was called "bridle or harness reins keeper man" (sènjóqî)—a man who leads or handles the reins. Owners' wives were known as "choked woman" (ṓpàmà), or "wife of a choked one."[29]

With the exceptions of retirement or cowardice, ownership of a sash was for life. If a sash owner was killed, a replacement was installed at the next initiation to fill his position. Any member not participating in a raid or war journey could loan his sash to another member who was going to battle. Owners frequently loaned their sashes to their society partners during dances or for use in warfare. Any occasion that was considered important, however, required the sash owner to participate and wear his own sash, lest he be accused of cowardice. If a member was found guilty of cowardice, he was stripped of his rank, and his sash was given to a braver man (Mooney 1898:285). During society initiations at the 1867 Sun Dance, some members who had been judged to have acted in a cowardly manner were degraded and their sashes given to other men deemed worthier (Mooney 1898:320). After serving as a sash owner, a member might give away his sash and office to another, something that usually accompanied retirement in old age. At the Dog Society initiations at the 1848 Sun Dance, Slow Running Wolf (Cûihâlâjè), then known as Crazy Old Man (Áulkáuiqáptàu), gave away his society sash.[30]

Sashes were remade only at specified renewal meetings, which generally coincided with initiations. By the time a meeting was held, society membership was usually greatly reduced through deaths. If a sash owner was killed, his sash was buried with him, leaving the position vacant. When any sashes were to be replaced, all were replaced, regardless of the number remaining and their present condition. Repair or replacement meetings were held during the period of preliminary men's society meetings before the Sun Dance. At this time a thorough inspection and overhauling of all society equipment was performed, including sashes, rattles, paintings, headdresses, and beadwork.[31] Old sashes of living members were placed in trees and left to the elements. Although the data are incomplete and not always in agreement, there seems to have been some association concerning the making of the Dog Society sashes by the Pehodlma, who were considered to be the best craft workers in the tribe. According to HeapoBears, when the society needed to renew its sashes, its members obtained elk hide from a shield owner and gave it to their wives from which to make sashes.[32] Yellow Wolf, a colt, stated that he did not know who made them but that the owner's wives did not make them. He maintained that the Pehodlma might tan the hides and might make some of the sashes but were not formally called together to do it.[33] Conversely, both Atah and Sangko indicated that the wives of the owners constructed the society sashes, including the actual beading and painting of the sashes.[34] Kintadl stated that the Pehodlma were the "Koitsenko of Women" among the Kiowa and that their chief function was to make the society sashes. She further suggested that members of the Pehodlma may have been picked by members of the Dog Society and possibly were their wives and daughters.[35] Whether some or all of the society members' wives belonged to the Pehodlma is unclear, but membership lists indicate that many of them were related to Dog Society members. This suggests a relationship between the highest-level male and female organizations, over which the socially prominent and wealthy held predominant control.[36]

Each member had a Dog Society bag (Qóichékàui or Qóichébìmkàui) in which he kept his society paraphernalia, including his sash, rattle, eagle-bone whistle, owl-feather headdress, paint, and other associated items (Lowie 1916b:848; Parsons 1929:94). In bad weather these bags were kept inside the owner's lodge, tied overhead on the west, or medicine, side of the lodge. In good weather women placed the bags on the outside of the lodge by standing on the cooking tripod inside the tipi and tying the bag under the top tipi pin, positioning the bag outside and just under the lodge smoke hole. The presence of such bags is said to have served as an indicator for locating members of the society within an encampment. During camp moves the society members' wives transported their husbands' society bags by tying them to the front of their mount's saddle, similar to medicine bundles. During raids members wore these bags under their right arms, and before a battle the equipment was put on with the sash end left hanging, ready to stake down if necessary at the appropriate place and time.

James Mooney obtained a model of a Dog Society bag, now in the Smithsonian Institution (no. 233123). It is a semirectangular, kidney-shaped rawhide container with a concave top and is laced up on either end. The top and side edges have a border of two blue stripes, between which horizontal red stripes are located on the sides alone. The central figure of the container is composed of two blue lines forming a vertical X, with a smaller red cross on each side of the figure. Parsons (1929:94) wrote that members had buffalo horns hanging over the entrances of their tipis that might have represented another form of societal identification, but she provided no further information. Although one 1935 consultant denied the presence of Dog Society shields, another elder stated that members owned shields that were painted solid red on both the cover and the inner shield. Mooney was unable to collect models of all Kiowa shields during his heraldry research, but I found no shields fitting this description in the Smithsonian collections.[37]

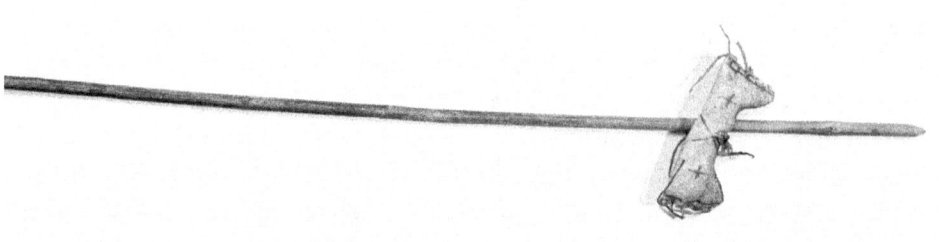

Model of a Kiowa Dog Society regalia bag.
National Anthropological Archives, no. 233131, Washington, D.C.

Society Dress

The earliest known image of Kiowa Dog Society dress is a portrait of Black Cap or Black Hat (Bóhònkǫ́gài) painted by George Catlin (Mooney 1898:268–269). Frizzlehead I, or Old Man Frizzlehead (Áulpépjè), identified this depiction to Mooney as showing the feather headdress and bone whistle of the society.[38] For meetings and initiations, members reportedly wore entire bison hides over their heads and bodies. Ledgerbook depictions of society dances suggest that these hides were omitted for dance activities. Using paint that was mixed with *kww.swbi*, a certain portion of bison fat, and kept in small cups, society members painted their entire faces and bodies, clothes, whistles, rattles, moccasins, and feathers red. Because such fat was used in ritual painting, a member could not eat it until after he had retired from the society. This taboo also applied to those who had contact with society members' bags, namely, their wives. A member's wife feared this portion of buffalo fat and would neither touch nor eat it, although the taboo did not apply to other family or tribal members. Members painted their faces with black stripes or with darker red stripes on a lighter red background. Illustrations from ledgerbook drawings and the 1935 Santa Fe fieldnotes show that the stripes were slightly curved, with one stripe on each side of a man's face, proceeding from the top of the forehead across the eyes and down the remainder of the face. The black paint was required to be obtained from a natural source, possibly charcoal. A black stripe was also painted around each wrist (Lowie 1916b:841; McCoy 1987:pl. 46).[39]

Members wore blue and white necklaces consisting of several strings of long bone beads, possibly made from bird leg bones. Attached to the center of the necklace was a red-painted whistle made from the wing bone of an eagle, which was coated with gum around the mouthpiece and pierced to emit a sound when blown. Whistles were held in the left side of the mouth during ceremonies and dances. Each member made a rattle of buffalo calf hooves (later deer hooves). Many other Plains military society rattles of this form were made of deer dewclaws. The rattles were attached to a stick approximately fifteen inches long and one inch in diameter that was covered with buckskin. Strings were tied along the distal end of the stick, and attached to them were fifteen to twenty hoofs that had been scraped clean, boiled until tender, cut in half, and dried. Rattles were carried in the right hand and shaken in time to the drumming as the members sang, producing a pleasing rattling sound. The handles of the rattles had designs beaded in blue and white beads.[40] According to Martinez (Lowie 1916b:849), these rattles were mandatory, and no modernization was allowed in their manufacture.

Members wore an *apwdl*, or owl-feather headdress, on the back of the head. According to Hunting Horse, this headdress represented a dead person, perhaps in association with the contrary and dangerous behavior practiced in battle. The headdress consisted of an owl wing and tail feathers that had been stripped partway down the quill, causing the fletchings to become curly and fluffy and forming a loose, fan-shaped arrangement. Such prepared feathers were common in the northern Great Plains in late-nineteenth-century "crow belts" and "mess bustles," which became a popular form of dress for the Omaha (War or Grass) Dance. The *apwdl* was attached to the scalp lock with a *qāuqápfádáun* or *jèdán* (sparrow hawk) feather or with a black eagle wing or tail feather placed through the center of the cluster of owl feathers. Like other society attire, the entire headdress was painted red with clay that served to stiffen it. Oral history and ledgerbook drawings support these descriptions. One Kiowa man with whom I visited was told by his grandfather, Goomdaw, that the society headdresses consisted of stripped owl feathers and two black and white eagle tail feathers extending back horizontally into the rest of the headdress.[41] A drawing of a Dog Society member by Wohaw (Harris 1989:53) shows a large, red-painted eagle tail feather extending horizontally back in the center of red-painted and stripped owl feathers.[42]

Depictions of the society have been preserved in several ledgerbook drawings. McCoy (1987:pl. 46) published a drawing of the society showing slight variations from the previously described dress; it illustrates the ritualized aspect of society partners. In this depiction, each sash wearer carries a dewclaw rattle in his left hand and a pipe with a Catlinite stone bowl in his right. The members standing behind all but one sash wearer each carry in their right hand the end of the sash of the man in front of him (presumably his partner), and in their left hand, a dewclaw rattle. Frank Given stated that in processionals, members wore buffalo hides over their heads and bodies, the chief a black robe and other members red robes. The ropes hung from the left shoulder down the back and "an attendant" (the partner) danced behind and to one side of the member. Although one drawing (Harris 1989:53) does not identify the figure as a Dog Society member (probably from the lack of a shoulder sash, the item of dress most art historians are familiar with), the left figure in the drawing is clearly dressed as a Dog Society member with dark eye, wrist, and ankle paint, a dewclaw rattle, red body paint, and a red-painted owl and eagle feather headdress.[43]

In a depiction of Kiowa and Navajo preparing for battle (Berlo 1996:147, fig. 70), one of the four Kiowa men wears a red shoulder sash and the society's red-painted,

The Kiowa Dog Society as depicted in a Kiowa ledgerbook drawing, 1870s. Julian Scott Ledger, plate 46, "Koitsenko." Reproduced from McCoy 1987, courtesy Morning Star Gallery, Santa Fe, New Mexico.

stripped-feather headdress. This drawing is significant because it indicates that these men were not all Dog Society members, and so the party was made up of members of several societies. Although there are indications that some military societies once raided and fought as composite units, this pattern appears to have been changing by the 1840s (Meadows 1995:392). Other depictions of the Dog Society are contained in the Silverhorn ledgerbooks at the Chicago Field Museum.

I have discussed the existence of "chapter societies," or societies found in multiple Plains tribal populations and sharing relatively similar dress, dance, and ritual styles, which occasionally danced together when visiting another tribe with a related society (Meadows 1999:55–57, 363). Although a comprehensive account of the extent and similarity of pan-Plains military chapter societies has not been undertaken, their existence is documented in both Native ledgerbook art and early ethnographic fieldnotes. Because so-called Dog Soldier societies are among the best documented types of military societies in Plains ledgerbook art, a brief comparison of Kiowa and Hidatsa Dog Societies, representing somewhat opposite ends of the Plains Indian spectrum, demonstrates the existence of this pattern. Like the Sun Dance, Plains military societies spread from the northern Great Plains to the Southern Plains populations. Great similarity is found in comparing Karl Bodmer's two watercolors of Pehriska-Ruhpa (Two Crows), the Hidatsa Crazy Dog Society chief, painted in about 1834 (Bowers 1963: pl. 3; Balantine and Balantine 1993:392; Time-Life Books 1993:81), with ethnographic descriptions of Kiowa Dog Society dress in the fieldnotes of James Mooney, the notes of the 1935 Laboratory of Anthropology Kiowa Field School, and ledgerbook drawings (Mooney 1898:284, 287; McCoy 1987:pl. 46; Harris 1989:53; Berlo 1996:147, fig. 70). The ethnographic and pictographic records of these two societies demonstrate numerous similarities in the material forms and ritual uses of eagle-bone whistles, hoof rattles, red sashes, owl-feather headdresses, red body and face paint, and linear black facial paint, as well as in expectations of bravery in battle.

Initiations

In contrast to the initiations of other Kiowa men's societies, Dog Society initiations were not held annually, and rarely were large groups of men inducted together.[44] By the time initiations and new sashes were to be made, the membership of the society had been greatly reduced through deaths in battle. During an initiation year, formal society meetings and initiations were conducted from the time of the Ride Around Camp held prior to the Sun Dance until the buffalo skin was placed on the center pole of the Sun Dance arbor. As in the other men's societies, older members decided on individuals they wanted to initiate and looked for them during this period. Because Dog Society initiations were infrequent and so important, the accompanying Sun Dances were frequently named after such events. Between 1832 and 1890, the Kiowa calendars record three such initiations, in the summers of 1846, 1848, and 1867, respectively (Mooney 1898:283–285, 287, 320). The summer of 1846 was recorded as the "Sun Dance when Hornless-Bull was made a Koitsenko" (Páugùhḗjèáôpàidèqàujò), and the 1848 Sun Dance was known as the "Koitsenko Initiation Dance" (Ốpàqàujò, lit. "Choking Rope Sun Dance"). The 1867 Sun Dance was named the "Sun Dance Where the Koitsenko Were Initiated" (Qóichḗgàuétốpàidèqàujò).

Membership in the society entailed such dangerous obligations in warfare and such lengthy initiation ordeals that men who suspected they might be recruited often avoided being found. When society members were known to be in camp and searching for recruits, young men often ran and hid. Young men in particular were said to have disliked joining because of the rigid rules and dangerous obligations. However, refusal was only temporary, because it was an honor to join and because, it was said, the society would find you sooner or later.[45]

When the society members located a man they wished to induct, they caught him and attempted to place a pipe in his hands. Upon recognizing their intentions, the candidate could attempt to resist by clenching his fists. As soon as the pipe touched his hands, however, he was made a member of the society and could offer no further resistance. Closing his fingers around the pipe terminated the initiate's right to resist membership (Parsons 1929:93). The reasons for this resisting behavior were twofold. First, acceptance of the pipe was avoided because a man felt unworthy of the honor offered him and feared that at some point his conduct might bring disgrace to the society. Unlike Charles Brant (1953:60), who attributed similar behavior by candidates of the Plains Apache Manatidie and Klintidie Societies to a lack of bravery and a shirking of responsibility, I believe modesty is probably a more accurate way to view the situation, because selected candidates knew they could not escape membership for long. Second, there was logic involved in temporarily postponing one's initiation. When the initiate was found, he henceforth had to attend the all-day and -night meetings and endure the "sitting ordeal" from that time until the initiation was concluded by the bringing of the releasing scalp or the placing of the buffalo on the center pole for the Sun Dance. Thus, the longer a man avoided recruitment, the shorter his initiation and the less discomfort he endured.[46]

The following two cases illustrate attempts to escape initiation. Hearing that the Dog Society was looking for him, Podlt'ai hid for three nights by sleeping in his father-in-law's tipi instead of his own. The old man finally chastised him by saying, "Stop hiding. It is an honor, and you won't be killed by the enemy." When Podlt'ai returned to his tipi, the society members found him and handed him a pipe to smoke, which they would have forced him to smoke if he had refused. After all present had smoked, they proceeded to the society meeting. On their way there Podlt'ai's father-in-law cried out, "If he is allowed to move and be comfortable, I will give a horse."[47] In another case, a man attempting to avoid membership hid in his tipi. His brother played a joke on him by entering the tipi with a stick of wood and attempting to make him touch it. Thinking it was a Dog Society member with a pipe, he resisted vigorously, and a virtual free-for-all ensued until the man realized that it was only his brother playing a joke on him.[48]

A man who was too old to go to war and was preparing to retire would likewise place a pipe in an initiate's hands, obligating him to become his successor. In some cases, men too old to engage in warfare had their sashes taken away publicly, but neither degradation of the owner nor cowardice on his part was indicated when this occurred. This method appears to have been the way to mandatorily retire a seasoned veteran, releasing him from his duties while allowing him to retire honorably and thus remain a member. After receiving a member's sash, an initiate gave the elder member gifts of blankets and other property. Thus membership required not only war honors but also wealth (Mooney 1898:285; Lowie 1916b:848).

In filling vacancies, colts who were considered worthy were promoted to regular member status, after which older and distinguished chiefs (qájáiqì, or men with at least one war honor) of other societies were sought to become regular members. Frizzlehead and Yellow Wolf stated that all members had to serve as colts but later implied differently and in some cases said they did not know which individuals had previously been colts. Therefore, it appears that not all members had to serve a period as colts. No specific war achievements were required for a colt to gain regular membership status, but colts were constantly urged to be as brave as possible, hence their frequent daring and reckless maneuvers in battle.[49]

The 1867 Initiation

The Sun Dance of 1867 marked the society's last initiation. Membership appears to have been very low by this time, for only one or two of the original sash owners were left, besides the two head society leaders and some retired members. A member of the remaining group—by requirement, an older member—vowed that new members would be taken in that summer. Unlike vows made during warfare or sickness, this form did not have to be made under stressful conditions. Members then decided whom they would take in, first as regular members, then as colts.⁵⁰

In 1935, Jane Richardson (Hanks) recorded the following description of the 1867 initiation, primarily from Frizzlehead II and Yellow Wolf, the last surviving members of the society. Both were inducted as colts at this time. Their accounts are supplemented by those of Marriott's consultants, who were of comparable age in 1935. The Dog Society met the night before the entry into the Sun Dance circle. Many Kiowa watched the meeting, including Frizzlehead and some of his companions. Packing A Quarter Of Meat (Thépòl) and White Tailed (Tónánthą́ijè), who were ordinary society members and not whipmen, came through the crowd with pipe in hand looking for someone. Packing A Quarter Of Meat suddenly announced, "Here he is," and made Frizzlehead touch the pipe with his left hand. After this Frizzlehead was led to the all-night meeting, where Old Man Saddle Blanket (Tàukàuiqáptàu) was the caller.⁵¹

Hearing of the society's meeting, Yellow Wolf also went to watch. A tipi had been erected with the sides rolled up and many back rests set up around the edges. Several prominent men in the tribe were sitting very still inside the lodge. Yellow Wolf was looking on when two men (probably Packing A Quarter Of Meat and White Tailed) grabbed his blanket and then caught his society partner, Kwwpa.te (possibly Càuáuvéjè, or Crow Appeared), Frizzlehead, and Black Headdress (Kóbóhòn) and asked them if they wanted to join as they handed them the pipe. All four were then led into the society tipi.⁵²

Individuals of at least eleven different statuses or categories were present at the initiation. These included (1) new colts, (2) old colts, who now received their sashes as owners for the first time, (3) assistant *cóm* (society partners) who received sashes as first-time owners because of the deaths of the previous owners, (4) assistant *cóm* of older sash owners, who received sashes because of the owner's retirement, (5) old sash owners who, having loaned their sashes to men who had been killed and lost them, received new sashes and were attended by their own assistant *cóm*, (6) new sash owners, (7) new assistant *cóm*, (8) old assistant *cóm* who were attending new owners, (9) old members who, having their sashes, were not required to partake in the sitting ordeal, (10) older retired members (*tál*), who ran the meetings and moved about freely, and (11) members' wives.⁵³

During initiations, the first six categories of participants were required to sit upright in the tipi with their heads erect, legs folded, and arms hanging down. They were required to remain in this "helpless" state unless called to dance by the whipmen. Members rested on pallets prepared by their wives. According to Spotted Bird, those who were required to perform the immobility ordeal had to remain seated with their arms folded until they were touched by a captive or by a captured garment or moccasin. Along with this ordeal was a greatly feared supernatural belief that served as a control mechanism and test for the initiates. If any initiate broke the rules of the ordeal, his body would swell up all over (Parsons 1929:93). Sash owners were not allowed to move and were attended to by their society partners. Categories 6, 7, and possibly 1 represent initiates who had been recruited from other societies.[54]

At this point in the initiation, the wife of each member who remained "helpless" during the ceremony stood behind her husband. Because Black Headdress was the only colt married during the 1867 initiation, his wife was immediately sent for. The wives' primary duties were to feed and change the position of their husbands during their immobility ordeal. Each wife rubbed her husband's back and limbs to relieve him from the aching produced by lengthy immobility, and she could either massage her husband's limbs as he sat or force him to stand while she pounded on his limbs until circulation was restored. During the ordeal, the initiate's wives wore red face paint and addressed their husbands in contrary fashion, asking them if they did "not want anything." Initiates were not allowed to ask for anything, requiring their wives to guess what their needs were. Occasionally an initiate might blow on his whistle and make a few requests using contrary speech, but the amount of speech used by initiates appears to have been kept to a minimum. An initiate's wife occasionally told him not to move, which allowed him to move to a very limited extent. Wives also had to know when a man needed to relieve himself and take him out to do so, because the initiate was not allowed to go on his own. If spectators were near, the man's wife held a blanket around her husband outside the lodge and then ushered him back inside. Colts also endured the ordeal of immobility, but theirs was much shorter in duration and less rigid than that required of a man receiving a sash.[55]

During one initiation, a man with two wives called upon his favorite to wait on him during his period of immobility. Loosing her temper, the second wife ran into the tipi and sat down by her husband to demonstrate her displeasure. No one could persuade her to leave, and she remained likewise immobile until her husband left the tipi.[56] Sangko and Frizzlehead indicated that an initiate might be allowed to move if a relative gave a horse or blanket and requested in contrary fashion, "Don't let him move," which gave him more mobility for the remainder of the evening but would require another gift for the next evening. Yellow Wolf denied that such action was possible, though Podlt'ai's father-in-law had made such an offer upon his initiation.[57]

Because of camp duties, the wives of the ten sash owners could not always remain the entire time with their husbands. If an initiate was unmarried or unattended by his wife, his partner attended him. In some instances both a man's wife and his society partner served him during his ordeal. A man could also ease his partner's ordeal by instructing him in contrary fashion not to dance. Spotted Bird said that while a colt sat immobile inside the initiation tipi, admirers of his wife could go to visit her, and if an admirer came into the tipi in which the initiate sat, he would say, "Here comes sapodl" (sàupól, owl), as an insult to him (Parsons 1929:93). According to Frizzlehead, this was a "very easy time for a woman to meet any lover she may have, and the would-be's are always on hand then." If a wife were faithful, she would inform her husband by saying in contrary fashion, "Sapodl [owl, i.e., this evil person] is not trying to meet me."[58]

During the 1867 initiation, Yellow Wolf sat between one of the whipmen and Giatogia, who was receiving a sash for the first time and was thus immobile. As the colts sat, older members sang and instructed them, occasionally coming over to raise an initiate's hand, requiring him to rise and dance. Older members confirmed membership by dancing around the initiate. In this initiation Giatogia danced with Yellow Wolf while Killed A Man (Qą́hį́hóljè), a whipman, danced with Frizzlehead. Killed A Man danced with several but not all of the initiates; different men danced with each initiate. Colts were reportedly not allowed to dance with sash recipients, which contradicts the account of dancing between Giatogia and Yellow Wolf, but because Giatogia was his paternal uncle, consanguineal relations may have been a prevailing factor in this instance. Yellow Wolf had a partner chosen for him by the society leaders at this meeting. After dancing with each other they always sat together, but there was none of the head bumping that characterized the initiation of society partners in other Kiowa men's societies.[59]

Sashes were placed on the recipients during the evening. Yellow Wolf and Frizzlehead could not recall exactly at which point the sashes were taken out of the bags or by whom they were conferred. While dancing, one member wore his sash while his partner held onto the other end. The two took turns wearing the sash. Only one member of each pair was the official sash owner, and he underwent the initiation ordeal while his assistant attended him. Frizzlehead stated that during the initiation the sash owner alone wore the sash, and after he was released his partner might borrow it to wear.[60] In 1935, Richardson recorded a membership roster for the 1867 initiation (see Appendix). Unfortunately, which members were "receiving a sash as owner" was unclear to the consultant and received no further inquiry.[61]

The Breakfast Dance and Release

The next morning, Old Man Saddle Blanket called for all the initiates' relatives to bring food for a feast and dance. As the oldest retired member, Old Man Saddle Blanket was chosen to offer the prayer. He painted Frizzlehead's face while Giatogia painted Yellow Wolf's face. The initiates were painted with *swtoi*, a type of bison fat–based red paint. Painters were required to be sash owners (or inferably former owners) but not necessarily retired members. All new members were painted at the same time on the morning before they came into the Sun Dance circle. The entire body of each member was coated with red paint, but whether the retired members painted the entire body or only the face of each member is unknown. At the 1867 initiation, Sitting Bear retired as the head society leader and gave his sash to his society partner, Crow Appeared (Càuáuvédài), who was required to sit rigidly as Sitting Bear moved about, serving as his society partner and directing the activities. Although contemporary Kiowa maintain that Sitting Bear was the last leader of the society, the last two surviving society initiates indicated that he in fact retired in 1867. Although he was officially retired, Sitting Bear's prominence in the society from 1867 until his death in 1871 suggests that he still held considerable status and prestige in the society.

At breakfast, a woman entered with meat, placed four pieces in Frizzlehead's mouth, and then took his hands and made him touch the meat, thereby releasing him from further immobility. Sash owners were fed by their wives and could not move until a scalp or any object that had been captured from an enemy was brought in for them to touch. According to Yellow Wolf, a freshly acquired scalp was required and was announced by the firing of guns, whereupon the colts, as a body, went out in a great rush to touch it.[62]

Following the face painting and the feast, members moved to the next encampment in the progression toward the final Sun Dance location or to the actual camp if it was already established. Although the colts were now released from immobility, the sash owners were not. They were given contrary instructions not to move or get on a horse, after which they were led on horseback by their partners on another mount. These members did not participate in the race to the center pole but entered as a group toward the back of the processional, among the women. Upon arriving at the east gate of the camp circle, the members went directly to a tipi set up in the middle of the camp circle. The sash owners sat down immediately, awaiting the releasing scalp that would be brought in one or two days later, and continued their immobility and contrary speech. If no scalp was brought, the members had to remain immobile until the buffalo hide was placed on the Sun Dance center pole. This could be a period of up to ten days, after which the Dog Society members went to obtain a scalp themselves.[63] According to Yellow Wolf, there had been some Sun Dances in which members had to endure the ordeal from the ride around camp until the time the buffalo hide was placed on the center pole, after which they had to venture on a journey to acquire their own releasing scalp.[64] Frank Given provided another account in which the "releasing" of the society took some time:

> Once on the way to a Sun Dance, the ropes were being renewed. All the work was completed, but no outsider had yet appeared. The society camped, with the wives of the members, away from the main camp. The wives assisted them to their horses and moved them to the Sun Dance camp. They were still helpless, until some Cheyenne came, bringing a scalp. This freed the society and the members could return to their homes. If no one had come during the Sun Dance they would have remained "paralyzed" throughout the entire ceremony.[65]

After the release, the dancers were painted and dressed in their society clothing. Once all was ready, a dance was held. With slow steps, the sets of partners danced, each assistant behind the sash owner, holding the end of his sash. One ledgerbook drawing (McCoy 1987:pl. 46) depicts this dance. Piatonma, one of Marriott's consultants, provided a description of the society's dance that resembles this stage of the ceremony:

> When all were ready the front of the tipi was opened to the top and the flaps laid back along the sides, so that each man came out standing erect. Following their

leader they formed a circle, blowing continuously on the whistles. . . . Dancing was always in a circle, a series of dances being performed around the entire circumference of the camp circle. It started in the tipi in which the members had been gathered and returned to it.[66]

The best description of a Dog Society dance comes from Frank Given, whose father, Sitting Bear, was the society leader. Given recounted:

> The dance-step of this organization was an alternate lifting up of feet, the arms being allowed to hang relaxed from the shoulders and the clenched fists swung at the sides. A circle was formed but did not revolve, the members dancing in place, pivoting from side to side as they swung. Several drummers and singers accompanied the dancers. After a feast they danced in a circle, forming here and there through the camp. Sometimes they danced inside the tipi, after the renewal of the ropes. At such times each man danced individually.[67]

To facilitate dances, the tipis of several members were combined into a composite, arborlike structure through the use of multiple three-pole tipi foundations and an unusually wide spreading of the secondary poles. Tipi covers were laid over this foundation, supported by the secondary poles. Upon the conclusion of the initiation, all members were released for regular daily activities.[68]

In comparison with older members, colts were formally forbidden to move for only one night but were nevertheless allowed minimal movement. Their ordeal was shorter and less rigid than that of sash owners. Sash recipients were prohibited from moving until a scalp came in, whereas new assistant *cóm*, old *cóm*, and the two whipmen were allowed to move at any time. Unless receiving a new sash, black sash owners were allowed unlimited movement, as were retired members, who directed the activities.[69]

Succession

Succession within the society appears not to have followed any regular pattern, but the accounts of Kiowa elders in 1935 varied concerning this topic. Frizzlehead II and Quoetone stated that sons usually did not replace their fathers—although an exception was Jóhâusàn (Son of Recess/Concavity In A Bluff, or Son of Bluff Recess), who succeeded his father, Jóhâudè (Recess/Concavity In A Bluff)—and older members did not try to get their sons into the society. According to Hunting Horse, however, members were replaced by a son or other close relative, who did not have to hold war honors (*qájáiqì*) but simply to be "fine men." Because Hunting Horse's older brother, Stood His Ground/Did Not Run (Càuéthḕdè), was a Dog Society member, this statement may be true, or it might reflect a change that had developed in the later years of the society. The statement apparently applied to the colts, because full members were required to be *qájáiqì*, and sash owners were usually great warriors (*qájáisàupàn*) or holders of at least four war deeds.[70] Henry Tsoodle Sr. said that the "Koitsenko was comprised mostly of chiefs. If there were others joining Koitsenko, they would be sons of members. But they took in others too."[71] All these accounts hold some validity, because the higher-ranking sash owners, society partner pairs, and older retired members consisted of many of the highest-ranking war chiefs. Other members could be qájáiqĩ recruited from other societies, whereas the colts were often inexperienced relatives of members.

When a sash owner died, his sash was buried with him. The surviving partner usually became his successor. But although the partner possessed all other society paraphernalia, he did not yet possess a sash, and he remained without a new partner and sash until the next sashes were remade and new initiations held.[72] The following cases illustrate the variety of relationships involved in membership and succession. In two examples, deceased members were replaced by their brothers: Killed One With His Hands (Máunjòfáhóljè) by his fifty-year-old brother, Yellow Bison Bull (Páugútqójè), and Many Camp Fires (Áiseàuidè or Iseeo) by a brother who took his name and position as a society whipman and feathered lance custodian. This replacement is puzzling, because the surviving partner and the replacement would have already been "brothers" through the "consanguineal" nature of the kinship of the prior set of society partners. In the 1867 initiation, Frizzlehead II and Yellow Wolf, the sons of two Dog Society partners, were both initiated. According to Yellow Wolf's account, his father was Bird Running (Thẹnéhâljè, an earlier one), a Jáifègàu whipman, whose brothers included Black Bear (Sétkǫ́gái), another Jáifègàu officer, and Giatogia, a Dog Society red blanket owner, who was Yellow Wolf's sponsor. Black Hat/Cap (Kóbóhòn), the son of the other retired member, Old Man Red Tipi, was also inducted into the society.[73]

Black Bird (Cűjòkǫ́gài), a stepson and nephew of Old Man Saddle Blanket (a retired Dog Society member who had married Black Bird's mother, the wife of his deceased brother), was initiated as a colt and later inherited his sash. Black Bird had joined no other society before his initiation as a colt. In another instance, Podlt'ai, the society partner of Jóhâusàn's son Warrior/Fighter (Câijàujè or Kyaitw.te), is reported to have received his partner's (red) sash and position.[74]

Two cases involved the passing of sashes between members. In one case, Never Got Shot (Háungúfâudè) gave a sash to Island (Ằujáujè or Wtwde), who was being inducted to replace the society partner of Never Got Shot. Thus Island was being initiated as a sash owner and not as a colt. Another account states that Packing A Quarter Of Meat gave his sash to Island at an initiation. According to Frizzlehead II, Never Got Shot was already a member, and his society partner had been killed some time back. At the request of Never Got Shot, Island was brought to the initiation from the Black Legs to replace the deceased man. Because Island was being initiated as a sash owner and not as a new member, or colt, it was necessary that someone give him a sash. Thus Packing A Quarter Of Meat gave his sash to Island and most likely retired at this time. In another case, Tabe'aide reportedly gave his sash to his partner, Yaikwwn. Although these examples are not completely consistent, kinship with a society member appears to have been a factor influencing membership, although distinguished battle valor appears to have remained a major determinant. The institution of society partners, however, did influence the replacement process.[75]

Society Partners

In the Dog Society the institution of *cóm*, or society partners, reached its most formal and ritualized level. This institution was tangibly expressed and symbolized through the sash and the associated rituals of initiation and sash transfer. Although the relationship of society partners did not involve the head bumping of the other men's societies, it still necessitated replacement when a vacancy occurred. When partners were selected, candidates were normally nonrelatives. Because the Dog Society was the highest-ranking Kiowa men's society by the mid-1800s, there was no further upward mobility or stealing of members once a man became a member. To be a regular member of the society (which was perhaps limited to sash owners and their assistants) was a higher honor than being a society chief in any of the other military societies. Unlike in the other Kiowa men's societies, vacancies in the Dog Society occurred only through death, retirement, or, more rarely, demotion of a member for cowardice.[76]

The symbolic importance of the sash and its transfer played a large role in society activities. Although one member of each partnership served as the sash owner (i.e., the formal or regular wearer of the sash), and his society partner served as his assistant, no hierarchical ranking or status distinction existed between the two partners.[77] The following are examples of what could and in some cases did arise between partners. I use the terms *sash owner* and *assistant* for purposes of clarification in these examples.

A very old man might retire and give his sash to his assistant, thereby making him the sash owner once he had completed the sitting ordeal. The retiring partner might suggest a person to become his former assistant's new partner. In 1867 Sitting Bear retired and gave his sash to his assistant and partner, Crow Appeared, who had to endure the sitting initiation in order to receive it. In this instance no new assistant *cóm* was brought in.

If a sash owner died from natural causes, his partner succeeded to the position of sash owner and after one to two years took a new assistant. If an assistant died from natural causes, the sash owner took a new assistant after one or two years. If a sash owner was killed while wearing the sash, it was buried with him, after which the surviving assistant became the owner and later took a new assistant. However, because it was prohibited to make a sash in the interim, successors had to wait until sashes for the whole society were officially made, at which time the surviving member of the first pair became the official sash owner.[78]

If an assistant was killed in battle while wearing the borrowed sash of his partner, it was buried with the assistant. After a year, the sash owner took a new society partner and assistant, but the owner could wear no sash until new ones were made at the next initiation. Unlike the new assistant, the sash owner then had to go through the sitting ordeal at the next initiation, even though he had previously performed it. If a colt borrowed a sash and was killed in battle, the sash was buried with the colt. The sash owner and his assistant then remained sashless until the next initiation, at which time the sash owner was required to perform the sitting ordeal again.[79]

These examples illustrate how a small but continuous entrance of members took place, which might explain the insistence by some 1935 informants that the society took in members every year, or at least frequently. These members entered as society partners to regular members and never as colts. The Dog Society frequently broke up society pairings in other men's societies to obtain a member for their own pairings. A man who lost his society partner to the Dog Society did not mind, because he generally did not desire membership for himself in that society. Former society partners maintained their social relations and probably their interfamilial relations. Whether this relationship carried over into economic and military relations is unknown, but it is unlikely, because the new pairing would undoubtedly have taken social and economic precedence over the old one. Nevertheless, the two men remained close friends. As Quoetone put it, "Once a kom, always a kom."[80]

For the "old colts," members who had been colts for a long time, society partners were chosen in the regular fashion. Either the man chose someone himself or the older men of the society suggested someone. The colts were not paired off as society partners but formed a collective group of *cóm*, which supported their role as replacements—hence their byname, "replacers" (*còthát*). Sashes were not received until the next initiation, during which time only some of the colts received sashes and thereby were no longer of colt status. Newly inducted colts never received sashes, and because sash renewal–initiation ceremonies might be many years apart, they often had to spend considerable time in the society before becoming sash owners. When colts did become sash owners, they were not paired with each other but sometimes with men who were distinguished warriors from other societies and who were of similar age. In addition, colts often served as replacements for Dog Society members who had died or been killed in battle, being paired with their survivors.[81] In one instance, Podlt'ai refused all potential suggestions for a partner and insisted on having Fighter/Warrior, his partner from a former society, brought in. Neither was a colt, so this was irregular. It is difficult to understand why a pair of partners from another society might have been reunited, unless membership in the Dog Society was low at this time and the number of colts, who generally received the higher positions before others, was insufficient.[82]

As in the other societies, property was commonly given away when members were inducted and society partnerships were formed. Frank Given explained in 1935: "After that they became close friends and exchanged gifts. As soon as an attendant was selected, he was named as the brother of the man who he accompanied. The pipe was given to the man when he became an attendant, and when he was taken into the society as a full member."[83]

Although regular members exchanged horses when a partnership was formed, colts did not exchange gifts with each other. Some elders in 1935 stated that sash owners might or might not give property to the person giving them their sash, but gifts seem to have been expected in return for the honor of receiving the sash and the position. Upon initial induction, each new member was required to give horses to a fellow society member or to an outsider. Colts were expected to give more, indicative perhaps of their low seniority. At Frizzlehead II's induction, his father, Old Man Frizzlehead, gave a horse to Wdlkwwn, an elderly Apache Klintidie Society member. At the same time, Sitting Bear gave two old men, Kiedodl and Tsentodl, each a horse. However, it is unclear in this exchange whether Sitting Bear gave these horses away because he was relinquishing his sash to Crow Appeared or, as Frizzlehead II stated, because Crow Appeared was being inducted and was a distant cousin of Sitting Bear's.[84] Although society partnerships were supposed to have been formed between unrelated men, there seem to have been some exceptions to this rule in the Dog Society, perhaps because the majority of members were drawn from the highest-ranking and wealthiest warrior families and because of the reduction in tribal population by the 1860s.

Behavior on War Parties

On war parties, the utmost in bravery was expected of Dog Society members. According to Spotted Bird (Parsons 1929:94), members wearing sashes could not turn back from a charge. A member was always expected to be the first into battle and the last to leave the enemy. Members were also obligated to form a rear guard. During a retreat a member reversed to face the enemy, with the sole intention of killing as many of the enemy as possible before being killed himself. Upon entering battle a member would dismount, sing the society song, and shoot an arrow through his sash, pinning himself to that location. This dictated that he remain at his position and fight until victory or death.[85]

There was, however, a release from this obligation (Lowie 1916b:848). According to Frizzlehead II, while riding into battle, someone would always call out *twgiaw'kw* (possibly a statement related to *thàugûgù*, a command to stake oneself down, from Thàugûgàu, "Those Who Stake Themselves Down"), to which the member replied *àhô, àhô* ("thank you, thank you"). In following their ritual contrary behavior, the opposite of the command would of course have been followed. According to Pia-tonma, the member's society partner or another member would shout this out, freeing sash wearers from having to stake themselves down in battle. If someone forgot to call this out, sash owners were obligated to stake themselves to the ground. If a member found himself in a dangerous spot, he would stake himself down in battle anyway, which required his society partner to rush to his side and make a stand with him to the death.[86]

According to Parsons (1929:94), if a sash wearer was killed in battle, his society partner was expected to take up the sash and wear it. A member who had staked himself down in battle could not ask to be released but could be freed by anyone who came and pulled up the arrow, physically releasing his sash and thus, symbolically, his obligation. In Parsons's account, in contrast to Lowie's (1916b:848), the rescuer did not have to be a fellow society member. A member's partner, while making a stand with him, could not pull up the arrow. Following the use of contrary speech, a rescuer would instruct the man "not to come," which then released both the sash wearer and his society partner to flee.[87]

The following cases illustrate this behavior. In a battle with the Ute, Island dismounted and shot an arrow through his sash, causing White Tailed (inferably his society partner) to rush to his side to be with him. Another warrior quickly released both of them. Se'tohi told of another case involving her husband, White Tailed. As a Kiowa party was being attacked and was retreating, White Tailed's horse began to tire. Covering the rear, White Tailed jumped from his horse, shot an arrow through his sash into the ground, and began to sing the "Tired of Living Song," which was sung when one prepared to die. Seeing his actions, Jòhâudè (Bluff Recess) rushed back to pull the arrow out. He then called out, "Don't run and don't jump on behind me," to which White Tailed responded in the customary opposite way, and the two rode safely away.[88]

The exact time at which a man staked himself down in battle appears to have been largely an individual decision, made when the sash owner was prepared to do so. According to White Fox, any sash owner could stake himself down and stand his ground, but this did not obligate the others to do so. Thus, such actions appear to have been individually based, not group-based actions related to a singular command.[89]

If a colt asked to borrow a sash, the owner could not touch it. The owner's wife took down the bag containing the sash, held it over burning incense, and took the sash out. She ran one end of the sash through one arm of her dress, across her chest, and out the other arm of her dress. She then gave the sash and the necklace whistle to the borrower and prayed for his safe return. When the sash was returned, the wife had to return it to the container, because the owner was again prohibited from touching it under these circumstances.[90]

A few instances involving the borrowing of a Dog Society sash are recorded. A young man who was a colt saw an enemy approaching. Putting on his father's black sash, he went forth and killed the enemy. Although the name of the man was not recorded, he was the son of the society chief, which narrows the possibilities greatly, the likely ones being that he was a son of Bluff Recess, of Son of Bluff Recess, or of Sitting Bear (Parsons 1929:94). Yellow Wolf, on his first war party after initiation into the society, borrowed a red sash and had such a close encounter in battle that he received a bullet hole through the sash. This event became a popular story in Kiowa oral history. According to Yellow Wolf, the bullet trailed along the sash, leaving burn marks down its length but not injuring him. In another battle, in which his society partner did not take part, Yellow Wolf had borrowed a sash from Giatogia. He rode double with his cousin, and the two dismounted and turned their mule loose to make a stand. Eventually they were forced to retreat to a hole in a riverbank, where they hid before later escaping. Thinking they had been killed, the rest of the party returned to camp, and people began to mourn for them. The two returned amid the mourning, and because Yellow Wolf was a young society member, his actions were highly praised.[91]

Society Songs

Kiowa Dog Society songs (Qóichẹ́dàugà) reflect the martial characteristics on which the Kiowa military society ethos was focused. Although many of these songs are no longer known, a qualitatively rich sample has survived that demonstrates the valor, bravery, and behavioral characteristics that served as society standards.

A party of ten Kiowa made up of five sets of brothers (possibly more), including the leader of the society, Jóhâusàn (son of Bluff Recess), was involved in the Hueco Tanks fight in 1839 near El Paso, Texas. After being attacked by Mexicans, the Kiowa were forced into a cave and trapped (Mooney 1898:301–305; Nye 1962:36–45). After ten days, out of food and water, the Kiowa decided to try to escape rather than remain and die. All but one of the Kiowa managed to escape in the dangerous attempt. Bluff Recess composed the following song while inside the cave to encourage his brother, Arose From The Sky. It typifies Dog Society behavior:

1. Pánbámhâjè ém bọ̀, deha okohie
 (Arose From The Sky, you, see, come out . . .),
 Arose From The Sky, I want to see you come out, the time has come
2. Kị́-fè + chán-dé-ą̀
 ([Our] fortification, [the enemy] nearing-is/are)
 The enemy is nearing our fortification/place of haven.[92]

Other cases reflect the bravery that was both expected of and shown by society members. A colt named Crow Appeared (Càuáuvéjè or Kwwpa.te) was a brave and confident young man who was not shy about getting up to dance when he was initiated and thereafter. In a fight with some Navajo he was painted red and wore a single eagle feather through his hair. One Navajo fought back with great fury. Crow Appeared rushed at the Navajo, who shot him laterally through the chest, killing him. Thereafter he was always talked about as a true Qóichẹ́gàu.[93] While starting out on the same war party, Crow Appeared (Càuáuvédài or Kwwp'e.dai) became sick and returned home. He gave his sash to his sister's son, Fish Hook (Hą̊upò̱, Metal Trap or Haunpo), a colt who distinguished himself by running over a Navajo in the fight.[94]

Although Dog Society membership brought the highest social status available to a Kiowa man, it also entailed the most dangerous activities. Members were frequently killed in battle in both offensive and defensive (rear guard) actions. The association between battle behavior, speech, dress, and the use of owl feathers—a sign of death—was frequently exhibited by society members. Because they assumed the most dangerous martial roles within the culture, death was an ever-present reality. The attitudes of society members regarding their role and the risk of death constitute the primary theme in their music, often expressed in emphatic statements that they will die.

The following two society songs demonstrate this devotion to dangerous duties and the recognition that upon death a man will become an owl:

> Song 1
> 1 Gûi-jè-dàum-gà à xő-thầu
>   (Another-land / I / lying-shall)
>   In another country/land I shall be lying.
> 2 Gûi-jè-dàum-gà yá̱-áun-gų̱-thầu
>   (Another-land / I-sounding-shall)
>   In another country/land I shall be sounding (i.e., hooting, meaning he will become an owl).
>
> Song 2
> 1 Já̱-êl bấu-dè-thầu-ẹ̀ áui-hyầu-yá̱-áun-thấu
>   (Star-big [i.e., morning star] / appears-shall-at that time / then-I-sound-shall)
>   When the morning star appears, then I shall make a sound.
> 2 Kí-thấ bấu-dè-thầu áui-hyầu-yá̱-áun-thấu
>   (Dawn-appears-shall / then-I-sound-shall)
>   When dawn appears, then I shall make a sound (indicating that he has become an owl).[95]

Perhaps the most representative and to this day the best-known Dog Society song is that sung by Sitting Bear just before his death in 1871 at Fort Sill. Although discrepancies exist concerning the exact content of the song he sang that day, Mooney (1898:329) provided the following, which is the generally accepted version:

> 1 I'ha hyo' o'ya i'ya i'ya' o i'ha ya'ya yo'yo
> 2 A'he'ya ahe'ya' ya'he'yo' ya e'ya he'yo e'he'yo
> 3 Qóichę́gàu án á ó-báui-hę̂-mà. Hàun-àn fái-dé-cì ó-báui-qầu
>   (Qóichę́gàu do die. Sun-alone / really-exists)
>   Qóichę́gàu do die/really die (emphatically). The sun exists forever.
> 4 Qóichę́gàu án á ó-báui-hę̂-mà. Hàun dáum-gáu-cì ó-báui-qầu
>   (Qóichę́gàu do die. Earth-alone / really-exists)
>   Qóichę́gàu do die/really die (emphatically). The earth exists forever.
> 5 I'ha hyo' o'ya i'ya i'ya' o i'ha ya'ya yo'yo
> 6 A'he'ya ahe'ya' ya'he'yo' ya e'ya he'yo e'he'yo

Charley White Horse gave the following as the song Sitting Bear sang as his death song in 1871 at Fort Sill. The song contains some of the same lyrics and closely resembles the preceding song in its representation of the society's values:

> 1 Háu à gôm-àl
>   (What if: living on or not [It matters little whether I live or not])

Although I go about [living],
2 Háu à ó-báui-gṳ̀-thàu
(If I live, I should not live forever)
I cannot live forever.
3 Ǫ́ dáum-gáu-cì
(But this earth will live forever)
The earth alone exists forever.
4 Háu à gôm-àl
Although I go about [living],
5 Háu à ó-báui-gṳ̀-thàu
I cannot live forever.
6 Ǫ́ fái-dé-cì ó-báui-fái-dè
(But summers will follow summers forever)
The sun alone exists forever.
7 Háu à ó-báui-gṳ̀-thàu
I cannot live forever.
8 Ǫ́ fái-qàu-dé-cì ó-báui-qàu
(But the sun remains up there forever)
The sun alone exists forever.[96]

Police Functions

Although the Dog Society could serve as hunt police during the Sun Dance period, it rarely did do. According to Frizzlehead II, the society once policed a hunt during a Sun Dance encampment. After a bison herd was sighted, the Sun Dance priest, Old Man Long Foot, decided it would be hunted the following day. He invited Sitting Bear and Old Man Red Tipi, who were not yet retired (thus this took place before 1867), and a number of men from the other societies to decide on the job of policing. Old Man Red Tipi called out for volunteers, and Many Camp Fires (Áiséàuidè or Iseeo), then a Dog Society whipman, accepted the duty for his society.[97] Neither the Jáifègàu nor the Black Legs Society, the usual hunt police, was reportedly angered or felt any infringement upon its rights. Frizzlehead II knew of no particular reason for the society's doing this, except perhaps to receive meat, even though hunt police received no more than anyone else. This event perhaps represents an exception to the norm, because it occurred before the ride around camp, and none of the other society leaders had yet been asked. Dog Society members were also said to have served as advisors and policemen on raiding parties and during the Sun Dance.[98]

Decline of the Society

The Dog Society last met five Sun Dances before the last one, which would have been either 1878 or 1879, depending on whether or not the incomplete Sun Dance of 1890 is counted. This meeting consisted of a feast sponsored by the wife of Horse Headdress/Cap (Chêbǫ̀hòn); she was a captive sister of Sangko's. Sangko reported that approximately ten to twenty elder members attended, dressed in their society regalia. Women came and stood behind the members, most likely their husbands, honoring them. No initiations were held at this time, the last ones having taken place in 1867.[99] Although all the men's societies focused on the relationship between social status, wealth, and warfare activities, the end of warfare clearly affected the Dog and related societies more quickly and to a greater degree than the other men's societies, for several reasons. The Dog Society was numerically smaller, had dangerously strict requirements, was composed largely of older members, held only occasional initiations, and met less frequently than other men's societies. Thus it had less a social function than other Kiowa men's societies did. Requiring war honors for membership, the Dog Society was more dependent on warfare than the other men's societies, and so it declined quickly with the end of warfare in 1875.

After the Dog Society ceased to meet, in 1878 or 1879, its remaining members soon joined other societies. Yellow Wolf rejoined the Black Legs; Frizzlehead II joined the Horse Headdresses and, after its cessation, the Black Legs. Previously, members would never have left the society except through death, because retired members retained membership and no higher-status society or position existed.[100]

The last major event involving the Dog Society took place at the unfinished 1890 Sun Dance. There, the Sons of the Sun (Fáiiyòi), a small anti-peyote group that formed in 1887, were preparing to be taken into the Dog Society as a group. Haumpo was a society member who also belonged to the Sons of the Sun. Although the society had not met in more than a decade, the Sons of the Sun were preparing to take part in the parade, after which all thirty members were to be inducted. Yellow Wolf had been training the Sons of the Sun in the society dance step, and the society paraphernalia had already been made.[101] Other society members, especially Frizzlehead II, were against it, because the whole group was to be taken in as full society members and not as colts. The outcome was never known. Fear of troops approaching from Fort Sill broke up the preparations for the Sun Dance, and another was never held.[102]

Today the Qóichę́gàu are still mentioned in conversations, particularly at society and dance events. Although interviews with contemporary elders produced little detailed information, the society is well remembered, and proud descendants of former society members are quick to point out their ancestors' membership. The Dog Society's bravery, sashes, contrary battle actions, and small number of sash owners are most frequently mentioned, and speeches at society functions praise the Dog Society for its martial bravery. The manner in which the society is spoken of marks it as a role model for military service. Although men no longer stake themselves down and perform contrary acts in battle, the demeanor and courage attributed to the Dog Society have become symbolic.

Because the society ceased around 1878–1879 and so little has been formally written about it, some misconceptions surround it in the contemporary Kiowa community, mostly concerning its size and membership. Most Kiowa today believe the society had only ten members. As previously mentioned, accounts from the last actual society members indicate that ten sash owners, their ten society partners, younger apprentice-like members (colts), and older retired members made up a body averaging forty or more members at any time.

Recently, members of some families have increasingly been making what are largely unverified public claims of Dog Society membership on the part of an ancestor.[103] Usually these involve historically well-known chiefs and warriors around whom recently formed descendants groups have developed. To some degree, an increasing correlation is appearing between having a noted warrior or chief as an ancestor and assuming that the ancestor was a Dog Society member. Indeed, great prestige accrues from having an ancestor with such an affiliation. Kiowa elders and past society members in the early 1900s clearly recounted that even regular members in the Dog Society (probably sash owners and their partners) ranked higher than members or leaders of any other society.

Not all such public claims can be validated, and an examination of an individual's multiple personal names is sometimes required. However, comparison of Kiowa names, birth dates from agency records, and archival membership lists obtained from the last Dog Society members (those from the 1867 initiation) show that certain well-known men were in fact not Dog Society members. Instead, they were leaders or members of other Kiowa military societies, themselves prominent positions.[104] These membership lists (see Appendix) may clarify as well as affect future claims concerning ancestors and society membership.

Some Kiowa have suggested that the Dog Society should be revived, with the ten highest-ranking Kiowa combat veterans as members, because there are several combat veterans who saw "considerable action." When asked who would be the most likely Dog Society member of recent times, most Kiowa say that it would have to be the late Pascal Poolaw, the most highly decorated American Indian veteran of the twentieth century. From the Kiowa viewpoint, the Qóichégàu continue to epitomize the greatest warriors of the past and the highest level of courage, service, and selflessness, traits that continue in the contemporary ideology and ethos of Kiowa military service.[105]

7

CÁUITÉMGÒP

The Kiowa Bone Strikers

The Cáuitémgòp was a Kiowa military society that, because of its extermination in battle, is the least known of all Kiowa men's societies.[1] The group was a contrary society, using contrary speech and action and being ritually prohibited from retreating in battle. It was known for its elevated and conspicuous bravery, ritual secrecy, antisocial nature, and use of large bone clubs as weapons. As the top-ranking Kiowa men's society prior to its cessation (after which the Dog Society apparently assumed this position), it policed communal bison hunts. It was exterminated in battle in the nineteenth century, most likely before 1840, because it does not appear in the Kiowa calendars. It was never revived, out of fear that if it were, its members would be killed again.

Hugh Scott's list of Kiowa men's societies in the 1890s includes the Cáuitémgòp: "6th—This used to be in existence in old times and was called Goy-e-tain (meaning unknown)."[2] The earliest detailed mention of the society comes from James Mooney's fieldnotes: "There was a something [of] a higher order = Ga-i-temgop. The name refers to an animal war club which they all carried, but [the society] was 'let go' because they [were] afraid, because [they] pledged not to run and on account the whole band [was] thus killed."[3] The relationship between the society's name and its use of clubs as insignia is further supported by Jack Doyeto's reference to the society as the "Tomahawk Society," made to Hugh Scott in 1897.[4]

Mooney indicated that the Cáuitémgòp was once the highest-ranking Kiowa military society: "They were chief of Yapahey [Yàpfàhêgàu, the Kiowa military societies] and could not run." The society also served as the hunt police.[5] Nothing more is known about its status and relations with other Kiowa societies.

Robert Lowie (1916b:841), too, noted the existence of the society:

There once existed in the time of one informant's great grandfather an additional men's society, the qo' + item "Kiowas Bone" (?). The members of this organization each represented a buffalo bull, except for the leader who, although also a man, represented a buffalo cow. The leader would stop to stand his ground and this obliged the others to do the same. Thus the entire group was killed, and because the people were afraid, the organization was no longer maintained.

Although one account attributes the society's cessation to declining membership because of its numerous organizational rules, accounts of the society's demise in battle are more common and are strongly supported.[6]

According to Kiowa elders in 1935, the society's name, Koitemgup or Goitemgup, meant "Kiowa Bone Strikers," referring to a certain portion of a bison's leg bone, approximately eight inches in length. Each member owned a club made from one of these bones. Contemporary Kiowa elders interpret the name of the society as Kiowa Bone Strikers, from Cáui (Kiowa), tém (a variant of tǫ̀sègàu, bone) and gòp (hit or struck). Mooney recorded both Cáuitémgàu (Kiowa Bone People) and Cáuitémgòp (Kiowa Bone Strikers) as names of the society.[7] In a statement pertinent to the basis of the society's name, Belo Cozad told Mooney that the society members carried only clubs into battle.[8] More detailed accounts of these clubs state that they were the length of canes and had the heads of horses, wolves, birds, and other animals carved into their ends. Being heavy, they had wrist straps and were used as war clubs. A member could not dance with his club held above his head unless he was a great warrior or chief. Similarly, younger men who were not high-ranking warriors were required to carry their clubs, tomahawks, and other weapons low while dancing and were subject to ridicule if they dared to raise them high.[9]

According to Hunting Horse, the Kiowa Bone Strikers Society had a special relationship with the bison, had around forty members, held a dance called Yǎuácùngà (meaning unknown), and had a leader named White Bear (not the White Bear of 1870s notoriety). Hunting Horse said that the leaders of the other societies belonged to this society, but this does not follow the general rules of membership for Kiowa men's societies and implies either that men could belong to more than one society at that time or that perhaps a special membership requirement for the leaders of the other societies existed. The only other known member of the society was Jòhâudè (Recess In The Side Of A Cliff, or Bluff Recess, also known as Páuthòcáui, or White-Faced Bison Bull), the father of Jòhâusàn (Son of Recess In The Side Of A Cliff, also known as Little Bluff Recess), the Kiowa tribal chief from 1833 to 1866 and leader of the Dog Society (Ewers 1978:14; Schneider 1982:8).[10]

The society functioned as police during the Sun Dance and was the only Kiowa military society known to have fought as an entire group in war—hence its extermination.[11] It practiced both contrary speech and a no-retreat rule in battle. Like other Plains military societies, after choosing a place in which to stand and fight until its warriors were either victorious or killed, the society danced as the enemy approached. Charley White Horse reported in 1935 that the society had a no-retreat rule and that "they died because no one told them 'not to run.'" Although no society ropes or sashes are known for the society, the no-retreat rule, as in the Dog Society, appears to have been associated with release in the form of a contrary verbal command. The Cáuitémgòp was not resuscitated, because of the danger that doing so posed to the tribe. By the third quarter of the nineteenth century, its demise may have influenced other Kiowa military societies no longer to go to war as entire societies.[12]

In 1936, Jack Doyeto gave Alice Marriott an account of the society's serving as hunt police. Camped near present-day Fort Cobb, Oklahoma, the Kiowa had declared a closed bison hunt, during which everyone had to remain in a central camp to avoid scaring the bison away. They were preparing to hunt a nearby herd when Fâbǒjè (Peahbo, or Large Mustang, the Comanche name of a Kiowa also known as Tâàuiqì, or Many Wives) disregarded the Cáuitémgòp police's orders and traveled onward to the southwest. Upon catching Large Mustang's party, the police punished it severely. The police shot the favorite horses of Large Mustang and his favorite wife, destroyed the clothes he wore, cut the packs off the remaining horses, destroyed the party's tipi poles, struck Large Mustang with bows, and finally whipped him. After returning to the main camp, the society danced before leaving to begin the hunt.[13] Although this account indicates that the society's demise took place after the Kiowa migrated to the southern Great Plains, the date of its demise is unknown.

Although the society ceased to exist long before the personal memory of any of the oldest 1935 Kiowa consultants (the eldest was born in 1844), and the names of only two members were known, these elders were well aware of the society's existence, its martial characteristics, and some of the society's songs, which were noted for their abrupt endings. Hunting Horse stated that the songs could be sung at any time but were usually reserved for times of great stress. He later said that Cáuitémgòpdàugà (Kiowa Bone Strikers songs) were not danced to at other society meetings because they belonged to that society.[14] The following society songs, taught by Jòhâudè to Jòhâusàn, were recorded from the latter's grandson Charley White Horse in 1935. They demonstrate the martial spirit of the society and its no-retreat rule:

1 Câi-jàu-gà yá ǫ́-dèp
   (Enemy-fighting / I / like)
   I love warfare.
2 Repeat.
3 É-hàu páu-thàu
   (Here, at this point / stop-shall)
   Now, over here, I will stop and make a stand.
4 É bà tǫ́-sè-sòm-dě-thàu
   (Here / you to I / bones-look at-shall)
   Here you will be to look at my bones.

According to White Horse, this song was very powerful and could have been composed only by a great warrior with great war power.[15]

Several elders indicated that the behavior and actions of the society were antisocial and somewhat harsh. One current Kiowa elder had been told by his grandmother that this society painted everything red like the Dog Society and was known to ingest something that made them act in a "mean and crazy manner." They would force everyone to leave the camp with all their dogs and horses. When the society was ready, its members came out into the camp. People watched from a distance as the men performed some activity in which they went from tipi to tipi throughout the camp. Another elder reported that after forcing everyone to leave camp with their horses and dogs, members went inside their lodges, washed and painted their bodies and faces in preparation for battle, and then came out and sang and danced.[16] In recounting the policing of Large Mustang, Jack Doyeto said that after beating him, the society members went off by themselves to dance before continuing the hunt. While the society danced, "no one would dare go near there to find out why they were dancing.... No one would go find out, because they were afraid of them."[17] Consequently, little is known of their activities. The following translation of one of their songs, provided by Yellow Wolf in 1935, illustrates the unusual behavior attributed to the society:

> He is mean,
> What is the matter with him?
> He has got some way,
> The boys whipped him and there is something over him.[18]

Victor Paddlety, in a 1976 tape recording of Kiowa history and names, provided part of one of the society's songs that refers to their antisocial behavior:

> 1 Cáui-tém-gòp, Cáui-tém-gòp
>   Kiowa Bone Strikers, Kiowa Bone Strikers.
> 2 Yá̱ jép-jè-dầu gàu
>   Even though I am related (have relatives),
> 3 Háun-àn à dầu nàu . . .
>   I don't want to be related (i.e., have any relatives).

Although the society's origins are unknown, the following song, collected in 1935, is said to refer to its origin. Two men from a raiding party saw a lone buffalo coming along a trail. Waiting out of sight to kill the creature, they heard the buffalo sing. This song was only partially recognizable to the elders I showed it to.

> 1 Dè gà zél-bè
>   (It / is / dangerous)
>   It is dangerous (for us).
> 2 Nàu á qá-côm-à̱
>   (And/ we / living-continuative)
>   We are living (the buffalo).
> 3 Nàu há-gà . . .
>   mwha'ggia po'dot'o
>   Can there be a time of peace?

4 Gudl'op'te ag'i dl yase
   Into the red clay gully walls they pour over.

This verse was interpreted to mean that it was dangerous for buffalo to be alive, because the hunters killed them by driving them over red clay walls, perhaps a reference to the common use of cliff drives in bison hunts of the pre-horse era. The second verse continues:

1 Páu-sạ̀-dàu bá ó-dè dé-hàup
  (Young buffalo bulls / you all / from there hitherward / right now)
  Young Bison Bulls, get over here (into the fight) right now.
2 Ę́-dé-chò g'iade e mo. lom gom
  (this way / . . .)
  This is the way you want to turn back (against the enemy).

This verse was interpreted as using the metaphor of a young male buffalo as a warrior and meaning that young men might easily be frightened in war. Therefore, the older men show the younger ones (personified as bison) how to turn back to face the enemy (the hunters). As the second verse is sung, the singer slowly turns around at the end, thus demonstrating the appropriateness of the war song by representing the practice of reversing his position in battle.[19]

Another society song recorded and translated in 1935 but no longer fully recognizable likewise challenges others to prove their bravery in battle:

1 Yan o~.de ha'oko, ha.tso omgia
  (Yắn . . . , hắchò áumgá)
  You have been boasting of bravery; something is happening now.
2. Tadly'ui epei nw ho'ko mo.mo
  (Tà-lyói é fè nàu . . .)
  (Boys, they became afraid of you . . .).
  Boys were afraid of you; frequently you bluffed them.

This song was interpreted as meaning, "As a young man you used to boast, but now that you are here in the real war, prove your valor. Now the test is here."[20]

Limited data inhibit a clear assessment of the Bone Strikers Society in the Kiowa military society system. If the presence of fictive society brothers could be confirmed, it would place the date of this institution farther back in time, possibly prior to the Kiowa migration to the southern plains. It is clear that the society was once the highest-ranking Kiowa men's society and provided integrative functions in policing, guarding camp movements, and guarding against attacks. Along with the Omaha Society, the Cáuitèmgòp is significant in illustrating the ongoing rise, spread, and decline of individual societies within a single tribal population, a process typical of pan-Plains military societies. Especially significant is that this society fought as a discrete unit.

Together with data from other tribes, this suggests an earlier and broader Plains pattern in which individual societies functioned as raiding or warfare units, a pattern that seems to have ended after about 1840. The Bone Strikers' ritual contrary behavior might also reflect a once more widespread characteristic of Plains men's military societies.

8

ÓHǪMÒGÀU
The Omaha Society

The Óhǫmò (Omaha) Society was the last men's society acquired by the Kiowa in the nineteenth century. Obtained from the Cheyenne in 1884, it was associated with a new and popular form of dance, music, and dress. Spreading across the Great Plains in the late 1800s, this dance came to be known by several names, including Omaha, Grass, War, Hot, Dream, and Drum Dance. The Omaha Society also brought the first feathered dance bustle to the Kiowa. Acquired shortly before the last Sun Dance, the society initially shared in the duties of the other men's societies and was centered on a celebration by combat veterans. With the end of warfare in 1875 and the decline in the number of combat veterans, the society gradually became a more social and honorific group focused on dancing but never forgetting its warrior origins. Its members originally performed what would today be called a western Plains form of the Straight Dance and added the Fancy Dance in 1917.

Throughout its existence, the Omaha Society has been the principal focus of Kiowa War dancing. It also contributed to the emergence of the Plains Indian powwow and the Straight and Fancy Dance styles of dancing in the modern powwow. Although non-societal-based powwows feature various styles of Omaha or War Dance music, the link between the Kiowa Omaha Society and War dancing continues in the annual Ohoma Lodge ceremonial, a formal society dance held every July. As one of four remaining Kiowa men's societies, the Omaha Society serves as the center of Kiowa War dancing and a core of ethnic identity for some Kiowa. It is the only Kiowa society that never stopped dancing during the period of U.S. government suppression from the 1880s through the 1930s.

The history and development of the Omaha Society are essential in understanding the evolution of past and present Plains, Prairie, Great Lakes, and pan-Indian dance and music, for the following reasons: it was the last and most widespread Plains Indian military society to diffuse in the late 1800s; it was the last Kiowa men's warrior society to be acquired; it represents the continued growth of Plains tribal military society complexes; and it was a major part of the War Dance complex, which led to the contemporary Plains Indian powwow. In this chapter I explore three primary subjects: the origin and diffusion of the Plains Omaha or War Dance of the late 1800s, the acquisition and development of the Kiowa Omaha Society from that time to the present, and the relationship of the Omaha Dance to the Plains Indian powwow.

The Origins and Diffusion of the Plains Omaha Dance

Most Plains Indian tribes had some ritualized combination of songs and dances for pre-warfare (War Journey) and post-warfare (Scalp and Victory Dance) activities. The relationship between the War Dance and the contemporary powwow involves a historically and culturally deep tradition that differs significantly from the popular non-Indian image of the dance. A number of ceremonial complexes (military society, Sun Dance, medicine bundle, Scalp and Victory Dance, Calumet Dance) existed on the Great Plains, some regional and others nearly pan-Plains. Several of these institutions contributed significantly to the contemporary powwow. The exchange of ceremonial dances, songs, forms of regalia, and their significances created a generally similar foundation that led to the development of the intertribal powwow.

Gloria Young (1981:103) reported that the War, Scalp, and Calumet Dances were already a "complex" at the time of European contact, were widespread among many tribes, and served various intertribal needs by the seventeenth century. She pointed out that in attempting to determine the roots of the modern powwow, one had to recognize that the War, Scalp, Calumet, Omaha, Drum, and Stomp Dances are all precursors of portions of the modern powwow. From the widespread presence of military societies in most Plains tribal communities and the subsequent development of the pan-Plains powwow, it is evident that dancing was an important activity affiliated with a wide variety of functions and ritual forms in the pre-reservation, reservation, and post-reservation periods. As Thomas Kavanagh noted (1982:13), "the powwow is the modern version of the Grass Dance, a secular dance which diffused widely across the Plains in the late 1800s." Thus, contemporary tribal and intertribal powwows are inextricably linked to the earlier Plains military societies. Two dance traditions in particular played seminal roles in the development of late-diffusing Plains military societies and the subsequent powwow: the dance known among tribes as the Iruska, Omaha, Grass, Hot, or War Dance, and the Drum or Dream Dance.

The Pawnee Iruska

The Omaha or Grass Dance is believed to have originated around 1820 with the Pawnee Iruska (The Fire Is In Me) Society, a medicine or doctoring society based on Pawnee cosmology that specialized in treating burns (Murie 1914:608–616; Wissler 1916:859–862). It once included ceremonies and ritual paraphernalia consisting of feathered bustles, whips, whistles, and ritual serving spoons. The Pawnee viewed the

Iruska Society as closely related to religion and cosmology. They maintained that a man named Crow Feather had received the dance through a vision, and while in a trancelike state he was given a porcupine and deer hair roach headdress and a crow bustle or belt. He was also given special medicine or spiritual powers that enabled him to pull chunks of meat from a boiling kettle without being burned, a ritual that was said to imitate the act of hunters removing steaming entrails from the stomachs of freshly killed game. Its originator, Crow Feather, is reported to have said, in relation to imitating an attack on an enemy through dance, "This will not be a social dance, neither will the members act as soldiers for the chiefs. We shall be known as medicinemen" (Murie 1914:616). Because society members had the ability to retrieve boiling meat from a kettle without injury and to overcome fire and the power of other medicines, the society's dance was also known as the "Hot Dance."

The two central items of Iruska regalia, the roach and the crow belt, were already common among several Plains Indian groups prior to the spread of the Omaha Dance. George Catlin depicted Lakota crow belts being worn in the Beggar's Dance of 1832, some thirty years before the Lakota obtained the rights to the Omaha Dance, regalia, and songs. Museums contain examples of round roaches from the Great Lakes region dating from 1800. The Lakota Kit Fox Society also used the roach prior to obtaining the Omaha Dance; it closely resembles that worn by a Lakota identified as an Omaha dancer in an early photograph (McCracken 1959:45; Philp 1977:62; Walker 1980; Browner 2002:22–23).

The Omaha Hethushka

In the 1830s the Pawnee gave or sold the Iruska Society and its dance to the Omaha and Ponca, who called it Hethushka and Helushka, or "Man Dance," respectively. The Omaha are also known to claim to have originated the dance. The Omaha Hethushka Society was originally a military or, as Alice Fletcher and Francis La Flesche (1911:459) distinguished it, a social society of the Omaha, Ponca, and their close Dhegihan cognates when they all lived together as a single tribe. Several anthropological works have addressed aspects of the origins and spread of the Omaha or War Dance (Wissler 1916; Vennum 1982; Powers 1990; Meadows 1995, 1999; Duncan 1997; Browner 2002). The dance became a widely diffused and relatively secular body of ritual among Plains, Prairie, and western Great Lakes tribes after about 1860.

The War Dance was often associated with the widespread Calumet ceremony, and its long existence has recently been suggested to extend well into pre-Columbian times. Jimmy Duncan (1997:11, 45–52) suggested that similarities of regalia and warfare motifs extend as far back as the Adena and Hopewell cultures of the Early and Middle Woodland periods in the Ohio Valley. The Omaha and Ponca maintain accounts of having originated in the Ohio River valley before moving to the eastern plains. Significant artistic themes in archaeological artifacts that are stylistically similar to late-nineteenth-century War Dance artifacts include effigy pipes and raptor motifs.

The well-known Adena pipe (Townsend 2004:31), made of pipestone and excavated from the Adena Mound in Ross County, Ohio, dates to between 100 B.C. and A.D. 100. The pipe depicts a male figure wearing a decorated waist garment, large earspools, and a headdress closely resembling a porcupine hair roach, with the pipe bowl extending upward from the top of the head, where a roach spreader would normally be. Attached to the belt on the back of the figure's waist is a fanlike splay of what appear to be ten tail feathers. Hanging from an attached base and positioned like a bird's spread-out tail, these feathers resemble historic versions of the Plains crow belt or feathered bustle. The roach and bustle are two of the core elements of historic War Dance regalia. Another important pipe is a Hopewell platform pipe (Jennings 1974:236A) depicting a bird, mostly likely a crow or raven, devouring a human face (possibly that of a fallen warrior), a later widespread Plains theme associated with several men's military societies. As part of the Southeastern Ceremonial Complex (Galloway 1989; Duncan 1997:47–52), the "seeds of the War Dance Complex" are also found in avian and avian-human themes in several regional foci of the Mississippian period (A.D. 800–1550). Although we cannot assume that these items held the same uses and meanings as their later historical counterparts, their marked physical similarities raise the possibility of some degree of connection through time.

For more than three centuries the term *War Dance* has been used extensively in the ethnographic literature, and it has become the generic term for all forms of the War Dance complex (Duncan 1997:5). Historical accounts of the Calumet ceremony begin in 1665 with Nicholas Perrot. Henri Joutel documented what he called a "War Dance" while he was a member of LaSalle's expedition in 1687 (Swanton 1942:187). Antoine Le Page Du Pratz (1942 [1774]:370–373) witnessed several such "war dances" between 1718 and 1734 along the Mississippi River valley. Edwin James (1823:235), a member of Stephen Long's expedition to the Rocky Mountains, provided the first extensive description of a War Dance among the Iowa and Otoe on October 3, 1819. Although these descriptions all share a war focus, how closely the dances resembled one another or the diffused Omaha Dance of the late 1800s is unclear. However, the dances seem to be related as parts of cultural traditions that contributed to the Plains War Dance complex of the late 1800s.

After European contact, Plains tribes were faced with adjusting to dramatic changes in subsistence strategies, to new diseases, and to population losses, disruptions in the dissemination of tribal religion and ritual knowledge, and new and spreading forms of warfare. Between 1855 and 1906, the Omaha and Ponca religion and the associated War ceremony began to decline and to be reformulated. By 1855, membership requirements in the Omaha Hethushka Society had changed from an emphasis on participation in ceremonially organized war parties that went out and sought enemies to an emphasis on defending the village and being a good provider. Duncan (1997:62) suggested that whereas the War ceremony had previously served within the larger Omaha religion to unify people in times of danger and channel warrior responses to group-oriented efforts in which individuals could obtain socially sanctioned war honors, the introduction of new forms of warfare centered on horses and guns undermined the ceremonial restrictions formerly placed on war. In time, the War ceremony became impractical in relation to new forms of warfare that were rapidly depleting the Omaha population and destabilizing the religion (Duncan 1997:63). Consequently, many Omaha sodalities and rituals, including those obtained from other tribes, were defunct by the 1870s (James Owen Dorsey, fieldnotes, 1873; Skinner 1915b:787). Similar developments are documented for the Kiowa, Plains Apache, and Comanche regarding changes in warfare followed by the decline and loss of military and shield societies during the reservation period (McAllister 1937:150; Meadows 1995, 1999).

Among the Omaha, the War Dance complex underwent a gradual change from being an integral part of the religious system to being a more secular and ethnic body of ritual. By 1860 the Omaha War Dance complex was being reinterpreted as a more secular dance form expressed as the Grass Dance, which attempted to "restate religious symbols from the old religion outside the previous restrictive structure" (Duncan 1997:64). Dorsey, in his 1872 fieldnotes, remarked that integral to this change was the retention of the memory of "old ways" and tribal values cherished by then middle-aged Indians from their childhood, a process also at work in most other Plains dance sodalities, which were becoming ethnic and honorific groups rather than active warrior societies at this time (Meadows 1999:375)—much as in the Kiowa Gourd Clan revival in 1957. The dance now served as a much broader source of ethnic revival and continuity, rather than as a strictly religious-ceremonial institution.

Fletcher (1893:26) noted that "a valiant record alone entitled a man to admission" in the Omaha Hethushka. Fletcher and La Flesche (1911:459; compare Duncan 1997:64) wrote of the key ideology behind the diffusion of the Grass Dance in the late 1800s: "It is said that the object in establishing the Hethu'shka society was to stimulate an heroic spirit among the people and to keep alive the memory of historic and valorous acts." Secularization was also a key to the rapid spread of the dance. The more secular features, less rigid membership requirements and rituals, and associated popular dance and dress styles prompted its rapid acceptance among many tribes during a period of great cultural change. As the Grass Dance spread, similar widespread introductions or revivals of the Ghost Dance, peyotism, Christianity, and hand games occurred, and older, traditional military societies declined (Meadows 1999:381–382).

By the time of James O. Dorsey's work among the Omaha and Ponca, the Hethushka had become a dancing and feasting society focused on both civic and martial aspects. It emphasized the recognition of war deeds, courage, and civic values and duties, ideals that continue to be associated with modern veterans. Members were younger warriors who had demonstrated themselves in battle, placed greater emphasis on the dancing and feasting aspects of the society, and were recognized for and advertised their warfare achievements by the use of special ritual forms of society regalia (Wissler 1917:865; Glazner 2002:20).

The Dakota and Lakota

In the early 1840s the Omaha sold the right to perform the dance and its songs to the Yanktonai Dakota, who later gave the rights to the ceremony to their Teton Lakota relatives. The Omaha or Grass Dance was most likely passed from the Omaha or Ponca to the Yankton Sioux during a period of alliance between the two groups against the Pawnee, from 1833 to 1842 (Fletcher 1892:143; Howard 1951:20). Both the Yanktonai and the Lakota called the dance the "Omaha Dance" for the people from whom they had acquired it. Around 1865 the Lakota began spreading the ceremony to other Northern Plains tribes, who began calling it the Grass Dance (Browner 2002:21–22). As it spread during the late nineteenth century, many tribes adopted the more secular form of the dance, focusing on the civic rather than the religious aspects of the War Dance. As Fletcher and La Flesche (1911:460) described it: "Although the Hethuska has a wide popularity, it is only in the tribes in which it originated that the religious rites and songs of the opening ceremonies are observed; outsiders omit these observances and make use only of the dramatic dance, the songs, and the feast."

During this time a number of cultural changes occurred, including the Ponca's receiving the Mawadani and Tokala Dances from the Dakota, who had abandoned them by 1855. A Dakota winter count records the acquisition of the Grass Dance in 1860, and it was noted as the principal dance among the Yankton in 1867 (Wissler 1916:865–866; Howard 1951:83; Powers 1973:24). Beginning by transmitting the dance to the Assiniboine in 1872, the Lakota and Dakota accelerated its diffusion to many other Plains populations over the next forty years (Wissler 1916:865–866; Vennum 1982:54; Duncan 1997:73). A comparison of ethnographic accounts of the dance shows that the ceremony was continually modified as each group reinterpreted it, altering it to fit the group's current cultural needs and tastes. The effect of the new Grass Dance on Plains communities was especially significant, because it replaced or superseded most of the previous military and dance society complexes from Canada to Oklahoma (Flannery 1947:6; Vennum 1982:59; Meadows 1999:382–384). By 1900 Lakota military societies were largely defunct, and the Grass Dance had acquired a primary social role while retaining serious ceremonial attributes (Wissler 1916:862). After the Ponca were removed to Indian Territory in 1877, they continued to pass the dance to neighboring tribes such as the Osage and Kaw. As other Central and Northern Plains tribes acquired the dance, some tribes, such as the Cheyenne and Kiowa, called it the Omaha Dance in recognition of its diffusion from the Omaha. When the Ponca performed the dance for the Comanche and Apache in 1919, the Kiowa, having already acquired the dance from the Cheyenne, declined the Ponca's offer to give the dance to them.[1]

The Bustle and Roach

As special forms of material culture widely understood to signify prestige and status associated with war rank, the porcupine hair roach headdress and the crow belt or bustle were primary influences from the Pawnee Iruska society that diffused to nearly all Plains tribes (Murie 1914:608). According to James Murie (1914:616):

> The headdress is the imitation of fire, the black hair for smoke. The feather represents the iruska man who understands fire. He is standing in the fire or has placed the fire about his whole body. The headdress represents the fireplace, the bone tube the medicine, and the feather, the man himself standing in the center of the fireplace. According to tradition, man came from an ear of corn and corn has life and life is fire. The original word for iruska is iriska (singular), iruska (plural), they are inside fire.

References to similar "fire tricks" among several other tribes and a similarity in the name of the dance among other groups (Omaha, Hethushka; Iowa, Heloka; Ponca, Hethushka; Kansa, Helucka; Dakota, Heyoka; Osage, I'nlonschka) point to the wide spread of the Iruska's central characteristics among other Plains tribes. As Tara Browner (2002:23–24) noted, this ritual act was common in many Plains and some northeastern Indian ceremonials, but often for different purposes and with different contextual meanings, depending on whether it was performed by a military, social, doctoring, or dream society. Although Clark Wissler (1916:859, 861) glossed the names Iruska, Hethushka, and Heyoka as having identical origins and meanings derived from the Pawnee Hot Dance ritual of extracting meat from a boiling kettle, he visited few of the groups he wrote about. Consequently, Browner's conclusion (2002:23, 27) that his assertion that the Dakota, Nakota, and Lakota had this ritual before the Pawnee seems both unlikely and inconsistent with the direction in which the dance spread. In addition, numerous pre-reservation warrior societies had similar dances and regalia, some being essentially "chapters" of the same society (Walker 1980:265; Meadows 1999:55–57) that had spread from tribe to tribe just as the Omaha Dance had. Whereas Murie (1914:608–616) and Wissler (1916:859–860) translated Iruska as "The Fire Is In Me," and Alice Ann Callahan (1990:19) translated the Osage I'nlonschka as "Playground of the Eldest." Kavanagh (1993:123n7) wrote that the exact meaning of the original name was unclear. What is clear is that these organizations made up a series of martial-oriented sodalities featuring highly ritualized dance performances. As Kavanagh (1993:109) described them:

> These were organizations of established warriors whose ceremonies were structured around a group of officials (including four officers chosen to wear the crow belts, feather bustles symbolizing crows flocking over a battlefield), a set of ceremonial and ritual acts involving the heroism of war deeds, and an accompanying feast. The feast was often placed in the center of the dance arena and "stalked" by the dancers, who used either their bare hands to retrieve pieces of

meat—thus the name "Hot Dance"—or the ritual forks carried by officers, who were comparable to the crow-belt wearers.

The Kiowa's Acquisition of the Omaha Society

The Kiowa originally called the Omaha tribe Ómàuhāugàu (Omaha People), and later Óhǫmògàu, both Kiowa pronunciations of the tribal name Omaha. With the acquisition of the Omaha Dance, the Kiowa adopted the name Óhǫmògàu for the society. In time, the name changed to Óhǫmò and then Óhǫmà. Today Kiowa refer to the society and dance as "Ohoma," "Ohomah," or "O-Ho-Mah Lodge." Although most Kiowa now use the gloss "War Dance" for the name of the society, the literal translation is Omaha, which I use here to refer to the society.[2]

Although the Kiowa Omaha Society became a new socioceremonial arena originally focused upon a series of martial- and warrior-related rituals, the Kiowa did not receive the society until after they were already well established on a reservation. Despite beliefs by some contemporary Kiowa that the Omaha Society participated in pre-reservation battles, the documented testimony of several Kiowa, including society members who lived during this period, counter these views. Recorded accounts state that both the Lakota and Cheyenne were responsible for introducing the dance to the Kiowa, but Kiowa elders always indicate that it was the Cheyenne who did so.[3] As will be demonstrated, although the Cheyenne played a larger and longer-lasting role than the Lakota, both were actually involved in the diffusion of the dance to the Kiowa.

Although most sources indicate that the society was introduced to the Kiowa in 1884, there is some discrepancy over the exact date. Silverhorn reported to James Mooney, "The Ohomo-guan [Omaha Dance] was introduced simultaneously and given to both Cheyenne and Kiowa in summer 1881 (Hot Sun Dance) by visiting Sioux who received a large number of horses for it. After then it began [to] supersede all Yapahey dances and [members of] different orders [of] Yapahey joined in it."[4]

No record of this 1881 visit by the Lakota is found in Mooney's *Calendar History of the Kiowa Indians* (1898:347). Other sources, however, state that the Cheyenne obtained it from the Lakota, who had previously obtained the dance from the Omaha around 1865.[5] Historical and ethnological sources indicate that a large party of Lakota came south to visit the Kiowa in the winter of 1883–1884. Intertribal visits by large contingents of people during the early reservation period reflect an earlier tradition of intertribal visits that continues in various forms to the present. Mooney recorded this visit (1898:352): "Anko notes also that a party of Dakota came down to dance with the Kiowa, indicated by the feather dance-wand at the side of the winter mark [in a calendar]." The visit was also described by Hugh Corwin (1962:169) and in an account from Gapkaugo, or Mrs. Hokeah, in 1935, who noted that the visiting tribe wore large earrings and performed the Omaha Dance for the Kiowa. From the Kiowa perspective, both the Lakota and the Cheyenne were known for their fondness for large earrings.[6] The next summer (1884), the Kiowa were visited by the Cheyenne, who, according to

Kiowa accounts, were then in the vicinity of present-day Gotebo and Hobart, Oklahoma. According to Kiowa elders, it was at this encampment that the Kiowa received the Omaha Society and Dance.

On the basis of a ledgerbook drawing made by Koba that depicts him wearing a Cheyenne-style bustle, which he made while he was a prisoner at Fort Marion from 1875 to 1878, Clyde Ellis (2003:53) raised the question of whether the Kiowa received the Omaha Dance from the Cheyenne at this time. The drawing depicts Koba wearing a bustle, holding a horned and feathered bonnet in his left hand, and standing in front of a horse. Koba's signature above the figure's head implies that it is a self-depiction. Brad Lookingbill (2006:194–195) also implied that the Kiowa Omaha Dance originated in the Cheyenne's performances of War Dances at Fort Marion and that the Kiowa learned the dance from the Cheyenne there. However, the dance was a pan-Plains phenomenon that is documented far beyond the prisoners and tribes involved at Fort Marion. In addition, Fort Marion predates the earlier eyewitness sources of acquisition by the Cheyenne and Kiowa dating to 1881 and 1884.

Although it is clear that many of the prisoners participated in dance exhibitions, mock buffalo chases, and Fourth of July celebrations at Fort Marion and in the surrounding area, the full content and context of these performances are unclear. At one point the prisoners, organized into two companies, one primarily of Cheyenne and Comanche and the other of Kiowa and Arapaho, were performing two dances a week, primarily to market the curios and crafts they produced. However, during much of their captivity they lacked traditional dance clothing and resorted to using unbleached muslin (for buckskin and turkey tail feathers), extended heron wings, and antler and horns for their "full war costume" (Lookingbill 2006:88–92). Only later, in 1878, was traditional buckskin clothing mentioned (Lookingbill 2006:160–161).

A potential problem exists in the accuracy of the names non-Indians used in describing the dances. One account (Lookingbill 2006:90) reports Kiowa Horse and Sheep Killing Dances (possibly Kiowa military society dances), a Comanche Swift Dance, and a Cheyenne Rabbit Dance. One program advertisement titled "Indian Sports and War Dances" included a so-called Osage War Dance (see Harris 1989:126; Viola 1998:96–99). Because the Kiowa had no Osage War Dance, and the Osage did not receive the formal War Dance (I'nlonschka) from the Kaw until 1884, it is unclear whether this performance was actually an Omaha-Grass Dance or some other form. The advertisement listed two mixed "companies" of Kiowa and Cheyenne dancers that, at least for this performance, did not include Koba. In Mooney's fieldnotes, Koba was listed as a member of the Horse Headdresses Society in the 1880s, before it ceased to function. Cheyenne ledgerbook drawings depict men wearing bustles on horseback in combat. The horse and rifle in the Koba drawing may represent a mock or simulated Indian attack, a popular form of entertainment in Wild West shows and related performances between 1880 and 1930. It is also unknown whether other Kiowa at Fort Marion wore bustles, presumably made by the Cheyenne, during these dances.

If the Cheyenne had the Omaha Dance before 1881, then the Kiowa prisoners undoubtedly learned of it, and probably other Cheyenne dances, during their stay at Fort Marion from 1875 to 1878 and probably participated in it. However, it seems unlikely that the dance was formally given to them at this time. Ideally, such a measure would have involved considerable political support from the Cheyenne Omaha Society and from within the Cheyenne tribe as a whole. The Kiowa at Fort Marion would also have been unable to reciprocate with a considerable exchange of horses upon receiving the dance. More important, accounts from Kiowa elders who witnessed the exchange place it on the reservation in 1884. The Fort Marion relationship was probably a significant factor leading to the gift of the dance from the Cheyenne to the Kiowa a few years after returning to Indian Territory.

According to Mrs. Hokeah, the Cheyenne performed the Omaha Dance for the Kiowa in a large tipi on the Kiowa-Comanche-Apache Reservation in 1884. The Cheyenne remained on the north side of the lodge while the Kiowa sat on the south side. While singing, one of the Cheyenne members, who wore an eagle feather on his head, danced over to the Kiowa group and placed the feather in the hair of one of them, thereby symbolizing his induction as a member. The Cheyenne took in several members this way and then asked whether any Kiowa chiefs were present. The Kiowa answered yes, to which the Cheyenne chief, singing the Chief's Song, danced over and placed a feather in the hair of a Kiowa chief named Kuelo (Cwélò, possibly Spanish for "neck" or "collar"). Kuelo, an agency policeman, reportedly was selected by the Kiowa as chief of the new society and received a drum from the Cheyenne at this time. All Kiowa men present were inducted as members. For each feather placed in a Kiowa's hair, a horse was reciprocated to the Cheyenne.[7]

Throughout the Great Plains, the ritual transfer of religious ceremonies and ritual societies, including the Hethushka, could be initiated in two ways. The first was as a gift to a visiting tribe or to individuals as a token of peace and friendship. This form of transfer was closely related to that of the Calumet ceremony, which the Omaha considered the "sister" ceremony of the War Dance. The second way was by formally requesting and purchasing the society and ceremony from another tribe (La Flesche 1939; Albers 1983; Duncan 1997:74). Although the Kiowa did not hold a Sun Dance in 1884, Mooney's quote of the Kiowa agent's report for August 28, 1884, is significant (1898:352):

> The Kiowas have danced less this year than usual, and they seem to have given up their annual medicine dance, for as yet they have said nothing about it. . . . They have generally gone out on the plains from 40 to 60 miles from the agency and been absent from five to six weeks. On several occasions since the buffalo disappeared, they have suffered very much from hunger while out, and I hope we have heard the last of the dance.

This account places the Kiowa in the area of the reservation where historical, ethnographic, and Kiowa accounts all indicate they received the ceremony from the Cheyenne.

While the Sun Dance was declining, a new dance was being delivered during the Kiowa's absence from the Indian agency. To the chagrin of the Indian agents, this dance would flourish throughout the first half of the twentieth century and continue to the present. It represented more than just another dance for the agents to try to terminate; it also represented their inability to suppress the Kiowa traditions of community, sharing, and nonmaterialistic concerns—their love of song, dance, intertribal visiting, honoring, and giving away. Much as the modification of the Hethushka Society into the War Dance provided a means of ethnic continuity for the Ponca during the difficulties of the reservation era, so it did for some Kiowa of the same time. Unlike the Sun, Ghost, and Scalp dances and peyotism, the War or Grass Dance appeared relatively secular and unthreatening to Anglos while it comprised a deep body of meaning and memories for Native participants (Wissler 1916; Duncan 1997:85). Because the dance met existing Indian needs and was perceived as largely unthreatening by non-Indians at this time, it is significant in understanding adjustments to the reservation period.

The Cheyenne also gave the Kiowa several dance articles and sets of clothing, including fully beaded moccasins, vests, cuffs, and broadcloth leggings with beaded strips. This style of clothing, which featured large areas of beadwork and was common to the Central and Northern Plains tribes, differed greatly with traditional Kiowa clothing of the period, which emphasized buckskin, earth paints, straight or twisted (rolled) buckskin fringe, and minimal beadwork, the latter used primarily as edge decoration. Early pictures of Kiowa Omaha Society dances (Boyd 1981:66) can easily be mistaken for Cheyenne or Lakota, because the Kiowa wear predominantly Northern Plains and Cheyenne-style clothing. One Kiowa related how older society members used to refer to their Omaha Society dance clothing of this era as "Nàu Sáqàulhòldà, our Cheyenne clothes." Family pictures from this period show that this style of clothing was prominent in Kiowa Omaha Dances from 1884 into the late 1920s.[8]

Central to the War and Grass Dance complex is the crow belt, or feathered bustle. A crow belt is a small waist bustle containing various feathers, usually from birds of prey, that hang downward from a central base of leather. Suspended from this base are two pendantlike trailers of cloth containing additional feathers and decorations attached at various points. A sash attached to the top of the base is tied around the waist like a belt, with the top of the bustle located at the center of the dancer's lower back.

Also received during this initiation was a feathered dance bustle (*tónchài*), which continues to hold a central part of the society's ceremonial.[9] Among the Kiowa, the *tónchài* is a "crow belt," the predecessor to the more circular "mess bustles" common among many Northern and Central Plains tribes from about 1870 to the 1940s and to the post-mid-1950s "traditional" or "swing bustles" used in powwows by contemporary "traditional dancers." Before the Kiowa acquired the Omaha Society from the Cheyenne, feathered bustles were unknown in Kiowa dances and military societies.[10]

The War Dance and Calumet ceremony were often related, especially in the ritual transfer of the War Dance as a gift to visiting tribes or as a token of peace (La Flesche

1939; Duncan 1997:74). In Plains Indian sign language, the Calumet Dance was called "Child Wave Feather Pipe."[11] Thomas Battey (1968 [1876]:130–134) reported that forty-five Pawnee visited the Kiowa from March 2 to 15, 1873. He did not indicate that a Calumet ceremony was conducted, but he described the formal making of peace and the conducting of elaborate gift exchanges between the Kiowa and the Pawnee. During these exchanges, "Kiowa fathers, each carrying a small child in his arms bearing a piece of stick in its little hands, young girls, and occasionally a woman" presented each Pawnee with a stick as a marker for a pony (Battey 1968 [1876]:131). This practice was typical of Calumet exchanges. Mooney (1898:336, 358) confirmed this visit and mentioned a dance performed in the winter of 1889–1890 by a contingent of Kiowa visiting the Comanche. The dance was known as Íàumcùngà (Offspring or Child Making Dance), the Kiowa name for the Calumet ceremony. According to Mooney, "the performance and dress somewhat resemble the Omaha dance, but only two men dance, while the rest sit around as spectators." He also noted the presence of the dance "among the Wichita and Pawnee and perhaps other tribes." The dance centered on the formal adoption of a child of the host group by the visiting group, along with an exchange of horses from the visitors for gifts supplied by the hosts. Child and sibling adoptions were a factor leading to the widespread diffusion of certain military and religious sodalities across the plains (Albers 1993). Scott recorded several Calumet ceremonies between the Kiowa and other Plains tribes.[12]

The Kiowa Omaha Society is similar in many aspects to the Ponca Hethushka and Osage I'nlonschka (Callahan 1990:7; Duncan 1997), in that the earlier associated military and police functions of men's military societies had been greatly reduced by the late nineteenth century, and a more social and ceremonial focus was developing. For the Kiowa, the introduction of the Omaha Society came after the cessation of Plains Indian warfare and bison hunting, and it functioned as a society in only two complete Sun Dances, those of 1885 and 1887. Indeed, many parallels are found in the functions, offices, traits, and ritual forms of the Omaha and Ponca Hethushka and the Kiowa Omaha Society, despite the changes involved in the diffusion of the dance from the Omaha to the Lakota, Cheyenne, and finally the Kiowa. These similarities include many of the features described for the Ponca Hethushka (Duncan 1997), including initial entry for anyone who had won war honors and performed dangerous duties, membership for socially prominent or well-thought-of men, the hosting of and giving of gifts to visiting tribes, the giving of charitable aid to the needy, and the performance of a role in providing the formal release of mourners to return to participation in public activities. Similarities in offices included having a single leader qualified to wear the crow belt, a specified number of advisors, a specified number of Tail dancers, whipmen with quirts as badges of office, cooks or servers, youth servants, a camp crier, society whistles and whistle songs, and the curation and use of a pipe. Other ritual similarities included a camp procession, entrance from the east, with the prevalence of pipe keepers and pipes upon entering, assigned seats around the arena, starting songs, sets of War Dance songs, the Kettle Dance, the ritual distribution of food by cooks or servers, giveaways and giveaway songs, charging songs symbolic in tempo of an attack on the enemy, trot dance or horse stealing songs, crow and thunder symbolism, and closing songs.

Other parallels are found in the circumstances and timing of the society's introduction to the Kiowa in 1884. Although many of the original Kiowa Omaha Society members were younger to middle-aged men with some combat experience, the introduction of the society came just nine years after the end of pre-reservation warfare, by which time the war records of warriors were frozen. Consequently, the relationship between the new Omaha Society and the existing Kiowa military society structure and martial ethos required modification. In essence, the introduction of the society during the reservation years provided a new forum for the maintenance of both an older, collective tribal warrior tradition and general Kiowa cultural forms that were rapidly being modified in the post-warfare period. For the Ponca and Kiowa, the War Dance served as a new arena for solidifying and reaffirming ethnic identity and, to a lesser degree, commemorating a past martial ethos (Dorsey, fieldnotes, 1872; Fletcher and La Flesche 1911:459; Duncan 1997:64). It represents one segment of the general late-nineteenth-century diffusion of the Grass Dance.

Major problems in researching the Kiowa Omaha Society are that what little has been written about it contains numerous historical inaccuracies and is highly romanticized, and current society leaders were not consulted in the research.[13] Maurice Boyd (1981:65) contended that "the Ohoma Society formerly was governed by a council of Kiowa war chiefs during the great days when the Kiowa roamed freely on the Plains." Because the Kiowa were permanently placed on their reservation in 1875, Boyd's statement is temporally impossible. Although some of the original members were younger warriors, comparison of their birth dates with the list of original society members collected by James Mooney in 1902 demonstrates that many were young men or boys in about 1875.[14] Henry Tsoodle Sr., born in 1869, explained in 1935: "The other groups [societies] are older than Ohoma. . . . It is since my time that we got it. The Cheyenne came over here among the Kiowa and picked out certain ones to join and taught them the dance. That's the way the society started."[15]

Functions and Organization of the Omaha Society

Although it was acquired late in the nineteenth century, the Omaha Society adopted most of the activities and functions characteristic of the other Kiowa men's societies. Again Boyd's account (1981:65) is misleading, for he states, "Originally the dance was not associated with any special time of year, nor was there any particular number of dancers, although today it is one of the traditional summer dances." Because the society was acquired while the Kiowa still maintained their Sun Dance, the society participated in all the usual society activities associated with the last Kiowa Sun Dances, including mourning rituals for the families of recently deceased members, Brush Dragging and other dances, and probably the sham battle and kick fight. In

1935, Gapkaugo (Mrs. Hokeah) described the society's participation in these activities: "They put on a dance every year at the Sun Dance. . . . It functioned in police duties, Sun dance, etc. just as the other societies."[16] Although it was initially associated with the Sun Dance, the society could have participated only in the last three Kiowa Sun Dances, those of 1885 and 1887 and the incomplete dance of 1890. Following the end of the Kiowa Sun Dance in 1890, Omaha dances began to be held in midsummer, usually around the Fourth of July, like other surviving Plains society dances.

The introduction of the Omaha-War-Grass Dance led to the decline of many of the older Plains men's societies, including those of the Kiowa. The Santa Fe Laboratory of Anthropology notes of 1935 indicate that while the other Kiowa societies were rapidly declining in popularity during the 1880s, the Omaha Society was increasing in popularity. Mrs. Hokeah said, "Their dance was more popular that that of any of the other societies (especially with the girls) and drew a large audience." Mooney's fieldnotes record several instances of Kiowa men leaving the older Kiowa military societies to join the Omaha Society—for example, Belo Cozad, who left the Mountain Sheep. Silverhorn stated that the Omaha Dance "began [to] supersede all Yapahey dances and different orders [of] Yapahey [i.e., members of different societies] joined in it."[17] The older practice of limiting membership to one society at a time continued. Members were also inducted according to older society practices. After initiates had been agreed upon, the society would wait until the man came to watch its dance, whereupon two men grabbed the initiate and escorted him into the dance arena, affirming his membership.[18]

The ceremonial organization of the Omaha Society was different from and much more complex than that of the other men's societies and reflected elements of its Omaha Hethushka origins. Parsons (1929) resided in 1927 in the Redstone community, which by then was the core residential area of Omaha Society members and from which the first detailed accounts of the society were recorded. The following description is from Parsons's work, supplemented by the accounts of elder Kiowa and other sources. According to Parsons (1929:92, 94) there were at least nineteen society leadership positions: a council of eleven chiefs, two Eagle Chiefs, two Crow Chiefs, two bustle keepers, and two whistle keepers. Reports of two whipmen indicate that a total of twenty-one ceremonial positions once existed in the society.

During meetings, a formally structured hierarchy of leadership positions was maintained, with eleven chiefs sitting in a crescent-shaped row along the west side of the lodge. The head leader (Óhǫ̀mòqàjàiqì, Omaha Chief, or tháumjóqî, first or head leader) sat in the middle of this row, with five elder subleaders on either side of him.[19] These leaders were commonly referred to as the council of chiefs and originally were all men who held at least one war honor, making them qájái. Boyd (1981:70) reported a hereditary council consisting of Joe Poolaw, Walter Kokoom, Linn Pauahty, Yale Spotted Bird, George Tsoodle, Mark Keahbone, Howard Geimausaddle, and James Silverhorn. All these men are now deceased, and current elders are unclear on what basis they were chosen as hereditary council members. The makeup of the original council of eleven chiefs is presently unknown; it most likely included ancestors of these eight men and others, because these men were all born after the acquisition of the society in 1884. Gregory Haumpy Sr., born in 1918 and a society whistleman since his youth, spoke of how he and Mark Keahbone, then the two whistlemen, "served" the four chiefs (in the late 1920s) during the meal inside the society tipi before society ceremonial dances. Haumpy said that the four chiefs were all old men who had been in pre-reservation battles.[20] Mac Whitehorse reported that Mark Keahbone often spoke of having had to "serve the chiefs" and that "there were several chiefs excluding the Eagle and Crow Chiefs" in the society, which supports the existence of the council.[21]

One of the primary offices of the society is that of bustle keeper (*tónchàiqì*), who wears the feathered bustle and serves as dance leader. According to Parsons (1929:92), the two "tsuntsaikya" (inferably the bustle keeper and his assistant) sat on the east side of the lodge during society meetings and served as dance managers. Tribal elders and current society bustle keeper Mac Whitehorse state that the bustle was originally given to Dąuàuiqį́ (Many Wounds), later known as Qódèbǫ̀hòn (Swift Fox Headdress/Cap) and better known as Gotebo, for whom the town of Gotebo, Oklahoma, is named.[22] To date there have been six society bustle keepers. Determining the dates of office for the six keepers is difficult. Gotebo converted to Christianity in January 1893, so it is likely that he gave up his position as bustle keeper around this time or shortly before. Botone succeeded him. A ledgerbook entry for July 1902 shows a picture of a man holding the society bustle and states, "Botone died in July," which correlates with cemetery records.[23] The table below provides a chronology of the Kiowa Omaha Society bustle keepers, their life spans, and their terms in office.[24]

Jane Richardson obtained a description of the original bustle from keeper Charley White Horse in 1935 and made a sketch of it. The bustle consisted of the head of an eagle (probably a golden eagle; some Plains tribes do not consider bald eagles honorable because of their scavenging habits) with yellow ribbons placed in its mouth, attached to a leather base. On either side of the eagle's head was an antelope horn. Be-

Chronology of Kiowa Omaha Society Bustle Keepers

Name	Life Span	Term of Office
Dąuàuiqį́ (Many Wounds, also known as Gotebo)	1847–1927	1884–c. 1892
Fǫ́tǫ́qį́ or Botone (Beaver Lake)	1870–1902	c. 1892–1902
Zépcàuiétjè (Big Bow III, or Aúgàutóyài, or Lone Traveler)	1861–1934	1902–c. 1915
Cûiqáujè (Wolf Lying Down, or Charley Tsalote)	1891–1963	c. 1915–c. 1921
Chȩ̂thàidè (White Horse III, or Charley Whitehorse)	1870–1949	c. 1921–1949
Matthew (Mac) Whitehorse (White Horse IV)	1917–	1952+

Sources: O-ho-mah Lodge Singers, *War Dance Songs of the Kiowa O-ho-mah Lodge Singers*, vol. 2 (Indian House Records, 1976), sleeve notes; Mac Whitehorse, personal communication, Apr. 3, 1991.

hind or perhaps attached to each horn was a spike consisting of an eagle wing feather with down feathers attached to the tips and bells along its length. Facing the bustle, a small bag of cedar was attached on the right side near the base of the antelope horn and eagle wing feather spike. Below the head was a fan-shaped cluster of golden eagle tail feathers. The lower part of the bustle consisted of two cloth trailers with attached eagle tail feathers.[25]

In the early 1940s a house fire destroyed Charley White Horse's residence west of Redstone and consumed two important Kiowa cultural items—the original Omaha Society bustle and one of the Kiowa Ten Medicine Bundles that had been handed down from White Horse's father-in-law, Páuqàusá (Stabbed A Bison Bull), or Rainy Mountain Charlie, a son of the noted war leader Mamanti. A new bustle was made by Steve and Jeanette Mopope and others. According to society bustle keeper Mac Whitehorse, the bustle leads the society. The great respect in which society members hold the bustle was poignantly described by Whitehorse, who told me of the advice he gives to members upon joining the society:

> When someone joins Óhọmò, I tell them, you join to follow that bustle, not to follow me or any other particular leader. The bustle, tónchài, it will be here when I am gone, as it has remained after former leaders. The bustle can be repaired and revived, the person cannot. So dance for that bustle . . . have respect for the bustle, it has come a long way. That bustle is leading Óhọmò. Many guys have been taken in [inducted into] Óhọmò, even after I was. Many of them are already gone, but that bustle is still here. There are prayers on that bustle. So I tell people to follow that bustle, it is leading Óhọmò.[26]

The society was originally divided into two grades based primarily on warfare status. Initially the two grades were also loosely divided and organized, both internally and relative to each other, by age, because of the late introduction of the society in 1884 and the cessation of warfare in 1875. Approximately thirty members known as Eagles (Cṹjòhį̀) sat on the north side of the lodge. At the head of this group sat two men known as Eagle chiefs (Cṹjòqàjàiqį̀), who had been wounded in battle. On the south side of the lodge sat a second group of members known as Crows (Màusáugàu). They likewise had two leaders, or Crow chiefs (Màusáuqàjàiqį̀). According to Charley White Horse (Parsons 1929:94), the Eagle and Crow chiefs sat at the tip of the crescent, inferably near the door at the east side of the lodge. This seating arrangement supports an account stating that originally the Eagles were men of combat status, whereas the Crows lacked combat status. The Eagles and Crows were graded by age in their seated positions, with the oldest members closest to the council of chiefs on the west side. Typically, the likelihood that a man possessed one or more war honors increased with age, so most members holding war honors—though by no means all—were older than those lacking them. On the east side of the lodge were the bustle keeper and his assistant, who served as dance leaders. The society also had two whipmen: Sétáfètjàui (popularly known as Afraid Of Bears) and Thḙnéjáidè (Bird Chief, lit. Brave Eagle), both pre-reservation veterans.²⁷ There were also two whistle keepers (jṓbájòqî), one on the north side of the lodge and one on the south, but their exact positions were not recorded. Parsons (1929:92, 94) reported that the Eagles and Crows had special singers and songs, to which each group danced separately at times.

Parsons (1929:92) wrote that there were two Eagle chiefs and two Crow chiefs at the heads of their respective groups, but on the same page she stated that a single leader sat at the end of each group. The latter statement coincides with the descriptions of Kiowa elders, who say that the chiefs were located next to the lodge door. The discrepancy may reflect the loss and subsequent compression of some offices. Parsons's descriptions indicate that the Eagle and Crow chiefs and the two whistle keepers were separate. By the late 1920s these four positions had been combined into two, and the Eagle and Crow chiefs were also both whistle keepers. A society drum keeper once existed, but the origins of this office and its succession of holders are unknown. George Bosin once kept a drum used by the society that contained a depiction of jagged lightning bolts around the edge with an eagle in the center clutching a lightning bolt in its talons. The reverse side portrayed a full moon with several stars. The side with the eagle was used for daytime dances, and the reverse side, for evening dances.²⁸ Konad (Qâuną̀, or Always Frowning, also known as White Buffalo) is reported to have served as drum keeper in the 1920s, but during much of Charley White Horse's tenure as bustle keeper (circa 1921–1948), no official drum keeper existed. Members report that Konad's grandson Marland (Konad) Aitsan was the last official drum keeper. After his death the official society drum began to be kept by the ceremonial chief. Recently there have been suggestions for reinstating the position of drum keeper. George Bosin served as the last Omaha Society camp crier, a position that has not been maintained.

Like the Mountain Sheep and Black Legs Societies, the Omaha Society had two female youth members. Boyd (1981:66) incorrectly attributed these positions to Cheyenne origins: "Following an ancient Cheyenne tradition, the Kiowa always select two women from aristocratic Kiowa families and permit them to occupy positions of honor during the men's dances." Some Cheyenne military societies did have society "princesses," but four, not two (Dorsey 1905:16). Because some pre-reservation Kiowa societies had two female positions (Meadows 1999:51–53), I believe this practice reflects an earlier Kiowa tradition. These female members served mainly in a symbolic and honorific position, dancing in place on the side of the arena. Their families sponsored feasts in their honor for the society at Sun Dances and at later annual society dances. The society's rules regarding marriage of these female members appear to have followed those of the older Kiowa men's societies. Female youth members were not allowed to have children and ceased to participate in the society's functions upon becoming pregnant or marrying. The society apparently did not practice the intersocietal exchange of gifts associated with the marriage of a female youth member. This may have resulted from a scarcity of existing societies to exchange gifts with after the mid-1880s, rather than from a significant change in practices.²⁹

Mrs. Tenedooah (Saioma) described the induction of the first two Omaha Society princesses, vividly illustrating the prestige and wealth displayed upon the induction of a favored girl:

> I have a daughter-in-law that was awday [âudê]. Her name was Gom'd'ai (White Back) [Gómthạimạ̀, or Mrs. J. O. Tenedooah], and her friend was Ehapedoma [Ȇhàpvèdònmàui, Searching For The Prettiest]. Both of them were very pretty girls, and awday too. They joined Ohomo. That's the lodge they joined. When they came for their dance and were going to join they were riding horses that were buckskins with black ears that were just alike. Those were the very best horses. A person who has a horse like that has high rank. They had on buckskin dresses covered with elk-teeth clear to their waists. That's the very highest. They had on tande—wildcat skins [thámdèl, mountain lion or cougar] for saddle blankets, too. . . . They had long earrings and pretty beads, and they both had beautiful hair. They had bells on their bridles, and all kinds of metal ornaments. Nowadays if anyone dressed that way she'd have to borrow a lot. But those girls didn't have to borrow, they had all those things. Their fathers were chiefs, but an awday didn't have to be a chief's daughter. . . . They gave mainly horses for a person that's joining one of those groups. The very best horses.[30]

The initiation of two new members together as friends or society partners followed the pattern of earlier Kiowa societies. Charley White Horse and Bert Geikaunmah, James Konad and Tom Tointigh, Allen Ware and James Silverhorn, Mark Keahbone and Frank Tongkeamha, and Russell Geimausaddle and Moses Botone were all inducted as society partners. Each set of partners had an individual song to which only they danced.[31] Although the existence of two Eagle and Crow chiefs would conform with the practice of partnership, other data appear contradictory. Mark Keahbone and Big Head II (also known as Komalty) were inducted as partners, with reciprocal kinship terms extended between their two families. However, when Keahbone became the Eagle chief, Big Head II was made Crow chief, so the two could no longer have sat together during ceremonials. By the early 1920s some of the original twenty-one ceremonial positions in the society had been eliminated or combined, probably because younger members lacked warrior status. The structure of the council of eleven chiefs does not seem conducive to society partner relationships in either number or seating arrangement (Parsons 1929:92, 94–95). Although society partners typically sat and danced together, the external origin of the dance and the formal orientation of the society offices may have altered this in some instances. However, the practice of society partners continued among regular members.

Songs and Dances

Although the entire repertoire of the original Omaha Society ceremonial is no longer known, a considerable body of society songs and dances from the early twentieth century remains. Many of them reflect the Omaha Hethushka Society origins. According to Boyd (1981:67), the content of each annual ceremonial varied as the council of chiefs selected the appropriate songs for each ceremonial. If this practice existed, it appears to have ceased with the end of the council. During the annual ceremonial, any of the following songs and dances might have been included in the performance: (1) Opening Song (Châtqàutèldǎugà), (2) Chief's Song (Qájáidǎugà), (3) Appeasement Prayer, (4) Feast or Kettle Song (probably Fídǎugà, or Eating Song), (5) Charging Song (a part of the Feast ceremony), (6) Tail Feather or Special Ritual Song (probably the Bustle Pickup Song), (7) Giveaway Song (Qíkódǎugà or Qícáudǎugà), (8) Mourning or Memorial Song (Câifêgàudǎugà, Mourning or War Dead Song), (9) Battle Story Song (Qóitąujéldǎugà, or Coup Recitation Song), used for picking up dropped feathers, (10) Pipe Dance Song (Sąujólcùndǎugà), (11) Song to Make Rain Go Away, and (12) Closing or Quitting Song (Fátcádǎugà). The Sit Down or Squat Dance (Tàucúndǎugà, lit. Kneeling Dance), which is probably the Charging Song described by Boyd (1981), is another known Omaha Society dance. Having a more northern plains origin, Kiowa Omaha Society songs are sung at a higher pitch than other types of Kiowa music, although they are performed at a lower pitch than among the Northern Cheyenne and Omaha. Brief descriptions of the significance and history of the preceding songs and dances as still known by Kiowa in the later twentieth century follow.[32] I use past tense for descriptions recorded in the past and for dances that are no longer held, and present tense for contemporary descriptions and practices.

The Opening Song (1) is used to begin each annual ceremonial. It is supposed to be sung only once a year as the first song on the first day of dancing. This song is not danced to; the dancers begin dancing upon the start of the second song.

When the Chief's Song (2) was sung, only the leaders danced—the bustle keeper and his assistant and the two whistle keepers. After this song, the families of the leaders had a giveaway, after which all other members could dance. This song was not the opening one of a dance session but was sung sometime during the dance.[33]

According to Boyd (1981:68), the Appeasement Prayer (3) was not a regular part of the ceremony but was offered to the "Earth-maker" when the tribe prayed for calm and peaceful weather during storm conditions.[34] The only times this prayer is known to have been performed was at Omaha Society dances held in 1920 at Edgar Keahbone's and in 1923 at Kiowa Jim Tongkeamha's. The society elders I interviewed did not recognize this prayer.

The Feast or Kettle Song (4) has not been performed since about 1929. It most likely was associated with the ritual serving of food, including the serving of dog as a part of the initiation common in the larger Plains Grass Dance ceremony.

The Charging Song (5) and dance recounts a battle, which is acted out by the Eagles and the Crows.

The Tail Feather Dance (6) appears to have been a later development, because Boyd (1981:70) reported that it involved two dancers with tail bustles. This implies that it originated after 1917, when the early Fancy Dance bustles appeared among the Kiowa.

The two dancers, possibly the whistle men, each carried a flute in one hand and an eagle tail fan in the other.

The Giveaway Song (7) was another special song of the Omaha Society. It was the only giveaway song and had no words. If a woman wanted to honor her brother, she would ask the singers to sing this song. The brother and his society partner danced, as did both their sisters. Any pair of society partners could dance as well. After the song, the crier, having previously been told a name by the man's sister, called out a person to whom the brother gave gifts. The family of the man's society partner also gave away gifts at this time.[35] The Giveaway Song belonged to the tribe, in the sense in that anyone who wanted to give away could do so during this song. Elders indicate that before the early 1960s, all giving away was done during this song. A person placed the goods he or she wished to give away in front of a dancer or another individual and then either placed a person beside the honoree to receive the gift or simply left the property on the dance ground to be claimed by anyone who desired it. Unlike in giveaways today, there was no speech making and no processional around the drum, and numerous persons often gave away during the same song.

The Mourning Song (8), now called the Memorial Song, had no words and was sung for a family that had lost a member during the previous year. After the society members had visited and cried with the family, they were given permission to carry on with their activities. Today the Memorial Song is often sung at the annual ceremonial in someone's memory.

The Battle Story or Coup Recitation Song (9) was a pantomime of the war deed or coup recitation once performed during Plains military society meetings. Members acted out their deeds in dance to the music. During brief pauses in the song, members approached the drum one at a time to recite their personal war deeds. Although this song and dance presumably played an important part in the society's ceremonies in its early days, it declined, probably by the 1920s, with the passing of pre-reservation combat veterans. This song was also sung to pick up dropped feathers.

The Closing Song (12) is supposed to be sung only as the last song on the last day of dancing. In the past, members are said to have danced out of the meeting tipi or dance arena during this song.[36]

Today only five of these songs and dances are a regular part of the Omaha Society ceremonial: the Opening Song, the Chief's Song, the Giveaway Song, the Mourning Song, and the Closing Song. Several other society songs, such as the Bustle Cedaring Song, the Bustle Pickup Song, songs for serving food, songs for smoking, the song for the Pipe Dance (which is described later), and the song for the Sit Down or Squat Dance, which are not mentioned in the earlier literature, hold prominent roles in current society ceremonials.

The Sit Down or Squat Dance reenacts a battle in which a Cheyenne warrior wearing a bustle was completely surrounded by Kiowa, who were shooting at him. He fought until he was finally killed. The dance represents the fight, and the fast drumming, the shooting. When the man is at last fatally wounded, the dancer "lies down" and ritually "dies" (as is signaled by the end of the music) by squatting down. Because the Kiowa and Cheyenne made peace in 1840, and the Cheyenne did not acquire the Omaha Society until sometime after 1865, it is unclear what this dance references — perhaps a pre-1840 event that was later incorporated into the Cheyenne or Kiowa version of the Omaha Society.[37]

Whereas most Kiowa military society songs are society or group songs, many Omaha Society songs are personal songs. Most elder society members have a personal song that was given to and shared with their society partner. Today members desiring a personal society song frequently ask society bustle keeper Mac Whitehorse, considered to be the most knowledgeable Omaha Society and Kiowa War Dance singer, to assign or compose a song for them. He generally composes a new song or allows people to choose a song from a large stock of old society War Dance songs no longer owned by anyone. When a person's Omaha Society song is sung, the person rises to dance, after which it is customary for him to go to the drum and give a gift of money to whoever started the song. A personal song is frequently requested by a society member or relative for any type of special event or giveaway for that member, and the songs are well known among society families. Some are quite old and have been "owned" or passed down several times. In order to keep the large number of personal songs active, many have been recycled — that is, reassigned to a new member after the death of the previous owner.[38] Today most personal songs belong to individuals and not to sets of society partners. Many of the songs recorded in the five commercial volumes entitled *War Dance Songs of the Kiowa O-ho-mah Lodge* are personal songs.

Society Dances in the Early 1900s

Kiowa Omaha Society dances continued to flourish between 1884 and 1935. Benjamin Kracht (1989, 1992, 1994) maintained that the Ghost Dance was a "vehicle" for the burgeoning society and the War Dance. Although dances were held during the years of the Kiowa Ghost Dance (1890, 1894–1917) and some people participated in both the Ghost Dance and the Omaha Society, Kiowa and society elders state that the society never danced at a Ghost Dance. Francis Tsonetokoy and Parker McKenzie, who witnessed several of the last Ghost Dances, said that no Omaha Society dances, powwows, or social dancing of any kind took place at the encampments they attended.[39]

By combining archival records with interviews of society and tribal elders, a general picture of the society's activities during this period can be reconstructed. During the 1920s, contingents of Cheyenne continued to visit and participate in Kiowa Omaha Society dances. U.S. Indian agents Ernest Stecker and C. V. Stinchecum attempted to stop society dances, resorting to withholding the government's 4 Percent Trust Fund annuity payments until dancers promised, by signing an affidavit, to stop dancing (Kracht 1989:820–875; Meadows 1995:153–163). Only then were Kiowa families provided with their annuities. Francis Tsonetokoy, who was blacklisted by the agency for attending dances even though he did not participate in them, and Parker McKenzie, who retired from the finance department at the Anadarko Agency, stated that many of the Kiowa who signed affidavits simply collected their money and headed for dances in Cheyenne country, where the "heat was off" at the time.[40]

Because of the frequent practice of giving away, the Omaha Society (having its own Giveaway Song) and War Dances in particular were singled out for attacks as agents attempted to teach the Kiowa to become Christian, materialistic, and individualistic, property-owning farmers. Yet despite these efforts the society refused to cease meeting or to give up its traditions. Elder society members indicate that they steadfastly resisted such coercive attempts to impede their cultural freedom. The lyrics of one song composed during this time, popularly called the "Resistance Song," demonstrate the society's stance regarding these attempts to suppress dancing:

> 1 Fòi bé áu-gá-kậu-jàu
> (Do not / you all / be hesitating [imperative])
> Do not hesitate (to dance)!
> 2 Dá bá tộ-pá-bà-hồ
> (You must / you all / legs-tied-go-ahead [imperative])
> Go ahead and be arrested/jailed![41]

To this day, society members are extremely proud of the fact that they are the only Kiowa society that never ceased meeting, a topic that is frequently and publicly raised by society members. In my conversations with society bustle keeper Mac Whitehorse, he was particularly proud of this resilience of the society's. Dorothy Whitehorse DeLaune spoke of the pride that members of the society take in this song and their reputation for having never stopped dancing: "Oh, the Resistance Song. That's my all-time favorite. When they would dance in secret . . . it says, 'Don't hold back,' it meant we'll keep dancing. You know, 'don't hold back, we'll go to jail.' But we'll keep dancing. . . . Never, never [did Ohoma stop]. That's what, it's so proud, you know it makes you so proud to claim allegiance to that organization for that reason alone."[42]

Later generations of Kiowa who grew up hearing about the government's attempts to suppress their ancestors' cultural freedom have continued their commitment to preserving the society and its associated ideals. Vanessa Jennings spoke of her grandfather Stephen Mopope, an Omaha Society member and one of the Kiowa Five artists, and of what the society traditions mean to her and her family. Her memories reflect the persistence of the generations of society members:

> When I was growing up, I grew up on stories about how they were deprived because they were heathens, they were not Christians. . . . I grew up on stories about my grandpa and them . . . my great-grandfather. You know, my great-grandfather was one of the ones who said, "If you want me to give up Ohoma, if you want me to give up my Ohoma ways, you'll have to kill me. Death is the only thing that will keep me from Ohoma," and so it's this kind of thinking, you know, that we were here, we never quit, you know, as "heathens" we are the ones

that saved something.... Ohoma is the one society that never had to be revived, we never quit.... My grandfather said, "I'm Ohoma, I could belong to anything I wanted to... but I'm Ohoma," he said, "and I'll be Ohoma until the day I die." And so it's that kind of respect for that society. That's something that I try to tell my sons about. You know, because that's important, because that man provided something for them to take care of them, so it's only right that they take care of it and get it ready for the next generation coming after.

But for myself, it's important for my family to take part and be a part of and be supportive, simply because if my grandfather were here, that's what my grandfather would have done. So for me it's important to live my life just as if my grandmother and grandfather were here beside me. Everything that I have was provided by them, and so it's important that I carry on the things that were important to them.[43]

Annual society encampments varied from year to year as different members sponsored dances on their allotments. Elders recall a number of locations where society dances were held. One early dance was held at Rainy Mountain during a grass payment that the Kiowa had gathered to receive.[44] Between 1915 and 1923 some dances were held at Kiowa Jim Tongkeamha's allotment, thirteen miles south of Carnegie. At the 1915 dance Agent Stinchecum came and asked that the dance be stopped, but the Kiowa would not relent.[45] The late John Emhoola Sr. recalled how he was inducted into the society at Kiowa Jim's place in 1916, when "there were a lot of members and the dances usually lasted for four days."[46]

Several Fourth of July society encampments were held at Konad's, between Washita and Redstone, between 1910 and 1925. The flourishing intertribal friendships and visitations and the growing enthusiasm for War dancing can be seen in the fact that Cheyenne, Arapaho, Ponca, Otoe, Osage, Pawnee, Comanche, Apache, and Taos Pueblo Indians attended these dances. Alice Littleman remembered attending the dances at her grandfather Konad's allotment; she often found coins and other items dropped at the old encampment site in the adjacent fields.[47] Like the societies of surrounding tribes, the Kiowa Omaha Society performed at the Dietrick's Lake Fair in 1923. Other dances were held at the homes of George Mopope, Edgar Keahbone, and Homer Buffalo, near Redstone, and at the allotments of Frank Bosin and Dǫ́gàdé (Standing In The Center, or Amy Dome-gatty), near Anadarko. By the 1920s the Redstone community dominated most Omaha Society activities and membership. Just as Black Legs Society dances of this period were focused on the Stecker area, so Gourd Dances were centered on the Cedar Creek area southeast of Carnegie, Oklahoma. The majority of active Ohoma Lodge membership still comes from the Redstone and Hog Creek communities.

One dance was held at the allotment of Red Buffalo, where the Kiowa tribal complex now stands, from which a good account of the Bustle Pickup ceremony has been preserved. Reflecting earlier traditions of all-night society meetings, the participants

Ohoma Society dance at the White Horse dance ground, about 1915. Charley White Horse wears the society bustle. Note the heavy presence of Cheyenne-style leggings.

in this dance followed the practice of placing an ax across the lodge door to prevent anyone from leaving until it was removed,. Members stayed up all night talking and visiting. Early in the morning, a crier proceeded around the camp announcing that the bustle would be picked up, a major society ritual. Horses and blankets were quickly placed along the perimeter of the dance ground to be given away to visitors. Charley Tsalote brought the bustle out and, after feinting with it four times, laid it down on the east side of the arena so that the top of the bustle faced east and the two waist ties formed a V toward the northeast and southeast. The Bustle Pickup Song was begun, gradually increasing in speed. Charley White Horse danced up to the bustle and, after making three feints toward it, quickly stepped in front of it. With the help of the assistant, who made sure it would not be dropped, he raised it and tied it as quickly as possible. When the bustle keeper picked up the bustle and tied it on, the men shouted and the women ululated. A rapid and successful pickup of the bustle was viewed as a good omen. After participants danced to several songs, White Horse took off the bustle and the assistant retired it to the tipi.[48] In other instances elders described the bustle keeper as approaching the bustle from the west, dancing around it four times, and then picking it up and tying it on. He was afterward followed by the dancers into the society tipi on the east side of the arena, where they prepared for some time and later danced out into the open to begin the formal dancing.[49]

During a dance at White Buffalo's in the 1920s, the society performed its mourning ritual in memory of Little Joe, or Hautago, a society member who had recently died and whose family had camped off to one side of the encampment. The society approached Little Joe's family singing as a group. After crying with the society members for a while, the family told them to go ahead and hold their dance, for the society "had wiped the tears away." Afterward the family fed the society members, and they returned to the main encampment. This account was obtained independently from several Kiowa elders and demonstrates the continuation of nineteenth-century society mourning practices.

Dances continued to be held on various Kiowa allotments until around 1930, when the dance began to be held annually at the home of Charley White Horse, near Redstone. Dances at this locale continued until 1978, when the annual dance was moved to the dance ground at Indian City U.S.A., south of Anadarko, Oklahoma, where it continues today.[50]

Omaha Society elders indicate that several aspects of the society were maintained into the early 1920s. Three- to four-day annual encampments including afternoon and evening dances continued to be held on the allotments of society members around the Fourth of July. Accounts of dances between 1915 and 1925 note the presence of two Tail dancers, a bustle keeper and his assistant, a drum keeper, and two whistle men, along with a Bustle Pickup ceremony as a prominent part of the society's dance. There are also eyewitness accounts of dances such as the Squat Dance that are no longer performed. Earlier Kiowa military society practices such as brush dragging, mourning, and society partners were common at this time.

Gregory Haumpy Sr. recalled participating in society ceremonials at Charley White Horse's home every July that included four days of afternoon and evening dancing. On the first day members met inside the society tipi, which had its sides rolled up and the society bustle hanging on the west side. Members discussed events that had taken place since the last year's meeting and then shared a meal, during which the whistle men served the society chiefs. During a special cedaring song, the bustle was taken down by the bustle keeper, who cedared it and then prayed. Afterward it was passed to each member, who could pray with the bustle and receive a blessing by rubbing himself with it. Mr. Haumpy described this part of the ceremonial:

> We take that bustle off that they got hanging up there and then we bring it down. And we were singing songs, see. Then we give it to the chief and he takes it and makes a motion with it. At the same time he's talking, praying. . . . They cedar it, the chief cedars it. When he gets through with that he sends it around, pass it around. Each member takes it. And when they get through with that singing and all of that, well, he passes it down. When it gets back up to the chief there, well, he hangs it up. You can touch it or take it and rub yourself all over [with the bustle] and at the same time you pray, you know. That's what it's for.[51]

Afterward a special song was sung to which all but the singers rose and danced out of the lodge and around the dance ground. During ceremonials at this time, women were not permitted to dance inside the arena but rose to dance in place in front of their seats, sitting down after each song. The singers remained in the lodge, where they continued singing, later coming out for the remainder of the program. Reflecting Kiowa martial traditions, Haumpy recalled that in addition to War dancing, the society held Round Dances, Victory Dances performed by remaining elder men who had seen combat, and women's Scalp and Victory Dances.[52]

Several Kiowa elders recall being inducted into the Omaha Society in 1929 at Charley White Horse's house. At this time only the bustle keeper and an assistant (which position probably became what is now known as the ceremonial chief) were on the west side of the meeting lodge. The Eagles and Crows sat on their respective sides of the lodge, with the Eagle and Crow chiefs on either side of the door and also serving as whistle keepers. Before the dance, new members were initiated inside the society tipi by the bustle keeper, Charley White Horse. The Bustle Pickup Song was sung, during which the bustle was raised and tied around the waist of the keeper. As part of the induction procedures, the initiates were served boiled dog, a common part of the larger Plains Omaha or Grass Dance ceremony and an occasional delicacy in Kiowa and Cheyenne diets. Gus and Dixon Palmer recalled that the bustle keeper said "Hoka-Nah-Soo" aloud before placing a piece of boiled dog meat in their and the other initiates' mouths, to which each replied, "Huhh."[53] The meaning of the term *Hoka-Nah-Soo* is no longer known by society elders but is believed to have originated with the Lakota. The bustle keeper then left the lodge while the other members remained inside. The bustle keeper alone then danced to the Opening Song. This song could be sung several times before ending, after which the Eagles, followed by the Crows, were permitted to tie on their own bustles (reflecting the influence of the early Fancy Dance), exit the society tipi, and begin dancing. At this time Mark Keahbone was the Eagle chief and Spencer Asah was the Crow chief.

During the 1920s the pronunciation of the society's name changed from Óhòmò to Óhòmà. Parker McKenzie remembered seeing, on the highway near Charley White Horse's home, a painted sign displaying the name "Ohoma" and an arrow pointing to the White Horse dance ground. This sign remained for several years during the 1920s. At this time younger Kiowa began pronouncing the society name as Óhòmà, and although current elders acknowledge the pronunciation as incorrect, it has continued as Ohoma, Ohomah, and O-Ho-Mah Lodge.[54]

As indicated by Parsons (1929:92, 94) and Kiowa elders, by the mid-1920s the organizational basis and leadership structure of the society had changed greatly from their original forms. The council of eleven chiefs and the two whipmen were no longer present, probably because of the decline in members with warrior status. That the council of chiefs was of *qájâi* status, usually translated as "chief," implies that all were of pre-reservation combat status. These members would have had to have been born around 1855 or earlier in order to have engaged in pre-reservation warfare, so all of them would have been seventy years of age or more by about 1925 and therefore deceased or too elderly to remain active. Although fourteen Kiowa served in World War I, only six went overseas, a few of whom saw actual combat.[55] Little further opportunity to acquire combat experience was available until World War II, and few veterans remained. Thus, the council of chiefs rapidly disappeared, with no veterans to fill its places. By 1927 Parsons (1929:92) noted that "O'humu is not organized as it used to be." As in the evolution of the Gourd Dance, the structure of the Kiowa Omaha Society and its relationship to the earlier military societies were significantly redefined by the mid-1920s. The introduction of Christianity, peyotism, and the Ghost Dance, along with Indian agency suppression, also affected the survival of the society.

Another significant structural change involved the position now known as the ceremonial chief. Today this man runs the preparatory meetings in the society tipi and the cedaring ceremonies and assists the bustle keeper during the annual ceremonial dance. By the 1920s this position appears to have combined previous positions in the original society structure, particularly the positions of Eagle chief and assistant bustle keeper. Mark Keahbone stated that he was made Eagle chief when his society partner was made Crow chief, and "we have a bundle of a certain plant and of feathers. I had to throw some of this plant on the fire and then hang the bundle behind the chief who kept it. What we did was very sacred" (Parsons 1929:92, 95). The references to the plant (cedar) and the bundle (bustle) and to tying it on the bustle keeper are clear. In addition, Mac Whitehorse was told by Mark Keahbone, the first known ceremonial chief, that he was chosen by the elders for the office when he was a fairly young man. Mark Keahbone served as ceremonial chief from about 1919 until 1984 and was succeeded by Ernie Keahbone, from 1984 to 1992, and then George Tahbone Sr., from 1992 to the present.[56]

But what was the overall response of the society to the decline of veterans and new socioreligious forms? Boyd (1981:65) stated that "with the beginning of reservation days, the Council of Chiefs evaluated the qualifications of anyone being considered for societal membership, and they placed emphasis on ancestral integrity since a new member was 'being put instead of' his ancestor." Although the Kiowa acquired the society during the reservation era, the remainder of this statement is fairly accurate. Even before 1900, many of the new society initiates were from "good families," as Kiowa often say, or families that were considered to be "prominent." This involved the traditional association of one's family in the set of Kiowa social classes. Favored boys (ą̂udę́tàlyòp) from socially high-status (ǫ̂dè and ǫ̂dègùfà) families made up the majority of initiates. As Weiser Tongkeamha explained, "First time was near Hobart. They mostly took in ą̂udę́tàlyì̀, firstborn boys, favored boys, and those from respectable families. These were the ones they wanted in Óhǫ̀mò."[57]

These procedures continued from the 1880s into the 1930s. Elders indicate that the majority of members were initially older men, but after a period of selected recruitment, membership was opened up to include younger men. One year in particular is remembered when an unusually large number of young men were initiated, after which a number of changes in dress, dance, and organization resulted. As Mac Whitehorse explained, "Before, we took in ą̂udę́ [favored] members mostly from well-off families. But today we take in those who are willing to learn and participate."[58]

Although views regarding society membership have changed, some people still believe in the older tradition of allegiance to a single society. As Vanessa Jennings described it:

> Quality is what they are looking for today. Do you care enough to devote a part of your life to the success of that society? Is that something that's important to you? Come in. This is where you can be seated.
>
> It is an honor, it isn't a right, it is an honor and a privilege to be seated at Ohomo.... At one time it was important for a man to pledge just to one society. But that's changed right now. Now you see a lot of young Kiowa men, you see a lot of men in general, like Comanches, and Apaches also ... all of a sudden it's important for them to join as many of the societies as they can, as many organizations as they can. But at one time not very long ago it was one society that you took a pledge to, but things change.
>
> When a man pledges to a society, it isn't just for the day, it isn't just for the moment. It isn't, "God, there's a lot of people here, you know I want people to see me." You know, that pledge is something to think about, because it's for the rest of your life. And for me, when a man pledges to a society, then that is as serious as a marriage vow. It's that serious, so unless it's something that's going to be too much trouble or you've got too many other things that you can't come. You know that vow is so serious that when that bustle keeper, when he calls for a singing or when he calls for a meeting, then if you want to have dinner with your girlfriend, then you have to cancel it. Or if you want to go and watch a ball game on TV and that bustle keeper has called for a meeting, you turn that TV set off and you get yourself over to that meeting place. That vow is that important.[59]

Membership is a serious obligation with long-term effects, for it involves a man's entire family. Ideally, family members are responsible for attending society functions and singing practices throughout the year, setting up the man's camp, cooking, attending each annual ceremonial, and holding a giveaway in his honor. In the early 1900s, society membership was almost totally Kiowa, but today a few Apache, Comanche, Caddo, Wichita, Anglo, and Hispanic members have been inducted, most of whom are married to Kiowa.

In researching this society, the themes I encountered most frequently in both archival and oral history sources were change and survival. As early as 1927, great change in the organization of the society were being mentioned. Parsons (1929:92) wrote: "Today all the Societies are extinct except Tainpaeko and O'humu. But O'humu is not organized as it used to be, and both groups are thought of merely as dance societies. Formerly they danced once during the summer, now they dance frequently, perhaps twenty times a summer, which to the older men cheapens the groups into mere 'shows.'"

In 1935 Piatonma (Mrs. Horse) told Marriott that although the young people referred to the Omaha Society dance as the "war dance," it was "a very showy dance" and "not the real war dance, when Kiowas wore very little but painted elaborately.

That's the real kind."⁶⁰ She was most likely contrasting the dances performed by pre-reservation military societies with the post-1884 Omaha-style War Dance.

One of the greatest changes in the society came when the Fancy Dance style of War dancing spread to the Kiowa. Francis Tsonetokoy recalled seeing the Fancy War Dance performed for the first time among the Kiowa by Steven Mopope and Chester Lefthand in 1917. In addition, dancing contests in the Kiowa-Comanche-Apache area are known from at least as early as 1894 (Brant 1969:83, 101). Another Kiowa elder remembered that dancing contests among the Kiowa were significant from 1918 onward, which coincides with the rapid diffusion of the Fancy Dance in Oklahoma.⁶¹

Previously, traditional Kiowa and Cheyenne dress of the late nineteenth century, which included large amounts of buckskin clothing, beadwork, and eagle feather bonnets, had dominated Omaha Society dancing. The choreography focused on "upright, straight War dancing"—as one person described it, "dignified and reserved, not too showy." Some elders described it as having the movements of a "strutting prairie chicken." During this time the society maintained only one bustle, worn by the bustle keeper. The original form of Kiowa War dancing was similar to contemporary Straight dancing but was performed with a more upright posture in what many Kiowa describe as a "dignified" manner.

As Browner (2002:30) noted, the demands of audiences at Wild West shows had a significant effect on the development of "fancy" War Dances that previously did not exist in Plains cultures. Audiences found the older War Dances an entertaining part of the programs, so William F. Cody asked dancers to "fancy it up." The result was the beginning of modern Fancy Dance style, which was performed strictly for entertainment and was unconnected to traditional Omaha or War Dance ritual. In addition, parades, which Kiowa military societies held at the Sun Dance, and grand entries, in which dancers entered the arena by dress and dance style or category, emerged during Fourth of July celebrations and Wild West shows (Browner 2002:30). Kiowa participation in dances at Fort Marion from 1875 to 1878 and in Texas also undoubtedly contributed to the increase of performance dancing. In Oklahoma the Fancy Dance or Fancy Feather Dance and dress style are often attributed to the influence of Gus MacDonald, a Ponca. After 1917, younger Kiowa Omaha Society members quickly became attracted to the faster "fancy" steps associated with the dance, which emphasized speed and intricacy of foot, head, and shoulder movements, and to the completely new and radical form of dress associated with the burgeoning Fancy Dance. Browner (2002:58) aptly described the factors that led to the Fancy Dance: "The men's style developed as a result of intersections between Traditional warrior society dances and Wild West shows, where dancing was performed as an exhibition event for audiences unfamiliar with the meanings behind more (comparatively) sedate styles of war dancing."

Among the Kiowa, this "early Fancy Dance" style is best represented by the paintings of the "Kiowa Five" artists, three of whom—Stephen Mopope, Spencer Asah, and

Jack Hokeah, all related to one another—were prominent dancers and Omaha Society members. Silverhorn influenced James Auchiah and Stephen Mopope (a grandson of Silverhorn's sister Kintadl), both of whom acknowledged Silverhorn as their first artistic influence. Jack Hokeah, a grandson of Silverhorn's brother Hau-vaught, may have also been influenced by Silverhorn. The frequent depictions of dancers in the works of the Kiowa Five reflect their membership in the society. Although Kiowa art scholars have focused much attention on Silverhorn, his artwork, and his influence on the Kiowa Five, one aspect has been largely overlooked. Silverhorn was also a fellow Omaha Society member, so shared membership in the War Dance society provided another connection between him, three of the Kiowa Five, and their art.

However, the Fancy Dance soon changed, adding sudden spinning moves, head and upper body movements, and a set of bustles as a part of the dance regalia. One elder who had witnessed society dances since around 1920 indicated that the dress style of the society changed before the dancing style did. Early Kiowa Omaha Society photographs illustrate these changes. Earlier pictures and older members in later pictures typically wear broadcloth leggings with geometrically beaded strips (some wear buckskin leggings), broadcloth breechclouts with floral beadwork, cloth or silk shirts, eagle feather bonnets or porcupine hair roaches with single eagle feathers, otter skin braid wraps, fully or heavily beaded moccasins, and knee bells. A few have fully beaded vests and metal and mescal bean bandoliers. Later pictures of early Fancy dancers are characterized by the presence of broadcloth aprons with floral beadwork; waist, back, and elbow bustles of eagle and brightly colored feathers; anklets of angora goat hair or beaded broadcloth sections; leg, knee, and ankle bells; long underwear or bare arms, legs, and torsos; often fully beaded moccasins, cuffs, armbands, waist belts, and harnesses; and roaches with single feathers, often with erect decorations made of stripped feathers. Many of the moccasins of this period are clearly of Cheyenne derivation.[62]

Although society members had already begun wearing individual waist and elbow bustles, long colored underwear, breechclouts with elaborate curvilinear beadwork, Cheyenne style beadwork, articles of 1920s Anglo "flapper" clothing, and items that became associated with the early Fancy Dance, the Omaha Society still danced "a straight War Dance." Elders indicate that the fancy footwork associated with the Fancy Dance was not present until a few years later and was largely because of the influence of two close friends who always danced together. These men were Chester Lefthand, an Arapaho married to a Kiowa, and Stephen Mopope, a Kiowa.[63] The Kiowa dubbed Lefthand Máunqúngài ("The Twister") for his revolutionary dancing style.[64] Following their introduction of the "Fancy War Dance" in the Kiowa community, it spread among the Kiowa and neighboring tribes with increasingly elaborate dress and rapid and intricate body and foot movements.

In 1936, Henry Tsoodle Sr. stated that the only Kiowa society still functioning was the Omaha and that its dress and dance styles contrasted greatly with those of earlier times:

> They used to dress very carefully in the finest, just like the others [societies], but with a lot of bells. But now they have added a lot. They used to wear one feather on their heads, with a crest made of a horse's mane—ok'oyk'okoy [qócáuiɔ̀pàul, roach headdress]. They didn't wear all those feather fans [bustles]. That's new. Tonsiai [tónchài]—ornament with two feathers worn down the back like a scarf. It hangs from the shoulders, and the feathers are on the ends. White Horse has one but he never wears it now. The dancing is different from what it used to be. There wasn't any of that quivering and carrying on [Fancy dancing]. Before it was serious. They were careful. Now there is a lot of putting on. Ohoma were in the same rank with the others [societies].[65]

Other external factors influenced the way the War Dance came to be performed. The introduction of the Fancy Dance style, the rising popularity of contest dancing, and increasing participation in nonsocietal events such as paid performances, shows, county fairs, and emerging powwows led to a dramatic increase in more secular War Dance performances during the 1920s. Similarly to the post-1957 Gourd Dance, two forms of the danced developed, a ceremonial form performed at annual society gatherings and a nonsocietal or popular form associated with powwows and shows. By the early 1940s the War Dance tradition had expanded to include heavy participation outside of societal contexts. Growth of the nonsocietal dances eventually distinguished the dance as significantly different from the formal and less frequently performed annual society ceremonial and helped foster the modern powwow. With reinforcement from celebrations held during World War II and the Korean War, veterans were propelled to the foreground of the powwow community, where they occupied many of the most prominent positions for decades. Indeed, most Kiowa powwows continue to focus on War Dance, veteran, and family songs.

Several families sponsored Omaha Society dances for returning World War II veterans who were society members. The society continued to foster martial themes through song, dance, and honoring. Bustle keeper Charley White Horse maintained a patriotic banner featuring a star for every society member in service. Kiowa elders composed several personal society songs with martial themes for Kiowa returning from World War II and later conflicts. Several of these songs refer to the bravery of the veterans, their status as chiefs, and thankfulness for their safe return. Others reference the Omaha Society by name, the good feelings associated with it, and the love of the songs and the way they make people feel upon hearing them.

The following two songs were composed for returning World War II veterans and demonstrate many of the themes found in Omaha Society songs. The first was composed by Jeanette Berry Mopope for her nephew, Army Air Corps veteran Gus Palmer Sr., and was presented during his homecoming celebration:

> 1 Mái-fâu-qì̃ jó-cà dáu áui-chàn
> (Máifâuqì̃ / home / we-he for us / again-came)
> Máifâuqì̃ came home (back) for us again.

2 Nàu è ǫ̏-dáu, nàu è ǫ̏-tą̏, nàu è ǫ̏-dáu
(And / we / felt elated or very happy; and / we / good-felt; and / we / were-felt elated or very happy)
And we were elated, and we felt good, and we were elated.[66]

When Roland Whitehorse returned from service in the 47th Infantry Regiment of the 9th Division, an honor dance was held for him at his father's home. As Dorothy Whitehorse DeLaune recalled, "Jeanette [Mopope], Momma [Laura Whitehorse], and all of them, they made a trail for him with blankets around the arena. And anybody was allowed to pick it up. They didn't call names. It was just a trail. He danced on it, around in a circle."[67] Martha Whitehorse Doyeto composed the following song for Roland Whitehorse while he was in service, and it was sung to honor him at this dance:

1 Háun-èm-í-dâu-qî́ á qá-jái-dầu
(Not-he-danger-male / he / chief-state of [lit. brave man])
Unafraid Of Danger, he is a chief (brave man).
2 Repeat.
3 Repeat.
4 Repeat.
1 Tén-á-zél-bé-dò á qá-jái-dầu
(Heart-he-strong-because [he is] / he / chief-state of)
Because he is strong hearted, he is a chief.
2 Háun-èm-í-dâu-qî́ á qá-jái-dầu.[68]

The following two Omaha Society songs show the deep affection and emotion associated with the society and its songs:

Song 1

1 Dấu-gá ę́ ǫ̏-dèp ę́-hàu-dè
(Song / to be liking / this one)
I like this song, this one (this is the song I like).
2 Repeat.
3 Ǫ̏-dé ǫ̏-dé dấu-gà à tháu-nàu
(Feel good / feel good / song / I / hear-and)
I feel good, I feel good when I hear this song, and . . .
4 Repeat line 1.[69]

Song 2

1 Ó-hò-mò-dầu-gà à tháu-chę̀.
(Ohomo-song / I / hear-when)
When I hear an Óhòmò song
2 Yą́ ǫ̏-dèp.
(I / good feel)

I feel good.
3 Repeat line 1.
4 Repeat line 2.
5 Repeat line 1.
6 Repeat line 2.
1 Ó-họ̀-mò-dầu-gà à tháu-chẹ̀.
2 Yá̱ ọ̄-dèp.[70]

In the late 1940s, anthropologist John Gamble was initiated into the society while conducting fieldwork on Kiowa dance and music. Gamble was an avid War dancer, and his statement that he was "initiated into the moribund Ohomo Society" (1952:20) reflects a period of decline with which the society was struggling to cope. In 1949, society bustle keeper Charley White Horse died. The society did not meet in 1950 and 1951, as it did between 1925 and 1927 after the death of the Crow chief Komalty (Parsons 1929:95).[71] When the society finally met, Frank Bosin and other elders decided that Mac Whitehorse, the son of the late bustle keeper, should succeed his father. In 1952 they brought him to a meeting and bestowed on him his father's position and Kiowa name, Chẹ̄thạ̀idè, or White Horse. Although Mac Whitehorse had not been active in the society in his youth, his singing ability and extensive knowledge of society and personal songs were major factors in the society's choosing him as bustle keeper. Whitehorse reflected upon his induction: "I took the bustle and led it the way he did. . . . I know the ceremonial songs and I know mostly everybody's [personal] song. And that's the reason why they took me, why they picked me, I thought. There were other guys [that were capable] too, but they picked me."[72]

Current Society Activities and Ceremonial

Although the Omaha Society has never ceased meeting since its origin in 1884, it is smaller than most of the other current Kiowa societies. Several Kiowa have stated that interest and participation in society activities have declined over the past twenty years and that the bustle keeper, Mac Whitehorse, has been the principal force keeping the society intact. Kiowa elders also say that Mac Whitehorse is unquestionably the most knowledgeable War Dance singer in the Kiowa tribe. His knowledge of Omaha Society, War Dance, and personal songs is indeed phenomenal. He knows not only the songs but also their histories, including who composed them and to whom they have belonged. Although he strongly encourages people to learn the songs and frequently puts them on tape, no successor to him is apparent. I have seen some instances in which Whitehorse was the only singer present who was able to start particular songs. With such reliance on his knowledge and singing talent, and in light of his advanced age, some people feel great concern for the future of the society.

Society and community members indicate that a resurgence in society participation took place during the mid-1990s, reflecting the observation by some Kiowa that Omaha Society families are noted for their internal strength and for remaining together through difficult periods. This revival of interest and participation was observable at meetings and dances during my fieldwork. A group that came to be known as the Reservation War Dancers separated from the Omaha Society, later splitting to produce a group known as the Kiowa Original Dancers. Both family-based organizations focused on War Dance performances, reportedly often for commercial purposes. However, the split seems to have had few long-term detrimental effects, because members of both groups continued to participate in society activities. They became relatively inactive by the late 1990s.

Although some families that have belonged to the society since its origins welcome the sudden renewal of interest by other Kiowa, they wonder what has kept them away for so long. Some Kiowa who have never ceased more "traditional" practices such as dancing, doctoring, praying before tribal bundles, and participation in the Native American Church have expressed amazement at the sudden interest and revival among families who are suddenly, as one person put it, "rediscovering their Indianness." Citing the society's longevity, a member of a six-generation Ohoma family commented, "We never quit as a society. We 'heathens' kept dancing . . . so that you royal 'full bloods' who have just now discovered that, 'Oh that's Kiowa. Hey, I have a right to that!' You know, we saved this for you all so that you could have something." This person offered similar observations concerning differences in the behavior of people who had not grown up with the "Ohoma Road":

> It seems like Ohoma now, there are so many people growing up now, they have no idea of the behavior that is a part of that and they've grown up outside of Ohoma and the only thing most of them know is contest powwows, you know, and that's just a world and a half away from Ohoma. That behavior is completely different. To me looking on, they do not have respect for each other. They don't talk good to each other, the right way. It's just completely different, and so when they come to Ohoma their manners are not very good.[73]

The Omaha Society today holds a single annual ceremonial. Every spring, shortly after the first thunder, bustle keeper Mac Whitehorse calls a meeting to cedar the bustle and offer prayers. A tipi in which to conduct the ceremony is set up in front of his house, near Stecker, Oklahoma. Wearing an eagle feather bonnet and carrying the bustle in his arms, Whitehorse leads a procession of men from in front of his house into the tipi. After he and the ceremonial chief address the members, each man is allowed to talk. The cedaring song is sung repeatedly while the bustle and each man are cedared. Whitehorse returns the bustle to the house, and after the men leave, the women are all invited in to speak, pray, and be cedared. Afterward a large meal is served and people visit throughout the afternoon.[74]

In the late spring and early summer, the society begins to hold weekly meetings and singing practices at member's houses or at St. Patrick's Catholic Mission in Anadarko. At meetings I attended, men sat on one side of the room and women on the other while a board composed of the bustle keeper, the ceremonial chief, and a treasurer sat at one end. After an opening prayer and a discussion of finances, fundraising, and initiations, duties are assigned in preparation for the annual summer ceremonial. Although the society co-hosts other dances throughout the year, it holds no benefit dances; all funds are raised through donations from members or during the society's annual dance. After all business has been completed, the women serve refreshments.

The remainder of each meeting consists of a singing practice of society songs, during which aspects of society history and customs may be discussed around the drum. Recently, great concern has been expressed over the shortage of society singers able to start certain songs. Remaining society members encourage the younger members to learn the songs well enough to lead them, in order to ensure the society's survival. Several younger people have become regular singers at the ceremonials.

The monthly meetings provide not only singing practice but also, as one elder put it, a means of "gaining momentum" for the upcoming ceremonial. At each meeting Mac Whitehorse places a bowl near the drum in which people can donate money. Throughout the evening, whenever an individual's song is sung, that member rises and dances in place beside the drum while his relatives join in behind him and offer money to honor him. The money is given to the priest of St. Patrick's for letting the society hold its meetings there.

The society holds its annual encampment and ceremonial on the last full weekend of July.[75] The preparatory and ceremonial details vary slightly from one year to another, and my description is an overall synthesis of the current ceremonial. Some families come to camp for the weekend of the ceremonial. A "sing," or a session of singing without dancing, is often held on the Friday evening. On Saturday, another singing practice is sometimes held in the morning and early afternoon. An open or intertribal program of social and War dancing makes up the evening program, from approximately 7:00 to 11:00 P.M.

The society ceremonial begins on Sunday afternoon around two o'clock. After the ceremonial chief has prepared the interior of the society lodge on the west side of the encampment, members are called to meet. They enter the lodge, are seated, and prepare for the formal War Dance ceremonial. Society members are not supposed to enter the lodge if they are angry or have outstanding disputes with anyone. Any ill feelings are supposed to be settled by both parties involved before entering the tipi, and ideally any member has the right to prevent another from entering until doing so. This practice is not always observed.

Out of respect for the ceremony and the society, I give only a brief account of the preparatory procedures. The bustle keeper makes opening remarks, followed by the ceremonial chief. At this time the history and traditions of the society are sometimes discussed. One of the most sacred and important parts of the ritual involves the offering of prayers inside the society lodge. Prayers are said for health and a good life for all, frequently for the entire world. During one ceremonial, individual members asked blessings and offered prayers for many parts of the world suffering from economic and social conflicts, civil unrest, or war, such as Bosnia, the Middle East, and China. Blessings are typically asked for others before asking for oneself. A pipe is lit using a coal that is handled with a split stick, and often the ceremonial chief offers a prayer. Traditionally the pipe is then passed around to each member, who, upon holding it, may speak if he so desires. In this widespread Plains tradition, to hold a pipe requires one to speak truthfully. In recent years the ceremonial chief has been noted simply to hold the pipe, point it at the next member, and ask him if he has anything he wants to say.

Cedar is then placed on coals in the fire, producing smoke. The Cedaring Song is sung for the society bustle, which is removed from an alter of sage on the west side of the lodge interior and then carried to the east side, where it is cedared. Outside, smoke can be seen coming from the top of the tipi while the singing and sounds of eagle bone whistles being blown emanate from within. Because many dancers today have bustles of their own, members are next allowed to cedar their own bustles, which usually have been hung inside the society lodge.

Mac Whitehorse explained the purpose of his efforts to maintain the society's ceremonial and its purpose: "Keeping with tradition and following the traditional ways of my father, Charley, has been the purpose of my continued effort to teach the younger generation. When someone joins O-Ho-Mah, you join to follow that Tone-tsi [bustle], not me or any particular leaders. Once a year we cedar and pray with it. If you are in need of cedaring and prayer, that is what the ceremonies are [for] on Sunday."[76]

The Pipe Dance

After the preparatory rituals are completed, members leave the lodge to perform the Pipe Dance. Although the origin of the Omaha Society Pipe Dance is no longer known, it is an old society dance and appears to have originated with the widespread Prairie-Plains Calumet ceremony. The Kiowa may have received it from the Pawnee in the winter of 1871–1872 (Mooney 1989:333; Marriott 1945:300–301). Hugh Scott recorded that the Kiowa gave the Pawnee many horses while the Pawnee put on a dance for the Kiowa and presented them with several pipes.[77] This dance used to be performed by ceremonial chief Mark Keahbone and others at ceremonials held at the old White Horse dance ground. Today, when the society has finished its preparations inside the society lodge, the members come out in order of age, from oldest to youngest. They are led by four young men, each of whom puts on a feathered bonnet and takes up a pipe. Symbolically this is viewed as a continuation of the prayers begun inside the society lodge.

At this time women, who are not allowed inside the tipi while the men are preparing, are permitted to enter for similar prayers and meditation. Like the men, they must not enter while harboring ill feelings or before settling any personal disputes. However, several women pointed out that this tenet is not always followed, because

Ohoma Society Pipe Dance, Anadarko, Oklahoma, July 25, 1993.

disputes between some women have continued for several years. Each woman is given a chance to address all in attendance and to pray aloud. One woman stated that the majority of women's prayers were for the health and success of others and generally not for themselves, unless someone was encountering a difficult period in her life. Children and grandchildren are frequently brought in by elders to be prayed for. After these prayers are finished, the ceremonial chief and an assistant pray for and cedar each woman and child.

Just before this point in the ceremonial, a member has placed a shovelful of hot coals from the fire inside the society lodge in the middle of the dance arena outside. The four male Pipe dancers dance into the arena clockwise from the southwest side, each carrying a pipe held horizontally to his chest.[78] Some pipe dancers say that they pray during this portion of the ceremony. Pausing to form a line, they dance in place on the west side of the arena while facing eastward. After the four dance a complete clockwise circle around the arena (which is not always a regular part of the dance), the fourth dancer to have entered stops on the north side, the third man on the east side, and so on for each cardinal direction. When all four men have reached their positions, they raise their pipes toward the center of the arena and dance a clockwise circle in place, turning inward to face each other. The men then dance toward the pile of coals in the center of the arena. In unison they make four feints toward and withdrawals from the coals, during which they bow toward the coals, lowering their pipes to symbolically light the tobacco in the bowls, then raising the pipes upward while dancing backward. Upon returning to their original positions, the dancers remain facing inward as they again complete a clockwise turn in place. Then they proceed clockwise, exiting on the southwest side of the arena. The last man in, the one on the north side, is the first to exit, followed by the third, or east, man, and so on. After the Pipe Dance, the four dancers remove their bonnets, replace them with their own porcupine hair roaches, and prepare for the society dance proper.

The Omaha Society Dance

With the entire society congregated on the southwest corner of the arena, the Kiowa Flag Song is sung. The ceremonial then begins with a processional or Opening Song led by the bustle keeper, followed by the ceremonial chief, who carries the bustle in his arms, and then by the other society members, who are dressed out for the ceremonial and dance along the south side of the arena. Women dance in place along the outside portions of the arena, where they remain during the entire ceremonial except to enter the arena for giveaways and specials to honor someone. Toward the end of the song the ceremonial chief ties the bustle around the waist of the bustle keeper. At the end of the song the dancers divide, with the Eagles proceeding to a row of wooden benches on the north side, the Crows to the south, and the Hawks—a relatively recent addition to the Eagles and Crows and not an original part of the society's structure—to the southwest. Citing her younger brother's inclusion, one woman stated that the Hawks had been in existence at least since the late 1950s but that the number of members of this group ebbed and flowed in comparison with that of the others.[79]

Whereas Eagles and Crows were originally differentiated primarily on the basis of warrior status and were seated by age, with the oldest members of each group nearest the council of chiefs on the west side of the arena, the three divisions are now determined solely by age. The Eagles include all adult male members, and the Crows comprise all male child members of about ten years old or younger. The addition of the Hawks came at the request of some youths who felt they were too young to be Eagles but too old to sit with the Crows. Thus the Hawks are generally between the ages of ten and fourteen. They sit on the southwest corner of the arena between the Crows to the south and the Eagles to the north. A male supervisor, or Hawk chief, has been instituted to go along with the older positions of Eagle and Crow chief.

The content of the program at this point has differed greatly in past years and has included Tail Dance songs, initiations, special honoring songs, families "reentering" the arena after the death of a relative, numerous giveaways, and regular War dancing. The style of War dancing performed by "Fancy dancers" and "Straight dancers" is of the old-fashioned, "straight up" Kiowa style and includes less crouching and bending over than does Osage and Ponca Straight dancing or the frequent fast spinning and whirling of contemporary Oklahoma Fancy dancing. Today most members don a variety of Fancy, Straight, and modern traditional dance clothing, with less Ponca-style clothing than in the Comanche War Dance Society.

In some years a set of songs has been sung during which only the bustle keeper danced in the middle of the arena while the other members danced in place on their respective sides. The point at which the bustle is retired from the arena varies but normally falls at this juncture of the program. In 1990, after four Tail Dance songs, the bustle was retired to the society tipi, where it remained for the rest of the afternoon. In 1991 it was placed on a pole inside the arena and just east of the drum for the remainder of the program, because the bustle keeper wanted to remain at the drum to reintroduce old society songs that were not commonly known to the younger singers. In 1992 the bustle keeper wore the bustle throughout the entire afternoon. Regardless of how long the bustle is worn during the dance, whenever the keeper must leave the arena, the ceremonial chief unties the bustle and holds it horizontally in his arms while dancing in place until the keeper returns. He reties the bustle on him, and both resume dancing.

Originally, only the single society bustle was worn during society ceremonials. After the introduction of the Fancy Dance, individual bustles began to be worn, but only after the bustle keeper had retired the society bustle during the ceremonial. However, with the rise of popular War dancing, every Fancy or Traditional dancer now has a bustle as part of his dress. I observed some years in which a few individuals wore bustles while the society bustle was being danced with during the ceremonial, which prompted discussion within the society. Typically, dancers leave their bustles inside the society lodge during the ceremony.

In other years a session of Tail Dance songs is sung. These differ from regular War Dance songs in that after the last verse is sung there is a brief pause, during which the dancers exit the floor and are seated. The tail, or last, portion of the song is then sung, during which one dancer from the Eagles and one from the Crows dance. These two dancers resemble the Tail dancers in societies such as the Osage I'nlonschka, positions that for the Kiowa Ohoma Lodge are the Eagle and Crow chiefs. The practice of Tail dancing has varied, but recently it has been a regular part of the ceremony.

Continuing the society's early martial focus, the Chief's Song was sung at the 1991 ceremonial for the induction of four Operation Desert Storm veterans. Wearing their uniforms, these men had bonnets placed on them and were led in a processional around the arena. Numerous shawls and blankets were placed at their feet to be given away, after which each veteran was asked to speak about his service in the war. The four veterans then led another processional as a Victory Song was sung.

Near the middle of the afternoon, new candidates are initiated into the society. Today the initiation song is called the "Tagging Song," a term of recent origin. During this song, new initiates are led by the bustle keeper in a dancing processional clockwise around the arena, followed by the ceremonial chief. The service records of new members who are veterans are read aloud over the public address system. Occasionally, two youths are still initiated into the society as partners and given a song to share if they desire it. Although songs were originally shared equally between partners, few do so today, because the social ties between such members and their families are not

Ohoma Society Initiation Dance led by Mac Whitehorse, Anadarko, Oklahoma, July 25, 1993.

nearly as strong as in the past. Some initiations of members as society partners have resulted in family arguments over the ownership and use of the two partners' society song.[80]

Following the initiation, members shake hands with the new initiates, whose families pledge money or beef for the next year's dance. Pledges may occur at any time during the afternoon when a family member wishes to honor and recognize a relative who is a society member. The pledges are collected before or at the next annual dance. Initiations for new society princesses may also take place at this point in the ceremonial. Although often running along particular family lines, society membership has never been truly hereditary. All members must either be selected by the society or approach the society for admission, and although candidates with military records are especially honored, veteran status is not required.

The remainder of the afternoon consists of regular War dancing interspersed with family specials and giveaways. Although the two whipmen are no longer maintained by the society, any member is said to be able to force another to dance by going in front of a seated dancer, tapping his foot in front of him, and then turning around. The seated dancer is then obligated to rise and dance. Later, Kiowa veterans perform the retreat of the colors during the Kiowa Flag Song.[81] After a dinner break, an evening powwow of Round dancing, two-step, and regular War dancing to Omaha Society songs is held. The Kiowa Black Legs Society co-hosts the evening program, which is reciprocated at Black Legs' dances.

The Óhǫmà Road

Today the organization and duties of the Omaha Society are split between the bustle keeper and the ceremonial chief. The bustle keeper cares for the bustle and serves as the dance leader, while the ceremonial chief focuses on directing the preparation in the society's lodge, the afternoon ceremonial dance, and the cedaring of family members and houses of recently deceased members. The ceremonial chief also now acts as the assistant to the bustle keeper in carrying the bustle and tying and untying it for him.

The respect and care given to the bustle by the society and its keeper, Mac Whitehorse, are truly admirable. The bustle is kept in a special room in Whitehorse's house that is reserved for this purpose. Mac Whitehorse showed me this room in 1990. The bustle is hung on the wall and kept covered with a cloth drawstring bag. Below it is an altarlike area where offerings may be left by members who visit the bustle to pray in private. For this role a traditional bustle keeper, like a medicine bundle keeper, is expected to remain at home most of the time, to be with the bustle and facilitate visitors. Another wall holds photographs of Kiowa singers, most of them society members. The other two opposite walls are covered with drumsticks of prominent Kiowa and Ohoma Society singers, each with a tag indicating the identity of the former owner. Recently the bustle has been restored to a more active role in society ceremonials. Just as Henry Tsoodle Sr. described for the mid-1930s, the bustle was not worn in society ceremonials from 1952 to the mid-1980s but was only opened in the society tipi, cedared, and put up before the dancing began. Since the mid-1980s the bustle keeper has worn the bustle during portions of the annual ceremonial.

The devotion given to the care of the society bustle is a reflection of the principles that form what society members refer to as the "Óhǫmà Road" or "Óhǫmò Road." During society activities, society members often express deep emotions in their speech and actions that reflect a high level of social and religious spirituality associated with the society. At society meetings, men and women frequently address those in attendance with expressions such as, "We know what the right way of doing this is," "That's the Óhǫmà way," and "We're Óhǫmà, we know what is expected of us." During one meeting a member stated, "We all know the Óhǫmà Road is not a social dance; there are prayers and much more associated with it." Much of the religious part of the society is associated with the society's bustle and with the prayers offered during the annual spring cedaring of the bustle and in the ceremonial lodge before the annual dance in July. As Mac Whitehorse told me, "There are prayers on that bustle. So I tell people to follow that bustle, it is leading Óhǫmà."[82]

The Óhǫmà Road is more than expected behavior and goodwill toward others. It is a society-based, collective, social, religious, and moral ethic—a way of life—that is intended to extend to, lead, and direct everyday life. It is the psychological outlook as well as the physical actions and behavior that a person should ideally practice in his or her interactions with others and the world. The morality embraced by the society is

Ohoma Society bustle worn by Mac Whitehorse, 1992.

intended for daily life. As one person whose grandparents were strong society members stated, "The way to lead a good life, how to treat yourself and others carries on to everyday life and not just at society activities."[83]

Gregory Haumpy Sr. described the interwoven socioreligious content of the society that reflects so much of Native American culture in general:

> There are a lot of prayers in Óhọ̀mà, a lot of prayers. Well, to me, it's kind of a religious dance and then it's a social dance, both of them together. See, you pray in there [inside the society tipi]. You pray about it and then you go out and you enjoy yourself. . . . But there's always a prayer brought in. God always comes in on that. They always talk to God before they dance and ask him to be kind, take care of them and all of that. All of that and then they go on with the dance. It's always been done.

Haumpy continued, explaining that the bustle, which is held during prayers but is not prayed to, can help one receive what he prays for: "It seems like it does. See, it must have helped me or something. See how old I am and what all the predicaments [medical condition] I have been through. All of that and I'm still here. There's something that happened that done me some good and I'm still here.... I know what I pray for I notice it comes about. I didn't realize it until later."[84]

Vanessa Jennings expressed her feelings concerning the Óhòmà Road and its relationship to an individual's life:

> Besides the morality, there is a self-respect, an esteem for your worth as a human being. What kind of life do you want to live, you know, it's all right here in your heart and that comes from those Ohoma teachings. We're doing this because that is the Ohoma way. This is the way we do things. There is this kindness, this generosity that goes with it.... It is a way for you to behave. There are ways for you to ask for things, there are ways for you to carry yourself. There is a way for you to dress and a part of this is things that are expected of you when you pledge yourself to Ohoma. And so that's what they're talking about, you know, all of these things. This way of living, this way of talking, everything. Everything is really structured, and it really is interesting, you know, because it really is beautiful.[85]

Rarely do people fully follow their own culturally prescribed ideals. Whereas all the Kiowa societies have a "road," a moral ethic and an etiquette for leading a better life, that exhibited by the Omaha Society is one of the more visible and encompassing ones I have witnessed. These qualities are visible at society meetings, at annual encampments, and throughout the families of society members. However, it must also be recognized that, as in all cultures, these behavioral qualities are ideal, and variation occurs with the constant ebb and flow of social relations that characterize life. Disagreements and hard feelings sometimes arise. Members sometimes stop associating with others or may withdraw their support in helping others. Some members or families may stay away from or sit out of society activities for a period of time. Individual and family-centered disagreements, arguments, gossip, denouncing letters to the editor in local newspapers, attempts to depose and undermine existing officers, avoidance of individuals, nonattendance of society functions, mediation, and reconciliation were all witnessed during my fieldwork. I also observed that most issues were either eventually resolved or forgotten to the degree that all involved resumed participation. And despite the temporary disturbances caused by fluctuating social relations, adherence to society ideology by others continues to pave the Óhòmò Road with a positive outlook for the future.

Currently there are more than eighty members of the society, of whom about thirty dancers dress out for the annual dance, the majority of them young men and boys. Many elder members attend as singers or spectators. Although participation fluctuates, a recent increase in interest and participation in society activities is visible.

Each year, two to eight new members are inducted. Many of them are young children. Several members have also recently been appointed to succeed to their ancestors' positions in the society. Barney Oheltoint Jr. and Robert Hatfield replaced Barney Oheltoint Sr. and Joe Poolaw as assistants to the ceremonial chief and bustle keeper, respectively. Terry Ware succeeded his grandfather Gregory Haumpy Sr. as a whistle keeper and was later followed by Tim Tsoodle.

The society has changed over the years, and some of its older aspects have not survived. Elders speak of how "the songs are sung faster today than in the past," dancers dance in circular progressions instead of along the edge of the arena, many of the organizational offices have not been maintained, and others have been combined into single positions. All organizations change over time, but a diachronic reflection is often necessary to recognize and account for the changes. Many Kiowa elders, both members and nonmembers, have criticized the Omaha Society, as they have other Kiowa societies, claiming that the members "aren't doing it right" or "they don't do like they used to, when I first saw it."

As in most cultures, many people fail to recognize that change is constant and apparent in any institution over a lengthy period. Of all Kiowa, Apache, and Comanche men's and women's societies, only the Kiowa Omaha Society did not cease functioning after the 1880s. Other societies had to be revived, sometimes twice, or were supplanted by nonindigenous dance forms. The Kiowa obtained the Omaha Society during a time of great cultural change, yet the society managed to adapt, flourish, and even supersede the older societies until their post–World War II revivals and subsequent growth.

One result of the longevity and flexibility of the Kiowa Omaha Society is that it has led to or influenced at least five different levels of the War Dance in which Kiowa participate. These include the original Kiowa Omaha Society, Oklahoma intertribal powwows and fairs, commercially oriented contest powwows such as Red Earth, and both American and European hobbyist powwows and contests that have been influenced by visits to the Kiowa community or in which Kiowa have participated or served as head staff.

The Emergence of the Plains Indian Powwow

The term *powwow* or *pow-wow* is believed to have derived from the Algonquian language family, from the Narragansett words *pau wau*, interpreted as "he/she dreams." According to Virgil Vogel (1970:126), the term was intended to refer to specific ritual actions performed during curing ceremonies, but non-Indians seem to have misinterpreted the term and adopted it to refer to the generic use of herbal remedies among settlers. The terms "pow-wow doctors" and "pow-wowing" became commonplace in Anglo American and Pennsylvania German folk medicine (Vogel 1970:126; Browner 2002:27). Later the term began to be used to refer to nearly any type of gathering of Indians, especially meetings and dances. Today, non-Indians use the word *powwow* as a colloquial term to refer to a number of group contexts, and both Indians and non-Indians use it in referring to contemporary, usually intertribal, dances.

Many works on the powwow have passed over the complex, multifaceted cultural and historical processes leading to its evolution, in order to focus on its spiritual qualities and on detailed descriptions of dance styles. Recently, Gloria Young (1981), Luke Lassiter (1998), Clyde Ellis (2002, 2003), Tara Browner (2002), and I (Meadows 1999) have begun to address both historical and performative aspects of Plains Indian military society and powwow dance traditions.[86] The modern powwow clearly has several influences that may be seen as points of origin, and several tribes claim to have held the first powwow. With several lines of diffusion, there appear to have been two primary phases in the diffusion of the Omaha Dance: an early phase that emphasized the ritual fire handling aspects, and a later, post-1860s phase characterized by a reduction of certain ritual aspects (such as restrictions on wearing bustles, which were formerly limited to a small number of men holding special status), a more secular nature, and some differences in functions (Ellis 2002:49–50). My purpose here is not to engage in the entirety of this tangled debate but to focus on the larger factors of the powwow's emergence as it relates to the Kiowa Omaha Society.

The Omaha-Grass-War Dance was one of two major dance traditions that contributed to the formation of the powwow. With increased intertribal visiting in the reservation period and the continued diffusion of the dance, marked similarities in ritual, regalia, ideology, and purpose developed in the late nineteenth century. With the end of warfare, the means to acquire the martial status that was so integral to the Plains military society complex disappeared. Warfare rank became frozen for combat veterans and unattainable for younger men. Significant shifts in reservation-era subsistence and martial culture resulted in significant structural and functional changes in sociocultural forms. The Omaha Dance became more social, with a gradual lessening of warfare requirements and a changing but ongoing body of elaborate ritual.

The other major dance tradition to diffuse widely in the late 1800s was the Drum or Dream Dance associated with the Great Lakes Midewiwin ceremony. Reverend Clay MacCauley first observed the Drum Dance among the Menominee at Kenosha, Wisconsin, around 1879 or 1880 and published the first public account of the dance in 1893. The Drum Dance spread quickly across the upper Midwest and Great Lakes region to the Sioux, Potawatami, Winnebago, and Ojibwa, who passed it to others by giving a drum, songs, and other presents to the recipients (Barrett 1911; Slotkin 1957; Young 1981:129–130; Ellis 2002:45).

Eventually, the Omaha and Drum or Dream Dance forms met and overlapped. Gloria Young (1981:153) wrote that the "grass or Omaha warrior societies which developed out of the old Iruska (the Pawnee form of the Omaha) met the Algonquian shamanism and Medicine Lodge among the easternmost Siouan tribes and created the environment out of which emerged the Drum dance." Clark Wissler (1916), James Slotkin (1957:16), Thomas Kavanagh (1993:111), and Young (1981) all reported that the Drum and Omaha Dances met and intermingled variously in Indian Territory by the 1880s and 1890s. The result was the emergence of two distinct forms of regional dress, dance, and song styles (Kavanagh 1993:111): an eastern or prairie version and a western or plains version.

The Prairie tribes of Oklahoma and Nebraska (Omaha, Osage, Otoe, Pawnee, Ponca, etc.) took the Omaha Dance, influenced by the Midewiwin and Dream-Drum dance complex, in one direction, with a ceremony focused on the use of a large drum and some revitalization features similar to those of the Ghost Dance. This form retained many of the ceremonial offices and ritual content, emphasizing the dance style now known as the Straight Dance, with a conservative dress and dance style. The prevalent toe-heel step and its motions are reminiscent of the feast-stalking aspects of the old Grass Dance (Kavanagh 1993:111), now interpreted by some dancers as tracking or searching for an enemy trail. Dispensing with the crow belt, this form centers on historic Prairie Indian tribal dress styles, including cloth shirts, wool leggings, vests, and breechclouts, often heavily adorned with strips of colorful appliqué ribbonwork and curvilinear, often floral beadwork, crossed bandoliers of beads, a porcupine hair roach or otter fur turban, an otter fur trailer, and German silver jewelry. The Fancy Dance, attributed to Gus MacDonald (Ponca), began around 1915.

The more western tribes (Kiowa, Cheyenne, Arapaho, Comanche, Apache) maintained a different form. Originally, a somewhat conservative Southern and Western Plains style was emphasized, with fringed and painted hide clothing, minimal beadwork, a basic toe-heel choreography, and a limited number of bustles. This form, without bustles, would later become the western Oklahoma style of the Straight Dance. The Cheyenne and Arapaho continued using heavily beaded items of dance regalia. After the introduction of the Fancy Dance among the Kiowa in 1917, that form developed into an increasingly elaborate version marked by individual embellishment through the enhancement of acrobatic spins, turns, and quivering shoulder movements. Accompanying this dance style was the development of individual feathered waist, shoulder, and arm bustles, matching harnesses of beadwork, and roaches. By the 1920s the Fancy Dance was emerging in several forms with developments in bustles, headdresses, flapper clothing, dance styles, and other accouterments. Although it was primarily a man's dance, some younger women have Fancy danced since the 1930s. Other Western Plains tribes such as the Comanche and Plains Apache received the dance from the Ponca and Pawnee, respectively, and soon after 1917 adopted the Fancy Dance form. Although the Comanche and Plains Apache obtained the Omaha Dance from Prairie tribes, it evolved to look more like the dance of their Western Plains neighbors. The mixing of the Omaha and Drum Dance complexes resulted in a new form that, although originating in earlier military society complexes, evolved into a new dance form that became the Oklahoma-style powwow.

As Plains tribes were forced onto reservations, they were quickly subjected to government efforts to eradicate their principal religious ceremonies. Policies were implemented in 1888 to end the Sun Dance, and later, to suppress social ceremonies such as society and intertribal dances. Enforcement varied, partly because of the extent of control the Bureau of Indian Affairs (BIA) could exert over a specific tribe. In 1902 the commissioner of Indian affairs issued the first of several edicts forbidding dancing. Viewing dances as detrimental to Indian development and assimilation, Indian Agency personnel intensified their efforts to stop dancing and its associated giveaways by threats, withholding of rations and annuities, freezing of bank accounts, and forcing of individuals to sign affidavits promising not to dance (see Kracht 1989:820–875; Meadows 1999:113–126). In 1921, Commissioner Charles H. Burke's Circular 1665, entitled "Indian Dancing," sanctioned both persuasive and punitive coercive measures against Indians in situations where dances were found to be "harmful" or "degrading." The basis of judgment clearly lay with the local Indian agents.

Several new arenas for Indian dancing emerged simultaneously in the late 1800s, further spreading the Omaha Dance. Following the Civil War, numerous "medicine shows" emerged, featuring sales of Indian and other medicinal remedies. Continuing until World War I, these spectacles toured the country advertising "real live Indians." They often included dramatic parades, exhibitions of "War Dances," and other aspects of the "Wild West." As Browner (2002:28) noted, although Indian dances were already a common form of entertainment, their incorporation with powwow doctors in medicine shows led to the association of the term *powwow* with the concept of Indian dancing. By the 1880s, some Indians began holding their own intertribal "Indian Medicine shows" across the Midwest without Anglo powwow doctors.

Many dances had to be conducted in secret or practiced in forms that the BIA had little ability to control, such as dancing at Wild West and medicine shows, county fairs, and exhibitions. Run by Anglo entrepreneurs, these venues were not subject to BIA policy and offered avenues in which Plains and other Indians could legally dance and earn incomes in an otherwise largely impoverished time. Between 1876 and 1930 Indians were actively sought out and hired to dance in Wild West shows, Fourth of July celebrations, traveling carnivals, fairs, exhibitions, and community gatherings. Performances ranged from international events such as the 1876 Centennial Celebration, the 1893 Chicago Columbian Exposition, the 1898 Omaha Exhibition, and the 1904 St. Louis World's Fair to the Wild West shows of William F. "Buffalo Bill" Cody and Pawnee Bill Lillie, the Miller Brothers' 101 Ranch Real Wild West Show, and Ringling Brothers, Barnum and Bailey Circus. More local and annual performances included those held at the Indian International Fair, Haskell Indian School, Dietrich's Lake, the Craterville Indian Fair (1924–1933), and the American Indian Exposition (1934–). The popularity of seeing Indian cultures led in part to the 1898 Omaha Exhibition, in which the U.S. government first sanctioned and funded Indians' performances (Browner 2002:29).

By 1890, fifty such shows were in existence, and between 1890 and 1917, nearly one hundred such shows were on the road annually (Ellis 2003:16, 95). The Omaha Dance was the primary style of dance being performed at rodeos, fairs, and other public events. In tribal communities, dances continued under the guise of homecomings, picnics, and celebrations. Dancing allowed Indian a means to continue activities focused on themes such as the warrior ethos, singing, and dancing that were both largely traditional and still important to them. Dancing also provided Indians with a means to flaunt government opposition in a nonviolent manner, with much-needed income for some as reservation economies and living conditions worsened because of legislative changes and economic shortages, and with opportunities for travel, adventure, and a reprieve from reservation conditions. Influenced by the popular image of the "vanishing Indian," curious non-Indians flocked to see the colorful and exotic performances, including "War Dances" from the recently conquered Wild West. National Park programs, early movies, and the adoption of Indian dancing and cultural themes by the Boy Scouts and the Order of the Arrow only spread the interest in Indian dancing (Ellis 2003).

Accompanying this evolution was a gradual shift from a more martially oriented ideology to a more pan-tribal one focused on widely shared values and Native constructs of tribal and Indian identity. Participation in dance societies and public dances in the form of powwows became a major means of emphasizing and maintaining ideas of family, community, sodality, faith, and culture on both the tribal and intertribal levels. In a time of tremendous cultural change, dancing provided important cultural forms that were familiar to participants. The transformation from military societies to tribal and intertribal powwows reinforced Indian identity by maintaining many traditions, including song, dance, prayer, social gatherings, feasting, generosity through giveaways, and prayerful and reflective aspects, in a form that was less threatening to whites than were some other traditions. The maintenance of traditional clothing, now primarily for use in dances and powwows, evolved into new tribal and regional styles that linked people to their past. Special regalia, dance, and songs, especially those with texts, continued as symbols of past tribal and martial heritage. The incorporation of numerous types of songs (Flag, Veterans, Scalp and Victory, Memorial, Round Dance), the public recognition of bravery, sacrifice, and service to one's people, and the celebration and commemoration of martial service and a warrior ethos—essentially equating pre-reservation warrior status with contemporary military service—continue as key foci in contemporary honor dances and powwows. As William Powers (2001:33) described it: "Nowhere else do we witness the full significance of these persistent symbols of fearless deeds in battle and accolades to the returning heroes than in the songs, dances, and attendant ceremonies related to what I call the continuing warrior tradition."

Strong anti-dance measures taken by the Bureau of Indian Affairs continued until shortly after World War I, when the widespread revival of dances to honor returning servicemen forced some agents to acquiesce. In 1926 the first large, intertribal, off-reservation powwow organized by Indians was held at Haskell Institute in Lawrence, Kansas. Indian Commissioner Burke failed to recognize that dances could hold both social and spiritual meanings, and his attendance at this dance implied that whereas "dancing for the entertainment of a white audience was acceptable, dancing for the purpose of religion on the reservation was not" (Browner 2002:30).

Sanctioned performances allowed Indian traditions such as singing and dancing to gain acceptability in American culture, even if they were largely relegated to forms of entertainment from an Anglo perspective. They also fostered broader intertribal exchanges and friendships and promoted modern Indian intertribalism. Whether performed in societal or entertainment contexts, dancing assumed an increasingly secular nature as part of a larger, evolving, pan-Plains dance culture. Often labeled "War Dance," the Omaha or Grass Dance was the form of Plains Indian dance most popularized by Wild West shows, which tended to hire young Indian men from Plains tribes, most of whom were already dancers. Through these public venues, the popularity and prevalence of the War Dance continued to grow among Indians and non-Indians alike from the late 1880s through the 1930s and beyond (Ellis 2002:48). As Christopher Glazner described it:

> By the turn of the twentieth century, the war dance under its various names had become a way to remember the actions of warriors after fighting on the Plains stopped and the opportunity to win war honors was no longer available. Over time, as the generation who had last seen combat grew older, many of the requirements of the societies grew lax; certain badges of office or articles reserved for warriors who had demonstrated specific heroic deeds began to be worn indiscriminately by most dancers who participated at the dances. Due to the dance's popularity, the requirement for war honors was relaxed entirely until eventually all men were welcomed to dance the Grass Dance.

While a few older Southern Plains military societies experienced brief revivals just before and after World War I, the Omaha Dance continued to flourish on two levels—in society contexts as annual ceremonials and in public contexts at powwows and as paid performances. Despite Indian Agency efforts to suppress dancing and giveaways, ceremonial, intertribal, and commercial dancing continued, and some tribes managed to establish tribal powwows in the 1920s. By 1925, many Indian dances were organized and controlled by Indians themselves and were beginning to be called powwows by both Indians and non-Indians. By the late 1920s, some of these Indian-sponsored dances had become annual events, such as the Ponca Powwow and the Haskell Powwow (Ellis 2003:119–121). Thus a parallel development of Indian dancing took place. Changing but still relatively conservative men's societies, focused on Omaha Society dances, continued in one direction, and varied forms of more public performances evolved to become the powwow by the 1930s (Ellis 2003:103–105).

The legalization of Indian religious ceremonies under the Indian Reorganization Act of 1934 changed the primary purpose of the powwow. While some War Dance societies continued to hold discrete ceremonials, by 1942 powwows, some of which had formerly been held to entertain non-Indians, shifted to being intertribal gatherings focused on Indian communities that wanted to honor outgoing and incoming servicemen. Increased numbers of honor dances in tribal communities during World War II and the Korean War and ongoing social dances and powwows in urban areas helped foster the revival of warrior societies and dancing in general. After World War II these events evolved into the modern form of the Plains powwow, which includes music, dance, parades (grand entries), contest dances, specialty dances, and spiritual overtones. The emergence of post–World War II powwow clubs and dances in urban areas filled some of the cultural void created with Indian relocation during the 1950s and 1960s. The modern powwow is an amalgam of military society dances featuring the Omaha Dance, Plains and Great Lakes ceremonials (the Calumet and Midewiwin ceremonies and the Drum or Dream Dance), reservation-era intertribal dances, Wild West and medicine shows, Fourth of July celebrations, paid exhibitions, World War I and II honor dances (sendoffs and homecomings) for veterans, and their postwar derivatives.

As Ellis (2002:14–15) observed, although powwows are derivative of society dances, many people participate in both forms, and the two kinds of events continue to influence each other in terms of songs, regalia, and traditions. Both societies and powwows continue to be associated with traditional tribal practices, purposes, and values, with tribal classifications of status, prestige, and power (Ellis 2002:24), and with an overall, collectively shared ideology, ethos, and associated symbols (Meadows 1999:24). To understand how these two distinct yet related dance traditions continue to evolve, it is necessary to remember that the relationship between the two forms is ongoing and that in some respects, "in its form, function, and history as a shared, pan-Plains phenomena, the contemporary powwow does not radically diverge from patterns and habits that were deeply established long before the powwow emerged" (Ellis 2002:24). Powwows also resemble military societies in that they provide structure, hierarchy, and a sense of shared ethnic identity, and as arenas of enculturation they aid in creating, maintaining, modifying, and revitalizing cultural values and practices that can serve as "cultural mooring posts" (Ellis 2001:25). Indeed, many of the ideals originating in military societies continue in similar or modified forms in the contemporary powwow.

The Kiowa Omaha Society and the Southern Plains Powwow

The eventual link between the Omaha Society dance and the modern powwow is that as the powwow burgeoned, the style of music associated with War Dance societies was quickly adapted to the Straight and Fancy Dances and became popular in nonsociety powwow contexts. In Kiowa powwows, the foundation for this genre of music and dance comes from the Omaha Society. Like Ponca Hethushka Society songs, Kiowa War Dance and Omaha Society songs, especially those without words, are now commonly used in the intertribal powwow.

The Kiowa Omaha Society was one of many tribal contributions to the larger, regionally diverse spread of the War Dance and powwow and was affected by many internal and external factors. As happened in other tribes, the Kiowa Omaha Society influenced the Kiowa and other powwows in several ways. First, it was the basis for the adoption of the widely diffused Omaha-Grass-War Dance among the Kiowa. Second, many of the active dancers who were being hired for commercial entertainment were members of this type of society. Third, as these dancers created new and more elaborate styles of dance, music and dress, such as the Fancy Dance and contest songs and dances, they incorporated elements of these changes into their local dance societies while performing them in external and nonsocietal contexts for increasingly commercial and intertribal social purposes. Thus two separate yet intermingled and to some degree mutually influential traditions have continued to evolve simultaneously.

Even as the Kiowa Omaha Society changed, it retained many ritual elements of its original structure, including an emphasis on recognizing a Kiowa social and warrior ideology and ethos from the past as constituted in newer forms under modern circumstances. It also became an important arena for displaying status and prestige through membership, leadership, skill in dancing and singing, the making of dance clothing, and the giveaway. As Regina Flannery (1947:65) noted among the Gros Ventre: "As the younger men had no chance to show their prowess in warfare and hunting there was a change of emphasis to recognition of superior singing and dancing ability as one of the roads to public approval." Although the spread of the War Dance hastened the decline of many older military societies across the plains (Meadows 1999:382–384), it also continued many forms of their martial ideology and material culture while fostering an increasing frequency of singing and dancing. Once warrior status was widely regained during World War II and the Korean War, this relationship helped to revive several men's societies.

During the late 1800s and early 1900s, many Indians maintained a strong desire to continue dancing. As a part of its larger goal of assimilation, the United States government undertook considerable efforts to suppress dancing but found itself without a legal basis to continue its efforts. At the same time, local entrepreneurs were eager to hire Indians for myriad entertainment purposes, and non-Indians were eager to pay to watch them perform. Many Indians found this arrangement useful as a means to earn income and travel. In turn, local Indian agents gradually acquiesced to increasing requests to participate in and or hold dances in order to gain bargaining power for achieving other reservation and post-allotment period goals. The Omaha Dance facilitated the continuation of many Plains and military society customs involving ideology (benevolence, generosity), the martial ethos (acknowledging military service, honoring veterans, emphasizing courage, self-sacrifice, and service), material culture (roach headdresses, bustles, otter hide breastplates and draggers, scalp feathers, war bonnets), and symbolism (acting out war deeds in dance; parading in ceremonies and powwows, much like past military society parades at the Sun Dance) (see Ellis 2003). With the growth of dancing and a focus on the War Dance, many Omaha Society and earlier Kiowa cultural forms were easily transferred to the emerging powwow.

Among groups adopting the Grass Dance, it is perhaps the ability to be flexible that best explains the dance's growth. For the Lakota, James Howard (1951:85) wrote, "This is probably one of the reasons this dance has survived while other ceremonials, far more important but less flexible, have through their very elaborateness and difficulty of performance, been dropped by the tribe." Concerning the secularization of the Grass Dance among the Lakota, Duncan (1997:79) also noted that the flexibility of the dance was largely responsible for its survival: "By 1900, the Grass Dance had changed from its original form among the Lakota Sioux, the societies were defunct, and the dance was primarily social.... The Grass Dance occupied a unique position in that it changed along with the rest of Lakota culture." Many of the same factors similarly affected the Ponca Hethushka and War Dance during the early twentieth century (Duncan 1997:80). It is the display of high esteem in which the society is held and the persistence in adapting and moving forward that reflects the spirit of the society, the Óhòmò Road, and what the original society traditions symbolize and hold for the Kiowa.

The Omaha Society is of great ethnological and historical interest to Plains Indian communities and scholars for three reasons. First, it was the last and best-documented nineteenth-century military society to diffuse across the Great Plains. Second, it was the origin of the later forms of the War Dance that spread to most Plains and Prairie tribes. Third, the society's dance represents a primary ancestral form that evolved into the modern powwow. As widely diffused phenomena, at least six identifiable levels or manifestations of the society exist that essentially demonstrate its evolution: (1) the original Pawnee Iruska Society, (2) the Omaha version of the society, (3) various diffused and altered society forms among individual Plains and Prairie tribes, (4) individual tribal-oriented powwows that evolved from distinct tribal War Dance societies, (5) larger, pan-tribal Plains powwows and contest powwows in more urban contexts, and (6) powwows adopted and performed by non-Indians.

Among the Kiowa, the Omaha Society has seen the evolution of three periods of distinct dress and dance. The first involved the use of large quantities of traditional Kiowa and Cheyenne clothing (wool and buckskin leggings, shirts, feathered bonnets), large quantities of Cheyenne beadwork on moccasins, legging strips, and vests, and a conservative and "upright" form of dance that is most accurately described as the Western Plains Indian form of the early Straight Dance, although as a category this name developed with the widespread emergence of powwows after the Korean War. This form was common from 1884 to the mid-1920s. The second period, which can be called the Fancy Dance period, began in 1917 and continues to the present. It included the emergence and use of individual bustles and other ornamentation associated with Fancy dancing, which dominated the dress and dance style of the Kiowa Omaha Society, although a few older people adhered to the previous style. Both the dress and dance of this form became more distinct and elaborate in the 1940s and again in the 1960s. The third period, which began in the 1970s, overlaps with the Fancy Dance period and also continues today. It can be called the Oklahoma Straight Dance period. The increasing use of Ponca- and Osage-style Straight Dance clothing, which emphasizes wool clothing with heavy ribbonwork decoration, and an increase

Stephen Mopope, Ohoma Society member and one of the Kiowa Five artists, in Fancy Feather–style dress, about 1950. Courtesy Vanessa Jennings.

in the lower and more "bent over" dance style of the northeastern Prairie tribes characterize this period.

Elders often voice the criticism that Ohoma members no longer dress and dance as they once did—originally and later as Fancy Dancers. Although true, these comments reflect the length of their life experiences while demonstrating the value of a more teleological approach in examining the entire evolution of a cultural form through anthropology and ethnohistory.

The Kiowa Omaha Society is also significant in demonstrating how a late-diffused society was adapted to the older military society system, contributed to the cessation of and superseded the older societies, continued into the present, and now functions on a supportive and noncompetitive co-hosting basis with the Kiowa Gourd Clan and the Kiowa Black Legs Society. The Omaha Society also serves several other functions similar to those of the other Kiowa men's societies. Although less so than the Black Legs, the Kiowa Omaha Society continues to honor veterans and maintain martial themes in surviving elements of the society's original organization, initiations, songs, use of war bonnets and the bustle, and certain dances. As one of the three major, active Kiowa men's societies, it holds a major ceremonial and is the origin of Kiowa War, Straight, and Fancy dancing. Society activities continue to provide an enculturative arena that fosters the maintenance and continuation of numerous sociocultural and religious forms of both the traditional Omaha Society (now the Ohoma Lodge) and Kiowa culture. These include song, dance, language, oral history, religion, cedaring, communal camping, kinship, generosity, and ethics. The society remains a distinct cultural form that integrates sizable segments of the Kiowa and neighboring tribes through membership, intermarriage, and co-hosting activities. It provides a unique form of ideology, the Óhòmò Road, and ethnic identity that is known on both Kiowa and intertribal levels.

9

KIOWA WOMEN'S SOCIETIES

During the second half of the nineteenth century, two Kiowa women's societies existed: the Calf Old Women and the Bear Women or Bear Old Women. Both were closely related to warfare and war power, serving largely as auxiliaries to Kiowa warriors, as sources of supernatural protection, and as charitable organizations. They functioned until around 1905. During World War II, three new Kiowa women's organizations formed to recognize Kiowa servicemen: the Kiowa War Mothers, the Carnegie Victory Club, and the Stecker Purple Heart Club. A fourth, the Kiowa Veterans Auxiliary, formed in 1958. These organizations continue to honor Kiowa veterans according to tribal tradition by helping to sponsor major tribal military society ceremonials, performing Scalp and Victory Dances, taking part in philanthropic activities to assist veterans, and enculturating younger Kiowa in traditional gender roles and ceremonial activities.

Although scholars have long recognized warfare as a significant part of historic Plains Indian cultures, they have tended to focus primarily on men's roles. It is well documented that women held important roles in supporting the military activities of men, especially through the holding of Scalp, Victory, and various social dances upon the successful return of a predominantly male raiding or war party (Grinnell 1910, 1983 [1915]:10–12, 20–22; Foreman 1954; Lowie 1982:106–107; Lang 1998). That women from many Native American cultures participated in warfare is less well known but is recorded in a small but growing body of literature. Their participation involved a variety of roles, including to encourage the men, carry medicine bundles, serve as camp administrators and cooks, serve as medicinal practitioners or healers (Lang 1998:176–178, 303–304), and look after the group's horses. In other instances women participated in attacks on other groups and in the defense of their own villages. The actions of some warrior women were dream or vision based, and instances of their success as warriors and war leaders are known (Lang 1998:304).

Recent literature has reassessed most aspects of Plains Indian women's lives, amply demonstrating that some Indian women, generally referred to by the term *warrior women*, periodically and in some cases regularly participated in raiding and warfare

(Foreman 1954; Albers and Medicine 1983; Lang 1998). Although data on some aspects of women's roles are limited and classifications often overlap, Sabine Lang (1998:306–308, 342–353) identified four types of alternative gender roles among pre-reservation Native American women. Female gender role crossing was more common than complete gender role change. In contrast to men-women—women who tended to follow male roles—"female warriors were generally women who strove for masculine prestige without giving up their gender status" (Lang 1998:303). That is, the transition of warrior women to more male roles involved temporary and periodic gender role changes that were generally warfare based. The correlation between social status, honor, and accomplishments in the male-dominated sphere of warfare and raiding permeated Plains cultures. Although fewer women than men pursued status in this domain, it nevertheless provided important opportunities to increase one's position in a culture in which martial success demonstrated the power of one's personal medicine and bravery and garnered social approval from both sexes. Whereas warrior women generally maintained feminine roles, including those of wives and mothers, the transition from feminine to masculine roles by men-women was generally a complete gender transition (Lang 1998:305–307).

Examples or warrior women are known among various Plains (Blackfeet, Cree, Crow, Ojibwa, Piegan), Southeast (Cherokee, Choctaw), Southwest (Apache, Navajo), Plateau (Klamath, Kutenai), Northwest Coast (Nootka, Tlingit), Great Lakes (Santee Dakota, Ottawa), and other Native populations (Lowie 1922:341, 364; Foreman 1954; Medicine 1983; Buchanan 1986; Ewers 1997:191–204; Martín 1997; Lang 1998; Perdue 1998:38–39; Aleshire 2001). Katherine Osburn (1998:22) described Ute women fighting alongside men in defensive engagements and a Ute women's auxiliary warrior sodality that helped redistribute goods procured during raids. This group had its "own songs and a victory dance, done with a lame step to symbolize a heavy load of spoils." Using a worldwide sample organized by region, David Jones (2000) examined women's martial roles. His account of the varied and vital roles performed by women in different forms of warfare counters the notion that only men are capable of participating in or assuming leadership positions in combat. Using numerous case studies from legends, historical incidents, and contemporary examples, his work chronicles female martial history, a largely neglected subject necessary to understanding the participation of both sexes in warfare.

Accounts of Plains warrior women date from 1751 to the beginning of the reservation period (about 1875–1890 for the last autonomous populations) and range from Texas to Canada. Accounts include the Arapaho, Arikara, Assiniboine, Blackfeet, Blood, Cheyenne, Comanche, Cree, Crow (involving a Gros Ventre captive), Eastern Dakota, Kiowa, Lakota, Ojibwa, Pend d'Oreille, Piegan, and Wichita (Medicine 1983; Ewers 1997; Lang 1998). At least three accounts of Kiowa women accompanying their husbands on raids or fighting alongside them are known. The fighting abilities of Big Bow and his wife were recorded on the Kiowa Battle Picture Tipi (Ewers 1978:16). Wilbur Nye (1962:95, 227–232) reported two other accounts, one involving the wife of Iseeo (the uncle of the later well-known scout), who accompanied him on a raid into Mexico in 1853, and a second involving Atah, who joined a party of thirty-seven men to avenge the death of her husband. An account involving two Comanche women wounded during a raid that later resulted in the formation of the Comanche Tuhwi Society has also been recorded (Meadows 1999:353).

Whereas much early literature focused on Plains Indian men's military societies (Wissler, ed., 1916), little attention was given to women's societies, which were fewer and typically more secretive. Because of this secretiveness, relatively few people in Native communities had knowledge of the women's societies' roles and activities that they might convey to ethnographers. Although no evidence concerning raiding or combat by any Plains women's society is known to exist, these groups actively performed other types of sodality-based functions associated with warfare and raiding, some of which have been revived and continue in modified form to the present. Brief scholarly works on Indian tribal chapters of the American War Mothers have been produced for the Northern Cheyenne (Anderson 1956) and the Otoe-Missouri (Schweitzer 1981, 1983).

Two nineteenth-century Kiowa women's societies that were closely related to warfare and war power were the Xálı̨chǫ̨hı̨̀ (Calf Old Woman) or Xálı̨chǫ̨hyòp (Calf Old Women) and the Ą̀unhádèmàimàu (Bear Women) or Sétchǫ̨hyòp (Bear Old Women). Both societies were founded after men seeking power dreamed of them. The Kiowa Bear Women Society is reported to have been formed later than the Calf Old Women.[1] Accounts from Kiowa elders in the mid-1930s indicate that the two women's societies were related to the men's organizations differently. In 1935, Old Lady Horse told Weston La Barre that

> the Bear Society is to be collated [correlated] with the Ten Medicine Society, and the Tsadlsonhyop with the men's societies with regard to number of leaders and several ritual points. But the members do not have pouches or medicines. However, they are like the Ten Medicine men in some ways, for instance a man would go to an individual bear member in a winter camp to get her to pray for him at war "so he can shine" at the next sundance.[2]

Jane Richardson reported that "there was a vague feeling that the Taime, [the] sun, and the Calf Old Women's Society comprised a male centered complex, so were more closely associated with men; [while] the bear, the Ten [Medicine] bags and [the] Bear Society were more associated with women." Alice Marriott also noted the latter association in her fieldwork.[3]

According to Kintadl, women obtained dą́udą́u, or supernatural power, through initiation into one of the two women's societies. Bear Society power was derived from the bear and the Ten Medicine Bundles. Although the concentration of power was tenfold or greatest during meetings, when all members were present, the power of the whole society was also apparently transferable through a single member.[4] There are indications that members of a women's society and their relatives worked collectively in preparing hides and constructing tipis. The Bear Women were noted for their unusual skill in tanning hides.[5] Unlike in some other tribes, transvestites are reported never to have belonged to the Kiowa women's societies.[6]

Adding to the paucity of ethnographic attention given to Plains women's societies is the fact that most early American anthropologists were male, which limited their degree of interaction with female consultants and led them to collect information largely from other men. As Robert Lowie noted at an early date, this resulted in a male-biased view of Plains Indian cultures. Many Plains women's societies were also smaller than the men's, more secretive, and thus more difficult to obtain information about. Prior to the Laboratory of Anthropology field school and Alice Marriott's fieldwork in the 1930s, scanty data had been collected on Kiowa women's societies. Although enough data exist to provide a general picture of the Calf Old Women Society, less is known concerning the Bear Women, whose membership was smaller and whose rituals were more secretive.

The Calf Old Women Society

The Calf Old Women or Calf Old Woman Society was associated with war power. Although the date of the society's origin is unknown, Atah (b. 1855) stated that her great-grandmother had been the society leader, possibly placing the group's existence into at least the late 1700s.[7] One of Marriott's consultants, however, indicated that the society was of relatively recent origin and was founded by a man who had received instructions to do so during a vision quest. According to Piatonma, the name of the society was a play on words meaning either "old woman calf" or "mothers-in-law." The former name is thought to have been associated with the liveliness of the members' dancing. According to Jerrold Levy (2001:912), the society served as a counterpart to the men's societies and was considered to be equal in status to the Jáifègàu. The Calf Old Women were associated with the ability to provide war power, so men frequently made vows to the society for various purposes. Because its primary function was to ensure martial success, it may be viewed as a women's auxiliary military society.

Vows, which resulted in the sponsoring of a meeting, were made for three primary purposes: to ensure success in warfare, to ensure a safe return from a war journey, and to give thanks for recovery from an illness. Individual men frequently sponsored society meetings before setting out on a war journey so that the society could pray for his success and health. A father might vow to sponsor a feast for the society upon the safe return of his son. A man might say, "Take this pipe. The next time I go on the warpath I want to be successful. I want to live to an old age and if I marry, may my children do so too." He might say, "If I am successful, and get a scalp, I will give a feast to the Old Women." Vows were occasionally made in nonmilitary situations, such as when a man dreamed of the society, or during a Sun Dance, when a man might pray to the society and pledge to feast its members at the next Sun Dance.

Although Mary Buffalo indicated that meetings could be held at any time, including winter, meetings were generally held during the Sun Dance period to facilitate the attendance of all members. As in the men's societies, meetings were announced and the women called to gather by a crier. The "pledge"—the man who had made the vow and sponsored the meeting—sat to the left of the lodge door, lit a pipe, and passed it to his left to the society leader, who prayed for his longevity. After smoking the pipe, the leader passed it around to the other members to smoke. Those who did not wish to smoke are said to have pretended to do so. The sponsor of the feast then set out on a war journey. Upon his successful return, the man called the society together again, lit a pipe, and presented it to the members. Each member again smoked in turn, praying for the warrior's longevity and honor. Members of the returning war party then brought water to the society members, who drank it and prayed again. When food was brought, the war party leader recited his deeds. Before eating, one of the society leaders cut a piece of each type of food present, buried it in the ground, and prayed over it (Lowie 1916b:849–850).[8]

Men also made vows for the safe return of their sons from war journeys or in thanksgiving for the recovery of a son, daughter, mother, or grandmother from an illness. These vows were made to induce the society to pray for the individual and to show the society the father's gratitude for his relative's recovery.[9] Although anyone could vow to sponsor a meeting, mostly men sought out the society for blessings or relief from sickness. If a medicine man failed to cure someone, the family might pray to the spirit of the Calf Old Women's Society, for it was believed that it was not the actual society but its collective spirit that healed a person.[10] Once, when Jack Sankadota was sick, his grandmother suggested that he go to a meeting of the society, to which his parents took him. When he entered the lodge, the women gave out a war whoop, sang, and then smoked a pipe. Sankadota proceeded from the southeast corner of the lodge to each member, who, being too old to stand up easily, rubbed the lower portions of his body. His family then presumably feasted the society.[11]

The majority of society members were elderly. The ages recorded for nineteen members during a meeting, counting clockwise, were 85, 81, 79, 78, 84, 60, 80, 84, 60, 80, 86, 82, 20–30, 30, 62, 62, 74, 50, and 40.[12] According to Kintadl, whose mother was the society leader, most women joined between the ages of sixty and sixty-five. However, one young girl named Stealing Horses From Another Tribe (Tsekonhyo) was inducted at the age of fourteen after her father pledged that she would join the society if she recovered from an illness. Because a vow had been made, the society could not refuse her admission. This case appears to have been an exception to the general rule for membership.[13] Lowie (1916b:849) stated that membership was by invitation to women who had given at least four public feasts, suggesting that members were from prominent families who were financially able to sponsor such gatherings.

Society membership was cross-band in composition and appears to have been inherited matrilineally. Mary Buffalo provided a list of nineteen, and later twenty-three, members. Lowie's inquiries (1916b:849) produced estimates of thirty-five to forty members. Membership was clearly dominated by particular family lines. Eight of nineteen members in Mary Buffalo's list were related to the informant, and at least two other members not related to her were related to other society members.[14]

Membership also appears to have been somewhat fixed, because a member's replacement was generally her oldest living direct female descendant. Mrs. Tenedooah stated that the order of preference in choosing a replacement was that of daughter, granddaughter, sister, and sister's daughter. There are also indications of inheritance of membership from a maternal aunt by a niece. Mary Buffalo gave similar statements. Kintadl, however, said that there was no daughter preference in the selection of new members. Despite the society's name, a member who became too old to participate was often succeeded by a young female relative in a manner perhaps resembling the retirement and occasional replacement of older members by their sons in the men's societies. Nevertheless, there is much to suggest that membership was held within a set number of specific lineages and was not always limited to elderly women. Several examples illustrate the tendency to maintain hereditary lines and induct younger women. In one case a granddaughter was inducted because the member's daughter was already deceased, and in another a member's eldest great-granddaughter was chosen to succeed her. One girl was known to have inherited membership in the society at the age of nineteen. Upon the death of the drum keeper, the position was filled by a female descendant of the deceased society leader and not by any of the elderly members already familiar with the ceremony.[15]

Mrs. Tenedooah (Saioma) indicated that membership in the society was decided by three women—two who sat on the west side of the tipi, each with a pipe, and one who sat beside the lodge door and suggested names.[16] This resembles the structure of Kiowa men's societies, in which two society leaders sat on the west side of the tipi while a whipman sat on either side of the lodge door. A seating schedule obtained from Mary Buffalo also demonstrates that two elder members sat on the west side of the society lodge. These descriptions suggest that the two women were the society leaders, because of their seating position and their custodianship of pipes.

The method used to induct new members also resembled that of the men's societies. Two women wearing buffalo hides inside-out approached a chosen inductee with a pipe, and upon touching it, she was obligated to join. Returning to the society tipi, the members passed the pipe around four times and smoked. Because the contents of the ceremony were reportedly well known outside of the society and were easily learned, there was no formal training period for new members. Unlike the Bear Women Society, the Calf Old Women Society had few secretive characteristics.[17] Instructions were then given for the procedures for prayer and dance. No special meetings were held for initiating members, which implies that new members were inducted during vowed meetings. Upon joining, the new member was required to give a substantial number of horses and quantities of bedding, dresses, and moccasins to the older members, again suggesting that members were from wealthy lineages that could afford such lavish giveaways.[18]

According to Levy (2001:912), the large initiation fee restricted membership to women of ôdè (affluent or aristocratic) status. Sangko also noted that only wealthy persons could belong to the society.[19] When Sun Dance Woman (Qáujómà) was initiated, she was brought to the society lodge, where she had to remain seated and silent until her female relatives came to give away a large quantity of horses, blankets, shawls and other goods in her honor. The two society leaders then rubbed their hands over the goods, themselves, and the initiate four times. Taking the pipe from her, they told her that she was free to move and talk, because she was now a member (Parsons 1929:96).

According to the accounts of elders, the exact order of activities during meetings varied, but the general sequence seems to have been smoking, being incensed with sage or cedar, singing, dancing, ritual running to four symbolic poles outside the lodge, more dancing, feasting, and finally more smoking and praying. Variations in accounts seem to derive from a dichotomy between descriptions of ceremonies performed when a man sponsored a meeting and descriptions of procedures for initiating new members. Meetings lasted from the morning through mid-afternoon, requiring less than a day of preparation. Kom'tu sponsored the last meeting of the Calf Old Women Society around 1905. The man who had vowed the meeting supplied the tipi in which the society met. His female kin prepared the lodge by clearing all household items out of it, cleaning the floor, and building a fire in the center. No special type of wood was required for the fire, and no special types of medicine were placed in the lodge.[20]

The Calf Old Women Society met more frequently that the Bear Women because it received the majority of requests regarding war power and journeys.[21] The society was known to possess a form of medicinal power that younger, sexually active women did not have.[22] When questioned about this, Jimmy Quoetone said he believed that the society's supernatural power had no connection with menopause, because the old and young members had the same amount of power.[23] Unfortunately, no women were asked about this association. Although members could call a meeting of their own society, no instance was ever known in which a Bear Women Society member called a meeting of the Calf Old Women.[24]

Meetings

For meetings, the members of the society lined up in a specified order outside the lodge, facing west. Each woman had a specific seating position in the lodge, which again suggests membership along family lines. Without first feinting three times, as was the practice in some other groups, the head woman entered the lodge, proceeded around the fire on the south side and clockwise to the east, and then sat just north of the door. The other members then proceeded one by one until the last member, carrying a drum, was seated just south of the door. When all were seated, the society remained silent and motionless until the man who had pledged the meeting entered.

Walking in a half circle to the south and west, the pledge took the pipe from its keeper on the west side of the lodge, the usual position associated with honor, pipes, and medicine and religious bundles.[25]

The pledge filled the pipe with tobacco he had brought and handed a brand from the fire to the drum keeper (*fáuljòmà*), who lit the pipe. He then held the pipe with both hands while the drum keeper, holding the stem to her lips, drew four puffs from the pipe and blew them upward, offering the smoke and prayers to the sun. Between each draw on the pipe the man tilted the pipe vertically, with the stem pointing upward. The drum keeper took four more draws, blowing them in the direction in which some of the Ten Medicine Bundles were located in the camp. If the bundles were scattered throughout the camp, then the draws of smoke were blown to the extreme left, half left, half right, and finally extreme right of where she was seated.[26]

Each woman then repeated this procedure in turn, with the first woman to enter being the last to smoke. After cleaning the pipe, the pledge proceeded clockwise, returned the pipe to the keeper on the west side of the lodge, and proceeded to the north and east, where he exited. This was the only regular time when a man (as a pledge) participated in the ceremony. However, the society once had a single male member, and one account mentions the inclusion of a favored boy, who might have served as an errand boy as in the men's societies.[27]

With the next part of the meeting, I move to a sensitive topic and body of ethnological material. A sparse but widespread body of knowledge concerning ceremonial sexual intercourse, both actual and symbolic, exists for many pre-reservation Plains Indian groups. In his synthesis of Plains Indian age-graded societies, Lowie (1916a) discussed the transfer of spiritual power through sexual intimacy for a number of Plains Indian men's military society complexes. Often this involved relations between the wife of a new initiate and an elder instructor or ceremonial father, who transferred power to the younger man through relations with his wife. Alice Kehoe (1970) later examined this phenomenon, which appears to have originated among the Mandan-Hidatsa and then spread to the Arapaho, Blackfeet, and Atsina as a part of their age-graded men's society complexes. Rituals including sexual elements have also been documented as taking place between the priest and the pledge's wife in the Arapaho and Cheyenne Sun Dances (Dorsey 1903:172–176, 1905:130–131) and in the Cheyenne ritual of "putting a woman on the prairie" as payment for men's society induction or as an offering to a men's society as punishment for adultery. Sexually oriented rituals were also found in the Plains Apache women's Izuwe Society (Meadows 1999:449n3). Clearly, such rituals were once linked to the religious (Sun Dance) and sodality (military society) structures of several Plains cultures.

According to descriptions provided by several of the last Kiowa women's society members and tribal elders in the 1930s, Calf Old Women Society meetings included some sexual-symbolic elements that were conducted in ceremonial contexts. The association of Native American women with concepts of fertility, procreation, social integration, strength, and the honoring of martial achievements permeates many

Native American tribal ideologies. Although these belief systems are especially visible in matrilineal societies, they are also present in patrilineal societies. Similar data regarding sexual and seemingly secretive and antisocial behavior are also found for the Plains Apache Izuwe Society (Meadows 1999:219–220, 449n73) and for some societies with medicinal-curing functions, such as the Iroquois False Face and Husk Face Societies (Fenton 1987). Southern Cheyenne elders have also described related materials concerning nineteenth-century women's sodalities.

Topics of a sexual nature are considered offensive by current Kiowa standards, but elders forthrightly described them in the 1930s. In reading this material, several things should be kept in mind: the data were collected from tribal members and firsthand participants themselves; a comprehensive study of sexuality and its relationship to symbolic and ritual contexts in Plains Indian sodality structures has not been undertaken; and although one might not fully understand these customs from the perspective of current concepts of appropriate behavior and morality, they undoubtedly were once significant for those who practiced them.

At this point in society meetings, the drum keeper began to sing and drum while individuals or groups of women began to dance in a circular fashion, facing inward and taking short, sideways steps. The dancing was reported to have been obscene, and according to Mary Buffalo, the Calf Old Women "had no shame." Reference to obscene actions is a common theme associated with the society, especially in terms of song and dance. Mary Buffalo said, "The Old Ladies are too old to think about sex, so they are entitled to act obscenely." La Barre noted that after his consultant and interpreter realized that he was not squeamish about the discussion of sexual matters, she responded quite naturally and directly about them.[28] Society songs had lyrics such as the following:

> I hear my sweetheart got killed.
> I wish I were out there.
> I'd put him on my back [followed by ululations].

and

> They killed my sweetheart in a battle and
> I wish I had been there to pick him up and
> throw him on my back
> and carry him away from the battlefield.

After the society members had smoked the pledge's pipe and all were incensed with burning cedar, sage, or sweet grass, they ceased dancing and exited the lodge. They proceeded outside approximately one hundred feet east of the tipi, where four sticks representing enemy men were secured in the ground. The members then danced, sang, and drummed toward the sticks, running around them on the fourth song. As in the men's societies' race to the miniature tipi made of sticks that was held upon arriving at the final Sun Dance encampment, the first member to reach the sticks knocked them down and ran back yelling. This ritual represented the killing of an enemy and symbolized the society's war power, which it could transfer to others to protect them in warfare. Possession of such power was the reason the society was so well respected, prayed to, and sought for aid.

All the members were supposed to take part in society meetings, but some of the older ones might send a daughter to represent them at a dance. The pledge's family provided a feast at noon. The pledge did not attend. Members shared the food and took the excess home with them.[29]

Water was then brought in and served to the members by a young female known as the water girl, who was usually related to one of the members. Mary Buffalo served in this position after her mother, then a member of the society, vowed a meeting on behalf of her recovery from illness. Before serving the water, the water girl said, "I'll give the Old Ladies a drink if my daughter gets well," to which they replied, "Thank you," as she brought it in. Standing, the water girl bent over holding the vessel until each member drank as much as she wanted, similarly to the carrying of the pipe by a man.[30] At this time each Calf Old Woman performed a procedure known as "transmitting her age" to the water girl. Each member prayed for the girl and then, beginning with her head, rubbed her all over her body in a downward manner to her ankles. During this procedure members made suggestive sexual remarks and prayed that the girl would have children and a successful marriage. They then "transmitted their old age," ensuring the girl a long and prosperous life—the primary motive behind their prayers. Mary Buffalo stated that when she served as the water girl she became afraid and fought with the Calf Old Women, who instructed her not to resist. Prayers for success in work also appear to have been made. When the society offered prayers for Red Dress (Hóldàgúlmà, b. 1863) as a child, one of the members prayed, "I hope you will become a good tanner like I was when I was young, have strong arms and never get tired."[31] After the last woman finished, the girl went outside the lodge, where she drank and anointed herself with some of the water kept for this purpose.[32]

Any remaining water was given to people to drink and anoint themselves with, usually relatives of society members who were either sick or desired the blessing to ensure future good health. This redistribution also suggests an organizational basis centered on certain families. Portions of the water were given to the person who had pledged the meeting and sometimes to nearby people who were sick or who had returned from a war journey, which might include members of the pledge's war party.[33]

The pledge of the meeting then provided a feast in gratitude for the women's power, which ensured his safe return from a war journey or recovery from an illness. Approximately seven large buckets of food prepared by the pledge's female relatives were placed just inside the lodge door between the drum keeper and another woman seated just north of the door. Although the society's power was believed to be responsible in the event of an unfavorable outcome, no sanctions were reported if the outcome was negative.[34]

Society meals consisted mainly of meat with side dishes of mesquite beans, grapes, plums, and other delicacies, depending on the time of year. Beginning with the drum keeper, each member picked up a small piece of meat, held it in the air while praying, and then buried it in the ground. This meat was sacrificed to the earth (dáum), sometimes also addressed as Mother (Câu), just as the sun (pài) was also sometimes addressed as Father (Jâu) or God (Dàuqį́).[35]

Next, the head or north woman, who sat on the north side of the lodge door, served each society member in a clockwise fashion, placing the bowl of food before her. She in turn made four sacrifices by burying pieces of meat in the ground. Last, the head woman placed the bucket before herself and sacrificed. After this solemn ritual, additional rounds of food were passed around the lodge clockwise, and the members ate in an uninhibited and festive mood with a great deal of talking and joking. Leftovers were placed in containers brought by the members and taken home. Like the previously distributed water, this food was believed to hold medicinal power. Before any of the leftover food was given to children, a piece of it was held aloft, prayed over, and buried in the ground, just as in the meeting.[36]

According to Mary Buffalo, the Calf Old Women Society once had a male member who served as a worker for the society by gathering wood, building fires, and cleaning up. This person was considered to be "different" from other males but was said not to have been a transvestite, as a few men were in some Plains societies. This male society member took part in nearly all aspects of the ceremony but played a role different from that of the women in later portions of the ceremony. Upon his death, no replacement was taken in.[37]

The male member was said once to have interrupted the society's singing of the "sweetheart song" when he called for the drum and instructed the others to listen as he sang:

> When I was young, I copulate with first girl.
> Girl cry and cry when deflowered.
> She put her feet straight up toward smoke hole.

At this time the man was "ceremonially attacked" by the society members.[38] Accounts from elders in 1935 attest to this man's possibly having been mentally retarded and at least having been foolhardy. According to Quoetone, this was the only male member ever in the society, and the women members considered him "crazy."[39]

Quoetone thought the man's membership might have been because he had two "sweethearts" who were sisters in the society and by this time must have been fairly old. The man went to the two sisters and asked them to ask their mother for moccasins (which she presumable made for him) and their father for arrows for him. He took these items on a war journey and was wounded in a battle. Upon his return he composed the following comical song:

> I went to battle with my sweetheart's mother's moccasins.
> I got wounded, these moccasins were all bloody.

> I went to battle with my sweetheart's father's arrows.
> I shot and shot, they are still sticking out in the battlefield.

One of the sisters in turn composed the following song:

> My sweetheart went to battle.
> He was wounded out there.
> I wish I were out there to rescue him.
> I would put him on my back and carry him to a safe place.[40]

Much of the society's seemingly obscene aspect may have been related to warfare, gender relations, and changes in age-status roles that were acted out in symbolic and ritualized fashion during society ceremonials. The large number of ceremonial traits focused on warfare themes and the "ceremonial attack" of the man by the female society members suggest the presence of a larger body of ritual behavior related to warfare and gender themes. The relatively greater freedom postmenopausal Plains women enjoyed in terms of female roles and actions concerning behavior, status, and the acquisition and use of medicine might also be related to these rituals. Cross-culturally, the presence of what would normally be considered antisocial behavior of a shocking nature in ritual forms is not uncommon, as in the sexual license of some Plains Indian men's military societies and the Cherokee Booger Dance.

Public Dancing and other Activities

Following the ceremonial portion of the meeting, members sometimes left the lodge to dance outside again, "with no shame." With their skirts lifted, members engaged in a variety of obscene remarks and actions. In 1935 Mary Buffalo demonstrated this dance for Weston La Barre. It referred to the absence of a young man (a son) who had lived with another tribe for a long time, in this case the Comanche. The dance consisted of a slow, circular, shuffling step. When the point nearest the Comanche camp was reached, the members raised their skirts in that direction, exposing themselves. The dance of the Calf Old Women involved the lifting of the right leg in a "staccato" movement that, although the women were old and slow, was supposed to imitate the movement of a frisky, limber young deer. A song was sung during which a deer call (ma . . . ma . . .) was given on each deerlike step (later said to have been given only four times) to cause the son to return, perhaps symbolically, to his mother and thus home, as quickly as a deer travels. This dance symbolized the society's focus on ensuring longevity and protection. According to an account collected by Hugh Scott in the 1890s, the groups danced in a circular fashion to the left (clockwise) while holding hands.[41]

During these outside dances, "everyone" was said to have watched and had a good time. Men watched but did not participate. Society members wore their best clothes, consisting of the black dresses with red sleeves known as "Red Wing [Sleeve] Dresses" (Xólgúlhòldà), which resemble the Red Sleeve Dresses (Màunkàugúlhòldà) worn during Scalp and Victory Dances. Members painted their faces with a red circle running across the forehead, by the ear, around the cheeks, and from the corner of the jaw to the edge of the chin. Inside this circle were four red stripes of paint on each cheek. A black vertical line was painted from the center of the forehead down the bridge of the nose, and the lips were painted black. Another account described black face paint extending from the upper lip downward, a blackened forehead, and a vertical black line extending halfway down the bridge of the nose. Although the meaning of the paint was no longer known, it was said not to have represented any animal. Members also wore men's earrings and cuirasses, apparently being free to do so because most were past the age of sexual activity.[42]

Thomas Battey (1968 [1876]:168), who witnessed an afternoon dance of the society during the 1873 Sun Dance, provided the earliest description of the society:

> The music consisted of singing and drumming, done by several old women, who were squatted on the ground in a circle. The dancers—old, gray-headed women, from sixty to eighty years of age—performed in a circle around them for some time, finally striking off upon a waddling run, one behind another; they formed a circle, came back, and, doubling so as to bring two together, threw their arms around each other's necks, and trudged around for some time longer; then sat down, while a youngish man circulated a pipe from which each in turn took two or three whiffs, and this ceremony ended.

Lowie (1916b:849) wrote that the group danced around in a circle with one leader on either end of the formation.

The other primary function of the society involved digging the hole for the center pole during the building of the Sun Dance Lodge and dancing around it after it was raised. They also prepared the floor of the Sun Dance lodge by cleaning it of all debris and digging the holes for the seventeen wall posts. During this time they sang to the Rabbits Society, which helped them collect and spread sand to form the floor of the enclosure.

1 Má-tàun-yi̧-gàu gàu tàl-yóp pái bát a̧ hàu
(Little Girls / and little boys / dirt / you all / bring)
Little girls and little boys, go and pack in dirt [imperative].

2 Jò̧-dôm bát áui-àum
(Floor / you all [imperative] / repair-fix or tidy up)
Fix up the floor.

3 À mâ-kàu-àun gàu qyáu-gà yá ó̧-dèp
(I / pitiable / and-but / love making / I / love-like)
I am pitiable, but I still love love-making.

Each morning afterward the Calf Old Women cleaned the floor and smoothed out the sand.[43]

Kiowa men's societies interacted closely with analogous societies of other tribes, but data concerning related Plains women's societies are presently lacking. Although a number of similarities existed between the Kiowa Calf Old Women and the Plains Apache Izuwe Society, whether the two interacted is unknown. Frizzlehead noted that Apache women did not participate in the spreading of the sand for the Kiowa Sun Dance lodge.[44]

The Bear Women or Bear Old Women Society

This society was known by two names. The first was Àunhấdèmàimàu (Bear Women), from àunhấdè (bear), mái (denoting women), and màu (denoting a group or collective form, similar to gàu). They are better known by the name Sétchǫ̂hyòp (Bear Old Women), from Sét (the name form for bear) and chǫ̂-hyòp (elderly women).[45] According to Marriott's consultants and Levy (2001:912), some Kiowa considered this society to have been related to the men's shield societies in general, with its closest relationship to the Tạimé (Sun Dance Bundle) Shields. By 1935 the circumstances of this connection were no longer remembered. Existing data suggest that this relationship became more focused toward the Ten Medicine Bundles than toward any shield society. Despite limited data, there appears to have been an intimate association between the Bear Women and the Ten Medicine Bundle keepers. Kintadl, the last Bear Women Society leader, stated that the society was essentially a women's auxiliary to the Ten Medicine keepers, having similar rituals, taboos, and number of members, although members did not have medicine bundles.[46] Quoetone also noted, as Donald Collier recorded it, that "the Bear Society was organized as a ladies' auxiliary to the [Ten Medicine] Keeper Soc. There are, eg., ten members, the ritual is similar etc., somewhat similar taboos."[47]

Atah stated, "They were organized in some way to be connected with the idols way back there.... The idol-keepers are afraid of bears in a medicine way," and, "This was about the time it all went away. They were important as bear women. Probably when the bear women were organized, they were originally related to the priests, but in later times with the change of membership they were not."[48] This is the only indication that the Bear Women may have been relatives of the Ten Medicine Bundle keepers. Marriott noted that her consultants and interpreters were reluctant and evasive in discussing the society. Some avoided even acknowledging its existence and would not provide detailed information until pinned down on the subject. All except Frank Given were noted as speaking of the society only in a manner that indicated fear.[49]

In discussing women's societies, Mrs. Tenedooah said, "The pipes belonged to the gods [bundles], and the women borrowed them for the occasion. It was only used for sacred purposes and was kept with the god. Each god had one pipe." However, she did not specify which society she was referring to.[50] In discussing the Bear Women with Frank Given, a Ten Medicine Bundle keeper whose first wife and half-sister were members of the society, Marriott noted, "I think he knows a great deal more about it, but doubt if I can ever get more out of him. There is some connection between the Bear Women and the Gods, and I do not think he will ever discuss either one with me."[51]

Interviews with Henry Tsoodle Sr., another Ten Medicine Bundle keeper, produced a similar avoidance of the subject: "There's very little known about the bear women. They meet at the sun dance, when the others do. No one can get near enough to their tipi to tell what's going on. People are kind of afraid of them, too. I don't know whether they dance or have a dinner, or what they do. It's forbidden to know much about them."[52]

The origin of the relationship between the Bear Women and the Ten Medicine Bundles is found in a well-known Kiowa legend. Although several versions of the story exist, Donald Collier recorded the fullest available account from Kintadl. Because she was the last leader of the society, her rendition may be the most accurate:

> Once there lived in a camp a beautiful young girl, her father's favorite. He had the habit of painting her face every morning before she went to get water. One day she came back, and the paint had been removed from her face. This happened several days, so the father became curious about how it came about. So one day he painted her face, then followed her as she went. He saw a great bear come up to her, hug her, and lick the paint off her face. He realized they were in love. He immediately went back to camp and told the camp crier to announce a bear hunt right away. Meanwhile, the bear went off into the thick timber. The girl, learning of the hunt, said to her father, "Father I want you to bring me a piece of the skin of that bear." The bear was surrounded in the timber by the hunters, and killed. A piece of the skin was brought to the girl, by the father, and she wore it on her body all the time. However, the bear, in hugging her, had given her power. One morning the young people in the camp were playing "Bear." This is a game where a semicircle of earth is heaped up, and balls of wet sand are laid in and around it, called fruit. One person is chosen bear, and chases the others who try to get the fruit, pick some up, and get back to "camp" without getting tagged, ie. "bitten." The one who has been bitten has to be the bear in her lair. During the game it became the turn of the young people [woman], Set'onyodl, to be the bear. She refused, but they insisted. She said she was afraid, but finally accepted. Before starting, she said to her younger sister, "the fourth time that I come out, you must run back to camp and hide in one of those holes in the ground where dogs with small pups are kept. You must run into the tipis, and get red earth paint. When you see me coming, you must not be afraid but must stand your ground and throw it in my face." Then they started to play. As the players came up to the lair, and were caught, the bear gave them a terrific bite. The second time it was worse. The third time they were scared to death, and the fourth time the woman had turned completely into a bear, who grabbed the children and killed them. Then she ran into camp and began to kill the whole camp. No arrows could touch her, so the people were all wiped out, except her sister,

who had followed her instructions. When the bear lunged at her, the younger sister stood her ground and threw the paint into the face of the bear. Instantly the bear turned back into a woman again. So the two went back to a large tipi to live, but the older one was a tyrant. She lay around across the door, and made her sister do all the work, and get the wood. As the girl came in she would stumble over the bear woman's feet, dropping the wood on them, then get beaten up for it. So they camped there.

One day the bear woman said to the other, "Take this tipi stake, painted red, and go get a rabbit with it. If you don't I will eat you." The younger one went out with a heavy heart. Now as it happened, the six brothers of the two had been out on a raiding party while all this happened, and were returning from it when they heard the girl crying in the woods. She told them, "Matonyodl [Wild Girl] has killed all the people, and will kill me if I don't get a rabbit with this stick." The brothers immediately started a rabbit hunt. The girl then told them that she had been told to kill the rabbit laterally, through the heart with the stake. One of the brothers then killed a rabbit laterally, but with a bow and arrow. The girl is afraid the deed will be discovered, but the brother tells her to set the dead rabbit up, and make four feints with the stake, throwing it the fourth time. When she does this, the stake goes through the rabbit as planned.

When the girl took the rabbit back to the older sister, she smelled the rabbit, and accused her younger sister of deceiving her. The girl then, to prove it was all right, laid the rabbit in the door, and standing at the west end of the tipi made three passes with the stake, throwing it on the fourth time. It went into the rabbit, so all was okay.

Now the brothers had told the girl to go around to all the empty tipis and collect all the needles. Seven rocks were to be placed outside around the tipi in a circle, with the needles in between. Matonyodl then sent her sister for wood, and stuck her foot out to trip her. When the wood was brought in, the girl had a stick ready, as her brothers had told her, so as she stepped in, she threw the wood on the tyrant and cracked her over the shins with the stick, then ran out, following the seven stones to where her brothers were. Then they started running, by shooting an arrow as far as they could. They'd land with the arrow, and then shoot again, so went at a great pace. Meanwhile the tyrant rolled around in pain, then started in pursuit. She fell into the needles, so had to stop to pull them all out.

But soon she caught up, and they noticed she had already turned back into a bear. The seven finally came to a huge rock, Tsoai [Xòâi, Up A Rock, or Rock That Grew Upward], Standing Rock, in Montana, and called on it for help. The rock told them to go around it four times, then come up on top. When they did this, the rock began to grow upwards. The bear came roaring up, and made a tremendous lunge for the seven. It missed the top of the rock by inches, so fell to the bottom, scratching the face with its claws as it went down. The seven went from there up to the stars. Not long afterwards a huge bear was killed with difficulty. That bear was Matonyal. The people took the claws and put one in each of the Ten Medicine bags. This is the origin of the ten.[53]

This story pertains to the Kiowa origin of Up A Rock (Xòâi), the mountain known today as Devils Tower in northeastern Wyoming. The story is often called the origin of the seven sisters, because the children became the Pleiades when they became stars. Kintadl mentioned that she had picked up "flints like bearclaws" at the foot of the rock. Some Kiowa elders have commented that the reason the Kiowa held a bear taboo in later times originated in this incident and that to kill or consume any part of a bear would be murder and cannibalism of one's kin.[54]

Membership and Power

The Bear Women Society consisted of ten members, a rule that, if infringed upon, was said to have caused a member to blow up because the group was so powerful (Lowie 1916b:849; Parsons 1929:96). Members were mature women, although later some younger women were taken in because they were said to have had "more power." Frank Given stated that whereas the leaders were always elders, other members were in their twenties and thirties. All members were said to have been "good women," inferably of outstanding social character and perhaps from prominent ǫ̀dè families.[55]

According to Levy (n.d.:20, 2001:915), bear power was controlled by this secret society, whose members were respected and greatly feared.[56] Their power was reportedly stronger even than that of the Ten Medicine Bundles. Even the Táimé was said to be afraid of it; hence the taboo of bear to all Kiowa. As Piatonma explained, "The young man prayed while on a raid. Something told him to pray to the Bear Women; they were stronger than the grandmothers [Ten Medicines]."[57] Bear Women had no power to cure illness from witchcraft, nor any rain power as the Ten Medicine keepers had.[58] Although all ten members were not always present at every meeting, the leader and the two door keepers were required to attend in order to facilitate the completion of a vow, suggesting that some meetings might have been held throughout the year. Because of band members' lack of proximity to one another, most meetings probably took place at the Sun Dance. Membership entailed two taboos: children and husbands could not hit or even feint hitting a member in the face, and food once placed on a member's plate could not be transferred to that of another.[59] Atah stated that the women could look at and talk about bears but could not wear bearskins.[60]

When a member became too old to participate, a substitute was named to replace her. Accounts by female consultants, which I give precedence over male accounts because of the great secrecy involved in society functions, indicate that replacements were required to be close relatives. Although sisters, daughters, and nieces were frequently chosen, any close female relative could be named. When a replacement was taken into the society, she stated, "I have taken my grandmother's place."[61] Piatonma believed that the Bear Women, like the Calf Old Women, were a hereditary group that chose its members carefully, implying that membership was dominated by a small number of affluent families.[62] Kintadl replaced her mother's sister, who had no daughters of her own. When she was between thirty-four and thirty-six (circa 1882–1884), she was sitting under a tree one day when, as in the men's societies, she was grabbed by the two sergeants at arms, Crossing/Bridge (Àunkímà) and Piayo'te (? Pȉyâujè, or At The Hilltop, also known as Dozite), and taken to a meeting. These two wore buffalo robes with the hair side out, concealing the pipe they carried. As in the men's societies, women were forced to touch the pipe, which obligated them to join. When the two members lit the pipe and asked the candidate to smoke, she could not refuse. The initiate acquired the supernatural power of the society at the moment of smoking. After the initiate was taken to the meeting lodge, she was quickly given instructions.[63]

Vows and Meetings

Unlike vows made for the Calf Old Women, those for the Bear Women were generally made in circumstances of extreme danger, such as being in a camp under attack or in a party about to be exterminated in battle. However, vows could also be made before setting out on an expedition. Unlike the situation with the Calf Old Women, vows were not made for recovery from illness. Similarly to the way requests were made to Ten Medicine Bundle keepers, a man sometimes approached a member of the Bear Women during the winter and asked her to pray for his success in war, "so he can shine at the next sundance."[64] Because most vows involving the Bear Women were made during war journeys, the society often had no knowledge of them until the pledge returned. Upon returning to camp, a man did not have to make his vow publicly known until he was ready to feast the society. On that day he sent the camp crier out to convene the society, which generally had no advance notice. In some instances advance notice of a potential meeting was given when a man leaving on a journey took a pipe to a member of the society to smoke and told her that if successful he would feast the society upon his return.[65]

According to Kintadl, the transfer of the society's power to the pledge occurred when the man told the Bear Women of his intentions, to which society members customarily replied, "Yes, yes," indicating that they understood his plans. To complete his vow, a feast including at least the leader and the two door keepers was required.[66] One such pledge came when a man dreamed of the Bear Women while on a raid. After praying for victory and a safe return, he counted coup and captured a young girl in the encounter. On returning he completed the vow by sponsoring a meeting of the society.[67]

Having vowed a meeting, the pledge prepared a lodge for the society, possibly under the direction of the "work woman"; meetings could be held in any of the member's lodges. The pledge built a small fire in the lodge and provided food prepared by his wife for a feast. Because even the pledge was not allowed to attend more than a brief portion of the meeting, much secrecy surrounds the society's activities. A society-owned pipe for which the work woman served as custodian was placed between the fire and the leader, with the stem facing south and the bowl facing north. One pipeful of mixed tobacco and sumac supplied by the work woman was smoked per meeting.[68]

After a crier announced a vow in camp, the women appeared at the designated location and formed a single-file, east-to-west line until all arrived. Curious about whether "they turned into bears," Piatonma watched the society prepare for a meeting as a child at the Wild Rice Sun Dance (probably 1870 or 1873, per Mooney 1989:327, 336–337). Members wore robes over their shoulders and carried objects under their arms and close to their chests, which they made efforts to conceal. When Piatonma asked a member about her object, "the woman laughed and said it was something sacred and was hard to see." These concealed objects may have been the Ten Medicine Bundles, because members were said not to have owned or maintained any bundles or medicine pouches of their own. If so, this would confirm the relationship between the society and the Ten Medicines mentioned by Kiowa elders in the 1930s.[69]

The leader squatted on her haunches before entering the lodge and pawed four times at the door while growling deep in her throat like a bear. Each member answered the leader, making four feints before entering on the fifth.[70] One elder indicated that the first member to enter sat just south of the door, the next to her left, and so on, with the other members passing in front of those already seated. Unlike the Calf Old Women, the Bear Women did not wait until the previous member had completed the circuit and was seated before they entered themselves. Each member was seated at a specified position determined by a number of tipi poles from the entrance (Marriott 1968:151).[71]

At meetings there were at least three offices: those of the leader, who sat at the west side of the lodge, the work woman, who sat just south of the door, and the cleanup woman, who sat just north of the door. Although it is unclear, the society leader probably had an assistant. Consultants indicated that the women's organizations had the same numbers of officers as the men's societies, which would make the number of Bear Women officers consistent with that of the Calf Old Women and may suggest the presence of society partners in the women's societies. Unfortunately, the details of these relationships in the women's societies are unknown.[72]

When all members had entered the lodge, the door was closed and barred with sticks, and one or two male guards were posted outside to keep people away. Members were not allowed to leave meetings, and children and young people were often sent out of the camp on meeting days (Levy 2001:915). If a man tried to enter, the women all growled like bears to scare him away. If he succeeded in getting in, the women forced him to eat until he became sick as punishment. One Kiowa cited this as another reason the group was feared. Henry Tsoodle Sr. reported a case in which a boy trying to watch a meeting was pulled in, after which the Bear Women stood up with their hands above their heads in imitation of bears. If a woman tried to enter, the others jumped on her and "clawed" her, obligating her to become a member, which might have been an arranged form of ritual induction. Meetings lasted from nine o'clock in the morning until evening, and the restrictions associated with meetings made membership arduous.[73]

Members sat with their robes covering their heads, faces bowed, and arms folded. Accounts of the ceremony do not specify the extent of the sponsor's participation, but it appears to have been brief. The sponsor arrived at the lodge door with a pipe and asked if the women were ready inside. After they covered themselves with bison robes, the leader granted the man permission to enter. He then lit the pipe with a coal from the fire and offered it to the leader. As he presented the pipe he said, "Smoke that I may kill, scalp, and subdue my enemy and become a great warrior, and [be] successful in all my undertakings. Pray that I may die of old age." The leader growled underneath her robe. As the man held the bowl down, she prayed for him and then took one draw from the pipe. The other members then growled and threw back their robes, after which the man carried the pipe around to each member, who prayed and smoked. The leader commanded the "bears" to look and breathe on the young man and to grant long life to him and his children.[74] After receiving their prayers and providing them with food, the pledge apparently left. Frank Given once feasted the society, departing after bringing food and water to the group, but he failed to mention the pipe, which other accounts indicate preceded the bringing of food.

The ceremony began with the work woman, who rose and, proceeding clockwise to the pipe, which had been filled with tobacco by the leaders, feinted four approaches. Standing on the north side of the leader, the work woman lit the pipe from the central fire. Feinting four times again, she presented it to the society leader on the fifth approach. The leader made several passes with the pipe upward and in other directions (possibly four), then took five draws from it. Having returned to her seat, the work woman received the pipe and smoked in the same manner.[75] She then passed the pipe around the lodge clockwise, and each member took five draws. Once it reached the last member, the cleanup woman, the smoking was reversed, moving counterclockwise back around the lodge, and then clockwise back to the leader seated at the west, where it stopped. The pipe made two and a half rounds after the leader initially smoked it, so the leader was the only person to smoke four times. She then emptied the ashes into the fire and placed the pipe behind her. It was said that it did not matter if the pipe went out during the smoking. Perhaps the ritual context was more important than the actual smoking.[76]

Prayers were then offered for the sponsor of the meeting. Around 11:00 A.M. the pledge brought in food for the feast, consisting of five courses placed in an east to west direction. The first dish was located closest to the fire and was required to be meat. The second was "choking berries" (probably chokecherries), followed by three other varieties of fruit. Bison tongues were a noted favorite of the society. Like the Calf Old Women, the Bear Women sacrificed food before eating during their meetings.[77] The leader or the work woman offered a bit of each type of food to the earth and then buried it. Proceeding clockwise, each member then took five dips into the food and passed it on to the next member. The cleanup woman placed the dishes on the north side of the door. Because one-half hour was required for each course, the feast was a lengthy process. No smoking or talking was allowed between the courses. According to Atah, "All food must be consumed. None may be removed. That is because bears are known to be hearty eaters."[78]

The pledge then brought water in a tin pail. During another meeting it was brought in by a young girl who was believed to be the pledge's daughter. This was the only water allowed all day, and because it was not allowed to remain inside, each woman, beginning with the one on the south, took five swallows, after which the water was removed, probably by the pledge or his appointee. Although no dancing took place in the lodge, singing followed the feast, each member keeping time to the music by beating on the ground with a stick of wild plum wood. Society songs were not allowed to be sung outside of meetings. The society song leader Tongoi (possibly Tâugàui, or Rattle) was replaced by Àunkímã upon her death. After another round of smoking and prayers, meetings were concluded. Members left in the order they entered, and the lodge owner cleaned up.[79]

Consultants in the 1930s stated that the Bear Women never danced in public, and little description of these activities survives. Private dances were formerly a part of the society's activities, but they lapsed in the organization's later years, which probably explains why some consultants said that no dancing was performed. Kintadl had been told of a dance the society performed in which the members danced in a circle and sang with their heads down in imitation of bears. There was no special costume, paint, or sacred color.[80] Other informants, however, stated that the leader wore a bear claw necklace and a square piece of hide, and the members painted their faces red, perhaps symbolic of the red paint and the bear's hide worn by the girl in the Devils Tower story. Parsons (1929:xv) also reported that members wore some special form of face paint.[81]

Although the Bear Women were considered sacred and were worshipped, this status was limited to meetings, during which only the pledge was allowed near them. Outside of these functions they were treated as regular people with no special taboos. Like the Sun Dance Bundle and the Ten Medicine Bundles, which were believed to possess some humanlike attributes, the Bear Women were afraid of bears. Although they could look at bears and talk about them, it was taboo to eat them, because the group's power was derived from the bear.[82] The last meeting of the Bear Women Society was held around 1905.[83]

Pehodlma: Industrious Women

Very little information concerning this group exists, because it ceased to function around the time the Kiowa entered a reservation in 1875. During my fieldwork I was unable to find anyone familiar with the group or who knew the actual pronunciation of the society's name. It consisted of around six (possibly more earlier on) middle-aged women who were noted as being extremely efficient in all domestic arts. Known as the "Qóichę̀gàu of women," they were especially noted as the best midwives, the best makers of war bonnets, bags, and painted parfleches, and the best hide tanners and cutters in the tribe. According to Kintadl, the group was not organized as a society, had no songs, no leader, no supernatural power (dą́udą́u), and no sanctity. These women provided girls and young women with training in various skills and were sought by others for help and advice in making tipis. Although no payment was involved for instruction in tanning hides, fees were paid to members who supervised tipi construction. When a young woman had enough hides to make a tipi, she often sought out a member, who was paid for supervising the fitting. This was considered the most critical part in constructing a tipi, since reportedly everyone could sew. Assisted by her female relatives, the sponsor feasted all who met to help in the construction.[84]

Members functioned as skilled midwives and were paid with meat, shawls, or cloth. They were assisted by medicine men only if complications set in. Members were picked by Dog Society members to tan and decorate the elk skin society sashes with beadwork and porcupine quills. The group worked all day inside a tipi with two male leaders. Individual Dog Society members came to instruct the group regarding the privately owned designs they desired to be placed on their sashes, each of which was decorated differently. Membership appears to have been hereditary, handed down from mother to daughter, but mothers had no say in inducting their own relatives. Kintadl thought that the members might have been the wives and daughters of Dog Society members. Because the group was so small and so little is known about it, it is difficult to ascertain its position and activities as a sodality. It appears to have been a smaller and less formally organized sodality similar to the Southern Cheyenne craft guild described by Marriott (1956).[85]

Summary of Pre-reservation Kiowa Women's Societies

Both the Calf Old Women and the Bear Women were believed to be sources of power for success and protection in warfare and were integrally linked to male martial success. The prayers of both societies were frequently sought and deemed effective. Prayers to the Bear Women were generally made before a war journey or while in battle. Prayers to the Calf Old Women were made before setting out on a war journey, by others for a relative on a war journey, for recovery of a member of either sex from illness, or simply to sponsor the group at a Sun Dance. Whereas the Calf Old Women were approached more frequently for vows related to illness and before war journeys, the Bear Women more often received vows made during sudden, life-threatening circumstances. Excepting the distinction concerning illness, it is possible that the other bases for vows applied to both groups. Structurally, the Calf Old Women Society was closer to the men's societies, with two officers on the west side and one on either side of the meeting lodge door. The Bear Women's organization is less clear. Although there are no clear references to society partners in the women's societies, the presence of an even number of members and indications of dualism in some seating arrangements suggest the possibility.

Membership in both societies appears to have been held within a few select families. In the Calf Old Women, the large number of relatives of Mary Buffalo, kin relations between other members of the society, examples of matrilineal succession, and the redistribution of leftover food and water and its blessed qualities to "kinfolk" all suggest membership in a limited number of lineages.

The data also suggest that membership in both women's societies was limited to members of wealthy, high-status families. Mrs. Tenedooah stated that no poor person could belong to the Calf Old Women Society. This is reflected in elder members' expectations of receiving considerable quantities of gifts from new initiates, and it supports Levy's assessment that membership was limited to persons from wealthy ǫ̀dè families. Based on status and thus wealth, this organizational standard probably held true for the Bear Old Women as well. Atah's comment, "Probably when the Bear Women were organized, they were originally related to the priests but in later times with the changes in membership they were not," is unclear. The statement does not clarify whether the alleged relationship was between the two collective groups, whether the Bear Women were originally female relatives of the bundle keepers, or both. Changes in Bear Women membership and, more important, bundle keeper genealogies demonstrate that bundle succession did not always follow direct hereditary lines, for several reasons. Thus the association between the two sodalities could easily have drifted away over time.

The exact date of origin for the Bear Women is unknown. The only membership roster for the society includes only the last members, and because ethnological and genealogical records prohibit a full reconstruction of either Bear Old Women Society members or Ten Medicine Bundle keepers, it is impossible to clearly establish this correlation. That there was once a biological relationship between the members of the two groups is quite possible, because many of the last Bear Women were from prominent, high-status families. Of interest is that Kintadl replaced her mother's sister as society leader, and her own mother had been the leader of the Calf Old Women Society. This clustering of high-status positions strongly correlates with high social status and wealth. Kintadl's father, Dáunfài, or Jòhâusàn II, was the nephew of the Kiowa tribal chief of the same name and a reputable warrior in his own right. He had at least four wives at one time and produced one of the largest Kiowa families during his time. Although current Kiowa elders recall little more than the names and existence of these societies, and little documentation exists, their basis and Kiowa women's auxiliary role in war power is clearly demonstrated. Traditional forms of honoring outgoing and successfully returning veterans through song and dance include Stirring Up Songs (Gúdáugá, the ancestral form of the contemporary 49 Dance), and women's Scalp and Victory (Áuldáucúngà), Shuffle (Tǫ́sódêcùngà), and later Round (Áuqóbêcùngà) dances, which were all performed in linear formations. Thus Kiowa women's societies and female relatives functioned significantly in traditional forms of encouraging, supernaturally protecting, and honoring male veterans.

Contemporary Kiowa Women's Societies

A Kiowa saying goes that when Kiowa warriors went to battle, their mothers were with them in spirit. In reviewing the Bear Old Women and Calf Old Women Societies of the nineteenth century, it becomes clear that prayers for the success, longevity, and safe return of warriors figured prominently in these organizations. Their cessation paralleled the decline in men's warfare following entrance onto the reservation in 1874–1875. After this time the role of women in supporting and recognizing Kiowa veterans is largely undocumented. However, despite the decline of organized women's societies, women's support role changed little qualitatively during the late nineteenth and early twentieth centuries. The revival of two men's societies in 1912, the burgeoning Omaha Society, powwows, and a brief period of sendoff celebrations and women's Scalp and Victory Dances for fourteen Kiowa servicemen in World War I continued the traditional dances to honor veterans and carried the Kiowa martial ethos into the twentieth century. These dances continued at annual Armistice Day encampments each November.

With the United States' entry into World War II, many more Kiowa served in the military and were viewed as continuing traditional male roles as warriors protecting their people and homeland. In turn, their service required traditional recognition in the form of honoring through song and dance. The role of Kiowa women in supporting veterans was reactivated, and dances held for departing and returning servicemen increased in frequency. Four Kiowa women's service organizations formed in response to World War II.

Although these organizations differed from the nineteenth-century women's societies in formation and ritual, they continued, in modern contexts, the traditional ideals associated with Kiowa women and the honoring of Kiowa warriors. Kiowa women did not revive their traditional societies so much as they syncretically reconfigured the core ideology that came from those organizations. In doing so, they continued a series of traditions that constitute an important part of the way many Kiowa women define their gender roles and ethnicity.

Numerous honor dances were held for outgoing and returning servicemen, leading to a dramatic increase in social powwows. As Ralph Kotay explained (Ellis 2003:21), "this powwow thing really got going when our boys came home from overseas in World War II. Those service clubs got going and sponsored dances for those boys, and then it just took off." Despite technological changes in warfare, the Kiowa have continued to honor and uphold their servicemen along largely traditional lines. Since World War II, the traditional role of Kiowa women's societies in supporting, praying for, blessing, and encouraging male veterans has been continued by the Kiowa War

Mothers, the Carnegie Victory Club, the Stecker Purple Heart Club, and the Kiowa Veterans Auxiliary.

Works on the role of contemporary Plains women's sodalities and veterans' issues have so far focused only on Native American chapters of the American War Mothers (Anderson 1956; Schweitzer 1981, 1983). Native American War Mothers chapters serve as bridges between the Indian and non-Indian world. In blending an Anglo American organizational structure with the goals, values, and rituals of traditional women's societies and tribal systems, War Mothers chapters provide arenas for participation and for the integration of women's veteran auxiliary groups into the dominant society while reinforcing and enhancing the culture and traditional women's roles of the respective tribal communities. In doing so, they foster and continue many important tribal values, especially the respect and honor shown to veterans and the redistribution of goods and services through philanthropy to veterans and their families. Although several Kiowa women's auxiliaries exist and each has distinct insignia, songs, and some ritual aspects, their values and roles are similar.

The Kiowa War Mothers

The American War Mothers is a nationally chartered nonprofit organization that was founded on September 29, 1917, and was incorporated by a congressional act on February 24, 1925. The organization functions on three levels: local chapters, state, and national. The national headquarters is located in Washington, D.C. A brief history of the group is given in its constitution and bylaws:

> We are a perpetual patriotic organization. We were established on September 29th, 1917, this date later known as Founder's Day. This great bond of women derived from the outstanding work they performed during World War I with the Food Conservation Committee and the State Council of Indiana. On August 16, 1918, the National Organization of American War Mothers was effected in a constitution and bylaws adopted. Between the lines of time in history many will be able to read a story of struggle, patience, self denial, and duty that brought us to the pinnacle of national recognition with a charter dated February 24, 1925. Covenant Law 453 from the United States Congress.
>
> The American War Mothers Organization is unique in that at its very inception it was a dying organization. At that time the membership was limited to mothers whose sons and/or daughters served in the Armed Forces between April 6, 1917, and November 11, 1918. Therefore it could exist only as long as any of the mothers survived. With the onslaught of World War II, Congress was petitioned to amend the charter to include mothers whose sons and/or daughters served in that war. Before World War II was officially ended, the Korean Conflict emerged, making it necessary to again amend the charter. It now includes

mothers of [veterans of] World War I, World War II, the Korean Conflict, and any future wars.[86]

Object:
The object of this organization shall be to keep alive and develop the spirit that prompts world service, to maintain the ties of fellowship born of that service, to assist and further any patriotic work, to inculcate a sense of individual obligation to the community, state, and nation, to work for the welfare of the Armed Forces of the United States, to assist in any way in their power, men and women, to serve the wounded or incapacitated in World Wars or conflicts of the United States, to foster and promote friendship and understanding between America and the Allies.[87]

As stated by the Kiowa chapter, the objects of the organization include the following: "(1) to keep alive and develop the spirit that prompted world service, (2) to maintain the ties of fellowship born of that service, (3) to assist and further any patriotic work, (4) to inculcate a sense of individual obligation to the community, state, and nation, (5) to work for the welfare of the Armed Forces, (6) to assist, within our ability, men and women who served and were wounded or incapacitated in war conflicts of the United States, and (7) to foster and promote friendship and understanding between the United States and the nations of the World."[88]

The constitution and bylaws of the American War Mothers say the following about membership:

The American War Mothers is limited to women and no woman shall be and become a member of this organization unless she is a citizen of the United States and unless her son, sons, or daughter, daughters or her legally adopted sons, sons or legally adopted daughter, daughters, adopted before their twelfth birthday, her step-son or sons, step-daughter or daughters who became her step children before their twentieth birthday served in the Armed Forces of the United States or its Allies in World War I, World War II, the Korean and Vietnam Conflicts or any subsequent wars or conflicts involving the United States [and] have an honorable discharge from service or [are] still in service. Amended and approved by the United States Congress, April 12, 1974.[89]

Membership in the Kiowa War Mothers is open to any enrolled Kiowa mother of an active male or female service person currently in good standing or of an honorably discharged male or female member of any of the four branches of the United States armed forces, whether he or she experienced combat or not.[90] The Kiowa War Mothers is primarily military service oriented. Past president Ruby Williams emphasized, "It's a patriotic organization and our work and everything pertains to the veterans and those that have served and those that are serving now. And all of our work is all directed in that way. It's a patriotic organization and it's for our veterans, men and women, the things that we do."[91]

Many women have had children serve in the military. However, in the Kiowa War Mothers' view, membership in the nationally based, chartered American War Mothers is the essential criterion differentiating their organization from other Indian and non-Indian service-oriented organizations and auxiliaries. Membership in the nationally chartered organization and the maintenance and observation of a formal charter, constitution, and bylaws are central to the American War Mothers' protocol and ideology. These features differentiate them from other service organizations and are frequently and proudly voiced by the members of Chapter 18, the Kiowa chapter. As one member said, having a son or daughter in service makes one a war mother, but only having a son or daughter in service and being a member of the national, chartered organization makes one an American War Mother: "You can be a war mother but you're not an *American War Mother* . . . because everything we have, our charter, our constitution and bylaws, all that goes back to the War Mothers and we are American War Mothers, not just because your son served over there, 'I am a war mother too,' you are not. That is, in our chapter or any other chapter unless you're affiliated with the [national] organization."[92]

The American War Mothers is also a nonpolitical organization. Its constitution and bylaws say, "This organization shall be non-political, non-sectarian, non-partitioned, non-partisan, and non-profit, and as an organization shall not promote the candidacy of any person seeking office." Its chapters must follow the precedents contained in the forty-two page *American War Mother Constitution and By-laws* and the fifty-six page "American War Mothers Ritual" booklet, published by the national organization. All members are required to have updated copies of both. A War Mothers National Board is composed of all previous national presidents. The national office also produces a newsletter focusing on national- and state-level changes and events. The American War Mothers' flower is the white carnation. Chapter officers include a president, vice president, treasurer, recording secretary, corresponding secretary, sergeant at arms, and historian. All offices are held for two-year terms that begin and end concurrently. The Kiowa chapter holds its elections during its September monthly meeting, and new officers are installed later that month or in early October. Kiowa Chapter 18 meetings are held from September through the following May, the peak period of chapter service-oriented activities. The Kiowa chapter also produces a monthly newsletter during this period. Officers cannot be reelected to the same office consecutively but may be elected to a different office or to the same office after an absence of one two-year term. A number of standing committees are also maintained, each with an acting chair.[93] Maintenance fees (dues) are payable annually on October 1. Chapter dues are $40, which is divided between the state and national organizations. Individual dues of $20 are divided for philanthropic use between the local chapter and the state and national levels.[94]

The War Mothers also occasionally accept women as Angel members. This position was created for people desiring to help or volunteer their efforts to the War Mothers but who either had no children or had no children who were veterans. For their devotion and service, such women were once called associate members, but the title was later changed to Angels. Angels are also found in other Indian as well as Anglo and African American chapters of the American War Mothers, and they participate in all activities. Recently, the Kiowa chapter has had three Angel members: Mildred Tsoodle, a navy veteran herself, Marie Lorrantz, whose grandmother Sally Kaulaity was an original Kiowa War Mother, and the late Carol Stockham, an army veteran.[95]

The Kiowa War Mothers is one of six all-Indian War Mothers chapters organized in the state of Oklahoma (Schweitzer 1981:4–8). Known as Chapter 18, the Kiowa chapter was the eighteenth chapter to join in Oklahoma and is known as the Kiowa War Mothers because all members are enrolled Kiowa.[96] Although it is most commonly referred to by the English name Kiowa War Mothers, I have occasionally heard elders use the Kiowa names Câijàuchàdàu (Fight/War Mothers) and Sólèchàdàu (Soldier Mothers).[97]

The Kiowa chapter received its charter from National War Mothers president E. May Hahn on February 10, 1944, at Mountain View, Oklahoma, where the Kiowa chapter headquarters was then located. A newspaper clipping announcing the formation of the chapter in February 1944 lists the Kiowa tribal population at 2,500, with 184 Kiowa then serving in the armed forces.[98] The Kiowa War Mothers is unique in that 98 percent of its charter members spoke only their native Kiowa, a fact of which they are especially proud. Many of the original members were also direct descendants of some of the most prominent nineteenth-century Kiowa war leaders. Because of the group's unique status, the War Mothers national president personally brought the national charter to the Kiowa chapter in Oklahoma. Today charters are typically mailed to the respective chapters.

The Kiowa chapter was formally organized at a meeting at the home of Lizzie Ahpeahtone near Mountain View, Oklahoma, to which Kiowa mothers brought items captured and sent home by their sons then serving in World War II. Having captured a sword near Rome, Italy, Private First Class Leonard Keahbone sent it home and requested a Sword Dance, which was performed at the meeting by Jasper Saunkeah. Lizzie Ahpeahtone and Jasper and Anna Saunkeah were instrumental in the formal organization of the group. Elected and installed at this meeting as officers were Ahoolah, or Lizzy Ahpeatone, president; Haubeiko, or Myrtle Paudlety Ware, of Anadarko, Effie Tonemah, or Effie Satepauhoodle Chanate, Lucy Saumpty Taua, or Lucy Goeins, and Amantomah, or Lizzie Unap, of Carnegie, vice presidents; May Sankadota Bohay, of Carnegie, recording secretary; Eliza "Sallie" Kaulaity, of Mountain View, treasurer; Taukobah, or Richenda Toyebo, sergeant-at-arms; and Padoti, or Mrs. David Paddlety, of Anadarko, chaplain. Other charter members included Anotesau, or Rose Saumpty Jay, Ianonen, or Eugenia Mausape, Ada "Mabel" Yeahquo, and Asequetah Eagleheart, all of Carnegie; Potsi, or Dora Jay, Martha Paddlety Bert, Katie "Anna or Annie" Keahbone Aunquoe, and Lillie Botone Tsonetokoy, of Mountain View; Sendaymah, or Libby "Sindy" Keahbone, and Frances Aunquoe, of Anadarko; Totsauah Red Horn, Rhoda Drywater, and Sadie Akoneto, of Fort Cobb; and Goomtigh, or Lottie Tanedooah, and Francis Bigbow Tahkopoodle.[99]

Kiowa War Mothers, 1944. Seated, left to right: Lizzie Bigbow Unap, Lucy Saumty, Magdalene Paddlety, Myrtle Paudlety Ware, Effie Genevieve Tonemah, May Sankadota Bohay, Lizzie Ahpeahtone, Sallie Kaulaity, Anne Katie Aunquoe, Eugenia Mausape, Sindy Keahbone, Frances Bigbow Aunquoe. Standing, left to right: Richenda Toyebo, Dora Jay, Rose Saumty Jay, Martha Paddlety Bert, Lily Botone Tsonetokoy, Mabel Ada Yeahquo, Lottie Tanedooah. Author's collection.

During World War II, all the charter Kiowa War Mothers had at least one son in service. In addition to other war-related functions in which the chapter participated, it held monthly business meetings at member's houses. Shortly after forming, the chapter donated $50 to the Red Cross, assisted it in wrapping bandages for use overseas, and raised another $50 for several Kiowa servicemen home on furlough.

Insignia

Like other Indian War Mothers chapters, the Kiowa chapter developed its own insignia in the form of a shawl. The Kiowa War Mothers are easily recognized by their distinct blue chapter shawls with red and white ribbonwork trim around the edges. The charter members obtained circular patches from the national office featuring the logo "American War Mothers" in red, white, and blue. The Kiowa War Mothers placed these on the backs of their shawls, adding "Kiowa Chapter 18" to the top of the patches and a red, white, and blue ribbon suspended from the bottom of the patch. Chapter shawls and insignia are worn primarily at Indian (Kiowa and other tribal chapter) functions but not at state and national meetings.[100]

Mothers who have lost a son or daughter killed in action, such as the late Mamie Boyiddle, are known as Gold Star mothers. Those who have had a son or daughter wounded in action, such as Violet Kauley and Carrie Sahmaunt, are called Silver Star mothers. According to one newspaper article, "the Gold Star Mothers group was formed after World War I as a way for women who had lost sons to handle their grief by consoling one another and doing volunteer work for veterans. The organization was named after the gold star that families hung in their windows in honor of the deceased veteran." In Long Beach, California, the War Mothers' national home, the Gold Star Manor is a 348-room apartment building with rates subsidized by the Department of Housing and Urban Development to assist low-income Gold Star Mothers aged sixty-two or older.[101]

Gold and Silver Star Mothers each receive a certificate, pin, and flower from the National War Mothers office. All Gold Star mothers are recognized in a ceremony at every national convention. Gold and Silver Star Mothers are also entitled to display their status with the title "Gold Star Mother" or "Silver Star Mother" on their blankets.[102]

Service Activities

One of the primary characteristics that differentiates the Kiowa War Mothers from other Kiowa women's organizations is the extent of its public military-service-oriented activities. The excellent service record of the Kiowa War Mothers chapter and its popularity have resulted in the organization's getting more requests for activities than it can possibly fill. In past years the chapter often received three or more requests for a single weekend. As a result, the War Mothers generally accept invitations only to activities that are service oriented, such as a service-oriented organization's activity or a dance for an individual service person. The War Mothers often receive requests to help with a dance for a veteran home on furlough, which is supported by the chapter. One member stated, "We are not what you call a powwow organization," but even this does not always prevent multiple invitations, such as from the Black Legs Society and for a service dance on the same weekend as the War Mothers state convention. In such cases a contingent of members goes to each event to represent the chapter.[103]

Eventually the chapter voted to co-host powwows with other organizations only if they were service-oriented organizations. The exceptions are the War Mothers' participation in the processional and camping at the annual ceremonial of the Kiowa Gourd Clan, which has many veteran members, and participation in various programs, pageants, and the grand entry of the annual American Indian Exposition. If an event is not service oriented, the War Mothers may accept a role as special guests, but not as co-hosts. Yet even in focusing on service-oriented events, the War Mothers are very active throughout the year.

The chapter frequently raises funds for incoming and outgoing veterans through food and craft sales held throughout the year. From September 1996 to September 1997 the Kiowa chapter undertook twenty-seven major projects, including co-hosting seven powwows, holding three benefit dances, sponsoring one catered meal, appearing on four radio programs, being interviewed for four newspaper articles, attending the state and national conventions, and holding an annual Thanksgiving dinner, an annual Veterans Administration (VA) hospital visitation, a pre–Mother's Day hospital visit and gift shop, an annual dance on Mother's Day, a prayer service for chapter mothers who were ill, and a family-style bingo night (in which people played for donated prizes while the money spent in purchasing bingo cards went toward the benefit cause) to defray travel costs for the national convention.[104]

A major activity of the War Mothers involves visiting veterans in VA hospitals and distributing care packages to them. Just before Mother's Day each year, contingents of members from every Oklahoma chapter of the American War Mothers go to the Oklahoma City VA Hospital, where they hold their annual Mother's Day Gift Shop. Gifts from members of all Oklahoma chapters are put in packages, and veterans are allowed to choose a gift for their mother, wife, or other female relative. For those who are unable to walk, gifts are placed on carts and taken to their respective hospital floors. If the mother or wife lives far away or out of state, the War Mothers wrap, label, and mail the packages for the veterans. One member remarked that although everyone begins the event in a happy, jolly mood, one sometimes cannot help leaving quiet, sad, and even depressed after visiting some of the more serious wards of the hospital. She said, "It broadens you in your thinking but gives you an incentive to go back and do more work."[105]

Every November the chapter meets at the Kiowa tribal complex to prepare care packages containing toiletries, socks, and so forth for veterans in VA hospitals. Although most gifts are donated by the members themselves, some are purchased with organization funds. Each year the chapter's hospitalization chair chooses a different VA hospital (such as those in Clinton and Duncan, Oklahoma) to visit, and care packages and poinsettias are distributed there. Around Christmas 1996, the War Mothers visited the Clinton, Oklahoma, VA hospital and took a contingent of dancers and singers who put on a program for the veterans, including War Mothers dances. Those who were able to walk were invited to join in and dance. The visit was so well received that the hospital wrote the chapter asking it to return.

Every Thanksgiving the Kiowa chapter hosts a Thanksgiving Veteran-Servicemen Dinner for all local veterans and their spouses. These dinners were originally held for all homeless veterans. The dinner was announced, and War Mothers drove and picked up homeless veterans and took them to the dinner. In time the dinner became an annual event. To reach as many veterans in as many communities as possible, the dinner is rotated to a different location every year. Dinners have been held in Anadarko, Carnegie, Hobart, Meers, Lawton, and Mountain View, Oklahoma. In past years the chapter also hosted a Christmas dinner, but it now makes an annual visit to a VA hospital. In some years a meeting with a gift exchange between the chapter mothers is held.

Contingents from the Kiowa chapter attend the Oklahoma state War Mothers meeting held every November 1 in Oklahoma City, where each president is required to give a report on her chapter's yearly activities. War Mothers chapters report their upcoming chapter events and current national events to one another at the state meetings and prepare for the annual national meeting. Contingents have also attended some of the national War Mothers conventions. Some Indian War Mothers chapters have put on cultural performances at state and national meetings, including Kiowa dances and an Osage style show. State and national American War Mothers meetings are attended by members from all over, both non-Indian and Indian.[106] The Kiowa chapter has also visited Arlington National Cemetery in Arlington, Virginia, the United Nations Cemetery in Honolulu, Hawaii, and the Oklahoma Governor's Mansion. Members also attend the biannual National War Mothers Convention held at different locations across the United States. Several members of the Kiowa chapter have also served as officers in the National Chapter of the American War Mothers.

Upon request, the War Mothers perform memorial services for deceased chapter members and deceased veterans. When a veteran dies, the War Mothers have a ceremony known as the "Ceremony for a Deceased Veteran" that the family may request, but it is not promoted by the organization. At the funeral of one Kiowa veteran and Black Legs Society member who had few surviving relatives, the Black Legs asked the War Mothers to receive his flag. They flew the flag at their next annual dance and now care for it. As part of the group's service orientation, memorial services for all deceased War Mothers are held at the chapter, state, and national levels of the War Mothers. The standard procedure for the memorial service is defined in the "American War Mothers Ritual" booklet. According to national policy, individual memorial services must not interfere with the funeral-day program. Although the chapter does not approach the family, if a family asks the chapter to perform a memorial service, it gladly does so, usually at the wake or before the actual burial- or funeral-day services.[107]

Fund-Raising

Fund-raising is a necessity for any charitable work and is a large part of the War Mothers' activities. Maintenance fees are kept by the local chapters and the state and national organizations and are used to help veterans. Like Easter Seals, Christmas cards with stamp seals portraying the American flag are sent out, for which donations are received. Benefit dances with reciprocal co-hosting between intertribal service groups and dance organizations are also major activities. Co-hosts general help supply a portion of and serve the evening meal and donate food baskets, shawls, blankets, and other items that the host group can raffle off. Co-hosts also participate in the dancing, and during their special (usually a dance led by the group or honoree, a speech, and a giveaway), any money received is generally given to the host organization toward its benefit goal.

When the Kiowa Tribe decided to build a veterans memorial at the Kiowa tribal complex in Carnegie, Oklahoma, the War Mothers held a benefit dance that raised more than enough money for the memorial. The War Mothers continue to raise funds for the memorial's maintenance as needed. On October 24, 1997, the Kiowa War Mothers (with co-hosts the Comanche Indian Veterans Association, the Apache Service Club, the Wichita Service Club, and the South-West Vietnam Era Veterans Organization) sponsored a benefit dance to raise funds for the "Moving Wall," a replica of the Vietnam Memorial in Washington, D.C., that was brought to Lawton, Oklahoma, from March 12 to 15, 1998. The South-West Vietnam Era Veterans Organization donated half of all proceeds from its concession stand to the War Mothers. As Carol Flores expressed it, "This wall, this traveling wall that's coming to Lawton, I guess because it's representing the United States, and being service connected, I think that's the reason why we all want to get involved in that."[108]

Meetings

As a patriotic support group, the Kiowa War Mothers holds monthly meetings that focus on a number of social and civic duties in support of veterans' interests.[109] The Kiowa chapter meets every second Tuesday afternoon of the month at a site chosen by the chapter president. Often these meetings are held at the Kiowa tribal complex in Carnegie or at the homes of members. The meetings include a very structured body of War Mothers' ritual and procedures as outlined in the "American War Mothers Ritual" booklet. Meetings open with prayers oriented toward veterans and their well-being. The opening ceremony is recited: "Mothers, we are again privileged to meet to honor the valor and courage of our beloved sons and daughters. They served, fought, and suffered and many of them died to uphold our national honor in order to hasten the day when the master's words 'peace be unto you' shall rule the world."[110]

The chapter chaplain then offers a prayer, after which the chair of the Americanism Committee leads the Pledge of Allegiance to the flag and a singing of "God Bless America." Next, a collective prayer is said aloud:

> Keep us, O God, from pettiness. Let us be large in thought, in word, in deed. Let us be done with fault-finding and leave off self-seeking. May we put away all pretence and meet each other face to face without self-pity and without prejudice. May we never be hasty in judgment and always [be] generous. Teach us to put into action our better impulses, straightforward and unafraid. Let us take time for all things and make us grow calm, serene, and gentle. Grant [that] we may realize it is the little things that create differences, that in the big things of life we are as one. And may we strive to touch and to know the great common human heart of us all. And O Lord God, let us not forget to be kind.[111]

The president then declares the chapter open for transacting business. The order of business followed is (1) a roll call of officers and chairmen, (2) a presentation of visitors by the president, (3) minutes of previous meetings, (4) the treasurer's report, (5) reception of any new members, (6) communications and bills read by the corresponding secretary, (7) reports of all officers, (8) reports of standing committees,(9) reports of temporary committees, (10) unfinished business, (11) new business, (12) a program and social hour, and (13) refreshments and fellowship, which close the afternoon.[112]

Past president Carol Flores said that the meetings were her favorite parts of being a War Mother: "I love the meetings because we talk about what we're planning to do, and to me it's exciting, to look forward to whatever events are upcoming and what we're going to plan to do for the veterans. . . . It's exciting to look forward to what we can do for others and not ourselves."[113]

Members also said they enjoyed the state and national meetings because of the opportunity to meet and visit with other Indian and non-Indian War Mothers from across the state and country.[114] Several non-Indian War Mothers have been invited to visit and participate in the Kiowa chapter's dances. Chapter members have also traveled to attend non-Indian War Mothers functions, which they said they greatly enjoyed. An especially close relationship exists between several of the Oklahoma Indian War Mothers chapters, who help one another by co-hosting one another's dances. As Carol Flores described it: "The other tribes, to me, they are real wonderful people. They put you first. And from what I hear we put them first too, so maybe it's the same."[115]

Membership

Membership is open to any Kiowa mother with children who are serving in or have been honorably discharged from the United States armed forces. New members may be inducted at any monthly meeting throughout the year. Induction involves an installation procedure, instruction concerning the constitution, bylaws, and rituals, and a reception. No giveaways are expected or required of new members. New members cannot hold office during their first year of service. Members are not recruited but must approach the group, express their interest, and request membership. Ruby Williams explained:

> We cannot approach a mother and say, we want you to be a member of our War Mothers. We don't do that. If a mother has a desire to become a member of our chapter, then she knows about our work . . . then she will approach one of the members or usually it's an officer or something. I've had many come to me that way. . . . She'll come and she'll state her desire that she would like to become a member of the Kiowa War Mothers.[116]

Members or officers visit with the prospective member. At the next monthly chapter meeting the prospect's name is announced and the chapter discusses the candidate and her son or daughter's military background. If the woman is accepted, she is invited to the next meeting, at which the president presents her to the chapter. A vote is then taken, which is usually unanimous. At the next monthly meeting the chapter chaplain and the chair of the Ways and Means Committee prepare an installation service to induct the new member; it can be led only by a president or past president. During the service the candidate takes vows, is told about the program, and is instructed to be supportive of the chapter. She is given a membership card containing her name, her child's name, branch of service, and number of years, the person she asked about joining, and the signatures of that chapter member and the current chapter president. The name the new member chooses to record at this time is permanently recorded in the national office, regardless of later marriages or name changes. The candidate is then told about the War Mothers' emblem, work, flower, and motto. Last, she is handed a white carnation by the installing officer, who tells her, "Now you are a member of the American War Mothers Kiowa Chapter 18. Now you have the right to wear our American War Mothers emblem." The chapter then greets the new member, which is followed by a social hour and refreshments.[117]

Although the group may not recruit people, women are sometimes encouraged to consider joining by their relatives. As in other Kiowa men's and women's societies, kinship is often important to the organization's long-term membership. Several War Mothers had female relatives who were members. Membership in the chapter averages around forty-five members.[118]

Dances

According to John Gamble (1952:40), the purpose of the Kiowa War Mothers was to recognize veterans and the mothers of veterans through dances. Although the group performs varied services, dances are an important facet of its activities. The Kiowa War Mothers hold an annual benefit dance on Valentines Day. A king and queen contest, games, and raffles are held to raise funds. The money from this benefit is used to fund the annual War Mothers dance on Mother's Day at Red Buffalo Hall in the Kiowa tribal complex. The funds pay for the meal, building rental, concessions, and other expenses. Because Mother's Day always falls on a Sunday, the War Mothers' annual dance is always a one-day event. Each year the chapter chooses one or more Kiowa veterans to honor and recites their service records during the dance. Past chapter president Carol Flores stated, "This is for the mothers because of their sons and daughters. That is their day."[119]

At around 1:00 P.M. the program starts with a prayer, introductions, the Kiowa Flag Song, and the presentation of the colors, followed by women's Scalp and Victory Dances. The War Mothers acknowledge that the Kiowa have always emphasized honoring veterans and that Scalp and Victory Dances are held today for the same reasons as in the past—because warriors and now soldiers are going to war and returning. Concerning the role of the War Mothers in these dances, Carol Flores explained, "Because of our sons, because we are American War Mothers, because of our service-connected sons or daughters, we have a right to get in [these dances]. We [also] have a right if we are descended from one of the warriors or one of the chiefs."[120]

An all–Gourd Dance program assisted by several co-hosting organizations continues throughout the afternoon. Any specials and giveaways are generally held during the afternoon to free up the evening program. Following a supper provided by the chapter, the War Mothers begin the evening program with a processional, followed by sets of War Mothers songs, the retreat of the colors, and an all–War Dance program until midnight. The combination of War Mothers observances and Mother's Day to honor mothers for their children's military service constitutes an interesting form of syncretism.

When recognizing one or more service persons, the chapter holds an honor dance with a serviceman carrying an American flag at the head of the processional. When more than one person is honored, the honorees follow behind the serviceman carrying the flag in a processional. The mother of the serviceman or servicewoman being honored usually addresses the crowd, much as in the speeches delivered after a giveaway for a warrior. This is usually followed by a session of War Mothers songs and dances, which are similar to Round Dances. Even at dances that they are not sponsoring, members always dance together as a unit and are easily recognized by their organizational shawls. War Mothers' dances are generally limited to the annual War Mothers Valentines Day Benefit Dance, the annual War Mothers dance in May, the annual Carnegie Victory Club Dance on November 11, the two Blacks Legs annual dances, and the Chief Satanta Descendants' annual powwow in June.

Songs

A large body of War Mothers songs (Câijàuchầudầugà, lit. Fight/ War Mothers Songs) was composed during World War II. War Mothers songs are similar to Round Dance Songs and are danced in the same manner, clockwise. During these songs, sons and daughters of War Mothers members and any service-connected men and women may come out and dance with the group. During my fieldwork, I collected tape-recordings and translations of nearly forty War Mothers songs.

Lewis Toyebo, who was a remarkably gifted composer but not a powwow-oriented person, is remembered for knowing many types of songs and for singing frequently around his home. As an adult, he publicly sang only Kiowa Christian hymns at church functions. During World War II, Lewis and his wife, Richenda's, son Ritchie Mitchell Toyebo served in the 89th Infantry Division in Europe, and Richenda became one of the charter members of the Kiowa War Mothers. It was during this period that Lewis Toyebo began composing veterans' songs for his son and all other Kiowa veterans. Richenda Toyebo also composed several personal songs for her son. Delores Toyebo Harragarra, Lewis and Richenda's daughter, allowed me to copy a tape-recording of these songs and helped translate them for me.[121] The combination of Lewis Toyebo's musical ability, Richenda Toyebo's charter membership in the Kiowa War Mothers, and their son's being overseas in service resulted in the composition of many beautiful songs now known as War Mothers songs. As Ruby Williams described them:

> The majority of them were composed by only one person. One man, and his name was Lewis Toyebo and he had a son that served in the war . . . in World

War II. . . . He was very fluent in Kiowa . . . and he was not what you would call a, now they use the term powwow person. . . . I guess just the loneliness and the thoughts and his meditation [inspired the songs]. They are just beautiful. There is not one that is [more] outstanding [than the others]. They all are, because of the thoughts that are there . . . they are in the songs. The words are beautiful and he composed most of them.[122]

According to the Toyebos' daughter, Delores, her father followed the war through radio and newspaper reports. He composed his songs during the war but independently of the campaign map showing the 89th Infantry's movements in France, Luxembourg, and Germany that now hangs in the Toyebo family dining room; it was sent to him after his son's discharge in 1946. It is also possible that because the Kiowa War Mothers was a new organization and his wife was a charter member, Toyebo was inspired to compose a body of songs so that the women would have their own organizational songs with which to honor returning veterans. More than one Kiowa elder has stated that when it came to Toyebo's composing songs, "it just came natural for him."[123]

With a parent's love and longing for his child, Lewis Toyebo was artistically inspired to revive and expand the traditional form of Kiowa war expedition songs while creating a new style focused on the modern warfare encountered in World War II. His songs represent an incredibly powerful musical form—not one or two songs but an entire genre of veteran's songs—created as a tribute to his son and to the military service of all Kiowa veterans in the Second World War. As Mildred Tsoodle Hamilton put it: "The original composer of the War Mothers songs, Lewis Toyebo, did not compose these songs for credit or recognition; neither did other traditional Kiowas before him. They were composed as traditional war expedition songs to give solace and strength and to convey pride. . . . These songs were exclusively for the Kiowa War Mothers, Chapter 18, of the American War Mothers during World War II."[124]

Toyebo's artistic and musical tribute continues today at War Mothers, Victory Club, and Kiowa Black Legs Society celebrations. As noted Kiowa singer Bill Koomsa Jr. described them, these songs reflect the continuity between traditional veterans' ideologies and contemporary military service: "There's a lot of songs, you know, that have words in them, the words have good meanings, good meanings. A lot of them are used during the veterans' dances, and they have good words in them about boys that have served in the service. They have words pertaining to the deeds that they did and coming back home and stuff like that."[125]

Because Toyebo did not attend powwows and dances, he rarely sang the songs in public, except at occasional memorial services. As he composed the songs, he gave them to the organization to honor veterans with and to help the members sustain themselves throughout the war. As Jim Anquoe, son of the gifted singer Jimmy Anquoe, explained to Clyde Ellis (2003:24): "Those songs they made were to soothe those women. When your son is in combat, you don't know whether he's going to survive or not. You can't help him. So what you can do is pray. It's the only tool you got. And they prayed hard. Those songs were like that." Toyebo did not claim the songs as his own or try to gain fame or wealth from them. Many of the songs were introduced to the Kiowa community by Jimmy Anquoe, another gifted Kiowa singer and song composer. Numerous elders, including other singers and relatives of both men, maintain that Toyebo introduced the songs to Anquoe, who was an active singer at powwows and other public dances, to be used in the Kiowa community. One of Anquoe's sons stated that his father and Lewis Toyebo often visited, sharing and collaborating on songs. Because Anquoe and his family commercially recorded a two-volume set of these songs (*Original Kiowa War Mother Songs*, 1985), many younger Kiowa believe that they are all of his composition.[126] Anquoe also composed a number of songs, some of which were eventually incorporated into the genre of War Mothers songs, such as the 45th Infantry Division "Thunderbirds" Song.[127] Suffice it to say that Toyebo composed the original body of War Mothers songs, which were given to the organization and popularized by Jimmy Anquoe and other singers, who subsequently composed other songs, including some in the same genre.

War Mothers songs have no designated titles and are sung in no particular order during dances; the head singer decides the order. During the 1990s the following song was often the first one sung during sets of War Mothers songs:

1 Thái-káu-ól-tâ-gàu hét-jáu è dè, hét-jáu è dè
  (Flag / still / it / standing or positioned; still / it / standing or positioned)
  The flag is still standing; it is still standing,
2 Repeat.
3 Repeat.
4 Repeat.
5 Áu-gàu-tâu jé-dàum-tài
  (Over there, over yonder / all-land-over)
  Over yonder, all over the world.[128]

Regarding the Kiowa War Mothers songs, past chapter president Carol Flores reflected:

They made some beautiful songs and it's all pertaining to their sons, grandsons, any service boy going off to war. Praying that they will come back safe, or being happy that they will come back home, or songs about them being home coming from service, coming from war and that we have been praying for you and we're happy that you're here, you know, and safe. Just the songs, all of it's pertaining to him going and coming back home safe.... And a lot of it, I guess, too, you would think about like a long time ago when in the 1800s and maybe the 1700s when they used to go on, you know, to war paths, to different tribes and different states and fighting and they sang these songs, those war songs. Then they came back and they did the Scalp Dance and the Victory Dance, and see, that's where all of that came in. So to this day ... all of it's bringing in these young men that have gone off to service in World War I, World War II, and [the] Vietnam Conflict.[129]

Flores described what she thinks about when she hears the songs:

> I think about especially the men that have gone on, got killed in action and maybe some missing in action. Mainly about my son, you know, because he was so young in joining.... I know you hope that they don't go off to war, but then if they do you're proud of them, you know. And not only my son but others, and sometimes they make you want to cry, and even now when you think about men, it's not only just the Kiowa, even non-Indians that are in Bosnia or whatever country they may be in ... I think about the others boys too because of their mothers or wives and families that they have to be away from.[130]

Translations of War Mothers Song texts reveal several consistent themes: the high esteem in which young Kiowa men are regarded as warriors, their willingness to travel far away, the prominence of the United States flag throughout the world, the joyous feeling of meeting returning servicemen, and the courageous deeds, fearlessness, and bravery displayed by Kiowa warriors in battle. As one Kiowa woman explained (Ellis 2003:24), "those songs brought my brother home from World War II and Korea, just like when my grandma sang for my grandpa way back there when he went away to fight the cavalry." The following War Mothers songs demonstrate these themes and the continued emphasis Kiowa place on honoring their veterans.

> *Song 1*
> 1 Cáui-jò-gǔ-dàu è jái-dàum, è jái-dàum, è qá-jái-dầu
>   (Kiowa-young men / they / brave / they [are] heroes)
>   Young Kiowa men, they are brave, they are heroes.
> 2 Repeat.
> 3 Cáui-jò-gǔ-dàu è jái-dàum, è qá-jái-dầu, è qá-jái dầu, è qá-jái-dầu
> 4 Táup-càu è dàum-tố-yà-dò[131]
>   (Far away / they / land / travel / because or why)
>   That's why they have traveled/been far away.
> 1 Repeat line 3.
> 2 Repeat line 4.
>
> *Song 2*
> 1 Áu-gáu-dàum-gà ọ̌-dé-jó-gúl bá àui-qầu-jè
>   (Our own-land / joyous, good or nice-young man / we / again-met)
>   In our own land, we met a joyous young man again.
> 2 Háun-dé-ọ̌-dè!
>   (It is exceptionally nice or good, or how wonderful it is)
>   How wonderful it is!

1 Repeat line 1.
2 Repeat line 2.[132]

Song 3
1 Cáui-jò-gǜ-dàu è cí̵-còt gàu táup-càu è dàum-tő-yà
   (Kiowa-young men-are / they / unafraid / and / far away / they / travel or foray)
   Young Kiowa men are unafraid and have traveled far away.
2 Repeat.
3 Cáui-jò-gǜ-dàu è cí̵-còt gàu táup-càu è dàum-tő-yà-nàu
   (Kiowa-young men-are / they / unafraid / and / far away / they / travel or foray / and)
   Young Kiowa men are unafraid and have traveled far away, and
4 È jái-dàum-hèl-gàu táup-càu è dàum tő-yà, gà sa̱u-mí̵
   (They / brave-reportedly-and / far away / they / travel or foray, it is / noteworthy or something).
   They are reportedly brave and travel far away; it is something.[133]

Lewis Toyebo composed the following song. His daughter, Delores Harragarra, stated that her father did not give a title or name to any of the War Mothers songs that he composed or explain the exact inspiration for any particular song. However, over time other Kiowa have begun informally to associate names or references with some of the songs, on the basis of their assumptions about a song's content. As with American popular music, people often make assumptions about the origin of a song on the basis of its lyrics, which may or may not correlate with the composer's intent. In some instances the exact context of these associations—whether a song was composed to reflect a particular battle or was based simply on combat in general—is unknown. Although the following song refers only to Kiowa men in combat, some Kiowa interpret it as referring to the D-Day invasion and describing the movement of troops and their taking of the Normandy beachhead on June 6, 1944, followed by the offensive advance of the Allied Forces on the German defenses. Although individual songs hold different meanings for different persons and groups, these interpretations are important to note, because they reflect the ongoing changes in meaning and reference of songs occurring in the Kiowa community.

Song 4
1 Cáui-jò-gǜ-dàu è jái-dàum-hèl è jái-dàum-hèl è ta̱u-jé-ba̱u-dà
   (Young Kiowa men / they / brave-reportedly / they / brave-reportedly / they / news-appeared)
   Young Kiowa men, they are reportedly brave, they are reportedly brave; news about them appeared,
2 Hé-gàu gà ái-qa̱u-jé-jó-àum-dè-hèl-nàu
   (And then / it is / smoky-together-into the midst / and)

And then, they reportedly came together (established a base) in the midst of the smoke, and

3 Cî-dè ét kóp-fé-hâ-fè-hèl-nàu
(Toward something moving toward you / they / in a run-charged-reportedly / and)
They reportedly charged at the approaching-charging enemy, and

4 Hàun ét î-dàu-hèl-nàu
(Not or without / they / afraid-reportedly-and)
They were reportedly unafraid (without hesitation), and

5 Gà ṣa̧u-mî
(It is / noteworthy, interesting, etc.)
It is noteworthy.[134]

1 Repeat line 2.
2 Repeat line 3.
3 Repeat line 4.
4 Repeat line 5.

One elder Kiowa woman described another War Mothers Song that some Kiowa refer to as the Iwo Jima Song because it references a flag-raising like the one atop Mount Suribachi:

It all pertains to our boys overseas and serving and the things that they go through, and there's one in particular—oh, there's a lot of them, and they're all beautiful. But the one in particular is that Iwo Jima [Song], you know, where they raised that flag and that. And it just tells about their bravery and what they did. . . . It says that through their bravery and their efforts that they are able to come together and raise the flag. And it's all through their bravery.[135]

Around 1994 Frank Kaubin composed the new War Mothers Club Song, which translates as follows:[136]

1 War Mothers, I'm proud of you—honor you.
2 It was your son who went on the war trail, across the ocean to fight.
3 Outstanding young men, they returned again for us and they were victorious; it is noteworthy.[137]

Operation Desert Storm

During Operation Desert Storm I lived in Oklahoma and had the opportunity to witness the response of the Kiowa and neighboring tribes to the war. During this time the Kiowa War Mothers were very busy with service-oriented activities, including meals and dances for outgoing and returning soldiers and several open prayer meetings for service personnel at the Anadarko Veterans of Foreign Wars office. Meetings included devotionals, singing of Indian hymns, and prayers for U.S. troops serving in Saudi

Arabia and elsewhere. The chapter was also active in decorating the streets of Anadarko with red, white, blue, and yellow ribbons to honor returning soldiers.[138] On February 9, 1991, I attended the Kiowa War Mothers' "Desert Storm Rally Powwow," held to raise funds for sending "care packages" to each Kiowa veteran in Saudi Arabia.

Carol Flores recalled the following about Operation Desert Storm: "We were really busy. That was really something. Everybody was excited during that time, and a lot of our Kiowa boys went, too. . . . There were several of the War Mothers, their sons went over."[139] Ruby Williams reflected on the chapter's activities during this time:

> We were really busy then. That was our busy time because our men were leaving and going. When they leave, well, if no one thinks about having anything for them [a send-off], then it's up to us to have something or provide something. When we do, it's not like a powwow, it's like a prayer service or something like that. To give them a good send-off and then to support them while they are there.[140]

In terms of support, morale, and community news, mail has always been important for veterans overseas. War Mothers members sometimes write notes at chapter meetings that are sent to servicemen and servicewomen wherever they are stationed. Desert Storm veteran Lowell Russell recalled receiving a package from the Kiowa War Mothers during Operation Desert Storm: "Mail was real important. I don't care if you got one letter. I mean, my gosh, somebody cares."[141] During Desert Storm the War Mothers frequently met to pack gifts for their relatives in service and to encourage one another by talking about their servicemen far away.[142] Ruby Williams described these efforts and some of the responses from veterans:

> Just through our work and the things that we do and the help that we give the servicemen and those that are going away. Even though we may be at a dance or whatever and if there's a serviceman there we don't neglect them, never. Because that's part of our work. So we recognize them and bring them, you know, it's in our minutes that we set aside so much money to give them, regardless [that] nobody [else] does, but we do. And then our prayers go with them and then during Christmas time we send gifts and packages to them, all of our boys, our Kiowa Chapter, to the boys that are from our Kiowa tribe. We do that every Christmas. . . . We got a check from some boy . . . he sent a personal check to us for one hundred dollars because he had received one of these packages. He said he was in a trench or something, soaking wet, and lo and behold he got one of our Kiowa War Mothers packages, Kiowa Chapter 18. We do things like that and we get some beautiful letters from the boys.[143]

Recent Awards

In the mid-1990s the Kiowa War Mothers received several awards for their service work. These included a state award for obtaining the largest number of new members, a state award for having the oldest state member (Carrie Sahmaunt, then ninety-two), and a fifty-year individual membership award to Elizabeth Two Hatchet of Hobart, Oklahoma. In 1998 Helen Marie Poolaw was elected the Oklahoma state president of the American War Mothers, overseeing ten state chapters. In September 2005 Poolaw was elected the 2006–2007 national chair of the American War Mothers, which has 340 active chapters nationwide. Poolaw was the first Kiowa and the second Native American to hold the position. On the east side of the Kiowa tribal complex, the Kiowa War Memorial was erected under the term of past chapter president Elva Mae Tsatoke. During Helen Poolaw's term as president, the Kiowa War Mothers implemented a series of brick plaques with the names, ranks, and branches of the servicemen. Leading to the memorial, this walkway is known as the "Warriors Sidewalk."[144]

The Carnegie Victory Club

The organization that became the Carnegie Victory Club was formed during World War II as a service-oriented association to honor and recognize veterans. At that time Pauline Beulah Zotigh (also known as Beulah Hall) saw groups preparing bandages from old sheets for the Red Cross to use overseas and became interested in such service-oriented activities. A local group of Kiowa women was soon invited to a powwow near Cushing, Oklahoma, that was being held for a young Indian serviceman. The powwow was sponsored by the local Armed Forces Service Club and was organized by local Indian parents who had family members in the armed forces. Upon returning to the Carnegie area, Hall and others began organizing local Kiowa women. Because of the Kiowa response to World War I and the beginning of World War II, the idea caught on quickly.[145]

Many Kiowa men were enlisting or being drafted for military service after 1941. World War I veterans encouraged the younger men but also warned them of the dangers. Hall's cousin Robert Koomsa and his cousin Frank Kaubin were two of the first Kiowa to enlist from the Carnegie area. Hall, her sister, Mary Hall Tofpi, and their parents organized the club, with Beulah as the first club president. Local Kiowa families joined the organization, which soon honored Robert Koomsa's enlistment with a farewell powwow. Later wounded in New Guinea, Koomsa was one of the first Kiowa in World War II to receive the Purple Heart.[146] The organization held its first celebration in 1943.

Veteran send-offs in the form of singing and dancing were major community social events and the primary stimulus behind the later expansion of powwows and society revivals in the 1950s. Martha Poolaw described the Victory Club's role during World War II:

> The Victory Club . . . is built on the same concept. That organization was started to . . . since the boys went away from home, they tried to keep contact with them, [to] have some type of contact with them at that time. When they came

home, maybe it was just one man that came home or maybe there were several, no matter what it was, back in those days they didn't have that many powwows at that time. And I can remember back when they didn't have very many things [dances], and when they did, it was a real big thing.[147]

During the war the organization focused on honoring departing and returning servicemen, maintaining communication with servicemen by sending care packages to Kiowa veterans overseas, and performing various civic duties to those who had lost loved ones. These services continue to the present.

After the war the club was given an official name for the first time: the Carnegie Victory Club. Each member wore a navy blue broadcloth club blanket bordered in red, white, and blue ribbon. In the center of each Victory Club blanket was a large V with a dot-dot-dash (Morse code for "victory") below it, sewn from red, white, and blue ribbon. Beulah Hall and Mrs. Pickler Boyiddle composed a song that was later introduced to the club by Leonard Cozad Sr. and that became the official Victory Club song. The Victory Club continues to honor veterans of all wars and is chartered as a nonprofit organization. As announced at the 2002 annual Veterans Day observance, "the purpose of the club was to recognize and honor veterans of all wars, men and women. Each year special honorees are selected by the organization to pay tribute to their families, friends, and relatives. The event is open to the public and all area veterans of the armed forces."[148]

The club's functions culminate in the sponsoring of an annual Veterans Day Celebration and Victory Club Armistice Day Powwow on November 10 and 11 at Red Buffalo Hall in the Kiowa tribal complex in Carnegie, Oklahoma. A special invitation is extended to all veterans and veterans' organizations. Prayers and recognition are offered for all past and present United States servicemen. A banner featuring multiple square pendants with the symbols of the Victory Club—red, white, and blue borders with the red, white, and blue letter V above the dot-dot-dash symbol—hangs across the room. A series of red, white, and blue cut-and-paste American flags and a letter from the Kiowa Head Start Program thanking the veterans for their service adorn another wall, reflecting the respect for veterans that is instilled in Kiowa youths at an early age. Several items of beadwork displaying American flags and military-related designs are often seen on people's dance clothing.

On the evening of November 10, a prayer is given, followed by a processional, Gourd dancing, princess promotions, the induction of new club members, Victory Club and War Mothers songs, War and social dancing, and a closing prayer.[149] On Veterans Day the program opens with a prayer and the flag-raising at 7:00 A.M., followed by speakers emphasizing veterans' contributions, the need to recognize them, and the role of the Victory Club. Thanks are offered for servicemen who returned safely and for those who made the supreme sacrifice for their tribe and country. Highly decorated veterans are frequently honored at this time and asked to give speeches as observances for all veterans are held. Just before 11:00 A.M. everyone assembles out-

Carnegie Victory Club Armistice observation, Kiowa tribal complex, Carnegie, Oklahoma, 11:00 A.M., November 11, 1997.

side at the Kiowa veterans memorial and flagpole. The singers carry out a large drum, and there the Armistice is observed, followed by the singing of two Kiowa Memorial Songs.[150] All return inside the building for the rest of the program. For the November 11, 1993, Victory Club Armistice Day Celebration, the agenda was as follows:[151]

    Flag-raising and prayer, 7:00 A.M.
    Morning program
    Victory Club members
    Speaker and color guard, 10:45 A.M.
    Observance, 11:00 A.M.
    Scalp, Victory, and Shuffle Dances, 11:15 A.M.–12:00 P.M.
    Prayer and noon meal, 12:00–1:00 P.M.
    Gourd dancing, 1:00–5:30 P.M.
    Prayer and evening meal, 5:30–7:00 P.M.
    War Mothers songs and War Journey Songs, 7:30–8:00 P.M.
    War and social dancing, 8:00–11:00 P.M.

Of particular importance during Victory Club celebrations are the honoring of past and present Kiowa veterans and Victory Club members throughout the day, the Scalp, Victory, and Shuffle Dances, and the War Mothers and War Journey songs, all of which are traditional Kiowa forms of honoring veterans. The program is somewhat flexible, and in some years two or more sets of War Mothers songs are sung after lunch, before the beginning of the Gourd Dance. During the 1997 Scalp Dance, emcee Martha Koomsa Perez announced:

> On this day, forever consecrated to our heroic dead and all men and women of all wars, we are able once again to express our sincere reverence, homage, and also to celebrate the victory declared for us on Armistice Day 1918 and the termination of World War I. This morning as you made your way down to the monument, the monument represents the resting place of many departed Kiowa men who served in all wars, and that to always remember that wherever the body of a comrade lies, there the ground is hallowed. Our presence here is calmly in commemoration of all these men, and there are women also. It is an expression of our tribute to their devotion of duty, to their courage, and to their patriotism by their services on land, on sea, and in the air, they have made us their debtors. The flag of our nation still flies over a land of free people. This hits home to all of us that are here this morning. We are all descendants of those who have danced these sacred dances of ours, many, many years, and for time, it is endless for us as Kiowa people. Endlessly we dance and carry on our tradition and our ceremonial way . . . these are our ceremonial dances. They are danced once or twice a year. And for those that aren't here with us, we wish that they were here to help us carry on this great tradition of ours.[152]

As in other Kiowa societies, the memory of ancestors and former club members is strongly and frequently expressed. Likewise, frequent references to ancestors and their relationship to Kiowa culture are major components of the emotion and spirit exhibited at Victory Club celebrations. Martha Koomsa Perez spoke of the importance of the original Victory Club members and what they left for the present generations of Kiowa to enjoy, cherish, and care for:

> The women that danced and danced very strongly . . . their names still ring in my ears: Old Lade Potiye, Laura Tahlo, . . . Mabel Hummingbird. So many of the elders have gone on and left us this to take care of, for us to take care of. That's why we continue to do this every year: Pearl Kerchee, Edna Pauahty, Mattie Hainta, Bessie Tanedooah, Julia Daingkau, Old Lady Berry, Sally Bointy, Lottie Whitefox, Mr. and Mrs. Jasper Reynolds, Mrs. David Mithelo, Ruth Ann Redbird, Dorothy Whitefox, Mrs. Sterling Wheat, Hattie Ako, . . . Mary Haumpy, Nellie Satepauhoodle, Martha Doyeto, Ruby Anquoe, Old Lady Joanna . . .[153]

Such sentiments were also expressed in a letter written to the Victory Club by Harlan Hall Zotigh, which was read during the 1997 observance:

> Today, the Victory Club's day of high spirits and honor, we look with happiness and strong hearts on this still beautiful land, our home. Somewhere in the winds of time all of the old time Victory Club songs can still be heard. We sing some of them today. The charter or original members will hear us in spirit. The veterans

of that long ago day will hear us in spirit too. Coming into this building, onto these grounds, Kiowa land. These very special Victory Club ceremonial grounds. The first steps of the president always sets the day's pace, as it is this day. As she makes her way, as is the old way of a half-century ago, we feel the spirit of Beulah Hall Taingyahigh with us today.

Every Victory Club song is a jewel in its own right. In the vast land that was the dominion of the Kiowa spirit, warriors, Kiowa warriors, always we honor first and in another time will listen, listen for the names of their grandchildren. Again leading the way will be grandparents, parents, aunts, nieces, nephews, cousins, sisters, brothers, uncles, and friends. Our lasting salute today then is for all who gave their all, first when the closing song is sung and the drum is put away for the next time, for the next year, prayer is intoned as we hold in precious memory those who wait on the other side.[154]

As described in chapter 4, the Scalp, Victory, and Shuffle Dances hold great significance for the Kiowa. As emcee Martha Perez announced during the Victory Dance portion of the celebration in 1997:

> These are women's dances. They are danced because they are Victory Dances. When the men went out on their war journeys and they returned home, they celebrated, they danced with victory. They showed off the scalps and the booty that they brought home. . . . And this is the significance of this dance. It's been with us for many, many years and we continue to carry it on. The people at this time rejoice, they celebrated in victory. The war mothers are proud, they are proud of the achievements of their loved ones. They dance and they dance and they dance to the victory and to uphold the honor of our young warriors and what they have brought home, especially their lives.[155]

Nearly all Victory Club members are descendants of earlier or charter members, and many of the organizational offices have been passed down through particular families. No head singer is appointed for the morning portion of the program, and most singers are descendants of past or present club members. During the morning program, Scalp, Victory, Shuffle, War Mothers, and War Journey Songs are sung. After supper the Victory Club opens the evening program with a processional. Members wear their club blankets, and each carries one of several small, forty-eight-star flags that have been handed down from the original club members. After the processional the club president collects the flags and keeps them until the next year's dance.

Several special recognitions are made throughout the Veterans Day program, including recognition of the first club president, Beulah Hall. The Fifty-Fifth Annual Armistice Day Celebration in 1997 was dedicated in her memory. The origin and historical development of the Victory Club is recited several times throughout the day by the emcee. Honorary female guests are also recognized several times throughout the day. Members of the Crow Tribe from Montana, who come down every year in early

November for a series of hand games against the Kiowa and neighboring tribes, always attend the Victory Club celebration and are brought into the center of the arena, where they are introduced and the service records of any veterans are read. A song is sung for them to dance to, and gifts are given to them. During the 1997 Veterans Day dance, the Crows reciprocated the honor and gifts they received by donating $800 in cash and pledging a bison for the next year's dance.

Other women's service organizations such as the Kiowa War Mothers, Kiowa Veterans Auxiliary (Kiowa Black Legs Auxiliary), Otoe War Mothers, Apache Service Club (Naishan Apache), Clinton Military Service Club (Cheyenne), Wichita Service Club, Kiowa Tia-Piah Society of Carnegie, and Kiowa Marine Veterans Auxiliary often co-host the Victory Club celebration. A special recognition for one of the co-hosts is also held. During the 1997 Veterans Day dance, the Apache Service Club was honored and the names of every Apache serviceman in the twentieth century was read off by the emcee as the Apache danced to the Apache Chief's Song.

The Victory Club's observances include a dedication of flowers to the sacrifice of past veterans. John Gamble (1952:41–42) noted that the Victory Club placed a vase of flowers by the flagpole near the arena late on the morning of November 11, and a prayer was made at approximately 10:50 A.M., the time of the Armistice. At the event Gamble observed, this was followed by what he listed as men's and women's Victory Dances, then women's Victory Dances.[156] At Victory Club celebrations I attended, an arrangement of red, white, and blue flowers was set at the front table near the emcee. Emcee Martha Koomsa Perez announced at the 1997 celebration:

> We place this symbol of purity; may each future generation emulate the unselfish courage of our men who fought for freedom. . . . In memory of the heroic dead who have fallen in defense of the United States of America we place this tribute of our devotion and everlasting remembrance . . . on behalf of all the ladies' auxiliaries in our organization, the veterans of foreign wars and of all wars of the United States. This emblem of eternity, its color that speaks life everlasting, thus do we immortalize the brave deeds of our soldiers, sailors, and marines who have given their lives on land and sea and in the air, their red, white, and blue flowers.[157]

After this dedication, the "Jr. Little Miss Victory Club," Isabella Poor Buffalo, was asked to place one red, one white, and one blue flower in the arrangement. The Victory Club Celebration continues with social and War dancing, concluding around midnight each year.

The Stecker Purple Heart Club

The Stecker Purple Heart Club was formed shortly after the United States entered World War II, its membership centered on the community of Stecker, Oklahoma.

During the war, many Kiowa servicemen were killed or wounded in action, and the largest number came from the Stecker area. These included Joe Domebo, Puppy Little Joe, George Neconie, Earl Palmer, Lyndreth Palmer (KIA), Wilson Palmer, Ernest Redbird, Jerry Redbone, Arthur Silverhorn, Chester Silverhorn, and Raymond Woodard, among others. The organization was formed to honor veterans who had been wounded in combat. As Orville Neconie explained, "Well, them boys that come home with that Purple Heart, see. Because one got it and another one got it and another one. I think there were the most Purple Heart holders in Stecker than in the other Indian centers, you know. This is why they named it that."[158] The organization was founded by the Domebo, Hummingbird, Odelty, Sankadota, and Silverhorn families—among them both Christian and Native American Church families—who sponsored dances to honor Kiowa Purple Heart recipients. A photograph of members in 1945 included Caroline Bosin, Virginia Bosin (club princess), Anna Chaino, Nancy Chaino, Rose Chaino, Agnes Domebo, Effie Domebo, Lou Daniel Domebo, Mary Domebo, Rose Mopope Domebo, Eula Geionety, Mrs. Hummingbird, Etta Mopope, Clara Rose Palmer Neconie, Anna Poolaw, Margaret Sankadota, and Hazel Tartsah.[159]

Mac Whitehorse explained some of the early history of the organization:

> The Purple Heart Club began at Stecker around 1941. From the Stecker area, the first Purple Heart recipients were Arthur Silverhorn and Earl Palmer. The dances were held at the Hummingbirds', the Silverhorns', and at different places in Stecker. Just to name some of the members, Ahboah, Big Joe, Little Joe, Bosin, Domebo, Doyebi, Geionety, Hummingbird, and Tartsah. The first club princess was Virginia Bosin. They didn't have a head staff at the powwows.[160]

During World War II the organization was active nearly every weekend as some local veteran left for or returned from service. Lula Geionety and Lucy Domebo composed several Purple Heart Club songs. Although elders indicate that the organization had around eight songs of its own, only one is still remembered; it is now used as the club song and for processionals. Composed by Lula Geionety and typical of other veterans songs used by the War Mothers and the Victory Club, this song references the bravery of Kiowa veterans:

1 Bét tháu-hâl-yĩ
   (You all / listen)
   You all listen!
2 Hè-gáu vău-táup-vâi-hĩ-yà
   (And then / across the ocean / keep fighting on-going)
   And then I am going across the ocean to fight (for my country).
3 Repeat line 2.
4 United States á áu-gà-jàu-dò, á dàum-áu-gà-bán-mà
   (United States / I / self possessive / because of / I / land-self possessive-going)

Because I do not want anyone to take the United States, because I do not want anyone to take our land, I am going.
1 Repeat line 1.
2 Repeat line 2.
3 Repeat line 2.
4 Gàu thái-káu-ól-tâ-gàu á áu-gà-jàu-dò, á xói-dè-thàu
   (And / the flag / I / self possessive / because of / I / fall [i.e., killed] / shall be)
   And because I do not want anyone to take our flag (I am going there to fight), even if I die.[161]

Although initially held for recipients of the Purple Heart, the organization's activities have broadened to include sponsoring dances to honor any service person. Dances sponsored by the Purple Heart Club in the Stecker community were held for three main events: the departure of a serviceman, the return of a serviceman, and the temporary furlough of a serviceman before going overseas. The dances began with dinners prepared by the organization's members, followed by Scalp, Victory, and Round Dances performed by the women. In the past, funds raised through sales and raffles of craftwork and through gifts, collections, and Blanket Dances (in which people place money on a blanket spread on the ground during a dance) was given to the service person being honored to use as he or she desired. Today, in addition to honor dances, prayer meetings are sometimes held for a soldier away on duty or home on leave.[162] Mary Neconie Shane described one such meeting held for her sons:

There's a lot of prayers of thanksgiving, there's a lot of singing, a lot of families get up and you know they testify how when they prayed they just had to have faith that this young man was going to come home safe. And actually we had a prayer service for both our sons because we had our oldest boy, he went to Korea, and just never had one for him, so I kind of combined them both. My brothers and sisters were there and it was really good because of that. Everybody comes out, and a lot of the people that were there were from the Stecker area, you know, so that was good.[163]

Originally, the Purple Heart Club's insignia was a purple blanket with white trim that club members wore like a shawl. Some of the blankets had an embroidered logo of the Purple Heart medal in the center. The blankets also featured the name, branch of service, and division of the club member's relative printed on the back. Servicemen who were being honored at these dances wore their military uniforms.

According to one Kiowa elder from Stecker, the Purple Heart Club held no dances during Operation Desert Storm because there were no servicemen from the Stecker area in that operation. The club did, however, help co-host the honor dances of other Kiowa women's organizations. Although the Purple Heart Club is smaller and less active today than the other women's societies, it still holds occasional dances to honor veterans. One dance I attended in 1994 was held to honor a highly decorated veteran. It included speeches about his rank and service, Gourd dancing, and Purple Heart Club and Veterans' songs with texts mentioning veterans' themes.[164]

Since the late 1950s, Purple Heart Club activities have increasingly been held outside the immediate Stecker area because of the relocation of many people to other areas for employment following World War II, the closing of the local school and church, and Stecker's becoming an unincorporated town. Ralph Kotay described how servicemen were honored in earlier times and how traditions have changed:

> In those days you can honor him, see . . . [when] you honor him, somebody will put a shawl on him while the dance is going on. They never stop the dance, and then somebody will throw some money in front of him, you know, to honor [him], that's the way it was at that time. But now it takes a whole hour to have one giveaway [laughing]. But these fellows, they keep on singing, keep on singing. [It was] like that [at] all the dances that we had of that time.[165]

Recently the organization has become more active again through the efforts of the Clara Neconie family and its relatives. Today the club uses a shawl designed by Tony Soontay consisting of a purple blanket with an outline of the state of Oklahoma, a star marking the location of Stecker, and the name Purple Heart Club. The organization currently has no officers, preferring to work through a cooperative structure of family and other members. Although the club currently holds no annual dance, it co-hosts other dances honoring veterans and occasionally sponsors a family-style bingo event for fundraising. Mary Neconie Shane commented, "They really do recognize the Purple Heart Club, like at different powwows, especially if it's for a veteran. We'll take our shawls and they'll recognize the Purple Heart Club, you know, because they know it's an old club."[166] With the exception of not holding benefit dances, the ideology and activities of the Purple Heart Club closely resemble those of the other Kiowa women's service organizations.

The Kiowa Veterans Auxiliary

The Kiowa Veterans Auxiliary (KVA) is the women's auxiliary to the Kiowa Black Legs Society and is composed of female relatives of the Black Legs Society members. The KVA provides refreshments at all Black Legs Society organizational meetings and hosts and participates in the Scalp, Victory, and War Mothers Dances at each of the two annual society ceremonials (see chapter 4). The KVA also prepares a large meal for the entire Black Legs encampment and all visitors, as well as during the smaller society meetings held in preparation for each ceremonial and for the annual Black Legs Society Christmas fellowship. KVA members also set up and run the camps at the Black Legs encampments and bring food to help feed the relatives of recently deceased members. Previously, officers in the KVA were elected, but beginning in the

Members of the Kiowa Veterans Auxiliary and Kiowa War Mothers at the Black Legs Society ceremonial, Indian City U.S.A., Anadarko, Oklahoma, about 1997.

mid-1980s, they began to be appointed by society leader Gus Palmer Sr. Like the other Kiowa women's organizations, the KVA emphasizes honoring veterans.[167]

Summary

In the nineteenth century the Kiowa had two women's societies that were closely related to warfare and war power: the Calf Old Women and the Bear Women. Both societies were founded by men who received dreams during vision quests, and both ceased functioning around 1905. Following a renewal of Scalp and Victory Dances associated with the return of fourteen Kiowa World War I veterans, these dances continued to be held upon people's return from service and during annual Armistice Day celebrations. The military service of nearly three hundred Kiowa men during World War II necessitated their honoring by Kiowa women through traditional song and dance, which facilitated the formation of four new women's organizations.

The four existing Kiowa women's organizations—the Kiowa War Mothers, the Carnegie Victory Club, the Stecker Purple Heart Club, and the Kiowa Veteran's Auxiliary—are attributable to two primary factors. The first is their origins in pre-reservation women's societies, which were integrally linked to ensuring success in warfare followed by participating in the honoring and celebration of returning warriors. The second is the return of warrior status through the large-scale participation of Kiowa men in World War II. Some of the Kiowa women's societies were formally revived during World War II and functioned prior to the men's societies that were revived in 1957 and 1958. They now play integral roles in contemporary veterans' and society dances.

The activities of these groups reflect both the degree of independence held by pre-reservation Kiowa women's societies and some of the changes in women's rights in what is still a predominantly male-dominated Kiowa culture—as, for example, in the War Mothers' practice of allowing only women at meetings. The War Mothers, Victory Club, and Purple Heart Club are independent organizations, not directly linked or subject to any male organization, whereas the Kiowa Veterans Auxiliary serves the Kiowa Veterans Association through the activities of the Black Legs Society. Kiowa women also indicate that the ability to form their own groups, elect officers, and conduct their own business meetings and fund-raisers, independent of the men's organizations, is important for members. Although several Kiowa women have served in the armed forces, no Kiowa women's veteran organizations have been formed.[168]

Kiowa women perceive a great similarity between past and present women's groups, that of honoring veterans. One woman stated that no one knows much about the Calf Old Women and Bear Women Societies, but in honoring veterans, the modern groups fill the void left by these older women's societies. Indeed, in comparison with Kiowa men's societies, I found little surviving data in interviews with elder Kiowa women about the women's societies. Kiowa veterans frequently acknowledge the traditional role of Kiowa women in honoring warriors and express gratitude for the efforts of the current women's service organizations, both privately and at public functions such as the annual Black Legs, War Mothers, and Victory Club dances. As Carol Flores explained, members receive great satisfaction from knowing they have helped the veterans:

> They appreciate what we do for them. They remember what the War Mothers have done, even before my time. If someone happens to get up there [at a dance] and wants to say a little something, they remember that when they were overseas how they got what you would say a care package from the War Mothers. . . . And when those men come back, well naturally . . . they might be home on leave or getting out of service and they appreciate us. They say, "We heard from the War Mothers. You know, we appreciate the War Mothers, because I received a care package or I received a letter," and how it makes them feel. They just appreciate what the War Mothers have done for them, how good it made them feel. And I've heard it so many times through different men. And it makes you feel good, even though maybe it wasn't during my time, it might have been through someone else.[169]

Since their revival, some Kiowa women's groups have been based in particular Kiowa communities—the Purple Heart Club around Stecker and the Victory Club around Carnegie and Mountain View. As larger and more pan-Kiowa organizations, the Kiowa Veterans Auxiliary and the Kiowa War Mothers are more widely based in membership. Dual membership is possible, and a few women now belong to more than one organization.

All the women's organizations are service oriented and hold the same traditional women's dances for servicemen, including women's Scalp and Victory, Shuffle, and Round (including War Mothers and Victory Club) Dances. Although some songs and dances are used by all the women's groups, each organization has its own group of regular singers and its own society or "club" songs with texts referencing veterans' themes.

The main difference between the Kiowa War Mothers and the Carnegie Victory Club is that the War Mothers is a chapter of a federally recognized, national, chartered, nonprofit organization that reports to Congress (which determines its continuation) annually, whereas the Victory Club is an individual, chartered, nonprofit Kiowa organization. Membership in the War Mothers requires military service by one's son or daughter, whereas the Victory Club is more broadly based, and a member may represent a more distant relative. The Victory Club, Purple Heart Club, and Kiowa Veteran's Auxiliary do not hold the dinners and perform the hospital and community work that the War Mothers do. Whereas the War Mothers' activities are structured along well-defined state and national levels of organization and periodically provide services to all veterans, the activities of the Victory Club, KVA, and Purple Heart Club are focused largely within the Kiowa Tribe, although the groups do co-host events with neighboring tribes. Organizations in which members have relatives in service usually sponsor celebrations for those relatives and are thus often community based. There is a tendency for men who have been honored by one of these organizations to attend the dances of that group, which usually contains most of his female relatives.

Some competition and rivalry exists between the women's groups, largely in the form of verbal assertions about one another's status. Members say that this rivalry is sometimes reflected in terms of groups jockeying to get ahead of others in line for processionals. Some women see the War Mothers, who have a generally fancier dress code and organizational shawl than the other groups, as elite or sometimes as looking down on the other women's groups, and some women describe the KVA as "little more than cooks." After a period of near inactivity, the Purple Heart Club is trying to increase its activities, and the KVA is not in the public spotlight as much as the War Mothers and the Victory Club. Although the contributions of the groups differ, each provides goods and services to the Kiowa and other communities, and all are dedicated to honoring veterans. The Black Legs ceremonials would not function as smoothly as they do without the dedication of the KVA women, who set up the camps and provide large meals for all. Without the War Mothers, numerous veterans would want for the lack of their contributions, and the Victory Club and Purple Heart Club provide dances that honor servicemen and servicewomen.

More important, these rivalries do not inhibit cooperation in activities. There is good rapport between the four Kiowa women's service organizations, which often serve as co-hosts at one another's dances and at the dances of other service-related organizations. The War Mothers have sold raffle tickets for the Victory Club at the latter's dance. There are also kin-based connections between members of the organizations. Families without female members in any of the women's service organizations frequently solicit a club to sponsor a dance in honor of their relative.

Although the activity level of the women's service groups fluctuates in accordance with the prevalence of military service and participation of community and tribal members, activities and dances sponsored by these groups have continued since World War II. According to some elders, the prominence of these organizations has periodically ebbed and flowed with fluctuations in membership, activities, the number of veterans in members' families, and resources. Whereas the Victory Club is said to have been the most influential group during World War II, the War Mothers has gained prominence in more recent years, and the Purple Heat Club has recently been increasing the frequency of its activities.

The organizations have combined pre-reservation women's roles in supporting men's martial activities with elements of Kiowa and Anglo women's service groups. Their continuity is culturally significant because they serve as the primary enculturative arena that belongs to and focuses on women and that continues to pass on a part of traditional Kiowa women's roles to younger generations. As an integral part of most Kiowa community celebrations, direct participation ensures the survival of traditional dances, martial ideology, use of the Kiowa language in songs, and women's roles. Participation further serves as a traditional form of maintaining and enhancing Kiowa women's roles and a distinct Kiowa ethnicity, through the expression of differences with other tribal and intertribal women's veterans auxiliaries but more importantly through songs, which describe the experiences of Kiowa veterans and the Kiowa community. While continuing several earlier women's traditions, these organizations also function as integrative sociocultural forms that have adapted to meet the contemporary needs of service personnel and the Kiowa community.

CONCLUSION

Kiowa military societies continue to hold great importance in the maintenance and continuation of Kiowa culture. Much as James Dempsey (1988:1, 1999) found among Northern Plains tribes, many Plains Indians have retained a warrior ethic or ethos despite lengthy government and missionary efforts to suppress it. Military service acquires a highly valued and socially praised status that, although now qualitatively different, continues in Kiowa culture. Although military-oriented institutions and cultural practices have changed through acculturation, they have also been perpetuated through the selective use of accommodation, adaptation, reorganization, revitalization, and syncretism. Dempsey's (1988:8) characterization of these developments among Northern Plains Indians closely resembles the way developments among the Kiowa and neighboring Plains groups might be characterized:

> While on the surface it appeared that the concerted efforts of the schools and government officials had extinguished the warrior ethic, in reality it had survived. Though diminished in intensity it had been partly redirected into religious ceremonies but still existed through such pursuits as parades, games, mock battles, counting coups, and the rituals of warrior societies. As an anthropologist commented about that period, "They bought medicine bundles, they joined societies; they honoured their sons and daughters with lavish payments in both horses and goods for ceremonial privileges." In short, the Indians preserved much of the old outlook in spite of government efforts to suppress [it].

Having interviewed Kiowa and observed and participated in their dances from 1989 to the present, I conclude by offering the following synopsis of Kiowa military societies and their ceremonials.

The frequent and heavy emphasis the Kiowa place on society dances and the honoring of veterans comes not from any inherent love of warfare. Some Kiowa veterans have expressed their dislike for but recognition of the necessity of military service and what they went through, and others have stated that they hope there are no future wars. First and perhaps foremost, these societies and dances are celebrations and expressions of the Kiowa's physical and cultural survival and freedom, as Kiowa and as Americans. Much of these expressions continues to be focused on song, dance, giving away, and public recognition of the warrior-veteran. Despite a markedly decreased land base and a troubled history with the United States government that continues to this day, Kiowa readily point out that their land is still Indian land. Indeed, existing trust status land has technically remained under Indian ownership. Kiowa also acknowledge that the United States still has a greater number of freedoms than anywhere else.

Second, the events held by present-day Kiowa societies are aimed at honoring those who were willing to defend their tribal (Kiowa) and national (United States) fellows, land, and freedoms. Centering primarily on song, dance, and ritual forms of recognition (honoring) and redistribution (giveaways), the societies and their ceremonies provide a source of social recognition and approval and martial celebration by recognizing veterans' efforts, the great distances they traveled, their absences from their families, tribes, and homelands, and their sacrifices in terms of combat, mental and physical wounds, and death. The women's Scalp and Victory Dances are physical manifestations of their appreciation of veterans' service and sacrifice.

Third, these events constitute a major form of socialization as public gatherings offering a sense of community fellowship and the opportunity to practice and enjoy Kiowa culture. These aspects are integral to the continuity of any group's ideology, ethos, and ethnicity.

Finally, these events constitute an important element of Kiowa enculturation through people's familiarization with, practice of, and continuity in varied aspects of Kiowa culture, and they provide a forum for the modification of existing culture and the introduction of new cultural forms. Although annual society ceremonials differ in certain aspects of their structural bases (whether a secular, military, or ethnic focus), each draws a considerable segment of the Kiowa population together around a sodality-based form of social organization aimed at maintaining important elements of Kiowa tribal culture. Assuming new cultural and ritual importances and foci, their roles and statuses are now qualitatively different, and in some ways greater, than in the pre-reservation era.

Kiowa military societies and their antecedents (multiple Gourd and War Dance associations, powwows) form the basis for all existing Kiowa ceremonial and powwow activities focused on dance. Two distinct forms of Kiowa Gourd and War Dances have evolved: society ceremonials performed annually or a few times a year, with restricted membership and more conservative dress, song, and dance, and powwow forms, which are more secular, tend to have fewer restrictions on membership, participation, and frequency, and may involve contests. Whereas Black Legs Society dances are limited to the group's ceremonials, varied combinations of Gourd, War, Round, Scalp and Victory, and War Mothers songs and dances compose the majority of all society or organizational annual powwows, benefit dances, memorials, and family and descendants group dances.

Kiowa society dances and powwows also provide the largest form of non-kin-based group activity in Kiowa society. In many cases they have diffused to or incorporated members of other tribes and non-Indians. As sodalities, they cross-cut kinship-based structures and organizations such as lineage-based family and descendants groups, and they provide larger and in some instances more frequent activities than some Native American Church meetings, hand games, sweat lodge meetings, and powwow organizations. The societies' events provide far-reaching integrative functions in the areas of social, cultural, and economic activities. Although non-kin-based, many sodalities contain sizable core families and receive support from multiple extended families, so they also provide a dual form of integration on both kinship and non-kinship levels. Although these societies did not qualitatively replace the structure and significance of the earlier Sun Dance on a religious level, to some degree they have evolved to replace the Sun Dance by fostering the largest pan-Kiowa or tribal-level aggregations through annual ceremonials and dances.

Because the more conservative societies each bring together a different segment of the Kiowa tribe, Kiowa culture in general and society-specific traditions or "roads" are maintained. Because most of these groups (except the three Gourd Dance societies) hold their annual dances at different times, they are mutually supportive overall and not directly competitive. Despite the severe initial factionalism of the Gourd Dance revival, the contemporary presence of multiple Gourd Dance groups is not really detrimental, for an adequate population, interest, and economic base exists to support all of them. However, a single, unified Gourd Dance sodality would undoubtedly be an impressive and politically influential organization.

The honoring of servicemen during World War II and the Korean War and a renewed pride in Indian ethnicity helped reinvigorate the Kiowa warrior ethos, resulting in the revival of two military societies and the resurgence of a third. This revitalization of a warrior ethos and related Kiowa traditions was subsequently maintained with service in Vietnam and the Middle East. Military service provided the most direct modern link to regaining traditional social status based on war deeds. In light of these developments, and much as John David Northcutt (1973:110) predicted, veteran status has returned as an important basis for social and political status in the Kiowa community.

The annual dances of the Black Legs Society, the Kiowa War Mothers, and the Carnegie Victory Club undeniably epitomize the martial ethos of past and present Kiowa military societies. Yet elements of a martially based ideology and the ritual symbols (songs, dances, material culture, customs) that reinforce traditional concepts of honoring warrior status also remain in the Kiowa Gourd Clan, the Ohoma Lodge, the Rabbits Society, and other dance organizations. Though clearly syncretic today, these groups still espouse many nineteenth-century Kiowa martial traditions. The elevation of this martial ideology into an ethos was observed during Operation Desert Storm in 1990 (Meadows 1999:173–174) and has been seen during Operation Enduring Freedom in Afghanistan since 2001 and in Iraq since 2003—both conflicts in which several Kiowa men and women have served. The honoring of veterans through send-offs and homecomings continues, even in peacetime, and all society and powwow organizations continue to honor veterans to some degree in their activities.

All the surviving Kiowa military and dance societies have changed in some ways.

The Black Legs Society has incorporated the red cape of Young Mustang. The Gourd Clan has added a society princess and, to its body of ceremonial war trophies, a fur crook (*pàubôn*) and a saber. Girls are now allowed to participate in Rabbit Dances. The Omaha Society has seen three distinct forms of dress and dance evolve, and the single society bustle has been followed by the development of individual bustles. Kiowa women's societies have blended aspects of pre-reservation women's societies with those of contemporary Anglo women's service auxiliaries. Powwows have incorporated public buildings, address systems, head staff positions, contest formats, and other relatively recent changes. Yet despite these developments, the organizations continue to carry forth many key elements of Kiowa culture, ideology, and ethos.

As major foci of traditional cultural activities, these organizations serve as important arenas of enculturation for a host of both Kiowa and society-specific traditions. Society activities provide the opportunity for the maintenance of ethnic and artistic expression (song, dance, ritual language, oral history), religious rituals (prayer, cedaring), kinship, economic redistribution (pledges, raffles, benefit dances, giveaways), socialization, and politics. They also provide public formats for related rituals such as naming ceremonies, historical and cultural speeches, adoptions, and performances by color guards, as well as for the revival of older tribal traditions and the introduction of new forms. Because of their high social status, their positions as elders, and sometimes their fluency in Kiowa, prominent society members are often sought out to perform other cultural activities outside of society contexts, such as at Native American Church meetings, naming ceremonies, blessings, and cedarings, and to pray, speak, or sing during public programs. These characteristics are typical of the society and powwow structures of neighboring Southern Plains tribes (Meadows 1999:172–176, 404–423).

On a regional level, the Kiowa are of great significance as the originators and driving force behind the post-1957 revival of Southern Plains military societies. The Kiowa have also established and maintained a strong position in the burgeoning post–World War II Southern Plains powwow community. This includes the spread of the War and Gourd Dances, the latter of which many non-Plains Indians and non-Indians use "to honor veterans," the use of the Black Legs as color guards at veterans and other cultural events, the presence of Kiowa societies in the annual American Indian Exposition parade, the widespread use of Kiowa head staff, singers, and songs at powwows throughout the country, the prominence and number of commercial Kiowa music recordings, and the number and achievements of dancers (especially Fancy Feather and Straight dancers) and artists. Song, dance, and dance societies are clearly some of the Kiowa's strongest markers in the contemporary Oklahoma, Plains Indian, and non-Indian communities.

Yet Kiowa military and dance societies suffer from numerous forms of ongoing, pervasive factionalism, most commonly over issues of leadership positions, elections, membership, behavior, and the control of and accountability for resources. Although the same issues exist in Anglo institutions, competition for limited resources and the relatively small but highly interrelated and kinship-based communities make the effects of Native factionalism more severe. But despite numerous internal and external problems in these organizations, it is important to recognize their strength, richness, and resilience. These organizations are often both origin and center of jealousy, factionalism, and struggle for power and control within the tribe. However, it should be remembered that although there are those engaged in personal, family, and even sodality-based disputes, other members and leaders manage to rise above the familism and factionalism. These people work to overcome infighting and conflict. By embracing traditional tribally shared values, they strive to reunify disputants to achieve greater harmony within the group and the successful completion of activities.

Finally, these organizations are also a source of release and healing for many people, in that they offer a therapeutic quality that is frequently needed and sought by individuals in these communities because of the everyday stresses and pressures stemming from poverty, low-quality housing, health problems, racism, and the policies of tribal and federal government bureaucracies. Like Christian and Native American Church services, hand games, and other Indian activities, society dances and powwows offer people a contemporary sociocultural activity with an enduring historical and cultural connection to their past while providing physical and psychological release from the vast array of problems they face in daily life. The songs accompanying each cultural activity and the wide array of personal, family, community, sodality, and tribal meanings they hold and convey form a large part of this release. Referencing those who came before them, people often speak of the emotional, spiritual, and actual physical relief from existing ailments they experience upon attending and participating in these activities or even upon simply hearing the songs.

Although military societies and powwows are only one arena of contemporary Southern Plains Indian life, they remain some of the richest and most traditional cultural and ceremonial forms in the lives of many contemporary Kiowa and other neighboring Southern Plains tribes.

APPENDIX
Kiowa Military Society Membership Rosters

The following lists are quoted directly from the primary sources, using the ethnographers' original diacritics and spellings of names. Data in brackets were added by the author.

Áljóyĩgàu (Mountain Sheep Society)

Henry Tsoodle Sr. provided the following list of Áljóyĩgàu members to participants in the Laboratory of Anthropology Kiowa Field School in 1935 (SFN, 571–573). Tsoodle became a member of the Áljóyĩgàu at the age of eighteen, after spending two years in the Black Legs Society. According to the members' ages he gave, this list dates to around 1880. The record is particularly valuable in that members are listed by their society partnerships (1 and 2, 3 and 4, etc.).

1. Bedlpan (Big Bow) [Bèlfân, or Sore Mouth], society leader, 40+
2. Yi/hato (Two Hatchet), [Yíhàutò, or Two Axes, also known as Two Hatchet], society leader, 40+
3. Aya/te [Âiájè, or Walking A Tree], whipman, 40+
4. HwB'skte [?], whipman, 30
5. Dadla [?], boy member, 18
6. Tso'odl [Xóól, or Packing Stones, Henry Tsoodle Sr.], boy member, 18 [nos. 15 and 16 may have succeeded 5 and 6 as boy members]
7. T'aGu'te [?], girl member, 8
8. Kw'Bai [Káupfài, or Against A Robe, Mrs. Neconie; b. 1871], girl member, 8
9. Jim Todo [Jòdôm, or Beneath A Lodge, Jim To-dome], 20
10. Banse, 30
11. Dwt'oba [Dáuthópá, or Leading A Group Singing, Dau-to-bi], 18
12. D'wsedl [?], 16
13. E'sa [Jim Asah], 19
14. Ba'tsadl [Báchàl or Batchaddle], 19
15. Guengudl (Red Horn) [Gúéngúl], boy member, 9–10

16. Tangudl [Jángúljè, or Red Feathered Bonnet Brow; probably Edgar Keahbone], boy member, 10
17. TonGwGw [?], 20
18. Gue.lo [Kuelo or Cwélò, possibly Spanish for neck/collar], 20
19. Na.Goi [also known as Padalti or Paddlety], 30
20. Ma.nhe [Máunhḗdè, or No Hand, also known as Kiowa Bill), 30
21. To/nkoi [Tónkòidè, or Angrily Counterattacked, Bob Koomsa], 16
22. Tsodaha [Xódáuhā́qî], 16
23. Yi.k'i [? Yíkị̀, or Two Shields], 17
24. Da./bin [Jábìntályî, or Big-Eyed Boy, Dau-bien], 17
25. GyayOntai [Câiàuntàidè, or Following The Comanche Way, Gei-one-ty], 30+
26. GodlBai [?], 30
27. Tene/aubo [Thḛnéánfǫ̂a̰, or Eagle Asounding Approaching], 20
28. WnGo'te [probably Àungópjè, or Paul Kicking Bird], 20
29. T'aikwGw, [probably Tháikóbáu, or Bearing A White Flag, Tigh-ko-bo], 30
30. SetanDo/an (Bear Speaking)[Sétjáujójáu, or Talking To Bears], 30
31. Koi'ma [?], 30+
32. Bwlte [Fáuljè, or Good Drummer/Singer, Paudle-ty], 30

Chḛ̀jánmàu (Horse Headdresses Society)

The following list of society members was recorded from Hunting Horse by members of the 1935 Laboratory of Anthropology Kiowa Field School (SFN, 561). Hunting Horse left the Rabbits Society to join the Horse Headdresses Society at the age of twenty. Five years later he left the latter to join the Omaha Society. The list appears to pertain to the years between 1877 and 1884, because the Cheyenne gave the Omaha Society to the Kiowa in 1884. Hunting Horse estimated that the society had forty to fifty members during this period and listed forty persons.

Cúnqàjài [Dance Chiefs or Leaders]
1. Dohwson (Little Bluff) [Jòhâusàn, or Little Bluff Recess or Concavity], also known as Daunpai [Dáunfài, or Against The Shoulder Blade Area]
2. Go.w/ta.gyE (Pretty Lance) [? Cáuáuthágài, or Good Crow, also known as Big Joe]
3. Ma/mide (Standing High) [Mâmèdḗjè, or One Who Is Standing Above]
4. Se/osa (Game with Cactus?) [Sḗáusàn, or Came With Peyote or Little Bringer/Introducer Of Peyote]

Chḛ̀tàjóqî̀ [Fox Pelt Keepers or Whipmen]
5. Tso./taide (Top of the Rock) [Xótáidè, or Atop A Rock, Tso-tigh]
6. Bo.itsede (White Horse) [Bóichḛ̀, or Shiny Horse, Bo-es-chay]

Fáuljògàu (Drum Keepers)
7. Te/pde.a (Coming Out Of The Sweathut) [Tépdḗą̀, or Standing Sweathouse, Tape-deah]
8. aA/kate (Spanish name?)
9. Pa/gadogudl (Single Young Man) [Fágàujògùl, or Lone Young Man, Pah-ko-to-quodle]

Regular Members
10. Dw/deko (Name Back) [Jáudèką́u, or Retained His Name A Long Time, Dau-ta-kan]
11. Guitende (Little Wolf Heart) [Cûitèndè, or Little Wolf Heart]
12. Te/Emtodoi (Left Everybody) [Jéèmtṓdâui, or Beats Them–Leads The Charge, Ta-em-to-da]
13. Pwko/gyai (Black Buffalo) [Páukǫ̀gài, or Black Bison Bull, Pau-kaung-ky]
14. Odla./te (Hair) [Áuljè, or Hair, Odle-ty]
15. Agi/Ete (Taking Out Feathers)
16. Tse.gya/ya (Stopping)
17. Pwtai/de (White Buffalo) [Páutháidè, or White Bison Bull, also known as Ko-nad]
18. Tse/k,ode (Stickers) [Sḗgàui, or Prickly Pear, Saing-ko]
19. Se/dlo.te (Joined Together) [? Tsa-lote]
20. Kwi/tan.de (Seeping) [Wéjàn or Que-ton, Kiowa corruption of a Comanche name, Discarded One]
21. Sa.tgy/an (Doorpole) [Chátgúnjè, or Lodge Entrance Pole]
22. T'oi/tap (Small Deer)
23. Bota./pde (Dried Hip)
24. Goyo/te (Howls Like A Wolf)
25. Se./no.de (?)
26. Goyete (Out Of The Throat)
27. KwaseBai (Comanche [for] Bobbed Tail) [Ísècwǎusè, or Bobtail Wolf]
28. E/ho.zepgua (Hit by Gun) [Éhá̰uzèpgṵ̀ą̀, or Hitting Them With A Gun]
29. Tene/to (Eagle Tail) [Thḕnétón, or Eagle Tail, Ta-ne-tone]
30. Tene/anboa (Approaching Bird) [Thḕnéánfǫ́ą̀, or Eagle Asounding Approaching, Ta-ne-an-pone]
31. Gu/eto (Wolf Tail) [Cûitònqĩ̀, or Wolf Tail or Wolf Den Digger, Jimmy Quoe-tone]
32. Gu/ek,w (Wolf Hide) [Cûikǎu, or Wolf Hide; ? Cûiqǎujè, Wolf Lying Down]
33. Sane/k,yAptw (Old Man Snake) [Sànéqáptàu, or Old Man Snake]
34. Oboi/tali (Real Boy) [Óbáuitàlyĩ̀, or Real Boy]
35. Tali/Ego (Since a Boy)
36. T'e/bodl (Calf, of the Meat) [Thépòl, or Packing A Calf Of Meat, Tay-bodle]
37. Gw/kidE (Ten) [Kǎuqĩ́gácútjè, or Return From Battle Marks; Gaw-ky]
38. Se/pdombegiai (Underneath the Rain)
39. SetO (Finding a Bear) [Séttàun, or Little Bear]
40. Senta/ (?)

Succession of leaders of Tse [Horse Headdresses Society]: Mapeita, Dohwte, Dohwsan, Go.w/ta.gyE.

Chę́jánmàu (Horse Headdresses Society)

The following list is from the fieldnotes of James Mooney, collected in 1902 (JMKFN, vol. 6, 183–184). Pa"go and Gui-p"aga were the last leaders of the society.

1. Maba" [Hǎubápjè, or Hillside/Slope, Hau-vaht]
2. Pa"go [Fágàujògùl or Lone Young Man]
3. Gui-pa"ga (present), [Cûifágàui, or Lonewolf, also known as Mammadety]
4. Ohe'-(hodla")
5. Goba" [Cóbě, or Captive, i.e., Wild Horse]
6. Kayanti [Qàuyâjè, or Descending Over A Bank]
7. Gya"togya [ʔGátǒgài, or Went By, Ended, Ceased To Be]
8. Kaleti [Qǎulę́jè, or One Who Bites, Joshua Kau-lai-ty]
9. Mai'-gadi [Máigàudę́, or High Ranking, George Mo-pope]
10. Kiabom [Qą̌hîfáákîbòm, or Rescued A Man, Keah-bone]
11. Petai [Féjàidè, or Unafraid Of Death, Jerry Paith-tite]
12. Zeba'-edal [Zêbàèlqî̧, or Big Arrows]
13. Kwetan [Wéjàn, or Discarded One, Qui-tan]
14. Apiatan [Áfîtą̀u, or Wooden Lance/Spear, Ah-peah-tone]
15. Ton'moi [Tónmàui, or Water Drinker, Tone-mah]
16. [blank]
17. Da-i-ton [Jack Doy-e-to]
18. Eho-da
19. Setpiatan [Sétfîtą̀u, or Bear Spear, Set-pe-ah-taw]
20. Podlha [Cûipòlâujè, or Large Wolf, George Poolaw]
21. Tongyamhe [Tǫ́càmhâ, or Arose From The Water, Tong-kea-mha]
22. Samti [Áqàjàisàumtą̌uą̌, or They Had Been Looking Upon Him With Honor, Billy Saum-ty]
23. Angoha [Ą́ugàuhą́u, or Carrying Something By Himself, Aun-ko-hau]
24. Ramti
25. Hina"gya"[ʔHîcài, or Close/Nearby, He-at-ke-ah]
26. Etsanti [Éxąnhólą̌, or Killed Them By Tricking Them, Lucius Ait-san]
27. Guata-ato [ʔ Cǔjòtòn, or Eagle Tail Feathers]
28. Pelo [Félǒ or Pedro, also known as Pe-dro, Pa-lo]
29. Ton-gyaguadal [Tóngàgúljè, or Red-Tailed Hawk]
30. Koga-i-tadal [Qócáuitàul, or Lean Elk, Jim Waldo]
31. Kia'tai [Qátáią̌, or Coming For Revenge, Ke-ah-tigh]
32. Ta"pdom [Tépdôm, or Inside A Sweatlodge, Tape-dome]
33. Tsen-tain-ti [Chę́thàidè, or (Charley White Horse]
34. Kale' (Calvin), [Ékàulę̌ą̌, or Coming Along Together, Calvin Kau-ley]
35. Tso-kon (Maba's br) [Xǒkǫ́, or Black Stone, Tso-kone]
36. Boin-edal (captive) [Bǫ́iêl, or Big White, Bo-yiddle]
37. Dop'a-in"-ti [Jǒvâuijè, or In The Middle Of The Camp, To-poie or Dupoint]

38. Ka-ikenhodal [Káuiqáunhól, or Dragonfly, Cha-nate] (boy name Tsenyyiate)
39. Giamosadla [Gîmàusàl, or Soliciting For Him, Gei-mau-saddle]
40. Set-ga-iki [? Bear]
41. Tsonkia-tain [Xǫ́gàthái̧, or White Plumes, Tsone-ke-ah-tine]
42. A'd"a'
43. Kantseha [Qàunchèhą̂ or Shorty, Oscar Ahpeahtone]

Tǫ̀kǫ́gàut (Black Legs Society)

The following list is from the fieldnotes of James Mooney, collected in 1902 (JMKFN, vol. 6, 181–183).

1. Gui-kati [Cûiqáujè, or Wolf Lying Down]
2. Badai [Fáibáudài, or Sun Arose, also known as Háunèmídâu, or Unafraid Of Danger]
3. Ekoyoti [Ékùiòtjè, or They Pulled Him Off, A-quo-yote]
4. Moakan/Hoakan [Máucîn or Joaquin]
5. Koga-i-den [Qócáuidén, or Elk Tongue]
6. Gui-ananti [Cûiánáunjè, or Wolf Howled]
7. Imkiati (old man) [Èmqí̧áumjè, or Aiming To Throw]
8. Konia-tain-ti [Qǫ́yí̧thái̧dè, or White Yearling Bison Bull]
9. Tenesake [? Eagle]
10. Tonkyaba' [Tócàbáudài, or Appeared From The Water, Tone-ke-ah-bo]
11. Ado-eetti [Ádàuiétjè, or Big Tree, A-do-ete]
12. Imota"a" [Èmáuthâą̂, or Arising Crying, also known as Frizzlehead II]
13. Iapa-gya [Ìvâigài, or Baby/Infant]
14. Maneytai-de [Máyí̧tèndè, or Woman's Heart]
15. Tene-guat-ti [Thęnécútjè, or Striped Eagle/Spotted Bird, Ta-ne-quoot]
16. Biago [Bíkǫ̀ or Viejo (Old), Be-ah-ko]
17. Semon [Sę́mâunjè, Sa-maun-ty]
18. Boiti alias Hoaunti [? Hóàundè or Hóàuntàlyî̧]
19. Samon' [Sę́mâun, the Kiowa pronunciation of his name, Ramón; Luther Sah-maunt (Samon)]
20. Gia"ko, alias Pa"o-se'npa [Qí̧kǫ́, Keah-ko or Harry Ware, also known as Pá̧upòsén, or Bison Bull Hair Tie, Pau-po-sy]
21. Domba-i [Jǫ̀bâu, or Bugle, Dome-bo]
22. Gui-ba [? Gûibáudèą̀, or Coming Along Behind, Gui-bau-de-a]
23. Kyuni"ada [Kyǫ̀ièdáujè, or Medicine Shield, Kau-ye-da-ty]
24. Gui-Konkga [Cûikǫ́gài, or Black Wolf]
25. Ta"onde [Tá̧àundè, or Wife Trailer, Ta-home]
26. Gunaoi-ti [Gúnááuidè, or Many Tipi Poles, also known as Áuljè or Hair, Odle-ty]
27. Do"pai" [Jópfài, or Up Against A Lodge, Tof-pi]
28. Gaa-ta"gya [Cáuáuthá̧gài, or Good Crow, Big Joe] (joined from Tainpeko)
29. Mo'tsatse [Màuchàchê or "Muchacho" or Boy, Mo-cha-chi, b. 1851]

30. Bot-aka'-i [Bótàukàuijè, or Wrinkled Stomach, also known as Aíséjè or Smokey]
31. Bina"kai [? Hîcài or Close/Nearby, He-at-ke-ah]
32. Tsena"
33. Gakin(ati) [Kǎuqígácútjè, or Return From Battle Marks, Gaw-ky]
34. Potsenkina [Pópchę̀qǐ, or Spotted Horse, Pope-tsait-ke] (Aiseeo's son Sp. Horse)
35. Guakoi' [Gútqóǐ, or Yellow Child, Quote-ko-ye]
36. Pekia = "Dead Man" [Féqą̌hǐ, or Dying Man, Pa-kei]
37. Pa'ggai [?Pą́igài, or In The Dust, Frank Given]
38. Te'ne'guadle [Thę̌négúljè, or Red Bird, Ta-ne-quodle]
39. Pada-i or Charley [Pádâui, or Twin, also known as Charley Oheltoint; Áutthą̂ui or High Forehead]
40. Gui-guakoti [Cûigùtqòjè, or Yellow Wolf, Quoe-quoot]
41. Konhati [Kǫ̀hápjè, Short Camper or Fond Of Briefly Staying With Others]
42. Zontom [Zǫ́tâm, or Driftwood, Zo-tom]
43. Pedom alias Doyopti [To-yop-te]
44. Ton-ola'
45. Gaap-iaton [Càuáufìtą̀u, or Crow Feathered Lance, also known as Heidsicki]. (He was a driver [whipman]—the drivers must have many coups to his credit).

Tǫ̌kǫ́gàut (Black Legs Society)

The following membership roster for the Black Legs Society was acquired from Henry Tsoodle Sr. by participants in the 1935 Laboratory of Anthropology Kiowa Field School (SFN, 568–69). It includes the members, their positions, and their approximate ages at the time Tsoodle joined the society. Judging from the ages of the members that he provided and their birth dates, this roster was current at or around 1880.

Officers
1. Patedlkya'ta or Se'kyata (Poor Buffalo), leader, near 80 [Páutáulqàptą̀u, or Old Man Lean Bison Bull]
2. Heidsick or Gw./pitan (Feathered Lance), leader, over 80 [Heidsicki or Càuáufìtą̀u, or Crow Feathered Lance]
3. Mw/gui [?], whipman, near 70
4. Kyatai/yakoma, whipman, near 70 [Qájáiácàumą̀, or Chiefs Call Him]
5. Po'tse (Spotted Horse) [Pópchę̀qǐ], boy member, 10
6. Tsadyialdte (Chasing Buffalo Calves), boy member, 10 [Xályìàljè, or Bison Calf Chaser] (These two boy members were inducted at the age of 8.)
7. Tai/ye'nte, girl member, 7
8. D'a/mdedlte, [Thámdéljè, or Panther], girl member, 7

Regular Members
9. Dena(h)ate, 20+
10. Zebatai (White Arrow) [Zêbàthài, or White Arrows], near 20

11. Tenesai (Blue Bird) [Thẹ̀nésâuhề or Thẹ̀nésàuihyề], 30
12. Tenegut (Spotted Bird) [Thẹ̀nécútjè], 40+
13. Sampn (Luther Samon) [Sẹ́mâun], 18
14. Psosepa (Harry Ware), 18 [Qíkố, Keah-ko or Harry Ware, probably also known by his father's name, Pấupòsén, or Bison Bull Hair Tie; Pau-po-sy]
15. Tenehadl (Bird Running) [Thẹ̀néhâljè], 40+
16. Eo.uta'a.dle or Eo.nte (Chasing Many Enemies), 18 [Ếọ̀tá̳âlề or Ếọ́jè, or Chased Them For The Joy Of It]
17. Tonkyabw [Tọ́càbáudài, or Appeared From The Water, Tone-ke-ah-bo], 20 (who received the pawbon from Yellow Wolf)
18. K'iataiba or T'oywde, 20 [Qáhị̂átáibàu, or Accompanying a Headman, Sam Kei-ti-bo]
19. T'oyi (Frizzlehead), 30 [probably Èmáuthâ̳a̳, or Arising Crying, also known as Frizzlehead II]
20. Tsent'ainte (White Horse) [Chẹ̀thá̳idè, or White Horse 1], 40+
21. Toyo'te, 28 or 29
22. Mwtsatse or Mwcace, 40 [Màuchàchê or "Muchacho" or Boy, Mo-cha-chi]
23. A'nysite (former boy member), 17
24. Tenegut (former boy member), 40 [Thẹ̀nécútjè, or Striped Eagle, Ta-ne-quoot]
25. Taon (taken in as boy member at the last Sun Dance), 8
26. Guekongi (taken in as boy member at the last Sun Dance), 8 [Cûikố̳gái, or Black Wolf]

Taon and Guekongi never had the chance to function in their positions, because of the incompletion of the last Sun Dance in 1890.

Tọ̀kố̳gàut (Black Legs Society), circa 1920s

From the author's fieldnotes: Frank Aulty, Bosin, Charley Domebo, Bert Geikaunmah, Hautogo–Little Joe, Joe Hummingbird, Big Joe (Cau-au-tagya), Old Man Jackson (Hawzipta), Naho (also known as Daingkau), Frank Odelty, Joe Poolaw, Guy Quoetone, Horace Quoetone, Jack Sankadota, Jim Tacone, Black Horse (Oscar Tahbone), Aunkoyday (a Mexican captive), Homer Buffalo, Belo Cozad, Daniel Boone, Rufus Tsoodle, Guy Quetone, Tenedoah.

Já̳ifègàu (Unafraid of Death or Skunkberry Society)

The following society membership list is from the fieldnotes of James Mooney, collected in 1902 (JMKFN, vol. 6, 179–180). The information was provided to Mooney by Paul Tsaitkopte.

1. Paul [Sétqópjè, or Mountain Bear, Tsait-kope-ta]
2. Badai [Fáibáudài, or Sun Appeared, also known as Háunèmídâu, or Unafraid Of Danger]. He was chosen by Tonkonko at Piho Gado San 1885 for their chief since Gaapitan who was getting too old. But they have had no other meetings since so chosen.
3. Koti [ʔKotay]

4. Ka-asyonti [Kǎuásândè, or Little Robes]
5. Odalpa, alias Set'tainte [Ôlpǎu, or Bison Bird, Odle-paugh] (son of old chief)
6. Domati [Domat]
7. Padalka [Pàulkǎujè, or Wooley Robe, also known as HeapoBears II] (son of Setdayaiti and inherits his name recently)
8. Makin, alias Luka (Mex.) [Màucîn or Joachin or Mokeen]
9. Ahende(la) [Áhę̀dè, or Storied To or They Are Telling Him, Ah-hai-tty]
10. Ekomdo (Two Bits) [Écàumdô, or Has His Weapon Ready, A-kone-to]
11. Piasedal [?]
12. Atsaiya [Áuchâią̀, or Peeping/Looking In, Mark Auchiah]
13. Tabeka-i, alias Eagle Heart [Thę̀néténjè, or Eagle Heart]
14. Giako (Mex.) [?Beahko or Viejo]
15. Guato-tende [Cújòténjè, or Eagle Heart, Ta-ne-tane] (Eagle Heart, he has given his name to 13)
16. Kodal-aka-i (old man) [Qólàukâui, or Wrinkled Neck]
17. Gui-imheti [Cûièmhèjè, or Wolf Arising, also known as Thę̀népíbę̀, or Hummingbird, Ta-ne-peah-by]
18. Setim-(guanmo) [Sétèmgúnmàu, or Bear Entering/Den]
19. Set-pago [Sétfǎgàui, or Lone Bear]
20. Sen-ko [Sę́gàui, or Prickly Pear, Seko or Saing-ko]
21. Eonhapa-a [Éàunhâfàui, or Trailing The Enemy, E-one-ah or Unap]
22. Yia-gui [Yígù, or Twice Missed, Yeah-guo]
23. Giakom [?]
24. Set-tadalti [Séttáuljè, or Lean Bear, also known as Átépjè, or Carried Them Out]
25. Adalton-edal [Àultòêl, or Big Head, also known as Komalty]
26. Adalpepti (old man) [Áulpépjè, or Bushyhead/Frizzlehead]
27. Anko' [Àunkóvàuigàdédè, or Standing In The Middle Of Many Tracks, Anko]
28. Imagomangu [?Em̀máunkâną̀, or Can't Get Hold Of It, an agency policeman]
29. Ten-pinaki [Ténfįqî, or Heart Eater, Tain-peah]
30. Tsen-etde [Chę̀étjè, or Big Horse, Jack Bointy]
31. Kopeki [Kófèqî, or Paralyzed, Ko-pe-ah-ki, a former boy member]
32. Kaandoti, [? Káutójè, or Leg Portion Of A Bison Robe]
33. [blank]
34. Tenpan [?]
35. Topa [Jófà, or Tied To The Lodge, Toh-pah]

Jáifègàu (Unafraid of Death or Skunkberry Society)

The following list of Jáifègàu members was collected from White Fox by participants in the 1935 Laboratory of Anthropology field school (SFN, 547). White Fox stated that the society was still meeting. He estimated that there were twenty active members but listed thirty-three members, some of whom presumably were inactive. The following members are listed by name, translation, band, agency name, and approximate current age:

1. Tso'odl (Packing Stone), Kogui, Tso-odl, Leader, about 70
2. Ta./lo (Looking [also known as Lone Bear]), Kogui, Tah-lo, also known as K'odadlk'ya'to (Old Wagon), about 80
3. T,o./kyamot (Get Off In Front) [also known as Blue Jay], Kogui, To-ga-mote, about 80
4. Da./gOmoi (Many Medicines), Kogui, Dau-go-mah
5. Te./nkoi (Rear Guard), Kogui, Bob Koom-sa
6. Pa.nt'a/iDe (White Cloud), Kogui, Henry Te-ne-doo-ah
7. Yi./Gu (Two Victory Paint), Kogui, Yeah-quo
8. W'dlGu.k'O (Yellow Hair), Kugui, Sam Top-pah
9. K'oGoi/sa (Elk Horse), Kogui
10. Se'maite (Bear In The Cloud), Kogui
11. Baitadlyi (Sun Boy), Kogui
12. Se'ze'dlbei (Fierce Bear), Kugui
13. P'a.i/gya (Dirt), Kogui, Frank Given or Set'a/gye (Sitting Bear), about 84
14. Bo.D'a.i. (Little White Beaver), Kinep, Po-tsi (Potighi)
15. E'madl/ko'ya (Turning Them Back), Koigu
16. Mw'tsa' (Leader In Front), Koigu
17. K'iata./iba (Man Wounded) or Coe/tai (Never Retreat), Koigu
18. K'iegya/Gut' (Victory Paint), Kei-kei-cut, Koigu
19. Bo/dlkya'ta (Old Snake), Koigu
20. Dw'kyato./yai (Walking Seeking Medicine), Jack Doy-e- to, Koigu
21. Te'n/boho.n (Tail Bonnet), Enis Haumpo, Kinep
22. Tene/ko.be' (Escaping Bird), Kogui
23. Tene/tEnde (Eagle Heart), Kogui, Ta-ne-tane
24. T'aikyu/hyd (Tall Whitey), Koigu, Tine-yu-yah
25. K'ydta.ica/n (Little Chief), Koigu
26. Swo/deto'n (Pretty Animal) [Sau-on-de-ton, or Squirrel Tail, possibly his son Robert Ah-si], Koigu
27. E'/pko'n (Charcoal) [Ape-kaum], Koigu
28. To'/ntozanma (Water Talking), Koigu
29. K'oa/noi (Many Knives), Koigu
30. To'/nkyame (Arose From The Water) [Ton-kea-mha], Kogui
31. WdlpeGu'it'a (White Fox), Odle-pah-quote, Koigu, age 67
32. Pa.t'okoi (Bald Face Buffalo) [Pau-to-koy, also known as Bo-hay]
33. Ze'Gwye (Big Bow), Koigu, Aung-ko-to-ye

Qóichégàu (Dog Society)

Jane Richardson (Hanks) obtained the following list of Dog Society members in 1935 during the Laboratory of Anthropology Kiowa Field School (SFN:1234–37). The information came primarily from Frizzlehead II and Yellow Wolf, the only surviving members of the society, with supplementation by other informants. The list includes members who were actually present at the initiation of 1867, when both Frizzlehead II and Yellow Wolf were inducted.

Membership is indicated by informant, coded as F for Frizzlehead II and Y for Yellow Wolf and by number for individual informants (1 = Frizzlehead, 2 = Seko, 3 = Gumdaw, 4 = HeapoBears, 5 = Guito, 6 = Kintadl, 7 = Lone Bear, 8 = Yellow Wolf, 9 = Hunting Horse). Society office, society partner (indicated by lowercase letter), and previous society are listed if known.

Society Leaders

a. FY (all) Set'angya [Sétągài, or Sitting Bear], b, ?, Called Tadlkyaptw [Tálqàptàu, or Retired Old Man] by YW [Yellow Wolf], a name assumed at the end of his life. Ten medicine keeper, no successor.

b. FY (all) Kwwp'e.dai [Càuáuvédài, or Crow Appeared], a, ?, Called Wsosema [Aúsǫchę̨mą̃, or Gray Mare] when old, Ten medicine keeper.

Whipmen

c. FY (2) Aiseoi [Áisęàuidè, or Many Camp Smokes], d, Jąifègàu, Seems to be a report of an "older" and a "younger" holding this position in succession (see below) as Ten Medicine keeper affirmed by (2), (6), denied by (1), ignored by Kosa, White Fox etc.

d. F Kyahihodlte [Qą̨hį̨hóljè, or Killed A Man], c, Mt. Sheep [d. 1869, a cousin of tribal chief Jòhâusàn's]

Red Sash (Blanket) Wearers

e. FY (2) (T)se'bǫhǫ [Chębǫ̀hòn, or Horse Hat], f, Black Legs, married sister of (2), possibly an old colt

f. FY Giatogia, e, ?, Not an old Colt, son of O't'oikyaptw [Aútthą̨uiqáptàu, or High Forehead Old Man, a name known to have been held by the father of Sun Boy], not a Dog Society member (7) [Possibly Gàjǫ̨̂âi, short for Sétgàjǫ̨̂âi, or Bear Running To Others, or Sétgàjǫ̨̂qı̨̃, or Ge-at-toke-ky (no. 18, father of Doyebi, in Kiowa Family Record, Fiscal Year 1901), and a known Dog Society member; see also JMKFN 11:100]

g. FY Honguebw.de [Háungúfâu, or Never Got Shot], h, (Y) Jąifègàu, g, (F). His own brother, Horse (9), gives him as Daimbega and does not mention this affiliation. Possibly the Dog Society member is another individual of the same family, of an older generation. This is more likely because the Jąifègàu was supposed to have sons too young to join any society, at the time they broke up. An old colt.

h. FY Wtwde [Ą̃ujáujè, or Island], g, (F,Y), Mt. Sheep; I, (F), Black Legs. [This is the name of the tribal chief deposed after the 1833 Cut Throat Massacre, possibly the same individual.]

i. Y (3) Tonant'aide [Tónánthą́idè, or White Tailed], h, j (F), Horse Headdresses (1) gives, in two places, two different *kom* to him. (It is not impossible, if one died). This is probably the person called "tonante," once by (1). [White Tailed was the father of Dupoint.]

j. FY (2) Tebodlte [Thépòl, or Packing A Calf Of Meat], I, (F) ?, Ten medicine keeper, Old Colt

k. FY (2) Kyaitw.te [Câijàujè or Warrior/Fighter], l, Jáifègàu, son of Dohausen, killed by Navajo. [Mooney, in his Kiowa Fieldnotes, MS 2531, vol. 11, National Anthropological Archives, reported killed by Utes in 1868.]
l. FY (2) Poda'tai, [?], k, Mt. Sheep, got Dohw's actual place in Koiseko according to Frizzlehead. It is doubtful, but possible that this is the same name as podlt'ai reported as a member by (2).
m. FY Yaikwwn [?], n, (F), ?; o, (Y). Frizzlehead's ie. (1's), judgement in this case seems better. Old Colt. Blanket sash owner (1).
n. F Tabe'aide [?], m, (F), ?, Blanket sash owner (1).
o. FY K'wde.te [?], p, (F), Jáifègàu; m, (Y).
p. F Tadliet'aide [Tàlyĭjáidè, or Brave Boy/Boy Chief], o, (F), ?. Old Colt [d. spring 1869, father of Donpai, d. 1892.]
q. F Yiehoto [Yíhǎutò, or Two Hatchets, lit. Two Axes], ?, Mt. Sheep, or Hwkw.tote [?] [d. circa 1899]
r. F Mwsot'aide [Mǎusàutháidè, or White Crow], ?, ?. Old Colt.
s. FY (2,9) Guetokogia [Cújòkǒgài, or Black Bird], t, (F), none. This is probably the one called Guekogiai, Dog Society member, and Ten medicine owner by (9). Stepson and nephew of (x). Old Colt.
t. F Twg'uetadli [Tàugûitàlyĭ, or Kiowa-Apache Boy], s, (F), Jáifègàu [reportedly a brother of Dragging Feathers]
u. F A.k'ue'te [Ákùijè, or Dragging Feathers], ?, Jáifègàu. Old Colt, society partner rumored to be Gwk'i, do not know if this is the same name as Gwk'iete, father of Lone Bear (7), whose society I do not have. Latter was surely not a Koitseko though, and the name Gwk'i never comes up again, so this must be in error. [Reportedly a brother of Kiowa-Apache Boy.]
v. Y Se'guekwde [?], ?, ?. Specifically denied by Frizzlehead who said he died lately, and never was a member.

The following two men were very old at the time of the 1867 initiation and had been members before, but had retired (were tadl [*tál*]) yet were present and very active in the ritual. They were both highly honored men.

w. F) Togudlkyaptw [Jògúlqáptàu, or Old Man Red Tipi], c, ?. Had been whipman with Iseeo (Many Camp Smokes) the elder, while Sitting Bear was society leader. Thought to have been of the same age as Sitting Bear, and was father of White Bear, society leader of Jáifègàu. Was one or two generations older than Frizzlehead II (age 80–85 in 1935). A former red sash owner and a Ten medicine keeper.
x. F) Twkoidekyaptw [Tàukàuiqáptàu, or Old Man Saddle Blanket], ?, ?. Another very old man. Was crier (?) for either the camp, or more particularly, for the Dog Society. At his B[rother]'s death, he married, see levirate, his B's wife, the M[other] of (s) above. To this step-son he gave his sash and his place (?). Also to (s)'s society partner (t).

Colt Members

The following were inducted as Colts at the 1867 initation.

aa. FY Kǫbǫhǫ [Kǫ́bǫ́hòn, or Black Headdress/Hat], a son of (w) (Old Man Red Tipi), according to the notes of La Barre from White Fox. Only one married.

bb. FY Tw.deywdlte [? Tâudèauljè, or The Other Scalp, reportedly a brother of Big Tree's father]

cc. FY Frizzlehead, or Emota, or Wdlpepde (2) [Èmáuthâą̂, or Arising Crying, also known as Áulpépjè, or Bushy Hair/Frizzlehead, son of Frizzlehead I, 1824–1907]. Called (a) father.

dd. FY Guegue or Yellow Wolf [Cûigùtqòjè, or Yellow Wolf]; society partner with (ee)

ee. FY Kwwpa.te [Càuáuvéjè, or Crow Appeared, not to be confused with (b)], *kom* of (dd), killed as a young man by the Navajo.

ff. FY Guikw [Cûiqáujè, or Wolf Lying Down; probably no. 101, Guoi-kau-ty, in Kiowa Family Record, Fiscal Year 1901]

gg. FY Hwpo [Hą́upòą̂ or Hą́upǫ̀, or Fish Hook, lit. Metal Trap], son of (b)'s [Crow Appeared's] sister.

hh. F How'kon [Hóàutkàun, or Traveling Behind/At The End] or Sankadoty [Xǫ́gàdáudè, or Medicine Plume or Down, San-ka-dota]

YellowWolf maintains that only seven colts were taken in, but Frizzlehead lists eight, possibly due to a replacement of (ee)'s untimely death.

Qóichę́gàu (Dog Society)

James Mooney in 1902 recorded the following list of the last five living members of the Dog Society, who had been intiated as colts (JMKFN, vol. 6, 178). The list correlates with the 1935 Laboratory of Anthropology list compiled by Jane Richardson.

1. Tsonhiada (second oldest) [Xǫ́gàdáudè, or Medicine Plume/Down, or Sankadota]. Previously a Jáifègàu.
2. Taimpe alias Set-adalka-i (oldest) [Jáifè, or Skunkberry, also known as Sétáulkáui, or Crazy Bear, also known as Hą́upòą̂, or Fish Hook, lit. Metal Trap] (number 1 and 2 were society partners)
3. Guhati [Cûiqáujè, or Wolf Lying Down; probably no. 101, Guoi-kau-ty, in Kiowa Family Record, Fiscal Year 1901]
4. Imo'ta"a" [Èmáuthâą̂, or Arising Crying, also known as Áulpépjè, or Bushy Hair/Frizzlehead; son of Frizzlehead I, 1824–1907]
5. Gui-guako'ti' [Cûigùtqòjè, or Yellow Wolf]

Additional Qóichę́gàu (Dog Society) Members

Several other society members were identified in the 1935 Laboratory of Anthropology fieldnotes. Although there is little or no chronological placement for many of these men, they represent Dog Society members before about 1867. The following were referred to as members once or more in passing, but except in a few cases the field school participants did not check them with Frizzlehead and Yellow Wolf. Most were dead by 1867. The following list quotes directly from the field school notes, with bracketed interpolations by the author.

1. Páuthòcáui, or Bald Faced Bison Bull, Pwto.koi, the father of Dohw, who was the head leader of the society.
2. Jòhâusàn, or Little Bluff Recess. Inherited the position of head society leader from his father. Died in 1866. Succeeded by Sitting Bear.
3. Tse'gyatogia, possibly a red sash owner [probably Chêgàtógài, Went By On A Horse].
4. Gw.ki, Káuqígácútjè, or Return From Battle Marks; Gaw-ky, or "Ten."
5. Guhwde. [This appears to be Gùhâudè, or Stabbed In The Ribs. If it is, this would have been an earlier Gùhâudè, because these names referred to members at or prior to 1867 and not to the later Wohaw.]
6. Cûiqáujè, or Wolf Lying Down, an earlier one than Guoi-kau-ty.
7. Gúlbímkàui, or Paint Bag (Gudlbimkw).
8. Podlt'ai.
9. Máunjòfáhóljè, or Killed An Enemy With His Hands, Montebahodl, name not recognized by (F). Oldest brother of Old Man Horse, and oldest son of Maientende [Woman's Heart; possibly Máunjòéhóljè, or Killed Them With His Hands].
10. Páugútqójè, or Yellow Bison Bull (Pwguek'o), second son of Maientende [Woman's Heart], put in to fill the place of his brother Montebahodl, on his death. He was a member, but was dead by 1867 (F), which correlates with the membership list.
11. Wdlkwwn, an Apache Koitsenko, very old in 1867 (F).
12. Fágáyíjè or Two Offerings–Sacrifices, Pangyagiate, Mooney's 1898:417, Sacrifice Man, killed in 1853.
13. Dabejaite, a paternal grandfather of Hodltagudl (Red Dress) [possibly Thápètáidè, or White Deer].
14. Càuéthẹ̀dè (Didn't Run or Stood His Ground, Father of Bof-peh-a).
15. Tone-tsa, the father of Onkima and Senkokyo. Also father of Cha-nate and Audle-sone-odle (KFR, 194, 198).
16. Cûihâlạ̀jè (Slow Running Wolf), also known as Áulkáuiqáptàu (Crazy Old Man). Gave sash away in 1848. JMKFN, vol. 6, 274, vol. 11, 138.

Óhọ̀mògàu (Omaha Society)

The following list of Omaha Society members is from James Mooney's 1902 fieldnotes (JMKFN, vol. 6, 185).

1. Tenetaidi [Thẹ̀néjáidè, or Bird Chief]
2. Hangun [Hạ́ugú, or Metal Horn, Silverhorn]
3. Imoa [Èmáuthâạ̀, or Arising Crying, E-mau-tah]
4. Epkon [Épkọ́, or Charcoal, Ape-kaum]
5. Angopti [Thẹ̀néàungópjè, or Eagle Striking With Talons, Kicking Bird II or Paul Kickingbird]
6. Zepko-setti (Ankotoya) [Ą́ugàutóyài, or Lone Traveler, Aung-ko-to-ye or Tom Little Bow]

7. Poton [Fótǫ́qī̀, or Beaver Lake, Po-tong-keah or Botone]
8. Patadal (nephew of old chief) [Páutáuljè, or Lean Bison Bull, also known as Poor Buffalo]. Possibly Duke Poor Buffalo b. 1879, son of chief Poor Buffalo.
9. Gonta-konkya [? Kòmjòkǫ́gài, or Black Owl]
10. Tsendon [? Chêjòqī̀, or Hunting Horse]
11. Set-angya (son of old chief) [Sétą́gài, or Sitting Bear, Frank Given]
12. Tene-hadalti [Thę̀néhâljè, or Running Eagle, Tene-haddle-ty]
13. Pa-guadal [Páugùljè, or Red Buffalo, Pau-quodle]
14. Gunhente [? Probably Páugų̀hèjè, or Hornless Bison Bull, the former name of two Kiowa men]
15. Ton-bon (Rotten Leg) [Tòbôn, or Spoiled Leg, D. K. Lonewolf]
16. Bot-talyi [Bóttàlyī̀, or Stomach Boy]
17. Dan-e [?]
18. Tsenon [?]
19. Set-zedalbe [Sétzèlbè, or Dangerous, Terrible, or Fierce Bear]
20. Kotebohon [Qǫ́dèbòhòn, or Swift Fox Headress, Kau-to-bone or Gotebo]
21. Guato-konkya [Cų́jòkǫ́gái, or Black Eagle]
22. Kinapai [Kį́fài, or Against The Shield, Ke-ah-vi]
23. Penti [?]
24. Pa-tainti [Páuthą́idè, or White Bison Bull, also known as Konad]
25. To-yati [also known as Sam Keitibo]
26. Tengu [?Den-gu, or Bow Handle Sinew]
27. Bila-ti (Belo) [Bélâuájềą̀, or They Caught Him By The Bridle, Belo Cozad]
28. Set-apeto [Sétáfètjàui, or Even The Bears Are Afraid Of Him, Sit-ah-pa-tah, known as Afraid of Bears]
29. Set-tainpe [Sétją́ifèjè, or Bear Unafraid of Death, Set-tain-pe-te; also known as Háupòą̀, or Metal Trap, Haun-po or Haun-po-ah, and Sétáulkáui, or Crazy Bear]
30. Guatsatti [Gúchátjè, or (Lower) Rib Cage Entrance, Guo-a-chet]
31. Gom-dati [Gómdáu, or Wind Medicine, Goom-do, Goomdaw]
32. Adalpa-guetain [Àulfàgûithą́idè, or White Coyote, Odle-pah-quote, also known as White Fox]
33. Set-tain [Sétthą́idè, or White Bear, a younger one]
34. Te'ne'ton (ti) [Thę̀nétón, or Eagle/Bird Tail, Ta-ne-tone]
35. De'ta"hadla" (only K living now) [Dêthà̀uhàlą̀, or They Had Been Listening To Him, also known as Bótpàulī̀, or Young Hairy Bellied Bison, also known as Old Man Skinny]
36. Kinahi-konyi [Qą́hį́qòyī̀, or Male Bison Yearling, Ke-in- kau]
37. Guhati [? Gùhâudè, or Stabbed Them In The Ribs, Wo-haw]
38. Gui-sabian [Cûisą̀ubī̀, or Wolf Quiver, Paul Tsaitkopeta]
39. Sekan [Sécáun, or Water Film; the later Tape-do?]
40. Anguaya [? Ángû, or Wise/Good Character; An-quoe]
41. Ta-kaita [Tàukàuidè, or Saddle Blanket; Max Frizzlehead]
42. Gyabian [Qábîn, or Carbine, also known as Elk Creek Charley]

Calf Old Women's Society

The following society members were given by Mary Buffalo to Weston La Barre on July 2, 1935 (SFN, 589–590). The list includes members in the year 1877. From the lodge door on the east and proceeding clockwise around the inside of the lodge, the members are listed in the order of their position during society functions. Kin relationships are expressed from the perspective of Mary Buffalo and are abbreviated as follows: M, mother; F, father; D, daughter; S, son; Z, sister; GM, grandmother; GGM, great-grandmother.

1. Syem'ote, Mary's father's sister, oldest member, drumkeeper, south door, 85
2. Kayohmte [Káuihyômjè, or Hide Scraping Tool, Kau-yone-ty or Mrs. Paudle-kaut], Mary's M's Dau in law (replaced GM E'ae), 18
3. E'se'nt, grandmother of no. 1, 79
4. Tso'Boek'a, Mary's sister. Z (replaced GGM Taeto'), young.
5. Sye'sonhi, no kin, cousin to no. 10, c. 78
6. Tope', no kin, cousin of no. 13, c. 84
7. Ka'sohodl, no kin, ?
8. Pekyma, Mary's F's Z, c. 60
9. Ko'yit, Mary's F's M's Z, c. 80
10. O'mati [Ǫ́mą́jè, or Personable/Nice Looking, O-ma-te], no kin, cousin of no. 13, c. 84
11. Po'guete, ?, c. 60
12. G'dltot'te, no kin, cousin to Sye'sonhi no. 5, c. 80
13. PoGy'seikea, ?, (society leader, pipe bearer), c. 83
14. A'mGote, Mary's M's F's second wife, c. 82
15. Tse'Gohya, no kin (Mary's F'F' D'D), c. 30
16. Sedlkisema, no kin, aunt to no. 19, cousin to no. 5 and 9, c. 62
17. Eto, Mary's M (sister to Snapping Turtle), c. 62
18. Tseton, Mary's GM, c. 74
19. AnGomodl, no kin, c. 50
20. Doaint, no kin, girl
21. Taimema [Tą́imémá or Taime (Woman), Ti-mah-ma], no kin
22. Ma.ku'et, no kin, niece of no. 13 (Head Woman, North door) c. 40

Former leaders: a great-grandmother of Atah
Former members: a grandmother of Atah, daughter of the above

Bear Women's Society

The following list of society members was collected by Jane Richardson on July 1, 1935, from Goutaha, or Mrs. Blue Jay, and from Kintadl. The list is the society's seating arrangement from the south side of the meeting lodge door to the northeast side of the door. However, the exact order of non-office-holding members is believed to be incorrect.

1. Onkima [Àunkį́mą̀ or Aun-ke-mah, Crossing or Bridge], Work Woman
2. Goutaha [Cą́ujàuháp or Kaun-to-hapt, Likes to Trade/Swap, Mrs. Blue Jay]
3. Zondo

4. Tongo [Tą̀ugàui, or Rattle, Tong-Kau-e]
5. Kintadl [Kį̀tàl or Kin-tadl, Moth] Society Leader
6. G'dlt'oto
7. I.Do'di
8. Dakoima [Probably Tháukáuimá̧, or Mexican/Mule] (replaced B'ot'ote)
9. Dozite (Cleanup Woman)
10. Tsoboete [Tso-bo-e or Xôbôi, Crystiline Rock]

Other members included Piayate, who served as a cleanup woman, and E'tso'da. Jack Doyeto's grandmother was once a leader of the society, sometime before Kintadl.

Pehodlma (Industrious Women)

The following list comes from the 1935 Laboratory of Anthropology fieldnotes (SFN, 574–576).

1. Ekin [possibly A-kein or Ékîn, Family 184 in Kiowa Family Record, Fiscal Year 1901]
2. Twikwde [Tháukáuidè, or Mexican, wife of Jóhâusàn]
3. Gúlvău [Red Water, lit. Red Stream]
4. Áljóchǫ̀hį̀ (Boss Old Woman), paternal grandmother of Kintadl
5. Eki.ni/dte (Kintadl's uncle's wife, no apparent relation to no. 1)

NOTES

Abbreviations

ADN   *Anadarko (Oklahoma) Daily News.*

AIEB   American Indian Exposition Guide Booklet, Anadarko, Oklahoma.

AMP   Alice Marriott Papers, Box 9, Western History Collections, University of Oklahoma, Norman.

AWMCB   *American War Mothers Constitution and Bylaws.* Privately published, Atlantic City, N.J., 1961.

DD   Doris Duke Oral History Collection, Western History Collections, University of Oklahoma, Norman. "T" indicates tape number. Numbers following the colon (e.g., T-32:18–32) are page numbers in the transcription of the tape-recorded interview.

HLS-1   Hugh L. Scott Ledgerbooks, vols. 1 and 2, circa 1892–1897, Fort Sill Museum Archives, Fort Sill Army Post, Lawton, Oklahoma.

HLS-2   Hugh L. Scott Papers, MS 4525, circa 1892–1897, National Anthropological Archives, Smithsonian Institution, Washington, D.C.

JMKFN   James Mooney Kiowa Fieldnotes, MS 2531, vols. 1, 6, 7 (Silverhorn Ledgerbook), and 11, 1891–1918, National Anthropological Archives, Smithsonian Institution, Washington D.C.

KFR   Kiowa Family Record, Fiscal Year 1901.

SFN   "Santa Fe Notes." Fieldnotes compiled in 1935 by Weston La Barre, William Bascom, Donald Collier, Bernard Mishkin, and Jane Richardson during the Kiowa Field School sponsored by the Laboratory of Anthropology, Santa Fe, New Mexico. The notes were later cut and pasted together by topic, and some sections were sourced with headings containing Roman numeral–Arabic numeral combinations. This version of the notes has no official page numbers, but Ben Kracht numbered the pages in a copy for reference purposes. I give those page numbers in the citations, along with the headings as they appear in the fieldnotes. This source includes La Barre's original 1935 Kiowa fieldnotes notebook, which I refer to as "La Barre Notebook."

Citations in the form "Mary Buffalo to Weston La Barre" (using note 1, chapter 1, as an example) refer not to correspondence but to interview material or other oral communication from one person to another.

Chapter 1. Pòlą́hyòp

1. Mary Buffalo to Weston La Barre, V-3, July 12, 1935, SFN, 935; Gueton (Quoetone) to La Barre, XI-1-3, July 24, 1935, SFN, 937.

2. Rev. J. J. Methvin to Lillian Gassaway, Sept. 23, 1937, Indian Pioneer Papers, 283–284.

Methvin's reference to filling the ranks of the Dog Soldiers refers to the military societies in general and not to the Kiowa Dog Soldier Society.

3. Seko (Sangko) and Gumdw (Goomdaw) to Jane Richardson, 1935, SFN, 1205–1206; Heapo-Bears to La Barre, 1935, SFN, 195; Silverhorn to Bernard Mishkin, V-4, July 1, 1935, SFN, 553; Frank Given to Alice Marriott, Aug. 1, 1935, AMP. Current Kiowa elders also confirm that originally only boys were actual Rabbits Society members. Methvin (Sept. 23, 1937, Indian Pioneer Papers, 283–284) states that both sexes belonged to the society, but all other Kiowa accounts state that only boys belonged.

4. Gumdw to Richardson, 1935, SFN, 1205; Donald Collier, IV-3, 4, 1935, SFN, 557.

5. Gumdaw (Goomdaw) and Seko to Richardson, 1935, SFN, 1205, 1206; HeapoBears to La Barre, 1935, SFN, 195.

6. Guiananti to James Mooney, May 1904, JMKFN, vol. 2. Guiananti lived from 1844 to Oct. 15, 1904.

7. Given to Marriott, Aug. 1, 1935, AMP; Piatonma (sometimes spelled Biatonma, also known as Mrs. Horse) to Marriott, July 16, 1936, AMP.

8. Gus Palmer Sr. to the author, Oct. 29, 1997.

9. "Kiowa Little Rabbits New Kids Care Center," ADN, June 23, 2000. This center is a satellite office of the Kiowa Head Start program in Carnegie.

10. Claude Jay to Charles Brant, Mar. 31, 1949, Western History Collections, University of Oklahoma, Norman.

11. Silverhorn to Mishkin, V-4, July 1, 1935, SFN, 553; Gumdw to Richardson, 1935, SFN, 1205. Because of the close interaction of Kiowa and Apache men's societies and the similarity between their children's Rabbits Societies, some of these symbolic associations may also have applied to the Kiowa Rabbits Society.

12. Seko to Richardson, 1935, SFN, 1205. The name Ko'go'ta', or Resistant To Pain, would be Qópcótjè.

13. Frizzlehead to Richardson, 1935, SFN, 1206, 1220; Luther Samon (Sahmaunt) to William Bascom, XIX-3, July 31, 1935, SFN, 264; HeapoBears to La Barre, SFN, 195.

14. Gumdaw to Richardson, 1935, SFN, 1205; Silverhorn to Mishkin, V-4, July 1, 1935, SFN, 553.

15. Gumdaw to Richardson, 1935, SFN, 1205; Silverhorn to Mishkin, V-4, July 1, 1935, SFN, 553; Parker McKenzie to the author, Oct. 4, 1993.

16. Richardson (probably from Seko), 1935, SFN, 1223; Gumdw to Richardson, 1935, SFN, 1206.

17. Samon to Mishkin, VIII-5, Aug. 1, 1935, SFN, 557.

18. Silverhorn to Mishkin, V-4, July 1, 1935, SFN, 553; Seko to Richardson, 1935, SFN, 1205; Given to Marriott, Aug. 1, 1935, AMP.

19. Seko to Richardson, 1935, SFN, 1205; Silverhorn to Mishkin, V-4, July 1, 1935, SFN, 553; HeapoBears to La Barre, 1935, SFN, 195.

20. Seko to Richardson, 1935, SFN, 1205. Although resembling a porcupine hair roach, the depiction in the Santa Fe Notes is of a circular headband with erect fibers.

21. Charley Apekaum and HeapoBears to La Barre, XIII-7 and XIII-8, 1935, SFN, 719, 781; Bert Geikomah and Mary Buffalo to La Barre, VI-7 and IV-11, 1935, SFN, 719–720; Charley Apekaum and Frizzlehead to Collier, V-15 and V-18, 1935, SFN, 718; White Buffalo to Collier, III-7, 1935, SFN, 715; Mrs. Hokeah to Collier, IV-19, 1935, SFN, 720; Given to Marriott, Aug. 1, 1935, AMP. Although the Kiowa were a nonagricultural group, they were undoubtedly familiar with wood, shell, and scapula bone hoes. The reference to hoes may indicate the use of wooden digging sticks or hoes made for this event.

22. Gus Palmer Sr. to the author, Oct. 29, 1997.

23. Ibid.; Monroe Tsatoke and White Horse to Richardson, IX-3 and IX-4, July 31 and Aug. 2, 1935, SFN, 1297.

24. Charley Apekaum and HeapoBears to La Barre, XIII-7 and XIII-8, 1935, SFN, 719, 781; Bert Geikomah and Mary Buffalo to La Barre, VI-7 and IV-11, 1935, SFN, 719–720; Charley Apekaum and Frizzlehead to Collier, V-15 and V-18, 1935, SFN, 718; White Buffalo to Collier, III-7, 1935, SFN, 715; Mrs. Hokeah to Collier, IV-19, 1935, SFN, 720; Given to Marriott, Aug. 1, 1935 AMP.

25. Francis Tsonetokoy to the author, Dec. 8, 1990. Team members included Steve Bohay (manager), John Emhoola Sr., Eddie Goombi, Mac Burgess (Comanche), Clouse Ahtone, Henry Ahtone, Mark Keahbone, John Chaino, Bill Koomsa Sr., William Wolf, Parker Brace, Allen Tsonetokoy, Jimmy Wolf, and Francis Tsonetokoy.

26. Oscar Tsoodle to the author, Oct. 13, 1990.

27. Author's fieldnotes and observations of Rabbit Dances, 1989–2007.

28. Gus Palmer Sr. and Parker McKenzie to the author, 1994. Several elders could not translate the line ôi yá fául-âu-chẹ̀, which is reputed to be in the language Séndè, the archaic form of speaking used by the Kiowa trickster. Although Greene (1993) translated this portion as "until you're tired and sleepy," the etymology is unclear.

29. Gus Palmer Sr. to the author, July 21 and Sept. 15, 1994; Parker McKenzie to the author. Regarding line 3, some Kiowa say ẹ̀ instead of chẹ̀. Line 4 translates as, "I gained the power of being favored."

30. Gà hâun-jàu-àl-bắu is grammatically correct; kàui-bá-tô-lè (butterfly) implies "awkwardly back and forth," as a butterfly flies. Gus Palmer Sr. to the author, July 21 and Sept. 15, 1994; Parker McKenzie to the author, Sept. 25, 1994.

31. Gus Palmer Sr. to the author, July 21 and Sept. 15, 1994; Parker McKenzie to the author, 1994. The line jò̱-sạ̀-nàu could not be clearly translated by elders but seems to denote "little tipi" or "house," as if "and I have a little [pitiable] dwelling." In line 2, àui-àum is pronounced àui-hyòm by some Kiowa.

32. Oscar Tsoodle to the author, Oct. 13, 1990.

33. Author's fieldnotes, 1995. Although only one of these persons belonged to an adult society (the Kiowa Gourd Clan), all agreed that membership in the Rabbits Society was an integral part of growing up as a Kiowa.

Chapter 2. Áljóyȋgàu

1. Author's fieldnotes; McKenzie n.d.b.

2. HLS-1, vol. 1, 192; Silverhorn to Mishkin, V-4, July 1, 1935, SFN, 550.

3. Jack Doyeto and Donety to H. L Scott, HLS-2; White Horse and Monroe Horse to Richardson, IX-3 and IX-4, July 31 and Aug. 2, 1935, SFN, 1304–1305. See also HLS-1, vol. 1, 192–193.

4. According to Charley White Horse, there were no actual Kiowa death songs, but a man might frequently sing in such instances. See also HLS-1, vol. 1, 192–193.

5. White Horse and Monroe Horse to Richardson, IX-3 and IX-4, July 31 and Aug. 2, 1935, SFN, 1304–1305. In this song, Rushed By Below refers to her brother's young widow. The reference is that because the widow is so young and does not yet know how to ululate properly, she might sound funny if she tries to do so, but because her brother's deed was so great, she would never be ridiculed for her inexperience.

6. Sangko, Guito (Quoetone), and Gumdw to Richardson, 1935, SFN, 1207; Little Henry (Tso'odl) to La Barre, XXI-5, Aug. 13, 1935, SFN, 571–572; Tso'odl to Marriott, July 10, 1936, AMP.

7. Gumdw to Richardson, 1935, SFN, 1207–1208; Tso'odl to Marriott, July 10, 1936, AMP.

8. Gumdw to Richardson, 1935, SFN, 1207–1208.

9. Seko to Richardson 1935, SFN, 1224; Tso'odl to Marriott, July 10, 1936, and Piatonma to

Marriott, July 16, 1935, AMP. Old men reportedly had trouble with their hair plates because their hair was often too thin to support the weight.

10. Given to Marriott, Aug. 1, 1935, AMP.

11. For a lengthier description, see chapter 4.

12. HeapoBears to Richardson, 1935, SFN, 1224; Silverhorn to Mishkin, V-4, July 1, 1935, SFN, 550; Tso'odl to Marriott, July 10, 1936, AMP.

13. Silverhorn to Mishkin, V-4, July 1, 1935, SFN, 551.

14. La Barre's depiction of the society's whip differs from the usual serrated club; it appears as a smooth-edged stick with a hole near the distal end through which several red-painted thongs are attached. La Barre Notebook, 3:22, SFN.

15. Gumdw to Richardson, 1935, SFN, 1217; Parsons 1929:93.

16. Richardson, 1935, SFN, 1218; La Barre Notebook, 3:14, SFN.

17. White Fox to La Barre, XI-9, XI-10, and XI-11, July 26, 1935, SFN; Gumdaw to Richardson, 1935, SFN, 1217.

18. Frizzlehead to Richardson, 1935, SFN, 1217. This man was probably Thḛnébáudài (Bird Appearing).

19. Given to Marriott, Aug. 1, 1935, AMP.

20. JMKFN, vol. 1, 63.

21. Seko to Richardson, 1935, SFN, 1219, 1233; Kintadl to Richardson, IV-6, July 5, 1935, SFN, 190.

22. Lone Bear to Richardson, VII-9, 1935, SFN, 174–175.

23. Nye (1968:373) reproduced a studio photograph of Enoch Smoky as a boy in Kiowa dress, holding a society whip in his left hand. Because his father was a Mountain Sheep Society whipman, this is likely one of the society's whips. Parsons's listing (1929:92) of Tahbai (Smoky) as a society whipman actually refers to Aíséjè (Smoky), who was enrolled as Ais-chant (KFR, 96) and best known as Smoky. He should not be confused with Black Bonnet Brow, the father of Kiowa George Poolaw, who was also known as Tábái (lit. Tobaccos) and was enrolled under the names Tan-ko-gai and Smoky (KFR, 133).

24. Lone Bear to Richardson, VII-9 1935, SFN, 174–175; see also Mooney 1898:425.

25. Gumdw to Richardson, 1935, SFN, 1207–1208.

26. HLS-2, Box 4, Kiowa File, "Story of Sheep Mountain."

27. Author's fieldnotes.

Chapter 3. Chḛjánmàu

1. JMKFN, vol. 6, 183; Parker McKenzie to the author, Mar. 2, 1993.

2. JMKFN, vol. 6, 183, and vol. 11, 98; Bert Geikaunmah to Julia Jordan and Timothy Baugh, July 28, 1967, DD T-32:18–32; Bert Geikaunmah to Julia Jordan and Timothy Baugh, July 6, 1967, DD T-74:3–8; author's fieldnotes. I have recorded three similar pronunciations of the society's name: Chḛjánmàu, Chḛtánmàu, and Chḛjángàu. On the basis of accounts of the derivation of the society's name from *ján*, for browband or headdress, the first appears to be correct.

3. HLS-1, vol. 1, 192. Although a Quahada Comanche camp is specified, the Quahada did not form as a distinct group until later. JMKFN, vol. 11, 98.

4. Guito to Richardson, 1935, SFN, 1208; Horse to Bascom, XIV-1, July 24, 1935, SFN, 552.

5. Gumdw to Richardson, 1935, SFN, 1208.

6. Hunting Horse to Bascom, XI-5, July 20, 1935, SFN, 561.

7. Silverhorn to Mishkin, V-6, July 1, 1935, SFN, 551.

8. Piatonma to Marriott, July 16, 1935, and Given to Marriott, Aug. 1, 1935, AMP.

9. Frizzlehead to Richardson, 1935, SFN, 1218. In 1935 Frizzlehead stated that the term *cúnqà*-

jàiqî, or dance leader, was used for the leader of the Ghost Dance (1890–1917) and that none of the men's military societies was then active.

10. Bascom (probably from Hunting Horse), XI-4, 1935, SFN, 562; Gumdaw and Frizzlehead to Richardson, 1935, SFN, 1215. Although one account states that all societies had the same officers, Hunting Horse's account and drawing (SFN, 562) are followed here. Hunting Horse's account does not mention the youth member positions.

11. Bascom (probably from Hunting Horse), XI-4, 1935, SFN, 562; Gumdaw and Frizzlehead to Richardson, 1935, SFN, 1215.

12. Bascom (probably from Hunting Horse), XI-4, 1935, SFN, 562; Gumdaw and Frizzlehead to Richardson, 1935, SFN, 1215.

13. Bascom, XI-4 (probably from Hunting Horse), 1935, SFN, 562–563; Lone Bear to Richardson, X-9, Aug. 12, 1935, SFN, 899–901; Frizzlehead to Collier, VIII-1, July 25, 1935, SFN, 843–847. The Calf Old Women Society and the Fáìiyoi (Sons of the Sun), a small anti-peyote group associated with war power that existed between 1887 and 1890, held a similar practice. No connection beyond a general offering to the sun before eating is known.

14. Bascom, XI-4 (probably from Hunting Horse), 1935, SFN, 563.

15. Hunting Horse to Bascom, XI-5, July 20, 1935, SFN, 562; Richardson (probably from Sangko), 1935, SFN, 1224; Piatonma to Marriott, July 16, 1935, and Given to Marriott, Aug. 1, 1935, AMP.

16. Hunting Horse to Bascom, XI-5, July 20, 1935, SFN, 562; Richardson (probably from Sangko), 1935, SFN, 1224; Piatonma to Marriott, July 16, 1935, and Given to Marriott, Aug. 1, 1935, AMP.

17. JMKFN, vol. 11, 98.

18. La Barre Notebook, 3:14, SFN; Bert Geikaunmah to Julia Jordan and Timothy Baugh, July 28, 1967, DD T-32:18–32; Bert Geikaunmah to Julia Jordan and Timothy Baugh, July 6, 1967, DD T-74:3–8; Piatonma to Marriott, July 16, 1935, AMP.

19. Richardson (probably from Sangko), 1935, SFN, 1224; Bascom, XI-4 (probably from Hunting Horse), 1935, SFN, 562; Piatonma to Marriott, July 16, 1935, AMP.

20. Piatonma to Marriott, July 16, 1935, AMP.

21. The La Barre Notebook, 3:14, SFN, however, says that only the Koitsenko used whistles.

22. La Barre Notebook, 3:14, SFN.

23. HeapoBears to La Barre, XIII-5, July 30, 1935, SFN, 557.

24. Frizzlehead to Richardson, 1935, SFN, 1217; Gumdw to Richardson, 1935, SFN, 1217; La Barre Notebook, 3, July 14, 1935, SFN.

25. Gumdw to Richardson, 1935, SFN, 1217; La Barre Notebook, 3, July 14, 1935, SFN.

26. Hunting Horse to Bascom, XI-5, July 20, 1935, SFN, 562.

27. Old Man Horse to Bascom, July 20, 1935, SFN, 561, 1233; HLS-1, vol. 1, 192; La Barre Notebook, 3:14, SFN; Bert Geikaunmah to Julia Jordan and Timothy Baugh, July 28, 1967, DD T-32:18–32; Bert Geikaunmah to Julia Jordan and Timothy Baugh, July 6, 1967, DD T-74:3–8; Issacs 1975.

28. JMKFN, vol. 6, 183. That Kicking Bird and Lone Wolf were simultaneously society leaders is interesting because they represented major peace and war factions of the tribe in the early 1870s. Whether this affected the longevity of the society is unknown.

29. Old Man Horse and Padalti (sometimes spelled Padlti) to Richardson, 1935, SFN, 1309.

Chapter 4. Tǫ̀kǫ́gàut

1. JMKFN, vol. 11, 98; letter from Gus Palmer Sr., commander, to the author, Sept. 29, 1990, on Kiowa Ton-Kon-Ko Black Legging Warrior Society, Kiowa Veterans Association and Auxiliary stationary. Gus Palmer Sr. served as the leader of the Black Legs and Rabbits Societies, for two years as the Kiowa chapter president of the Native American Church, for two years as Kiowa tribal chair,

and for two years as Kiowa tribal director for the American Indian Exposition. Palmer was also a member of the Kiowa Gourd Clan and the Omaha Society.

2. Although Boyd (1981:71) states that the Black Legs and other Kiowa military societies were organized in 1838 after a great battle with the Cheyenne and Arapaho, there is no strong evidence to support this regarding the Black Legs. Although the battle between the Kiowa and Cheyenne-Arapaho in 1838 is well documented and led to the 1840 alliance of the five major Southern Plains tribes, it is usually associated with the origin of the Kiowa Jáifègàu and the Gourd Dance.

3. HLS-1, vol. 1, 77–78.

4. Ibid.

5. JMKFN, vol. 6, 181, and vol. 11, 98; HLS-1, vol. 1, 193. Mooney also indicated that members did not wear leggings in their dances and that some but not all painted their legs black below the knee.

6. Little Henry to La Barre, Aug. 13, 1935, SFN, 571; George Hunt and Little Henry to La Barre, La Barre Notebook, 3:14, SFN; White Fox to La Barre, July 26, 1935, SFN, 550; Monroe Horse and White Horse to Richardson, IX-3, 4, July 31, 1935, SFN, 1290; Richardson n.d., from Kintadl; Piatonma to Marriott, July 16, 1935, AMP. Several persons stated in 1935 that the members of various societies could be identified in a war party by their insignia. This may refer more to officers (whipmen or certain lance carriers), who carried specified items of society insignia, than to regular members.

7. Richardson, 1935, SFN, 1218.

8. Kavanagh (1996:182) described the gifts given by Juan Bautista de Anza to Ecuaracapa in 1786 and by Fernando de Chacón, who, in the name of the king, recognized the newly elected Kotseteka Comanche leader Canaguaipe in 1797 "by turning over to him the symbols: a cane with silver head, a medal of the same, and . . . a scarlet cloak."

9. Author's fieldnotes; Two Hatchet 1984. The closest drawing resembling the cape worn in a photograph of Charley White Horse (Boyd 1981:68) and identified as Young Mustang's is a black-and-white depiction (Harris 1989:69). However, the drawing cannot be positively identified as representing the same cape as that shown in the photograph reproduced by Boyd.

10. Author's fieldnotes.

11. Berlo (1996:146–149) published four of these drawings with commentary and wrote, "The series of eleven drawings (along with three given at the same time to Williams College, from which Barber graduated in 1857) were made by a Kiowa artist for Barber in 1880. Although the artist's name is unknown, the caption to cat. no. 70 suggests that he drew himself in the scene."

12. Author's fieldnotes. A Kiowa consultant also gave me a version of this ledgerbook drawing and identified Feathered Headdress. The drawing appears to be from the original ledgerbook, because it lacks the editorial cropping of the Maurer version. Rev. George Saumpty, a grandson and namesake of Feathered Headdress, provided related information; George Saumpty to the author, July 16, 1990. See also Mooney 1898:396.

13. In reviewing McCoy's *Kiowa Memories*, Silberman (1988:286) attributed some of the drawings to the "Koitsenko and Black Legs Soldier Societies" but gave no supporting evidence or indication of which drawings he was referring to, although the Koitsenko drawing is identified.

14. Richardson n.d.; Weiser Tongkeamah and George Saumpty to the author, July 16, 1990; Oscar Tsoodle to the author, Oct. 13, 1990.

15. This closely resembles descriptions of Apache Manatidie dances (Meadows 1999).

16. HeapoBears to Richardson, 1935, SFN, 1224; White Horse and Monroe Horse (Tsatoke) to Richardson, July 31 and Aug. 2, 1935, SFN, 1293–1294; Richardson n.d.

17. Piatonma and Given to Marriott, July 16 and Aug. 1, 1935, AMP.

18. HeapoBears to Richardson, 1935, SFN, 1224; White Horse and Monroe Horse (Tsatoke) to Richardson, July 31 and Aug. 2, 1935, SFN, 1293–1294; Richardson n.d.

19. HeapoBears to Richardson, 1935, SFN, 1224; White Horse and Monroe Horse (Tsatoke) to Richardson, July 31 and Aug. 2, 1935, SFN, 1293–1294; Richardson n.d.

20. La Barre Notebook, 3, SFN.

21. Bascom, XI-4, 1935, SFN, 526; Richardson n.d.

22. Lone Bear to Richardson, VII-22, 1935, SFN, 560; Richardson n.d; Samon to Bascom, XIX-3, July 31, 1935, SFN, 264.

23. Alice Marriott, "The Sacred Spear of the Kiowa Indians, AMP, Box 8, 5–8.

24. Gus Palmer Sr. and Parker McKenzie to the author, 1992.

25. Given to Marriott, Aug. 1, 1935, and July 21, 1936, George Poolaw to Marriott, May 28, 1936, Tso'odl to Marriott, July 11 and 13, 1936, and Saioma to Marriott, May 30, 1936, AMP.

26. HLS-1, vol. 1, 193; Yellow Wolf to Bascom, July 2, 1935, SFN, 552.

27. George Poolaw to Marriott, May 28, 1936, Tso'odl to Marriott, July 11 and 13, 1936, Given to Marriott, Aug. 1, 1935, and July 21, 1936, and Saioma to Marriott, May 30, 1936, AMP.

28. George Poolaw to Marriott, May 28, 1936, Tso'odl to Marriott, July 11 and 13, 1936, Given to Marriott, Aug. 1, 1935, and July 21, 1936, and Saioma to Marriott, May 30, 1936, AMP.

29. George Poolaw to Marriott, May 28, 1936, Tso'odl to Marriott, July 11 and 13, 1936, Given to Marriott, Aug. 1, 1935, and July 21, 1936, and Saioma to Marriott, May 30, 1936, AMP.

30. George Poolaw to Marriott, May 28, 1936, Tso'odl to Marriott, July 11 and 13, 1936, Given to Marriott, Aug. 1, 1935, and July 21, 1936, and Saioma to Marriott, May 30, 1936, AMP.

31. George Poolaw to Marriott, May 28, 1936, Tso'odl to Marriott, July 11 and 13, 1936, Given to Marriott, Aug. 1, 1935, and July 21, 1936, and Saioma to Marriott, May 30, 1936, AMP.

32. Alice Marriott, "The Sacred Spear of the Kiowa Indians, AMP, Box 8, 5–8.

33. Saioma to Marriott, May 30, 1936, Poolaw to Marriott, May 28, 1936, and Tso'odl to Marriott, July 11 and 13, 1936, AMP.

34. La Barre Notebook, 3:14, SFN.

35. Richardson, 1935, SFN, 1217, 1244; Richardson n.d. See note 69, this chapter.

36. Alice Marriott, "The Sacred Spear of the Kiowa Indians, AMP, Box 8, 5–8.

37. Richardson, 1935, SFN, 1218; Given to Mishkin, I-8, Aug. 22, 1935, SFN, 289; Kintadl to Richardson, I-6, 1935, SFN, 395; Yellow Wolf to Bascom, III-3, July 2, 1935, SFN, 529.

38. Given to Marriott, Aug. 1, 1935, and July 21, 1936, and Tso'odl to Marriott, July 11 and 13, 1936, AMP.

39. Guito to Richardson, 1935, SFN, 1208. The 1935 Laboratory of Anthropology Kiowa Field School focused on recording pre-reservation culture and life-style, which ended in 1875, through elder consultants born between 1848 and the 1870s.

40. Little Henry (Henry Tsoodle Sr.) to La Barre, XXI-1, Aug. 13, 1935, SFN, 568–569.

41. Ibid.

42. The description of this summer's circumstances corroborates Mooney's account (1898:347) of the 1881 Sun Dance, which was held on the North Fork of the Red River, beyond the "end of the [Wichita] Mountains." It was known as the "Hot Dance" for being held in August instead of June, because of the inability to secure a bison bull until then.

43. JMKFN, vol. 6, 179, 181.

44. HeapoBears to Richardson, X-11, 1935, SFN, 680.

45. Author's fieldnotes.

46. Gus Palmer Sr. to the author, July 18, 1990. The name appears to be Bôhį̀ (Real or Original Bo, i.e., Very Strong) and may refer to the words bô-gàu (bow) and hį̀ (real or original), hence Original Bow. Mooney (1898:411) reported Bo to have been a mythic dwarf of great strength, so the name also meant "Very Strong."

47. Author's fieldnotes; Parker McKenzie to the author, Jan. 30, 1993; Gus Palmer Sr. to the

author, Feb. 5, 1993; McKenzie 1988:5, n.d.b. The interpretation "turning or becoming red when angry" in not conveyed in this form of the name.

48. Author's fieldnotes; Two Hatchet 1984.

49. Gus Palmer Sr. to the author, Oct. 13, 1990; Mac Whitehorse to the author, May 12, 1993.

50. Gus Palmer Sr. to the author, Oct. 13, 1990; Mac Whitehorse to the author, May 12, 1993; Two Hatchet 1984; Ananthy Odlepaugh Ledgerbook. The Odlepaugh Ledgerbook was reportedly drawn by Cáulánàundáu̱a̱ or Cáulánàundáumà (Standing In The Footprints Of Bison). Born in 1859, she was enrolled as Aun-au-dah-ah (KFR, Family 334) and was the wife of Odlepaugh. One descendant of Mrs. Odlepaugh's stated that he believed she did not start the ledgerbook but later took it up and maintained it (author's fieldnotes, July 8, 2004). Recent information (Scott Tonemah Papers) indicates that the ledgerbook was actually compiled by Tonemah (Tónmàui, or One Who Is Drinking Water) and later came into the custodianship of Mrs. Odlepaugh.

51. Parker McKenzie to the author, Jan. 30, 1993; KFR. Some family members place his birth in 1850 or 1851. Goule-Hay-Ee Story, copy in the author's possession.

52. JMKFN, vol. 7, 25, 27.

53. JMKFN, vol. 1, 32.

54. Kiowa Agency Files; Two Hatchet 1984; Kiowa tribal census, 1895; KFR; Parker McKenzie to the author, 1994.

55. JMKFN, vol. 7, 25, 27.

56. Gus Palmer Sr. to the author, Mar. 5, 1992; Two Hatchet 1984. Palmer was a great-grandson of Young Mustang's. The Kiowa hearsay tense is similar in use to the adverb "reportedly" in English. The song is in a hearsay tense; hence the use of *hèl* in the first two lines. It switches back to present tense in the last line; hence the use of *góbàu* instead of *góbèhèl*. Some people believe James Two Hatchet obtained the song from a recording at the Smithsonian Institution and reintroduced it to the Black Legs Society in 1984 or 1985. I have been unable to locate such an archival version of the recording.

57. Richardson, 1935, SFN, 1212–1213.

58. A family dispute exists among the descendants of Young Mustang's two children. Essentially the dispute is between the Mopope-Palmer and Keahbone-Anquoe families, both of which are large and influential. The Palmers, descendants of George Mopope, revived the Black Legs Society and have controlled much of its leadership since 1958. The Anquoes are descendants of Sain-day-ma (Sendehmah), or Sindy Keahbone, wife of Edgar Keahbone. In the mid-1990s, the descendants of their daughter, Anna Keahbone Anquoe, wife of the late Jimmy Anquoe, formed a descendants group called the Goule-Hae-Ee Descendants, later led by Nora Keahbone Antelope. Although some of the Anquoe family have made public and written claims concerning Goule-Hae-Ee (Anquoe 1991a), their participation in the Black Legs Society was minimal during much of the revival and during the 1990s. Their residence in Tulsa is an issue of contention to other Kiowa who see themselves as remaining in the home area. Led by Jack Anquoe, the Anquoe family is well known for its family singing group, commercial recordings, participation in the Tulsa Powwow, and extensive travel of the powwow circuit. More recently, members of the Keahbone family formed the Ghoul-Hay-Ee Descendants Organization, which has been active in promoting oral and written accounts of their ancestor. Since 1995 new information and detailed descriptive accounts of Young Mustang have continued to surface. This side of the family has been criticized by others who allege that it is exaggerating and in some cases even "making up" accounts in order to increase the importance of its apical ancestor and in turn make itself better known. Recent accounts that I collected were highly varied. Some maintain that Young Mustang was not only Spanish but of royal Castilian stock and that his carriage, coat of arms, and suit of armor have been located in a museum in Spain. One descendant commented that this was unlikely, because he was a two- or three-year-old boy when

he was captured in Texas. At the fall 2001 Black Legs ceremonial, Nora Antelope introduced Young Mustang's "flag" and stated that he "was coming out of the closet" for all to know. Although some details in accounts are reliable and easily correlated with birth dates, Kiowa calendars, and historical events, others are totally unreliable, placing people and events at historically impossible times, far beyond people's known lifetimes. During my fieldwork I saw Young Mustang's historical importance rise significantly within a few years, from that of a captive ancestor who was known to be a warrior, with a notable war action to his credit, to that of a dynamic apical ancestor with a rapidly growing body of oral history that has taken on a nearly mythical quality. That several elder descendants refute many of the most recent claims suggests factors perhaps based in part on intralineage factionalism over a sort of ancestor control. Reflecting a growing current trend, one newspaper article recently listed Goule-hay-ee as a "Koisenk[o]" member, which he was not ("Goule-hey-ee Descendants to Honor Their Princesses," ADN, Jan. 19, 2001). His membership in this society is not given in the lists of James Mooney or the Santa Fe Notes.

From an etic perspective, this kind of ancestor promotion is interesting in two ways. First, it reflects an apparent need to reaffirm and strengthen an existing lineage with what is considered to be perhaps the most important aspect of its past. Second, it demonstrates a continued emphasis on presenting oral history without any means to back it up. In the past, witnesses were commonly called to affirm or refute a warrior's claims. The subject of these claims, Young Mustang, is of course so far removed in time that no firsthand witnesses exist. The presentation of recent claims is affected by both an unfamiliarity with and, in some cases, a lack of concern with credible alternative sources. Many of these sources, such as calendars, were produced by elder Kiowa, and others, such as interviews and firsthand fieldnotes, were recorded from elder Kiowa, who were undoubtedly more familiar with the person and events in question. These are sources that could be used to support, refute, clarify, or fix a temporal basis for an account. Although Kiowa sometimes use such sources (such as Mooney's *Calendar History of the Kiowa Indians* [1898]), even in public settings including Black Legs ceremonials, more often they do not. As is customary, polite patience prevails, and people are rarely interrupted while speaking in public during dances and ceremonials, regardless of the degree to which those in attendance agree with or believe what they are saying.

59. Piatonma and George Hunt to Marriott, July 22, 1935, AMP.

60. Gus Palmer Sr. learned this song from Bert Geikaunmah. Gus Palmer Sr. to the author, Mar. 5 and May 13, 1992. The syllable *gà* denotes "sing it"; *gá* denotes "sing it for you." Parker McKenzie to the author, 1992.

61. Piatonma and George Hunt to Marriott, July 22, 1935, AMP. Although Marriott's fieldnotes contain the actual account, she incorrectly combined young Sitting Bear's death with that of Lone Wolf's son Sitting In The Saddle (Marriott 1945:106–111), who was killed with his cousin Wolf Heart during a separate journey in 1873 (Nye 1937:182–184).

62. Piatonma and George Hunt to Marriott, July 22, 1935, AMP.

63. Piatonma and George Hunt to Marriott, July 22, 1935, AMP. Piatonma noted the difference between the deaths of the sons of Sitting Bear and Lone Wolf. Whereas the former was willing to help and protect the other young men involved in his party, the latter turned on his party, accusing its members of being cowards and of not having saved his life. Victor and David Paddlety gave me independent accounts of these events, which they learned from their maternal grandmother Kintadl, who referred to Sitting Bear as her uncle. Author's fieldnotes.

64. HLS-1, vol. 1, 192–193.

65. Guito to Richardson, August 1935, SFN, 1201; Kintadl to Richardson, IV-6, July 5, 1935, SFN, 190; JMKFN, vol. 6, 179, 181. Poor Buffalo and Sun Appearing never became society partners, which may suggest that they were somehow related to each other.

66. JMKFN, vol. 6, 179, 181.

67. Ibid.

68. Gumdaw to Richardson, 1935, SFN, 1233. Squirrel Tail was reportedly half white. Because his father was reported to have been a society leader, this implies that his mother was an Anglo captive. His parents died before allotment, and their names were not recorded.

69. Seko and Frizzlehead to Richardson, 1935, SFN, 1219, 1231; Mrs. Hokeah to Collier, IV-7, July 19, 1935, SFN, 42; Horse to Collier, IX-1, IX-6, Aug. 6 and 13, 1935, SFN, 201, 218; Yellow Wolf to Bascom, IV-3, July 2, 1935, SFN, 1033. Auchiah (n.d.) reported that White Bear was a Black Legs member, but he is usually associated with the Jáifègàu (see Mooney 1898; Parsons 1929:92; Boyd 1981:71). Yellow Wolf was reportedly the youngest leader in the society and was said to have been shot at so closely one time that his quiver caught fire and his red sash was burnt black (Auchiah n.d.). This is incorrect: he was inducted into the Dog Society before joining any other society, and a red sash is usually associated with Dog Society membership. He joined the Black Legs after the Dog Society disbanded. Yellow Wolf was known to have been the pàubôn keeper at one time. A replica of the lance is now maintained by the Yellowwolf family and displayed with the Kiowa Gourd Clan trophies each July.

70. Bert Geikomah and Mary Buffalo to La Barre, IV-5-6, 1935, SFN, 761; HeapoBears to Richardson, 1935, SFN, 1259.

71. Frizzlehead to Richardson, 1935, SFN, 1218; Guy Quetone to Julia Jordan, Apr. 18, 1968, DD T-246:9-11, 19-25; Guy Quetone to Julia Jordan, Mar. 23, 1971, DD T-637:5.

72. Author's fieldnotes.

73. Domebo Calendar, DD T-214 and T-216:38.

74. Domebo Calendar, drawings 89-106, DD T-214 and T-216:38. Although Guy Quoetone, in the Doris Duke files, disagrees with the ordering of some of the other calendar entries, there is good evidence to support this year as the date of the society's reorganization.

75. Domebo Calendar, DD T-216:3, Guy Quetone to Julia Jordan, Mar. 23, 1971, DD T-637:5.

76. Author's fieldnotes; Joyce Auchiah Daingkau to the author, July 20, 1990; Leonard Cozad Sr. to the author, Mar. 17, 1991. The birth dates for Mrs. Oyeby (1875) and Mrs. Whitefox (1877) suggest that these women might have been the last society princesses in the late 1880s (KFR).

77. Guy Quetone to Julia Jordan, Apr. 18, 1968, DD T-246:9-11, 19-25; Guy Quetone to Julia Jordan, Mar. 23, 1971, DD T-637:5. Quetone gave two dates for the time of his induction, 1910 and 1911, at the annual Ghost Dance encampment on the Washita River west of Carnegie, but later he stated that he was inducted during or just after the end of World War I (1917-1918). The former statements differ from those of later eyewitnesses to the Ghost Dance, who stated that no society or social dances were held there.

78. Guy Quetone to Julia Jordan, Apr. 18, 1968, DD T-246:23.

79. Guy Quetone to Julia Jordan, Apr. 18, 1968, DD T-246:21; Leonard Cozad Sr. to the author, Mar. 17, 1991; author's fieldnotes. Boyd (1981:73) associated the wearing of black long underwear with the Black Legs at this time. He might have confused the wearing of such dress by the increasingly popular "fancy" War dancers with bustles, such as those who participated at the Craterville and Dietriech Lake fairs.

80. Guy Quetone to Julia Jordan, Apr. 18, 1968, DD T-246:9; Guy Quetone to Julia Jordan, Mar. 23, 1971, DD T-637:4-11.

81. Guy Quetone to Julia Jordan, Apr. 18, 1968, DD T-246:9; Guy Quetone to Julia Jordan, Mar. 23, 1971, DD T-637:4-11; author's fieldnotes.

82. Guy Quetone to Julia Jordan, March, 23, 1971, DD T-637:4-8; Silverhorn to Mishkin, II-12, July 3, 1935, SFN, 531; author's fieldnotes.

83. Tongkeamha's father, Kiowa Jim, ceased participating in traditional dance activities following the death of his son Frank in December 1926. In 1927 he joined the Saddle Mountain Baptist

Church, where he became a deacon. Tongkeamha noted that although new members were being inducted into the Black Legs during these years, anyone who wanted to participate was allowed to do so. Weiser Tongkeamha to the author, July 16, 1990, and Feb. 2, 1991.

84. Harry Domebo to the author, Oct. 2, 1990; Leonard Cozad Sr. to the author, Mar. 17, 1991. Alice Littleman also reported some of these men as members she saw at Black Legs dances during her childhood. Alice Littleman to the author, May 2, 1992.

85. Alice Littleman to the author, May 2, 1992.

86. Oscar Tsoodle to the author, Oct. 13, 1990, and Mar. 5, 1992.

87. George Saumty to the author, July 16, 1990.

88. Oscar Tsoodle to the author, Oct. 13, 1990, and Mar. 5, 1992.

89. Oscar Tsoodle to the author, Oct. 13, 1990, and Mar. 5, 1992.

90. Laura Sankadota Tahlo to the author, July 9 and 12, 1992; Ralph Kotay to the author, Apr. 4, 2008.

91. Author's fieldnotes.

92. Atwater Onco to the author, Oct. 15, 1997.

93. Author's fieldnotes, June 28, 2001; see also Anquoe 1991a.

94. Gus Palmer Sr. to the author, Oct. 29, 1997.

95. Gus Palmer Sr. to the author, July 22, 1996. In June 1993 the Occitan Nation in Mountauban, France, presented Vanessa Santos Jennings, a relative of Lyndreth Palmer's who was then visiting France, with several gifts in honor of him. Included were a clay plaque of France, a brass medal from the mayor of Mountauban, a red cloth bundle containing sage, and another containing a flicker feather and consecrated soil from France. She donated these items to the Kiowa Tribal Museum. On the same occasion, Gus Palmer Sr. visited his brother's grave and sang three songs for him: a memorial song composed by Lewis Toyebo, the Black Legs Society funeral song, and another Black Legs Society song. Gifts were given to the French people in a giveaway held by the family. A special Catholic mass was also held in France in memory of Lyndreth Palmer during this visit.

96. Gus Palmer Sr. to the author, Oct. 29, 1997.

97. Some members maintain that originally in 1958 all members had to be combat veterans but that active combat service was later waived, and honorably discharged veterans could join if they had an ancestral society member. However, the only available membership lists were compiled for the years between about 1880 and 1900 by James Mooney in the 1890s and by the Laboratory of Anthropology Kiowa Field School in 1935 and were not in the possession of the current society. Therefore, this precedent appears not to be firmly followed. Kiowa tribal enrollment and any form of active or honorably discharged military service are now required for membership. For example, one veteran who is half Kiowa but enrolled in another tribe was denied membership unless he switched enrollment, which he did not.

98. Author's fieldnotes; see also Bantista 1983:5.

99. David Pinezaddleby is remembered for teaching the younger veterans the Shuffle Dance songs, and Bert Geikaunmah, for the Turn Around or Reverse Dance. Gus Palmer Sr. to the author, May 16, 1990, May 13 and Oct. 1, 1992.

100. "Black Leggings Ceremonial to be held at Indian City, U.S.A.," ADN, May 15, 2003.

101. The term *traditional* is a subjective one that applies only in reference to a specified time and context, but it is useful in discussing cultural change because all cultures create, borrow, and modify as needed.

102. Atwater Onco to the author, Oct. 15, 1997.

103. Although Kiowa do recognize and maintain distinctions between "traditional" and "Christian," to some degree these terms are only broad labels by which the Kiowa and non-Indians distin-

guish major differences between the two social groups. Both Christian and non-Christian Kiowa have maintained numerous cultural forms such as language, kinship, joking patterns, foods, songs, and storytelling, which may be referred to as traditions. Kiowa and non-Indians loosely use the term *traditionalist* to refer to those who maintain or participate in one or more older traditions such as dancing, powwows, society dances, hand games, peyote, and traditional doctoring. "Christian" Kiowa are generally persons whose social lives are structured more toward church-oriented activities and whose doctrines often discourage or prohibit participation in the preceding activities. The latter are clearly becoming more syncretic since the 1960s.

104. Author's fieldnotes, 1997.

105. Ibid.

106. Ibid.

107. Ibid.

108. Author's fieldnotes, Oct. 15, 1997.

109. Author's fieldnotes, Rainy Mountain Kiowa Indian Baptist Church services, Nov. 9 and Dec. 7, 1997; Delores Harragarra to the author, Nov. 9 and Dec. 7, 1997.

110. Author's fieldnotes; Gus Palmer Sr. to author, Aug. 1, 1991.

111. Moira Harris (1989:98) incorrectly stated that the Black Legs wore red capes in the nineteenth century. Although there are reports that the original cape and a replica given to the society by the Mexican army are in the possession of members of the society (Bantista 1983:6; Kracht 1989:969), society and family members state that the original cape and lance were never returned after Charley White Horse died, and their whereabouts remain unknown. They may have perished when White Horse's house burned in the 1940s.

112. Author's fieldnotes.

113. Richardson n.d.; author's fieldnotes. Current Black Legs Society member and artist Sherman Chaddlesone has produced a ledgerbook-style painting of the society (Red Earth Indian Center 1995) similar to the drawing in the Scott ledgerbook (McCoy 1987). Kiowa-Navajo artist and Black Legs Society member Dennis Belindo (Jones 1995:17) has painted a work titled *Black Leggings* in which each dancer carries a rawhide rattle. However, rattles have never been associated with this society.

114. Author's fieldnotes.

115. JMKFN, vol. 1, 50–52. Mooney noted about Sleeping Bear: "Besides his comradeship, he may have been connected by marriage with Dohausan, who, about the time of the peace, took a Cheyenne wife, who died soon after, leaving a son to grow up in her own tribe." The son might have been from this union. Little Bluff died in 1866, and Sleeping Bear, in 1867.

116. JMKFN, vol. 1, 50–52. For other accounts of this tipi, see Greene 1993 and Greene and Drescher 1994:421–423.

117. Gus Palmer Sr. and Dixon Palmer to the author, Aug. 23, 1992.

118. Gus Palmer Sr. to the author, Oct. 29, 1997.

119. Evalu Ware Russell to the author, Nov. 6, 1997.

120. Chief Stumbling Bear Dedication Ceremonies Program, National Indian Hall of Fame, Anadarko, Oklahoma, Oct. 8, 1994; ADN, Oct. 9, 1994.

121. "Kiowa Indian Hall of Fame to Present Posthumous Awards at Honor Dance," ADN, Dec. 27, 2002.

122. Author's fieldnotes, Black Legs ceremonial, Oct. 8, 2006; *Lawton Constitution*, Nov. 18, 2005; ADN, Nov. 28, 2005.

123. Author's fieldnotes; Gus Palmer Sr. to the author, Mar. 29, 1991.

124. Gus Palmer Sr. to the author, Oct. 29, 1997.

125. The following section is written from observations of thirty-two performances of society

ceremonials between 1989 and 2007, a videotape of the October 1984 ceremonial, and interviews with society and tribal members.

126. Author's fieldnotes, Oct. 13, 1997.

127. Author's fieldnotes, 1995.

128. Gus Palmer Sr. took the time to sing, record, translate, and provide the background of each song's history and composition for me. Parker McKenzie assisted me in transcribing them into his Kiowa orthography. The texts vividly demonstrate the cultural and martial themes associated with this veterans' society.

129. This observation is based on my attendance of Black Legs Society ceremonials and some preparatory meetings and singing practices between 1989 and 2007.

130. Author's fieldnotes, 1995.

131. Gus Palmer Sr. to the author, July 21, 1993, and Sept. 15, 1994.

132. Gus Palmer Sr. to the author, July 21, 1993, and Sept. 15, 1994. *Ám* denotes emphasis.

133. Gus Palmer Sr. to the author, Feb. 4 and Oct. 25, 1994. The expression *chól* is from the adverb *chólhàu*, "surely," or "in that way or manner"; *a̧ugî* is a verb meaning "think about" or "consider it as such"; *féldò̧* is a verb meaning "thinking," "think of," "pondering."

134. Gus Palmer Sr. to the author, Feb. Apr. 1994.

135. David Paddlety to the author, Nov. 5, 1997.

136. Author's fieldnotes, 1997.

137. One member said that these speeches were necessary because of the relatively small attendance at meetings held prior to society ceremonials.

138. Gus Palmer Sr. to the author, Feb. 5, 1994; Meadows 1999:164.

139. Blas Preciado to the author, Dec. 4, 1997.

140. Atwater Onco to the author, Oct. 15, 1997.

141. Among the Comanche (Wallace and Hoebel 1952:270), the Scalp and Victory Dance was distinguished by the presence of either scalps alone or plunder and captives alone. A dance with scalps became a Scalp Dance, whereas a dance with only plunder, captives, or both was a Victory Dance. Whether the Kiowa used this dichotomy is unknown.

142. Author's fieldnotes, Jan. 17, 1998. This reflects Native people's keen power of observation. Intimately familiar with the tradition, they contribute to a deeper level of ethnography.

143. Evalu Ware Russell to the author, Nov. 6, 1997.

144. Martha Poolaw to the author, Aug. 3, 1995.

145. Ibid.

146. Atwater Onco to the author, Oct. 15, 1997.

147. Evalu Ware Russell to the author, Nov. 6, 1997. The film *Strangers in Their Own Land* (1993) contains a segment showing Mrs. Russell dancing the Scalp and Victory Dance and her son's induction into the Black Legs Society.

148. Blas Preciado to the author, Dec. 4, 1997.

149. Vanessa Jennings to the author, Oct. 11, 1997.

150. Atwater Onco to the author, Oct. 15, 1997.

151. Vanessa Jennings to the author, Oct. 3, 2002.

152. Author's fieldnotes. One woman noted that when asked to join in, some women decline on the basis of not wanting to mess up their hair and makeup. Although individuals have many cultural and personal reasons for not participating, such as a recent death in the family, I have heard some people decline on this basis. Consequently, in some years only a few adult women participate.

153. Sherman Chaddlesone to the author, July 8, 2004.

154. Author's fieldnotes. Some women attribute these efforts at control and assertion of ownership or having the right to particular cultural forms to factors of Anglo ideology and assimilation.

155. Morgan 1991b; ADN, Jan. 26–27, 1991; Gus Palmer Sr. to the author, July 10, 1990. Palmer remembered Mrs. Jennings reviving the use of these dresses, making several of them for other women. He recalled that her grandmother, Jeanette Berry, had one of these dresses. See Jennings 2002 on the history of these dresses in her family.

156. Morgan 1991b; ADN, Jan. 26–27, 1991; Gus Palmer Sr. to the author, July 10, 1990.

157. See Petersen 1971:42, 81, 139, and Harris 1989:71, 74, 76, 97. Wohaw provided six views of these dresses from drawings he made at Fort Marion, one of which was worn by a captive. Petersen (1971:287) used a figure of a Red Sleeve Dress in her pictographic dictionary but did not identify it as such, labeling it only "panel set into side of dress," in reference to the red gussets. Two of the six views (Harris 1989) are also found in Berlo's book (1996:171, pl. 98, and 175, pl. 101).

158. Vanessa Jennings to the author, Feb. 5, 1994; Meadows 1999:164–166.

159. Atwater Onco to the author, Oct. 15, 1997.

160. Evalu Ware Russell to the author, Nov. 6, 1997.

161. Vanessa Jennings to the author, Oct. 11, 1997.

162. Author's fieldnotes, Oct. 12, 2003.

163. Richardson n.d.

164. Charley Apekaum and White Buffalo to La Barre, 1935, SFN, 706; author's fieldnotes.

165. Gus Palmer Sr. to the author, Oct. 29, 1997.

166. Richardson n.d.; author's fieldnotes.

167. Author's fieldnotes, 1995–1997; Gus Palmer Sr. to the author, Mar. 29, 1991.

168. Gus Palmer Sr. to the author, July 21, 1993.

169. In essence, Onco practiced good ethnohistory, combining archival records, participant-observation fieldwork through informal visits and interviews, and personal experience—an approach little different from mine.

170. Gus Palmer Sr. to the author, May 13, 1992, and July 21, 1993. This song is based on the one composed by Sitting Bear for his son, Sitting Bear II, and shows how a song may have some of its lyrics changed to make a new song.

171. Author's fieldnotes.

172. David Pinezaddleby and Charley White Horse taught the Shuffle Dance Songs to the society. Gus Palmer Sr. to the author, May 13, 1992, and July 21, 1993.

173. Author's fieldnotes.

174. Gus Palmer Sr. to the author, May 13, 1992, and Sept. 15, 1994.

175. Gus Palmer Sr. to the author, Sept. 15, 1994. In the third line of the song, *dé* is an abbreviation of *háun-dé* (really, in reality). The parent term is *háun-gáu* (something, anything). That pronoun forms do not occur twice in the same expression also indicates that *dé* is not a pronoun form. Parker McKenzie to the author, June 17, 1998.

176. Gus Palmer Sr. to the author, July 22, 1996.

177. Author's fieldnotes, 1997.

178. The two Turn Around or Reverse Dance songs were learned from Bert Geikaunmah. Gus Palmer Sr. to the author, May 13, 1992.

179. Author's fieldnotes. As the dance increases in intensity, the changes in dance direction often take place more frequently than solely when the inside and outside men meet up. In such cases Kiowa tend to comment quickly on the mistakes in choreography and to chuckle among themselves, viewing them largely as unimportant mistakes that occur under the overwhelming spirit of the dance.

180. Reuben Topaum, public coup recitation, Kiowa Black Legs Society fall ceremonial, Oct. 13, 1991. Reuben Topaum to the author, Aug. 31, 1994. Topaum was a squad leader and sniper in L Company, 2nd Battalion, 179th Infantry Regiment, 45th Infantry Division. Besides the Purple

Heart and Bronze Star Medal, he received the European Theater Badge, the Combat Infantry Badge, and the Good Conduct Medal (ADN, Dec. 6, 2001, and Dec. 27, 2002).

181. Larry Kaulaity, public coup recitation, Kiowa Black Legs Society fall ceremonial, Oct. 7, 1990.
182. Atwater Onco to the author, Oct. 15, 1997.
183. Author's fieldnotes, Oct. 13, 1997.
184. Blas Preciado to the author, Dec. 4, 1997.
185. The only exception I know of was when the song was sung at the fall 2007 ceremonial.
186. Gus Palmer Sr. to the author, Feb. 4, 1994. Bert Geikaunmah provided this song and told Palmer that it was an old Black Legs Society song. Because of the irregularity with which the song is sung, younger members are often unfamiliar with it.
187. Author's fieldnotes.
188. Gus Palmer Sr. to the author, Oct. 29, 1997.
189. To prevent bias, I met requests for archival information, mainly photocopied archival materials, after completing my interviews and initial observations of society functions.
190. Martha Poolaw to the author, Aug. 3, 1995.
191. Author's fieldnotes, Nov. 1997. One younger veteran voiced considerable displeasure over the inclusion of non–combat veterans but later stated that he had only four days of combat experience.
192. Author's fieldnotes, 1997.
193. David Paddlety to the author, Nov. 5, 1997.
194. Evalu Ware Russell to the author, Nov. 6, 1997.
195. Author's fieldnotes, 1997.
196. Author's fieldnotes, July 2004.
197. Sherman Chaddlesone to the author, July 8, 2004.
198. ADN, May 15, 2002.

Chapter 5. Jáifègàu

1. HLS-1, vol. 1, 192; JMKFN, vol. 6, 180.
2. Parker McKenzie to the author, Mar. 2, 1993; Atwater Onco to the author, Nov. 9, 1993; Kiowa Tai-Piah Society 1990.
3. There are no known independent two-syllable words involving the syllables *jai-fe* in the Kiowa language (McKenzie 1991). Four known words involve the syllables *fe-gau*: *fȇ-gáu*, a collective noun for "the dead"; *fè-gáu*, an adverb for "once again"; *fẹ̀-gàu*, a triplural noun for turkeys; and *fȇ-gàu*, a noun or verb for "would not straighten" or "resistant to being made straight." Of these, only *fȇ-gáu* (the dead) correlates with other known Plains military society names.
4. *Rhus trilobata*, also known as squawbush, polecatbush, skunkberry, and fragrant sumac, is a scraggly, upright shrub growing up to two meters in height, with clustered, fuzzy red fruit. It is common to much of the southern Great Plains and Mexico, including the Texas Panhandle (Barkley 1986:571–573; Powell 1988:258). According to Barkley (1986:572), the fruit ripens between May and September. Mooney (1898:424) described Skunkberry Creek as a southern tributary of the South Canadian near Lathrop, Texas, possibly White Deer Creek.
5. Issacs 1975. Several Kiowa elders and society members who have been active since the revival of the dance in 1957 state that the meaning behind the society name was never explained to them.
6. McKenzie 1991; Kiowa Tai-Piah Society 1990; author's field notes.
7. JMKFN, vol. 11, 98.
8. This assertion is based on a sample of more than 2,100 Kiowa personal names collected by

the author and examination of military society names among several Plains populations. Author's fieldnotes; JMKFN, vol. 1, 94, and vol. 11, 156, 177, 196, 206; Parker McKenzie to the author, Apr. 11 and Oct. 2, 1993. Mike Sheets (correspondence to the author, July 5, 2000) reported being given the translation "Unafraid Of Death" as the society name by Kiowa elders Atwater Onco, Melvin Queton, and Spencer Queton.

9. Howard (1965:110–111) noted that his consultants knew little of these defunct societies. In his discussion of the Omaha Hand Game and Gourd Dance (Howard 1950:41), he described the dancing of the Gourd Dance by two members of the losing hand game team after each complete game: "This dance, in the case of the men, is the same as the Hethushka or 'war dance' in choreography, except that the dancers must keep time to the drum and singing with the gourd rattles which they carry." It is difficult to compare his information with earlier descriptions of Omaha dances, because he did not describe the exact choreography of the dance.

10. Some earlier Plains Indian societies with "no-flight" or contrary characteristics were severely defeated in battle or exterminated and were not revived because of their losses. These included the Kiowa Bone Strikers, the Lakota No-Flight Society (Wissler 1912:30), several Pawnee societies (Murie 1914:567–582), and possibly the Comanche Los Lobos Society (Meadows 1999:370–371).

11. Milton Toyebo and Yale Spottedbird to Boyce Timmons, June 19, 1971, DD T-651:13–16. Although Lassiter (1998) used the term "Rattle Dance," obtained from Billy Evans Horse, Horse was the only elder I interviewed who used that term. Billy Evans Horse to the author, Jan. 24, 1995. Scott (HLS-1, vol. 1, 192) listed "Rattle" and "Rattle Foot" as the name of the society. Yale Spottedbird used the names "Rattle Clan" and "Gourd Clan" interchangeably.

12. See also Kiowa Gourd Clan 1976:7.

13. The use of "Wolf Songs" associated with preparations for war journeys and of wolf cries at the conclusions of military society songs is a widespread Kiowa (Black Legs Society), Pawnee, Cheyenne, and Plains Indian tradition. See Hoebel 1978:78; Meadows 1991.

14. Kiowa Gourd Clan 1976:7; Kiowa Tai-Piah Society 1990. This was the only account I collected that referred to a Rattle Dance, or Tàucùngà (Gourd [i.e., Rattle] Dance), and suggested that it preceded the Jáifègàu. I have located no documentation indicating the presence of any other type of society from which the Jáifègàu might have developed. I have also found no documented association or mention of the Rattle Dance outside the context of its being a nickname for the type of dance practiced by the Jáifègàu. Lassiter (1997:88) referred to the dance as Ton-goon-get. The correct pronunciation is Tàucùngà. This is not to say that there are no spiritual or religious aspects to Plains military society dances, for there are; it is simply to distinguish between primarily religiously oriented dances such as the Sun Dance and more martial and socially oriented military society dances.

15. Author's fieldnotes, Oct. 13, 1989. This version indicates that the Kiowa acquired the dance after migrating to the southern plains.

16. These alleged adoptions refer to the vocables and general style of Bowstring Society music rather than to the adoption of any Bowstring songs with Cheyenne lyrics. The inference is that the Kiowa learned the general style and subsequently expanded on it. Six Kiowa men were killed in this fight; the number of Apache and Comanche casualties is unknown.

17. When asked about the absence of Cheyenne lyrics in their Gourd Dance songs, Cheyenne state that contemporary Cheyenne Gourd Dance songs are too fast for Cheyenne words, reflecting the fact that the Kiowa version became the post-1957 revived form.

18. JMKFN, vol. 7, 4. The Mary Buffalo calendar (winter 1836–1837) states, "Tsent'ainta organized." The name in this entry clearly does not resemble Jáifègàu, but it does resemble two other names, the personal name Sétthájdé (White Bear) and the society name Chějánmàu (Horse Headdresses Society). However, the historically well-known White Bear (circa 1820–1878), known by the name Big Ribs as a youth, would have been too young to have organized or held a leadership

position in a society at this date (see Nye 1962:103–104). If the name is intended to be White Bear, it may refer to an earlier White Bear to whom there are references in Kiowa history. If this name is intended to refer to the Horse Headdresses Society—which the first portion seems to indicate, because *tsen* is the common English spelling for *chę̀* (horse)—then this is the first recorded reference to the origin of that society. Many of the entries in the Mary Buffalo calendar and a few in the George Hunt calendar precede the accounts in the Mooney and George Poolaw calendars by two years but are generally in the same chronological order and thus correlate when examined. George Hunt's entry for 1835, for example, correlates with other calendar entries for 1837, and so forth.

19. HLS-1, vol. 2, 169.

20. Noyes (1993:278) reported that a contingent of Kiowa-Apaches visiting an Arapaho camp, apparently aided by an Arapaho man married to a Kiowa-Apache woman, informed the leaders that the Kiowa and Comanche wanted peace with the Cheyenne and their allies, which led to the 1840 peace alliance made near Bent's Fort.

21. JMKFN, vol. 7, 5. Silverhorn's depiction of a society rattle constructed from a can is probably indicative of the style common to his generation and the time he drew the calendar (1902), because earlier accounts indicate that the society's rattles were constructed from rawhide. The use of Anglo-produced metal food cans for rattles undoubtedly became more common after the Kiowa entered the reservation in 1875.

22. Author's fieldnotes. Geographical and floral information concerning *Rhus trilobata* is from Barkley 1986:572.

23. Milton Toyebo and Yale Spottedbird to Boyce Timmons, June 19, 1971, DD T-651:14–16. Because military societies came and went during the nineteenth century, this may demonstrate the formation of a new sodality. What membership the original members then had in the Kiowa military society system is unknown. This reference to White Bear appears to have been to an earlier individual of that name; the historically prominent White Bear (circa 1820–1878) was probably too young to have participated in this fight. He came to prominence in the society and as a young warrior in the 1850s (see Nye 1962:103–104). Society members and membership rosters report several earlier leaders of the society older than the later White Bear.

24. This stance reflects the slight ethnocentrism that is found in all human cultures and still permeates Southern Plains intertribal rivalries.

25. Milton Toyebo and Yale Spottedbird to Boyce Timmons, June 19, 1971, DD T-651:13–16; author's fieldnotes Kiowa and Cheyenne. I do not maintain that myth and oral history are irrelevant, for in many cases they contain important historical elements. However, myths are often difficult to place temporally. I believe a combination of extensive fieldwork emphasizing oral history interviews and archival research into earlier Kiowa oral history produces a more thorough and well-rounded account of the events surrounding the society and dance. Many of the oral histories were collected directly from Kiowa elders, but they are located, unfortunately, in museums far from the Kiowa community. Copies of them are expensive to acquire, and they often require special permission to access. That these sources are primary documents collected from the last generation of Kiowa active in these traditions merits their inclusion in any examination of the subject.

26. The association between a belief in God and a belief that all things are God given is fairly elementary, and in my experience is typical not just of Kiowa but of many people who believe firmly in God. Lassiter (1998:248 n.4) stated, "Because this revival was founded on song, one of the new foundations is a strong belief in the power of Kiowa culture." I cannot see that this belief is new, because every group, even under circumstances of external coercion, believes in the rightness and strength of its own ways, as is evidenced by the continuation of culture and by the way various cultures' names for themselves are often slightly ethnocentric toward other cultures. These patterns continue today (Meadows 1999:414–415). Some Kiowa are concerned not with the origin or diffu-

sion of the dance but only with its present form as a Kiowa dance. Lassiter refrained from pursuing data related to nineteenth-century origins and diffusion (see Lassiter 1998:243 n.1).

27. See also Lassiter 1998:248 n.4, which mentions this duality of focus between song and older society martial themes.

28. Sangko to Marriott, Aug. 19, 1935, AMP; HLS-1, vol. 1, 77–78. John (1985:387) wrote that "it was in the first half of 1806 that the Kiowa and Comanche celebrated the enduring peace between those two markedly different nations."

29. JMKFN, vol. 6, 179.

30. White Fox to La Barre, XI-9, 10, 11, July 26, 1935, SFN, 547–550; Lone Bear to La Barre, 1a-5, June 28, 1935, SFN, 542; Lone Bear to Richardson, VII-22, 1935, SFN, 560.

31. HeapoBears to La Barre, XIII-2, 1935, SFN, 677; HLS-2, 102.

32. Lone Bear to Richardson, VII-22, 1935, SFN, 558–560; Mary Buffalo to La Barre, IV-4, July 11, 1935, SFN, 676–677, 760; Hodltagudlma to Collier, I-24, 1935, SFN, 677; HeapoBears to La Barre, XIII-2, 1935, SFN, 677.

33. Given to Marriott, Aug. 1, 1935, AMP.

34. Given to Marriott, Aug. 1–2, 1935, AMP.

35. Lone Bear to Richardson, VII-22, 1935, SFN, 558–560; Mary Buffalo to La Barre, IV-4, July 11, 1935, SFN, 676–677, 760; Hodltagudlma to Collier, I-24, 1935, SFN, 677; HeapoBears to La Barre, XIII-2, 1935, SFN, 677; Lone Bear to Richardson, VII-7, VII-9, 1935, SFN, 170, 176.

36. Given to Marriott, Aug. 1, 1935, and Piatonma to Marriott, July 16, 1935, AMP; Lone Bear to Richardson, VII-7, VII-9, 1935, and VII-12, July 15, 1935, SFN, 129, 170, 176.

37. Bill Koomsa Jr. to the author, Jan. 24, 1995.

38. White Horse and Monroe Horse to Richardson, 1935, SFN, 1291–1292; HLS-1, vol. 1, 192. White Horse was originally a member of the Jáifègàu and later joined the Omaha Society. He said that this song could be sung at any time by members of the society and might be considered the favorite or most important of all their songs. Today this song and several related versions of it are considered family songs belonging to the descendants of White Bear. The song is usually sung at a dance when requested by descendants. Bill Koomsa Jr. to the author, Jan. 24, 1995.

39. Hunting Horse and Padalti to Richardson, 1935, SFN, 1310. Today this song is known as Hunting Horse's song.

40. Frizzlehead to Richardson, 1935, SFN, 1233; White Fox to La Barre, XI-9, 10, 11, July 26, 1935, SFN, 549; Seko to Richardson, 1935, SFN, 1223. Frizzlehead II, also known as E-mau-tah (Èmáuthââ, or Arising Crying), was the son of Áulpépjè, or Bushy Hair (1824–1907), popularly known as Frizzlehead. Frizzlehead I was once the principal leader of the Jáifègàu. Regarding the owl feather headdress, Richardson wrote: "Kohw.k'odlte [Crow Neck] had one, and this was the thing that Odlpw got. These owl feather headdresses (apawdl: no name for the wearers), were inherited, but the actual descent of one is unknown. When the daimbega are painted red in this fashion, they do an 'old style dance.'" Seko to Richardson, 1935, SFN, 1223.

41. Piatonma to Marriott, July 16, 1935, AMP.

42. One account states while the Kiowa were camped at present-day Randlett Park in Anadarko, Oklahoma, White Bear pulled Sun Boy out of his tipi and beat him. Whether the drawing was connected to this event is unknown.

43. School for Advanced Research, Santa Fe, New Mexico, Accession Files SAR 1990.19, n.d.

44. White Fox to La Barre, XI-9, 10, 11, July 26, 1935, SFN, 548–549; HeapoBears to La Barre, XIII-5, July 5, 1935, SFN, 557; Given to Marriott, Aug. 1, 1935, AMP.

45. Given to Marriott, Aug. 1, 1935, AMP. Feder (1982:pl. 37) also provided a photograph of this rattle. An excellent example of the shift to decorated metal can rattles is one from the Mandan Kit Fox Society in the American Museum of Natural History (Time-Life 1993:78–79).

46. HeapoBears to La Barre, XIII-5, July 5, 1935, SFN, 557; White Fox to La Barre, XI-9, 10, 11, July 26, 1935, SFN, 548; Lone Bear to La Barre, 1a-5, June 26, 1935, SFN, 542; Given to Marriott, Aug. 1, 1935, AMP.

47. White Fox to La Barre, XI-9, 10, 11, July 26, 1935, SFN, 549; Richardson, SFN, 1218.

48. Special Agent H. T. Ketcham to Governor John Evans, Apr. 4, 1864, in Annual Report of the Commissioner of Indian Affairs, 1864, 401–402; HeapoBears to La Barre, XIII-5, 1935, SFN, 557. Piatonma to Marriott, July 17, 1935, AMP; Given to Marriott, Aug. 1, 1935, AMP.

49. HeapoBears to La Barre, XIII-5, July 30, 1935, SFN, 557; Ananthy Odlepaugh Ledgerbook.

50. Cecil and Jenny Horse to Julia Jordan, July 26, 1967, DD T-25:24–25; Given to Marriott, Aug. 1, 1935, AMP.

51. JMKFN, vol. 6, 180, notes only the rope belonging to White Bear; see also HLS-1, vol. 1, 193.

52. Nye 1962:103–104; Lone Bear to Richardson, VII-20, 1935, SFN, 905–908; Given to Marriott, Aug. 1, 1935, AMP; Kiowa Gourd Clan 1976. Boyd (1981:116–117) incorrectly attributed White Bear's rescue to Sitting Bear and Lone Wolf. In another publication, Boyd (1983:226–227) attributed the rescue to A-mau-tah, or Frizzlehead II, who reportedly chased the Mexican, and to Lone Wolf, who cut the rope to free White Bear. Because A-mau-tah was born in 1860, this incident clearly points to his father, Frizzlehead I (1824–1907). According to Taybodle in the 1890s (see Nye 1962:103–104), it was Frizzlehead I who rushed in with his lance and saved White Bear from being dragged to death.

53. The name *aúfégúl* (lit. "red otter") is actually the Kiowa name for the mink, so called for its reddish fur. The Red Otter, or Mink, depicted by Berlo (2000:38–39) would be an earlier Red Otter (1828–1880; JMKFN, vol. 1, 67), because the later Red Otter was born in 1854, died prior to allotment, and was not a known Dog Society member. The varied accounts may simply reflect the ways different participants remembered the event and to whom they attributed the rescue. From the variety of accounts, Frizzlehead I, Red Otter I, and Lone Wolf (d. 1878) may all have been involved in the counterattack to rescue White Bear. This event is an excellent example of the failure of most scholars to cross-check data concerning tribal censuses, birth and death dates, and the succession of Indian names and incorporate them into historical accounts.

54. Ananthy Odlepaugh Ledgerbook; Taybodle to Scott, HLS-1, vol. 1, 13, 18, 42.

55. Given to Marriott, Aug. 1, 1935, AMP.

56. Ibid.

57. Given to Marriott, Aug. 1, 1935, Atah to Marriott, Jan. 31, 1936, and Tso'odl to Marriott, July 11, 1936, AMP.

58. Frizzlehead to Richardson, 1935, SFN, 1216; Lone Bear to Richardson, VII-20, 1935, SFN, 905–908; Given to Marriott, Aug. 1, 1935, Atah to Marriott, Jan. 31, 1936, and Tso'odl to Marriott, July 11, 1936, AMP.

59. JMKFN, vol. 1, 71–72.

60. Frizzlehead to Richardson, 1935, SFN, 1216; Tso'odl to Marriott, July 11, 1936, AMP. White Bear's lance reportedly had no specific location in the meeting formation, but judging from the structure of other societies, it was probably located with him on the west side, because of his office.

61. Frizzlehead to Richardson, 1935, SFN, 1216.

62. JMKNF, vol. 11, 152. Corwin (1971a:148) wrote that Red Bonnet Brow's lance had a Mexican steel blade for its tip.

63. JMKFN, vol. 7, 13.

64. Ibid.

65. JMKFN, vol. 7, 29.

66. Lone Bear to Richardson, VII-20, 1935, SFN, 905–908; HeapoBears to Richardson, X-11, 1935, SFN, 755. Attotain (White Cow Bird) was a brother of Sun Boy's and Pagotogoodle's (Lone Young Man).

67. Lone Bear to Richardson, VII-20, 1935, SFN, 905–908.

68. Ibid.

69. Ibid. The name was recorded as *pot'e.to*. Although the exact etymology is unknown, the first syllable denotes beaver. A similar gift was given to White Bear's eldest son, Tsal-aut-te, who was also a Jáifègàu member and later took his father's name, White Bear. The name Tsal-aut-te is often popularly translated as Cry of the Wild Goose. The name Sáláutjè or Sáláutsàn is the Kiowa personal name form for The Curlew or Little Curlew (i.e., the upland field plover). McKenzie n.d.b; Parker McKenzie to the author, Apr. 4, 1993, and Sept. 5, 1994.

70. Lone Bear to Richardson, X-7, Aug. 12, 1935, and VII-20, 1935, SFN, 254, 905–908; Tso'odl to Marriott, July 13, 1936, AMP.

71. Lone Bear to Richardson, VII-20, 1935, SFN, 905–908; JMKFN, vol. 7, 33. Photographs taken in the early 1900s show Bison Bird holding this lance in a group of Kiowa. These photos prove to be stills from the film *Old Texas*, originally produced by Charles Goodnight in 1916. The film contains footage of the same group of Kiowa performing during a visit at Goodnight's ranch in Texas, with Bison Bird holding this lance. *Old Texas*, Panhandle-Plains Museum, Canyon, Texas.

72. Lone Bear to Richardson, VII-22, 1935, SFN, 558–559. This account states that the rope was tied around a "water drum" and used in Omaha Society meetings. However, the society had no direct link to the Native American Church or the use of water drums in peyote meetings. Thus it might have been used to secure a rawhide head to a drum in that society.

73. Given to Marriott, Aug. 1, 1935, Atah to Marriott, Jan. 31, 1936, and Tso'odl to Marriott, July 11, 1936, AMP.

74. Frizzlehead to Richardson, 1935, SFN, 1216.

75. Richardson, 1935, SFN, 1216.

76. Frizzlehead to Richardson, 1935, SFN, 1233.

77. Kintadl to Richardson, IV-4, 1935, SFN, 436; Frizzlehead and Gumdw to Richardson, 1935, SFN, 1218; Luther Samon (Sahmaunt) to Mishkin, VIII-5, Aug. 1, 1935, SFN, 506. Mooney (1898:392) noted that Comalty was the nephew of the elder Big Head and the second to hold that name. Parsons (1929:xxii, 92) listed Comalty as having been born in 1869 and as the third to bear the Big Head name. See note 71, chapter 8, for information about Comalty. It is important to recognize that there were at least three known Kiowa named White Bear in the nineteenth century. The first lived early in the 1800s. The second is the historically well-known White Bear, who was born about 1820–1830 and died in Texas in 1878. The third was his son, who died in 1894. In Parsons's account (1929:91–92), it is unclear whether Big Head was speaking of men who were society leaders when he was (1913–1922), in earlier years, or both, because some of the death dates of these individuals preceded these years.

78. JMKFN, vol. 6, 179.

79. Rueben Topaum to the author, Aug. 31, 1994.

80. This picture was in the *Kiowa Indian News*; see Poolaw 1981.

81. Lone Bear to Richardson, 1935, SFN, 560; White Fox to La Barre, XI-9, XI-10, and XI-11, July 26, 1935, SFN, 548; Gumdw to Richardson, 1935, SFN, 1228.

82. Domebo Calendar, DD T-214 and T-216; Ananthy Odlepaugh Ledgerbook; Frizzlehead to Richardson, 1935, SFN, 1218; Parker McKenzie to the author, 1991, 1994; Francis Tsonetokoy to the author, Dec. 8, 1990.

83. Domebo Calendar, drawings 89–106, DD T-214 and T-216.

84. Ananthy Odlepaugh Ledgerbook; Parker McKenzie to the author, 1991, 1994; Francis Tsonetokoy to the author, Dec. 8, 1990.

85. Kiowa Bill, who took his allotment southeast of present day Hobart, Oklahoma, was close friends with Red Buffalo, on whose allotment the Kiowa tribal complex now stands on the west side of Carnegie, Oklahoma. After dances ceased around the Hobart area and became centered on the Carnegie area, Kiowa Bill remarried, and Red Buffalo gave him forty acres of land to live on near Carnegie. He moved there in the 1920s. Atwater Onco to the author, Aug. 30, 1994.

86. Grace Tsonetokoy to the author, July 11, 1991, photo courtesy of Grace Tsonetokoy; author's fieldnotes.

87. Ananthy Odlepaugh Ledgerbook; Fred Tsoodle to the author, June 14, 2001.

88. Alice Marriott, "Kiowa Giveaway and Dance," AMP, Miscellaneous Folder.

89. Grace Tsonetokoy to the author, July 11, 1991; clipping from Carnegie, Oklahoma, newspaper, April 1929. Mrs. Lone Bear was reportedly hard of hearing, and although she was warned not to leave the room, she attempted to retrieve a folded tipi cover from another room for extra protection and was swept away. Some Kiowa maintain that Lone Bear's admonition has held true, for the Kiowa Warrior Descendants, who continue to dance at this location, have continually suffered organizational problems. This event was also recorded for the spring of 1929 in the Ananthy Odlepaugh Ledgerbook.

90. Oscar Tsoodle to the author, Oct. 13, 1990.

91. According to one elder Kiowa woman whose mother attended the dance at Jack Bointy's in 1926 and told her of what transpired, the Ponca taught their Soldier Dance to the Kiowa, and it became known as the Round Dance among the Kiowa. Author's fieldnotes, 1998.

92. "Kiowa Giveaway and Dance," AMP.

93. Ibid.

94. White Fox to La Barre, XI-9, XI-10, and XI-11, July 26, 1935, SFN, 547; Lone Bear to La Barre, 1a-5, June 28, 1935, SFN, 542.

95. Henry Tsoodle Sr. to Marriott, July 10, 1936, AMP.

96. Oscar Tsoodle to the author, Mar. 4, 1992. See also Poolaw 1981.

97. Fred and Peggy Tsoodle to the author, July 21, 2004.

98. Ibid.

99. Ibid.

100. Fred and Peggy Tsoodle to the author, June 14, 2001.

101. Jerrold Levy to the author, June 26, 1990.

102. Bill Koomsa and Billy Evans Horse to the author, Jan. 24, 1995. Issacs (1975) and Poolaw (1981) noted the inclusion of other societies' songs in modern-day Gourd Clan music.

103. Author's fieldnotes and tape-recordings, Kiowa Gourd Clan ceremonials, 1990, 1991, 1993, 1995.

104. Bill Koomsa and Billy Evans Horse to the author, Jan. 24, 1995.

105. This song is a good example of the way lyrics in songs are altered and are sometimes ungrammatical in composition, relative to speech. In speaking, the expression would be "Jáifègàu hâbé ém ǫ̂tâgûnjàu," but in singing, the pronoun form ém (they) is omitted.

106. Author's fieldnotes. Several elders indicated that songs from other societies had been brought into the modern Gourd Dance, both because of their similarity and in order to keep them alive.

107. Author's fieldnotes.

108. This is not to say that Indian music is any easier to learn or physically easier to sing than other types of music.

109. Whistler was a Sauk and Fox. See Hatton 1989 for the program's origins and development.

110. On clear days I could receive this program in Norman, Oklahoma, and on Saturday mornings I often listened to it while driving to Anadarko, in order to hear the music and the announcements of that weekend's events.

111. Fred Tsoodle to the author, July 21, 2004.
112. Oscar Tsoodle to the author, Mar. 5, 1992.
113. Kiowa Gourd Clan (1976); author's fieldnotes.
114. Author's fieldnotes. Apparently, political conflict resulted in Bill Koomsa Sr.'s being elected vice president instead of president and in his early resignation. Some elders have indicated that Koomsa, the son of an influential and knowledgeable singer and Gourd dancer, Bob Koomsa, and a grandson of White Bear's, was more familiar with the Gourd Dance traditions and thereby more qualified to lead the revival. Some Kiowas say that Hainta's relationship as a son-in-law of Daugomah's swayed a major portion of the vote for the presidency in his favor, because many of the older men involved and consulted during the revival were relatives of Daugomah's. Poolaw (1981) noted other factors told to him by Bill Koomsa Sr., pertaining to Koomsa's separation from the society. These included jealousy and Koomsa's determination to allow only Kiowa to dance, to dance only during the daytime, and not to allow dancing on the Fourth of July.
115. Author's fieldnotes, 2004. When I asked this man whether membership in the Black Legs Society elevated a person's social status, he replied, "Yes, it does, but it's not designed that way. Again, I guess mostly it's a celebration. It's a reunion of all the veterans in the tribe, and a celebration that we went out and did this thing and came back. We're here to celebrate with each other."
116. Author's fieldnotes, 2004.
117. Lassiter (1995:254) wrote, "The Red Wolf story is not about the origination of the Taimpego Society per se; but because it is about receiving song, it is about the origin of the Gourd Dance." He amplified (1995:289): "Indeed, the Taimpego Society's origin story holds little importance for most Gourd Dance practitioners because, philosophically, it has little to do with the contemporary Gourd Dance experience. Not only are the dance's practitioners and contexts vastly different, but the Gourd Dance's revival reformulated the Rattle Dance on completely different foundations than those grounding the nineteenth century's Taimpego Society. One of these new foundations is the strong belief in the power of Kiowa culture. For example, both the Kiowa Gourd Clan Ceremonials' (Kiowa Gourd Clan 1976) and Kiowa Tia-Piah Society's (Kiowa Tia-Piah 1990) publications locate the dance's origin in the Red Wolf legend; the Taimpego Society is hardly mentioned, if at all, in telling contrast with scholars' literature. The Kiowa Gourd Clan Ceremonials (Kiowa Gourd Clan 1976) treat the revival as the conscious retention and perpetuation of 'Kiowa ways' through the dance, rather than as a continuation of the Taimpego Society. Hence the currency of the Red Wolf legend. At the same time, however, many distinct practices, tenets, and themes of the Taimpego Society continue to center the dance's history for many Gourd Dance practitioners, especially Kiowa at the annual celebrations (e.g., the display of war trophies)." In addition, numerous martial themes are found in Gourd Dance song texts (see also Lassiter 1998:163–168).
118. Bill Koomsa Jr. to the author, Jan. 24, 1995; Meadows 1999:138; author's fieldnotes. While visiting the Lone Bear dance ground one day by himself, Leonard Cozad Sr. was thinking of the elders when these words came to him and he composed this song. For a discussion of the cultural importance of the song, see Lassiter 1993.
119. Author's fieldnotes.
120. Author's fieldnotes, July 4, 1991.
121. Oscar Tsoodle to the author, Oct. 13, 1990.
122. Bill Koomsa Jr. to the author, Jan. 24, 1995.
123. Oscar Tsoodle to the author, Oct. 13, 1990.
124. Robert J. Stahl suggested that "Gourd Dance regalia was 'invented' by studying turn-of-the-century photographs of Kiowa, Comanche, and Plains Apache peyotists" (Kracht 1994:334). I disagree, because elder Kiowa still clearly distinguish between Gourd Dance and Native American Church (peyotist) attire and because early-twentieth-century photographs of Kiowa Gourd Dancers

(see Poolaw 1981) show an absence of shoulder blankets, red and blue blankets, and gourd (plant) rattles. Although the dress styles of both the Gourd Dance and the Native American Church have changed and are relatively similar, I find no clear basis for this diagnosis in my own interviews with elder Kiowa, Comanche, and Apache. Although each has influence the other, it is apparent that the large number of Native American Church members involved in the revival of the Gourd Dance heavily influenced post-1957 Gourd Dance dress.

125. Author's fieldnotes, 1990–1998. Although the Kiowa Ten Medicine Bundles were collectively given a sweat bath and opened, cleaned, and repaired at each Sun Dance, there is no mention in the pre-reservation ethnographic fieldnotes of any association with or annual visit to the Kiowa bundles by the society.

126. Author's fieldnotes, Oct. 13 and Nov. 22, 1999.

127. Author's fieldnotes, Oct. 13 and Nov. 22, 1999.

128. Author's fieldnotes, Apr. 10, 1993; "Cedar Ceremony Is Set for Sunday," ADN, Feb. 18, 2000; "Cedaring Rites Set for Sunday," ADN, Feb. 15, 2002.

129. Author's fieldnotes, Kiowa Gourd Clan ceremonial, July 4, 1991.

130. Martha Poolaw to the author, Aug. 3, 1995.

131. Atwater Onco to the author, Oct. 15, 1997.

132. Vernon Tsoodle to the author, July 16, 2004.

133. In the past there were two of these curved staffs in the Kiowa tribe, one associated with the Black Legs Society and one associated with Se/osa (Séáusàn, Little Bringer/Introducer of Peyote) of the Horse Headdresses Society. Yellow Wolf, who was once a curved lance keeper in the Black Legs Society, remade and sold one of these lances to Tócàbáudài (Appeared From The Water), another Black Legs member, after the Dog Society became defunct.

134. This is in contrast to Kracht's assertions (1994:334).

135. Author's fieldnotes, 1990.

136. Family members state that an older form of this song belonged to another, now extinct society (possibly the Horse Headdresses) and was adopted as a family song by the Tanedooah family. New words were added, and the Kiowa Gourd Clan adopted that form as a recruiting song. The old form is still used as the Tanedooah family song. Bill Koomsa and Billy Evans Horse to the author, Jan. 24, 1995.

137. At one performance of the Rattle Song at a Tia-Piah Society of Colorado benefit dance, the Kiowa leaders sang the entire song through and the drum did not join in. Author's fieldnotes, Nov. 18, 1995.

138. The more traditional emphasis on a gradual increase in the speed and tempo of songs throughout a dance is in direct contrast with practices in more pan-Indian dances, in which singers often perform Kiowa songs at a much faster speed throughout the entire dance. This contrast comes from the distinction between the types of men's society meetings that involved feasts and were associated with the Sun Dance encampment. The first was the afternoon kífákùgà (daytime feasts) or kíqàlfígà (invited [to eat] feasts), which had the sides of the tipi rolled up and were open to the public. The second form consisted of the dáucâum meetings, in which the lodge door was closed and roll call was taken, and the gíkúgà (regular nightly feasts), both of which lasted all night. Since the form of dancing performed today by the Gourd Clan as well as the Black Legs Society falls into the daytime feast category, it is standard to stop at dark. Lassiter (1997:82) used the term *bawl dawgeah*. The name of the dance is a single word, and the correct pronunciation is Fáuldàugà. There are three distinct *p* sounds in the Kiowa language; the soft *p* is represented in the McKenzie Kiowa orthography by the letter *f* (Meadows and McKenzie 2001).

139. Oscar Tsoodle to the author, Oct. 13, 1990.

140. Atwater Onco to the author, Aug. 30, 1994. See also Lassiter 1998:175–176.

141. Author's fieldnotes.

142. Ibid.

143. Ibid.

144. Tai-Piah Society 1990; "Powwows and Handgames," ADN, June 30, 2000.

145. Author's fieldnotes; ADN, Aug. 30, 2001. The Kiowa Warrior Descendants advertised their Twenty-eighth Annual Labor Day Powwow in 2000 (ADN, Aug. 28, 2002).

146. Author's fieldnotes, 1991, 1997.

147. White Fox to La Barre, XI-9, 10, 11, July 26, 1935, SFN, 549.

148. Author's fieldnotes, Kiowa Gourd Clan ceremonial, July 4, 1993.

149. Author's fieldnotes, 1997.

150. One elder Kiowa women stated that although she went along with the male dominance of traditional ceremonies, she refused to do so in her everyday life and work.

151. Author's fieldnotes, 1997.

152. All powwows, benefits, and hand games are regularly listed in the *Anadarko Daily News* under "Powwows and handgames." Most benefit dances include sales of dinners and Indian tacos, raffles, cake walks, blanket dances, and other specials for fund-raising.

153. Author's fieldnotes.

154. Billy Evans Horse to the author, Jan. 24, 1995.

155. Author's fieldnotes, 2004.

156. Ibid.

157. Although guests are always welcome as spectators, Kiowa's opinions on the inclusion of non-Kiowa and especially of non-Indians in the Gourd Dance vary greatly. Although some Kiowa wholeheartedly embrace the interest shown by outsiders, others are strongly opposed to it. Among the Kiowa I spoke with who were concerned about or opposed such participation, common complaints were about placing too much emphasis on protocol, such as certain ways to walk around the drum, about initiation rights and fees, and about "trying to hard to be Indian." Another was about the use of Gourd Dance organizations for personal profit through the holding of leadership positions. Perhaps most offensive are people in non-Indian organizations who claim to have "the authority to do such and such" according to rights allegedly given to them by someone claiming the authority to do so, along with people who, from a lack of understanding of change and adaptation, are in a state of static, frozen, nineteenth-century romanticism. They believe they are "experts" and try to tell the Kiowa, including the direct descendants of Jáifègàu members, how to dance the Gourd Dance. Such hobbyists demonstrate their failure to understand the complex mechanics of culture change among those they so badly want to emulate. In discussing Anglo attempts to correct Indians about what is and is not tradition, Kiowa often use expressions such as "trying to out-Indian us" or "trying to out-tradition us," followed by much laughter. See Lassiter 1995:35–36n.3 for a similar example. Similarly, a Crow Sun Dance priest told me how an Anglo tried to "out-Indian us" by coming to him and telling him how to correctly run his own sweat lodge. Author's fieldnotes, 1997.

158. Author's fieldnotes, Kiowa Tia-Piah Society ceremonial, July 4, 1992.

159. "Powwows and Handgames," ADN, Mar. 1, 2000, 4.

160. Several dancers I spoke with in a large Midwestern hobbyist club, who model their dress and dance styles after the Kiowa and Comanche, indicated that they really had no understanding of the dance's history but simply enjoyed dancing and making the clothes.

161. Author's fieldnotes, 2004.

162. The race issue is a useful trump card that is always available in any interracial or interethnic relationship. It is emotionally harmful and a stance against which one has little recourse. This is a common occurrence that I have witnessed and experienced in working in Native American, Asian, and Anglo societies.

163. Lassiter (1995:18–34) discussed the Joe True syndrome and his experiences at length.
164. Author's fieldnotes, 2004.
165. Author's fieldnotes.
166. Ibid.
167. Ibid.
168. Author's fieldnotes, 2004.
169. The strength of Ellis's 1990 article lies in his discussion of the role of the Gourd Dance revival in broader Native trends and as an agent of cultural reintegration. As a historical work, this article definitely contributes to knowledge of the Gourd Dance. Some historical and ethnological inaccuracies are present, however, because of Ellis's reliance on one Kiowa consultant, his limited interviews and fieldwork at that time (see also Ellis 1996:232), the view of historians concerning ethnographic fieldwork, his limited knowledge of primary ethnological documentary sources, and his lack of familiarity with nineteenth-century military societies. Acquisition of such data and an ethnohistorical approach would have clarified many points, thereby preventing his statement (Ellis 1990:21) that "indeed, the tangled history of these early types of the dances makes it difficult to ascertain with any degree of certainty their precise role and function in the cultural life of the various tribes," which was clarified in Meadows 1995 and Meadows 1999.
170. Author's Cheyenne fieldnotes, 1994. Whereas Lassiter (1998:243) chose to refrain from exploring questions of nineteenth-century origins in favor of current popular views concerning Gourd Dance origins, I have chosen to address both in an attempt to provide a more thorough temporal account of the dance and its evolution.
171. Author's Comanche and Cheyenne fieldnotes.
172. Gregory Haumpy Sr. to the author, Apr. 2, 1998.
173. Albert Bronaugh to the author, July 7, 2004.
174. Ibid.
175. Observe the root word *fẽgà* in the following sentences: *Né dáuchái nàu à fẽgàọ̀tạ̀* (You prayed for me and I became spiritually pleased); *Dáuqí ẹ́ gúibàu* (I was spiritually downcast and God revived me); *Pànmái yạ́ fẽgàcạ̀umẽ̀* (He [God] showed me the spirit way to heaven). The expressions *fẽgàjò* (with spirit) and *fẽgàdọ̀gà* (within the spirit), from Kiowa Christian hymns, also exemplify this association between spirit and soul.
176. Residing at the University of Oklahoma from 1989 to 1995 allowed me to conduct year-round field research and to attend and participate in many Kiowa Gourd Dances. Additional research from October 1997 to May 1998 and two six-week ethnographic field schools I directed in 2004 and 2006 provided other data. During this time I attended several annual dances and numerous benefit dances of the Kiowa Gourd Clan, Kiowa Tia-Piah Society of Carnegie, Kiowa Tia-Piah Society of Oklahoma, and the Kiowa Warrior Descendants, as well as other, non-society-sponsored Gourd Dances. Attendance and participation at Comanche, Apache, and Cheyenne Gourd Dances provided other data and experiences for comparison and contrast.
177. Gregory Haumpy Sr. to the author, Apr. 2, 1998.
178. Ibid.
179. Martha Koomsa Perez, Carnegie Victory Club Veterans Day Celebration, Red Buffalo Hall, Carnegie, Oklahoma, Nov. 11, 1997.
180. Parker McKenzie and Gus Palmer Jr. to the author; author's fieldnotes.
181. Author's fieldnotes.
182. Ideally, Kiowa like to have enough singers to have a full drum. Although there is no set number of singers, and the required number depends on the abilities of the singers who are present, sometimes a less than desired or scheduled number of singers is present or the singers have less than the desired ability, and this is often commented upon. Some singers, upon arriving at a dance

and seeing few other singers, quickly leave before they are obligated to sit at the drum. In some instances a weak drum does the best it can. Once, a major Veterans Day celebration had to be canceled because of insufficient singers.

183. See also Lassiter 1995:226, 267.
184. Author's fieldnotes, 1995.
185. Atwater Onco to the author, Aug. 30, 1994; Meadows 1999:154.
186. Tim Tsoodle to the author, July 23, 2004.
187. Gregory Haumpy Sr. to the author, Apr. 2, 1998.
188. Billy Evans Horse to the author, Jan. 24, 1995.
189. Oscar Tsoodle to the author, Oct. 13, 1990.
190. Atwater Onco to the author, Aug. 30, 1994; Meadows 1999:155.
191. Author's fieldnotes, 1995.
192. Parker McKenzie to the author, May 13 and July 11, 1993; Francis Tsonetokoy to the author, Dec. 8, 1990. McKenzie, who camped at and witnessed four Ghost Dances between 1907 and 1917, stated that the sweating of the bundles was regularly done in the morning. The Ghost Dance ceremonies generally began around noon and continued throughout the afternoon, concluding before dark.
193. Author's Southern Cheyenne fieldnotes, Sept. 21, Oct. 9, Dec. 9, and Dec. 10, 1992; ADN, June 7 and 22–23, 2002.
194. Author's Southern Cheyenne fieldnotes, Sept. 21, Oct. 9, Dec. 9, and Dec. 10, 1992; ADN, June 7 and 22–23, 2002.
195. Author's fieldnotes.
196. Author's fieldnotes, 1995.
197. Author's fieldnotes.
198. Oscar Tsoodle to the author, Oct. 13, 1990.
199. Billy Evans Horse to the author, Jan. 24, 1995; Meadows 1999:155.
200. Bill Koomsa to the author, Jan. 24, 1995; Meadows 1999:157–158.
201. Billy Evans Horse to the author, Jan. 24, 1995; Meadows 1999:158.
202. Author's fieldnotes. The descriptive terms *vocable* and *nonvocable* are simply an improvisation Kiowa use for purposes of clarity and discussion.
203. Author's fieldnotes, 1997.
204. Author's fieldnotes; Eric Lassiter, personal communication.
205. I have observed some Kiowa and Comanche who are strong Gourd Dance practitioners but who have been away from public dances or ceremonies for an extended period experience, emotionally and to some degree physically, what I call "song deprivation" (having anxiety, cravings, etc.).
206. Albert Bronaugh to the author, July 7, 2004.
207. Tim Tsoodle to the author, July 23, 2004.
208. Anne Yeahquo to the author, July 1995; Meadows 1999:161.

Chapter 6. Qóichégàu

1. Tso'odl to Marriott, July 13, 1936, and Given to Marriott, Aug. 1, 1935, and July 21, 1936, AMP.
2. HLS-1, vol. 1, 192–193. On the basis of these data, I have modified the translation of the society's name from that in my earlier work (Meadows 1999:41).
3. Frizzlehead to Richardson, 1935, SFN, 1243.
4. White Fox to La Barre, XI-9, 10, 11, July 26, 1935, SFN, 547.
5. JMKFN, vol. 11, 98.
6. Parker McKenzie to the author, May 13 and Sept. 5, 1993.

7. Parker McKenzie to the author, May 13 and Sept. 5, 1993.

8. While acknowledging the data obtained from the earlier generation of Kiowa interviewed on this subject, I present this discussion to allow readers to examine the data for themselves, as well as to provide examples of the difficulty involved in such research, especially with a tonal language, and of the possibilities produced by combining ethnohistorical data with contemporary fieldwork and linguistic analysis.

9. Frizzlehead and Guito to Richardson, 1935, SFN, 1243; Sangko to Marriott, Jan. 29, 1936, AMP. See also Mary Buffalo's account (Nye 1962:3–9). This Frizzlehead is E-mau-tah (Arising Crying), born in 1860 (KFR, 34), the son of the earlier Bushy Haired or Frizzlehead (KFR, 32; 1824–Feb. 18, 1907).

10. Silverhorn to Mishkin, V-7, 8, 9, July 2, 1935, SFN, 544–545. Fágàujògùl is not to be confused with the later Pagotogul (1848–1910), who was a brother of Sun Boy and White Cow Bird (see Nye 1962:158). On the basis of one of Marriott's calendar entries (1945:7, 294), Lowie (1953:361) suggested that the society was first organized in 1846, although he noted that this was a possible reorganization. The data indicate an earlier origin for the society and thus simply an initiation in 1846 (see Mooney (1898:283–285).

11. Silverhorn to Mishkin, V-7, 8, 9, July 2, 1935, SFN, 544–545. Nye (1962:3–9) recorded a longer version of this story from Mary Buffalo that closely agrees with Silverhorn's account, with additional circumstances concerning the return of Lone Young Man's daughter, who had been captured by the Comanche.

12. Frizzlehead and Seko to Richardson, 1935, SFN, 1243.

13. Guito to Richardson, 1935, SFN, 1243.

14. Gumdaw to Richardson, 1935, SFN, 1243.

15. Kintadl to Richardson, VIII-13, 1935, SFN, 546; Frizzlehead and Yellow Wolf to Richardson, 1935, SFN, 1244.

16. JMKFN, vol. 6, 178; Parker McKenzie to the author, Apr. 4 and June 16, 1993.

17. Frizzlehead, Seko, and Yellow Wolf to Richardson, 1935, SFN, 1245; Piatonma to Marriott, July 16, 1935, and Given to Marriott, Aug. 1, 1935, AMP.

18. Frizzlehead and Yellow Wolf to Richardson, 1935, SFN, 1244.

19. Frizzlehead and Yellow Wolf to Richardson, 1935, SFN, 1212, 1244. Richardson recorded, "Very old men, who have retired by giving their sashes away to a younger member. They are subsequently known as tadl (grandmother). The term is not to be confused with tadl, meaning a 10-medicine owner, though I see no way of distinguishing the 2 terms." Her notes indicate some degree of uncertainty on her part about the varied uses of this term. She also noted: "tadl—one who has retired. This term applies to every kind of retirement, eg. the gudlguet who had given his right to paint away, a topadoki, a koiseko who had transferred his sash to another" (SFN, 1211). Although tál is also the single and dual form of reference for one's paternal grandmother—one name for the Ten Medicine Bundles—the relationship is unclear.

20. JMKFN, vol. 6, 178.

21. Sangko to Marriott, Aug. 19, 1935, AMP.

22. Richardson, 1935, SFN, 1243; Silverhorn to Mishkin, V-3, July 1, 1935, SFN, 544.

23. Frizzlehead, Seko, and Yellow Wolf to Richardson, 1935, SFN, 1244, 1252; Given to Marriott, Aug. 1, 1935, AMP.

24. Frizzlehead, Seko, and Yellow Wolf to Richardson, 1935, SFN, 1240–1242.

25. Frizzlehead and Yellow Wolf to Richardson, 1935, SFN, 1241; Sangko to Marriott, Jan. 27, 1936, AMP; HLS-1, vol. 1, 192–193.

26. Frizzlehead and Yellow Wolf to Richardson, 1935, SFN, 1241; Sangko to Marriott, Jan. 27, 1936, and Atah to Marriott, Jan. 31, 1936, AMP; HLS-1, vol. 1, 192–193.

27. Sangko to Marriott, Jan. 27, 1936, and Given to Marriott, Aug. 1, 1935, AMP.

28. Frizzlehead and Yellow Wolf to Richardson, SFN, 1240; HLS-1, vol. 1, 192–193. The different enumerations of the society's sashes may represent several possible inconsistencies. Either some of the sashes were no longer extant at the time a particular description was recorded or the larger figures represent a later expansion of the society's membership. Although Mooney's account does not match that of the 1935 Santa Fe field school, his account should be given greater credence than the 1935 accounts, because he resided longer among the Kiowa and was in close contact with many of the last pre-reservation warriors who had firsthand knowledge of the society. There are two major reasons the Laboratory of Anthropology fieldnotes may hold strength in stating that there were ten red elk-skin sashes. First, the Kiowa have always associated the number ten with the Dog Society, in reference, I believe, to the ten regular sash owners. The use of the term "Ten Bravest" by the Kiowa is most likely not simply a romantic lamentation for a past society but a historical reference that upon further investigation holds truth. Second, the Santa Fe study was the most thorough one regarding Kiowa societies in the nineteenth century. The lack of correlation with some of the respective categories of sashes may represent the absence of sashes or difficulties in translation. Although it is difficult to decipher all these inconsistencies at this time, I am inclined to defer to Mooney's account for the previously listed reasons.

29. Frizzlehead, Guito, and Yellow Wolf to Richardson, 1935, SFN, 1241.

30. Gaapitan to Mooney, 1902, JMKFN, vol. 6, 274.

31. Given to Marriott, Aug. 1, 1935, and Sangko to Marriott, Jan. 27, 1936, AMP.

32. HeapoBears to Richardson, X-18, Aug. 5, 1935, SFN, 595.

33. Yellow Wolf to Richardson, 1935, SFN, 1244; Kintadl to Richardson, V-III-10, 1935, SFN, 575.

34. Sangko to Marriott, Jan. 27, 1936, and Atah to Marriott, Jan. 31, 1936, AMP.

35. Kintadl to Richardson, VIII-10, 1935, SFN, 575.

36. Hodltagudlma to Collier, I-25, July 2, 1935, SFN, 574; Mrs. Hokeah to Collier, IV-9, July 19, 1935, SFN, 574–575; Kintadl to Richardson, VIII-10, SFN, 575–576.

37. Sangko to Marriott, Jan. 27, 1936, and Given to Marriott, Aug. 1, 1935, AMP. During a fellowship at the Smithsonian in April 1991, I examined and photographed Mooney's Kiowa shield models and found none resembling the description of these shields.

38. Frizzlehead I to Mooney, JMKFN, vol. 1, 64a.

39. Frizzlehead, Seko, and Yellow Wolf to Richardson, 1935, SFN, 1243.

40. Frizzlehead and Yellow Wolf to Richardson, 1935, SFN, 1242; Silverhorn to Mishkin, V-3, July 1, 1935, SFN, 540, 544.

41. Frizzlehead and Yellow Wolf to Richardson, 1935, SFN, 1242; author's fieldnotes, Dec. 1997.

42. According to Hunting Horse, a Ten Medicine Bundle keeper named Gorget (Qólyìjè) received a vision in 1864 that was in some way related to the Dog Society. Although this date for the origin of the Qóichégàu disagrees with those given by other informants, Hunting Horse's descriptions of Dog Society dress and initiations match those of other consultants and sources. He maintained that the dress code and initiation process of the society began at the 1864 Sun Dance. This appears to be either a mistranslation or incorrect data, because Catlin's 1834 painting of Black Cap and Kiowa calendar drawings of the 1846 and 1848 Sun Dances depict this style of dress (Mooney 1898:284, 287). The inference is that some new dance or dress aspect may have been added to the society at this time. Hunting Horse to Collier, Aug. 15, 1935, SFN, 567–568.

43. Given to Marriott, Aug. 1, 1935, AMP. Although Wohaw (b. 1851) could have been inducted during the society's last initiation in 1867, he is not listed on the society's membership rosters. An earlier "Guhwde" (Gùhâudè, an abbreviated name form referencing Stabbed In The Ribs And

Removing A Portion Of Meat) is listed as a society member (see Appendix). Because Wohaw was known as Gùhâudè, this person may have been a relative of the same name.

44. Frizzlehead, Seko, and Yellow Wolf to Richardson, 1935, SFN, 1245.

45. Frizzlehead, Seko, Gumdw, and Yellow Wolf to Richardson, 1935, SFN, 1248.

46. Frizzlehead, Seko, Gumdw, and Yellow Wolf to Richardson, 1935, SFN, 1248; Given to Marriott, Aug. 1, 1935, AMP.

47. Seko to Richardson, 1935, SFN, 1248.

48. Ibid.

49. Frizzlehead and Yellow Wolf to Richardson, 1935, SFN, 1248.

50. Ibid., 1244, 1249.

51. Ibid., 1249.

52. Ibid.

53. Ibid.

54. Ibid.; Hunting Horse to Collier, Aug. 15, 1935, SFN, 567–568; Piatonma to Marriott, July 16, 1935, AMP.

55. Frizzlehead and Yellow Wolf to Richardson, 1935, SFN, 1248; Hunting Horse to Collier, Aug. 15, 1935, SFN, 567–568; Piatonma to Marriott, July 16, 1935, and Given to Marriott, Aug. 1, 1935, AMP.

56. Piatonma to Marriott, July 16, 1935, AMP.

57. Frizzlehead and Seko to Richardson, 1935, SFN, 1250. Who received the goods was not recorded.

58. Frizzlehead to Richardson, 1935, SFN, 1250; Hunting Horse to Collier, Aug. 15, 1935, SFN, 567–568.

59. Frizzlehead and Yellow Wolf to Richardson, 1935, SFN, 1250. See the appendix for information about Giatogia.

60. Frizzlehead, Yellow Wolf, and Hunting Horse to Richardson, 1935, SFN, 1250.

61. The members listed by the informant as receiving sashes for the first time (b, e, f, g, h, k, l, o, t, u, v) correlated only three times (e, g, u) with the list of "old colts" for 1867 (g, j, m, p, r, s, u, e), with which it should have matched exactly. In addition, (e) was not considered to be an old colt by Frizzlehead II. Frizzlehead, Yellow Wolf, Seko, Guito, and Hunting Horse to Richardson, 1935, SFN, 1237–1252. Richardson noted that she considered her list to be "sloppily taken, and unchecked."

62. Yellow Wolf and Frizzlehead to Richardson, 1935, SFN, 1251–1252.

63. Ibid.

64. Yellow Wolf to Richardson, 1935, SFN, 1251.

65. Given to Marriott, Aug. 1, 1935, AMP.

66. Piatonma to Marriott, July 16, 1935, AMP; Frizzlehead to Richardson, 1935, SFN, 1246.

67. Given to Marriott, Aug. 1, 1935, AMP.

68. Frizzlehead and Yellow Wolf to Richardson, 1935, SFN, 1252–1253.

69. Ibid.

70. Frizzlehead, Guito, Yellow Wolf, and Hunting Horse to Richardson, 1935, SFN, 1239–1240.

71. Tso'odl to Marriott, July 13, 1936, AMP.

72. Frizzlehead, Guito, Yellow Wolf, and Hunting Horse to Richardson, 1935, SFN, 1239–1240.

73. Ibid.

74. Frizzlehead to Richardson, 1935, SFN, 1239–1240. This account refers to Podlt'ai's replacing Warrior as a red blanket sash owner. Sitting Bear succeeded Little Bluff Recess as society chief and black sash owner.

75. Frizzlehead to Richardson, 1935, SFN, 1240.
76. Frizzlehead, Guito, Yellow Wolf, and Hunting Horse to Richardson, 1935, SFN, 1239–1240, 1245.
77. Frizzlehead, Guito, Yellow Wolf, and Hunting Horse to Richardson, 1935, SFN, 1239–1240, 1245–1246.
78. Yellow Wolf and Frizzlehead to Richardson, 1935, SFN, 1246.
79. Yellow Wolf and Frizzlehead to Richardson, 1935, SFN, 1246–1247.
80. Yellow Wolf, Frizzlehead, and Guito to Richardson, 1935, SFN, 1245–1248.
81. Yellow Wolf and Frizzlehead to Richardson, 1935, SFN, 1245–1247.
82. Yellow Wolf, Guito, and Frizzlehead to Richardson, 1935, SFN, 1247. These consultants thought that because Podlt'ai was the son of the earlier Dog Society leader Jòhâusàn (Little Bluff Recess), the members did not want to refuse his request. However, this seems to be an error, because Câijàujè (Warrior/Fighter), the son of Little Bluff Recess, was the society partner of Podlt'ai. Podlt'ai, therefore, should not also have been a son of Little Bluff Recess and an actual brother to Warrior/Fighter, because of the requirements of nonconsanguineality between society partners.
83. Given to Marriott, Aug. 1, 1935, AMP.
84. Frizzlehead to Richardson, 1935, SFN, 1239, 1252.
85. Frizzlehead to Richardson, 1935, SFN, 1252.
86. Frizzlehead to Richardson, 1935, SFN, 1253; Piatonma to Marriott, July 16, 1935, AMP.
87. Frizzlehead to Richardson, 1935, SFN, 1253.
88. Frizzlehead and Gumdw to Richardson, 1935, SFN, 1253.
89. White Fox to La Barre, XI-9, 10, 11, July 26, 1935, SFN, 550.
90. Frizzlehead to Richardson, 1935, SFN, 1253.
91. Yellow Wolf to Richardson, 1935, SFN, 1253; Yellow Wolf to Bascom, III-5, July 2, 1935, SFN, 546; Piatonma to Marriott, July 16, 1935, AMP. Although Yellow Wolf is reported to have been fighting the Osage, the peace between the Osage and Kiowa and the late date of this account (post-1867) suggest that it was likely another tribe.
92. SFN, 1300–1301. In the McKenzie Kiowa orthography, the symbol + denotes a pronoun form that is understood but not voiced in speaking and thus not written. In this case the pronoun form é is implied.
93. Frizzlehead and Yellow Wolf to Richardson, 1935, SFN, 1237, 1253.
94. Frizzlehead to Richardson, 1935, SFN, 1254. The names Kwwpa.te and Kwwp'e.dai refer to different men. Their names were derived from the same root, a common occurrence in Kiowa names.
95. Andrew Stumbling Bear and Charley Apekaum to Richardson, 1935, SFN, 1325.
96. Charley White Horse to Richardson, 1935, SFN, 1301. George Hunt, who also sang Sitting Bear's song, gave a shorter variation of this version that did not include all the lines (Rhodes 1954).
97. This was not the later Iseeo (formerly Tahbonemah) who was a Fort Sill L-Troop Scout but was likely his uncle, from whom the later Iseeo received his name.
98. Frizzlehead to Richardson, 1935, SFN, 1254.
99. Frizzlehead, Seko, Gumdw, and Yellow Wolf to Richardson, 1935, SFN, 1244, 1252–1254.
100. Frizzlehead, Seko, Gumdw, and Yellow Wolf to Richardson, 1935, SFN, 1244.
101. Frizzlehead to Collier, VIII-1, June 25, 1935, SFN, 843–847; Lone Bear to Richardson, X-9, Aug. 12, 1935, SFN, 899–901. Haumpo (Metal Trap, Fish Hook) was also known by other names.
102. Frizzlehead to Collier, VIII-1, July 25, 1935, SFN, 843–847; Lone Bear to Richardson, X-9, Aug. 12, 1935, SFN, 899–901.
103. Many of these claims are made at public dances and in local newspaper articles.

104. See ADN, May 24, 2000. Although some people maintain that Lone Wolf belonged to the Dog Society, membership rosters acquired from the last society members by Mooney and the 1935 Santa Fe field school indicate that he was a leader of the Horse Headdresses.

105. Author's fieldnotes. Much of this ideology and respect for the society is observable in speeches, conversations, and mannerisms at Black Legs Society functions and in conversations with society members.

Chapter 7. Cáuitémgòp

1. Silverhorn to Mishkin, V-3, July 1, 1935, SFN, 553. See Meadows 1999:370–371 for a discussion of warfare and raiding ventures conducted by single military societies among several Plains tribes before about 1840. Murie (1914:567–582) discussed several Pawnee societies that were exterminated in warfare.

2. HLS-1, vol. 1, 192–193.

3. JMKFN, vol. 6, 178.

4. Donety and Jack Doyeto to H. L. Scott, "History of the Chief Pe-a-vo-co," HLS-2.

5. JMKFN, vol. 11, 95; HeapoBears and Kuito to Mishkin and Collier, Aug. 2, 1935, SFN, 504.

6. Jack Doyeto to Alice Marriott, July 23, 1936, AMP.

7. Monroe Horse and White Horse to Richardson, 1935, SFN, 1302; Lone Bear to La Barre, Ia-3 June 27, 1935, SFN, 683; Parker McKenzie to the author, Mar. 2, 1993; Gus Palmer Sr. to the author, Jan. 19, 1991, and Oct. 1, 1992; JMKFN, vol. 11, 98. Palmer obtained his information on the society from Eugenia Ianonen Mausape.

8. JMKFN, vol. 11, 95.

9. HeapoBears to La Barre, XIII-5, July 30, 1935, SFN, 557.

10. HeapoBears to Collier, VI-7 1935, SFN, 667; Monroe Horse and White Horse to Richardson, IX-3, 4, July 31 and Aug. 2, 1935, SFN, 302; Old Man Horse (Hunting Horse) to Bascom, XI-6, July 20, 1935, SFN, 556.

11. Silverhorn to Mishkin, V-3, July 1, 1935, SFN, 553; HeapoBears and Kuito to Mishkin and Collier, Aug. 3, 1935, SFN, 504, 667; Frizzlehead to Mishkin, VII-22, July 30, 1935, SFN, 555.

12. Old Man Horse to Bascom, XIV-2, July 4, 1935, SFN, 553; Old Man Horse and Padalti to Richardson, 1935, SFN, 1302, 1311, 1325–1326; Lone Bear to La Barre, Ia-3, June 27, 1935, SFN, 683; Silverhorn to Mishkin, V-3, July 1, 1935, SFN, 553.

13. Jack Doyeto to Alice Marriott, July 23, 1936, AMP; Donety and Jack Doyeto to H. L. Scott, "History of the Chief Pe-a-vo-co," HLS-2. Fâbò (Peahbo, or Large Mustang, also known as Táàuiqî, or Many Wives), is said to have had ten wives. The society then returned to the camp on the hill east of Henry Tenedaw's (Tenedooah's) allotment and danced.

14. Hunting Horse and Padalti to Richardson, 1935, SFN, 1311–1312, 1325–1326.

15. Monroe Horse and White Horse to Richardson, 1935, SFN, 1302.

16. Gus Palmer to the author, Jan. 19, 1991; Paddlety 1976. Victor Paddlety obtained this information about the society from his grandmother Kintadl.

17. Jack Doyeto to Alice Marriott, July 23, 1936, AMP; Marriott Shield Society paper, 41, AMP; Donety and Jack Doyeto to H. L. Scott, "History of the Chief Pe-a-vo-co," HLS-2; Gus Palmer Sr. to the author, Jan. 19, 1991; Paddlety 1976.

18. Yellow Wolf to Bascom, III-6, July 2, 1935, SFN, 916.

19. Old Man Horse and Padalti to Richardson, 1935, SFN, 1311–1312.

20. Old Man Horse and Padalti to Richardson, 1935, SFN, 1325–1326.

Chapter 8. Óhǫ̀mògàu

1. Alfred Chalepah (Apache) attended this encampment and dance at Apache Jim Wettseline's home near Apache, Oklahoma, during which time the Apache received a drum from the Ponca. According to Chalepah, the late Harry Buffalohead (Ponca) told him that his grandfather had said that this occurred in 1921. Alfred Chalepah to the author, Dec. 2, 1993. Abe Conklin (Ponca-Osage) told me of this visit and of the Kiowa's decline of the Ponca's offer of the dance. Abe Conklin to the author, Oct. 23, 1993. Both the Apache and Comanche report having acquired the dance earlier. The Apache originally acquired it from the Pawnee when the two tribes "became friends," whereas the Comanche report obtaining it from the Ponca in the 1800s (Meadows 1999:216–219, 288–289). Although this may have been a renewal for the Comanche, it was a completely separate acquisition for the Apache, who had already received the dance from the Pawnee. See also Duncan 1997:86. The Comanche report initially obtaining the dance after a battle with the Ponca, and later from a group of Ponca visiting in southwestern Oklahoma who performed the dance for the Apache and Comanche in 1919. The Comanche call their society the Wearers of Yellow Headgear or Yellow Roaches. Acquiring the dance from the Pawnee, the Plains Apache called it the Pawnee Dance (Meadows 1999:216–219, 288–289, 357–361).

2. Tso'odl to Marriott, July 10, 1936, AMP; author's Cheyenne fieldnotes, 1992; McKenzie n.d.a. The Southern Cheyenne also use the name Ohomo in referring to the Omaha tribe proper and its version of the Omaha Dance. In Kiowa, "War Dance" is Câicùngà (War, Fight Dance).

3. Oscar Tsoodle to the author, Mar. 4, 1992; Mac Whitehorse to the author, 1990–1995; Gus Palmer Sr. to the author, 1990–1994; Weiser Tongkeamha to the author, July 17, 1990, and Feb. 2, 1991; Harry Domebo to the author, June 18, 1993; Alice Littleman to the author, July 23, 1991, and May 2, 1992; Vanessa Jennings to the author, 1991–1998.

4. Silverhorn to Mooney, JMKFN, vol. 6, 165.

5. Mrs. Hokeah (Gapkaugo) to Collier, IV-24, July 18, 1935, SFN, 554; White Horse to Richardson, SFN, 1308.

6. Mrs. Hokeah to Collier, IV-24, July 18, 1935, SFN, 554. One Kiowa name for the Cheyenne was Tháusépgàu, "Pierced Ears." The Sioux tribes, particularly the Lakota, were most commonly known as Qólpàgàu, "Necklace People" (McKenzie n.d.a). Petter (1913–1915:779) stated that the Omaha Dance Society "started some 24 years ago" among the Cheyenne. Because this suggests that the Cheyenne obtained the dance in 1889, his account may be a few years too late, for the Kiowa data indicate that they obtained the dance from the Cheyenne in 1884.

7. Mrs. Hokeah to Collier, IV-24, July 18, 1935, SFN, 554. Collier's notes read, "The ohomo society danced the first time when G [Gapkaugo] was 14 years old (this places it about 1884)." KFR, Family 350, records the birth date of Gapkaugo, or Mrs. Hokeah, as 1869, correlating with the date of 1883–1884 as the date of the acquisition of the society. According to Weiser Tongkeamha, the Cheyenne chief who brought the ceremony to the Kiowa was known as Woman's Saddle. However, this appears to be a Kiowa name, and I have been unable to locate any Cheyenne by this name. Weiser Tongkeamha to the author, Feb. 2, 1991.

The original Gwe-lo (Kuelo, Kwelo, Cwélò) was an adopted captive of unspecified descent who was noted as a brave man. Mooney wrote that the name was of Mexican origin. Kwelo II was also known as Kope-ta, abbreviated from Kópjéhóljè (Killed An Enemy In A Painful Manner). Mooney recorded that he was a brother of Ankima, was the son or nephew of the Kiowa Kobe or Wild Horse, and was a former police captain (JMKFN, vol. 11, 123). He was listed as Kope-ta, or Strong Whip, in the 1880 census (no. 108) and as a lieutenant in the police force. He is known to have served on the Kiowa police force from June 30, 1880, to June 30, 1882, and again in 1895 (McKenzie n.d.c). He was listed in the 1895 census (no. 465) as age forty-two, so he was born around 1853. He died before 1900.

To-ome was also known as Kuelo. KFR, Family 344, lists a To-ome who died before 1900. To-ome, or Kuelo, was the father of Edward Yeahquo, born in 1886. According to Gertrude Yeahquo Hines, a daughter of Edward Yeahquo's, her grandfather Kuelo (also known as To-ome) died while her father, Edward, was a young child, and her grandmother Taum-gope was remarried to his brother, Yeah-quo (b. 1861). They had their first child, Helen Blanche Yeahquo, in 1899. Yeah-quo resided in the Carnegie area and is known by elders today as Kuelo. Gertrude Hines to the author, Aug. 2, 1993; KFR 1901. Judging from the ages of the persons involved and the fact that Kiowa elders in 1935 stated that Kuelo held chieftain status, Kuelo II was the person associated with receiving the Omaha Society from the Cheyenne in 1884; Yeah-quo and possibly To-ome were too young, because southern Plains warfare ended in 1875.

8. An examination of many family photographs owned by Vanessa Jennings shows the large quantity of Cheyenne-style clothing in Kiowa Omaha Society dress well into the 1920s. See also Jennings and Jennings 2000.

9. The exact etymology of *tónchài* is unclear. The first syllable is clearly "tail," whereas the second syllable may be derived from *chál* (at or around the waist), which applies to the way a bustle is worn.

10. Among the Ponca, members of the second order (*nika gahi xude*, or "gray chiefs") of the War ceremony were tattooed and won the right to wear the crow belt by carrying sacred bundles into battle. Whipmen and hunt police wore crow belts during bison hunts so that they might be easily identified (Duncan 1997:57, 58). Crow belts are also commonly depicted in Lakota and Cheyenne ledgerbook drawings, including warfare scenes. The Chicago Field Museum has a late-nineteenth-century crow belt on a Kiowa mannequin as a part of its permanent display. However, the presence in this bustle of owl feathers, which became highly taboo to the Kiowa in the late 1800s, as well as the fact that the only mess bustle maintained by the Kiowa was the Ohomo Society bustle, which burned in 1941, suggests that this bustle is more likely an Arapaho or Cheyenne one.

11. Isseo to Scott, HLS-1, vol. 1, 176.

12. Isseo to Scott, HLS-1, vol. 1, 176–182. These Calumet ceremonies included the following, only some of which can be temporally placed: (1) Pawnee to Wichita, circa 1870s; (2) Wichita to Kiowa, when Heidsicki was a boy (circa 1826–1830); (3) Wichita to Tohausen (Donpai); (4) Arapaho to Kiowa; (5) Osage to Kiowa, between the time when the Kiowa and Osage made peace (1834) and Iseeo's birth (1849); (6) tribe with heads shaved like the Osage and called Ollar-ho (possibly the Àláhògàu or Quapaw) to Zabile and the Kiowa; and (7) Zabile and the Kiowa to Attocknie and the Comanche two years later.

13. See Boyd 1981:65–70. Boyd did not consult the society bustle keeper, Mac Whitehorse, and the ceremonial chief, Mark Keahbone, during his research for this work. Mac Whitehorse to the author, Dec. 1, 1990.

14. JMKFN, vol. 6, 185.

15. Tso'odl to Marriott, July 10, 1936, AMP; Mrs. Hokeah to Collier, IV-24, July 18, 1935, SFN, 554.

16. Mrs. Hokeah to Collier, IV-24, July 18, 1935, SFN, 554.

17. Kintadl to Richardson, July 22, 1935, SFN, 414; Mrs. Hokeah to Collier, IV-24, July 18, 1935, SFN, 554; Belo Cozad to James Mooney, JMKFN, vol. 6, 11; Silverhorn to Mooney, JMKFN, vol. 6, 165.

18. Kintadl to Richardson, July 22, 1935, SFN, 414; Mrs. Hokeah to Collier, IV-24, July 18, 1935, SFN, 554.

19. Mrs. Hokeah to Collier, IV-24, July 18, 1935, SFN, 554.

20. Gregory Haumpy Sr. to the author, Apr. 2, 1998.

21. Mac Whitehorse to the author, July 13, 1993. Whitehorse has been the bustle keeper and leader of the Ohoma Lodge since 1952 and has served as the Kiowa tribal director at the American

Indian Exposition. Many Kiowa have stated that Whitehorse, with his vast repertoire of War Dance songs, is the most knowledgeable Kiowa War Dance singer.

22. Author's fieldnotes; Mac Whitehorse to the author, Nov. 4, 1990; Gus Palmer Sr. (from Lewis Toyebo), July 9, 1992; Delores Toyebo Harragarra to the author, Oct. 30, 1997.

23. Ananthy Odlepaugh Ledgerbook.

24. O-ho-mah Lodge Singers, *War Dance Songs of the Kiowa O-ho-mah Lodge Singers*, vol. 2 (Indian House Records, 1976), sleeve notes; Mac Whitehorse to the author, Apr. 3, 1991. The fourth keeper, Charley Tsalote, is known to have suffered from epilepsy, which appears to have attributed to his short term as bustle keeper.

25. White Horse to Richardson, 1935, SFN, 1308.

26. Mac Whitehorse to the author, Apr. 3, 1991, and Jan. 24, 1995.

27. Mrs. Hokeah to Collier, IV-24, July 18, 1935, SFN, 554.

28. Mac Whitehorse to the author, Jan. 24, 1995. This drum was buried with George Bosin at the time of his death.

29. Sangko to Marriott, Jan. 28, 1836, AMP. According to Sangko, the Omaha Society princesses were allowed to marry someone inside or outside the society, which deviates significantly from the norm. The tradition against marrying within the same society in which one has served as a princess is still well known among Kiowa societies. This could reflect a mistake in transcription.

30. Saioma (Mrs. Tenedooah) to Marriott, July 14, 1936, AMP. Information from contemporary Ohoma Society elders supports this account. Author's fieldnotes.

31. Weiser Tongkeamah to the author, Feb. 2, 1991; Mac Whitehorse to the author, May 12, July 13, and Aug. 9, 1993.

32. These descriptions combine archival and published data with data from my interviews with Kiowa including Mac Whitehorse, Gregory Haumpy Sr., Gus Palmer Sr., Dixon Palmer, Harry Domebo, Weiser Tongkeamah, John Emhoola Sr., Rev. George Saumpty, Alice Littleman, Dorothy Whitehorse DeLaune, and Vanessa Jennings. Author's fieldnotes, 1989–2008.

33. White Horse to Richardson, 1935, SFN, 1308. In earlier times the council of eleven chiefs and the Eagles would also likely have danced to this song, because they were all of chief or veteran status. Boyd (1981:69) reported the presence of a second Chief's Song that had less ritual significance.

34. This practice may relate to the Kiowa tradition in which, when a severe storm or tornado was approaching, a man (often a bundle keeper) took a pipe and smoked and prayed toward the storm, asking it to go in another direction. The term *Earth-maker* is the translation of one of the Kiowa terms for God or Creator, Dàumâuiàmdàuqî (lit. Land-all-maker, creator-power-male personification).

35. See note 32, this chapter.

36. See note 32, this chapter.

37. See note 32, this chapter; also, Jim Anquoe, telephone conversation with the author, June 28, 2001.

38. For example, I have on several occasions heard the Ohoma song of Wallace (Frank) Tongkeamah (also known as Frank James Tongkeamha) requested and sung; it is still well known more than eighty years after his death in 1926. Although his song and his position as whistle keeper were inherited that year by Gregory Haumpy Sr. (b. 1918), the song is still often referred to as Frank Tongkeamha's song. Because Haumpy inherited the position at such a young age, his parents held a dance for him in Carnegie, Oklahoma, when he was fifteen (in 1933) at which the position was reannounced, his song was sung, and his family gave away a beef, four horses, shawls, and other goods. Weiser Tongkeamha to the author, Feb. 2, 1991; Mac Whitehorse to the author, July 13, 1993; Gregory Haumpy Sr. to the author, Apr. 2, 1998. See also O-ho-mah Lodge Singers 1976, 1994.

39. In attempting to link the Kiowa Grass Dance to the Southern Cheyenne and Arapaho Crow Dance, Kracht (1989, 1994:329) contended that there was a direct link between the Ghost Dance and the Omaha Society: "Since the Ghost Dance was associated with other traditional activities like dancing, it served as a vehicle to perpetuate the Grass Dance, a precursor of the War Dance." Although all these dances are variants of the Omaha Dance, I disagree with this idea for three reasons. First, the Kiowa's acquisition of the Omaha Dance (1883–1884) preceded that of the well-documented Ghost Dance (1890) by some six years. Second, if the Ghost Dance served as a vehicle to perpetuate the Grass (War or Omaha) Dance, then it did so as a stimulus to perpetuate more "traditional" or old-time activities such as dancing in a general sense, possibly as conservative efforts against Anglo acculturative pressures. My elder consultants who saw the last several Ghost Dances said that there were no Omaha Society activities in or at the Ghost Dance in later years (1910–1917). In describing the activities held at Ghost Dances, they indicated that no other type of dancing occurred outside of the actual Ghost Dance, which was held each afternoon from approximately one o'clock until sundown. Because the Omaha Society was burgeoning at this time, it had no immediate or competitive incentive to separate from the Ghost Dance (if it was ever associated with that dance). Third, Kracht (personal communication, May 16, 1998) did not interview the Omaha Society leaders or any actual eyewitnesses to the Ghost Dance. In light of statements by society leaders, accounts of Ghost Dance eyewitnesses, and the larger pattern of Kiowa military society history discussed in this work, I am inclined to follow these sources. Parker McKenzie to the author, Nov. 17, 1990, and Mar. 14 and July 17, 1995; Mac Whitehorse to the author, May 12, 1993; Francis Tsonetokoy to the author, Dec. 8, 1990; George Tsoodle to the author, July 1991. Probably what Kracht meant was that the Ghost Dance, as a symbol of "Indian" and "traditional" activities, including dancing, became a vehicle to perpetuate other, independent forms of dancing and powwows, because it was a form of Native activity embraced by more conservative Kiowa in opposition to the growing Christian Kiowa community between 1893 and 1917. Indeed, Kiowa labeled by the agency as the "Dance crowd" were those associated with more conservative cultural forms such as society and powwow dancing, giveaways, peyote, hand games, and the Ghost Dance. Several Omaha Society members participated in the Ghost Dance, but as individuals and not as a collective. Although Omaha Society dances and Ghost Dances both took place during this period, they were held as separate functions and at different locales.

40. The 4 Percent Trust Funds were closed on Oct. 31, 1920, with a final payment of $299 per person. A 5 Percent Trust Fund continued until 1926. Parker McKenzie to the author, July 30, 1990, and Feb. 19, 1998; Francis Tsonetokoy to the author, Dec. 8, 1990.

41. Mac Whitehorse to the author, Oct. 9, 1993; Gus Palmer Sr. to the author, Feb. 4 and Sept. 15, 1994.

42. Dorothy Whitehorse DeLaune to the author, July 9, 2004.

43. Vanessa Jennings to the author, Feb. 5, 1994.

44. Author's fieldnotes.

45. Author's fieldnotes.

46. John Emhoola Sr. to the author, July 23, 1991.

47. Alice Littleman to the author, July 23, 1991.

48. Mac Whitehorse to the author, July 13, 1993; Harding Bigbow to the author, Feb. 7, 1992. Bigbow described a similar bustle pickup ceremony he witnessed.

49. Harry Domebo to the author, June 18, 1993.

50. Some people maintain that this change was caused by one of White Horse's family member's taking control of the family house on the property, thereby forcing White Horse to move to another home near Stecker, Oklahoma. Author's fieldnotes.

51. Gregory Haumpy Sr. to the author, Apr. 2, 1998.

52. Ibid.

53. Gus Palmer Sr. to the author, Jan. 19 and July 9, 1991. Parker McKenzie stated that as a youth he occasionally ate boiled puppy prepared by his grandmother, that it was considered a delicacy, and that it was common for members of his grandparents' generation occasionally to prepare such a meal. Author's fieldnotes.

54. Parker McKenzie to the author, Aug. 3, 1992.

55. Parker McKenzie to the author, Apr. 17, 1992.

56. Mac Whitehorse to the author, Dec. 1, 1990. Several society elders stated that Mark Keahbone, at that time the oldest society member, often attempted to relay important elements of the society's history and ritual during society meetings but was regularly interrupted by his son, who inhibited him from doing so. Other elders reported that when the late Weiser Tongkeamha attempted to sing and reintroduce old Omaha songs to the society, he was likewise interrupted by this man, who shut off the tape recorder on which he was recording the songs for the society. Consequently, society elders report that much of the older ritual knowledge associated with the society, the position of ceremonial chief, and many songs were lost with their deaths. Author's fieldnotes.

57. Weiser Tongkeamha to the author, Feb. 2, 1991.

58. Mac Whitehorse to the author, Apr. 3, 1991.

59. Vanessa Jennings to the author, Feb. 5, 1994.

60. Piatonma to Marriott, July 25, 1935, AMP.

61. Francis Tsonetokoy to the author, Dec. 8, 1990; author's fieldnotes. Born in 1910, Alfred Chalepah, the oldest living Apache during my fieldwork, also reported that Mopope and Lefthand introduced the Fancy Dance and the use of bustles when he was a young boy. Alfred Chalepah to the author, Dec. 2, 1993.

62. These descriptions are based on observations of the photograph collection of Vanessa Jennings.

63. Francis Tsonetokoy to the author, Dec. 8, 1990, and Apr. 3, 1991; Harry Domebo to the author, June 18, 1993.

64. Harry Domebo to the author, June 18, 1993.

65. Tso'odl to Marriott, July 10, 1935, AMP.

66. Gus Palmer Sr. to the author, Feb. 4, 1994.

67. Dorothy Whitehorse DeLaune to the author, July 9, 2004.

68. Mac Whitehorse to the author, May 12, 1993; author's fieldnotes, Ohomah Lodge singing practice, Dec. 2, 1993.

69. Gus Palmer Sr. to the author, Feb. 4, 1994. Barney Oheltoint Sr. composed this song.

70. Gus Palmer Sr. to the author, Sept. 15, 1994; author's fieldnotes, Ohomah Lodge singing practice, St. Patrick's Catholic Mission, Anadarko, Oklahoma, Feb. 3, 1994.

71. Because Komalty's life span, 1851–1920, does not correspond to the death date of 1925 that Parsons gave for him (1929:xxii, 95), her reference to Komalty might pertain to another person who inherited his home, or it might simply reflect inaccuracies in the dates she collected.

72. Mac Whitehorse to the author, Dec. 1, 1990.

73. Author's fieldnotes.

74. Author's fieldnotes, Ohoma Lodge cedaring ceremony, March 18, 2007.

75. The following description is from the author's fieldnotes and observations of ten annual society ceremonials and four singing practices between 1990 and 2008. I am especially grateful to Mac Whitehorse for letting me videotape several years of society ceremonials and tape-record several singing practices to aid me in my fieldwork.

76. "Powwows and Handgames," ADN, July 18, 2001.

77. HLS-1, vol. 1, 112–114, 176–182.

78. The directions of entry and exit into the arena are affected by the architecture of the dance ground. Large concrete bleachers on the west and south sides of the arena limit entry to the southwest and southeast corners. In recent years, the pipes and bonnets for the Pipe Dance have been supplied by Carl and Vanessa Jennings.

79. Author's fieldnotes. Boyd (1981:66) incorrectly reversed these positions and did not include the Hawks.

80. These disputes are usually between the families of the members and not between the actual members themselves. Author's fieldnotes.

81. O-ho-ma Lodge Singers 1976, vol. 2, sleeve cover.

82. Mac Whitehorse to the author, 1991, 1995.

83. Author's fieldnotes.

84. Gregory Haumpy Sr. to the author, Apr. 2, 1998.

85. Vanessa Jennings to the author, Feb. 5, 1994.

86. From her critique of Wissler's (1916) emphasis on tracing the diffusion of regalia and selected ceremonial objects and actions but not examining music styles, Browner (2002:20–27) concluded that there are in fact two forms of the Grass Dance in the contemporary powwow. The first is the ancestral version that led to the contemporary Northern Men's Traditional Dance, a more controlled, straight form of dancing using large single bustles of natural feathers. The second is the contemporary Northern Plains Grass Dance, which includes no bustle but features fringed jumpsuits and fancy footwork with backward dancing, crossing of the legs, and rotating in circles on the toe of one foot.

Chapter 9. Kiowa Women's Societies

1. Given to Marriott, Aug. 1, 1935, AMP.

2. Old Lady Horse to La Barre, Aug. 12, 1935, SFN, 577; AMP, File D.

3. Kintadl to Richardson, VI-10, 1935, SFN, 588; Old Lady Horse to La Barre, Aug. 12, 1935, SFN, 577; AMP, File D.

4. Kintadl to Richardson, VI-7, 1935, SFN, 955.

5. Mary Buffalo to La Barre, V-I and I-1, July 1 and July 3, 1935, SFN, 462, 464; Saioma to Marriott, May 30, 1936, AMP.

6. Quoetone to Mishkin, VI-9, July 17, 1935, SFN, 373.

7. Atah to Marriott, Jan. 31, 1936, AMP.

8. Kintadl to Richardson, I-8, 1935, SFN, 586; HeapoBears to Richardson, X-18, Aug. 5, 1935, SFN, 902; Sangko to Marriott, May 3, 1936, AMP.

9. Mary Buffalo to La Barre, II-6, July 2, 1935, SFN, 589–590.

10. Jack Sankadota to Mishkin, II-3, July 5, 1935, SFN, 587.

11. Ibid.

12. Mary Buffalo to La Barre, II-6, July 2, 1935, SFN, 593; Given to Marriott, Aug. 1, 1935, AMP.

13. Kintadl to Richardson, I-8, 1935, SFN, 586.

14. Mary Buffalo to La Barre, II-6, July 2, 1935, SFN, 589, 594. Although many of the members were related to one another, Buffalo stated that membership existed in different and unrelated families, which may reflect her lack of recognition of an association between kin relations and membership or of some of the more distant kin relations between other members.

15. Mary Buffalo to La Barre, II-6, July 2, 1935, SFN, 594; Kintadl to Richardson, I-8, 1935, SFN, 587; Saioma to Marriott, Jan. 27 and May 30, 1936, AMP.

16. Saioma to Marriott, May 30, 1936, AMP.

17. Saioma to Marriott, May 30, 1936, AMP.
18. Kintadl to Richardson, I-8, 1935, SFN, 586–587; Mary Buffalo to La Barre, II-6, July 2, 1935, SFN, 594; Saioma to Marriott, Jan. 27 and May 30, 1936, AMP.
19. Sangko to Marriott, May 3, 1936, AMP.
20. Mary Buffalo to La Barre, II-6, July 2, 1935, SFN, 598–590; Alice Marriott, "Old Women's Society" manuscript, AMP.
21. Kintadl to Richardson, VI-10, 1935, SFN, 588.
22. Mary Buffalo to La Barre, II-6, July 2, 1935, SFN, 594.
23. Gueton to La Barre, XI-2, July 24, 1935, SFN, 595.
24. Kintadl to Richardson, VI-10, 1935, SFN, 587.
25. Mary Buffalo to La Barre, II-6, July 2, 1935, SFN, 590, 594; Kintadl to Richardson, I-8, 1935, SFN, 587.
26. Kintadl to Richardson, I-8, 1935, SFN, 587; Mary Buffalo to La Barre, II-6, July 2, 1935, SFN, 590–591.
27. Mary Buffalo to La Barre, II-6, July 2, 1935, SFN, 591.
28. Mary Buffalo to La Barre, II-6, July 2, 1935, SFN, 591; Mary Buffalo to La Barre, II-4, July 6, 1933, SFN, 596.
29. Mary Buffalo to La Barre, II-6, July 2, 1935, SFN, 591–592.
30. Given to Marriott, Aug. 1, 1935, Piatonma to Marriott, July 16, 1935, and Saioma and Sanko to Marriott, Jan. 27 and Jan. 29, 1936, AMP.
31. Holtagulma to Collier, I-25, July 2, 1935, SFN, 588; Mary Buffalo to La Barre, II-6, July 2, 1935, SFN, 592.
32. Mary Buffalo to La Barre, II-6, July 2, 1935, SFN, 592; Holtagulma to Collier, I-25, July 2, 1935, SFN, 588.
33. Mary Buffalo to La Barre, II-6, July 2, 1935, SFN, 592.
34. Ibid.
35. Ibid., 592–593.
36. Ibid., 592.
37. Ibid., 593. According to this account, the man served as a center of attention when the women stripped him of his clothes. Despite the name Calf Old Women, the members removed their own clothing or raised their skirts, after which they exposed themselves and sometimes menstruated, urinated, defecated, masturbated or even copulated with the male member. I cannot speak to the validity or the context of this account. Although the translators in 1935 were greatly reluctant to relate this material, Mary Buffalo urged them to translate it in full detail.
38. Mary Buffalo to La Barre, II-4, July 6, 1933, SFN, 596. Accounts state that at this time the Calf Old Women raised their skirts and said, "Our friend been 'taken,' we kill him," upon which they held the man's arms, legs, and hair and sat on his face until he became sick. The women stripped the man of his clothes and stimulated him sexually, but because he was "too old," he was unable to respond.
39. Ibid. Translator Ned Brace stated that during meetings, the society members played with the man, "felt him all over," and possibly tickled him but did not copulate with him.
40. Gueton (Quoetone) to La Barre, XI-2, July 24, 1935, SFN, 595–596.
41. Mary Buffalo to La Barre, II-6, July 2, 1935, SFN, 593–595; HLS-1, vol. 1, 193.
42. Mary Buffalo to La Barre, II-6, July 2, 1935, SFN, 594–595; Tso'odl and Piatonma to Marriott, July 16, 1935, and July 10, 1936, AMP; HLS-1, vol. 1, 193.
43. Charley Apekaum and HeapoBears to La Barre, XIII-7 and XIII-8, 1935, SFN, 715; Bert Geikomah and Mary Buffalo to La Barre, VI-7 and IV-11, 1935, SFN, 719; Charley Apekaum and Frizzlehead to Collier, V-15 and V-18, 1935, SFN, 718–720; White Buffalo to Collier, III-7, 1935, SFN,

715; Mrs. Hokeah to Collier, IV-19, 1935, SFN, 781. For a lengthier discussion of this process and its ceremonial aspects, see chapter 1. White Horse and Monroe Tsatoke to Richardson, 1935, SFN, 1297.

44. Frizzlehead to Collier, July 25, 1935, SFN, 120.

45. Goutaha to Richardson, II-1, July 1, 1935, SFN, 583.

46. Kintadl to Richardson, VI-2, 1935, SFN, 576; Collier, 1935, SFN, 842; Kintadl to Richardson, VI-7, 1935, SFN, 818; Old Lady Horse to La Barre, XVIII-1, Aug. 12, 1935, SFN, 577.

47. Quoetone to Collier, CII-14, July 30, 1935, SFN, 842.

48. Atah to Marriott, Jan. 31, 1936, AMP.

49. Jack Doyeto to Marriott, July 23, 1936, and Atah to Marriott, Jan. 26, 1936, AMP.

50. Saioma to Marriott, May 30, 1936, AMP.

51. Given to Marriott, Aug. 1, 1935, AMP.

52. Tso'odl to Marriott, July 10, 1936, AMP. Marriott noted: "Tsoodle was probably evading here. There is evidently some relationship between the bear women and the gods, and he is a priest. He always avoids discussion of bears, and any mention of the gods is impossible. His extreme conservatism is making him even more rampant than F. G. [Frank Given], who would, I believe, discuss such matters freely, were he not afraid of T [Tso'odl]."

53. Kintadl to Richardson, VI-2, 1935, SFN, 786–788.

54. Ibid.

55. Kintadl to Richardson, I-5, 1935, SFN, 576; Holtagulma to Collier, I-25, July 2, 1935, SFN, 577; Old Lady Horse to La Barre, XVIII-1, Aug. 12, 1935, SFN, 577; Given to Marriott, Aug. 1, 1935, AMP.

56. Holtagulma to Collier, I-25, July 2, 1935, SFN, 577.

57. Piatonma to Marriott, Aug. 23, 1935, AMP.

58. Kintadl to Richardson, VI-9, 1935, SFN, 578.

59. Kintadl to Richardson, VI-9 and I-5, 1935, SFN, 578, 579.

60. Atah to Marriott, Jan. 31, 1936, AMP.

61. Saioma to Marriott, July 13, 1936, AMP.

62. Piatonma to Marriott, Aug. 23, 1935, AMP.

63. Kintadl to Richardson, VI-9 and I-5, 1935, SFN, 578, 585.

64. Old Lady Horse to La Barre, XVIII-1, Aug. 12, 1935, SFN, 577.

65. Kintadl to Richardson, VI-9 and I-5, 1935, SFN, 578; Old Lady Horse to La Barre, XVIII-1, Aug. 12, 1935, SFN, 579.

66. Kintadl to Richardson, VI-9, 1935, SFN, 578.

67. Piatonma to Marriott, Aug. 23, 1935, AMP.

68. The sumac was prepared by being cooked in grease, dried, ground up, mixed with tobacco, and then stored in a beaded tobacco pouch. Kintadl to Richardson, I-4, 1935, SFN, 581; Goutaha to Richardson, II-1, July 1, 1935, SFN, 582.

69. Piatonma to Marriott, Aug. 23, 1935, AMP.

70. Jack Doyeto to Marriott, July 23, 1936, AMP.

71. Kintadl to Richardson, I-4, 1935, SFN, 581–582; Given to Marriott, Aug. 1, 1935, AMP; Old Lady Horse to La Barre, XVIII-1, Aug. 12, 1935, SFN, 579.

72. Kintadl to Richardson, I-4, 1935, SFN, 581–582.

73. Ibid.; Old Lady Horse to La Barre, XVIII-1, Aug. 12, 1935, SFN, 584; Tso'odl to La Barre, Aug. 16, 1935, SFN.

74. Piatonma to Marriott, Aug. 23, 1935, AMP.

75. Kintadl to Richardson, I-4, 1935, SFN, 581–582; Goutaha to Richardson, II-1, July 1, 1935, SFN, 582–583.

76. Kintadl to Richardson, I-4, 1935, SFN, 581–582; Goutaha to Richardson, II-1, July 1, 1935, SFN, 582–583; Jack Doyeto to Marriott, July 23, 1936, AMP.

77. Bascom, Aug. 20, 1935, SFN, 1122; Atah to Marriott, Jan. 31, 1936, AMP.

78. Kintadl to Richardson, I-4, 1935, SFN, 581–582; Goutaha to Richardson, II-1, July 1, 1935, SFN, 582–583; Atah to Marriott, Jan. 31, 1936, AMP.

79. Goutaha to Richardson, II-1, July 1, 1935, SFN, 582–583; Atah to Marriott, Jan. 31, 1936, AMP.

80. Kintadl to Richardson, I-5 and VI-2, 1935, SFN, 576, 585; Atah to Marriott, Jan. 31, 1936, AMP.

81. Old Lady Horse to La Barre, XVIII-1, Aug. 12, 1935, SFN, 584; Tso'odl to La Barre, Aug. 16, 1935, SFN.

82. Jack Doyeto to Marriott, July 23, 1936, and Given to Marriott, July 17, 1936, AMP.

83. Jack Doyeto to Marriott, July 23, 1936, and Given to Marriott, July 17, 1936, AMP.

84. Hodltagudlma, Mrs. Hokeah, and Kintadl to Richardson and Collier, 1935, SFN, 574–576.

85. Ibid. This is the only reference I have found of Kiowa practicing quillwork.

86. Carol Flores to the author, Oct. 16, 1998; Kiowa War Mothers exhibit, Kiowa Tribal Museum, Carnegie, Oklahoma; AWMCB; Charter Amended by Act of Congress, September, 1942; Charter Amended by Act of Congress, June, 1953, Revised April, 1974.

87. AWMCB; Carol Flores to the author, Oct. 16, 1998.

88. AIEB 1990, 1996.

89. AWMCB; Carol Flores to the author, Oct. 16, 1997, and Mar. 2, 1998. If a member fails to pay her dues by the following January 1, she retains membership but is considered not in good standing and forfeits the right to vote. The loss of voting privilege continues until dues are paid in full, with an extra dollar for lateness. The renewal must go through the state and national offices. Only after the renewal is recorded with the national office, a process that may take up to a month, may a member vote again.

90. Carol Flores to the author, Mar. 2 and Oct. 16, 1998; Ruby Paukei Williams to the author, Oct. 28, 1997.

91. Ruby Paukei Williams to the author, Oct. 28, 1997.

92. Author's fieldnotes, October 1997. Recently, one woman was allowed to join through her son's participation in the National Guard. A letter verifying his membership in the National Guard was required. Although some disagreement concerning this policy exists, members have continued to follow the policy as long as it is official American War Mothers' policy.

93. Carol Flores to the author, Mar. 2, 1998. The War Mothers' standing committees include those on Americanism, Budget and Finance, By-Laws, Carnation, Civil Defense, Emblems, Gold and Silver Star, Hospitalization, Legislation, Liaison, Magazine, Membership, Memory Tree and Memorials, Public Relations, Rehabilitation and Welfare, VAVS Representatives or Alternates, and Ways and Means.

94. Carol Flores to the author, Oct. 16, 1997.

95. Ruby Paukei Williams to the author, Oct. 28, 1997.

96. Carol Flores to the author, Oct. 16, 1998; Ruby Paukei Williams to the author, Oct. 28, 1997. Other Oklahoma Indian chapters of the American War Mothers include the Otoe, Osage (Grey Horse), Pawnee, and Comanche War Mothers. From 1995 to 1997 the Comanche chapter experienced problems with membership and retention of its state registration and national charter.

97. Author's fieldnotes.

98. AIEB 1990, 1996; Kiowa War Mothers exhibit, Kiowa Tribal Museum, Carnegie, Oklahoma; "Kiowa Tribe's War Mothers Form Chapter," *Daily Oklahoman*, circa 1944, AMP.

99. "Kiowa Tribe's War Mothers Form Chapter," *Daily Oklahoman*, circa 1944, AMP; Parker

McKenzie to the author, July 30, 1991. McKenzie provided a photograph, identifications, and birth dates of the original Kiowa War Mothers.

100. Carol Flores to the author, Oct. 16, 1998; Ruby Paukei Williams to the author, Oct. 28, 1997. Non-Indian groups do not have shawls but may put the same national patches on jackets and other items.

101. Carol Flores to the author, Oct. 16, 1998; Ruby Paukei Williams to the author, Oct. 28, 1997; "Gold Star Mothers Keep Vigil over Servicemen in Iraq," ADN, Apr. 1, 2003.

102. Carol Flores to the author, Oct. 16, 1998; Ruby Paukei Williams to the author, Oct. 28, 1997.

103. Author's fieldnotes.

104. Carol Flores to the author, Mar. 2 and Oct. 16, 1998.

105. Author's fieldnotes.

106. Non-Indian members in Oklahoma are primarily Anglos.

107. Ruby Paukei Williams to the author, Oct. 28, 1997; Carol Flores to the author, Mar. 2, 1998.

108. Carol Flores to the author, Oct. 16, 1998.

109. Kiowa War Mothers meetings are open to female visitors, but because they are not open to males, I was unable to attend a chapter meeting. However, past chapter presidents Carol Flores and Ruby Williams were very helpful in explaining the agenda and activities of their meetings.

110. Carol Flores to the author, Oct. 16, 1998.

111. Ibid.

112. Ibid

113. Ibid.

114. There are several Anglo War Mothers chapters throughout Oklahoma and at least three African American chapters, one in Enid and two in Oklahoma City.

115. Carol Flores to the author, Oct. 16, 1998.

116. Ruby Paukei Williams to the author, Oct. 28, 1997.

117. Ibid.

118. In 1990 the Kiowa chapter had forty-four members, including four associate members, now known as Angels. As of April 1997 there were forty-seven members, three of whom were Angels. Christine Two Hatchet Kaulaity and Belle Geionety Kayitah to author, 1990; Carol Flores to the author, Oct. 16, 1998; AIEB 1990, 1996.

119. Carol Flores to the author, Oct. 16, 1998.

120. Carol Flores to the author, Mar. 2 and Oct. 16, 1998.

121. Delores Toyebo Harragarra to the author, Oct. 30, 1997. I am indebted to Harragarra for her assistance with these songs.

122. Author's fieldnotes.

123. Delores Toyebo Harragarra to the author, Mar. 14, 2004; author's fieldnotes.

124. "Mildred Tsoodle Hamilton," ADN, Feb. 18, 1991, 8.

125. Bill Koomsa Jr. to the author, Jan. 24, 1995.

126. Author's fieldnotes. As discussed in chapter 4, Toyebo composed and sang the memorial song for Lyndreth Palmer, the first Kiowa killed in twentieth-century warfare, in December 1944. The controversy over whether Lewis Toyebo or Jimmy Anquoe composed the large number of War Mothers Songs continues to this day. However, several things indicate that Toyebo was responsible for the original composition of most of them. First, examination of the song texts indicates that the versions of many of them as now sung and sold by the Anquoe family on commercial tapes (*Original Kiowa War Mother Songs*, 1985) differ significantly from the earlier tape-recordings of Lewis and Richenda Toyebo. Second, numerous elder singers, men's society leaders, War Mothers, and male

and female tribal elders (relatives and nonrelatives of both Toyebo and Anquoe) state that although Jimmy Anquoe was an incredibly gifted singer and did compose some of the songs later on, Toyebo composed the vast majority of them and even passed many of them on to Anquoe, giving him permission to sing them at Kiowa public functions. Some elder Kiowa have told me that Jimmy Anquoe himself acknowledged this to them personally. See also Hamilton 1991:8.

127. Author's fieldnotes. Glazner (2002:64) noted that Mr. and Mrs. Toyebo, Mr. and Mrs. Anquoe, and others sang War Mothers Songs together on the "Indians for Indians" radio program (no. 236) on January 22, 1946.

128. Author's fieldnotes.

129. Carol Flores to the author, Oct. 16, 1998.

130. Ibid.

131. In regular speech, *dàumtóyàdò* would be *dàumzémàdò*.

132. Author's fieldnotes.

133. Lines 1 through 3 are in the present tense; line 4 is in hearsay tense. Agreement of tenses may be reached by either the addition of *cícòthèl* (instead of *cícòt*), which would make the first three lines agree in hearsay tense, or the deletion of *hèl* ("reportedly") in *jáidàumhèlgàu* in line 4. Again, *dàumtóyà* should be *dàumzémà*, because it involves the irregular use of the triplural (three or more) "they."

134. In line 1 the expression *tạu-jé-bàu-dè-hèl* is in the hearsay tense.

135. Ruby Paukei Williams to the author, Oct. 28, 1997.

136. The War Mothers had a prior club song, but the composer, stating that his sons had asked him to get it back, unexpectedly asked to take the song back. Although this was considered highly inappropriate and unheard of in Kiowa custom, the War Mothers granted the unorthodox request in order to keep everyone happy and sought a new club song. Author's fieldnotes, Oct. 1997.

137. Ruby Paukei Williams to the author, Oct. 28, 1997.

138. ADN, Feb. 12 and Mar. 9–10, 1991.

139. Carol Flores to the author, Oct. 16, 1998.

140. Ruby Paukei Williams to the author, Oct. 28, 1997.

141. Lowell Russell to the author, Nov. 6, 1997.

142. Etter 1991; author's fieldnotes.

143. Ruby Paukei Williams to the author, Oct. 28, 1997.

144. Ibid.; *Kiowa Indian News*, Dec. 5, 2006.

145. Author's fieldnotes, Carnegie Victory Club Veterans Day Celebration, Red Buffalo Hall, Carnegie, Oklahoma, Nov. 11, 1997.

146. Ibid.

147. Martha Poolaw to the author, Aug. 3, 1995.

148. Author's fieldnotes, Carnegie Victory Club Veterans Day Celebration, Red Buffalo Hall, Carnegie, Oklahoma, Nov. 11, 1997; "Powwows and Handgames," ADN, Nov. 9–10, 2002.

149. Author's fieldnotes, Carnegie Victory Club Veterans Day Celebration, Red Buffalo Hall, Carnegie Oklahoma, Nov. 11, 1993.

150. The second of these songs is the same Memorial Song sung at the Black Legs ceremonials, which was composed by Lewis Toyebo in memory of Lyndreth Palmer.

151. Carnegie Victory Club Veterans Day Celebration flier and author's fieldnotes, Nov. 11, 1993.

152. Author's fieldnotes, Carnegie Victory Club Veterans Day Celebration, Red Buffalo Hall, Carnegie, Oklahoma, Nov. 11, 1997.

153. Ibid.

154. Harlan Hall Zotigh to the Carnegie Victory Club, letter read Nov. 11, 1997, at the Carnegie

Victory Club Veterans Day Celebration, Red Buffalo Hall, Carnegie, Oklahoma. Zotigh, a disabled veteran, was unable to attend this celebration and sent the letter asking for special prayers for himself and a fellow serviceman who was ill.

155. Author's fieldnotes, Carnegie Victory Club Veterans Day Celebration, Red Buffalo Hall, Carnegie, Oklahoma, Nov. 11, 1997.

156. Gamble (1952:41–42) also noted that the program often varied during the time of his fieldwork.

157. Author's fieldnotes, Carnegie Victory Club Veterans Day Celebration, Red Buffalo Hall, Carnegie, Oklahoma, Nov. 11, 1997.

158. Orville Neconie and Mary Neconie Shane to the author, July 14, 2004.

159. Harry Domebo to the author, June 28, 1993. This photograph and list of members is on display in the Kiowa Tribal Museum in Carnegie. An additional photograph and name list was provided by Mary Neconie Shane, July 14, 2004.

160. Mac Whitehorse, tape-recording provided by Mary Neconie Shane and Orville Neconie, July 14, 2004.

161. Ibid.

162. Orville Neconie and Mary Neconie Shane to the author, July 14, 2004.

163. Mary Neconie Shane to the author, July 14, 2004.

164. Harry Domebo to the author, June 28, 1993.

165. Ralph Kotay to the author, July 14, 2004.

166. Mary Neconie Shane to the author, July 14, 2004.

167. Author's fieldnotes, 1997.

168. Kiowa women who have served in the armed forces include Wanada Whitefox, Hazel Tsalote, and Carol Chaino Stockham (U.S. Marine Corps); Mildred Tsoodle Hamilton, Geneva Sahmaunt Foote, and Clarissa Palmer Campbell (U.S. Navy); Evelyn White Tingley, Emelia Standing, Kay Standing Sotes, and Angela Delon (U.S. Army); Elva Tapedo Tsatoke (U.S. Army Air Force); and many other younger Kiowa women.

169. Carol Flores to the author, Mar. 2, 1998.

BIBLIOGRAPHY

Archival Sources

Alice Marriott Papers (AMP). Western History Collections, University of Oklahoma, Norman.
Box 8. "The Sacred Spear of the Kiowa Indians" (manuscript); Kiowa Clippings File: "Kiowa Tribe's War Mothers Form Chapter," *Daily Oklahoman*, ca. February 1944, p. 6A.
Box 9. Small expanding folder: File C, Kiowa fieldnotes; File D, Kiowa Dancing and Shield Societies fieldnotes; Miscellaneous Folder: Kiowa Dancing and Shield Societies manuscripts, "Kiowa Giveaway and Dance" (paper).
Anadarko Daily News (ADN). Anadarko, Oklahoma. Miscellaneous news articles.
Ananthy Odlepaugh Ledgerbook. Fort Sill Museum Archives, Lawton, Oklahoma, MS:D-1049.
Annual Reports of the Commissioner of Indian Affairs, 1846–1906. Washington D.C.: U.S. Government Printing Office.
Bureau of Indian Affairs, Anadarko Agency. Letter to M. Pickering, Kiowa Agency, Anadarko, Oklahoma, Apr. 22, 1938, re: National Folk Festival. Manuscript in Decimal File .072, Fiestas and Festivals, 1936–1939, Anadarko Area Office: General Correspondence. Records of the Bureau of Indian Affairs, Record Group 75, National Archives, Fort Worth, Texas.
Doris Duke Oral History Collection (DD). Tapes 25, 32, 74, 214, 216, 246, 637, 651: interviews conducted with Kiowa consultants, 1967–1971. Western History Collections, University of Oklahoma Libraries, Norman.
Grace Lone Bear Tsonetokoy. Photograph of Kiowa Gourd Dance, Lone Bear Dance Ground, 1921. Copy in author's possession.
Hugh L. Scott Ledgers, vols. 1 and 2 (HLS-1). Circa 1892–1897. Fort Sill Museum Archives, Fort Sill Army Post, Lawton, Oklahoma.
Hugh L. Scott Papers, MS 4525 (HLS-2). Circa 1892–1897. National Anthropological Archives, Numbered Manuscripts, Records, and Papers, Smithsonian Institution, Washington, D.C.
Indian Pioneer Papers. Western History Collections, S-149. University of Oklahoma, Norman.
James Mooney Kiowa Fieldnotes, Manuscript (MS) 2531 (JMKFN), vols. 1, 6, 7 (Silverhorn Ledger), and 11, 1891–1918. National Anthropological Archives, Numbered Manuscripts, Records, and Papers, Smithsonian Institution, Washington D.C.
James Owen Dorsey, fieldnotes, 1872–1873. Microfilm. Office of Anthropology Archives, Smithsonian Institution, Washington D.C.
Kiowa Agency Files. National Anthropological Archives, Smithsonian Institution, Washington, D.C. General records of the Kiowa Agency, Anadarko, Oklahoma, 1907–1939. Documents are arranged topically in a decimal-subject classification system and listed by item number, year, and topic file number, such as 104547-1913-063. Principal topics are 062, Feasts–Fiestas–Festivals; 063, Dances; 066, Forms of Government–Indian Judges; 126, Liquor Traffic–Cocaine–Drugs–Mescal; 810, Teaching and Training–School Curriculum; 816, Religious Training; 816.2, Missions–Missionaries–Churches; and 820, Pupils. See also Kracht 1989.

Kiowa Family Record, Fiscal Year 1901 (KFR). Prepared by Parker McKenzie. Copy in author's possession.

"Santa Fe Notes" (SFN). Fieldnotes compiled in 1935 by graduate students in the Kiowa Field School sponsored by the Laboratory of Anthropology, Santa Fe, New Mexico. The students were Weston La Barre, William Bascom, Donald Collier, Bernard Mishkin, and Jane Richardson, under the direction of Alexander Lesser. The notes are now in the Weston La Barre Papers, Series 1: Kiowa Studies, National Anthropological Archives, Smithsonian Institution, Washington, D.C. They include La Barre's original 1935 Kiowa fieldnotes notebook.

School for Advanced Research (SAR), Santa Fe, New Mexico. Accession Files SAR 1990.19, n.d. (ledgerbook drawings).

Scott Tonemah Papers. Courtesy of Mrs. Doris Tonemah and Anne Yeahquo. Copies in possession of the author.

Books, Articles, and Similar Materials

AIEB (American Indian Exposition Guide Booklet)
    1958   *American Indian Exposition.* Anadarko, Okla., August.
    1968   *American Indian Exposition.* Anadarko, Okla., August.
    1989   *American Indian Exposition.* Anadarko, Okla., August.
    1990   *American Indian Exposition.* Anadarko, Okla., August.
    1996   *American Indian Exposition.* Anadarko, Okla., August.

Albers, Patricia C.
    1993   Symbiosis, Merger, and War: Contrasting Forms of Intertribal Relationship among Historic Plains Indians. In *The Political Economy of North American Indians*, ed. John H. Moore, 94–132. University of Oklahoma Press, Norman.

Albers, Patricia C., and Beatrice Medicine
    1983   *The Hidden Half: Studies of Plains Indian Women.* University Press of America, Washington, D.C.

Aleshire, Peter
    2001   *Warrior Woman: The Story of Lozen, Apache Warrior and Shaman.* St. Martin's Press, New York.

American War Mothers
    1961   *American War Mothers Constitution and By-laws.* Privately published, Atlantic City, N.J.

Anderson, Robert
    1956   The Northern Cheyenne War Mothers. *Anthropological Quarterly* 29(3):82–90.

Anquoe, Mary A.
    1991a   Research Facts. *Anadarko Daily News*, Jan. 24, 1991.
    1991b   Ruffled Feathers. *Anadarko Daily News*, Mar. 12, 1991.

Auchiah, James
    n.d.   Miscellaneous unpublished papers. Copies in possession of the author.

Balantine, Betty, and Ian Balantine, eds.
    1993   *The Native Americans: An Illustrated History.* Turner Publishing, Atlanta, Ga.

Bantista, Rudy
    1983   *Kiowa Black Leggings Warrior Society: Twenty Fifth Anniversary.* Anadarko, Okla.

Barkley, T. M., ed.
    1986   *Flora of the Great Plains.* University Press of Kansas, Lawrence.

Barrett, Samuel A.
    1911   Dream Dance of the Chippewa and Menominee Indians of Northern Wisconsin. *Bulletin of the Public Museum of the City of Milwaukee* 1:251–406. Milwaukee, Minn.

Battey, Thomas C.
    1968 [1876]   *The Life and Adventures of a Quaker among the Indians.* Corner House Publications, Williamstown, Mass.

Beatty, John Joseph
    1974   *Kiowa-Apache Music and Dance.* University of Northern Colorado, Museum of Anthropology, Ethnology Series 31. University of Northern Colorado, Greeley.

Berlo, Janet Catherine, ed.
    1996   *Plains Indian Drawings 1865–1935: Pages from a Visual History.* Harry N. Abrams, New York.
    2000   Artists, Ethnographers, and Historians: Plains Indian Graphic Arts in the Nineteenth Century—and Beyond. In *Transforming Images. The Art of Silverhorn and his Successors*, ed. Robert G. Donnelley, 26–45. University of Chicago Press, Chicago.

BIA (Bureau of Indian Affairs)
    1945   *Indians in the War.* U.S. Department of the Interior, Haskell, Kans.

Biolsi, Thomas
    1984   Ecological and Cultural Factors in Plains Indian Warfare. In *Warfare, Culture, and Environment*, ed. Brian Ferguson, 141–168. Academic Press, New York.

Bittle, William E.
    1962   The Manatidie: A Focus for Kiowa Apache Tribal Identity. *Plains Anthropologist* 7(17):152–163.

Bowers, Alfred W.
    1963   *Hidatsa Social and Ceremonial Organization.* Bulletin of the Bureau of American Ethnology 194. Smithsonian Institution, Washington, D.C.

Boyd, Maurice
    1981   *Kiowa Voices*, vol. 1: *Ceremonial Dance, Ritual and Song.* Texas Christian University Press, Fort Worth, Tex.
    1983   *Kiowa Voices*, vol. 2: *Myths, Legends and Folktales.* Texas Christian University Press, Fort Worth, Tex.

Brant, Charles S.
    1953   Kiowa Apache Culture History: Some Further Observations. *Southwest Journal of Anthropology* 9:195–202.
    1969   *Jim Whitewolf: The Life of a Kiowa Apache Indian.* Dover Publications, New York.

Browner, Tara
    2002   *Heartbeat of the People: Music and Dance of the Northern Pow-wow.* University of Illinois Press, Urbana.

Buchanan, Kimberly Moore
    1986   *Apache Women Warriors.* Texas Western Press, University of Texas at El Paso.

Burroughs, Jean M.
    1974   Chief Satanta and His Bugle. *Southwest Heritage* 4:21–28.

Callahan, Alice Ann
    1990   *The Osage Ceremonial Dance I'n-Lon-Schka.* University of Oklahoma Press, Norman.

Carlson, Gustav G., and Volney H. Jones
    1939   Some Notes on Uses of Plants by the Comanche Indians. *Papers of the Michigan Academy of Science, Arts, and Letters* 25:517–542 (printed 1940).

Clark, W. P.
    1885   *The Indian Sign Language.* L. R. Hamersley, Philadelphia. Reprint, 1982, University of Nebraska Press, Lincoln.

Collier, Donald
- 1938 Kiowa Social Organization. Master's thesis, Department of Anthropology, University of Chicago.

Corwin, Hugh D.
- 1962 Fifty Years with the Kiowa. Unpublished manuscript in possession of the author.

Corwin, Hugh D., ed.
- 1971a The A-Nanthy Odle-paugh Kiowa Calendar. *Prairie Lore*, January, 130–153.
- 1971b The A-Nanthy Odle-paugh Kiowa Calendar. *Prairie Lore*, October, 107–125.

Dempsey, James L.
- 1988 Persistence of a Warrior Ethic among the Plains Indians. *Alberta History* 36(1):1–10. Calgary.
- 1999 *Warriors of the King: Prairie Indians in World War I*. University of Regina, Canadian Plains Research Center, Saskatchewan, Canada.

Denton, Joan Frederick, and Sanford L. Maudlin Jr.
- 1987 Kiowa Murals: Behold I Stand in Good Relation to All Things. *Southwest Art*, July, 68–75.

Donnelley, Robert G.
- 2000 *Transforming Images: The Art of Silverhorn and His Successors*. With Contributions from Janet Catherine Berlo and Candace S. Greene. University of Chicago Press, Chicago.

Dorsey, George A.
- 1903 *The Arapaho Sun Dance: The Ceremony of the Offerings Lodge*. Field Columbian Museum Publication 75, Anthropological Series vol. 9, no. 2. Chicago.
- 1905 *The Cheyenne: 1. Ceremonial Organization*. Field Columbian Museum Publication 99, Anthropological Series vol. 9, no. 1.

Dorsey, James Owen
- 1884 Omaha Sociology. In *Third Annual Report of the Bureau of American Ethnology, 1881–1882*, 205–370. Smithsonian Institution, Washington, D.C.

Driver, Harold E.
- 1961 *Indians of North America*. University of Chicago Press, Chicago.

Duncan, Jimmy W.
- 1997 Hethushka Zani': An Ethnohistory of the War Dance Complex. Master's thesis, Northeastern State University, Talequah, Okla.

Dunn, Dorothy
- 1969 *1877: Plains Indian Sketch Book of Zo-Tom and Howling Wolf*. Northland Press, Flagstaff, Ariz.

Ellis, Clyde
- 1990 Truly Dancing Their Own Way: Modern Revival and Diffusion of the Gourd Dance. *American Indian Quarterly* 14(1):19–33.
- 1993 A Gathering of Life Itself: The Kiowa Gourd Dance. In *Native American Values: Survival and Renewal*, eds. Thomas E. Schirer and Susan M. Branstner. Lake Superior State University Press, Sault Ste. Marie, Mich.
- 1996 *To Change Them Forever: Indian Education at the Rainy Mountain Boarding School, 1893–1920*. University of Oklahoma Press, Norman.
- 2002 The Sound of the Drum Will Revive Them and Make Them Happy: Nineteenth-Century Plains Society Dances and the Roots of the Powwow. Unpublished paper; copy in possession of the author.
- 2003 *A Dancing People: Powwow Culture on the Southern Plains*. University Press of Kansas, Lawrence.

Etter, Jim
 1991 Mothers Still Support Kiowa Warriors. *Sunday Oklahoman* (Oklahoma City), Feb. 10, 1991, A14.

Ewers, John C.
 1975 Intertribal Warfare as the Precursor of Indian-White Warfare on the Northern Great Plains. *Western Historical Quarterly* 6:397–410.
 1978 *Murals in the Round: Painted Tipis of the Kiowa and Kiowa-Apache.* Smithsonian Institution, Washington, D.C.
 1980 Climate, Acculturation, and Costume: A History of Women's Clothing among the Indians of the Southern Plains. *Plains Anthropologist* 25(87)63–81.
 1997 Women's Roles in Plains Indian Warfare. In John C. Ewers, *Plains Indian History and Culture: Essays on Continuity and Change*, 191–204. University of Oklahoma Press, Norman.

Feder, Norman
 1982 *American Indian Art.* Harrison House/Harry N. Abrams, New York.

Fenton, William N.
 1987 *The False Faces of the Iroquois.* University of Oklahoma Press, Norman.

Ferguson, Brian R., ed.
 1984 *Warfare, Culture, and Environment.* Academic Press, New York.

Flannery, Regina
 1947 The Changing Form and Functions of the Gros Ventre Grass Dance. *Primitive Man* 20(3):39–70.

Fletcher, Alice C.
 1892 Haethushka Society of the Omaha Tribe. *Journal of American Folklore* 5:135–144.

Fletcher, Alice C., and Francis La Flesche
 1911 *The Omaha Tribe.* Twenty-Seventh Annual Report of the Bureau of American Ethnology, 1905–1906. Smithsonian Institution, Washington, D.C.

Foreman, Carolyn Thomas
 1954 *Indian Women Chiefs.* Zenger Publishing, Washington, D.C.

Galante, Gary
 1994a *The Kiowa Ledger Book.* Exhibition brochure. Montclair Art Museum, Montclair, N.J.
 1994b A Very Fine Ledger Book of Drawings. In *Fine American Indian Art,* Sotheby's auction catalogue (May). New York.

Galloway, Patricia, ed.
 1989 *The Southeastern Ceremonial Complex: Artifacts and Analysis.* University of Nebraska Press, Lincoln.

Galvin, John, ed.
 1970 *Through the Country of the Comanche Indians in the Year 1845: The Journal of a U.S. Army Expedition Led by Lt. James E. Abert.* John Howell Publishers, San Francisco.

Gamble, John I.
 1952 Kiowa Dance Gatherings and Costumed Dancers. Master's thesis, Washington University, St. Louis.

Gelo, Daniel J.
 1986 Comanche Belief and Ritual. Ph.D. diss., Department of Anthropology, Rutgers University.

Glazner, Christopher G.
 2002 Honoring Our Warriors: Southern Plains American Indian Music for War Veterans. Senior thesis, University of Texas, Austin. www.mit.edu/~glazner/thesis/thesis.html.

Goldfrank, Esther S.
  1945 *Changing Configurations in the Social Organization of a Blackfoot Tribe during the Reserve Period.* J. J. Augustin, New York.
Goldstein, Kenneth
  1972 On the Application of the Concepts of Active and Inactive Traditions in the Study of Repertoire. In *Towards New Perspectives in Folklore*, eds. Americo Paredes and Richard Bauman, 62–76. University of Texas Press, Austin.
Greene, Candace
  1993 The Tepee with Battle Pictures. *Natural History* 102(10):68–76.
  2000 Changing Times, Changing Views: Silver Horn as a Bridge to Nineteenth- and Twentieth-Century Kiowa Art. In *Transforming Images: The Art of Silverhorn and His Successors*, ed. Robert G. Donnelley, 15–26. University of Chicago Press, Chicago.
  2001 *Silver Horn: Master Illustrator of the Kiowas.* University of Oklahoma Press, Norman.
Greene, Candace S., and Thomas D. Drescher
  1994 The Tipi with Battle Pictures: The Kiowa Tradition of Intangible Property Rights. *Trademark Reporter* 84(4):418–433.
Grinnell, George Bird
  1910 Coup and Scalp among the Plains Indians. *American Anthropologist* 12:296–320.
  1983 [1915] *The Fighting Cheyennes.* University of Oklahoma Press, Norman.
Grobsmith, Elizabeth S.
  1981a *Lakota of the Rosebud: A Contemporary Ethnography.* Holt, Rinehart and Winston, New York.
  1981b The Changing Role of the Giveaway Ceremony in Contemporary Lakota Life. *Plains Anthropologist* 26(91):75–79.
Hail, Barbara
  2000 *Gifts of Pride and Love: Kiowa and Comanche Cradles.* Haffenreffer Museum of Anthropology, Brown University, Bristol, R.I.
Hamilton, Mildred Tsoodle
  1991 There Is a Kiowa Way and a Pow-wow Way. *Anadarko Daily News*, Feb. 18, 1991, 8.
Harrington, John P.
  1928 *Vocabulary of the Kiowa Language.* Bulletin of the Bureau of American Ethnology 84. Smithsonian Institution, Washington, D.C.
Harris, Moira F.
  1989 *Between Two Cultures: Kiowa Art from Fort Marion.* Pogo Press, St. Paul, Minn.
Hatton, Orin T.
  1989 Indians for Indians Hour Collection: 1943–1950. In *Songs of Indian Territory*, ed. Willie Smyth, 59–62. Center of the American Indian, Oklahoma City, Okla.
Haynie, Nancy Anne, ed.
  1984 *Native Americans and the Military: Today and Yesterday.* U.S. Army Forces Command Public Affairs, Command Information Branch, Fort McPherson, Ga.
Hoebel, E. Adamson
  1978 *The Cheyennes: Indians of the Great Plains.* Holt, Reinhart and Winston, New York.
Holm, Tom
  1996 *Strong Hearts, Wounded Souls: Native American Veterans of the Vietnam War.* University of Texas Press, Austin.
Howard, James H.
  1950 The Omaha Hand Game and Gourd Dance. *Plains Archaeological Conference News Letter* 3:39–42. Omaha, Neb.

1951 Notes on the Dakota Grass Dance. *Southwest Journal of Anthropology* 7(1):82–85.
1955 The Pan-Indian Culture of Oklahoma. *Scientific Monthly* 18(5):215–220.
1965 *The Ponca Tribe*. Bulletin of the Bureau of American Ethnology 195. Smithsonian Institution, Washington, D.C.
1976 The Plains Gourd Dance as a Revitalization Movement. *American Ethnologist* 3(:2):243–59.
1983 Pan-Indianism in Native American Music and Dance. *Ethnomusicology* 27(1):71–82.

Humphrey, Norman D.
1941 A Characterization of Certain Plains Associations. *American Anthropologist* 43:428–436.
1942 Police and Tribal Welfare in Plains Indian Cultures. *Journal of Criminal Law and Criminology* 33:147–161.

Issacs, Tony
1975 *Kiowa Gourd Dance*, vol. 2, record sleeve. Indian House Records, Taos, N.M.

James, Edwin
1823 *Account of an Expedition from Pittsburg to the Rocky Mountains, Performed in the Years 1819 and 20, under the Command of Major Stephen H. Long*. 2 vols. N. C. Carey and I. Lea, Philadelphia.

Jennings, Carl, and Vanessa Jennings
2000 Kiowa Dance Aprons that Appear in Photographs belonging to the Mopope Family Dated 1914–1922, Redstone Community, Located between Anadarko and Fort Cobb, Oklahoma. Paper presented at the Kiowa Beadwork Seminar, Tulsa, Okla., Feb. 26–27. Copy in the author's possession.

Jennings, Jesse D.
1974 *Prehistory of North America*. 2nd ed. McGraw-Hill, New York.

Jennings, Vanessa
2002 The Tradition of the Kiowa Battle Dress and Aw-Day-Tah-Lee in My Family. *Whispering Wind* 32(3):8–16.

John, Elizabeth A. H.
1985 An Earlier Chapter of Kiowa History. *New Mexico Historical Review* 60:379–397.

Jones, David E.
1968 Comanche Plant Medicines. *Papers in Anthropology* (University of Oklahoma, Department of Anthropology) 9:1–13.
1972 *Sanapia: Comanche Medicine Woman*. Holt, Rinehart and Winston, New York.
2000 *Women Warriors: A History*. Brassey's Press, Dulles, Va.

Jones, Ruth Blalock
1995 Like Being Home: Oklahoma Indian Art. *Gilcrease Journal*, Oklahoma Indian Art edition, 3(2):6–21.

Kavanagh, Thomas W.
1982 The Comanche Pow-wow: Pan-Indianism or Tribalism? *Haliksa'i* (University of New Mexico Anthropology Society) 1:12–27.
1993 Southern Plains Dance: Tradition and Dynamics. In *Native American Dance: Ceremonies and Social Traditions*, ed. Charlotte Heth, 105–123. National Museum of the American Indian, Smithsonian Institution, Washington, D.C.
1996 *Comanche Political History: An Ethnohistorical Perspective 1706–1875*. University of Nebraska Press, Lincoln.
2008 *Comanche Sourcebook: Notes of the 1933 Santa Fe Laboratory of Anthropology Field Party Recorded by Waldo R. Wedel, E. Adamson Hoebel, and Gustav G. Carlson*. University of Nebraska Press, Lincoln.

Kehoe, Alice B.
    1970   The Function of Ceremonial Sexual Intercourse among the Northern Plains Indians. *Plains Anthropologist* 15(48):99–103.

Kiowa Gourd Clan
    1976   Ceremonials booklet. July 1–4. Privately published.
    1996   Ceremonials booklet. July 2–4. Privately published.

Kiowa Tai-Piah Society
    1990   *24th Annual Celebration Booklet.* July 1–4. Privately published.

Kracht, Benjamin R.
    1989   Kiowa Religion: An Ethnohistorical Analysis of Ritual Symbolism, 1832–1987. Ph.D. diss., Southern Methodist University, Dallas, Tex.
    1992   The Kiowa Ghost Dance, 1894–1916: An Unheralded Revitalization Movement. *Ethnohistory* 39(4):452–477.
    1994   Kiowa Powwows: Continuity in Ritual Practice. *American Indian Quarterly* 18(3):321–348.

Kroeber, Alfred R.
    1907   *The Arapaho.* Bulletin of the American Museum of Natural History 18. New York. Originally published in three parts in 1902, 1904, and 1907.

La Barre, Weston
    1938   *The Peyote Cult.* New Haven Press, Hamden, Conn.
    1989   *The Peyote Cult.* 5th ed. University of Oklahoma Press, Norman.

La Flesche, Francis
    1939   *War Ceremony and Peace Ceremony of the Osage Indians.* Bulletin of the Bureau of American Ethnology 101. Smithsonian Institution, Washington D.C.

Lang, Sabine
    1998   *Men as Women, Women as Men: Changing Gender in Native American Cultures.* University of Texas Press, Austin.

Lasko, Steven B.
    1997   A Strong and Humble People: An Ethnicity Study of the Apache Tribe of Oklahoma. Master's thesis, Department of Anthropology, University of Oklahoma, Norman.

Lassiter, Luke Eric
    1992   Rattles, Song, and Spirit: The Kiowa Gourd Dance. Unpublished paper, University of North Carolina. Copy in possession of the author.
    1993   They Left Us These Songs . . . That's All We Got Now: The Significance of Music in the Kiowa Gourd Dance and Its Relation to Native American Cultural Continuity. In *Native American Values: Survival and Renewal,* eds. Thomas E. Schirer and Susan M. Branstner, 375–384. Lake Superior State University Press, Sault Ste. Marie, Mich.
    1995   Towards Understanding the Power of Kiowa Song: A Collaborative Exercise in Meaning. Ph.D. diss., University of North Carolina, Chapel Hill.
    1997   Charlie Brown: Not Just Another Essay on the Gourd Dance. *American Indian Culture And Research Journal* 21(4):75–103.
    1998   *The Power of Kiowa Song.* University of Arizona Press, Tucson.

Le Page Du Pratz, Antoine Simone
    1942 [1774]   *The History of Louisiana.* Louisiana State University, Baton Rouge.

Levy, Jerrold E.
    1959   After Custer: Kiowa Political and Social Organization from the Reservation Period to the Present. Ph.D. diss., University of Chicago.
    2001   Kiowa. In *Handbook of North American Indians,* vol. 13: *Plains,* part 2, ed. Raymond J. DeMallie, 907–925. Smithsonian Institution, Washington, D.C.

n.d. Kiowa. Draft of chapter for *Handbook of North American Indians*, vol. 13: *Plains*. Copy in the author's possession.

Liberty, Margot
- 1973 The Urban Reservation. Ph.D. diss., Department of Anthropology, University of Minnesota.
- 1980 The Sun Dance. In *Anthropology on the Great Plains*, eds. W. Raymond Wood and Margot Liberty, 164–178. University of Nebraska Press, Lincoln.

Lookingbill, Brad D.
- 2006 *War Dance at Fort Marion: Plains Indian War Prisoners*. University of Oklahoma Press, Norman.

Lowie, Robert H.
- 1913 Dance Associations of the Eastern Dakota. *Anthropological Papers of the American Museum of Natural History* 11(2):102–142.
- 1916a Plains Indian Age-Societies: Historical and Comparative Summary. *Anthropological Papers of the American Museum of Natural History* 11(8):877–992.
- 1916b Societies of the Kiowa. *Anthropological Papers of the American Museum of Natural History* 11(11):837–853.
- 1922 The Religion of the Crow Indians. *Anthropological Papers of the American Museum of Natural History* 25(2):309–444.
- 1941 Property Rights and Coercive Powers of Plains Indian Military Societies. *Journal of Legal and Political Sociology* 1:59–71.
- 1953 Alleged Kiowa-Crow Affinities. *Southwestern Journal of Anthropology* 9(4):357–368.
- 1956 Notes on the Kiowa Indians. *Tribus: The Journal of Ethnology and Its Related Sciences* (Linden Museum, Stuttgart, Germany) 4:131–38.
- 1982 *Indians of the Plains*. University of Nebraska Press, Lincoln.
- 1983 *The Crow Indians*. University of Nebraska Press, Lincoln.

Lurie, Nancy Oestreich
- 1971 The Contemporary American Indian Scene. In *North American Indians in Historical Perspective*, eds. Eleanor Burke Leacock and Nancy Oestreich Lurie, 418–480. Waveland Press, Prospect Heights, Ill.

Mails, Thomas E.
- 1973 *Dog Soldiers, Bear Men and Buffalo Women: A Study of the Societies and Cults of the Plains Indians*. Prentice Hall, Englewood Cliffs, N.J.
- 1998 *Dog Soldiers: Societies of the Plains*. Marlowe, New York. Originally published as *Dog Soldiers, Bear Men and Buffalo Women: A Study of the Societies and Cults of the Plains Indians*.

Marriott, Alice
- 1945 *The Ten Grandmothers*. University of Oklahoma Press, Norman.
- 1956 Trade Guild of the Southern Cheyenne Women. *Oklahoma Anthropological Society Bulletin* 4:19–27.
- 1968 *Kiowa Years: A Study in Culture Impact*. Macmillan, New York.

Martín, Jo
- 1997 Women Warriors: Secret Weapon of the Apaches. *New Mexico Magazine*, August, 90–96.

Maurer, Evan M.
- 1977 *The Native American Heritage: A Survey of North American Indian Art*. Art Institute of Chicago, Chicago.

McAllister, Gilbert J.
- 1935 Kiowa-Apache Social Organization. Ph.D. diss., University of Chicago.

- 1937 Kiowa-Apache Social Organization. In *Social Anthropology of North American Indian Tribes*, ed. Fred Eggan, 99–169. University of Chicago Press, Chicago.
- 1970 *Daveko: Kiowa-Apache Medicine Man*. Bulletin of the Texas Memorial Museum 17. Austin, Tex.

McCoy, Ronald
- 1987 *Kiowa Memories: Images from Indian Territory, 1880*. Morning Star Gallery, Santa Fe, N.M.

McCracken, Harold
- 1959 *George Catlin and the Old Frontier*. Dial Press, New York.

McKenzie, Parker P.
- 1988 Kiowa Monosyllables. Unpublished manuscript. Copy in possession of the author.
- 1991 Kiowa Disyllables. Compilation of more than twelve thousand two-syllable Kiowa words. Unpublished manuscript. Copy in possession of the author.
- n.d.a Kiowa Names of Indian Tribes. Unpublished manuscript. Copy in possession of the author.
- n.d.b Vocabulary of Kiowa Terms for Mammals, Birds, Insects, Reptiles, and Fishes. Unpublished manuscript. Copy in possession of the author.
- n.d.c Kiowa Police at the Kiowa, Comanche and Wichita Agency, 1880 to 1895. Unpublished manuscript. Copy in possession of the author.
- n.d.d Early Years of the American Indian Exposition. Unpublished manuscript. Copy in possession of the author.
- n.d.e Kiowa Medical and Disease Terms. Unpublished manuscript. Copy in possession of the author.

McLeod, William Christie
- 1937 Police and Punishment among Native Americans of the Plains. *Journal of Criminal law, Criminology, and Police Science* 28:181–201.

Meadows, William C.
- 1991 Tonkonga: An Ethnohistory of the Kiowa Black Legs Society. Master's thesis, University of Oklahoma, Norman.
- 1995 Remaining Veterans: A Symbolic and Comparative Ethnohistory of Southern Plains Indian Military Societies. Ph.D. diss., University of Oklahoma, Norman.
- 1999 *Kiowa, Apache, and Comanche Military Societies: Enduring Veterans, 1800 to the Present*. University of Texas Press, Austin.

Meadows, William C., and Parker P. McKenzie
- 2001 The Parker P. McKenzie Kiowa Orthography: How Written Kiowa Came into Being. *Plains Anthropologist* 46(177):233–248.

Meadows, William C., and Gus Palmer Sr.
- 1992 Tonkonga: The Kiowa Black Legs Military Society. In *Native American Dance: Ceremonies and Social Traditions*, ed. Charlotte Heth, 116–117. National Museum of the American Indian, Smithsonian Institution, Washington, D.C.

Medicine, Beatrice
- 1983 Warrior Women: Sex Role Alternatives for Plains Indian Women. In *The Hidden Half: Studies of Plains Indian Women*, eds. Patricia C. Albers and Beatrice Medicine, 267–280. University Press of America, Washington, D.C.

Merriam, Alan P.
- 1964 *The Anthropology of Music*. Northwestern University Press, Evanston, Ill.

Merrill, William L.
- 1977 An Investigation of Ethnographic and Archaeological Specimens of Mescal Beans (Sophora

secundiflora) *in American Museums*. Research Reports in Ethnobotany, Contribution 1. Museum of Anthropology, University of Michigan, Ann Arbor.

Methvin, Rev. J. J.
- 1927 *Andele, or the Mexican Kiowa Captive*. Anadarko, Okla.

Mishkin, Bernard
- 1940 *Rank and Warfare among the Plains Indians*. American Ethnological Society Monograph 3. J. J. Augustin, New York.

Momaday, N. Scott
- 1976a *The Names: A Memoir*. University of Arizona Press, Tucson.
- 1976b *The Gourd Dancer*. Harper and Row, New York.

Mooney, James
- 1896 *The Ghost Dance Religion and the Sioux Outbreak of 1890*. Fourteenth Annual Report of the Bureau of American Ethnology, 1892–1893, part 2, 641–1110. Smithsonian Institution, Washington, D.C.
- 1898 *Calendar History of the Kiowa Indians*. Seventeenth Annual Report of the Bureau of American Ethnology, part 1, 129–468. Smithsonian Institution, Washington, D.C.
- 1907 The Cheyenne Indians. *Memoirs of the American Anthropological Association* 1, part 6, 357–442. Menasha, Wis.
- 1912 Military Societies. In *Handbook of American Indians North of Mexico*, ed. Frederick W. Hodge, 861–863. Bulletin of the Bureau of American Ethnology 30. Smithsonian Institution, Washington, D.C.

Moore, John Hartwell
- 1987 *The Cheyenne Nation: A Social and Demographic History*. University of Nebraska Press, Lincoln.

Morgan, Vanessa Paukeigope
- 1991a Respect Ancestors. *Anadarko Daily News*, Feb. 5, 1991, 8.
- 1991b Battle Dresses to Be Worn at Black Leggings Event. *Anadarko Daily News*, Oct. 12–13, 1991, 1–2.

Murie, James R.
- 1914 Pawnee Indian Societies. *Anthropological Papers of the American Museum of Natural History* 9(7):543–644.

Newcomb, W. W. Jr.
- 1950 A Re-examination of the Causes of Plains Warfare. *American Anthropologist* 52:317–330.

Nettl, Bruno
- 1983 *The Study of Ethnomusicology: Twenty-nine Issues and Concepts*. University of Illinois Press, Urbana.
- 1985 *The Western Impact on World Music*. Schirmer Books, New York.

Northcutt, John David
- 1973 Leadership among the Kiowa, 1833–1973. Master's thesis, University of Oklahoma, Norman.

Noyes, Stanley
- 1993 *Los Comanches: The Horse People, 1751–1845*. University of New Mexico Press, Albuquerque.

Nye, Colonel Wilbur S.
- 1937 *Carbine and Lance: The Story of Old Fort Sill*. University of Oklahoma Press, Norman.
- 1962 *Bad Medicine and Good: Tales of the Kiowas*. University of Oklahoma Press, Norman.
- 1968 *Plains Indian Raiders: The Final Phases of Warfare from the Arkansas to the Red River*. University of Oklahoma Press, Norman.

Ortner, Sherry B.
   1973   On Key Symbols. *American Anthropologist* 75(5):1338–1346.
Osburn, Katherine M. B.
   1998   *Southern Ute Women*. University of New Mexico Press, Albuquerque.
Paddlety, Victor
   1976   Tape recording of Kiowa history and names. Copy in author's possession.
Parsons, Elsie Clews
   1929   *Kiowa Tales*. Memoirs of the American Folk-Lore Society 22. New York
Perdue, Theda
   1998   *Cherokee Women*. University of Nebraska Press, Lincoln.
Petersen, Karen Daniels
   1971   *Plains Indian Art from Fort Marion*. University of Oklahoma Press, Norman.
Petter, Rodolphe C.
   1913–1915   *English-Cheyenne Dictionary*. "Printed Entirely in the Interest of the Mennonite Mission among the Cheyenne Indians of Oklahoma and Montana." Valdo Petter, Kettle Falls, Wash.
Philp, Kenneth R.
   1977   *John Collier's Crusade for Indian Reform, 1920–1954*. University of Arizona Press, Tucson.
Poolaw, Newton
   1981   Revival of the Taipay Society. *Kiowa Indian News* (Carnegie, Okla.), April, 2.
Powell, A. Michael
   1988   *Trees and Shrubs of Trans-Pecos Texas*. Big Bend Historical Association, Big Bend, Texas.
Powell, Peter J.
   1981   *People of the Sacred Mountain: A History of the Northern Cheyenne Chiefs and Warrior Societies, 1830–1879, with an Epilogue, 1969–1974*. 2 vols. Harper and Row, San Francisco.
Powers, William K.
   1973   The Sioux Omaha Dance. *American Indian Crafts and Culture* 4(2):24–33.
   1980   Plains Indian Music and Dance. In *Anthropology of the Great Plains*, eds. W. Raymond Wood and Margot Liberty, 212–229. University of Nebraska Press, Lincoln.
   1990   *War Dance: Plains Indian Musical Performance*. University of Arizona Press, Tucson.
   2001   *The Lakota Warrior Tradition: Three Essays on Lakotas at War*. Lakota Books, Kendall Park, N.J.
Red Earth Indian Center
   1995   Four Generations: Mopope, Palmer, Jennings and Morgan. Pamphlet. Red Earth Indian Center, Kirkpatrick Center Museum Complex, Oklahoma City, Okla.
Rhodes, Willard
   1954   *Kiowa*. Recording with written booklet. Music of the American Indian from the Archive of Folk Culture, Library of Congress, Washington, D.C.
Richardson, Jane
   1940   *Law and Status among the Kiowa Indians*. American Ethnological Society, Monograph 1. New York.
   n.d.   Miscellaneous Notes on Kiowa Tonkonga Society, Taken from Kintadl during the 1935 Santa Fe Laboratory of Anthropology Kiowa Field School. Copy in possession of the author.
Robinson, Charles M. III
   1997   *Satanta: The Life and Death of a War Chief*. State House Press, Austin, Tex.
Schneider, Mary Jane
   1982   Connections: Family Ties in Kiowa Art. In *Pathways to Plains Prehistory: Anthropological*

Perspectives of Plains Natives and Their Pasts, eds. Don G. Wycoff and Jack L. Hofman, 7–18. Oklahoma Anthropological Society, Memoir 3. Duncan, Okla.

Schultes, Richard Evans
- 1937 Peyote and Plants Used in the Peyote Ceremony. *Harvard University Botanical Museum Leaflets* 4(8):129–152.

Schweinfurth, Kay Parker
- 2002 *Prayer on Top of the Earth: The Spiritual Universe of the Plains Apache*. University Press of Colorado, Boulder.

Schweitzer, Marjorie M.
- 1981 The Otoe-Missouria War Mothers: Women of Valor. *Moccasin Tracks* 7(1):4–8.
- 1983 The War Mothers: Reflections of Space and Time. *Papers in Anthropology* (Department of Anthropology, University of Oklahoma) 24(2):157–171.

Scott, Hugh Lenox
- 1928 *Some Memories of a Soldier*. Century, New York.

Silberman, Arthur
- 1988 Review of *Kiowa Memories: Images from Indian Territory, 1880*, by Ronald McCoy. *Plains Anthropologist* 33(120):285–287.

Skinner, Alanson
- 1915a Societies of the Iowa. *Anthropological Papers of the American Museum of Natural History* 11(9):679–740. New York.
- 1915b Ponca Societies and Dances, *Anthropological Papers of the American Museum of Natural History* 11(9):777–801. New York.

Slotkin, James S.
- 1957 *The Menominee Powwow: A Study in Cultural Decay*. Milwaukee Public Museum Publications in Anthropology 4. Milwaukee, Minn.

Smith, Marian W.
- 1938 War Complex of the Plains Indians. *Proceedings of the American Philosophical Society* 78:425–464.

Stahl, Robert J.
- 1989 Joe True: Convergent Needs and Assumed Identity. In *Being and Becoming Indian: Biographical Studies of North American Frontiers*, ed. James A. Clifton, 276–289. Dorsey Press, Chicago.

Stewart, Omar C.
- 1987 *Peyote Religion: A History*. University of Oklahoma Press, Norman.

Swanton, John R.
- 1942 *Source Materials on the History and Ethnography of the Caddo Indians*. Bulletin of the Bureau of American Ethnology 132. Smithsonian Institution, Washington, D.C.

Szabo, Joyce
- 1994 Shields and Lodges, Warriors and Chiefs: Kiowa Drawings as Historical Records. *Ethnohistory* 41(1):1–24.

Time-Life Books
- 1993 *The Way of the Warrior*. Alexandria, Va.

Townsend, Richard F., ed.
- 2004 *Hero, Hawk, and Open Hand: American Indian Art of the Ancient Midwest and South*. Yale University Press, New Haven, Conn.

Tsonetokoy, Dewey D.
- 1988 1830s, Golden Age of Kiowas. In *Anadarko Daily News Visitors Guide*. Anadarko, Okla.

Two Hatchet, James
- 1984 Tape-recorded speech delivered at Kiowa Black Leggings Ceremonial, Anadarko, Okla-

homa, May. Copy of recording courtesy of Gus Palmer Sr.; transcript of speech courtesy of Benjamin Kracht. Copies in author's possession.

Vennum, Thomas
- 1982 *The Ojibwa Dance Drum: Its History and Construction*. Smithsonian Institution Press, Washington, D.C.

Vestal, Paul, and Richard Evans Schultes
- 1939 *The Economic Botany of the Kiowa Indians as It Relates to the History of the Tribe*. Botanical Museum, Cambridge, Mass.

Viola, Herman J.
- 1998 *Warrior Artists: Historic Cheyenne and Kiowa Indian Ledger Art Drawn by Making Medicine and Zotom*. National Geographic Society, Washington, D.C.

Vogel, Virgil
- 1970 *American Indian Medicine*. University of Oklahoma Press, Norman.

Voget, Fred
- 1964 Warfare and the Integration of Crow Indian Culture. In *Explorations in Cultural Anthropology*, ed. Ward Goodenough, 483–509. McGraw Hill, New York.

Walker, James
- 1980 *Lakota Ritual and Belief*. Eds. Raymond J. DeMallie and Elaine A. Jahner. University of Nebraska Press, Lincoln.

Wallace, Anthony F. C.
- 1956 Revitalization Movements. *American Anthropologist* 58:264–281.

Wallace, Ernest, and E. Adamson Hoebel
- 1952 *The Comanche: Lords of the South Plains*. University of Oklahoma Press, Norman.

Wissler, Clark
- 1912 Societies and Ceremonial Associations of the Oglala Division of the Teton-Dakota. *Anthropological Papers of the American Museum of Natural History* 11(1):1–100.
- 1916 General Discussion of Shamanistic and Dancing Societies. *Anthropological Papers of the American Museum of Natural History* 11:859–876.

Wissler, Clark, ed.
- 1912–1916 *Societies of the Plains Indians*. Anthropological Papers of the American Museum of Natural History, vol. 11.

Wright, Muriel H.
- 1946 The American Indian Exposition in Oklahoma. *Chronicles of Oklahoma* 24(3):158–165.

Young, Gloria
- 1981 Powwow Power: Perspectives on Historic and Contemporary Intertribalism. Ph.D. diss., University of Indiana, Bloomington.

Zotigh, Dennis
- 1991 *Moving History: The Evolution of the Powwow*. Center of the American Indian, Kirkpatrick Center Museum Complex, Oklahoma City, Okla.

Films and Audio Recordings

Strangers in Their Own Land. Commercial film, 1993. Strangers In Their Own Land Inc., Oklahoma City, Okla.

Canyon Records, Phoenix, Ariz.
- *Kaulaity and Cozad*
- *Kiowa Black Leggings Society Songs* (CR-6167)
- *Kiowa Dance Group Singers*
- *Kiowa Scalp and Victory Dance Songs* (CR-6166)

Gourd Dance Songs of the Kiowa (CR-6148)
  Koomsa Tribal Singers
  Kiowa! (CR-6145)
  Various Artists
  Kiowa "49" and Round Dance Songs (CR-6087)
  Kiowa Gourd Dance Songs (CR-6103)
Indian House Records, Taos, N.M.
  Kiowa 49, War Expedition Songs. IH-2505.
  Kiowa Black-Leg Warriors Society Songs. SC-305 (1964). Reissued by American Indian Soundchiefs, 1994.
  Kiowa Gourd Dance, vols. 1 and 2. IH 2503, IH 2504 (1975).
  O-ho-mah Lodge Singers. *War Dance Songs of the Kiowa O-ho-mah Lodge Singers*, vols. 1 and 2. IH 2508, IH 2509 (1976).
  O-ho-mah Lodge Singers. *Songs of the O-Ho-Mah Lodge, Kiowa War Dance Society*, vols. 3 and 4. IH2510 and 2511 (1994).
  Soundchief Singers. *Kiowa Warriors Dance Songs* and *Kiowa War Expedition Songs*. SC-131.
Independent Recordings
  Anquoe Family. *Original Kiowa War Mother Songs*, vols. 1 and 2 (1985). James and Anna Anquoe Family. Produced by J. W. Carter, Tulsa, Okla.

INDEX

Note: Individuals are listed alphabetically by English translation of their Kiowa names (e.g., Bird Appearing) or by Agency surname, followed by English given name (e.g., Ahboah, Sam).

Adena culture, 255–56; effigy pipe and, 256
Afghanistan, military service in, 67, 75, 105, 365
Afraid Of The Bears, 268
Against The Shoulder Blade (Dáunfài), 37, 329
Ahboah, Fannie, 55
Ahboah, Sam, 59
Ahpeahtone, 85
Ahtape, Clyde, 148
Aitsan, Amos, 77
Aitsan, Marland Konad, 269
Alabama-Koasati Tribe, 186–87
Albers, Patricia, 115–16
American Indian Exposition, 61, 62, 147–48, 152, 299, 366
American Legion Posts, 63, 67. *See also* Veterans of Foreign Wars posts
Anko (Kiowa calendar keeper), 260
Anquoe, Jack, 61
Anquoe, Jim, 343
Anquoe, Jimmy, 61, 65, 80, 343–44
Anquoe, Kenneth, 61
Anquoe, Leonard, 61
Apache Blackfeet Society (Manatidie), 9, 47–48, 80, 89, 229
Apache Izuwe Society, 314–15
Apache Klintidie Society, 117, 229, 239
Apache Rabbit Society (Katsowe), 14, 16
Apache Tribe of Oklahoma (Naishan Dene, Plains Apache), 47–49, 217, 258
Arapaho Indians, 48, 218; Bitahi'nena Society, 44
Arose From The Sky, 241
Asah, Spencer, 278, 281
Atah, 225, 310, 320, 323, 329

Auchiah, Celia, 63
Auchiah, James, 124, 139, 152, 169, 282
Aunkoyday, 55, 57

Bantista, Rudy, 77
Bear Old Women Society (Sétchǫ̂hyòp), 307–10, 320–27, 328–30; meetings, 324–27; members, 383–84; membership, 323; name 320; power, 323–24; Up A Rock Story (Devil's Tower), 321–23, 327; vows, 324. *See also* Kiowa Military Societies
Bear Shields, 141
Bear Unafraid Of Death, 115
Bent/Warped By Heat, 138
Big Arrows, 143
Big Bow, Abel, 148
Big Bow, Nelson, 169
Big Bow II (b. 1833), 29–30, 71;
Big Bow III (Lone Traveler), 143, 146, 267
Big Head. *See* Friendship Tree
Big Meat, 26–27
Big Tree, 37
Bird Appearing, 30
Bird Chief, 268
Bird Running, 142, 236
Bison Bird (Odlepaugh), 140–41
Bison Bull Recess, 47
Black Bear, 138–39, 142, 236
Black Bird, 236
Black Cap/Hat, 226
Black Goose, 142
Black Headdress, 231, 236
Black Horse I, 136, 138, 142
Black Horse II, 42, 55, 57, 142
Black Legs Society (Tǫ̀kǫ́gàut), 28, 39–112,

445

Black Legs Society (Tòkôgàut) (continued) 137–38, 143, 148, 150, 154–55, 174, 198, 205, 269, 292, 306, 364–66; Auxiliary, 357–58; cedaring ritual, 83; cessation, 49, 54–55; Chief's Song, 96, 104; Christianity and martial ethos, 65–68; community functions, 103–104; coup recitations, 100–101, 107; current activities, 103–12; current ceremonial, 78–112; dances, 43–44, 57, 93–103; dress, 40–43, 56–58, 68–70; early members, 373–75; Empty Saddle Ceremony, 95; ethnological significance of, 39, 108–12; Excite/Stirring To Action songs, 94; fiftieth anniversary ceremonial, 105–107; fiftieth anniversary veteran's song, 98–99; flag songs, 97–98; funeral rites and song, 103–104; initiations, 55–59, 92–93, 95–96, insignia (pàubôn, whips), 41, 44–48, 68, 73, 107–108; Kiowa Warrior (helicopter), 75, 107; leaders, 49–54, 55–56, 76–78; ledger drawings of, 41–43; lodge / tipi, 70–74, 105–106; meetings, 44–45, 56; membership, 48–49, 57; memorial songs, 81–82, 95; name, 39–40, 61–62; origins, 40; red capes, 41; Reverse Dance, 28, 43–44, 57, 59, 99–103, 107; revivals of, 19, 54–61; role in Kiowa society, 60; Shuffle Dance, 44, 58–59, 86, 96–97; social status, 58; songs, 68; Up and Down dance, 97; veteran recognition, 74–76. *See also* Kiowa Military Societies

Blackmon, John P., 55
Black Turtle, 49
Bluff Recess (Jòhâudè), 235, 240, 241, 248–49. *See also* Son of Bluff Recess
Bodmer, Karl, 228
Bohay, 146
Bohee / Bohi (Very Strong), 49, 51, 68
Bointy, Bill, 169
Bointy, Jack (Big Horse), 143–46
Bointy, Vincent, 169
Boone, Daniel, 55
Bosin, Frank, 57, 275, 285
Bosin, George, 269
Botone (Beaver Lake), 141, 267
Botone, Fred, 148
Botone, Moses, 152, 270
Boyiddle, Mrs. Pickler, 350
Brace, Ned, 144

Brant, Charles, 229
Bronaugh, Albert, 191–93, 213
Brown, General Charles, 167
Buffalo, Homer, 57, 65, 275
Buffalo, Mary, 121, 139, 310–12, 315–18, 329, 383
Buffalo Calf Tongue, 140
Burke, Charles H. 299–300

Calf Old Women Society (Xálīchôhyòp), 18–19, 307–10, 310–20, 328–30; dances, 318–19; feasts, 316–17; initiations, 312–13; meetings, 313–18; members, 383; membership, 311–12; name of, 310; offerings, 317; role in Sun Dance, 319–20; sexual symbolism, 314–18; songs, 315–17; vows, 310–11. *See also* Kiowa Military Societies
Calumet Dance, 254–56, 262–64, 288, 302
Cannon, T. C., 75
Carnegie Victory Club, 64, 78, 80, 85–86, 89, 147, 197, 349–54; celebrations by, 350–54; early members of, 352; insignia of, 350
Catlin, George, 255
Chaddlesone, Alice, 77
Chaddlesone, Sherman, 90–91, 105, 111–12
Chapter Organizations. *See* Military Societies
Charlie Brown (song). *See* Komalty Family Song
Cheyenne Indians, 47–48, 70, 120–25, 188, 207; 1840 peace with Kiowa-Comanche-Apache, 122; Gourd Dance, 204–206; Omaha Dance, 253, 304; 258, 260–65; Sacred Arrows, 204–205; Sun Dance, 204–205; 1838 Wolf Creek Fight, 121–25. *See also* Cheyenne Military Societies
Cheyenne Military Societies: Bowstrings 47, 120–25, 204, 314; Dog Soldiers 122, 205; Elkhorn Scrapers, 205; Hoof Rattlers, 47; Kit Foxes, 205; society "princesses," 269
Chief, Kiowa concept of, 27, 219
Chief Sa-tan-ta Descendants, 172–73
Chieftain Park, 20
Childers, Lt. Col. Ernest, 74
Christianity, effects on Indian culture, 65–68; and martial ethos, 65–68
Cody, William F., 281, 299
Comanche Indians, 188, 207, 217, 258; Big Horse Society, 130; Buffalo Dance, 130;

Little Ponies, 9; Los Lobos, 117; Tuhwi Society, 9, 80, 89; War Dance Society, 190, 290
Coup Recitations. *See* Black Legs Society
Cozad, Belo, 29, 57, 248, 266
Cozad, Charles, 74
Cozad, Leonard Sr., 61, 63, 98, 114, 148, 197, 350
Craterville Indian Fair, 299
Crazy Old Man. *See* Slow Running Wolf
Creek Where The Cheyenne Were Annihilated, 120–21
Crossing / Bridge, 324, 327
Crow Appeared (Càuáuvédài), 233
Crow Appeared (Càuáuvéjè), 231, 237, 239, 241
Crow Indians, 34, 353–54; Big Lodge Ceremony, 201
Crow [Feathered] Lance (Heidsick), 53–54

Dakota War Dance, 258
Dancing, before warfare, 121
Daugamah / Daugomah, 65, 148, 152
Daunfai / Done-pi. *See* Against The Shoulder Blade
Daveko (Plains Apache), 49
DeLaune, Dorothy Whitehorse, 274, 284
Dietrich's Lake Fair, 275
Dohau. *See* Bluff Recess
Dohausan / Dohausen. *See* Son of Bluff Recess
Domebo, Alice Soontay, 55
Domebo, Andy, 55
Domebo, Charley, 57
Domebo, Harry, 57
Dome-gatty, Amy, 275
Donety, 31
Dorsey, James O., 257
Doyebi, Ernest, 61
Doyebi, Hugh, 61, 74
Doyebi, Nathan, 61
Doyeto, Jack, 247, 249–50
Doyeto, Martha White Horse, 284
Duncan, Jimmy, 211, 255, 304
Dupoint, Herbert, 63
Dupoint, Joe "Fish", 20

Eagleheart (John Topaum), 143, 144
Ellis, Clyde, 143, 261

Emhoola, John Sr., 275
Eni'ede, 142
Entering Wolf, 26
Ethnohistorical approach, 9–11

Factionalism. *See* Kiowa Military Societies
Favored boys and girls, 5–6
Fearless Charger. *See* Sun Appeared; White Horse, Roland
Feather Headdress, 43, 54
Fish Hook (Haunpo / Haumpo), 241, 244
Flannery, Regina, 303
Flores, Carol Tapedo, 339–41, 344–45, 348, 359
Fort Marion, Florida, 261–62, 281
Forty-Fifth "Thunderbird" Division, 344, 398
Forty-Nine (49) Dance, 66, 146
Friendship Tree (Komalty, Big Head), 36, 43, 133, 134, 270
Friendship Tree I, 142
Friendship Tree II, 142–43, 285
Frizzlehead I, 136–37, 142, 226, 239
Frizzlehead II (Arising Crying), 40, 55, 85, 132, 137, 142–43, 217, 219–20, 224, 230–33, 235–36, 239, 243–44, 320, 377, 380

Gamble, John, 285, 354
Garza, Annette Emhoola, 77
Gawky, 54
Geikaunmah, Bert, 33, 36, 37, 57, 61, 65, 104, 270
Geimausaddle, Howard, 266
Geimausaddle, Russell, 266
Geionety, Lula, 355
Giatogia, 232–33, 236, 240
Gift Dance. *See* Omaha Society
Giveaway. *See* Omaha Society
Given, Frank, 28, 43, 46, 47, 134–37, 141, 222, 227, 234, 235, 238, 320, 323, 326
Glazner, Christopher, 154, 197, 301
Good Crow (Big Joe), 37, 55, 57
Goomdaw / Gumdaw (Wind), 14, 17, 29, 227, 378
Gotebo (Many Wounds), 267
Goule-Hae-Ee Descendants, 52, 107
Gourd Dance, 33, 37, 283; Anglo Gourd Dance organizations, 180; Anglo interest in, 178–87; Anglo use of "Tia-Piah" name, 180,

Gourd Dance (*continued*)
183–86; appropriation of, 175–87; current issues, 178–87; diffusion of, 168–73, 175–87; economic importance of, 175–77; Indian Gourd Clans, 186–87; Kiowa basis of revival, 18; secularization of 175–87. *See also* Kiowa Gourd Clan, Unafraid of Death Society, *individual tribes*
Goutaha (Mrs. Blue Jay, Mrs. Togamote), 383
Grass Dance, 211. *See also* Omaha Dance, Omaha Society
Gray Thunder, 121
Gros Ventre Indians, 303
Guito. *See* Quoetone, Jimmy

Hainta, Taft, 151–52
Hainta Family, 163
Hair plates (hair metal), 28
Hamilton, Glen, 153
Hamilton, Mildred Tsoodle, 343
Harragarra, Delores Toyebo, 342, 343, 346
Haskell Institute, 299–301
Hatfield, Robert, 296
Haumpy, Bruce, 169
Haumpy, Gregory, 190, 196–97, 202, 267, 277, 294–96
Haumpy, James, 148, 152
Heapobears I, 50
Heapobears II, 14, 16, 49, 126, 133, 135, 378
Heart Eater, 70–71
Hidatsa Indians, 228
Hokeah, Harry, 148
Hokeah, Jack, 282
Hokeah, Mrs. (Gapkaugo), 260, 262, 266
Honoring (of Veterans), 301, 364–65
Hopewell Culture, 255–56
Hornless Bull, 229
Horse, Billy Evans, 177, 197, 208–209
Horse, Cecil, 136
Horse, Curtis, 153
Horse Headdresses Society (Chèjánmàu, Crazy Horses), 33–38, 133–34, 144, 146, 148–49, 244, 261; dances and dress of, 36; early members of, 370–73; leaders of, 37; meetings of, 34–36; membership and status in, 34; names of, 33; songs of, 37–38. *See also* Kiowa Military Societies
Howard, James, 157, 188, 303–304

Hueco Tanks Fight (1839), 241
Hummingbird, Joe, 57
Hunt, George, 121, 139
Hunting Horse (Tsatoke), 34, 227, 235, 248–49, 370, 378

Indian City U.S.A., 64–65, 277
Indian Reorganization Act (1934), 301
Indians For Indians Hour, 151
Iowa Indians, 34; military societies of, 116–18, 129; War Dance of, 256
Iraq, military service in, 67, 75, 105, 365
Island, 236

Jackson, Charlie (Hawzipta), 57
Jay, Claude, 16
Jennings, Vanessa, 88, 90, 91–93, 274, 280, 295

Kauahquo Family, 169
Kaubin, Frank, 75, 97–98, 347, 349
Kaulaity, Adam, 63, 153
Kaulaity, Jesse, 153
Kaulaity, Joe, 152
Kaulaity, Larry, 101
Kaulaity, Lynetta Gay, 171
Kaulaity, Walter, 153
Kauley, Violet, 336
Kavanagh, Tom, 259–60
Kaw Indians (Kansa), War Dance of, 258, 261
KCA (Kiowa, Comanche, Apache), historical relations, 3–4
Keahbone, Edgar, 14, 19, 130, 138, 271, 275
Keahbone, Ernie, 279
Keahbone, Leonard, 334
Keahbone, Mark, 266, 267, 270, 278–79, 288
Keahbone, Sindy, 50–51, 61
Ketchum, H. T. (Special Agent), 135
Kicking Bird (Eagle Striking With Talons), 37, 54
Killed A Man, 222–23
Killed One With His Hands, 236
Kintadl (Kital or Moth), 40, 41, 43, 54, 70, 93, 97, 225, 282, 309, 312, 320, 321–24, 328, 378, 383
Kiowa Apache. *See* Apache Tribe of Oklahoma
Kiowa Battle Picture Tipi, 70–72. *See also* Black Legs Society

Kiowa Bill Maunhede, 143, 144
Kiowa Bone Strikers (Cáuitémgòp), 247–52; cessation, 247–49; clubs, 247–48; name, 247–48; significance of, 251–52; songs, 249–51. See also Kiowa Military Societies
Kiowa Calendars (pictographic calendars), 55, 120–22, 125, 135–36, 138–39, 143–45, 229, 267
Kiowa Five (Artists), 281–82
Kiowa Gourd Clan, 110, 145, 147–214, 306, 366; benefit dances of, 160, 176–77; Brush Dance, 149, 161–62; Buffalo Dance, 149, 168; bugle calls, 166; consolidation (theory of), 150–51; current ceremonial 20–22, 159–68; dances, 103; diffusion of, 168–73, 175–87; dress, 156–59; ethnic significance of, 190–214; factionalism within, 168–73; Fast Paced Songs (Fáuldåugà), 167; functions, 173–75; giveaways, 164–65; initiations, 165–66; leadership, 151–53; martial aspects; name, 151–52; 154–55; mescal bean bandoliers, 157; music, 148–51, 155, 163–64; 166–68, redefinition of Jáifègàu, 154–56, 158; religious significance of, 200–206, 213; red and blue blankets,157–58; Red Wolf, 164, 207; respect for elders, 153, 155, 208–209; revival of, 8, 147–53, 177; role and impact of, 173–214; spirit, 193–98; themes of, 153–56, 183; trophies, 162–63; visits to Ta̢imé and Ten Medicine Bundles, 159. See also Kiowa Gourd Dance, Unafraid of Death Society
Kiowa Gourd Dance, 33, 37, 79, 113, 118–20, 364, 366; anthropological classifications of, 188–91; diffusion of 212–13; elevation in status of, 204; medicinal qualities of music, 193, 211–12; music and ethnic identity, 191–214; music and spirit, 103–95, 208; revival, 188–91; songs, 198–214; songs and language retention, 189, 198–200; spirit as a dialectical process, 195–98; spiritual and religious significance of, 200–206
Kiowa Indian Agency, cultural suppression by, 60, 273–75
Kiowa KIA (Killed In Action), 73, 105–106
Kiowa ledger books, 41–43, 133, 226–28
Kiowa Military Societies: characteristics of, 3–4; community associations, 8, 275; dance activities (basis of), 364; decline of, 266; defacto age-grading, 4; dog taboos, 17; enculturation (role in), 364–67; factionalism in, 366–67; functions, 3–4, 7; general characteristics, 4–7; inactivity (post 1890), 10–11; lances, 5, 37; name (Yàpfàhêgàu), 4, 266; offices, 5–6; rank and social status, 4–5; revivals, 8–9, 19; significance of, 363–67; society partners, 6; songs, 11; sources on, 10–11; warrior/martial ethos, 3, 80, 363; whips, 5–6, 29, women's societies, 328–30, 358–61. See also Bear Old Women Society, Black Legs Society, Calf Old Women Society, Horse Headdresses Society, Kiowa Bon Strikers, Mountain Sheep Society, Omaha Society, Pehodlma Society, Rabbits Society, Sentinel Dogs Society, Unafraid of Death Society
Kiowa Original Dancers, 286
Kiowa Sun Dance, 15, 17–20, 37, 126, 160, 200–202, 210, 229, 234, 266, 319–20; Brush Dragging and 7; cessation of, 62; government suppression of, 298; Kick Fight and, 7
Kiowa Tia-Piah Society (formerly Tia-Piah Society of Carnegie), 20, 168–72,178–80, 206; Anglo participation in, 178–80; Brush Dance, 170, bugle calls, 170; Chieftain Park, 169, 180; Rabbit Dances, 169; trophies, 170
Kiowa Tribe: Flag Song, 80; Ghost Dance, 54–55, 143, 204, 211, 273; sodalities, 3–7; Sons of the Sun, 244; Ta̢imé and keeper, 40, 127, 159, 309; Ten Medicine Bundles, 7, 14, 16, 66, 159, 202, 204, 219, 268, 309, 320, 323–27; 1838 Wolf Creek Fight, 121–25
Kiowa Veterans' Association, 63. See also Black Legs Society, Kiowa Military Societies
Kiowa Veterans' Auxiliary, 63–64, 357–58. See also Black Legs Society, Kiowa Military Societies
Kiowa War Mothers, 64, 80, 85–86, 89–90, 110, 331–49, 365; awards, 348–49; background, 331–35; dances, 341–42; fundraising, 338–39; insignia, 335–36; meetings, 339–40; membership, 340–41; name, 334; original members, 334–35; service activities, 336–38, 347–48; songs, 342–47

Kiowa Warrior Descendants, 80, 168, 171, 175
Kiowa Women's Societies. *See* Kiowa Military Societies, Military Societies
K'la/noi, 143
Koba, 261
Kodaseet, Gary, 153
Kokoom, Rev. Walter, 77, 266
Komalty. *See* Friendship Tree
Komalty Family Song, 167–68
Kom'tu, 313
Konad (White Buffalo), 269, 275–77
Konad, James, 270
Koomsa, Bill Jr., 129, 149, 155, 156–57, 208, 343
Koomsa, Bill Sr., 147, 152, 153, 168, 197
Koomsa, Robert (Bob), 349
Korean War, 60, 61, 74, 105, 109, 147, 154–55, 175, 283, 301, 303, 365
Kosan (Cosan), 119, 147
Kotay, Ralph, 124, 330, 357
Kracht, Benjamin, 273, 385
Kuelo, 226

Lakota Indians: Beggar's Dance, 255; Kit Fox Society, 255; War Dance 255, 258, 260, 303–304
Large Mustang / Horse (Pahbo), 41–43, 54, 249
Lassiter, Luke E., 9, 143, 171–74, 189–90, 192, 194, 198–99, 203, 206–207
Lean Bear (Settaulje or Poor/Thin Bear), 37, 143
Lefthand, Chester, 281–82
Leg Portions Of A Robe, 140
Levy, Jerrold, 217
Little Bluff (Jòhâu). *See* Bluff Recess
Little Bluff Recess (Jòhâusàn). *See* Son of Bluff Recess
Little Bow (Keinkau), 143, 146
Little Bringer/Introducer of Peyote, 37
Littlechief, James, 148
Littlechief, Tom, 169
Little Joe (Hautago), 55, 57, 276–77
Little Joe, Puppy, 61
Littleman, Alice, 57, 275
Littleman, Steve, 78
Lone Bear, 30, 128, 137, 138, 141, 143–45, 378; family, 171

Lone Bear Dance Ground, 64, 143, 145, 171; 1929 tornado and, 145
Lonewolf (the former Mammedety) 37
Lone Young Man I, 217–19
Lone Young Man II, 37
Lookingbill, Brad, 261
Lowie, Robert, 216, 219, 247
Luluing. *See* Ululation
Lurie, Nancy, 188

MacDonald, Gus, 281, 298
Mamanti, 54
Many Camp Fires (Iseeo/Aiseauide): (I), 222, 236, 243; (II), 236; (III, the scout), 236
Marriott, Alice, 122, 145–46, 223, 234
Martinez, Andres (Andale or Andele), 15, 56, 220, 227
McAllister, J. Gilbert, 16
McKenzie, Parker Paul, 11, 144, 193–94, 216–17; 273–74, 278
Methvin, Rev. J. J., 14
Military Societies, of Plains Indians, 3–4; chapter organizations, 228; men's, 115, 117, 188, 207, 228, 253; structure of, 172; studies of, 7–11; warfare role, 307–10; women's, 307–10, 314
Momaday, N. Scott, 75, 119, 166
Montgomery, Jack, 75
Mooney, James, 39–40, 44, 50, 113–14, 120, 137, 215–17, 225–26, 228, 242, 247, 266
Mopope, George, 50–51, 61, 275
Mopope, Jeanette Berry, 93, 268, 283–84
Mopope, Stephen, 268, 274, 281–82, 305. *See* Kiowa Five
Morgan, Gabriel, 69, 77
Morgan, Seth, 69
Mountain Sheep Society (Áljóyĭgàu), 25–31, 51–52, 99, 144, 148–49, 266, 269; dances and dress of, 28; early members of, 369–70; insignia of, 29; leaders of, 29–30; Love Sticks of, 29; meetings of, 28; membership and status in, 27–28; mention of, 34; names of, 25; role in Kiowa society, 31; Sheep Mountain, 25–26, 30; songs of, 26–27, 31. *See also* Kiowa Military Societies
Mwtsa, 143
Music, medicinal qualities of, 193, 211–12, 367

Naho (Daingkau), 57
Naishan Dene. *See* Apache Tribe of Oklahoma
Native American Church and Peyotism, 66, 145, 153, 156–58, 190, 202, 211, 286, 367
Navajo Indians, 205, 227, 241
Neconie, George, 74
Neconie, Orville, 355
Nettl, Bruno, 150
Never Got Shot, 236
No Moccasins, 37
Not Afraid Of Them, 141

Odlety, Frank, 56–58
Oheltoint, Barney Jr., 296
Oheltoint, Barney Sr., 296
Oheltoint, Charley, 57
Ohoma / Ohomo Lodge. *See* Omaha Society
Old Man Long Foot, 54, 243
Old Man Red Tipi, 137–41, 220, 236, 243
Old Man Saddle Blanket, 231, 233, 236
Omaha Dance (Hethushka; Grass, Hot, War Dance), 253–68, 296–306; crow belts, 254–55, 259–60; flexibility of, 303–304; names of, 254–60; origins and diffusion, 254–60; porcupine hair roaches, 254–55, 259–60; possible archaeological links, 255–56; Wild West show influence, 260–62
Omaha Society (Óhǫ̀mǫ̀gàu), 37, 57, 60, 66, 103, 141, 155, 174, 190, 198, 205, 211, 227, 253–306, 365–66; allegiance to, 274, 280, 286; bustle cedaring ceremony, 277–78, 286–88; bustle keepers, 267–68, 293; bustle pick-up ceremony, 275–76, 278; bustles, 259–60, 263, 267–68, 293–94; ceremonial chief, 293; changes in, 256–58, 295–96, 306; Cheyenne clothing, 263; Chief's Song, 291; current ceremonial, 285–92; dances, 79, 270–84; dress, 261, 263, 281–82; dress and dance periods, 304–305; Eagle and Crow Divisions, 268–70, 290; early accounts of, 256–83; early members, 381–82; Fancy Dance, 281–83, 290–91, 298, 304–306, 290, 298; forms of, 304; functions, 265–66; giveaways, 272, 274; Hawks, 290; hereditary council, 266, 279; initiations and membership 270, 278, 291–92, 295–96; lodge/tipi, 287–88; mourning ritual, 276–77; names for, 260,

278; Ohoma Road (ethic), 293–95, 306; organization of, 264–70, 276, 278–79; origins, 260–65; persistence of, 273–75, 296; prayers, 286–88, 293–94; princesses, 269–70; Resistance Song, 274; role of in Southern Plains powwow, 302–306; significance of, 251, 253–54, 304–306; singing practices, 286–87; social status, 279; society partners, 270, 273; songs, 270–74, 283–86, 291; Straight Dance, 290, 298; Tail Dance, 286, 291; War Dance, 146. *See also* Kiowa Military Societies, Omaha Dance, Powwows
Omaha Tribe: Gourd Dance of, 187; military societies, 116–17
Onco, Atwater, 61, 66, 77, 84, 87–89, 92, 95, 102, 160–61, 175, 201, 203
Onco, Eddie, 77
Operation Desert Storm, 61, 67, 92, 105, 109, 291, 347–48, 356
Ortner, Sherry, 209
Osage Indians, 40; War Dance, 259, 261, 264, 290, 304
Otoe Indians: Gourd Dance, 145–46, 187; War Dance, 256
Oyeby, Suzie, 56

Packing A Quarter Of Meat, 49–52, 54, 136, 231, 236
Paddlety, Rev. David, 77, 82
Paddlety, Victor, 250
Palmer, Christian, 77
Palmer, Dixon, 61, 65, 68, 71–73, 107, 278
Palmer, George, 61, 63, 68, 72–73
Palmer, Gus Sr., 15–16, 18–20, 22, 61–63, 65, 68, 73, 76, 78–80, 83, 93–94, 96, 104, 108, 278, 283–84, 358
Palmer, Lyndreth, 62, 63, 82
Palmer, Tugger, 76, 107
Palmer, William (Choctaw Bill), 62, 82
Paralyzed, 143
Parker, Quanah, 55
Parsons, Elsie Clews, 114, 266
Pauahty, Lynn, 169, 266
Pawnee Iruska (War Dance), 254–55, 264, 289, 304
Pehodlma Society, 224–25, 327–28; members of, 384. *See also* Kiowa Military Societies
Perez, Martha Koomsa, 197–98, 352–54

Piatonmah (Mrs. Horse or Old Lady Horse), 8, 41, 43, 53, 135, 234, 239, 280–81, 309, 323, 325
Piayo'te, 324
Pinezaddleby, David, 63, 65
Plains Apache. *See* Apache Tribe of Oklahoma
Podlt'ai, 230, 236, 238
Ponca, Helushka (War Dance), 255–58, 263–65, 281, 290, 304; military societies, 116–17; Ponca Powwow, 301
Poolaw, Helen Marie, 349
Poolaw, Joe, 57, 266, 296
Poolaw, Kiowa George, 46, 47
Poolaw, Martha Nell, 87, 108–109, 160, 349–50
Poolaw, Pascal Cletus, 74, 86, 92, 245
Poolaw, Robert Sr., 87, 108–109
Poor Buffalo (Lean Bison Bull), 53
Poor Buffalo, Isabella, 354
Porcupine Bear, 122
Powers, William, 189–90, 300
Powwows, 175–77, 296–306; commercial venues, 299–302; conflict within, 286–87; contests, 281, 286; Drum-Dream dance, 297–98; early intertribal dances, 297, 300–301; emergence of (Plains Indian powwow), 296–302; explanation of term, 296; influences in development of, 297–302; medicine shows, 299; Midewiwin Ceremony, 297–98; mixing of Plains-Prairie traditions in Indian Territory, 297–98, 302; powwow clubs, 302; powwow doctors, 296; Southern Plains powwows, 302–306. *See also* Kiowa Military Societies, Omaha Society, Omaha Dance
Preciado, Blas, 76, 83, 88, 103
Purple Heart Club. *See* Stecker Purple Heart Club

Quetone, Allen, 63, 75–76, 108
Quoetone, Guy, 55, 56
Quoetone, Jimmy (Guito), 217, 219, 235, 238, 312, 317, 320, 378

Rabbits Society (Pòláhyòp), 13–24; 150–51, 161, 174, 365; activities of, 17–19; current society, 19–23; functions of, 15–17, 22–24; name of, 13; origins of, 13–14; role in Kiowa culture, 22–24; songs of, 20–22. *See also* Kiowa Military Societies
Rainy Mountain Kiowa Indian Baptist Church, 67–68
Redbird, Ernest Sr. 63, 65
Red Bonnet Brow, 54, 137–38
Red Buffalo, 37, 275–76
Red Dress, 316
Red Horn, 143
Red Otter, 136
Red Sleeve Dresses, 70, 89–91, 133, 318
Red Wing Dresses, 318
Red Wolf, 143
Reservation War Dancers, 286
Rushed By Below (Dombetai), 26–27
Russell, Evalu Poolaw Ware, 74, 77, 86, 88, 92, 111
Russell, Lowell, 92, 348

Saddle Blanket, 30–31
Sahmaunt, Carrie, 336, 349
Sahmaunt, Luther (Samon), 15, 40
Sahmaunt, Norman L., 76
Sangko (Prickly Pear), 7, 16, 29, 132, 217, 221, 223, 225, 232, 244, 313, 378
Sankadota, Howard, 59
Sankadota, Jack, 55, 57, 59, 311
Sankadota, Jasper, 59, 169
Satepauhoodle, Sam, 152
Satepeahtaw, 37
Satethieday Khatgomebaugh (White Bear's People/Descendants), 172–73
Saumty, Rev. George, 58–59
Saunkeah, Jasper, 334
Saynday (the Kiowa Trickster), 20
Scalp and Victory Dances, 26, 57–58, 84–93, 110, 254, 278, 364
Scott, Hugh L., 30, 33, 40, 45–46, 113, 117, 120–21, 215–16, 222–23, 247
Scout Dogs Society (Qóichégàu, Sentinel Dogs Society), 20, 43, 45–48, 51–52, 71, 117, 125–26, 133, 136, 141–42, 215–45, 247–49, 328; behavior on war parties, 239–41; contrary speech of, 221; decline of, 243–44; dress/regalia, 225, 226–28; early history of, 217–19; early members, 377–81; feasts, 221–22; initiations, 229–35; ledger drawings of, 226–28; membership, 219–21; member-

ship issues, 245; name, 215–17; offices and sashes, 222–26, 237–38; origins, 217; owl feather headdresses, 136, 227; police functions of, 243; significance of, 219, 244–45; society bags, 225–26; society partners, 237–39; songs, 241–43; succession of, 235–37. *See also* Kiowa Military Societies
Searching For The Prettiest, 270
Shane, Mary Neconie, 356–57
Shawnee Indians, 177
Short, R. G., 77
Silverhorn, 34, 51, 57, 122, 133, 217, 260, 266, 282
Silverhorn, James, 266, 270
Silverhorn, Lizzie Oyeby, 55
Sitting Bear I, 52–53, 220, 233, 235, 237, 239, 240, 242–43
Sitting Bear II, 52–53, 79, 96
Sitting On A Tree, 71
Skunkberry Society. *See* Unafraid of Death Society
Skunkberry Creek, 114
Sleeping Bear, 70
Slow Running Wolf (Crazy Old Man), 224
Smoky (Tobaccos), 30
Smoky, Old Lady, 47
Sodalities, 3
Songs. See *Individual Kiowa Military Societies and Dance Societies*
Son of Bluff Recess (Jòhâusàn / Dohausan), 37, 40, 42, 54, 70, 71, 235, 240, 248–49. *See also* Bluff Recess
Soontay, Tony, 357
Southeastern Ceremonial Complex (Mississippian Period), 256
Spotted Bird, 216, 219, 231–32, 239
Spottedbird, Yale, 122, 169, 266
Spotted Faced [Horse] (Davis), 30
Squirrel Tail, 54
Stahl, Robert, 181
Standing, McKinley, 77
Standing Ready To Strike (Mrs. Lonebear), 65, 145
Stealing Horses From Another Tribe, 311
Stecker, Ernest, 55, 273
Stecker Purple Heart Club, 80, 354–57; early members, 355, insignia, 356–57; name, 355; Purple Heart recipients, 355; songs, 355–56

Stinchecum, C. V., 273, 275
Stirring Up Songs (War Journey songs), 329
Stood His Ground/Did Not Run, 235
Stumbling Bear (Bear That Runs Them Over), 54, 75
Sun Appeared (Fearless Charger, Haunemidau), 54, 142. *See also* White Horse, Roland
Sun Boy, 133, 140
Sun Dance. *See* Kiowa Sun Dance
Sun Dance Woman, 313
Supernatural Power (dáudáu), 309, 328

Tabe'aide, 236
Tadli'ekoi, 142
Tahbone, George Sr., 107, 279
Tahlo, Laura Sankadota, 59
Tahlo, Oscar, 61. 65
Tahlo, Paul, 61
Takone, Jim, 57, 59
Tanedooah, Henry, 152, 65
Tanedooah, John Oliver, 20, 148
Tanedooah, Mrs. John Oliver (White Back), 270
Tanedooah, William, 148–49, 152
Tapedo, Elva Mae, 86
Tartsah, Jimmy, 81
Tenedooah (Tanedooah), 57
Tenedooah ,Mrs. (Saioma), 46, 47, 270, 312, 320, 329
Texas Tia-Piah Society, 170. *See also* Gourd Dance (Anglo organizations)
The Other Scalp, 37
Tia-Piah Park, 169
Tia-Piah Society. *See* Kiowa Tia-Piah Society
Tia-Piah Society of Oklahoma, 167, 168, 169–71, 179; Tia-Piah Park and, 169
Tofpi, Harry Lee, 154
Tofpi, Mary Hall, 349
Tofpi, Rogers, 148, 152
Tointigh, Tom, 270
Tonekeahbo, 48
Tonemah, Quay, 148, 152
Tonemah, Scott, 63, 77, 154, 174
Tongkeamha, Frank, 270
Tongkeamha, Kiowa Jim, 56, 57, 271, 275
Tongkeamha, Weiser, 57, 279
Topaum, Allie, 143
Topaum, Rueban, 75, 101, 143

Toyebo, Lewis, 81–82, 342–47
Toyebo, Milton, 118
Toyebo, Richenda Sitapatah, 342
Toyebo, Ritchie Mitchell, 342
True, Joe, 181–82
Tsaitkopeta, Paul, 126, 143, 375
Tsalote, Charley, 267, 276
Tsatoke, Elva Mae, 349
Tsatoke, Lee, 61
Tsatoke, Monroe, 43
Tsonetokoy, Francis, 144, 273, 281
Tsoodle, Fred, 146–48, 152–53
Tsoodle, Henry Jr., 152
Tsoodle, Henry Sr., 40, 47, 49, 53, 137–39, 141, 144, 146, 147, 235, 265, 282–83, 293, 321, 325, 369, 374
Tsoodle, Mrs. Henry Sr., 147
Tsoodle, James Henry, 152
Tsoodle, Navy Paul "George", 144–45, 152, 266
Tsoodle, Oscar, 20, 23, 58, 59, 75–76, 145, 152, 156, 158, 160, 167, 202, 206
Tsoodle, Peggy, 67–68, 148
Tsoodle, Rufus, 57
Tsoodle, Tim, 153, 202, 213, 296
Tsoodle, Tomascine, 152
Tsoodle, Vernon, 153, 163, 166
Tsotigh, Huberta Jean, 171
Turkey Trot Dance, 56
Two Hatchet, 30
Two Hatchet, Elizabeth, 349
Two Hatchet, James, 50–51

Ululation, 92
Unafraid of Death Society (Jáifègàu, Skunk-berry Society), 19, 36, 44, 60, 113–214; 280, 310; activities, 126–28; age, 125; Brush Dance, 146; Buffalo Dance, 128, 130; cessation, 143; dances, 128–31; 1921 dress,131–42; early members, 375–77; Fast Paced Songs (Fáuldåugà), 129–30; Gourd Dance, 144–45; insignia, 131–32, 136–42; lances, 137–42; leaders, 142–43; ledger drawings of, 133; organization, 126; mescal beans, use of, 131–32; names, 113–15, 117, 125; National Folk Festival Program, 146; Old Man Songs, 129; origins, 118–25; Rattle Dance, 117–19; rattles, 133–34; Red Wolf (mythological figure), 118, 124–25, 129; revival of, 19, 143–44; sashes/ropes, 136–37, 140; significance of, 113; similarity to other societies, 115–17; skunkberries, 113–15, 122, 124; songs, 124, 128–31; Wolf Songs, 124. *See also* Kiowa Military Societies, Kiowa Gourd Clan
Urban Relocation Program, 187

Veterans of Foreign Wars (VFW) posts, 63, 67, 108; dissatisfaction with, 67
Vietnam War, 61, 74, 105, 107

Walking On A Tree, 16, 30
War Dance. *See* Omaha Dance, Kiowa Omaha Society
Ware, Allen, 270
Ware, Emma, 77
Ware, Joshua J., 75–76, 105
Ware, Lt. Col. Lawrence, 74, 77
Ware, Presley, 77
Ware, Terry, 296
War Journey Songs. *See* Stirring Up Songs
War Mothers. *See* Kiowa War Mothers
Warrior / Fighter, 236, 238
Warrior / Martial Ethos. *See* Kiowa Military Societies
Warrior Societies. *See* Military Societies
Wdlkwwn, 239
Whetseline, Rhea, 77
Whistler, Don, 151
White Bear I, 248
White Bear II, 122, 128, 130, 133, 135–42, 148, 153, 163–64, 166, 170, 172; bugle of, 135–37; zébàut or fletched lance of, 137–41
White Bear III, 143
White Bear Descendants,
White Buffalo, 37.
White Cow Bird, 140–41
White Fox, 65, 85, 132, 143, 146, 147, 152, 173, 240, 376
White Fox, Mrs. (Tahlomah), 56
White Horse, 30, 91
White Horse, Charley, 43, 50, 65, 130, 242, 248–49, 267–70, 276–78, 283, 285, 288
White Horse, Laura, 284
White Horse, Mathew (Mac), 267–68, 273–74, 279, 285–88, 292–93, 355
Whitehorse, Roland (Fearless Charger or Haunemidau II), 284

INDEX

White Tailed, 231, 240
Wild West Shows, 281, 299, 301
Williams, Ruby Paukei, 332, 340, 342–43, 348
Wohaw, 227
Wolf Lying Down, 130
Wolf That Howled, 15
Woman's Heart, 54
Wooly Haired, 54
World War I, 60, 80, 85, 105, 278, 301, 330–32, 358
World War II, 60–61, 65–66, 68, 74, 98, 105, 108–109, 147, 155, 175, 283, 301–303, 330–32, 334–35, 342–47, 358–61, 365–66
Wtote, 54

Yaikwwn, 236
Yàpfàhêggàu. *See* Kiowa Military Societies

Yeahquo, Anne L., 214
Yellow Bison Bull, 236
Yellowhair, Jeff, 105
Yellow Wolf I, 71
Yellow Wolf II, 40, 48, 220, 224–25, 230–34, 236, 240–41, 244, 250, 377, 380
Yellow Wolf Family, 163
Yost, Anthony Little Calf, 105
Young, Gloria, 254
Young Mustang (Gúlhèì), 49–52, 61, 68, 79, 97, 366. *See also* Goule-hae-ee Descendants

Zotam, Paul, 136
Zotigh, Harlan Hall, 352–53
Zotigh, Harry Hall, 148
Zotigh, Pauline Beulah Hall, 349–50, 353